FAMILY FAVORITES

FAMILY FAVORITES

For Everyday Meals & Special Occasions

Conversion Tables

Volume measure
(liquids)

US		Metric
1/8 tsp		0.5 ml
1/4 tsp		1 ml
1/2 tsp		2 ml
3/4 tsp		3 ml
1 tsp		5 ml
2 tsp		10 ml
3 tsp		15 ml
1 tbsp		15 ml
4 tsp		20 ml
2 tbsp	1 oz	30 ml
3 tbsp		45 ml
4 tbsp	2 oz	60 ml
1/4 cup	2 oz	60 ml
5 tbsp		75 ml
1/3 cup		80 ml
1/2 cup	4 oz	125 ml
2/3 cup		160 ml
3/4 cup	6 oz	180 ml
1 cup	8 oz	250 ml
1 1/4 cups	10 oz	300 ml
1 1/2 cups	12 oz	375 ml
1 3/4 cups	14 oz	425 ml
2 cups	16 oz	500 ml
2 1/2 cups	20 oz	625 ml
3 cups	24 oz	750 ml
3 1/2 cups	28 oz	875 ml
4 cups	32 oz	1 L
5 cups		1.25 L
6 cups	48 oz	1.5 L
8 cups	64 oz	2 L

Weight measure

US		Metric
1 oz		30 g
2 oz		60 g
3 oz		90 g
4 oz	1/4 lb	115 g
5 oz		140 g
6 oz		165 g
7 oz		190 g
8 oz	1/2 lb	225 g
9 oz		270 g
10 oz		280 g
12 oz	3/4 lb	350 g
16 oz	1 lb	450 g
	1 1/2 lb	675 g
32 oz	2 lb	900 g
	2 1/4 lb	1 kg
	3 lb	1.4 kg
	4 lb	1.8 kg
	4 1/2 lb	2 kg
	5 lb	2.2 kg
	10 lb	4.5 kg

Cans

US	Metric
5 oz	142 ml
8 oz	227 ml
10 oz	284 ml
12 oz	341 ml
14 oz	398 ml
19 oz	540 ml
28 oz	796 ml

Length measure

US	Metric
1/8 inch	0.25 cm
1/4 inch	0.5 cm
1/2 inch	1.25 cm
1 inch	2.5 cm
1 1/2 inches	3.75 cm
2 inches	5 cm
3 inches	7.5 cm
4 inches	10 cm
5 inches	12.5 cm
6 inches	15 cm
7 inches	18 cm
8 inches	20.5 cm
9 inches	23 cm
10 inches	25 cm
11 inches	28 cm
12 inches	30.5 cm

Temperature

°F	°C
200°	95°
212°	100°
225°	105°
250°	120°
275°	135°
300°	150°
325°	160°
350°	175°
375°	190°
400°	205°
425°	220°
450°	230°
475°	245°
500°	260°
525°	275°
550°	290°

Published by Mint Publishers, Bedford, New York, (1997)
ISBN 1-55120-016-3

INTRODUCTION

FAMILY FAVORITES

It's the end of a long day, you're tired, at least one member of your family wants to know "What's for dinner?", and you could use a little inspiration in the kitchen. Here's the energy boost you need.

Family Favorites is filled with ideas for delicious and practical meals for your family and friends. You'll find hundreds of new and exciting recipes, plus menu ideas, cooking tips and shortcuts. Recipes are easy to follow. Ingredients are readily available. Nutritional analyses are provided for each and every recipe to enable you to balance your meals and encourage your family's better health.

The recipes in *Family Favorites* have been collected from hundreds of good cooks, the result of countless hours of experimentation, testing and tasting. They have been reviewed and edited by Judi Olstein, the author of *American Family Cooking, The Great American Baking Book, New American Cuisine* and *Desserts*. Judi runs Della Robbia Foods, a specialty bakery supplying restaurants and gourmet stores in the New York area.

Family Favorites will surely become your constant kitchen companion. Use it and reap the praise!

The Editor

TABLE OF CONTENTS

FAMILY FAVORITES is uniquely constructed as a meal. In order, the chapters will bring you from appetizers to desserts, passing through the entrées, light refreshments, main dishes, side dishes, salads and cheeses.

So as to facilitate easy and quick reference, FAMILY FAVORITES has filed its recipes into two different indexes:

- the Main Index, page 466, classifies the recipes by chapters and alphabetical order,

- the Supplementary Index, page 474, groups together certain recipes with common ingredients.

In both instances, you will find that the recipes reserved for microwave cooking are identified by the microwave icon.

EATING AND HEALTH

Food: What's in it for you?
All the foods we eat supply us with energy, expressed in terms of calories or kilojoules. Energy needs differ with each individual, depending on height, age, weight, sex, bone structure and the intensity of physical activity, either in sports or manual labor.

If we store more energy than we need, our body mass increases. Conversely, if we eat less than our body needs, our stored fat is used up and we lose weight.

Food contains glucids (sugars), proteins, lipids (fats), vitamins, minerals, dietary fibers and water. However, only the glucids, proteins and lipids produce energy.

GLUCIDS

Glucids are also called sugars or carbohydrates. They represent the main source of energy for the human body. You'll find them mainly in fruits and fruit juices, vegetables, milk, yogurt, bread, cereals, rice, pasta, potatoes and legumes (broad beans, etc.). Other major sources of glucids are white and brown sugars, honey, molasses, syrups, jams, candies, and other sugar treats. However, this second group contains virtually no vitamins, minerals or dietary fibers, and is therefore very low in nutritional value.

PROTEINS

Proteins help us build, repair, and renew body tissue. They form antibodies, elements in the blood that help us fight infection. Meat, poultry, fish and eggs are the main sources of protein. Milk and dairy products, as well as nuts, seeds, and legumes also supply protein.

LIPIDS

We're more familiar with the term "fats" than lipids. Despite their high calorie quotient, lipids help us absorb essential substances for good health, such as vitamins A, D, E and K. Consuming lipids gives us a feeling of having eaten well (satiety), and helps maintain our body temperature.

Cholesterol is a component of lipids, and our bodies need it to function properly. Among other things, cholesterol plays a part in manufacturing Vitamin D and certain hormones. It also acts as a building block for cellular membranes. However, high levels of blood cholesterol can, in the long run, cause hardening of the arteries and cardiovascular diseases.

Here are a few recommendations designed to help lessen the danger of developing cardiovascular problems.

- Achieve and maintain an ideal weight for health.
- Stop smoking.
- Exercise regularly.
- Increase your intake of dietary fibers, particularly those found in legumes, barley, oats and fruit.
- Cut down your total intake of fats.

WHERE DO WE FIND FATS?

Fats are found in oils, butter, margarine, vegetable fat and meat. Watch out for disguised sources of fat, such as nuts, sauces, certain cheeses, delicatessen meats, pies, cakes and pastries.

VITAMINS AND MINERALS

Vitamins and minerals are necessary for good health. We have to get a sufficient amount of them in our food, since our bodies can't manufacture them, for the most part. Actually, they are all present in food, although in varying quantities. Let's look at how some of them work.

VITAMIN A

- Aids night vision.
- Keeps skin and mucous membranes healthy.
- Helps normal development of bones and teeth.

VITAMIN B (Thiamin, Riboflavin and Niacin)

- Helps the body use energy contained in food.
- Encourages normal growth and appetite.
- Helps the nervous system function properly.

VITAMIN C

- Helps heal lesions and maintains healthy gums.
- Keeps the walls of blood vessels in good condition.

VITAMIN D

- Helps the body use calcium and phosphorus to build and maintain healthy bones and teeth.

CALCIUM

- Helps build and maintain healthy bones and teeth.
- Helps normal coagulation of blood and normal functioning of the nervous system.

IRON

- Helps build red corpuscles needed for carrying oxygen.

COMBINATIONS THAT PROMOTE HEALTH

CALCIUM AND VITAMIN D

Vitamin D helps the body absorb calcium. For this reason, milk is an ideal food, because it contains both Vitamin D and calcium.

IRON AND VITAMIN C

Vitamin C helps the absorption of iron. If you are serving iron-rich liver, for example, include in the same meal a food rich in Vitamin C (tomato juice, broccoli, orange, grapefruit, kiwi, cantaloup or strawberries).

DIETARY FIBERS

Dietary fibers are vegetable components that aren't digested by the body. They help us feel full after a meal, and prevent or correct constipation. The fibers in such foods as legumes, barley and fruit are known to help decrease blood cholesterol levels. There are a number of other sources of fiber, including vegetables, breads, and whole-grain cereals.

WATER

The human body is 65% water. This water acts as a means of transportation for nutritive elements, and helps the body eliminate waste matter. Water also acts as a body temperature regulator.

All foods contain a certain percentage of water. As a general rule, the higher this percentage, the less energy (i.e., fewer calories) the food provides.

ALCOHOL

Alcoholic drinks supply the body with a great deal of energy, despite their low nutritional value. Alcohol is also recognized for its ability to stimulate the appetite as well as reduce the speed of reflex actions or the ability to concentrate, particularly on an empty stomach. Drinks before a meal are a good example of this phenomenon. Alcohol abuse can damage the nervous system, cause ulcers, or lead to cirrhosis of the liver, a chronic liver disease. In the long run, alcohol abuse can lead to substituting alcohol for more nutritious food, and result in social and economic problems.

A QUESTION OF WEIGHT?

Many people are dissatisfied with their present weight and would like to become thinner. It's a preoccupation especially common among women, and the reason is not hard to understand. Advertising is constantly pitching the image of the gracefully slender young woman. But losing weight for the purpose of looking like a model is not always very realistic. Some women even adopt dietary habits that are quite dangerous for their health.

HOW MUCH SHOULD YOU WEIGH?

According to the new concept of "healthy weight," each person has his or her optimum weight range. To find out whether your present weight falls within this range, calculate your BMI (Body Mass Index) according to the charts on the right and on the opposite page. This index applies to men and women between the ages of 20 and 60. It can apply to the under-20 group as well, as long as body growth is complete (from 18 up). The BMI doesn't apply to children, adolescents, pregnant women, or people over 65.

Calculating your BMI makes it possible to determine the risk of developing health problems associated with obesity or excessive thinness. If your BMI is outside the healthy weight range, you should consult a physician and dietician/nutritionist to help change certain eating and living habits.

BODY MASS INDEX

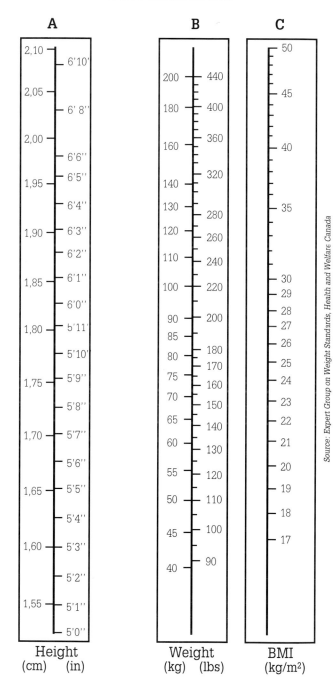

Height (cm) (in) Weight (kg) (lbs) BMI (kg/m²)

Source: Expert Group on Weight Standards, Health and Welfare Canada

How to find your BMI

1) Mark an X at your height on line A
2) Mark an X at your weight on line B
3) Take a ruler and join the two X's
4) To find your BMI, extend the line to line C.

IF YOUR BMI IS

▪UNDER 20:

A BMI under 20 may be associated with health problems for some individuals. It may be a good idea to consult a dietician and physician for advice.

▪Between 20-25:

This zone is associated with the lowest risk of illness for most people. This is the range you want to stay in.

▪Between 25-27:

A BMI over 25 may be associated with health problems for some people. Caution is suggested if your BMI is in this zone.

▪Over 27:

A BMI over 27 is associated with increased risk of health problems such as heart disease, high blood pressure and diabetes. It may be a good idea to consult a dietician and physician for advice.

DIET FOODS

Many people wrongly believe that diet food means slimming food. Eating diet food doesn't necessarily lead to weight loss, since the energy component in the particular food may not be reduced.

By definition, a diet food is one in which a single or several components, such as sugars, fats, salt, or calories, have been altered. In some countries, manufacturers are obliged by law to label diet products under specific headings, for example:

REDUCED SUGAR FOODS

These are reduced in glucids (sugars) but not in calories.

Examples: Biscuits, candies and chocolate

SUGARLESS FOODS

These contain a negligible quantity of sugar and a maximum of one calorie per 3 1/2 oz (100 mL).

Examples: Sugarless soft drinks

REDUCED CALORIE FOODS

Food in this category supplies a maximum of half the normal calories.

Example: Reduced calorie puddings

LOW CALORIE FOODS

These supply a maximum of 15 calories per serving as listed on the label.

Examples: Low calorie jams and jellies

LOW SODIUM FOODS

This category must not contain more than half the normal sodium content.

Examples: Low sodium peanut butter, soups, tomato juice

LOW FAT FOODS

This heading includes food with reduced cholesterol levels.

Example: Egg Beaters

These few explanations will help you understand that diet foods aren't simply slimming foods. What's more, they aren't essential for losing weight.

WHAT ABOUT LIGHT FOODS?

The term "light" is not subject to the same regulations as "diet" in describing foods. Manufacturers are merely obliged to state how the product has been lightened whether in texture, taste, fats, calories and so on. It's worth noting that if only the taste is light, the product's energy value is not reduced.

Read the labels. This is the only way to find out the nutritional value and to compare different products. You should be aware that sometimes it's better to buy the regular product than a light version.

BUYING HEALTHY FOOD...

How to Balance Menus?

To guarantee good nutrition, you must eat foods from the following groups every day.

MILK AND MILK PRODUCTS

- Children under 11, 2 to 3 servings
- Teenagers, 3 to 4 servings
- Pregnant and nursing women, 3 to 4 servings
- Adults, 2 servings

Examples of 1 serving:

- 1 cup (250 mL) milk
- 3/4 cup (180 mL) yogurt
- 1 1/2 oz (45 g) Cheddar or soft cheese

BREADS AND CEREALS

- 3 to 5 servings of whole or enriched grains

Examples of 1 serving:

- 1 slice of bread
- 1/2 cup (125 mL) cooked cereal
- 3/4 cup (180 mL) ready-to-eat cereal
- 1/2 to 3/4 cup (125 to 180 mL) cooked rice or pasta
- 1 muffin or roll

FRUITS AND VEGETABLES

- 4 to 5 servings (including at least 2 servings of vegetables)

Examples of 1 serving:

- 1/2 cup (125 mL) vegetables or fruits (fresh, frozen, or canned)
- 1/2 cup (125 mL) juice (fresh, frozen or canned)
- 1 medium potato, carrot, tomato, peach, apple, orange or banana

MEAT, FISH, POULTRY OR SUBSTITUTE

- 2 servings

Examples of 1 serving:

- 2 to 3 oz (60 to 90 g) cooked lean meat, fish, poultry or liver
- 1 cup (250 mL) cooked legumes
- 2 oz (60g) Cheddar cheese
- 2 eggs

We suggest choosing foods that are low in fat, sugar and salt.

BUYING HEALTHY FOOD AND BUDGETING FOR IT

- Plan your menus in relation to weekly specials.
- Draw up your shopping list at home, and stick to it once you're in the store.
- Read product labels. Buy the food, not a brand name or a game inside a pretty package.
- Buy large packages rather than small if you have the space to store them and expect to use up the contents within a short time.
- Buy fresh fruits and vegetables in season, or use frozen or canned if they aren't available.
- Keep impulse buying to a minimum by avoiding impromptu visits to the supermarket between regular marketing days.
- Don't do your grocery shopping when you're hungry.

READING LABELS

All food products containing more than one component (soups, biscuits, cereals, and so on) must list the ingredients. However, the packaging of 100% pure, unsweetened orange juice, for example, will merely describe the single product.

Manufacturers must list ingredients in order of quantity, starting with the highest amount.

There are various ways of describing ingredients. For example, words describing sugar content include honey, malt syrup, corn syrup, and molasses. You should also look for words ending in OSE, as these generally describe sugar components. Examples include glucose, dextrose, fructose, lactose, maltose, saccharose, and levulose, among others.

It is worth noting that all these forms of sugar are energy foods with 4 calories per 0.035 oz (1 g).

People who want to avoid salt should look for the words LOW SODIUM on labels.

HELPFUL SLIMMING HINTS

- Whole milk can be replaced with skimmed or partially skimmed milk.

- Try replacing mayonnaise with plain yogurt in dips and salad dressings.

- Choose cheeses made with skimmed or partially skimmed milk, and therefore with a reduced calorie content.

- Go easy on deep-fried or sauce-covered foods.

- Chill stocks and sauces. The fat content rises to the surface and can be easily removed.

- Contrary to what most people believe, cooking with wine doesn't mean adding surplus calories to your food. Recipes usually call for dry wine. When boiled, the alcohol evaporates, leaving only the low-calorie wine.

FOOD MYTHS

Grapefruit makes fats dissolve.

FALSE. No food can do this, even if it is acidic. In any case, how can a food containing glucids (sugars) help in losing weight? The only way to lose weight is to reduce consumption of calories to less than your energy requirements, so that the body will be forced to burn up its fat reserves.

Bread, potatoes and pasta must be cut out of the diet of anyone wanting to lose weight.

FALSE. It's more often the abuse of these foods and their garnishes—butter, margarine, jams, cream sauces, and sour cream— that turn them into high calorie foods.

In any case, you shouldn't forget that bread, potatoes, and pasta are important sources of vitamins and minerals.

Gelatin hardens your nails.

FALSE. Gelatin is a protein which is digested in the same way as proteins from other sources. Therefore it doesn't directly affect anything so specific as fingernails.

Butter and margarine supply exactly the same number of calories.

TRUE. However, there is a major difference between the two. Butter contains cholesterol, whereas margarine contains none.

GLOSSARY

AL DENTE Italian culinary term used to describe pasta that is cooked but remains slightly resistant.

ALMONDS, ROASTED whole or slivered almonds lightly browned in the oven.

ARRANGE (1) to place a food decoratively on a serving dish or plate ; (2) to lay denser or thicker parts of a food towards the outside of a dish, with thinner parts towards the center, for even cooking.

AU GRATIN French culinary term defining saucy dishes, sprinkled with bread crumbs or grated cheese, then usually browned under a hot broiler.

BAIN MARIE term referring to the method of gently cooking food in a water bath. A bain marie is made by placing a pan or dish of food in a larger, shallow pan and then adding enough water to the larger pan to come about halfway up the sides of the smaller dish.

BASTE to spoon or pour a liquid (cooking juices, wine, oil, etc.) over meat or other food to prevent it from drying out while cooking and to add flavor.

BLANCH to cook a food in lightly-salted boiling water for a few minutes to make it tender, remove the bitter or strong taste, or make it easier to peel.

BLEND to stir, beat, or otherwise combine ingredients to produce a homogeneous mixture.

BLENDER electric utensil designed to chop or purée a food. Usually not recommended for dry foods.

BLIND BAKED term used to describe a prebaked, unfilled pie shell. The blind-baked pie shell may be baked further after filling, or not, depending on the recipe.

BONE to remove bones from meat, fish or poultry.

BRAISE to cook food, previously browned or not, over low heat, in a little liquid in a covered pan.

BROCHETTE the French term for a skewer; also refers to food cooked on a skewer, or *en brochette*.

BROWN to cook food in fat, over high heat, until it reaches the desired color.

CARAMELIZE (1) to coat the inside of a pan with caramel ; (2) to cover food with melted caramel ; (3) to broil a mixture of butter and sugar until it melts and turns a golden-brown color.

CHOP to cut food into small pieces using a knife, blender or food processor.

CLARIFY to separate and remove solids and sediments from a liquid to make it clear. Butter is clarified by heating it and pouring off the clear yellow fat, leaving behind the milk solids.

COAT to dip food into, or sprinkle with, cream, sauce, frosting, etc. until food is fully covered.

COOL to refrigerate or let stand food at room temperature, until it is no longer warm to the touch.

CUBED to cut into 1-inch (2.5 cm) cubes.

CREAM, TO to make food soft and smooth by beating with a whisk, spoon, or with a mixer.

CROUTON (1) a small cube of bread toasted or fried, or (2) a slice of bread, rubbed with seasonings then toasted (often cut into fancy shapes).

CURDLE to separate into lumpy curds and liquid. Foods tend to curdle when they are exposed to prolonged or too high heat, or in the case of milk, combined with acids.

CURE to preserve meats and fish by smoking, salting, drying or a combination of two or three.

DEEP-FRY to cook food in enough hot oil for food to float on it.

DEGLAZE to pour a liquid into a pan used for frying meat or vegetables, then to scrape bottom of pan to mix liquid with drippings. This provides the base for a sauce.

DEGREASE to remove the fat, in part or in full, from the surface of liquids (cooking juices or broth), either by skimming it off, or sucking it up with a paper towel or bulb baster.

DICED to cut into ⅛- to ¼-inch (0.25 to 0.5 cm) cubes.

DILUTE to mix a solid with a liquid, or to mix two liquids, in order to lessen the consistency or the strength of a food.

DISSOLVE to fully decompose a solid food by mixing with a liquid.

DRAIN to remove all liquid from a food, and if necessary to pat food dry.

DREDGE to coat food with a dry ingredient such as seasoned flour, by tossing the food in a bowl or a bag.

DRIPPINGS fat and cooking juices rendered by meat or poultry during cooking, often used as the base for a sauce.

FLAMBÉ to add alcohol to a dish, then set it alight ; flames are either extinguished after 30 seconds by covering pan, or allowed to extinguish by themselves if not specified in the recipe. This technique is used to add a subtle flavor to a dish or for a spectacular presentation.

FOLD to delicately blend a fragile food into a heavier mixture without breaking or mashing.

FOOD PROCESSOR a multi-purpose electric utensil with a variety of attachments that can chop, slice, mix, mince and so on.

FRICASSEE to cook meat first in fat or vegetable oil and then gently in liquid along with aromatic vegetables.

FRILL paper decoration used to cover bone tips of a leg of lamb or poultry.

GARNISH to decorate a dish with a complementary and attractive food, such as parsley, lemon wedges, sliced radishes and fresh herbs.

GLAZE (1) to coat with a glossy mixture ; (2) melted mixture of flavored jam or jelly used to coat pastries for a glossy finish.

GRATE to reduce food to a fine powder or thin slivers.

HERB BOUQUET a combination of parsley, thyme, and bay leaf used in flavoring soups, stews, and other dishes. When fresh, the herbs are tied together with string, and removed when the cooking is done. A dried bouquet is wrapped in cheesecloth for easy removal. Other combinations of herbs may also be commercially available.

JULIENNED food cut into slivers about 2-4 inches (5-10 cm) long by 1/8-inch (0.25 cm) thick.

KNEADED BUTTER equal parts of cold butter and flour creamed together.

MACERATE to soak foods in a liquid ; term usually reserved for fruit soaked in alcohol or liqueur.

MARINADE liquid mixture of a fat element, an acid element and condiments, in which food is soaked to absorb flavor, become more tender or keep longer.

MEDLEY mixture of diced vegetables and/or fruit.

MELON BALLER utensil designed to shape vegetables and fruit into small, decorative balls.

MINCE to cut solid food into tiny pieces.

MIXER utensil designed to beat, knead or mix ingredients to a smooth consistency.

PAN-BROIL to cook food (usually meat) in a hot skillet that may or may not contain fat.

PARBOIL to partially cook food in boiling water. The cooking is usually completed by another method.

PARE to remove the thin skin of a fruit or a vegetable.

PINCH a very small amount, usually less than 1/8 teaspoon.

POACH to cook partially or completely by submerging food in a gently boiling liquid.

PREPARE to remove all fat, gristle and other unnecessary parts of meat, poultry or fish prior to cooking.

PUNCH DOWN to deflate risen dough by pushing it down with the fist.

PURÉE to mash solid foods with a blender, food processor, sieve or other kitchen utensil until smooth.

RAMEKIN small, ovenproof dish — sometimes called a custard cup — in which individual servings can be cooked.

REDUCE to partly boil down a liquid, over high heat and in an uncovered pan, in order to thicken it and concentrate its taste.

RENDER to cook food until it releases its fat as liquid.

ROUX French culinary term defining a mixture of flour and butter, browned over moderate heat, and used to thicken sauces.

SAUTÉ to brown a food in oil, butter or a mixture of both, in order to seal in juices.

SCALOPPINE this refers to thin boneless slices of meat, usually veal. These cuts of meat can also be called scallops, for example *veal scallops*.

SEAR to cook briefly over very high heat to seal the juices in meat.

SEED to remove seeds.

SHALLOTS of the shallot " family ", 2 varieties are here called for : (1) the green onion, a young or spring onion with a small white bulb and long green stem, and (2) the French (dry) shallot, a small dried onion with reddish-brown skin that has a slight garlic taste. In recipes specifying only " shallot ", choose either variety according to preference.

SHRED to cut food into slivers.

SIFT to remove lumps and earate dry ingredients by passing them through a mesh sifter or strainer.

SIMMER to heat a liquid just below boiling point, so that the surface trembles but does not bubble.

SKIM to remove fat or scum from the surface of a liquid using a spoon.

SKIN to remove the skin of poultry or fish prior to cooking.

STIR-FRY to cook food in a skillet or wok, tossing or stirring quickly.

TENDER-CRISP doneness of vegetables that are cooked enough to be tender on the surface but crisp in the middle.

THICKEN to give a liquid more body by blending in beaten egg, kneaded butter or cornstarch, stirring constantly to keep it smooth.

TOSS (1) to mix foods lightly, using spoons or forks in a lifting motion ; (2) to turn over food in a pan by flipping food into the air.

TRUSS to secure poultry with string or with small skewers, either to hold its shape while cooking or to seal in stuffing.

WELL cavity made in flour to pour in liquid ingredients.

SOUPS & APPETIZERS

Soups and appetizers set the pace for the balance of the meal. For this reason it is important to choose dishes which are complementary to the cuisine to follow.

Whether you desire a smooth and creamy soup or one that is clear but substantial, there are several delicious soups in these pages suitable to both the occasion and your taste buds.

The appetizers sections feature a variety of hot and cold menu items. These dishes may be served as feature dishes at luncheons or afternoon teas, or as appetizers during more formal occasions. Whatever your requirements, you are sure to find many wonderful dishes to enhance any event.

The idea of finger foods is said to have begun in Russia when small portions of food were served before the formal dinner was to begin. Today, finger foods form a very important part of the entertaining menu. Whether you are serving finger foods for a casual affair or gourmet delights for a formal evening's entertainment, you are sure to find what you desire in this chapter.

Finger Foods

Tomatoes Tapenade

24 APPETIZERS	
24	cherry tomatoes
1/4 cup	(60 mL) black olives
1	anchovy fillet
1	garlic clove, finely chopped
1 tsp	(5 mL) olive oil
2 tsp	(10 mL) parsley, chopped
1 tsp	(5 mL) capers, chopped
1/4 tsp	(1 mL) onion salt
	dash of Worcestershire sauce
	fresh ground pepper

- Cut a 1/4-inch (0.5 cm) slice off the top of each tomato, reserving caps. With a small spoon or knife, scoop out enough tomato pulp to allow stuffing. Set aside.
- Finely chop olives, anchovy and garlic. Mix well. Fold in remaining ingredients.
- Fill each tomato with 1 tsp (5 mL) olive stuffing. Top with reserved caps. Serve.

Recipe shown above

VARIATION
- Use pimento-stuffed olives. Add 1 tbsp (15 mL) grated Parmesan to stuffing.

NUTRITION	
CALORIES PER SERVING: 39	
FAT: 1 *g*	CAL. FROM FAT: 18%
PROTEIN: 1 *g*	CHOLESTEROL: 0 *mg*
SODIUM: 101 *mg*	CARBOHYDRATES: 8 *g*

Small Cheese Puffs

36 APPETIZERS	
1/2 cup	(125 mL) butter
1/2	onion, sliced
1/2 cup	(125 mL) flour
2 1/2 cups	(625 mL) milk
2 cups	(500 mL) Gruyère cheese, grated
1 tsp	(5 mL) salt
1/2 tsp	(2 mL) pepper
36	puffs *(p. 356)*

- In a skillet, melt butter. Over low heat, cook onion without browning 3 minutes. Discard onion.
- Sprinkle melted butter with flour, mixing until flour is absorbed. Cook 1 minute. Fold in milk. Stirring constantly, continue cooking until sauce thickens.
- Stir in cheese and seasonings. Once cheese has fully melted, remove from heat. Let stand until mixture sets.
- Puncture a small hole in the side of each puff. Using a pastry bag with a plain nozzle, stuff cheese mixture into puffs. Refrigerate 1 hour.
- Meanwhile, preheat oven to 350 °F (175 °C).
- Transfer cheese puffs to a baking sheet. Cover with aluminum foil. Bake 20 minutes, removing foil after 15 minutes. Serve piping hot.

NUTRITION	
CALORIES PER SERVING: 324	
FAT: 23 *g*	CAL. FROM FAT: 64%
PROTEIN: 6 *g*	CHOLESTEROL: 16 *mg*
SODIUM: 249 *mg*	CARBOHYDRATES: 24 *g*

Tuna Balls

24 APPETIZERS	
8 oz	(225 g) cream cheese, softened
1/2 cup	(125 mL) canned tuna, drained
1/4 cup	(60 mL) mayonnaise
1 tsp	(5 mL) tarragon
	pinch of pepper
1/4 cup	(60 mL) toasted almonds

- In a bowl, combine first 5 ingredients. Mix to a firm paste.
- Shape into 24 balls. Roll in toasted almonds. Refrigerate 1 hour. Serve.

NUTRITION	
CALORIES PER SERVING: 63	
FAT: 6 g	CAL. FROM FAT: 84%
PROTEIN: 2 g	CHOLESTEROL: 12 mg
SODIUM: 54 mg	CARBOHYDRATES: 1 g

Egg Balls

24 APPETIZERS	
6	hard-boiled eggs
1 tsp	(5 mL) parsley, chopped
1 tbsp	(15 mL) onion, chopped
1/2 cup	(125 mL) ham, finely chopped
1/4 cup	(60 mL) mayonnaise
	salt and pepper
	pecans, chopped

- Finely mince or chop hard-boiled eggs. Add parsley, onion, ham and mayonnaise, mixing well. Season to taste.
- Shape into 24 balls. Roll in chopped pecans. Refrigerate 1 hour. Serve.

NUTRITION	
CALORIES PER SERVING: 45	
FAT: 4 g	CAL. FROM FAT: 79%
PROTEIN: 2 g	CHOLESTEROL: 48 mg
SODIUM: 76 mg	CARBOHYDRATES: 0 g

Raspberry-Cheese Dip with Fresh Fruit

ABOUT 2 CUPS (500 ML)

6 oz	(165 g) cream cheese, softened
1 tbsp	(15 mL) brown sugar
1/2 tbsp	(2 mL) ground ginger
1 tbsp	(15 mL) red wine vinegar
1 cup	(250 mL) raspberries, crushed
	fresh fruit, in bite-size pieces

- In a bowl, mix first 4 ingredients. Blend in raspberries. Refrigerate 30 minutes.
- Serve dip with fresh fruit skewered onto long toothpicks.

NUTRITION	
CALORIES PER 1/3 CUP SERVING: 305	
FAT: 10 g	CAL. FROM FAT: 28%
PROTEIN: 3 g	CHOLESTEROL: 31 mg
SODIUM: 100 mg	CARBOHYDRATES: 54 g

Chicken Salad in Mini Pita Breads

24 APPETIZERS

12	mini pita breads
1 cup	(250 mL) cooked chicken, diced
1	green onion, chopped
1	garlic clove, chopped
1/4 cup	(60 mL) tomatoes, diced
2 tbsp	(30 mL) mayonnaise
1 tbsp	(15 mL) orange juice

- Cut each pita bread into half-moons. Set aside. Mix remaining ingredients. Season to taste. Spoon chicken salad into each small pocket. Serve.

NUTRITION	
CALORIES PER SERVING: 107	
FAT: 2 g	CAL. FROM FAT: 17%
PROTEIN: 5 g	CHOLESTEROL: 5 mg
SODIUM: 180 mg	CARBOHYDRATES: 17 g

Oyster Crackers

20 APPETIZERS

3 1/2 oz	(104 g) canned smoked oysters
3 tbsp	(45 mL) mayonnaise
1 tbsp	(15 mL) chili sauce
4	drops of Tabasco sauce
2	lettuce leaves
20	crackers
3	thin lemon slices

- Drain oysters on a paper towel. Set aside.
- Blend mayonnaise with chili and Tabasco sauces.
- Cut lettuce into 20 cracker-size pieces. Set aside.
- Cut lemon slices into triangles.
- Spread each cracker with 3/4 tsp (3 mL) sauce. Cover with lettuce. Top with one oyster. Garnish with lemon. Serve.

NUTRITION	
CALORIES PER SERVING: 35	
FAT: 2 g	CAL. FROM FAT: 50%
PROTEIN: 1 g	CHOLESTEROL: 3 mg
SODIUM: 57 mg	CARBOHYDRATES: 4 g

Prosciutto Breadsticks

24 APPETIZERS

24	very thin slices of Prosciutto ham
2 tbsp	(30 mL) Dijon mustard
24	sesame breadsticks

- Spread each slice of Prosciutto with a thin coat of mustard.
- Mustard side in, tightly roll ham slices around breadsticks, so ham will not come loose. Serve.

NUTRITION	
CALORIES PER SERVING: 44	
FAT: 1 g	CAL. FROM FAT: 29%
PROTEIN: 3 g	CHOLESTEROL: 7 mg
SODIUM: 310 mg	CARBOHYDRATES: 4 g

Surprise Snails Kabobs

12 APPETIZERS

36	snails
3 tbsp	(45 mL) butter, melted
1	garlic clove, chopped
1 tsp	(5 mL) parsley, chopped
	pinch of pepper
36	spinach leaves, stalks removed

- In a microwave-safe dish, combine snails, butter, garlic, parsley and pepper. Cook 1 minute, on HIGH. Let stand 2 minutes.
- Meanwhile, in a saucepan filled with lightly-salted boiling water, blanch spinach leaves 30 seconds or so. Remove spinach. Immerse in a bowl of ice-cold water. Drain well. Pat dry.
- Wrap each snail in a spinach leaf. Thread onto long toothpicks or small wooden skewers, 3 escargots per kabob.
- Cook in microwave oven 45 seconds, on HIGH. Let stand 1 minute. Serve.

NUTRITION	
CALORIES PER SERVING: 38	
FAT: 3 g	CAL. FROM FAT: 70%
PROTEIN: 3 g	CHOLESTEROL: 8 mg
SODIUM: 32 mg	CARBOHYDRATES: 1 g

Vegetable Kabobs with Blue Cheese Dip

12 APPETIZERS

6	zucchini rounds
12	broccoli florets
12	cauliflower florets
12	cherry tomatoes
12	button mushrooms

Dip

1/2 cup	(125 mL) firm-style plain yogurt
1 tbsp	(15 mL) Blue cheese, crumbled
1 tsp	(5 mL) lemon juice
	dash of Worcestershire sauce
	salt and pepper

- Cut zucchini rounds into half-moons.
- In a saucepan filled with lightly-salted boiling water, blanch broccoli and cauliflower florets 1 minute. Add zucchini. Continue cooking 30 seconds or so.
- Remove vegetables from saucepan. Immerse in a bowl of ice-cold water. Once cool, drain well. Pat dry.
- Thread one of each vegetable onto small skewers. Set aside.
- In a food processor, blend dip ingredients.
- Serve kabobs with dip on the side.

NUTRITION	
CALORIES PER SERVING: 118	
FAT: 2 g	CAL. FROM FAT: 11%
PROTEIN: 9 g	CHOLESTEROL: 2 mg
SODIUM: 92 mg	CARBOHYDRATES: 23 g

Clockwise from upper left :
Vegetable Kabobs with Blue Cheese Dip,
Surprise Escargot Kabobs, Oyster Crackers,
Chicken Salad in Mini Pita Breads

Pâté-stuffed Mushrooms

24 APPETIZERS	
24	large mushrooms
4 oz	(115 g) liver pâté, softened
1	shallot, finely chopped
2 tbsp	(30 mL) bread crumbs
1/2 cup	(125 mL) Brick cheese, grated

- Preheat oven to 400 °F (205 °C).
- Remove mushroom stems, reserving caps. Coarsely chop stems.
- In a bowl, mix stems with liver pâté, shallot and bread crumbs.
- Stuff mushroom caps with pâté mixture. Sprinkle with cheese. Cook in oven 5 minutes. Serve.

NUTRITION	
CALORIES PER SERVING: 35	
FAT: 2 g	CAL. FROM FAT: 53%
PROTEIN: 2 g	CHOLESTEROL: 14 mg
SODIUM: 52 mg	CARBOHYDRATES: 2 g

Apricot-glazed Ham Meatballs

24 APPETIZERS	
1 lb	(450 g) ground ham
2	eggs
1 cup	(250 mL) corn flakes, crumbled
2 tbsp	(30 mL) onion, finely chopped
1 tsp	(5 mL) parsley
	pinch of seasoning salt
3/4 tsp	(3 mL) mustard
1/2 cup	(125 mL) commercial barbecue sauce
1 cup	(250 mL) apricot jam

- Preheat oven to 350 °F (175 °C).
- In a bowl, mix first 7 ingredients. Shape into 1-inch (2.5 cm) balls.
- Transfer to a buttered roasting pan. Lightly brown in oven 15 minutes.
- Meanwhile, blend barbecue sauce and apricot jam. Set aside.
- Remove meatballs from oven. Coat with sauce. Continue cooking 5-10 minutes. Serve meatballs with individual toothpicks.

NUTRITION	
CALORIES PER SERVING: 80	
FAT: 1 g	CAL. FROM FAT: 16%
PROTEIN: 5 g	CHOLESTEROL: 24 mg
SODIUM: 368 mg	CARBOHYDRATES: 13 g

Cheese Twists

48 APPETIZERS

2 cups	(500 mL) cheese, grated
2 cups	(500 mL) all-purpose flour
6 tbsp	(90 mL) corn oil
1/4 tsp	(1 mL) salt
	pinch of cayenne
1 cup	(250 mL) cold water
1	egg yolk
1 tbsp	(15 mL) milk
	paprika

- Preheat oven to 375 °F (190 ° C).
- In a bowl, mix first 5 ingredients. Gradually blend in water, stirring to a soft dough.
- With a rolling pin, flatten dough into a rectangle, 1/8-inch (0.25 cm) thick. Cut into strips, 6-inch (15 cm) long by 1/2-inch (1.25 cm) wide. Twist.
- In a small bowl, beat together egg and milk.
- Transfer cheese twists to a greased baking sheet. Brush with egg mixture. Sprinkle with paprika. Lightly brown in oven 15-20 minutes. Serve hot or cold.

NUTRITION	
CALORIES PER SERVING: 54	
FAT: 3 *g*	CAL. FROM FAT: 57%
PROTEIN: 2 *g*	CHOLESTEROL: 9 *mg*
SODIUM: 41 *mg*	CARBOHYDRATES: 4 *g*

Golden Cheese Toast

12 APPETIZERS

1 cup	(250 mL) Cheddar cheese, grated
2	eggs, beaten
1 tsp	(5 mL) Worcestershire sauce
1/4 tsp	(1 mL) salt
1/2 tsp	(2 mL) dry mustard
12	bread slices
6	bacon slices

- Preheat oven to 475 °F (245 ° C).
- In a bowl, mix first 5 ingredients. Set aside.
- With a glass or pastry cutter, cut bread into 3-inch (7.5 cm) rounds. Spread with cheese mixture.
- Cut bacon slices in half. Top each bread round with a half-slice of bacon. Cook in oven 15 minutes or until bacon is crisp. Serve.

NUTRITION	
CALORIES PER SERVING: 134	
FAT: 6 *g*	CAL. FROM FAT: 43%
PROTEIN: 6 *g*	CHOLESTEROL: 43 *mg*
SODIUM: 301 *mg*	CARBOHYDRATES: 13 *g*

Assembling Canapés

- Preheat oven to BROIL.
- Lightly butter bread slices. Toast in oven 2 minutes or so per side.
- Add topping. Remove crusts to make straight, even sides.
- Cut each toast slice into 4 small, equal triangles.

Vegetable Canapés

24 APPETIZERS

3 tbsp	(45 mL) carrot, grated
3 tbsp	(45 mL) green bell pepper, chopped
3 tbsp	(45 mL) tomato, diced small
1/4 cup	(60 mL) cream cheese, softened
2	dashes of Worcestershire sauce
	salt and pepper
6	bread slices, toasted
24	celery slices, cut diagonally
4-6	mushrooms, minced

- Mix first 5 ingredients. Season to taste with salt and pepper. Spread mixture on toast. Cut into canapés.
- Garnish each canapé with a celery slice and a mushroom slice. Serve.

NUTRITION	
CALORIES PER SERVING: 28	
FAT: 1 g	CAL. FROM FAT: 34%
PROTEIN: 1 g	CHOLESTEROL: 3 mg
SODIUM: 55 mg	CARBOHYDRATES: 4 g

Shrimp Canapés

24 APPETIZERS

1/2 cup	(125 mL) shrimp, chopped
3 tbsp	(45 mL) cream cheese, softened
1 tbsp	(15 mL) chili sauce
1 tsp	(5 mL) horseradish in vinegar
	salt and pepper
6	bread slices, toasted
24	baby shrimp
24	fresh parsley sprigs

- Mix first 4 ingredients. Season to taste with salt and pepper. Spread mixture on toast. Cut into canapés.
- Garnish canapés with shrimp and parsley. Serve.

NUTRITION	
CALORIES PER SERVING: 45	
FAT: 1 g	CAL. FROM FAT: 21%
PROTEIN: 4 g	CHOLESTEROL: 20 mg
SODIUM: 80 mg	CARBOHYDRATES: 5 g

Liver Pâté Canapés

24 APPETIZERS

1 1/2 cups	(375 mL) liver pâté
6	bread slices, toasted
12	small gherkins

- Spread pâté on toast. Cut into canapés.
- Slice gherkins in half lengthwise. Cut each half into a decorative fan shape. Garnish canapés. Serve.

NUTRITION	
CALORIES PER SERVING: 67	
FAT: 4 g	CAL. FROM FAT: 52%
PROTEIN: 2 g	CHOLESTEROL: 33 mg
SODIUM: 195 mg	CARBOHYDRATES: 6 g

Cheese and Spinach Canapés

24 APPETIZERS

3/4 cup	(180 mL) cream cheese, softened
1/4 cup	(60 mL) goat cheese, softened
1/3 cup	(80 mL) spinach, finely shredded
2 dashes	Worcestershire sauce
6	bread slices, toasted
6	cherry tomatoes

- Mix first 4 ingredients. Season to taste with salt and pepper. Spread mixture on toast. Cut into canapés.
- Garnish each canapé with a tomato wedge. Serve.

NUTRITION	
CALORIES PER SERVING: 58	
FAT: 3 g	CAL. FROM FAT: 50%
PROTEIN: 2 g	CHOLESTEROL: 10 mg
SODIUM: 71 mg	CARBOHYDRATES: 6 g

Sausage Canapés

24 APPETIZERS

1/4 cup	(60 mL) mustard
6	bread slices, toasted
6-12	salami slices
1/3 cup	(80 mL) mayonnaise
24	black olives, sliced

- Spread mustard on toast. Cover with salami. Cut into canapés.
- Using a pastry bag, pipe decorative lines of mayonnaise onto canapés. Garnish with 4 olive slices. Serve.

NUTRITION	
CALORIES PER SERVING: 81	
FAT: 6 g	CAL. FROM FAT: 68%
PROTEIN: 3 g	CHOLESTEROL: 10 mg
SODIUM: 272 mg	CARBOHYDRATES: 4 g

Cucumber Canapés

24 APPETIZERS

1/2	cucumber
1/2 cup	(125 mL) cream cheese, softened
2 dashes	Worcestershire sauce
3/4 tsp	(3 mL) chives
6	bread slices, toasted
24	fresh dill sprigs

- Set aside 12 thin slices of cucumber. Peel remainder. Remove seeds. Mash. Mix with cheese and seasonings. Spread mixture on toast. Cut into canapés.
- Garnish each canapé with a half-slice cucumber and a dill sprig. Serve.

NUTRITION	
CALORIES PER SERVING: 35	
FAT: 2 g	CAL. FROM FAT: 48%
PROTEIN: 1 g	CHOLESTEROL: 5 mg
SODIUM: 57 mg	CARBOHYDRATES: 4 g

Smoked Salmon Canapés

24 APPETIZERS

1/4 cup	(60 mL) mayonnaise
6	bread slices, toasted
6	smoked salmon slices
1/4 cup	(60 mL) onion, chopped
3 tbsp	(45 mL) capers
1 tbsp	(15 mL) lemon juice

- Spread mayonnaise on toast. Cover with salmon. Cut into canapés.
- Garnish each canapé with chopped onion and 3-4 capers. Lightly sprinkle with lemon juice. Serve.

NUTRITION	
CALORIES PER SERVING: 42	
FAT: 2 g	CAL. FROM FAT: 52%
PROTEIN: 2 g	CHOLESTEROL: 2 mg
SODIUM: 112 mg	CARBOHYDRATES: 3 g

W hat is more comforting than a steaming bowl of soup on a cold winter day?

Soups may be served in the summer or winter. In fact, all of the cream soups found in this section can be served cold. Leek Soup (p. 30) is a good example of this versatility.

Soups are ideal to use up leftover meat, noodles, rice, and cooked vegetables. They are easy to freeze and can be prepared in advance.

To reduce the sodium and fat content in soups, use home-made soup stock that you have defatted.

Good Health Soup

4 SERVINGS

2	zucchini, diced
2	medium-size potatoes, peeled, diced
2	medium-size onions, diced
2	carrots, peeled, diced
	water
2 cups	(500 mL) chicken broth
	salt and pepper
	fresh parsley sprigs

- In a large saucepan, cover vegetables with water. Bring to a boil. Cover. Over low heat, simmer 10 minutes. Remove from heat. Let stand to cool slightly.

- In a food processor, purée mixture. Add chicken broth. Season to taste with salt and pepper.

- Return soup to saucepan. Reheat. Serve garnished with a parsley sprig.

NUTRITION	
CALORIES PER SERVING: 175	
FAT: 2 g	CAL. FROM FAT: 12%
PROTEIN: 6 g	CHOLESTEROL: 6 mg
SODIUM: 91 mg	CARBOHYDRATES: 36 g

Leek Soup

6 SERVINGS

2 tsp	(10 mL)	butter
3		leeks, minced
1		small onion, minced
2		potatoes, peeled, diced
1		celery stalk, minced
2 cups	(500 mL)	chicken broth
		salt and pepper
2 cups	(500 mL)	milk
		parsley, chives or fresh basil, chopped

- In a saucepan, melt butter. Lightly cook vegetables.

- Add chicken broth. Season to taste with salt and pepper. Bring to a boil. Cover. Over low heat, simmer 15 minutes or until vegetables are tender.

- Meanwhile, in a small saucepan, heat milk without boiling. Set aside.

- With a pestle, mash vegetables. Fold in warm milk. Simmer 10-15 minutes. Sprinkle with chopped parsley. Serve.

Recipe shown above

VARIATION
- Replace milk with tomato juice.

NUTRITION	
CALORIES PER SERVING: 190	
FAT: 16 g	CAL. FROM FAT: 26%
PROTEIN: 7 g	CHOLESTEROL: 19 mg
SODIUM: 116 mg	CARBOHYDRATES: 30 g

Green Soup

6-8 SERVINGS

6 cups	(1.5 L) chicken broth
4	carrots, peeled, coarsely chopped
	whites of 3 leeks, washed, chopped
1	onion, chopped
2 cups	(500 mL) fresh spinach, chopped
1	lettuce, chopped
4	potatoes, peeled, diced
2	turnips, peeled, chopped
1	parsnip, peeled, chopped
	salt and fresh ground pepper
1 cup	(250 mL) skim milk
2	shallots, chopped (optional)

■ In a saucepan, heat broth. Add vegetables. Bring to a boil. Cover. Over low heat, simmer 20 minutes or until vegetables are tender. Let stand to cool slightly.

■ In a blender, purée mixture. Season to taste with salt and pepper. Return soup to saucepan. Reheat.

■ Pour into soup tureen. Swirl milk into mixture. Sprinkle with chopped shallots, if desired. Serve.

NUTRITION	
CALORIES PER SERVING: 251	
FAT: 4 g	CAL. FROM FAT: 13%
PROTEIN: 9 g	CHOLESTEROL: 10 mg
SODIUM: 131 mg	CARBOHYDRATES: 250 g

Fennel Soup

6 SERVINGS

¹/₂ cup	(125 mL) onions
1 cup	(250 mL) carrots
1 cup	(250 mL) fennel bulb
2	potatoes, peeled
¹/₄ cup	(60 mL) butter
4 cups	(1 L) chicken or beef broth
	salt and pepper
	milk
2 tbsp	(30 mL) chives, chopped

■ Coarsely chop vegetables. Set aside, reserving potatoes separately.

■ In a saucepan, melt butter. Add vegetables, except potatoes. Over low heat, cook 15-20 minutes until tender but not browned.

■ Add broth and potatoes. Season to taste with salt and pepper. Bring to a boil. Cover. Over low heat, simmer until potatoes are tender.

■ In a blender, purée mixture. Add enough milk to make a thick, creamy soup. Return to saucepan. Reheat without boiling. Sprinkle with chopped chives. Serve.

NUTRITION	
CALORIES PER SERVING: 248	
FAT: 13 g	CAL. FROM FAT: 47%
PROTEIN: 8 g	CHOLESTEROL: 36 mg
SODIUM: 170 mg	CARBOHYDRATES: 26 g

Creamy Winter Vegetable Soup

6-8 SERVINGS	
1 tbsp	(15 mL) butter
¹/₂ cup	(125 mL) carrots, diced
¹/₂ cup	(125 mL) turnip, diced
¹/₂ cup	(125 mL) potatoes, peeled, diced
¹/₂ cup	(125 mL) celery, diced
¹/₂ cup	(125 mL) chicken broth
1 ¹/₂ cups	(375 mL) milk
¹/₄ tsp	(1 mL) nutmeg
	salt and pepper
1 tbsp	(15 mL) sugar
1	egg yolk
	chervil, chopped

- In a saucepan, melt butter. Stirring often, cook vegetables 4-5 minutes.
- Add chicken broth, milk, nutmeg, salt, pepper and sugar. Bring to a boil. Cover. Over low heat, simmer 20 minutes, stirring occasionally.
- In a blender, purée mixture. Return to saucepan. Reheat.
- In a bowl, beat egg yolk. Fold into soup. Sprinkle with chervil. Serve.

NUTRITION	
CALORIES PER SERVING: 75	
FAT: 4 g	CAL. FROM FAT: 46%
PROTEIN: 3 g	CHOLESTEROL: 37 mg
SODIUM: 76 mg	CARBOHYDRATES: 8 g

Carrot and Parsnip Soup

6-8 SERVINGS	
¹/₄ cup	(60 mL) butter
1	medium-size onion, sliced
1	small garlic clove, chopped
5 cups	(1.25 L) water
1 ¹/₂ cups	(375 mL) carrots, sliced
1 cup	(250 mL) parsnip, minced
¹/₄ cup	(60 mL) long-grain rice
2 tbsp	(30 mL) chicken broth concentrate
	salt and pepper
	parsley, chopped

- In a saucepan, melt butter. Sauté onion and garlic.
- Add remaining ingredients, except parsley. Bring to a boil. Cover. Over low heat, simmer 20-30 minutes.
- In a blender, purée mixture. Sprinkle with chopped parsley. Serve.

NUTRITION	
CALORIES PER SERVING: 102	
FAT: 6 g	CAL. FROM FAT: 50%
PROTEIN: 1 g	CHOLESTEROL: 15 mg
SODIUM: 744 mg	CARBOHYDRATES: 12 g

Cream of Lettuce Soup

6 SERVINGS	
3 tbsp	(45 mL) butter
2	onions, chopped
3 cups	(750 mL) faded lettuce, hand-torn
3 tbsp	(45 mL) rice, cooked
10 oz	(280 g) frozen green peas
4 cups	(1 L) chicken broth
1 tbsp	(15 mL) dill, chopped
	salt and pepper
	pinch of nutmeg
	peel of ½ lemon, grated
1 cup	(250 mL) heavy cream
1	lemon, thinly sliced
	fresh dill sprigs

- In a saucepan, melt butter. Sauté onions. While stirring, add lettuce. Continue cooking until limp.
- Fold in rice, peas and broth. Season with dill, salt, pepper, nutmeg and lemon peel. Bring to a boil. Cover. Over low heat, simmer 20 minutes.
- In a blender, purée mixture. Return to saucepan. Reheat. Fold in cream. Garnish with thin lemon slices and dill sprigs. Serve.

VARIATION
- Without reheating, refrigerate puréed vegetables 1 hour. Add cream and garnish. Serve chilled.

NUTRITION	
CALORIES PER SERVING: 353	
FAT: 24 g	CAL. FROM FAT: 54%
PROTEIN: 9 g	CHOLESTEROL: 78 mg
SODIUM: 206 mg	CARBOHYDRATES: 37 g

Cauliflower and Shallot Soup

8 SERVINGS	
2 tbsp	(30 mL) butter
1	small onion, minced
3	potatoes, peeled, minced
1	small cauliflower, in florets
	salt and pepper
6 cups	(1.5 L) chicken broth, heated
½ tsp	(2 mL) basil
½ tsp	(2 mL) thyme
1	bay leaf
¼ cup	(60 mL) shallots, chopped

- In a saucepan, over moderate heat, melt butter. Add onion. Cover. Cook 3-4 minutes until tender but not browned.
- Add potatoes and cauliflower. Continue cooking 1-2 minutes. Season with salt and pepper.
- Pour in broth. Add mixed herbs. Bring to a boil. Cover. Over low heat, simmer 40 minutes.
- In a blender, purée mixture. Adjust seasoning. Sprinkle with chopped shallots. Serve.

VARIATION
- Replace cauliflower with broccoli, and shallots with chopped parsley.

NUTRITION	
CALORIES PER SERVING: 184	
FAT: 6 g	CAL. FROM FAT: 29%
PROTEIN: 5 g	CHOLESTEROL: 17 mg
SODIUM: 97 mg	CARBOHYDRATES: 30 g

Cream of Beet Soup

4-6 SERVINGS

3 tbsp	(45 mL)	butter
1/4 cup	(60 mL)	shallots, chopped
8 oz	(225 g)	beet leaves
8 oz	(225 g)	watercress
2 tbsp	(30 mL)	flour
2 cups	(500 mL)	milk
1 tbsp	(15 mL)	fresh parsley, chopped
1/2 tsp	(2 mL)	salt
1/4 tsp	(1 mL)	thyme
1/4 tsp	(1 mL)	marjoram
		fresh ground pepper

- In a large, microwave-safe saucepan, spread butter. Sprinkle with shallots. Top with beet leaves and watercress. Cover saucepan with plastic wrap. Cook 4 minutes, on HIGH.

- Remove from oven. Stir. Continue cooking 1-2 minutes or until vegetables are tender.

- In a blender, purée mixture. Return to saucepan. Stirring constantly, fold in flour. Add remaining ingredients.

- Simmer 8 minutes, on MEDIUM. Stir once during cooking. Serve.

NUTRITION	
CALORIES PER SERVING: 121	
FAT: 8 *g*	CAL. FROM FAT: 61%
PROTEIN: 4 *g*	CHOLESTEROL: 26 *mg*
SODIUM: 323 *mg*	CARBOHYDRATES: 8 *g*

Recipe shown above

Cream of Turnip Soup

4-6 SERVINGS

1 1/2 cups	(375 mL)	turnips, diced
1 cup	(250 mL)	potatoes, peeled, diced
2 cups	(500 mL)	water
1		bay leaf
		salt and pepper
1		egg yolk
1/4 cup	(60 mL)	light cream
		fresh parsley sprigs

- In a saucepan, cover vegetables with water. Bring to a rolling boil. Season with bay leaf, salt and pepper. Reduce heat. Simmer 10 minutes. Remove bay leaf.

- In a blender, purée mixture. Return to saucepan. Set aside.

- In a bowl, beat together egg yolk and cream. Fold into vegetables. Over low heat, while stirring, reheat without boiling. Garnish with parsley sprigs. Serve.

NUTRITION	
CALORIES PER SERVING: 72	
FAT: 3 *g*	CAL. FROM FAT: 37%
PROTEIN: 3 *g*	CHOLESTEROL: 42 *mg*
SODIUM: 73 *mg*	CARBOHYDRATES: 10 *g*

Homestyle Cream of Tomato Soup

4 SERVINGS

6	tomatoes, peeled, chopped
	or
12 oz	(375 mL) canned tomatoes, drained
1 tbsp	(15 mL) butter
1	onion, finely chopped
1	garlic clove, minced
2 tbsp	(30 mL) tomato paste
½ tsp	(2 mL) sugar
	salt and pepper
¼ tsp	(1 mL) thyme
½ cup	(125 mL) vegetable or chicken broth
½ cup	(125 mL) light cream
	tomato, sliced
	basil and fresh parsley, chopped

■ To peel fresh tomatoes, arrange in a microwave-safe bowl. Cover with hot water. Seal bowl with plastic wrap. Bring to a boil, on HIGH. Remove. Peel tomatoes under running cold water.

■ In a second bowl, mix butter, onion and garlic. Cook in oven 1 minute, on HIGH.

■ Remove from oven. Add tomatoes, tomato paste, sugar and seasonings. Continue cooking 7 minutes, on HIGH. Stir once.

■ In a blender, purée mixture. Fold in broth and cream. Serve hot or chilled, garnished with a tomato slice, basil and parsley.

NUTRITION	
CALORIES PER SERVING: 183	
FAT: 10 g	CAL. FROM FAT: 42%
PROTEIN: 5 g	CHOLESTEROL: 28 mg
SODIUM: 217 mg	CARBOHYDRATES: 25 g

Cream of Potato Soup

4-6 SERVINGS

3 cups	(750 mL) water
3 cups	(750 mL) potatoes, peeled, diced
2	onion slices
2 tbsp	(30 mL) butter
3 tbsp	(45 mL) flour
2 cups	(500 mL) condensed milk
½ tsp	(2 mL) celery salt
	salt and pepper
1 tbsp	(15 mL) parsley, chopped

■ In a large saucepan, combine water, potatoes and onion. Cook until vegetables are tender.

■ Strain vegetables, reserving 2 cups (500 mL) cooking liquid. Pass vegetables through a sieve in order to obtain 2 cups (500 mL) pulp. Set aside.

■ In a double-boiler, melt butter. Sprinkle with flour. Mix until well-blended. Slowly fold in milk and reserved cooking liquid. Simmer until mixture thickens.

■ Add vegetable pulp, stirring constantly. Season to taste with salt and pepper. Sprinkle with parsley. Serve very hot.

NUTRITION	
CALORIES PER SERVING: 190	
FAT: 7 g	CAL. FROM FAT: 31%
PROTEIN: 6 g	CHOLESTEROL: 21 mg
SODIUM: 253 mg	CARBOHYDRATES: 28 g

Spinach Soup with Dumplings

6 SERVINGS	
1	knob of butter
1	onion, finely chopped
10 oz	(280 g) fresh or frozen spinach
3/4 cup	(180 mL) all-purpose flour or wheat flour
1	egg
4 cups	(1 L) milk
	salt and pepper

- In a saucepan, melt butter. Sauté onion. Add spinach. Cover. Over moderate heat, continue cooking until spinach is tender. Stir occasionally.

- Meanwhile, pour flour into a mixing bowl. Make a well in the center. Place egg into the well. With a fork, mix egg and flour. Shape into dumplings.

- Add milk to cooked spinach. Stirring constantly, bring milk to a foam. Season.

- Add dumplings one at a time. Cover. Remove from heat. Let stand 5 minutes. Serve.

NUTRITION	
CALORIES PER SERVING: 205	
FAT: 8 g	CAL. FROM FAT: 36%
PROTEIN: 10 g	CHOLESTEROL: 57 mg
SODIUM: 177 mg	CARBOHYDRATES: 24 g

Pesto Soup

6 SERVINGS	
3 cups	(750 mL) vegetable broth
1 cup	(250 mL) chicken broth
1/2 cup	(125 mL) vermicelli
1/2 cup	(125 mL) fresh basil leaves
3 tbsp	(45 mL) pine nuts
3	garlic cloves
1 tbsp	(15 mL) Parmesan cheese, grated
2 tsp	(10 mL) olive oil
	dash of Worcestershire sauce
	salt and pepper

- In a saucepan, bring both broths to a boil. Add vermicelli. Simmer 10 minutes.
- Reserve 2 basil leaves and 2 tsp (10 mL) pine nuts for decoration.
- In a food processor, combine remaining basil leaves and pine nuts with garlic, Parmesan and oil. Process. Blend into broth. Simmer 5 minutes.
- Meanwhile, finely shred reserved basil leaves. In a bowl, mix with pine nuts. Set aside.
- Season soup with Worcestershire sauce, salt and pepper. Sprinkle with basil and pine nut garnish. Serve.

NUTRITION	
CALORIES PER SERVING: 131	
FAT: 5 g	CAL. FROM FAT: 28%
PROTEIN: 6 g	CHOLESTEROL: 3 mg
SODIUM: 182 mg	CARBOHYDRATES: 24 g

Chicken-Liver Soup

6 SERVINGS	
3 cups	(750 mL) chicken broth
1 cup	(250 mL) beef broth
3 tbsp	(45 mL) brown rice
4 oz	(115 g) chicken livers
2 tsp	(10 mL) olive oil
1	garlic clove, chopped
2 tbsp	(30 mL) onion, chopped
1/2 tsp	(2 mL) coriander, chopped
	dash of Worcestershire sauce
	sea salt
	fresh ground pepper

- In a saucepan, bring both broths to a boil. Add rice. Simmer 10 minutes or so.
- Meanwhile, trim chicken livers, removing all fat. Cut livers into 4 pieces. Set aside.
- In a skillet, heat oil. Sear chicken livers 4 minutes. Stir in garlic, onion and coriander. Continue cooking 3 minutes or so.
- Add liver mixture to broth. Simmer 10 minutes. Season with Worcestershire sauce, salt and pepper. Serve.

NUTRITION	
CALORIES PER SERVING: 124	
FAT: 6 g	CAL. FROM FAT: 39%
PROTEIN: 7 g	CHOLESTEROL: 92 mg
SODIUM: 68 mg	CARBOHYDRATES: 13 g

Creamy Cabbage Soup

6 SERVINGS	
1	small cabbage
1	medium-size onion
1 1/2 cups	(375 mL) cold water
1/2 tsp	(2 mL) sugar
1/2 tsp	(2 mL) salt
3 tbsp	(45 mL) butter
1/4 cup	(60 mL) flour
2 1/2 cups	(625 mL) milk
	pepper, to taste

- Chop cabbage and onion. In a saucepan, mix vegetables with water, sugar and salt. Bring to a boil. Let reduce 30 minutes or until liquid has almost all evaporated. Remove from heat. Set aside.

- In a second saucepan, melt butter. Mix in flour. Over low heat, fold in milk, stirring constantly. Cook until mixture thickens slightly. Season.

- Pour milk soup over cabbage, mixing gently. Serve hot.

NUTRITION	
CALORIES PER SERVING: 163	
FAT: 9 g	CAL. FROM FAT: 50%
PROTEIN: 6 g	CHOLESTEROL: 29 mg
SODIUM: 312 mg	CARBOHYDRATES: 15 g

From top to bottom :
Creamy Cabbage Soup,
Chicken-Liver Soup,
Pesto Soup

Asparagus Velouté with Croutons

	6 SERVINGS
1 lb	(450 g) asparagus, cut in ½ inch lengths
3 tbsp	(45 mL) butter
½ cup	(125 mL) onions, minced
½ cup	(125 mL) white of leek, julienned
5 cups	(1.25 L) chicken broth, heated
	salt and pepper
½	French baguette
2	garlic cloves
¼ cup	(60 mL) light cream

■ Clean asparagus, reserving tips for decoration.

■ In a saucepan, melt butter. Cook vegetables 2-3 minutes. Cover with hot chicken broth. Season lightly. Bring to a boil. Cover saucepan. Over low heat, simmer 20 minutes.

■ Meanwhile, cut baguette into rounds. Toast in oven. Rub croutons with garlic. In a saucepan filled with lightly-salted boiling water, blanch reserved asparagus tips 1 minute.

■ Fold cream into vegetable broth. Mix until well-blended. Adjust seasoning. Garnish with tips. Serve velouté with croutons on the side.

NUTRITION	
CALORIES PER SERVING: 269	
FAT: 12 g	CAL. FROM FAT: 40%
PROTEIN: 8 g	CHOLESTEROL: 33 mg
SODIUM: 365 mg	CARBOHYDRATES: 34 g

Recipe shown above

Cream of Carrot Soup

	6 SERVINGS
6 tbsp	(90 mL) unsalted butter
2 cups	(500 mL) carrots, diced
½ cup	(125 mL) leeks, minced
¼ cup	(60 mL) onions, minced
10 cups	(2.5 L) chicken broth
¼ cup	(60 mL) rice flour or potato flour
	salt, to taste
½ tsp	(2 mL) pepper

■ In a saucepan, melt half the butter. Cook vegetables until tender but not browned. Add chicken broth. Bring to a boil. Cover. Over low heat, simmer 1 hour.

■ In a bowl, pour 1 cup (250 mL) hot broth. Blend in rice flour. Let stand to cool. Pour slowly into soup, stirring constantly.

■ In a blender, purée soup. Return to saucepan. Adjust seasoning. Simmer 1-2 minutes until creamy smooth. Dot with remaining butter. Serve hot.

NUTRITION	
CALORIES PER SERVING: 229	
FAT: 15 g	CAL. FROM FAT: 54%
PROTEIN: 5 g	CHOLESTEROL: 41 mg
SODIUM: 95 mg	CARBOHYDRATES: 23 g

Vegetable Chowder

4-6 SERVINGS	
2	cubes chicken broth
2 ½ cups	(625 mL) boiling water
3 cups	(750 mL) turnips, minced
2	potatoes, peeled, diced
¼ cup	(60 mL) butter
1	onion, chopped
2	shallots, chopped
3 tbsp	(45 mL) flour
3 cups	(750 mL) milk
	salt and pepper

- Dilute broth cubes in water. Add turnip and potatoes. Bring to a boil. Cover. Over low heat, simmer 15 minutes.

- In a saucepan, melt butter. Sauté onion and shallots 4 minutes. Sprinkle with flour. Mix until well-blended. Slowly fold in milk, stirring constantly. Simmer 10 minutes until mixture thickens.

- Stir into vegetables, mixing until smooth. Season. Serve.

NUTRITION	
CALORIES PER SERVING: 259	
FAT: 12 g	CAL. FROM FAT: 41%
PROTEIN: 8 g	CHOLESTEROL: 37 mg
SODIUM: 596 mg	CARBOHYDRATES: 32 g

Garbanzo Bean Soup

6-8 SERVINGS	
1 tbsp	(15 mL) vegetable oil
⅓ cup	(80 mL) celery, finely chopped
⅓ cup	(80 mL) carrots, finely chopped
⅓ cup	(80 mL) onions, finely chopped
2	garlic cloves, minced
4 cups	(1 L) vegetable broth
2 cups	(500 mL) canned garbanzo beans, drained
1 tbsp	(15 mL) chili sauce
1 tbsp	(15 mL) lemon juice
1 tsp	(5 mL) curry
½ tsp	(2 mL) salt
½ cup	(125 mL) cheese, grated

- In a saucepan, heat oil. Lightly brown vegetables and garlic. Set aside.

- In a second saucepan, mix broth and garbanzo beans. Bring to a boil. Cover. Over low heat, simmer 15 minutes or so.

- Add vegetables and seasonings. Over low heat, continue cooking 30 minutes.

- Pour with grated cheese into soup bowls. Serve.

NUTRITION	
CALORIES PER SERVING: 164	
FAT: 6 g	CAL. FROM FAT: 25%
PROTEIN: 8 g	CHOLESTEROL: 8 mg
SODIUM: 486 mg	CARBOHYDRATES: 29 g

Green Pea Soup

8 SERVINGS	
¼ cup	(60 mL) butter
4 cups	(1 L) lettuce, hand-torn
1	medium-size onion, minced
1 tbsp	(15 mL) flour
1 tsp	(5 mL) sugar
¼ tsp	(1 mL) parsley, chopped
¼ tsp	(1 mL) ground coriander
42 oz	(1.3 L) canned chicken broth
2 ¼ cups	(560 mL) frozen green peas
1 cup	(250 mL) milk
	fresh mint leaves

- In a saucepan, melt butter. Stirring often, lightly brown lettuce and onion.
- Fold in remaining ingredients, except milk and mint leaves. Bring to a boil. Cover. Over low heat, simmer 15 minutes. Reserve a few green peas for decoration.
- In a blender, purée mixture, 1 cup (250 mL) at a time. Return to saucepan. Fold in milk. Reheat without boiling. Serve, garnished with a few green peas and a mint leaf.

NUTRITION	
CALORIES PER SERVING: 166	
FAT: 9 g	CAL. FROM FAT: 47%
PROTEIN: 6 g	CHOLESTEROL: 26 mg
SODIUM: 147 mg	CARBOHYDRATES: 18 g

Hearty Split Pea Soup

6-8 SERVINGS	
2 tbsp	(30 mL) corn oil
2	medium-size onions, minced
1 tsp	(5 mL) celery seeds
1	bay leaf
1 cup	(250 mL) dried split peas
½ cup	(125 mL) hulled or pearl barley
10 cups	(2.5 L) chicken broth
3	carrots, minced
1	potato, peeled, diced
½ tsp	(2 mL) basil
	salt and pepper
2 tbsp	(30 mL) parsley, chopped (optional)

- In a saucepan, heat oil. Lightly brown onions. Add celery seeds, bay leaf, split peas and barley.
- Pour broth into mixture. Bring to a boil. Cover. Over low heat, simmer 75 minutes.
- Add carrots, potato and basil. Continue cooking 15-20 minutes. Season with salt and pepper. Sprinkle with chopped parsley, if desired. Serve.

VARIATION
- Replace chicken broth with any cooking liquid or homemade broth.

NUTRITION	
CALORIES PER SERVING: 328	
FAT: 10 g	CAL. FROM FAT: 25%
PROTEIN: 13 g	CHOLESTEROL: 16 mg
SODIUM: 102 mg	CARBOHYDRATES: 52 g

Red Lentil Soup

8 SERVINGS

1 cup	(250 mL) canned red lentils
4	bacon slices, diced
1	onion, finely chopped
1	garlic clove, minced
1	sweet red pepper, diced
1	celery stalk, finely sliced
6 cups	(1.5 L) chicken broth, degreased
1	bay leaf
	pinch of curcuma
	pinch of thyme
	salt and pepper

Garnish (optional)

sweet gherkins, very finely chopped

parsley, chopped

hard-boiled egg, chopped

onion, finely chopped

▪ Rinse lentils. Drain well. Set aside.

▪ In a saucepan, brown diced bacon until crisp. Remove bacon from saucepan. Drain on a paper towel to soak up as much fat as possible. Set aside.

▪ Remove bacon fat from saucepan, except 1 tbsp (15 mL). While stirring, fry onion, garlic, sweet red pepper and celery 2 minutes. Pour in chicken broth. Bring to a boil. Add lentils and seasonings. Cover. Over low heat, simmer 1 hour, stirring occasionally. Add diced bacon.

▪ If desired, in a small bowl, mix garnish ingredients. Sprinkle over soup. Serve very hot.

Recipe shown above

VARIATION

● For a creamy soup, purée mixture in a blender, before adding diced bacon. Return to saucepan. Heat through. Add bacon and garnish, if desired.

NUTRITION	
CALORIES PER SERVING: 283	
FAT: 7 *g*	CAL. FROM FAT: 20 %
PROTEIN: 17 *g*	CHOLESTEROL: 35 *mg*
SODIUM: 334 *mg*	CARBOHYDRATES: 45 *g*

Sweet-and-sour Soup

6 SERVINGS

3 cups	(750 mL) chicken broth
1 cup	(250 mL) vegetable broth
2 tsp	(10 mL) peanut oil
1/2 tsp	(2 mL) sesame oil
1/4 cup	(60 mL) carrots, julienned
1/4 cup	(60 mL) turnip, julienned
1/4 cup	(60 mL) broccoli florets
1/4 cup	(60 mL) Chinese mushrooms
1	garlic clove, chopped
1 tbsp	(15 mL) rice vinegar
1 tbsp	(15 mL) soy sauce
1/4 cup	(60 mL) tofu, diced
3 tbsp	(45 mL) pickles in vinegar, julienned
	salt and pepper

- In a saucepan, bring both broths to a boil. Reduce heat. Simmer 10 minutes.

- Meanwhile, in a skillet, heat both oils. Sauté vegetables and garlic 2 minutes or so, until vegetables are just tender-crisp. Set aside.

- Pour rice vinegar and soy sauce into broth mixture. Simmer 5 minutes.

- Add sautéed vegetables, tofu and pickles. Season to taste. Serve.

Recipe shown above

VARIATIONS
- Replace vegetable broth with tomato juice, as shown opposite.
- Replace Chinese mushrooms with quartered oyster mushrooms, as shown bottom right.

NUTRITION	
CALORIES PER SERVING: 102	
FAT: 5 *g*	CAL. FROM FAT: 36%
PROTEIN: 4 *g*	CHOLESTEROL: 7 *mg*
SODIUM: 336 *mg*	CARBOHYDRATES: 15 *g*

Minestrone

8 SERVINGS

Meatballs

8 oz	(225 g) ground beef and veal
2 tbsp	(30 mL) onion, chopped
1	garlic clove, chopped
2 tbsp	(30 mL) Italian bread crumbs
1	small egg yolk
	pinch of basil
	pinch of oregano
	pinch of parsley
	salt and pepper

Soup

2 tbsp	(30 mL) olive oil
¹/₄ cup	(60 mL) canned red kidney beans
¹/₄ cup	(60 mL) celery, sliced diagonally
¹/₄ cup	(60 mL) cabbage, shredded
¹/₄ cup	(60 mL) turnip, diced small
3 tbsp	(45 mL) onion, chopped
1	garlic clove, chopped
2 cups	(500 mL) beef broth
14 oz	(398 mL) canned Italian tomatoes
1	bay leaf
1	clove
	salt and pepper
3 tbsp	(45 mL) Parmesan cheese, grated

▪ In a bowl, mix meatball ingredients to a stiff paste. Shape into olive-sized balls.

▪ In a saucepan, heat oil. Brown meatballs. Remove cooked meatballs from saucepan. Set aside.

▪ Rinse kidney beans. Drain well. Set aside.

▪ In the same saucepan, add fresh vegetables and garlic. Cook 5 minutes. Stir in beef broth and tomatoes. Bring to a boil. Over low heat, simmer 20 minutes, stirring from time to time.

▪ Add meatballs, beans, bay leaf and clove. Simmer 10 minutes. Season. Ladle into soup bowls. Sprinkle with 1 tsp (5 mL) or so Parmesan. Serve.

VARIATIONS

• Replace meatballs with 1 ¹/₂ cups (375 mL) cooked macaroni.

• Replace beef broth with chicken broth, and canned tomatoes with fresh tomatoes, previously blanched then peeled.

NUTRITION	
CALORIES PER SERVING: 171	
FAT: 11 g	CAL. FROM FAT: 59%
PROTEIN: 9 g	CHOLESTEROL: 56 mg
SODIUM: 209 mg	CARBOHYDRATES: 8 g

Oyster Chowder

<table>
<tr><td colspan="2" align="center">4-6 SERVINGS</td></tr>
<tr><td>36</td><td>oysters, in their juice</td></tr>
<tr><td>3 cups</td><td>(750 mL) milk</td></tr>
<tr><td>1 cup</td><td>(250 mL) light cream</td></tr>
<tr><td>1</td><td>medium-size onion, chopped</td></tr>
<tr><td>2</td><td>celery stalks, minced</td></tr>
<tr><td>2</td><td>parsley stalks, chopped</td></tr>
<tr><td></td><td>white pepper, to taste</td></tr>
<tr><td>1/4 cup</td><td>(60 mL) butter</td></tr>
<tr><td></td><td>celery salt</td></tr>
<tr><td></td><td>paprika</td></tr>
</table>

- With a fine sieve or cheese-cloth, strain oysters, reserving juice and oysters separately.
- In a saucepan, blend milk and cream. Add onion, celery, parsley and pepper. Simmer a few minutes without boiling.
- Pass milk and cream through a sieve. Return to saucepan. Add oyster juice. Set aside.
- In a large skillet, over moderate heat, melt butter. Add oysters. Cook 1 minute until oysters swell.
- Add oysters to creamy mixture. Heat through until oyster sides ripple.
- Ladle into warm soup bowls. Sprinkle with celery salt and paprika. Serve.

NUTRITION	
CALORIES PER SERVING: 348	
FAT: 23 g	CAL. FROM FAT: 56%
PROTEIN: 16 g	CHOLESTEROL: 111 mg
SODIUM: 477 mg	CARBOHYDRATES: 24 g

Shrimp Chowder

<table>
<tr><td colspan="2" align="center">6 SERVINGS</td></tr>
<tr><td>4 cups</td><td>(1 L) water</td></tr>
<tr><td>1</td><td>medium-size onion, chopped</td></tr>
<tr><td>1</td><td>small leek, chopped</td></tr>
<tr><td>2</td><td>celery stalks, diced</td></tr>
<tr><td>1</td><td>carrot, diced</td></tr>
<tr><td>1</td><td>medium-size potato, peeled, diced</td></tr>
<tr><td>8 oz</td><td>(225 g) salmon, diced</td></tr>
<tr><td>1 lb</td><td>(450 g) baby shrimp</td></tr>
<tr><td>1/4 tsp</td><td>(1 mL) cayenne</td></tr>
<tr><td></td><td>salt and pepper</td></tr>
<tr><td>1/4 cup</td><td>(60 mL) heavy cream</td></tr>
</table>

- In a large saucepan, bring water to a boil. Add vegetables. Cook 10 minutes.
- Add diced salmon. Simmer 5 minutes. Fold in shrimp and seasonings. Continue cooking 2 minutes.
- Stir in cream, mixing until well-blended. Reheat without boiling. Serve.

NUTRITION	
CALORIES PER SERVING: 215	
FAT: 6 g	CAL. FROM FAT: 27%
PROTEIN: 25 g	CHOLESTEROL: 148 mg
SODIUM: 195 mg	CARBOHYDRATES: 14 g

Smoked Cod Soup

8 SERVINGS

¼ cup	(60 mL) butter
2	onions, chopped
1 tbsp	(15 mL) flour
4 cups	(1 L) boiling water
¾ cup	(180 mL) celery, chopped
2 cups	(500 mL) potatoes, peeled, diced
2 cups	(500 mL) smoked cod, diced
3 cups	(750 mL) tomato juice
⅛ tsp	(0.5 mL) pepper
	parsley, to taste
	thyme, to taste

■ In a saucepan, melt butter. Cook onions 5 minutes. Sprinkle with flour. While stirring, continue cooking until well-blended.

■ Add remaining ingredients. Bring to a boil. Reduce heat. Simmer 30 minutes. Serve.

NUTRITION	
CALORIES PER SERVING: 190	
FAT: 8 g	CAL. FROM FAT: 39%
PROTEIN: 13 g	CHOLESTEROL: 29 mg
SODIUM: 869 mg	CARBOHYDRATES: 16 g

Seafood Chowder

8 SERVINGS

¼ cup	(60 mL) butter
1	onion, minced
2	celery stalks, minced
10 oz	(284 mL) canned sliced mushrooms
1 lb	(450 g) scallops, diced
1 lb	(450 g) halibut, diced
8 oz	(225 g) salmon, diced
1 lb	(450 g) cod, diced
2 cups	(500 mL) water
10 oz	(284 mL) canned lobster or crab bisque or canned fish soup
5 oz	(142 mL) canned clams, in their juice
1 lb	(450 g) cooked shrimp
2 cups	(500 mL) milk

■ In a saucepan, melt butter. Lightly cook onion, celery and mushrooms. Add fresh fish. Continue cooking 5 minutes.

■ Pour in water. Bring to a boil. Add bisque, clams in their juice and shrimp. Bring back to a boil.

■ Fold in milk. Continue cooking 5 minutes without boiling. Serve very hot.

NUTRITION	
CALORIES PER SERVING: 336	
FAT: 12 g	CAL. FROM FAT: 32%
PROTEIN: 47 g	CHOLESTEROL: 199 mg
SODIUM: 603 mg	CARBOHYDRATES: 8 g

Crab Chowder

6 SERVINGS

2 tbsp	(30 mL) butter
	whites of 3 leeks, minced
3 cups	(750 mL) chicken broth
4	potatoes, peeled, sliced
2 cups	(500 mL) milk
5 oz	(142 mL) canned crab meat
2 oz	(60 mL) dry sherry
1/2 oz	(15 mL) kirsch
	salt and pepper
	chives, chopped

- In a saucepan, melt butter. Cook leeks until tender. Add broth and potatoes. Bring to a boil. Cover. Over low heat, simmer 20 minutes.
- In a blender, purée mixture. Return to saucepan.
- Fold in milk, crab, sherry and kirsch. Reheat without boiling. Season with salt and pepper. Sprinkle with chopped chives. Serve.

NUTRITION	
CALORIES PER SERVING: 328	
FAT: 9 g	CAL. FROM FAT: 26 %
PROTEIN: 14 g	CHOLESTEROL: 49 mg
SODIUM: 229 mg	CARBOHYDRATES: 46 g

New England Clam Chowder

6-8 SERVINGS

19 oz	(540 mL) canned clams, in their juice
2 tbsp	(30 mL) butter
1	medium-size onion, minced
4 cups	(1 L) boiling water
3/4 tsp	(3 mL) salt
1/2 tsp	(2 mL) pepper
1	medium-size potato, peeled, diced
1 cup	(250 mL) light cream
1 cup	(250 mL) milk
	cornstarch (optional)
	paprika

- Strain clams, reserving 1 cup (250 mL) juice (add water if juice is insufficient).
- In a saucepan, melt butter. Cook onion until transparent. Add clams. Continue cooking 5 minutes. Transfer mixture to a bowl. Set aside.
- In the same saucepan, combine boiling water, clam juice, salt and pepper. Simmer 25 minutes. Add potato. Continue cooking 5 minutes.
- Fold in cream and milk. Reheat without boiling. Add clam mixture. Simmer 5 minutes.
- If soup needs to be thickened, add cornstarch mixed with a little water. Sprinkle with a pinch of paprika. Serve.

NUTRITION	
CALORIES PER SERVING: 142	
FAT: 10 g	CAL. FROM FAT: 61 %
PROTEIN: 3 g	CHOLESTEROL: 734 mg
SODIUM: 407 mg	CARBOHYDRATES: 11 g

Cheesy Fish Soup

6 SERVINGS

1 lb	(450 g) fresh or frozen fish fillets (cod, sole, etc.)
1 lb	(450 g) fresh or frozen shrimp
2 tbsp	(30 mL) butter
1/4 cup	(60 mL) onion, finely chopped
1 cup	(250 mL) carrots, finely chopped
1/3 cup	(80 mL) celery, diced
1/4 cup	(60 mL) flour
1/2 tsp	(2 mL) salt
	pinch of paprika
2 cups	(500 mL) chicken broth
3 cups	(750 mL) milk
1/2 cup	(125 mL) processed cheese spread

- If using frozen fish and shrimp, thaw first.
- Dice fish fillets. Mix with shrimp. Set aside.
- In a saucepan, melt butter. Sauté vegetables until onion is transparent. Add flour, salt and paprika.
- Gradually stir in chicken broth and milk. Continue stirring until mixture thickens.
- Add fish and shrimp. Simmer 5 minutes or until fish is cooked. Fold in cheese. Stir until cheese has melted. Serve very hot.

NUTRITION	
CALORIES PER SERVING: 347	
FAT: 14 g	CAL. FROM FAT: 37%
PROTEIN: 37 g	CHOLESTEROL: 188 mg
SODIUM: 592 mg	CARBOHYDRATES: 17 g

Creole Bouillabaisse

6 SERVINGS

1 lb	(450 g) fresh or frozen fish
1/4 cup	(60 mL) oil
2	onions, chopped
1	celery stalk, diced
2	green bell peppers, diced
3-4	garlic cloves, chopped
2 tbsp	(30 mL) parsley, chopped
2 tbsp	(30 mL) oregano
2 tbsp	(30 mL) marjoram
1	bay leaf
1/4 cup	(60 mL) flour
19 oz	(540 mL) canned tomatoes
3 cups	(750 mL) chicken broth

- If using frozen fish, thaw first.
- Cut fish into 1-inch (2.5 cm) cubes. Set aside.
- In a heavy-bottomed saucepan, heat oil. Sauté onions, celery, bell peppers, garlic and seasonings a few minutes.
- Stir in flour. Add tomatoes and chicken broth. Bring to a boil, while stirring.
- Add fish. Cover. Over low heat, simmer 15 minutes or until fish flakes easily. Stir occasionally. Adjust seasoning. Serve very hot.

NUTRITION	
CALORIES PER SERVING: 264	
FAT: 12 g	CAL. FROM FAT: 41%
PROTEIN: 18 g	CHOLESTEROL: 39 mg
SODIUM: 271 mg	CARBOHYDRATES: 22 g

Hot or Cold Vichyssoise

6 SERVINGS	
1 tsp	(5 mL) peanut oil
1	medium-size onion, chopped
4 cups	(1 L) water
2 cups	(500 mL) potatoes, peeled, diced
1 cup	(250 mL) leeks, sliced
	sea salt, to taste
	mixed herbs, to taste
2 tbsp	(30 mL) fresh chives, chopped
1/4 cup	(60 mL) fresh parsley, chopped

- In a saucepan, heat oil. Sauté onion a few minutes.
- Add water and vegetables. Bring to a boil. Cover. Over low heat, simmer 30 minutes.
- In a blender, purée mixture. Season with sea salt and mixed herbs. Serve hot or chilled, sprinkled with chives and parsley.

NUTRITION	
CALORIES PER SERVING: 83	
FAT: 2 g	CAL. FROM FAT: 25 %
PROTEIN: 2 g	CHOLESTEROL: 0 mg
SODIUM: 32 mg	CARBOHYDRATES: 14 g

Green Bell Pepper Soup

4 SERVINGS	
3	green bell peppers, finely chopped
1 tbsp	(15 mL) corn oil
1	large onion, chopped
1	small celery stalk, chopped
1 cup	(250 mL) vegetable broth
1 cup	(250 mL) beef broth
1/4 tsp	(1 mL) oregano
1/2 tsp	(2 mL) basil
4 tsp	(20 mL) whole wheat flour
2 cups	(500 mL) skim milk
	salt and pepper

- Set aside 2 tbsp (30 mL) chopped green bell peppers for decoration.
- In a saucepan, heat oil. Sauté vegetables. Add both broths and mixed herbs. Over low heat, simmer 10 minutes.
- In a blender, purée mixture. Return to saucepan.
- In a bowl, blend flour and milk. Fold into soup. Over low heat, while stirring, reheat without boiling. Season with salt and pepper. Serve hot or chilled, sprinkled with chopped green bell peppers.

NUTRITION	
CALORIES PER SERVING: 131	
FAT: 4 g	CAL. FROM FAT: 25 %
PROTEIN: 7 g	CHOLESTEROL: 2 mg
SODIUM: 179 mg	CARBOHYDRATES: 21 g

Pumpkin Soup

4 SERVINGS	
2 tbsp	(30 mL) butter
2 tbsp	(30 mL) flour
1	celery stalk, diced
1	potato, peeled, diced
1	onion, chopped
1 cup	(250 mL) pumpkin pulp, diced
1 cup	(250 mL) chicken broth
1 tbsp	(15 mL) lemon juice
3	drops of Tabasco sauce
1/4 tsp	(1 mL) paprika
	pinch of nutmeg
1/4 tsp	(1 mL) ground clove
1 cup	(250 mL) milk
	salt and pepper
1/4 cup	(60 mL) heavy cream

- In a saucepan, melt butter. Sprinkle with flour. Make a roux. Add vegetables and pumpkin, mixing well. Fold in remaining ingredients, except cream. Over low heat, simmer until potato is cooked.
- In a blender, purée mixture. Fold in cream, mixing well. Serve hot.

VARIATION
- Refrigerate purée. Once cold, fold in cream. Serve chilled.

NUTRITION	
CALORIES PER SERVING: 268	
FAT: 15 g	CAL. FROM FAT: 47 %
PROTEIN: 6 g	CHOLESTEROL: 47 mg
SODIUM: 167 mg	CARBOHYDRATES: 30 g

Yocoto Soup

6-8 SERVINGS	
1 cup	(250 mL) plain yogurt
1 cup	(250 mL) milk
2	cucumbers, peeled, diced
2	tomatoes, diced
2 tbsp	(30 mL) fresh parsley, chopped
2 tbsp	(30 mL) olive oil
	a few leaves of fresh basil, chopped
2 tbsp	(30 mL) chives, chopped
	salt and pepper

- In a food processor, blend yogurt and milk.
- Transfer mixture to a large bowl. Add remaining ingredients. Season to taste.
- If needed, refrigerate soup. Serve chilled.

NUTRITION	
CALORIES PER SERVING: 94	
FAT: 6 g	CAL. FROM FAT: 50 %
PROTEIN: 3 g	CHOLESTEROL: 8 mg
SODIUM: 57 mg	CARBOHYDRATES: 9 g

From top to bottom :
Pumpkin Soup,
Green Bell Pepper Soup,
Yocoto Soup

The cold appetizers presented here are both delicious and easy to prepare. They are sure to have a place at any buffet and reception.

Some of the recipes in this section are also low in fat and calories. Two examples of this type are Cossack-style Borscht and Cucumber in Minty Sauce (p. 54). We are sure you will find all of the recipes both delicious and satisfying.

COLD APPETIZERS

Bell Pepper Cheese Balls

9 SERVINGS	
1 lb	(450 g) bacon
1 lb	(450 g) Cheddar cheese, grated
8 oz	(225 g) cream cheese, softened
1	green bell pepper, coarsely chopped
1	sweet red pepper, coarsely chopped
¼ cup	(60 mL) fresh parsley, chopped
¼ cup	(60 mL) nuts, finely chopped
	crackers

- In a frying pan, cook bacon until crisp. Drain on a paper towel to soak up as much fat as possible.
- In a bowl, combine bacon, both cheeses and bell peppers. Divide into 3 equal parts.
- In a food processor, mix each third to a ball. Shape total mixture into one big ball or several smaller ones. Set aside.
- In a large bowl, combine parsley and nuts. Dredge each ball with mixture. Seal in plastic wrap or aluminum foil. Refrigerate at least 24 hours. Serve at room temperature with crackers.

NUTRITION	
CALORIES PER SERVING: 622	
FAT: 15 g	CAL. FROM FAT: 74%
PROTEIN: 31 g	CHOLESTEROL: 121 mg
SODIUM: 1134 mg	CARBOHYDRATES: 8 g

Nutty Ricotta Entrée

4 SERVINGS	
1 cup	(250 mL) Ricotta cheese
⅓ cup	(80 mL) dates, finely chopped
⅓ cup	(80 mL) nuts, finely chopped
⅓ cup	(80 mL) raisins, finely chopped
2 tbsp	(30 mL) mayonnaise
	lettuce leaves

- In a large bowl, mix all ingredients, except lettuce. Refrigerate at least 1 hour before serving.
- Remove from refrigerator. Serve on a bed of lettuce.

NUTRITION	
CALORIES PER SERVING: 309	
FAT: 21 g	CAL. FROM FAT: 57%
PROTEIN: 10 g	CHOLESTEROL: 34 mg
SODIUM: 95 mg	CARBOHYDRATES: 25 g

Marinated Cauliflower

6 SERVINGS	
1 cup	(250 mL) plain yogurt
1 tsp	(5 mL) Worcestershire sauce
1 tbsp	(15 mL) fresh parsley, chopped
¼ tsp	(1 mL) oregano
¼ tsp	(1 mL) garlic, minced
¼ tsp	(1 mL) paprika
	pinch of thyme
3 cups	(750 mL) cauliflower florets

- In a food processor, blend all ingredients, except cauliflower, to a marinade. Set aside.
- In a saucepan filled with lightly-salted boiling water, blanch cauliflower 1 minute. Remove from saucepan. Immerse in a bowl of ice-cold water. Drain well.
- Pour marinade over cauliflower. Refrigerate 3 hours. Serve.

NUTRITION	
CALORIES PER SERVING: 37	
FAT: 1 g	CAL. FROM FAT: 30 %
PROTEIN: 2 g	CHOLESTEROL: 5 mg
SODIUM: 41 mg	CARBOHYDRATES: 5 g

Asparagus Rolls

6 SERVINGS	
12	whole wheat bread slices, crusts removed
4 oz	(113 g) cream cheese, softened
12	asparagus tips, cooked
3 tbsp	(45 mL) Parmesan cheese, grated
4 tsp	(20 mL) parsley, chopped
1	egg, lightly beaten

- Preheat oven to 375 °F (190 °C).
- With a rolling pin, flatten each bread slice. Spread with cream cheese. Place an asparagus tip at one end of each slice. Roll. Set aside.
- In a large bowl, mix Parmesan and parsley. Set aside.
- Lightly brush each asparagus roll with beaten egg. Roll in Parmesan and parsley mixture. Cut into 3 rounds.
- Transfer rolls to a non-stick baking sheet. Cook in oven 7-8 minutes. Let stand to cool 15 minutes. Serve.

NUTRITION	
CALORIES PER SERVING: 341	
FAT: 13 g	CAL. FROM FAT: 32 %
PROTEIN: 17 g	CHOLESTEROL: 53 mg
SODIUM: 560 mg	CARBOHYDRATES: 46 g

Cucumber in Minty Sauce

4 SERVINGS

2	firm cucumbers, peeled
1/2 cup	(125 mL) plain yogurt
2 tbsp	(30 mL) fresh chives, finely chopped
2 tbsp	(30 mL) fresh mint, finely chopped
	salt and pepper
4	green cabbage leaves

▪ Slice cucumbers in half lengthwise. Remove seeds. Cut into thin slices. Set aside.

▪ In a bowl, mix yogurt, chives and mint. Season. Gently fold in cucumber slices. Refrigerate at least 30 minutes.

▪ Cover 4 salad plates with a green cabbage leaf. Spoon cucumber mixture into the middle. Serve.

NUTRITION	
CALORIES PER SERVING: 59	
FAT: 1 g	CAL. FROM FAT: 19%
PROTEIN: 3 g	CHOLESTEROL: 4 mg
SODIUM: 65 mg	CARBOHYDRATES: 10 g

Recipe shown above left

Cossack-style Borscht

6-8 SERVINGS

14 oz	(398 mL) canned beets, drained — reserve 1 cup (250 mL) juice
2	envelopes unflavored gelatin
1 cup	(250 mL) beef broth
1/4 cup	(60 mL) spinach, finely shredded
1 tbsp	(15 mL) lemon juice
1/2 cup	(125 mL) plain yogurt
	fresh chives, chopped

▪ In a medium-size saucepan, pour beet juice. Sprinkle with gelatin. Over low heat, stir until gelatin dissolves. Remove from heat. Set aside.

▪ In a food processor, combine beets and beef broth. Process until smooth. Fold beet purée into gelatin mixture. Add spinach. Sprinkle with lemon juice. Transfer to a soup tureen. Cover. Refrigerate until borscht has half-set.

▪ Decorate with a swirl of yogurt. Sprinkle with chopped chives. Serve.

VARIATION

• Transfer borscht to a mold. Refrigerate until mixture has set. Garnish with yogurt and chopped chives.

NUTRITION	
CALORIES PER SERVING: 122	
FAT: 1 g	CAL. FROM FAT: 9%
PROTEIN: 3 g	CHOLESTEROL: 4 mg
SODIUM: 198 mg	CARBOHYDRATES: 26 g

Recipe shown above right

Hearts Vinaigrette

4-6 SERVINGS	
¹/₂ cup	(125 mL) olive oil
2 tbsp	(30 mL) wine vinegar
1	onion, finely chopped
1	garlic clove, minced
¹/₂ tsp	(2 mL) basil, chopped
	salt and pepper
10 oz	(284 mL) canned artichoke hearts, quartered
10 oz	(284 mL) canned palm hearts, sliced
	lettuce leaves
	fresh parsley

- In a bowl, whisk first 6 ingredients until smooth. Gently mix in artichoke and palm hearts.

- Marinate in refrigerator at least 3 hours, stirring occasionally.

- Spoon over a bed of lettuce. Garnish with parsley. Serve.

NUTRITION	
CALORIES PER SERVING: 256	
FAT: 18 g	CAL. FROM FAT: 60%
PROTEIN: 4 g	CHOLESTEROL: 0 mg
SODIUM: 100 mg	CARBOHYDRATES: 23 g

Stuffed Oranges

2 SERVINGS	
2	large oranges
1	apple, julienned
1	carrot, coarsely grated
¹/₄ cup	(60 mL) celery, minced
2 tbsp	(30 mL) raisins
2 tbsp	(30 mL) pistachios
¹/₂ tsp	(2 mL) salt
¹/₄ cup	(60 mL) sour cream
¹/₄ cup	(60 mL) plain yogurt

- Slice tops off oranges. With a spoon, scoop out pulp without breaking skin. Set aside orange shells. Dice pulp.

- In a bowl, combine orange pulp and remaining ingredients, mixing well. Set aside.

- With a small knife, cut a zigzag edge around orange shells. Spoon stuffing into oranges. Serve.

NUTRITION	
CALORIES PER SERVING: 235	
FAT: 10 g	CAL. FROM FAT: 33%
PROTEIN: 5 g	CHOLESTEROL: 16 mg
SODIUM: 588 mg	CARBOHYDRATES: 38 g

Carrot and Apricot Molds

6 SERVINGS	
1/4 cup	(60 mL) cold water
1 tbsp	(15 mL) unflavored gelatin
1 1/4 cups	(300 mL) pineapple juice
1/2 tsp	(2 mL) salt
1/4 cup	(60 mL) lemon juice
2 tbsp	(30 mL) sugar
1 cup	(250 mL) canned apricots, drained, diced
1 cup	(250 mL) carrots, grated
	lettuce leaves (optional)
	carrot sticks

- In a saucepan, sprinkle water with gelatin. Over low heat, dissolve gelatin. Add pineapple juice, salt, lemon juice and sugar. Let stand to cool slightly.
- Fold apricots and carrots into mixture. Pour into molds. Refrigerate 1 hour.
- Unmold on a bed of lettuce, if desired. Serve with carrot sticks.

NUTRITION	
CALORIES PER SERVING: 77	
FAT: 1 g	CAL. FROM FAT: 1%
PROTEIN: 1 g	CHOLESTEROL: 0 mg
SODIUM: 197 mg	CARBOHYDRATES: 19 g

Antipasto

8 SERVINGS	
10 oz	(284 mL) canned palm hearts, sliced
10 oz	(284 mL) canned miniature corn, sliced
10 oz	(284 mL) canned artichoke hearts
1/2 cup	(125 mL) black olives
1/2 cup	(125 mL) sweet red pepper, cut into strips
1/2 cup	(125 mL) green bell pepper, cut into strips
1/2 cup	(125 mL) fresh mushrooms, sliced
	lettuce leaves

Dressing

1/4 cup	(60 mL) red wine vinegar
3/4 cup	(180 mL) olive oil
1 tsp	(5 mL) Dijon mustard
1 tsp	(5 mL) salt
1/2 tsp	(2 mL) sugar
1/2 tsp	(2 mL) black pepper
1/2 tsp	(2 mL) basil
1/2 tsp	(2 mL) oregano
1	garlic clove, crushed
2 tbsp	(30 mL) water

- Mix all vegetables, except lettuce.
- In a blender, whip dressing ingredients. Pour over vegetables. Marinate in refrigerator 12 hours.
- Spoon antipasto over a bed of lettuce. Serve.

NUTRITION	
CALORIES PER SERVING: 272	
FAT: 22 g	CAL. FROM FAT: 67%
PROTEIN: 4 g	CHOLESTEROL: 0 mg
SODIUM: 412 mg	CARBOHYDRATES: 19 g

Russian Salad

6 SERVINGS	
6	ripe medium-size tomatoes
1/3 cup	(80 mL) cucumber, diced
1/3 cup	(80 mL) canned green peas, drained
1/4 cup	(60 mL) unsweetened pickles, minced
2 tbsp	(30 mL) capers
	dash of vinegar
	salt and pepper
1/2 cup	(125 mL) cooked chicken, cold, diced
1/4 cup	(60 mL) mayonnaise
	lettuce leaves
	fresh parsley, finely chopped

- Slice tops off tomatoes. With a spoon, scoop out pulp. Set aside.

- In a bowl, carefully mix 1/3 cup (80 mL) tomato pulp with remaining ingredients, except lettuce and parsley. Stuff mixture into tomato shells. Arrange on a bed of lettuce. Garnish with parsley. Serve.

NUTRITION	
CALORIES PER SERVING: 141	
FAT: 9 g	CAL. FROM FAT: 56%
PROTEIN: 6 g	CHOLESTEROL: 13 mg
SODIUM: 287 mg	CARBOHYDRATES: 11 g

Apple Cole Slaw

4 SERVINGS	
2 cups	(500 mL) red cabbage, grated
1/2	apple, finely chopped
2 tbsp	(30 mL) green bell pepper, finely chopped
1/2 cup	(125 mL) plain yogurt
2 tbsp	(30 mL) sugar
1/4 tsp	(1 mL) celery seeds
	salt and pepper

- In a medium-size bowl, mix cabbage, apple and bell pepper. Set aside.

- In a second bowl, whisk remaining ingredients until smooth. Pour over cole slaw, mixing gently. Refrigerate 1 hour or so. Serve.

NUTRITION	
CALORIES PER SERVING: 60	
FAT: 1 g	CAL. FROM FAT: 15%
PROTEIN: 1 g	CHOLESTEROL: 4 mg
SODIUM: 61 mg	CARBOHYDRATES: 12 g

Ham-and-Cheese Wheels

8 servings	
8 oz	(225 g) cream cheese, softened
¼ cup	(60 mL) green onions, minced
1 tbsp	(15 mL) fresh parsley, chopped
¼ cup	(60 mL) mayonnaise
24	ham slices

- In a bowl, mix all ingredients, except ham. Spread mixture on ham slices. Roll. Cut each slice into ¾-inch (1.5 cm) thick rounds.
- Divide among individual salad plates. Serve with fresh vegetables.

NUTRITION	
CALORIES PER SERVING: 298	
FAT: 21 g	CAL. FROM FAT: 65%
PROTEIN: 24 g	CHOLESTEROL: 87 mg
SODIUM: 1544 mg	CARBOHYDRATES: 2 g

Recipe shown above

VARIATIONS
- Replace mayonnaise with chili sauce, as shown opposite.
- Replace ham with smoked turkey, as shown bottom right.

Stuffed Pasta Shells

4 SERVINGS

16	jumbo pasta shells
1 cup	(250 mL) cooked chicken, chopped
1 tbsp	(15 mL) onion, minced
1 tbsp	(15 mL) bell pepper, minced
1 tbsp	(15 mL) celery, minced
3 tbsp	(45 mL) mayonnaise
	paprika (optional)
	fresh parsley, chopped (optional)
	lettuce leaves
4	tomato slices
	olives

- In a saucepan filled with lightly-salted boiling water, cook pasta shells.

- Meanwhile, in a bowl, mix chicken, onion, bell pepper, celery and mayonnaise. Set aside.

- Drain cooked pasta shells well. Stuff with chicken mixture. Sprinkle with paprika or parsley, if desired.

- Cover 4 salad plates with a bed of lettuce leaves. Place 4 pasta shells in the center of each. Serve with a tomato slice and olives.

NUTRITION	
CALORIES PER SERVING: 269	
FAT: 14 g	CAL. FROM FAT: 47%
PROTEIN: 15 g	CHOLESTEROL: 33 mg
SODIUM: 176 mg	CARBOHYDRATES: 21 g

NUTRITION	
CALORIES PER SERVING: 309	
FAT: 24 g	CAL. FROM FAT: 67%
PROTEIN: 11 g	CHOLESTEROL: 55 mg
SODIUM: 531 mg	CARBOHYDRATES: 16 g

Stuffed Peaches

4 SERVINGS

4 oz	(115 g) cream cheese, softened
5 oz	(140 g) canned turkey flakes
2 tbsp	(30 mL) red onion, chopped
¼ cup	(60 mL) mayonnaise
	salt and pepper
28 oz	(796 mL) canned peach halves, drained
	lettuce leaves
	fresh parsley sprigs

- In a bowl, blend first 5 ingredients.

- Stuff mixture into peach halves. Transfer to a bed of lettuce. Garnish with fresh parsley. Serve.

Recipe shown above left

Delicious Triangles

4-6 SERVINGS

12	ham slices
12	cheese slices
	pickled vegetables

- On a plate, lay a ham slice. Cover with a cheese slice. Repeat, using all slices to form a stack. Cover with plastic wrap. Refrigerate 3 hours.

- Remove from refrigerator. Cut into triangles. Arrange with pickled vegetables on small salad plates. Serve with individual toothpicks.

NUTRITION	
CALORIES PER SERVING: 264	
FAT: 17 g	CAL. FROM FAT: 58%
PROTEIN: 23 g	CHOLESTEROL: 65 mg
SODIUM: 566 mg	CARBOHYDRATES: 5 g

Recipe shown above right

Avocado Pear Surprise

4 SERVINGS

1	green bell pepper
1	sweet red pepper
2	avocados
3/4 cup	(180 mL) ham, chopped
3/4 cup	(180 mL) mayonnaise
1 tsp	(5 mL) ketchup
	salt and pepper
3 tbsp	(45 mL) pimento-stuffed olives, sliced

- Reserve a few strips of green and red bell peppers for decoration. Mince remainder. Set aside.
- Slice avocados in half lengthwise. Remove pits. With a spoon, scoop out flesh without breaking skin. Set aside avocado shells.
- In a bowl, mash avocado flesh. Mix in remaining ingredients, except bell pepper garnish and olives. Stuff avocado shells with mixture.
- Transfer each avocado pear to an individual salad plate. Garnish with bell pepper strips and olive slices. Serve.

NUTRITION	
CALORIES PER SERVING: 473	
FAT: 49 g	CAL. FROM FAT: 87%
PROTEIN: 7 g	CHOLESTEROL: 27 mg
SODIUM: 774 mg	CARBOHYDRATES: 9 g

Recipe shown above

Pork in Aspic

6 CUPS (1.5 L)

4 lbs	(1.8 kg) pork shoulder
1 1/4 lbs	(565 g) pork hocks
2	large onions, sliced
1	leek, diced
2	garlic cloves, minced
1/4 tsp	(1 mL) cinnamon
1 tsp	(5 mL) savory
1/4 tsp	(1 mL) ground clove
2 tbsp	(30 mL) cider vinegar
6 cups	(1.5 L) water
	salt and pepper
1	envelope unflavored gelatin

- In a saucepan, combine all ingredients, except gelatin. Bring to a boil. Cover. Over low heat, simmer 2-3 hours.
- With a sieve, strain meat over a medium-size saucepan. Sprinkle cooking juices with gelatin. Over low heat, dissolve gelatin. Set aside.
- Dice meat. Place in a mold. Cover with gelatin mixture. Refrigerate 24 hours. Unmold. Serve.

NUTRITION	
CALORIES PER SERVING: 522	
FAT: 30 g	CAL. FROM FAT: 47%
PROTEIN: 35 g	CHOLESTEROL: 170 mg
SODIUM: 249 mg	CARBOHYDRATES: 17 g

Ham Mousse

4-6 SERVINGS

6 ¹/₂ oz	(184 g) canned ham flakes
8 oz	(225 g) cream cheese, softened
¹/₂ cup	(125 mL) shallots, minced
¹/₂ cup	(125 mL) celery, minced
1 cup	(250 mL) sour cream
	pinch of paprika
¹/₄ cup	(60 mL) cold water
1	envelope unflavored gelatin
	crackers

▪ In a bowl, crumble ham flakes with a fork. Fold in cream cheese and vegetables. Add sour cream and paprika, mixing until well-blended. Set aside.

▪ In a small saucepan, sprinkle cold water with gelatin. Over low heat, dissolve gelatin. Fold into ham mixture. Pour resulting mousse into an oiled mold. Refrigerate at least 4 hours.

▪ Serve with crackers, rusks, croissants or chips.

NUTRITION	
CALORIES PER SERVING: 490	
FAT: 29 *g*	CAL. FROM FAT: 52%
PROTEIN: 13 *g*	CHOLESTEROL: 70 *mg*
SODIUM: 1024 *mg*	CARBOHYDRATES: 45 *g*

Beef Mousse

4-6 SERVINGS

1 cup	(250 mL) cooked roast beef, chopped
8 oz	(225 g) cream cheese, softened
¹/₂ cup	(125 mL) celery, minced
¹/₂ cup	(125 mL) shallots, minced
1 cup	(250 mL) mayonnaise
¹/₄ tsp	(1 mL) curry
	salt and pepper
	lettuce leaves
	fresh parsley

▪ In a bowl, combine all ingredients, except lettuce and parsley, mixing well. Pour into an oiled mold. Refrigerate at least 4 hours.

▪ On a serving dish, unmold cold mousse over a bed of lettuce. Garnish with parsley. Serve.

NUTRITION	
CALORIES PER SERVING: 447	
FAT: 46 *g*	CAL. FROM FAT: 89%
PROTEIN: 9 *g*	CHOLESTEROL: 67 *mg*
SODIUM: 376 *mg*	CARBOHYDRATES: 4 *g*

Shrimp Mold

8 oz	(225 g) cream cheese, softened
2 cups	(500 mL) shrimp, chopped
1/4 cup	(60 mL) shallots, minced
1 cup	(250 mL) plain yogurt
1/2 cup	(125 mL) cold water
1	envelope unflavored gelatin

- In a bowl, mix cheese, shrimp, shallots and yogurt until well-blended. Set aside.

- In a small saucepan, sprinkle water with gelatin. Over low heat, dissolve gelatin. Blend into shrimp mixture. Pour into a mold. Cover. Refrigerate at least 8 hours.

- In a bowl filled with hot water, dip bottom of mold 10 seconds. Unmold. Serve.

Recipe shown above

VARIATION
- To first mixture, add 1/4 cup (60 mL) chili sauce, as shown opposite.

NUTRITION	
CALORIES PER SERVING: 187	
FAT: 11 g	CAL. FROM FAT: 54%
PROTEIN: 9 g	CHOLESTEROL: 73 mg
SODIUM: 162 mg	CARBOHYDRATES: 13 g

Pineapple Islands

4 SERVINGS	
7 oz	(198 g) canned tuna, drained, crumbled
7 oz	(198 g) canned salmon, drained, crumbled
1/4 cup	(60 mL) celery, minced
3	shallots, minced
1	garlic clove, minced
	fresh parsley, finely chopped
2 tbsp	(30 mL) mayonnaise
1/2 tbsp	(7 mL) lemon juice
4	canned pineapple slices, drained

- In a bowl, mix ingredients, except pineapple. Refrigerate 2 hours.
- Place a pineapple slice on each of 4 salad plates. Using an ice-cream scoop, top with fish salad. Serve.

VARIATIONS
- Replace canned fish with meat or fish leftovers, cooked then chopped. Replace pineapple with tomato slices.

NUTRITION	
CALORIES PER SERVING: 351	
FAT: 10 g	CAL. FROM FAT: 24%
PROTEIN: 25 g	CHOLESTEROL: 45 mg
SODIUM: 509 mg	CARBOHYDRATES: 45 g

Smoked Oyster Pears

4 SERVINGS	
8 oz	(225 g) cream cheese, softened
2 tsp	(10 mL) vodka
1 tsp	(5 mL) lemon juice
4 3/4 oz	(134 mL) canned smoked oysters, drained
28 oz	(796 mL) canned pear halves, drained
	pimento-stuffed olives, sliced

- In a bowl, mix cheese, vodka and lemon juice. Fold in oysters.
- Stuff pear halves with oyster mixture. If needed, use a spoon to dig a larger cavity in the center of pear halves. Garnish with sliced olives. Serve.

NUTRITION	
CALORIES PER SERVING: 310	
FAT: 22 g	CAL. FROM FAT: 65%
PROTEIN: 7 g	CHOLESTEROL: 81 mg
SODIUM: 324 mg	CARBOHYDRATES: 19 g

Crab Ball

6-8 SERVINGS	
1 lb	(450 g) canned crab meat, drained, crumbled
8 oz	(225 g) cream cheese, softened
1 tbsp	(15 mL) onion, minced
1 tbsp	(15 mL) lemon juice
2 tsp	(10 mL) prepared horseradish (optional)
½ tsp	(2 mL) Worcestershire sauce
½ tsp	(2 mL) Tabasco sauce
½ cup	(125 mL) walnuts, chopped
¼ cup	(60 mL) fresh parsley, finely chopped
	crackers

- In a bowl, mix first 7 ingredients. Shape mixture into one large ball or several smaller ones. Refrigerate at least 2 hours.

- In a large bowl, mix walnuts and parsley. Roll crab ball in mixture. Serve with crackers.

NUTRITION	
CALORIES PER SERVING: 286	
FAT: 15 g	CAL. FROM FAT: 47%
PROTEIN: 16 g	CHOLESTEROL: 75 mg
SODIUM: 634 mg	CARBOHYDRATES: 22 g

Spicy Crab-stuffed Avocados

4 SERVINGS	
½ cup	(125 mL) mayonnaise
½ cup	(125 mL) celery, minced
¼ cup	(60 mL) pickled hot peppers, minced
¼ cup	(60 mL) fresh parsley, finely chopped
1 tbsp	(15 mL) prepared mustard
	a few drops of Tabasco sauce
	a few drops of Worcestershire sauce
	pinch of salt
	juice of ½ lemon
6 oz	(180 g) canned crab meat
2	ripe avocados
	fresh watercress
	cherry tomatoes
	black olives

- In a bowl, mix first 8 ingredients and 2 tsp (10 mL) lemon juice. Cover. Refrigerate.

- Drain crab meat. In a bowl, crumble into flakes. Refrigerate.

- Peel avocados. Slice in half lengthwise. Remove pits. Dip cut sides into remaining lemon juice.

- Cover 4 salad plates with a bed of watercress. Place avocado halves in the center. Stuff with crab meat. Spoon spicy mayonnaise on top. Garnish with tomatoes and olives. Serve.

NUTRITION	
CALORIES PER SERVING: 413	
FAT: 37 g	CAL. FROM FAT: 75%
PROTEIN: 13 g	CHOLESTEROL: 47 mg
SODIUM: 495 mg	CARBOHYDRATES: 15 g

Smoked Salmon Mousse

6 SERVINGS	
8 oz	(225 g) smoked salmon
2 tbsp	(30 mL) onion, chopped
8 oz	(225 g) cream cheese, softened
2	anchovy fillets
1	garlic clove, chopped
2 tsp	(10 mL) parsley, chopped
¼ tsp	(1 mL) onion salt
	dash of Worcestershire sauce
2 tbsp	(30 mL) lemon juice
	fresh ground pepper
	lettuce leaves

■ In a food processor, mix all ingredients, except lettuce, to a smooth mousse. Refrigerate 12 hours.

■ Spoon mousse into a pastry bag with a flutted nozzle. Pipe onto lettuce leaves.

VARIATIONS
• Use other varieties of smoked fish.

NUTRITION	
CALORIES PER SERVING: 186	
FAT: 15 g	CAL. FROM FAT: 72%
PROTEIN: 11 g	CHOLESTEROL: 51 mg
SODIUM: 528 mg	CARBOHYDRATES: 3 g

Stuffed Tomatoes

4 SERVINGS	
4	medium-size tomatoes
8 oz	(225 g) canned salmon, skin and bones removed
1 cup	(250 mL) cooked rice
½ cup	(125 mL) mayonnaise
	juice of ½ lemon
2 tbsp	(30 mL) parsley, chopped
2-3	drops of Tabasco sauce
	salt and pepper
2	hard-boiled eggs
	fresh parsley sprigs
2	pitted black olives, halved

■ With a knife, slice tops off tomatoes. Scoop out pulp. Set aside tomato skins.

■ Chop tomato pulp. In a bowl, mix with salmon, rice, mayonnaise, lemon juice, parsley and seasonings. Stuff tomato skins with mixture. Set aside.

■ Separate egg whites and yolks. Pass egg yolks through a sieve. Set aside.

■ Finely chop egg whites. Sprinkle each stuffed tomato with islands of egg whites and yolks. Garnish with a parsley sprig and a half-olive. Serve.

NUTRITION	
CALORIES PER SERVING: 577	
FAT: 32 g	CAL. FROM FAT: 46%
PROTEIN: 30 g	CHOLESTEROL: 132 mg
SODIUM: 847 mg	CARBOHYDRATES: 55 g

Norwegian Salmon

10-12 SERVINGS

1	3-4 lb (1.4-1.8 kg) whole salmon
1/4 cup	(60 mL) coarse salt
1/2 cup	(125 mL) dill, chopped
2 oz	(60 mL) cognac
	juice of 1 lemon
	water

Sauce

1 cup	(250 mL) heavy cream
1/4 cup	(60 mL) Dijon mustard
	salt and pepper
	parsley, chopped

- Slice salmon in half lengthwise. Remove backbone. Do not peel skin.

- In a dish, place salmon cut side up. Rub coarse salt into fish. Sprinkle with dill, cognac and lemon juice. Cover bottom of dish with water, surrounding but not topping fish. Refrigerate 2 days.

- Turn over salmon. Stir marinade. Refrigerate 2 more days.

- In a bowl, mix sauce ingredients. Carve marinated salmon into diagonal slices. Spoon sauce over fish. Serve at once.

NUTRITION	
CALORIES PER SERVING: 266	
FAT: 13 *g*	CAL. FROM FAT: 46%
PROTEIN: 31 *g*	CHOLESTEROL: 106 *mg*
SODIUM: 2087 *mg*	CARBOHYDRATES: 3 *g*

Shrimp New Orleans

4 SERVINGS

1 cup	(250 mL) baby shrimp
19 oz	(540 mL) canned pineapple chunks, in their juice
1/4 cup	(60 mL) oil
2 tbsp	(30 mL) prepared mustard
1 tbsp	(15 mL) lemon juice
1 tsp	(5 mL) Worcestershire sauce
2	green onions, minced
	lettuce leaves

- In a bowl, mix all ingredients, except lettuce. Marinate in refrigerator 1 hour.

- Cover 4 salad plates with a bed of lettuce leaves. Spoon marinated shrimp in the middle. Serve.

NUTRITION	
CALORIES PER SERVING: 716	
FAT: 15 *g*	CAL. FROM FAT: 48%
PROTEIN: 8 *g*	CHOLESTEROL: 38 *mg*
SODIUM: 148 *mg*	CARBOHYDRATES: 28 *g*

Salmon and Scallop Ceviche

4 SERVINGS	
8 oz	(225 g) fresh salmon fillets
8 oz	(225 g) fresh scallops
1/2 cup	(125 mL) lemon juice
1/2 cup	(125 mL) lime juice
1 cup	(250 mL) cherry tomatoes, halved
1/2	red onion, diced
1	canned hot green peppers, drained, diced
1/4 cup	(60 mL) olive oil
3 tbsp	(45 mL) lime juice
1 tbsp	(15 mL) fresh coriander, finely chopped
1	garlic clove, minced
1/2 tsp	(1 mL) oregano
	salt and pepper

lettuce leaves

fresh coriander sprigs

- With a pair of small pliers, remove salmon bones. Cut flesh into 1/2-inch (1.25 cm) cubes.

- In a small glass bowl, combine salmon, scallops, lemon and lime juices. Cover. Refrigerate 5 hours or until flesh turns opaque. Stir occasionally.

- Remove from refrigerator. Drain well. Mix in remaining ingredients, except lettuce and coriander sprigs. Cover. Refrigerate 1 hour.

- Arrange on a bed of lettuce. Garnish with coriander. Serve.

NUTRITION	
CALORIES PER SERVING: 278	
FAT: 16 g	CAL. FROM FAT: 51%
PROTEIN: 22 g	CHOLESTEROL: 48 mg
SODIUM: 181 mg	CARBOHYDRATES: 13 g

Scallop Entrée

4 SERVINGS	
3 tbsp	(45 mL) olive oil
1 tbsp	(15 mL) tarragon vinegar
	salt and pepper
5 oz	(142 mL) canned mandarin orange sections, drained
1 cup	(250 mL) cooked scallops

- In a bowl, whisk oil, vinegar and seasonings until smooth. Fold in mandarin oranges and scallops. Marinate in refrigerator 1 hour.

- Divide scallops and mandarin oranges among 4 salad plates. Serve.

NUTRITION	
CALORIES PER SERVING: 164	
FAT: 11 g	CAL. FROM FAT: 58%
PROTEIN: 10 g	CHOLESTEROL: 20 mg
SODIUM: 142 mg	CARBOHYDRATES: 7 g

Deviled Egg Trio

4 SERVINGS

6	eggs
3 tbsp	(45 mL) mayonnaise
2 tsp	(10 mL) chili sauce
	salt and pepper
1 tsp	(5 mL) chives, chopped
1	garlic clove, chopped
	salt and pepper

Garnish

1 tsp	(5 mL) pink peppercorns
1 tsp	(5 mL) capers
4	anchovy fillets

- In a saucepan filled with lightly-salted boiling water, cook eggs 10 minutes. Cool under running cold water. Shell. Slice in half lengthwise. With a spoon, carefully remove yolks, reserving egg whites.
- Combine egg yolks with remaining ingredients, mixing well.
- Pour mixture into a pastry bag with a fluted nozzle. Pipe into egg whites.
- Garnish 4 egg halves with pink peppercorns, 4 with capers, and 4 with anchovies.
- On 4 salad plates, arrange 3 deviled eggs, one of each type.

NUTRITION	
CALORIES PER SERVING: 179	
FAT: 16 *g*	CAL. FROM FAT: 77%
PROTEIN: 9 *g*	CHOLESTEROL: 282 *mg*
SODIUM: 382 *mg*	CARBOHYDRATES: 1 *g*

Poached Egg in a Cone

4 SERVINGS

4 cups	(1 L) water
2 tbsp	(30 mL) vinegar
4	eggs, at room temperature
3 tbsp	(45 mL) mayonnaise
1/2 tsp	(2 mL) prepared horseradish
	salt and pepper
4	lean ham slices

- In a saucepan, bring to a boil water and vinegar.
- Meanwhile, break each egg into an individual cup. One by one, carefully tip eggs into boiling water. Poach 5 minutes or so. With a slotted spoon, remove eggs. Immerse in a bowl of ice-cold water. Set aside.
- In a second bowl, blend mayonnaise and horseradish. Season. Set aside.
- Roll ham slices into cone shapes. Place an egg inside each cone. Top with 2 tsp (10 mL) horseradish mayonnaise. Serve.

NUTRITION	
CALORIES PER SERVING: 176	
FAT: 14 *g*	CAL. FROM FAT: 73%
PROTEIN: 11 *g*	CHOLESTEROL: 200 *mg*
SODIUM: 570 *mg*	CARBOHYDRATES: 1 *g*

Liver Pâté Tart

6 SERVINGS

3/4 cup	(180 mL) canned beef consommé, undiluted
1 oz	(30 mL) port wine
2 tsp	(10 mL) unflavored gelatin
3 tbsp	(45 mL) cold water
1 cup	(250 mL) liver pâté
1	shortcrust pastry, baked (p. 334)
4-5	smoked turkey slices
10-12	pimento-stuffed olives, sliced
2	hard-boiled eggs, sliced

- In a saucepan, over low heat, warm consommé. Add port. Set aside.
- In a bowl, let gelatin foam in cold water. Add to consommé, mixing well. Let stand to cool slightly.
- Meanwhile, in a food processor, soften liver pâté.
- Spread an even layer of liver pâté into pie crust. Cover with turkey slices. Top with olive and egg slices. Pour lukewarm consommé over tart in order to cover garnish. Refrigerate 3 hours. Serve.

NUTRITION	
CALORIES PER SERVING: 324	
FAT: 21 *g*	CAL. FROM FAT: 59%
PROTEIN: 15 *g*	CHOLESTEROL: 159 *mg*
SODIUM: 1034 *mg*	CARBOHYDRATES: 17 *g*

Caviar Tart

6 SERVINGS

3/4 cup	(180 mL) canned seafood bisque, undiluted
1 oz	(30 mL) vodka
2 tsp	(10 mL) unflavored gelatin
3 tbsp	(45 mL) cold water
1 cup	(250 mL) smoked salmon mousse (p. 65)
1	shortcrust pastry, baked (p. 334)
4-5	smoked salmon slices
1	hard-boiled egg, sliced
2 tbsp	(30 mL) caviar

- In a saucepan, over low heat, warm bisque. Add vodka. Set aside.
- In a small bowl, let gelatin foam in cold water. Fold into bisque, mixing well. Let stand to cool slightly.
- Meanwhile, in a food processor, soften salmon mousse.
- Spread an even layer of mousse into pie crust. Cover with smoked salmon slices. Top with egg slices and caviar. Pour lukewarm bisque over tart in order to cover garnish. Refrigerate 3 hours. Serve.

NUTRITION	
CALORIES PER SERVING: 262	
FAT: 13 *g*	CAL. FROM FAT: 49%
PROTEIN: 16 *g*	CHOLESTEROL: 78 *mg*
SODIUM: 810 *mg*	CARBOHYDRATES: 16 *g*

O ver the next few pages you will experience the features of hot, lighter menu items such as Broccoli Quiche (p. 73), Chicken-stuffed Mushrooms (p. 77) and Lobster Newburg (p. 82). These menu selections will fit perfectly into your needs and those of the guests you are serving.

These dishes may be served not only as the feature menu item for a luncheon or light dinner, but may be offered as hot appetizers for a formal dinner. You may choose to select various items as features for a sports party, ladies' afternoon luncheon or whenever the occasion dictates lighter, but hot menu delights.

HOT APPETIZERS

Zucchini Squares

8 SERVINGS

3 cups	(750 mL) zucchini, grated
2 cups	(500 mL) carrots, grated
1	medium-size onion, finely chopped
½ cup	(125 mL) Parmesan cheese, grated
4	eggs, beaten
½ cup	(125 mL) vegetable oil
1 cup	(250 mL) whole wheat flour
¼ tsp	(1 mL) salt
¼ tsp	(1 mL) pepper
¼ tsp	(1 mL) parsley, chopped
¼ tsp	(1 mL) basil

- Preheat oven to 350 °F (175 °C). Butter a 9 x 13-inch (23 x 33 cm) baking dish. Set aside.

- In a bowl, mix all the ingredients. Pour into baking dish. Bake in oven 10 minutes.

- Remove from oven. Cut into 24 squares. Serve hot.

NUTRITION	
CALORIES PER SERVING: 256	
FAT: 18 g	CAL. FROM FAT: 62%
PROTEIN: 8 g	CHOLESTEROL: 97 mg
SODIUM: 222 mg	CARBOHYDRATES: 17 g

Vegetable Pie

6-8 SERVINGS

⅓ cup	(80 mL) margarine
1 ½ cups	(375 mL) mushrooms, minced
1 ¼ cups	(300 mL) salted crackers, crumbled
½ cup	(125 mL) onions, sliced
1	zucchini, minced
2	tomatoes, thinly sliced
3	eggs, beaten
1 tbsp	(15 mL) all-purpose flour
1 cup	(250 mL) milk
¼ tsp	(1 mL) salt
¼ tsp	(1 mL) pepper
¼ tsp	(1 mL) basil
	fresh parsley, finely chopped
2 tbsp	(30 mL) Parmesan cheese, grated

- Preheat oven to 350 °F (175 °C).

- In a skillet, melt margarine. Sauté mushrooms. Add salted crackers, mixing well.

- Line a deep 9-inch (23 cm) pie plate with mixture, spreading over bottom and along sides. Cover with onion and zucchini slices. Top with tomato slices. Set aside.

- In a bowl, mix eggs with remaining ingredients, except Parmesan. Pour into crust. Sprinkle with Parmesan. Bake in oven 25-35 minutes. Serve hot.

Recipe shown above

VARIATIONS

- Replace zucchini with any other vegetable. Blanch firm vegetables such as turnip, beet, carrot, etc. beforehand.

NUTRITION	
CALORIES PER SERVING: 208	
FAT: 11 g	CAL. FROM FAT: 48%
PROTEIN: 6 g	CHOLESTEROL: 74 mg
SODIUM: 185 mg	CARBOHYDRATES: 21 g

Broccoli Quiche

6-8 SERVINGS	
2 cups	(500 mL) broccoli florets
1/4 cup	(60 mL) margarine or butter
1 cup	(250 mL) onions, chopped
1/2 cup	(125 mL) fresh parsley, chopped
1/4 tsp	(1 mL) basil
1/4 tsp	(1 mL) oregano
1/2 tsp	(2 mL) salt
1/2 tsp	(2 mL) pepper
2 cups	(500 mL) Mozzarella cheese, grated
2	eggs, beaten

1	package commercial crescent roll dough, thawed
2 tsp	(10 mL) Dijon mustard

- Preheat oven to 375 °F (190 °C).
- In a saucepan filled with lightly-salted boiling water, blanch broccoli 1 minute. Remove from saucepan. Immerse in a bowl of ice-cold water. Drain well. Set aside.
- In a frying pan, melt margarine. Sauté onions. Season with mixed herbs, salt and pepper, stirring well. Set aside.

- In a bowl, mix broccoli, Mozzarella and eggs. Add onion mixture. Set aside.
- Line a quiche mold or pie pan with crescent dough. Be sure to cover sides in order to form a lip. Brush with mustard.
- Pour broccoli mixture into pan. Bake in oven 20 minutes or until a knife inserted in the middle comes out clean. Serve.

NUTRITION	
CALORIES PER SERVING: 207	
FAT: 15 g	CAL. FROM FAT: 46 %
PROTEIN: 31 g	CHOLESTEROL: 66 mg
SODIUM: 364 mg	CARBOHYDRATES: 8 g

Bacon-wrapped Plantain Bananas

6-8 SERVINGS	
3	plantain bananas, peeled
1 lb	(450 g) bacon

- Slice bananas lengthwise then across, in slices 1-inch (2.5 cm) thick by 2-inch (5 cm) long. Set aside.
- Cut bacon slices into 3 pieces. Wrap banana slices in bacon. Fry in a pan. Serve hot.

NUTRITION	
CALORIES PER SERVING: 380	
FAT: 28 g	CAL. FROM FAT: 66 %
PROTEIN: 18 g	CHOLESTEROL: 48 mg
SODIUM: 907 mg	CARBOHYDRATES: 14 g

Asparagus Mimosa

4 SERVINGS

24	asparagus tips
3 tbsp	(45 mL) butter
1	hard-boiled egg, finely chopped
	pinch of ground nutmeg
2 tbsp	(30 mL) fresh parsley, finely chopped

- Peel asparagus. Cut into 6-inch (15 cm) lengths. Clean well. Tie in a bunch. Stand in a saucepan filled with lightly-salted boiling water. Cook 10 minutes.
- Meanwhile, warm 4 salad plates in oven.
- Remove asparagus from saucepan. Drain well. Transfer to warmed salad plates. Set aside.
- In a skillet, melt butter. Add egg. Season with nutmeg. Stirring skillet, toss 30 seconds. Pour over asparagus. Sprinkle with parsley. Serve at once.

NUTRITION	
CALORIES PER SERVING: 230	
FAT: 14 g	CAL. FROM FAT: 48%
PROTEIN: 17 g	CHOLESTEROL: 68 mg
SODIUM: 116 mg	CARBOHYDRATES: 18 g

Asparagus au Gratin

4 SERVINGS

12 oz	(341 mL) canned asparagus tips, drained
3 tbsp	(45 mL) butter
1 tbsp	(15 mL) all-purpose flour
1 1/2 cups	(375 mL) milk
	salt and pepper
1/3 cup	(80 mL) Emmenthal cheese, grated
1 tbsp	(15 mL) bread crumbs
	pinch of nutmeg
1/4 tsp	(1 mL) thyme

- Preheat oven to 400 °F (205 °C).
- In a baking dish, arrange asparagus. Set aside.
- In a skillet, melt 1 tbsp (15 mL) butter. Sprinkle with flour. While stirring, cook 2 minutes. Fold in milk. Stirring constantly, continue cooking 6 minutes until sauce is creamy smooth. Season.
- Pour sauce over asparagus. Dot with remaining butter. Top with cheese, then bread crumbs. Season with nutmeg and thyme. Cook in oven 20 minutes or until cheese and bread crumbs make a golden crust. Serve.

NUTRITION	
CALORIES PER SERVING: 198	
FAT: 15 g	CAL. FROM FAT: 66%
PROTEIN: 8 g	CHOLESTEROL: 44 mg
SODIUM: 547 mg	CARBOHYDRATES: 10 g

Crispy Eggplant

4-6 SERVINGS

½ cup	(125 mL) bread crumbs
½ cup	(125 mL) wheat germ
¼ tsp	(1 mL) salt
	pinch of cayenne
¼ tsp	(1 mL) basil, thyme or mixed herbs
2	eggs
1	eggplant, sliced
½ cup	(125 mL) cheese of your choice, grated or sliced

- Preheat oven to 350 °F (175 °C). Oil a cookie sheet. Set aside.

- On a plate, combine bread crumbs, wheat germ and seasonings.

- In a bowl, beat eggs. Dip in eggplant slices. Dredge with seasoned bread crumbs. Transfer to a cookie sheet. Cook in oven 20 minutes.

- Remove from oven. Top with cheese. Continue cooking until golden brown. Serve.

VARIATION

- In hamburger buns, serve cooked eggplant without cheese topping. Garnish with lettuce, tomato slices and mayonnaise.

NUTRITION	
CALORIES PER SERVING: 146	
FAT: 6 g	CAL. FROM FAT: 37%
PROTEIN: 8 g	CHOLESTEROL: 71 mg
SODIUM: 246 mg	CARBOHYDRATES: 16 g

Tomato Fondue

6 SERVINGS

28 oz	(796 mL) canned whole tomatoes
5	garlic cloves, crushed
1	green bell pepper, chopped
½ tsp	(2 mL) Tabasco sauce
	salt and pepper
1 lb	(450 g) Brick cheese, sliced
1	French baguette, cut into cubes

- In a large microwave-safe bowl, mix first 5 ingredients. Cook 10 minutes, on HIGH.

- Remove from oven. Blend in cheese until smooth. Serve very hot. Serve bread cubes separately.

NUTRITION	
CALORIES PER SERVING: 520	
FAT: 25 g	CAL. FROM FAT: 43%
PROTEIN: 26 g	CHOLESTEROL: 71 mg
SODIUM: 1198 mg	CARBOHYDRATES: 48 g

Veggie Pâté

	6 SERVINGS	
3/4 cup	(180 mL) whole wheat flour
1/2 cup	(125 mL) ground sunflower seeds
1 cup	(250 mL) hot water
2 tbsp	(30 mL) lemon juice
1/4 cup	(60 mL) sunflower oil
2/3 cup	(160 mL) nutritional yeast (from health food store)
1	garlic clove, minced
2	onions, minced
1	carrot, minced
1	celery stalk, minced
1	raw potato, peeled, grated
1/4 cup	(60 mL) Tamari sauce
1 tsp	(5 mL) basil
1/2 tsp	(2 mL) thyme
1/4 tsp	(1 mL) sage

■ Preheat oven to 350 °C (175 °C).

■ In a large bowl, mix ingredients. Pour into a 4 x 8-inch (10 x 20.5 cm) loaf pan. Bake in oven 45-60 minutes. Let stand to cool. Unmold. Slice. Wrap in aluminum foil. Reheat in oven. Serve hot.

Note : Veggie Pâté may be frozen up to 2 months.

NUTRITION	
CALORIES PER SERVING: 282	
FAT: 13 *g*	CAL. FROM FAT: 39 %
PROTEIN: 12 *g*	CHOLESTEROL: 0 *mg*
SODIUM: 702 *mg*	CARBOHYDRATES: 33 *g*

Cheesy Spinach Rice

	6-8 SERVINGS	
10 oz	(280 g) frozen spinach, thawed, stalks removed
2	eggs, beaten
13 oz	(369 mL) canned evaporated milk
2/3 cup	(160 mL) instant rice
8 oz	(225 g) processed cheese, diced
1/2 tsp	(2 mL) salt
1/4 tsp	(1 mL) pepper
1/4 cup	(60 mL) onion, chopped

■ In a 5-cup (1.25 L) microwave-safe casserole dish, place spinach. Cover. Cook in oven 5-6 minutes, on HIGH. Drain. Set aside.

■ In a 10-cup (2.5 L) microwave-safe bowl, mix eggs, milk, rice, cheese, salt and pepper. Cook 2 minutes, on HIGH. Stir. Continue cooking 3-4 minutes or until cheese has melted.

■ Fold in onion and spinach. Pour mixture into a 10 x 6 x 2-inch (25 x 15 x 5 cm) microwave-safe baking dish. On HIGH, cook 10-12 minutes or until a knife inserted in the middle comes out clean. Serve.

NUTRITION	
CALORIES PER SERVING: 225	
FAT: 14 *g*	CAL. FROM FAT: 54 %
PROTEIN: 26 *g*	CHOLESTEROL: 71 *mg*
SODIUM: 1198 *mg*	CARBOHYDRATES: 48 *g*

Crusty Mushroom Toast

4-6 SERVINGS	
1 tbsp	(15 mL) oil
8 oz	(225 g) mushrooms, sliced
2-3	shallots, minced
2 tbsp	(30 mL) parsley, chopped
3 tbsp	(45 mL) butter
3 tbsp	(45 mL) flour
1 ½ cups	(375 mL) milk
	salt and pepper
16	French baguette rounds
1 ½ cups	(375 mL) cheese, grated

- Preheat oven to 350 °F (175 °).

- In a frying pan, heat oil. Sauté vegetables and parsley. Set aside.

- In a saucepan, melt butter. Sprinkle with flour. Cook 2 minutes, while stirring. Fold in milk. Stirring constantly, continue cooking 6 minutes or until sauce is thick and creamy. Add sautéed mushrooms. Season. Set aside.

- On a non-stick cookie sheet, place baguette rounds. Coat with mushroom sauce. Sprinkle grated cheese on top. Cook in oven 5 minutes or until cheese has melted and starts to brown. Serve.

NUTRITION	
CALORIES PER SERVING: 464	
FAT: 22 g	CAL. FROM FAT: 42%
PROTEIN: 17 g	CHOLESTEROL: 53 mg
SODIUM: 762 mg	CARBOHYDRATES: 50 g

Chicken-stuffed Mushrooms

4-6 SERVINGS	
24	large mushrooms
4 oz	(115 g) cooked chicken, diced
6 tbsp	(90 mL) bread crumbs
2 tsp	(10 mL) fresh parsley, finely chopped
	salt and pepper
2 tbsp	(30 mL) butter
2 tsp	(10 mL) onion, finely chopped
¾ cup	(180 mL) Cheddar cheese, grated

- Preheat oven to 425 °F (220 °C).

- Remove mushroom stems, reserving caps.

- Finely chop stems. In a bowl, combine with chicken, bread crumbs and parsley. Mix in seasonings.

- In a skillet, melt butter. Cook onion 3-4 minutes. Add to chicken mixture. Stuff into mushroom caps. Sprinkle with cheese.

- On a non-stick cookie sheet, arrange stuffed mushrooms. Cook in oven 8-10 minutes. Serve hot.

NUTRITION	
CALORIES PER SERVING: 197	
FAT: 12 g	CAL. FROM FAT: 51%
PROTEIN: 13 g	CHOLESTEROL: 41 mg
SODIUM: 239 mg	CARBOHYDRATES: 12 g

Spinach Crêpes

6 SERVINGS

	6 crêpes (p. 380)
1 ½ cups	(375 mL) spinach, finely chopped
	cinnamon

Cheese sauce

2 tbsp	(30 mL) butter or margarine
1	small onion, finely chopped
2 tbsp	(30 mL) all-purpose flour
1 cup	(250 mL) partly-skimmed milk
	salt and pepper
½ cup	(125 mL) Cheddar cheese, grated

- Preheat oven to BROIL.

- On a non-stick baking sheet, arrange crêpes. Cover with spinach. Season with a pinch of cinnamon. Roll or fold into a square. Set aside.

- In a skillet, melt butter. Cook onion. Sprinkle in flour. While stirring, cook 2 minutes. Over moderate heat, fold in milk. Stirring constantly, continue cooking until creamy smooth. Season. Add cheese. Stir until cheese has melted.

- Spoon cheese sauce over each crêpe. Broil in oven 2-3 minutes. Serve at once.

Recipe shown above

VARIATIONS
- Replace spinach with blanched cauliflower florets, as shown opposite, blanched broccoli florets, or well-drained canned beets, as shown bottom right.

NUTRITION	
CALORIES PER SERVING: 181	
FAT: 8 *g*	CAL. FROM FAT: 40%
PROTEIN: 7 *g*	CHOLESTEROL: 25 *mg*
SODIUM: 398 *mg*	CARBOHYDRATES: 21 *g*

Cheesy Rice Cakes

4 SERVINGS

¼ cup	(60 mL) oil
1	onion, finely chopped
2 cups	(500 mL) short-grain rice, cooked
2	eggs, beaten
⅔ cup	(160 mL) Gruyère cheese, grated
2 tbsp	(30 mL) all-purpose flour
1 tsp	(5 mL) curry
	salt and pepper
3 tbsp	(45 mL) bread crumbs

▪ In a skillet, heat 1 tbsp (15 mL) oil. Sauté onion. In a bowl, mix onion with rice, eggs, Gruyère, flour and seasonings. With dampened hands, shape into 8 tightly-packed patties. Dredge with bread crumbs.

▪ Over moderate heat, in the same skillet, heat remaining oil. Fry patties 10 minutes each side. Serve.

VARIATIONS
• Use different cheeses.

NUTRITION	
CALORIES PER SERVING: 402	
FAT: 23 *g*	CAL. FROM FAT: 51%
PROTEIN: 12 *g*	CHOLESTEROL: 112 *mg*
SODIUM: 181 *mg*	CARBOHYDRATES: 37 *g*

Chow Mein

6-8 SERVINGS

3 tbsp	(45 mL) cornstarch
⅓ cup	(80 mL) soy sauce
10 oz	(284 mL) canned water chestnuts, drained, sliced
19 oz	(540 mL) canned bean sprouts, drained
7 oz	(198 g) canned mushrooms, in their juice
2 cups	(500 mL) cooked leftover meat, diced
2 cups	(500 mL) celery, cut into ½-inch (1.25 cm) diagonal slices
1 cup	(250 mL) onions, minced
	cooked rice or fried noodles

▪ In a 10-cup (2.5 L) microwave-safe casserole dish, dilute cornstarch in soy sauce. Mix in remaining ingredients, except rice. Cook 10 minutes, on HIGH. Remove from oven. Stir once. Continue cooking 10-12 minutes or until mixture thickens. Remove from oven. Let stand 5 minutes.

▪ Ladle over a bed of rice or fried noodles. Serve at once.

NUTRITION	
CALORIES PER SERVING: 394	
FAT: 18 *g*	CAL. FROM FAT: 40%
PROTEIN: 19 *g*	CHOLESTEROL: 30 *mg*
SODIUM: 1052 *mg*	CARBOHYDRATES: 42 *g*

Fiesta Nachos

4-6 SERVINGS

1 tsp	(5 mL) vegetable oil
1	garlic clove, minced
14 oz	(398 mL) canned red kidney beans, drained
1 tsp	(5 mL) chili powder
1/4 tsp	(1 mL) cumin
	dash of Tabasco sauce
	pepper
36	2 1/2-inch (6 cm) round tortillas
3	tomatoes, chopped
1	green bell pepper, chopped
1 tbsp	(15 mL) pickled jalapeño pepper, finely chopped (optional)
1 cup	(250 mL) Cheddar cheese, grated

- In a microwave-safe casserole dish, combine oil and garlic. Heat 35 seconds, on HIGH. Remove from oven. Mix in beans and seasonings, except pepper. Cover. Cook 2-3 minutes. Stir halfway through cooking.

- In a food processor, purée mixture. Season with pepper. Spread each tortilla with 1 tsp (5 mL) mixture. Transfer to two 12-inch (30.5 cm) microwave-safe platters. Sprinkle with tomatoes, bell pepper and jalapeño pepper, if desired. Cover with cheese.

- On MEDIUM, cook in oven around 3 minutes or until cheese has melted. Serve.

NUTRITION	
CALORIES PER SERVING: 273	
FAT: 10 g	CAL. FROM FAT: 32%
PROTEIN: 12 g	CHOLESTEROL: 20 mg
SODIUM: 521 mg	CARBOHYDRATES: 35 g

Hot Chunky Crab Dip

4 SERVINGS

8 oz	(225 g) cream cheese, softened
4 oz	(113 g) canned crab meat, drained
2	shallots, finely chopped
2-3	drops of Worcestershire sauce
1 tbsp	(15 mL) lemon juice
	salt and pepper, to taste
	garlic, to taste
	fresh vegetables and crackers

- Preheat oven to 300 °F (150 °C).

- In an ovenproof casserole dish, mix all ingredients, except vegetables and crackers. Cover. Cook in oven 20 minutes.

- Transfer dip to a chocolate-fondue dish. Serve hot with a platter of fresh vegetables and crackers.

NUTRITION	
CALORIES PER SERVING: 235	
FAT: 20 g	CAL. FROM FAT: 76%
PROTEIN: 10 g	CHOLESTEROL: 87 mg
SODIUM: 309 mg	CARBOHYDRATES: 4 g

Parmesan Fondue

8 servings	
6 tbsp	(90 mL) butter
³/₄ cup	(180 mL) flour
1 ¹/₄ cups	(300 mL) milk
1	egg yolk
¹/₂ cup	(125 mL) Gruyère cheese, grated
¹/₂ cup	(125 mL) Parmesan cheese, grated
	salt and pepper
¹/₂ tsp	(2 mL) paprika
1	egg white
¹/₈ tsp	(0.5 mL) oil
1 cup	(250 mL) bread crumbs
1 tbsp	(15 mL) Parmesan cheese, grated
¹/₂ cup	(125 mL) flour

- In a bowl, mix first 6 ingredients. Season. In a skillet, over low heat, cook until cheese has melted and paste thickens. Spread evenly in a square 8-inch (20.5 cm) dish. Refrigerate 6 hours.
- Preheat oven to 350 °F (175 °C).
- In a bowl, lightly beat together egg white and oil.
- Mix bread crumbs with 1 tbsp (15 mL) Parmesan.
- Remove paste from refrigerator. Cut into 16 squares. Dredge each square with flour. Dip in egg mixture. Dredge with bread crumbs. Transfer to a non-stick baking sheet. Cook in oven 20 minutes. Serve hot.

NUTRITION	
CALORIES PER SERVING: 296	
FAT: 16 g	CAL. FROM FAT: 49 %
PROTEIN: 11 g	CHOLESTEROL: 68 mg
SODIUM: 408 mg	CARBOHYDRATES: 27 g

Cheese Rolls

4-6 servings	
2 cups	(500 mL) all-purpose flour
4 tsp	(20 mL) baking powder
1 tsp	(5 mL) salt
1 tbsp	(15 mL) butter, softened
1 tbsp	(15 mL) shortening
1 cup	(250 mL) milk
1 cup	(250 mL) yellow Cheddar cheese, grated

- Preheat oven to 350 °F (175 °).
- In a large bowl, sift flour, baking powder and salt twice. Set aside.
- In a second bowl, cream butter and shortening. Alternating with milk, fold in dry ingredients until smooth. With a rolling pin, flatten into a ³/₈-inch (1 cm) thick rectangle.
- Sprinkle with cheese. Roll. Cut into 1-inch (2.5 cm) thick rounds. Transfer to a non-stick baking sheet. Bake in oven 30-40 minutes or until golden brown. Serve warm.

NUTRITION	
CALORIES PER SERVING: 290	
FAT: 12 g	CAL. FROM FAT: 38 %
PROTEIN: 10 g	CHOLESTEROL: 30 mg
SODIUM: 754 mg	CARBOHYDRATES: 35 g

Scallops on a Bed of Vegetables

4 SERVINGS

5 tbsp	(75 mL) butter
8 oz	(225 g) medium-size scallops
1 tbsp	(15 mL) shallot, chopped
1/3 cup	(80 mL) carrot, julienned
1/3 cup	(80 mL) zucchini, julienned
1/3 cup	(80 mL) celery, julienned
1/3 cup	(80 mL) sweet red pepper, julienned
1/3 cup	(80 mL) green bell pepper, julienned
	salt and pepper
	juice of 1/2 lemon
1/2 tsp	(2 mL) parsley, chopped

▪ In a skillet, melt 2 tbsp (30 mL) butter. Add scallops. Cook 2 minutes. Mix in shallot. Continue cooking 2 minutes. Make sure scallops are cooked all over. Set aside.

▪ In a saucepan, melt remaining butter. Sauté julienned vegetables 2 minutes. Season with salt and pepper.

▪ Cover 4 salad plates with a bed of vegetables. Spoon scallops into middle. Sprinkle with lemon juice and parsley. Serve.

NUTRITION	
CALORIES PER SERVING: 191	
FAT: 15 g	CAL. FROM FAT: 67%
PROTEIN: 10 g	CHOLESTEROL: 57 mg
SODIUM: 293 mg	CARBOHYDRATES: 6 g

Lobster Newburg

6 SERVINGS

6	bread slices, toasted, buttered
1 tbsp	(15 mL) butter
2 tsp	(10 mL) all-purpose flour
1 cup	(250 mL) heavy cream
1 cup	(250 mL) cooked lobster meat, diced
2	egg yolks
1 oz	(30 mL) sherry
1/2 oz	(15 mL) cognac
	pinch of salt
	pinch of paprika
	pinch of cayenne

▪ With a pastry cutter or a small knife, cut bread slices into fancy croutons. Set aside.

▪ In a small saucepan, melt butter. Sprinkle with flour, mixing well. Fold in cream. Bring to a boil. Over high heat, boil 30 seconds. Stir in lobster. Set aside.

▪ In a small bowl, beat together egg yolks, sherry and cognac. Season. Pour into saucepan, mixing well. Over very low heat, cook 2 minutes.

▪ Place croutons on individual salad plates. Spoon lobster mixture on top. Serve.

NUTRITION	
CALORIES PER SERVING: 280	
FAT: 19 g	CAL. FROM FAT: 64%
PROTEIN: 9 g	CHOLESTEROL: 148 mg
SODIUM: 287 mg	CARBOHYDRATES: 15 g

Flaky Crab Turnovers

6 SERVINGS

1	onion, finely chopped
6	mushrooms, minced
1/4 tsp	(1 mL) tarragon
8 oz	(225 g) crab meat or pollock
8 oz	(225 g) baby shrimp
1/2 cup	(125 mL) slivered almonds
3/4 cup	(180 mL) white wine
1/4 cup	(60 mL) light cream
1 lb	(450 g) flaky pastry (p. 335) or commercial pastry dough
1/4 cup	(60 mL) milk
	cheese sauce (p. 78)

▪ Preheat oven to 400 °F (205 °C).

▪ In a saucepan, mix first 7 ingredients. Bring to a boil. Reduce heat. Simmer until liquid has reduced to three-quarters. Fold in cream. While stirring, continue cooking 3 minutes or until creamy smooth.

▪ With a rolling pin, flatten dough. Cut into six 5-inch (12.5 cm) squares. Spoon 1-2 tbsp (15-30 mL) seafood mixture into the middle of each square. Fold into triangles. Pinch edges to seal tightly.

▪ Transfer turnovers to a non-stick baking sheet. Brush with milk. Bake in oven 12 minutes.

▪ Serve at once, topped with cheese sauce.

NUTRITION	
CALORIES PER SERVING: 553	
FAT: 31 g	CAL. FROM FAT: 52%
PROTEIN: 25 g	CHOLESTEROL: 147 mg
SODIUM: 712 mg	CARBOHYDRATES: 40 g

Crab and Cheese Delight

4 SERVINGS

10 oz	(284 mL) canned crab meat or canned crab and pollock, crumbled
1/4 cup	(60 mL) mayonnaise
1	small onion, finely chopped
	salt and pepper, to taste
1/4 tsp	(1 mL) lemon juice
4	French baguette rounds
1/2 cup	(125 mL) Mozzarella cheese, grated

▪ In a bowl, mix first 5 ingredients. Refrigerate 2-3 hours.

▪ Preheat oven to 400 °F (205 °C).

▪ Spread baguette rounds with chilled seafood mixture. Sprinkle with cheese. Transfer to a non-stick baking sheet. Cook in oven 7 minutes or so.

▪ Increase oven temperature to BROIL. Continue cooking 2 minutes or until is cheese golden brown. Serve.

NUTRITION	
CALORIES PER SERVING: 530	
FAT: 19 g	CAL. FROM FAT: 33%
PROTEIN: 26 g	CHOLESTEROL: 73 mg
SODIUM: 1081 mg	CARBOHYDRATES: 62 g

Clockwise from upper left :
Flaky Crab Turnovers, Crab and Cheese Delight, Scallops on a Bed of Vegetables

Imperial Tuna

4 SERVINGS

7 oz	(198 g) canned white tuna, drained, crumbled
1	onion, finely chopped
1	garlic clove, crushed
1/4 tsp	(1 mL) lemon juice
1/4 tsp	(1 mL) Worcestershire sauce
1 tsp	(5 mL) fresh parsley, finely chopped
	salt and pepper
1 cup	(250 mL) béchamel sauce, hot
4	pastry shells
1/4 cup	(60 mL) Parmesan cheese, grated

- Preheat oven to BROIL.
- In a saucepan, mix all ingredients, except pastry shells and cheese. Over low heat, warm mixture. Pour into pastry shells. Sprinkle with cheese.
- Broil in oven 3-4 minutes. Serve.

NUTRITION	
CALORIES PER SERVING: 441	
FAT: 26 g	CAL. FROM FAT: 53%
PROTEIN: 22 g	CHOLESTEROL: 42 mg
SODIUM: 581 mg	CARBOHYDRATES: 29 g

Coquilles St-Jacques

4 SERVINGS

2 tbsp	(30 mL) butter
1/2 cup	(125 mL) mushrooms, minced
1/2 cup	(125 mL) shallots, chopped
2 cups	(500 mL) béchamel sauce, hot
1 lb	(450 g) seafood (shrimp, scallops, clams, etc.)
1 cup	(250 mL) mashed potatoes, hot
2 tbsp	(30 mL) butter, melted
2 tsp	(10 mL) lemon juice

- Preheat oven to BROIL.
- In a saucepan, melt butter. Lightly cook mushrooms and shallots. Add béchamel sauce and seafood. Simmer 3 minutes. Set aside.
- Meanwhile, pour mashed potatoes into a pastry bag with a fluted nozzle. Pipe a crown of potatoes around edge of 4 scallop shells. Spoon seafood mixture into the middle. Lightly sprinkle seafood with lemon juice. Brush potato crown with melted butter.
- Broil in oven until lightly browned. Serve.

NUTRITION	
CALORIES PER SERVING: 371	
FAT: 22 g	CAL. FROM FAT: 52%
PROTEIN: 21 g	CHOLESTEROL: 98 mg
SODIUM: 450 mg	CARBOHYDRATES: 24 g

Shrimp Puffs

4 SERVINGS

2	slices of white bread, crusts removed, hand-torn
1	egg, lightly beaten
1/3 cup	(80 mL) mayonnaise
8 oz	(225 g) baby shrimp, chopped
1/4 cup	(60 mL) sweet red pepper, finely chopped
1/4 cup	(60 mL) onion, finely chopped
1 tsp	(5 mL) Dijon mustard
1/4 tsp	(1 mL) fresh ground pepper

- Preheat oven to 375 °F (190 °C).

- In a bowl, combine bread, egg and mayonnaise until smooth. Blend in remaining ingredients.

- Shape mixture into 1 1/2-inch (3.75 cm) balls. Arrange on a non-stick baking sheet. Bake in oven 25 minutes or until golden brown. Serve.

NUTRITION	
CALORIES PER SERVING: 247	
FAT: 18 g	CAL. FROM FAT: 64%
PROTEIN: 14 g	CHOLESTEROL: 138 mg
SODIUM: 285 mg	CARBOHYDRATES: 8 g

Salmon Hot Dog Rolls

12 SERVINGS

7 oz	(198 g) canned solid salmon, crumbled
1 cup	(250 mL) mild Cheddar cheese, grated
3	hard-boiled eggs, mashed or diced
2 tbsp	(30 mL) green bell pepper, finely chopped
2 tbsp	(30 mL) onion, minced
2 tbsp	(30 mL) green relish
1/2 cup	(125 mL) mayonnaise
12	hot dog buns

- Preheat oven to 400 °F (205 °C).

- In a bowl, mix first 7 ingredients. Stuff hot dog buns with mixture. Wrap individually in aluminum foil.

- Place on a baking sheet. Cook in oven 15-20 minutes. Serve.

NUTRITION	
CALORIES PER SERVING: 269	
FAT: 15 g	CAL. FROM FAT: 50%
PROTEIN: 11 g	CHOLESTEROL: 68 mg
SODIUM: 483 mg	CARBOHYDRATES: 23 g

Jiffy Pizza

6 SERVINGS

1	commercial 10-inch (25 cm) pizza crust or
1	flat Italian bread
¹⁄₂ cup	(125 mL) tomato sauce
1 cup	(250 mL) cooked ham, diced
¹⁄₄ cup	(60 mL) sweet red pepper, sliced
¹⁄₄ cup	(60 mL) green bell pepper, sliced
¹⁄₂	Spanish onion
¹⁄₂ tsp	(2 mL) basil
¹⁄₂ tsp	(2 mL) oregano
1 cup	(250 mL) Cheddar or Mozzarella cheese, grated

■ Preheat oven to 400 °F (205 °C).

■ Place crust on a pizza sheet. Brush with tomato sauce. Cover with ham and vegetables. Season with mixed herbs. Top with cheese.

■ Place pizza in the center of the oven. Cook 12 minutes or until cheese browns lightly. Serve.

VARIATIONS
• Add sliced mushrooms.
• Use low-fat cheese for a health bonus !

NUTRITION	
CALORIES PER SERVING: 349	
FAT: 12 g	CAL. FROM FAT: 31 %
PROTEIN: 16 g	CHOLESTEROL: 33 mg
SODIUM: 1099 mg	CARBOHYDRATES: 43 g

Stuffed Salad Rolls

5 SERVINGS

3 tbsp	(45 mL) oil
8 oz	(225 g) ground pork
8 oz	(225 g) ground veal
1	onion, finely chopped
10 oz	(284 mL) canned chicken and rice soup
	salt and pepper
2 tbsp	(30 mL) dry mustard
2 tsp	(10 mL) soy sauce
¹⁄₂ tsp	(2 mL) ketchup
10	bread rolls

■ In a saucepan, heat oil. Add meat. Cook 10 minutes, stirring occasionally. Mix in onion. Continue cooking 4 minutes. Fold in remaining ingredients, except bread rolls. Bring to a boil. Reduce heat. Simmer until liquid has evaporated. Mix well. Let stand to cool slightly.

■ Preheat oven to 350 °F (175 °C).

■ Stuff bread rolls with mixture. Wrap individually in aluminum foil. Place directly on oven rack. Warm 10 minutes. Serve.

NUTRITION	
CALORIES PER SERVING: 457	
FAT: 24 g	CAL. FROM FAT: 47 %
PROTEIN: 28 g	CHOLESTEROL: 83 mg
SODIUM: 729 mg	CARBOHYDRATES: 31 g

Veal Meatballs in Peach Sauce

8 SERVINGS	
1 1/2 lbs	(675 g) ground veal
1	onion, chopped
1	egg, beaten
1/2 cup	(125 mL) soft part of bread, hand-torn
	salt and pepper
1 tbsp	(15 mL) oil

Sauce

1/2 cup	(125 mL) chili sauce
1 tbsp	(15 mL) lemon juice
1/4 cup	(60 mL) brown sugar
2 tbsp	(30 mL) dry mustard
1 tsp	(5 mL) soy sauce
19 oz	(540 mL) canned peach slices, in their syrup

- Preheat oven to 350 °F (175 °C).
- In a large bowl, mix first 5 ingredients. Shape into meatballs. Set aside.
- In a skillet, heat oil. Brown meatballs. Transfer to an ovenproof covered casserole dish. Set aside.
- In a bowl, mix sauce ingredients, except peaches. Pour over meatballs. Cover. Cook in oven 30-40 minutes.
- Remove from oven. Add peach slices in their syrup. Continue cooking 15 minutes.
- Spoon meatballs over a bed of rice. Serve.

NUTRITION	
CALORIES PER SERVING: 490	
FAT: 9 g	CAL. FROM FAT: 17 %
PROTEIN: 23 g	CHOLESTEROL: 92 mg
SODIUM: 171 mg	CARBOHYDRATES: 77 g

Spicy Spareribs

4-6 SERVINGS	
2 lbs	(900 g) spareribs
	salt and pepper
1	small onion, chopped
2	garlic cloves, chopped
2	celery stalks, minced
3/4 cup	(180 mL) ketchup
1 cup	(250 mL) water
2 tbsp	(30 mL) white vinegar or lemon juice
2 tbsp	(30 mL) Worcestershire sauce
2 tbsp	(30 mL) brown sugar
1 tsp	(5 mL) prepared mustard

- Preheat oven to 350 °F (175 °C).
- In a saucepan filled with lightly-salted boiling water, cook spareribs 15 minutes. Remove from saucepan. Drain well. Transfer to a baking dish. Season with salt and pepper. Set aside.
- In a bowl, mix remaining ingredients. Pour over spareribs. Cook uncovered in oven 1 hour. Serve.

NUTRITION	
CALORIES PER SERVING: 339	
FAT: 22 g	CAL. FROM FAT: 59 %
PROTEIN: 17 g	CHOLESTEROL: 73 mg
SODIUM: 551 mg	CARBOHYDRATES: 18 g

Quail Fricassée in Orange Sauce

4 SERVINGS	
4	quails
2 tbsp	(30 mL) peanut oil
3 tbsp	(45 mL) honey
1	garlic clove, chopped
1 tbsp	(15 mL) lemon juice
¹/₂ cup	(125 mL) oranges, peeled, pith removed, sectioned, in their juice
¹/₂ cup	(125 mL) chicken broth
¹/₄ cup	(60 mL) heavy cream
	salt and pepper

- Bone quails into 4 pieces, as shown in technique opposite. Set aside.

- In a skillet, heat oil. Lightly brown quails on one side. Turn over. Mix in honey and garlic. Pour lemon juice and oranges in their juice over quails. Continue cooking.

- Once liquid has almost all evaporated, add chicken broth. Let liquid reduce by half. Fold in cream. Season with salt and pepper, mixing well. Continue cooking 30 seconds. Transfer to a serving dish. Serve.

NUTRITION	
CALORIES PER SERVING: 391	
FAT: 26 g	CAL. FROM FAT: 59%
PROTEIN: 23 g	CHOLESTEROL: 105 mg
SODIUM: 115 mg	CARBOHYDRATES: 18 g

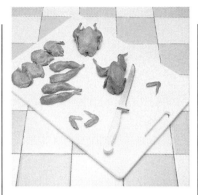

- *Cut off wing tips.*

- *Slit quails down both sides of bone. Gently detach each breast without breaking wing joint.*

- *Bend thighs outward. Remove.*

Savory Liver

6 SERVINGS	
1 lb	(450 g) veal liver, thinly sliced
2 tbsp	(30 mL) all-purpose flour
1 cup	(250 mL) shortening
1	onion, minced
¹/₂	green bell pepper, minced
10 oz	(284 mL) canned tomato soup
1 cup	(250 mL) water
1 tsp	(5 mL) lemon juice

- Dredge liver slices with flour. Set aside.

- In a skillet, melt shortening. Add liver, onion and bell pepper. Sear livers. Fold in tomato soup, water and lemon juice. Cover. Over low heat, simmer 30 minutes or until liver is tender. Serve.

NUTRITION	
CALORIES PER SERVING: 456	
FAT: 38 g	CAL. FROM FAT: 75%
PROTEIN: 15 g	CHOLESTEROL: 234 mg
SODIUM: 377 mg	CARBOHYDRATES: 14 g

Sausage Rolls

4 SERVINGS	
2 tsp	(10 mL) butter
8	pork-veal sausages
3 tbsp	(45 mL) all-purpose flour
1 lb	(450 g) flaky pastry (p. 335) or commercial pastry dough
¹/₂ cup	(125 mL) liver pâté
2 tbsp	(30 mL) hot mustard

- Preheat oven to 400 °F (205 °C).

- In a frying pan, melt butter. Add sausages. Cook around 4 minutes or until half-done.

- Flour work surface. Roll out pastry. Cut into eight 3-inch (7.5 cm) squares. Spread each square with an even layer of liver pâté. Brush with hot mustard.

- Place a sausage at one end of each square. Roll. Tightly seal pastry. Transfer rolls to a non-stick baking sheet. Lightly brown in oven 10 minutes or so. Serve.

NUTRITION	
CALORIES PER SERVING: 845	
FAT: 63 g	CAL. FROM FAT: 67%
PROTEIN: 18 g	CHOLESTEROL: 176 mg
SODIUM: 849 mg	CARBOHYDRATES: 52 g

From top to bottom :
Sausage Rolls, Savory Liver,
Quail Fricassée in Orange Sauce

SWEET INTERMISSION

What does one follow the soup or appetizer with before serving the main course? To enjoy the main course to its fullest, the distinctive flavors of previous dishes must be removed from the taste buds. The best way to achieve this is to serve a light, refreshing ice, sorbet or fresh fruit.

Family Favorites presents a selection of just right refreshments guaranteed to stimulate the appetite. Choose from such selections as Grapefruit-Vodka Sherbet (p. 92) or Frosted Berries (p. 95). No matter what you choose, be certain that your guests' taste buds will be enraptured.

Grapefruit-Vodka Sherbet

10-12 SERVINGS	
3 cups	(750 mL) grapefruit juice
2 oz	(60 mL) vodka
2 tbsp	(30 mL) sugar
	fresh mint leaves

- In a large bowl, mix first 3 ingredients. Pour into an airtight container. Freeze 12 hours or until mixture is almost solid.

- In a food processor, beat until nearly smooth. Freeze once more.

- Remove from freezer 15 minutes before serving. If desired, beat once more for a creamier sherbet. Serve in frosted cups. Garnish with a mint leaf.

VARIATIONS

APPLE SHERBET
- Replace grapefruit juice with apple juice, and vodka with calvados.

ORANGE SHERBET
- Replace grapefruit juice with orange juice, and vodka with orange liqueur.

LEMON SHERBET
- Replace grapefruit juice with lightly-sweetened lemonade, and vodka with tequila.

NUTRITION	
CALORIES PER SERVING: 43	
FAT: 1 g	CAL. FROM FAT: 2%
PROTEIN: 0 g	CHOLESTEROL: 0 mg
SODIUM: 1 mg	CARBOHYDRATES: 8 g

- *In a food processor, beat until nearly smooth.*

- *For a creamier texture, beat once more in food processor, 15 minutes before serving.*

Muscadet Wine Sherbet

8 SERVINGS	
	juice of 6 oranges
	juice of 4 lemons
1 1/2 cups	(375 mL) sugar
2/3 cup	(160 mL) Muscadet wine
1	egg white
1/4 tsp	(1 mL) cinnamon
1 cup	(250 mL) fresh grapes

- In a saucepan, mix half the fruit juices with sugar. Bring to a boil. Over moderate heat, simmer 5 minutes. Let stand to cool slightly. Fold in remaining juices and wine. Pour into an airtight container. Freeze until mixture is almost solid.

- In a mixer bowl, combine egg white and cinnamon. Beat until stiff peaks form. Set aside.

- Remove mixture from freezer. In a food processor, beat until smooth. Gently fold in egg white. Freeze 3 hours.

- Remove from freezer 15 minutes before serving. If sherbet is too hard, beat a second time in food processor for a creamier texture. Serve in frosted cups. Garnish with fresh grapes.

NUTRITION	
CALORIES PER SERVING: 230	
FAT: 1 g	CAL. FROM FAT: 2%
PROTEIN: 2 g	CHOLESTEROL: 0 mg
SODIUM: 11 mg	CARBOHYDRATES: 56 g

Honeydew Granita

8-10 SERVINGS	
1	honeydew melon, peeled, cut into pieces
2 tbsp	(30 mL) liquid honey
1/2 cup	(125 mL) sugar
3/4 cup	(180 mL) white wine
	fresh mint leaves

- In a food processor, purée honeydew melon flesh. Transfer to a bowl. Set aside.

- In a small saucepan, over low heat, dissolve honey and sugar in wine. Fold into melon purée. Mix with a wooden spoon. Pour into a roasting pan. Freeze 24 hours.

- Remove from freezer. With a metal spoon, scrape granita into crystal-like flakes. Pour into frosted cups. Garnish with a mint leaf. Serve at once.

NUTRITION	
CALORIES PER SERVING: 85	
FAT: 1 g	CAL. FROM FAT: 1%
PROTEIN: 0 g	CHOLESTEROL: 0 mg
SODIUM: 7 mg	CARBOHYDRATES: 19 g

*From left to right :
Grapefruit-Vodka Sherbet,
Muscadet Wine Sherbet,
Honeydew Granita*

Fruity Rum Delight

6 SERVINGS

1 tbsp	(15 mL) butter
3	oranges, peeled, cut into 1/2-inch (1.25 cm) thick slices
3	bananas, peeled, cut into 1/2-inch (1.25 cm) thick slices
	brown sugar, to taste
	cinnamon, to taste
3 oz	(90 mL) rum
	ice cream

▪ Set oven rack as close as possible to top element. Preheat oven to BROIL.

▪ Cut six 10-inch (25 cm) squares of aluminum foil. Butter center of each square. Cover with 2 orange slices. Divide banana slices among servings. Sprinkle with brown sugar, cinnamon and 1/2 oz (15 ml) rum. Seal aluminum squares.

▪ Cook in oven 5 minutes. Let stand to cool. Top each fruity rum delight with a scoop of ice cream. Serve.

VARIATIONS
● Replace rum with your choice of alcohol.
● Replace ice cream with your choice of sherbet (pp. 406-407).

NUTRITION	
CALORIES PER SERVING: 260	
FAT: 9 g	CAL. FROM FAT: 35%
PROTEIN: 3 g	CHOLESTEROL: 35 mg
SODIUM: 81 mg	CARBOHYDRATES: 36 g

Fruit au Gratin

4 SERVINGS

4 cups	(1 L) strawberries, raspberries, blueberries, peaches, cantaloupe, cut into pieces
3 tbsp	(45 mL) sugar
6 oz	(180 mL) Grand Marnier
6	egg yolks
1 tbsp	(15 mL) cold water
2 tbsp	(30 mL) light cream
2 tbsp	(30 mL) sugar

▪ In a large bowl, combine fruit, sugar and Grand Marnier. Macerate 30 minutes. Strain fruit, reserving syrup. Set aside.

▪ Preheat oven to BROIL.

▪ In a double-boiler, combine egg yolks, water and cream. Whisking rapidly, heat to a thick, creamy sauce. Gradually stir in syrup. Set aside.

▪ Butter a baking dish. Pour in fruit. Cover with sauce. Sprinkle with sugar. Caramelize under broiler. Serve hot for best results.

VARIATIONS
● Replace cantaloupe with honeydew, fruit with seasonal varieties, and Grand Marnier with your choice of liqueur.

NUTRITION	
CALORIES PER SERVING: 362	
FAT: 10 g	CAL. FROM FAT: 32%
PROTEIN: 5 g	CHOLESTEROL: 324 mg
SODIUM: 15 mg	CARBOHYDRATES: 42 g

Frozen Fruit Cups

10-12 SERVINGS	
2 lbs	(900 g) seedless green grapes
	fresh mint leaves

- In an airtight container, place grapes. Cover. Freeze 24 hours.
- Transfer grapes to frosted cups or emptied-out fruit shells. Garnish with fresh mint. Serve at once.

VARIATIONS
- Replace green grapes with blackberries, quartered strawberries, a melon shaped with a melon baller or chunks of kiwi.

Recipe shown above

- Replace mint leaves with lemon grass.

NUTRITION	
CALORIES PER SERVING: 31	
FAT: 1 g	CAL. FROM FAT: 2%
PROTEIN: 0 g	CHOLESTEROL: 0 mg
SODIUM: 5 mg	CARBOHYDRATES: 8 g

Frosted Berries

10-12 SERVINGS	
8 oz	(225 g) raspberries
8 oz	(225 g) strawberries, quartered
8 oz	(225 g) blueberries
8 oz	(225 g) blackberries
2 cups	(500 mL) white wine
1/4 cup	(60 mL) icing sugar

- In a large bowl, place fruit. Cover with wine. Mix well. Macerate at least 3 hours. Drain.
- On a cookie sheet, spread fruit in a single layer. Freeze until quite firm. Transfer to an airtight container. Freeze until time to serve.
- Arrange fruit in frosted cups or emptied-out fruit shells. Sprinkle with icing sugar. Serve.

NUTRITION	
CALORIES PER SERVING: 70	
FAT: 1 g	CAL. FROM FAT: 6%
PROTEIN: 1 g	CHOLESTEROL: 0 mg
SODIUM: 3 mg	CARBOHYDRATES: 11 g

Recipe shown above

- *Cut a fine slice off bottom of each apple to prevent rolling.*

- *Slice tops off apples, taking care not to damage caps.*

- *With a melon baller, remove apple core and pips without breaking skin.*

- *Immerse apple shells and caps in ice-cold water mixed with 1 tsp (5 mL) sea salt. Soak 1 minute. Remove. Shake off any excess water. Freeze apples and mint leaves 24 hours.*

- *Midway through meal, remove apples from freezer. Pour 1 oz (30 mL) liqueur into the center of each apple. Crown with a mint leaf. Cover with cap.*

Trou Normand

4 SERVINGS	
4	apples
4 cups	(1 L) ice-cold water
1 tsp	(5 mL) sea salt
4	fresh mint leaves
4 oz	(125 mL) liqueur, of your choice

- Cut a fine slice off bottom of each apple to prevent rolling. Slice tops off apples, taking care not to damage caps.
- With a melon baller, remove apple core and pips without breaking skin.
- Immerse apple shells and caps in ice-cold water mixed with sea salt. Soak 1 minute. Remove apples. Shake off any excess water. Freeze apples and mint leaves 24 hours.
- Midway through meal, remove apples from freezer. Pour 1 oz (30 mL) liqueur into the center of each apple. Crown with a mint leaf. Cover with cap. Serve at once.

VARIATIONS
- Replace apples with pears.
- Replace liqueur with brandy.

MELON TROU NORMAND
- For a spectacular presentation, serve in a melon !

- *With a sharp knife, slice top off melon, leaving a zigzag edge. Scoop out fibrous center and seeds. Rinse in cold water. Pat dry inside of melon.*
- *With toothpicks, decorate melon by pinning small fruit to skin, without piercing through.*
- *Fill melon with your choice of liqueur. Serve guests by ladling alcohol into frozen apple " goblets " !*

NUTRITION	
CALORIES PER SERVING: 141	
FAT: 1 g	CAL. FROM FAT: 5 %
PROTEIN: 0 g	CHOLESTEROL: 0 mg
SODIUM: 478 mg	CARBOHYDRATES: 19 g

Recipe shown opposite page

MAIN DISHES

The main course of every meal should be an expression of the heart of the host or hostess. *Family Favorites* will provide the inspiration to create meals with heart.

Within the following chapters you will find meals of the heart and some that are good for the heart as well.

The main course is where most people obtain the majority of their nutritional needs. Meat, fish and seafood are all excellent sources of protein, minerals such as iron and zinc, and complex vitamins. So *Family Favorites* is what's good for you too.

Chicken and other poultry remain the mainstay of most family menus throughout the world. The most inexpensive of meats, chicken is also the most versatile. Chicken, duck, and turkey are used in more ways than may be culinarily imagined.

Whenever a menu selection is in question, turn to poultry for your inspiration. Some individuals may not care for fish, pork, or even beef, however most guests enjoy a finely prepared feature such as Honey-glazed Chicken (p.112) or Turkey Croquettes (p.119). Just vary your menu selection, show a little creativity and enjoy.

POULTRY

- *Remove chicken wings. Slit chicken down the backbone. Detach breast by pressing knife against carcass and gently sliding down.*

- *Fold breast away from carcass without removing skin from breast. Carefully insert blade under carcass to cut skin attached to bottom.*

- *Once both breasts are detached, remove carcass. Lay chicken flat. Slice tips off legs. Bone legs* (see p. 108).

Cranberry Chicken

6 SERVINGS	
2 tbsp	(30 mL) oil
1	small onion, chopped
8 oz	(225 g) ground pork
1/4 cup	(60 mL) ground ham
3 oz	(90 g) cranberries
	peel of 1/2 orange or lemon
1 tbsp	(15 mL) mixed herbs (parsley, tarragon, chives)
1 tbsp	(15 mL) fresh thyme, chopped
	salt and pepper
1	egg, separated
1	3 1/2-lb (1.6 kg) whole chicken, boned

- Preheat oven to 375 °F (190 °C).

- In a skillet, heat oil. Sauté onion 2 minutes. Let stand to cool.

- In a large bowl, mix onion with remaining ingredients, except egg white and chicken. Set aside.

- In a mixer bowl, beat egg white until stiff peaks form. Gently fold into stuffing. Set aside.

- On a large sheet of aluminum foil, place chicken, skin side down. Cover with stuffing. Fold chicken sides around stuffing in order to form a large roll. Tuck in both ends.

- Transfer chicken to a roasting pan. Seal aluminum foil. Cook in oven 2 hours. Remove aluminum foil. Roast 10 minutes. Serve.

VARIATIONS
- Replace cranberries with fresh or frozen red currants.

- Add one whole egg to stuffing.

NUTRITION	
CALORIES PER SERVING: 542	
FAT: 29 g	CAL. FROM FAT: 50 %
PROTEIN: 59 g	CHOLESTEROL: 217 mg
SODIUM: 352 mg	CARBOHYDRATES: 7 g

Homestyle Chicken

4 SERVINGS

1	3-4 lb (1.4-1.8 kg) chicken
	salt and pepper
2 cups	(500 mL) homemade or commercial ketchup, with vegetable chunks
2 tbsp	(30 mL) whole wheat flour

- Preheat oven to 350 °F (175 °C).

- In an ovenproof covered casserole dish, place chicken. Season with salt and pepper. Coat with ketchup. Cover. Cook in oven 1 hour.

- Remove chicken and cooking juices from casserole dish. Set aside chicken.

- Using a sieve, strain cooking juices over casserole. Sprinkle with flour. Over moderate heat, stir until sauce thickens.

- Place chicken in sauce. Continue cooking 20 minutes or until chicken is done. Serve with mashed potatoes and a green salad, if desired.

NUTRITION	
CALORIES PER SERVING: 735	
FAT: 45 *g*	CAL. FROM FAT: 56 %
PROTEIN: 59 *g*	CHOLESTEROL: 282 *mg*
SODIUM: 908 *mg*	CARBOHYDRATES: 16 *g*

Chicken in the Pot

4 SERVINGS

1 tbsp	(15 mL) butter
2	onions, minced
1	celery stalk, diced
	salt and pepper
1	2 ½-3 lb (1.2-1.4 kg) chicken, prepared
1 ½ cups	(375 mL) chicken broth, heated
	parsley, chopped

- In a large stove-top casserole dish, melt butter. Cook onion and celery until tender but not browned.

- Meanwhile, season chicken cavity with salt and pepper. Place chicken over vegetables. Pour in broth. Cover. Over low heat, cook 2 hours. If needed, add more broth so liquid does not reduce. Sprinkle with parsley 15 minutes before the end of cooking.

- Remove chicken and vegetables from casserole dish. Drain well. On a serving dish, arrange chicken on a bed of vegetables. Surround with diced turnip and carrots, if desired.

VARIATIONS

- Add soy sauce and chopped shallots to cooking liquid. Arrange chicken on a bed of vegetable rice.

- Add ½ cup (125 mL) white wine and 1 tsp (5 mL) rosemary to cooking liquid. To vegetables, add 10 oz (280 g) canned mushroom caps, well-drained.

NUTRITION	
CALORIES PER SERVING: 596	
FAT: 40 *g*	CAL. FROM FAT: 60 %
PROTEIN: 46 *g*	CHOLESTEROL: 224 *mg*
SODIUM: 286 *mg*	CARBOHYDRATES: 13*g*

Chicken in Peach Sauce

4 SERVINGS	
2 tbsp	(30 mL) butter
4	chicken breasts
2	onions, minced
1	garlic clove, chopped
1/2	green bell pepper, diced
14 oz	(398 mL) canned peach halves, drained — reserve 1/2 cup (125 mL) syrup
10 oz	(284 mL) canned cream of mushroom soup
2 tsp	(10 mL) basil
	slivered almonds (optional)

▪ In a covered skillet, melt butter. Sear chicken breasts 2-3 minutes each side. Halfway through cooking, add onions, garlic and bell pepper. Remove chicken. Degrease skillet.

▪ Return chicken to skillet. Mix in peach syrup, cream of mushroom and basil. Cover. Over low heat, simmer 30 minutes. Fold in peaches. Warm a few minutes. Garnish with almonds. Serve on a bed of rice, if desired.

VARIATIONS
- Replace cream of mushroom soup with cream of chicken soup.
- Replace basil with 1 tsp (5 mL) savory.

NUTRITION	
CALORIES PER SERVING: 265	
FAT: 11 g	CAL. FROM FAT: 36%
PROTEIN: 13 g	CHOLESTEROL: 42 mg
SODIUM: 396 mg	CARBOHYDRATES: 31 g

Béarnaise Chicken Breasts

6 SERVINGS	
3 tbsp	(45 mL) butter
1	onion, finely chopped
8 oz	(225 g) chicken livers
2 oz	(60 mL) dry sherry
1 tsp	(5 mL) paprika
	salt and pepper
6	bread slices, toasted, crusts removed
3	chicken breasts, halved
	juice of 1 lemon
	sesame seeds

▪ In a skillet, melt 1 tbsp (15 mL) butter. Lightly brown onion. Add livers, sherry and half the paprika. Cook 2 minutes. Season with salt and pepper.

▪ In a food processor, chop liver mixture until smooth. Spread over toast. Set aside.

▪ Preheat oven to 375 °F (190 °C).

▪ In a saucepan, melt remaining butter. Baste chicken breasts. Place on a baking sheet. Season with salt, pepper and remaining paprika. Sprinkle with lemon juice. Cook in oven 30 minutes. Halfway through cooking, sprinkle with sesame seeds.

▪ Around 5 minutes before the end of cooking, place garnished toast in oven.

▪ Remove both chicken and toast from oven. Place a half chicken breast on each garnished toast. Coat with cooking juices. Serve.

NUTRITION	
CALORIES PER SERVING: 330	
FAT: 11 g	CAL. FROM FAT: 31%
PROTEIN: 36 g	CHOLESTEROL: 246 mg
SODIUM: 6329 mg	CARBOHYDRATES: 19 g

Spicy Orange Chicken

2 SERVINGS	
	juice of 1 lemon
	juice of 1 orange
1 tsp	(5 mL) black tea
1 tsp	(5 mL) paprika
1 tsp	(5 mL) garlic salt
2	chicken breasts, boned
2 tbsp	(30 mL) butter
1	onion, chopped
2	garlic cloves, chopped
3 tbsp	(45 mL) plain yogurt
	peel of 1 orange
	salt and pepper

- In a bowl, mix first 5 ingredients. Coat chicken breasts with mixture. Marinate in refrigerator 1 hour.
- Drain chicken, reserving breasts and marinade separately.
- In a skillet, melt butter. Brown onion and garlic. Add chicken. Sear on both sides. Pour in marinade. Over very low heat, simmer 20 minutes. Remove chicken from skillet. Keep warm in oven.
- Add yogurt and orange peel to cooking juices. Over moderate heat, simmer 1 minute. Adjust seasoning. Pour over chicken. Serve with mixed vegetables, if desired.

NUTRITION	
CALORIES PER SERVING: 431	
FAT: 15 g	CAL. FROM FAT: 31%
PROTEIN: 55 g	CHOLESTEROL: 163 mg
SODIUM: 1390 mg	CARBOHYDRATES: 21 g

Sweet-and-sour Chicken

4 SERVINGS	
1 cup	(250 mL) ketchup
1 cup	(250 mL) water
1 tbsp	(15 mL) Worcestershire sauce
1/4 cup	(60 mL) brown sugar
2 tbsp	(30 mL) vinegar
1 tbsp	(15 mL) prepared mustard
	salt and pepper
1/4 cup	(60 mL) butter
4	chicken breasts
2	medium-size onions, sliced
1 cup	(250 mL) celery, sliced

- Preheat oven to 350 °F (175 °C).
- In a bowl, blend first 6 ingredients to a smooth sauce. Season. Set aside.
- In an ovenproof skillet, melt butter. Brown chicken breasts all over. Remove chicken from skillet. Set aside.
- In chicken cooking fat, fry onions and celery 2-3 minutes. Fold in sauce. Simmer 10 minutes.
- Add chicken breasts. Cook uncovered in oven 1 hour or so, stirring occasionally. Serve with mashed potatoes or rice, if desired.

NUTRITION	
CALORIES PER SERVING: 377	
FAT: 13 g	CAL. FROM FAT: 31%
PROTEIN: 28 g	CHOLESTEROL: 96 mg
SODIUM: 1061 mg	CARBOHYDRATES: 38 g

Maple Chicken Breasts

6 SERVINGS

1/2 cup	(125 mL) butter, melted	
1 tbsp	(15 mL) powdered mustard	
6	chicken breasts	
4 oz	(115 g) solid pork fat or bacon, sliced	
1	onion, sliced	
1 cup	(250 mL) maple syrup	
2 cups	(500 mL) boiling water	
1 cup	(250 mL) ketchup	
3 tbsp	(45 mL) vinegar	
3	cloves	
1	bay leaf	
	pinch of thyme	

- Preheat oven to 325 °F (160 °C).

- Mix butter and mustard. Brush over chicken breasts. In a buttered ovenproof dish, place chicken. Top each breast with a slice of pork fat and a slice of onion. Coat with maple syrup. Cook uncovered in oven 90 minutes. Baste regularly with cooking juices. Remove chicken from dish. Keep warm in oven.

- Degrease cooking juices. Deglaze with boiling water. Add remaining ingredients. Boil to a thick, smooth sauce.

- Pass sauce through a sieve. Coat chicken. Cook in oven 5-10 minutes. Serve.

NUTRITION	
CALORIES PER SERVING: 570	
FAT: 27 g	CAL. FROM FAT: 42 %
PROTEIN: 33 g	CHOLESTEROL: 122 mg
SODIUM: 1019 mg	CARBOHYDRATES: 51 g

Traditional Chicken

6 SERVINGS

6	chicken breasts	
1/4 cup	(60 mL) flour	
6 tbsp	(90 mL) olive oil	
	salt and pepper	
5 cups	(1.25 mL) chicken broth, heated	
20	small onions, blanched, drained	
1/4 tsp	(1 mL) basil	
1 tsp	(5 mL) thyme	
1 tsp	(5 mL) chervil	
1	bay leaf	
2 tbsp	(30 mL) parsley, chopped	
8 oz	(225 g) mushrooms	
2	egg yolks, beaten	
1/3 cup	(80 mL) heavy cream	

- Preheat oven to 350 °F (175 °C).

- In a saucepan filled with cold water, boil chicken 5 minutes. Drain. Pat dry. Dredge chicken with flour.

- In a casserole dish, heat oil. Sear chicken all over. Season with salt and pepper. Cook in oven 10 minutes. Add broth, onions, mixed herbs and parsley. Cover. Cook in oven 1 hour. Halfway through cooking, add mushrooms.

- In a bowl, beat together egg yolks and cream. Set aside.

- Remove chicken from casserole dish. Fold egg mixture into cooking juices. Heat through without boiling. Pour over chicken. Serve on a bed of tomato-flavored rice, if desired.

NUTRITION	
CALORIES PER SERVING: 494	
FAT: 26 g	CAL. FROM FAT: 46 %
PROTEIN: 34 g	CHOLESTEROL: 165 mg
SODIUM: 821 mg	CARBOHYDRATES: 35 g

Chicken in Beer Sauce

4 SERVINGS

3 tbsp	(45 mL) butter
4	chicken breasts, skinned
1 cup	(250 mL) beer
1 cup	(250 mL) chicken broth
1 tsp	(5 mL) thyme
	salt and pepper
2 tbsp	(30 mL) butter, softened
2 tbsp	(30 mL) all-purpose flour

- In a skillet, melt butter. Over moderate heat, sauté chicken breasts 8-10 minutes.
- Add beer, chicken broth and seasonings, mixing well. Cover. Over low heat, cook 45-50 minutes.
- Blend butter and flour. Set aside.
- Remove chicken from skillet. Add kneaded butter to cooking juices. While stirring, cook until sauce thickens. Pour over chicken. Serve with rice, mixed vegetables and a broccoli floret, if desired.

NUTRITION	
CALORIES PER SERVING: 435	
FAT: 18 g	CAL. FROM FAT: 40%
PROTEIN: 53 g	CHOLESTEROL: 171 mg
SODIUM: 350 mg	CARBOHYDRATES: 9 g

Creole Chicken

4 SERVINGS

1 1/2 cups	(375 mL) canned whole tomatoes
5 1/2 oz	(156 mL) tomato paste
2 tbsp	(30 mL) onion, finely chopped
1/4 tsp	(1 mL) salt
1/4 tsp	(1 mL) sugar
1 tbsp	(15 mL) vegetable oil
4	chicken breasts
1/2 cup	(125 mL) green bell pepper, chopped
1/2 cup	(125 mL) mushrooms, minced
1/4 cup	(60 mL) onion, chopped
6	green or black olives, minced
1	garlic clove, chopped
1 tsp	(5 mL) parsley, chopped
	pinch of thyme
1/2 oz	(15 mL) dry sherry
	cooked rice

- In a large saucepan, combine first 5 ingredients. Over low heat, simmer 15-20 minutes.
- Meanwhile, in a frying pan, heat oil. Sear chicken breasts 3 minutes each side.
- Place chicken in tomato mixture. Add remaining ingredients, except rice. Over low heat, simmer 30 minutes or until chicken is cooked. Arrange on a bed of rice. Serve.

NUTRITION	
CALORIES PER SERVING: 472	
FAT: 7 g	CAL. FROM FAT: 13%
PROTEIN: 34 g	CHOLESTEROL: 65 mg
SODIUM: 743 mg	CARBOHYDRATES: 67 g

Chicken Legs with Rice Vermicelli Stuffing

- Lay chicken legs very flat. Slice tips off chicken legs. Make an incision across bones lengthwise.

- Scrape bones in order to partly detach them.

- Slide knife under bones. Remove completely.

4 SERVINGS

4	chicken legs
2 tbsp	(30 mL) peanut oil
1/4 cup	(60 mL) carrot, julienned
1/4 cup	(60 mL) leek, minced
1/4 cup	(60 mL) turnip, julienned
1/4 cup	(60 mL) onion, chopped
1 cup	(250 mL) cooked rice vermicelli
1	garlic clove, chopped
2 tbsp	(30 mL) sesame seeds
1 tsp	(5 mL) sesame oil
	salt and pepper
2 tbsp	(30 mL) butter
1 tsp	(5 mL) lemon juice
1/2 cup	(125 mL) oranges, peeled, pith removed, sectioned, in their juice
1/2 cup	(125 mL) chicken broth
1/4 cup	(60 mL) heavy cream

- Preheat oven to 350 °F (175 °C).

- Bone chicken legs as shown in technique opposite. Set aside.

- In a skillet, heat peanut oil. Fry vegetables 1 minute. Add rice vermicelli, garlic, sesame seeds and oil. Mix without cooking. Off heat, season with salt and pepper. Stuff each leg with 1/2 cup (125 mL) vermicelli stuffing. Roll sausage-like. Tie with a string.

- In an ovenproof skillet, melt butter. Sear chicken rolls all over. Cook in oven 20 minutes.

- Meanwhile, in a saucepan, combine lemon juice, oranges in their juice and chicken broth. Bring to a boil. Over low heat, simmer 5 minutes. Stir in cream. Continue cooking 10 minutes.

- Remove chicken legs from oven. Cut string. Slice each leg into 5-6 rounds. Coat with sauce. Serve.

NUTRITION	
CALORIES PER SERVING: 638	
FAT: 42 g	CAL. FROM FAT: 60%
PROTEIN: 35 g	CHOLESTEROL: 177 mg
SODIUM: 256 mg	CARBOHYDRATES: 29 g

Snap, Crackle, Pop Chicken Legs

6 SERVINGS	
2	eggs
¼ cup	(60 mL) milk
	salt and pepper
4	chicken legs, skinned
1 cup	(250 mL) commercial puffed rice, ground
1 tbsp	(15 mL) peanut oil
1 tbsp	(15 mL) butter
3 tbsp	(45 mL) water
1 ½ cups	(375 mL) commercial barbecue sauce
2 tbsp	(30 mL) parsley, chopped

- Preheat oven to 350 °F (175 °C).
- In a bowl, beat together eggs, milk, salt and pepper. Dip chicken legs in mixture. Roll in ground puffed rice. Set aside.
- In an ovenproof skillet, heat oil and melt butter. Gently brown chicken legs on both sides. Cook in oven 15 minutes.
- Remove chicken legs from skillet. Set aside.
- Degrease skillet. Deglaze with water. Add barbecue sauce. Simmer to a smooth sauce. If sauce needs to be thickened, add cornstarch mixed with a little water. Spoon sauce over chicken. Sprinkle with parsley. Serve.

NUTRITION	
CALORIES PER SERVING: 123	
FAT: 7 g	CAL. FROM FAT: 51%
PROTEIN: 4 g	CHOLESTEROL: 68 mg
SODIUM: 587 mg	CARBOHYDRATES: 11 g

Saucy Mushroom Chicken

4 SERVINGS	
4	chicken legs, skinned
2 tbsp	(30 mL) flour
2 tbsp	(30 mL) butter, melted
½ cup	(125 mL) white grape juice
⅓ cup	(80 mL) chicken broth
½ tsp	(2 mL) tarragon
¼ tsp	(1 mL) ground marjoram
2	garlic cloves, crushed
1 cup	(250 mL) mushrooms, sliced
½ cup	(125 mL) sour cream
¼ cup	(60 mL) shallots, chopped

- In a microwave-safe dish, arrange chicken legs star-like, with meaty ends pointing outward. Cover dish with plastic wrap. With a fork, puncture a few holes. Cook chicken in oven 5 minutes, on HIGH. Turn over halfway through cooking. Remove chicken. Drain.
- In a bowl, blend flour and butter. Fold in grape juice, chicken broth, mixed herbs, garlic and mushrooms. On HIGH, cook 6 minutes or until mixture turns to a thick sauce. Stir once during cooking. Add sour cream and half the shallots. Pour over chicken.
- Cook 8-10 minutes, on HIGH. Garnish with remaining shallots. Cover. Let stand 5 minutes. Serve.

NUTRITION	
CALORIES PER SERVING: 336	
FAT: 18 g	CAL. FROM FAT: 47%
PROTEIN: 31 g	CHOLESTEROL: 142 mg
SODIUM: 202 mg	CARBOHYDRATES: 13 g

Delectable Chicken Legs

---
6 SERVINGS
---

4 tsp	(20 mL) butter
2	bacon slices, in pieces
6	whole chicken legs
5	shallots, chopped
	salt and pepper
1/2 tsp	(2 mL) tarragon
1/2 cup	(125 mL) milk
10 oz	(284 mL) canned cream of chicken soup

▪ In a skillet, melt butter. Cook bacon until golden brown. Add chicken legs and shallots. Fry lightly. Season. Cover. Over low heat, continue cooking 40 minutes.

▪ In a bowl, blend milk and cream of chicken until smooth. Pour over chicken. Simmer 15 minutes. Serve.

NUTRITION	
CALORIES PER SERVING: 399	
FAT: 26 g	CAL. FROM FAT: 60%
PROTEIN: 33 g	CHOLESTEROL: 153 mg
SODIUM: 425 mg	CARBOHYDRATES: 6 g

Mexican Chicken Legs

---
6 PORTIONS

6	whole chicken legs
1 cup	(250 mL) ketchup
1 cup	(250 mL) water
1/4 cup	(60 mL) vinegar
1/4 cup	(60 mL) Worcestershire sauce
	pinch of cayenne
1 tbsp	(15 mL) brown sugar
1 tbsp	(15 mL) butter
1 tsp	(5 mL) salt
1 tsp	(5 mL) celery salt
1 tsp	(5 mL) chili powder
2 tbsp	(30 mL) lemon juice

▪ Preheat oven to 325 °F (160 °C).

▪ In an ovenproof dish, place chicken legs. Set aside.

▪ In a bowl, mix remaining ingredients. Pour over chicken. Cook uncovered in oven 2 hours. Serve on a bed of rice, if desired.

NUTRITION	
CALORIES PER SERVING: 395	
FAT: 23 g	CAL. FROM FAT: 52%
PROTEIN: 32 g	CHOLESTEROL: 145 mg
SODIUM: 1351 mg	CARBOHYDRATES: 16 g

Foil-wrapped Chicken Surprise

6 SERVINGS

6	chicken legs
1	small envelope cream of mushroom soup
1/2 tsp	(2 mL) poultry seasoning
2 tbsp	(30 mL) dried parsley
1 1/3 cups	(330 mL) quick-cooking rice
2	green bell peppers, sliced into rounds
3	tomatoes, halved
3/4 cup	(180 mL) light cream
1 1/3 cups	(330 mL) water

- Preheat oven to 325 °F (160 °C).
- Line a baking dish with aluminum foil. Place chicken legs inside. Set aside.

- In a bowl, mix cream of mushroom, seasonings and parsley. Sprinkle half over chicken. Surround chicken with rice, bell peppers and tomatoes. Season with remaining mushroom mixture. Set aside.
- In a bowl, blend cream and water. Pour over chicken. Seal aluminum foil. Cook in oven 2 hours.
- Open aluminum foil. Roast chicken 30 minutes. Serve.

VARIATIONS
- Replace legs with a whole chicken or other chicken parts.
- Replace tomatoes with carrot slices and diced turnip.

NUTRITION	
CALORIES PER SERVING: 503	
FAT: 28 g	CAL. FROM FAT: 51%
PROTEIN: 34 g	CHOLESTEROL: 160 mg
SODIUM: 332 mg	CARBOHYDRATES: 27 g

Crispy Fried Chicken

4 SERVINGS

4	whole chicken legs
1	onion, chopped
	salt and pepper
1 cup	(250 mL) flour
1/2 tsp	(2 mL) salt
1/2 tsp	(2 mL) parsley
1/8 tsp	(0.5 mL) pepper
1/8 tsp	(0.5 mL) cayenne
1/8 tsp	(0.5 mL) chili powder
1/8 tsp	(0.5 mL) garlic salt
1/8 tsp	(0.5 mL) onion salt
1/4 tsp	(1 mL) paprika
1/4 tsp	(1 mL) barbecue seasoning
1/4 tsp	(1 mL) celery salt
1	egg
2 tbsp	(30 mL) milk
4 cups	(1 L) peanut oil

- In a saucepan filled with boiling water, place chicken and onion. Season with salt and pepper. Boil 10 minutes. Let stand to cool.
- In a bag, combine flour and spices.
- In a bowl, beat together egg and milk. Dip in chicken legs. Transfer to bag of seasoned flour. Toss chicken in order to coat evenly. Set aside.
- In a large deep-fryer, heat oil to 400 °F (205 °C). Fry chicken legs until golden brown. Serve with honey or barbecue sauce.

NUTRITION	
CALORIES PER SERVING: 588	
FAT: 36 g	CAL. FROM FAT: 56%
PROTEIN: 36 g	CHOLESTEROL: 186 mg
SODIUM: 710 mg	CARBOHYDRATES: 28 g

Honey-glazed Chicken

4 SERVINGS	
1	3-lb (1.4 kg) chicken, quartered
2 tbsp	(30 mL) butter
2 tbsp	(30 mL) honey
1 tbsp	(15 mL) soy sauce
1	garlic clove, finely chopped
¹/₂ cup	(125 mL) fruit relish

- Preheat oven to 350 °F (175 °C).
- In a covered ovenproof dish, place chicken, skin down. Set aside.
- In a small frying pan, melt butter. Add remaining ingredients, except relish. Mix to a smooth sauce. Remove from heat. Fold in relish.
- Pour half the sauce over chicken. Cover. Cook in oven 40 minutes.
- Remove chicken from oven. Turn over. Coat with remaining sauce. Continue cooking uncovered in oven 20-30 minutes. Serve.

NUTRITION	
CALORIES PER SERVING: 558	
FAT: 24 g	CAL. FROM FAT: 39 %
PROTEIN: 61 g	CHOLESTEROL: 201 mg
SODIUM: 743 mg	CARBOHYDRATES: 23 g

Coq au Vin

4 SERVINGS	
1	3-4 lb (1.4-1.8 kg) chicken, cut into 10 pieces
¹/₂ cup	(125 mL) flour
¹/₄ cup	(60 mL) butter
	salt and pepper
2 oz	(60 mL) cognac
¹/₄ tsp	(1 mL) thyme
2	bay leaves
1 tbsp	(15 mL) curry
2 cups	(500 mL) red wine
4	bacon slices, diced
12	small onions
12	mushrooms
	toasted bread, cut into triangles

- Dredge chicken pieces with flour. Set aside.
- In a large skillet, melt butter. Lightly brown chicken. Season with salt and pepper. Pour in cognac. Flambé 30 seconds. Add mixed herbs. Top up chicken with wine. Cover. Over low heat, simmer 40 minutes.
- Meanwhile, in a second skillet, lightly fry bacon. Add onions. Cover. Over low heat, cook onion until tender but not browned. Add mushrooms. Continue cooking 2 minutes.
- On a warm serving dish, arrange chicken pieces on a bed of fried vegetables. Coat with cooking juices thickened with cornstarch, if desired. Garnish with toast triangles. Serve.

NUTRITION	
CALORIES PER SERVING: 1038	
FAT: 52 g	CAL. FROM FAT: 51 %
PROTEIN: 55 g	CHOLESTEROL: 248 mg
SODIUM: 1378 mg	CARBOHYDRATES: 59 g

Chicken in White Sauce

4 SERVINGS	
1 tbsp	(15 mL) vegetable oil
3 tbsp	(45 mL) butter or margarine
1	3-lb (1.4 kg) chicken, cut into pieces
3 tbsp	(45 mL) flour
1/3 cup	(80 mL) white wine or cider
2 cups	(500 mL) water
1	egg yolk, beaten
	salt and pepper
1/4 tsp	(1 mL) paprika
1 tsp	(5 mL) parsley, chopped

- In a skillet, heat oil and melt butter. Sear chicken pieces all over. Remove from skillet.
- Sprinkle chicken cooking fat with flour. Gradually mix in wine and water. While stirring, cook to a thick creamy sauce.
- In a bowl, mix egg yolk and 2 tsp (10 mL) heated sauce. Slowly fold into remaining sauce. Return chicken to skillet. Season. Cover. Over low heat, simmer 1 hour.
- Serve with small boiled potatoes seasoned with paprika, and diced carrots, if desired.

NUTRITION	
CALORIES PER SERVING: 642	
FAT: 47 g	CAL. FROM FAT: 69%
PROTEIN: 43 g	CHOLESTEROL: 281 mg
SODIUM: 299 mg	CARBOHYDRATES: 5 g

Deviled Chicken Fricassée

4 SERVINGS	
3 tbsp	(45 mL) corn oil
4	chicken breasts, skinned, diced
	salt and pepper
1	green bell pepper, cut into strips
1	sweet red pepper, cut into strips
1	red onion, minced
3	canned miniature corn, drained
1/4 tsp	(1 mL) thyme
1/4 tsp	(1 mL) parsley, chopped
1	small hot pepper, diced (optional)

- In a pan, heat oil. Add chicken. Season with salt and pepper. Cook 10 minutes.
- Add vegetables, thyme and parsley. Continue cooking 5 minutes.
- Sprinkle with diced hot pepper, if desired. Serve with noodles in soy sauce, if desired.

NUTRITION	
CALORIES PER SERVING: 374	
FAT: 13 g	CAL. FROM FAT: 33%
PROTEIN: 54 g	CHOLESTEROL: 130 mg
SODIUM: 197 mg	CARBOHYDRATES: 8 g

Recipe shown above

Chinese-style Veggie Chicken

6 SERVINGS	
1 cup	(250 mL) broccoli florets
1 cup	(250 mL) cauliflower florets
1 cup	(250 mL) celery, cut into diagonal slices
2 tbsp	(30 mL) cornstarch
2 tbsp	(30 mL) corn syrup
1 tbsp	(15 mL) soy sauce
1/2 cup	(125 mL) chicken broth
3 tbsp	(45 mL) corn oil
1 cup	(250 mL) mushrooms, quartered
1 cup	(250 mL) tomatoes, diced
1 lb	(450 g) cooked chicken leftovers, cut into strips

- In a saucepan filled with lightly-salted boiling water, blanch broccoli, cauliflower and celery 1 minute. Set aside.
- In a saucepan, mix cornstarch, corn syrup, soy sauce, chicken broth and oil. Cook to a smooth sauce.
- Fold in vegetables and chicken strips. Over low heat, simmer 5-10 minutes, stirring occasionally. Serve on a bed of rice, if desired.

NUTRITION	
CALORIES PER SERVING: 304	
FAT: 16 *g*	CAL. FROM FAT: 47%
PROTEIN: 26 *g*	CHOLESTEROL: 65 *mg*
SODIUM: 267 *mg*	CARBOHYDRATES: 14 *g*

Almond Chicken Stir-fry

4 SERVINGS	
4 tsp	(20 mL) cornstarch
2 tbsp	(30 mL) soy sauce
1 lb	(450 g) chicken breasts, cut into strips
1/2 cup	(125 mL) chicken broth
2 tbsp	(30 mL) vegetable oil
2 cups	(500 mL) celery, minced
2 cups	(500 mL) snow peas, cut into diagonal slices
1 cup	(250 mL) carrots, minced
1-2	large onions, minced
2	garlic cloves, chopped
2 tbsp	(30 mL) water
	salt and pepper
2 tbsp	(30 mL) toasted sliced almonds

- Dilute 1 tbsp (15 mL) cornstarch in soy sauce. Coat chicken with mixture. Set aside.
- Dilute remaining cornstarch in chicken broth.
- In a wok, heat oil. Stir-fry chicken 4 minutes or until chicken turns white. Remove from wok.
- In chicken cooking fat, stir-fry vegetables and garlic 1 minute. Pour in water. Cover. Cook 2 minutes.
- Add thickened broth and chicken. Continue cooking 3-4 minutes or until sauce reaches boiling point and vegetables are just tender-crisp. Season. Sprinkle with toasted almonds. Serve on a bed of rice, if desired.

NUTRITION	
CALORIES PER SERVING: 298	
FAT: 12 *g*	CAL. FROM FAT: 35%
PROTEIN: 27 *g*	CHOLESTEROL: 54 *mg*
SODIUM: 861 *mg*	CARBOHYDRATES: 22 *g*

Chicken Shepherd's Pie

6 SERVINGS

2 tbsp	(30 mL) butter
2	chicken breasts, cubed
³/₄ cup	(180 mL) onions, chopped
1 cup	(250 mL) mushrooms, minced
1 ¹/₂ lbs	(675 g) ground pork
¹/₄ cup	(60 mL) white wine
³/₄ cup	(180 mL) beef broth
¹/₂ tsp	(2 mL) salt
¹/₂ tsp	(2 mL) pepper
	pinch of thyme
1 tbsp	(15 mL) parsley, chopped
2 tbsp	(30 mL) cornstarch
¹/₄ cup	(60 mL) chicken broth
2	shortcrust pastries
	(p. 334)

- In a casserole dish, melt butter. Lightly brown cubed chicken. Add vegetables and pork. Over moderate heat, cook 10-15 minutes.
- Pour in wine and beef broth. Season. Cook 2-3 minutes.
- Dilute cornstarch in chicken broth. Pour over chicken, mixing well. Continue cooking until sauce thickens. Let stand to cool.
- Preheat oven to 350 °F (175 °C).
- Line a 9-inch (23 cm) spring-form pie pan with crust. Pour chicken mixture into pan. Cover with remaining crust. Bake in oven 30-40 minutes. Serve.

Note : if crust browns too quickly, cover with aluminum foil.

NUTRITION	
CALORIES PER SERVING: 681	
FAT: 43 g	CAL. FROM FAT: 58 %
PROTEIN: 43 g	CHOLESTEROL: 172 mg
SODIUM: 416 mg	CARBOHYDRATES: 28 g

Tender-crisp Chicken Croquettes

4 SERVINGS

2 tbsp	(30 mL) butter
2 tbsp	(30 mL) flour
1 cup	(250 mL) milk
	pinch of onion salt
2 tsp	(10 mL) parsley, chopped
	salt and pepper
¹/₄ cup	(60 mL) flour
¹/₄ cup	(60 mL) salted crackers, crumbled
4	chicken breasts, boned, ground
1	egg, beaten
4 cups	(1 L) oil for frying
	commercial barbecue sauce

- Preheat oven to 400 °F (205 °C).
- In a saucepan, over low heat, melt butter. Sprinkle with flour. Cook 2-3 minutes. Whisking vigorously, stir in milk until mixture turns to a smooth, creamy sauce. Season with salt and pepper. Continue cooking 5 minutes.
- In a bowl, mix flour and crumbled salted crackers.
- Add chicken to sauce, mixing well. Shape into 12 patties. Dip in beaten egg. Dredge with breading.
- In a deep-fryer, heat oil to 400 °F (205 °C). Fry patties to a nice golden brown color. Drain well. Coat with barbecue sauce. Serve.

NUTRITION	
CALORIES PER SERVING: 398	
FAT: 21 g	CAL. FROM FAT: 48 %
PROTEIN: 32 g	CHOLESTEROL: 134 mg
SODIUM: 719 mg	CARBOHYDRATES: 20 g

Carrot Chicken Wings

4 SERVINGS	
2 tbsp	(30 mL) vegetable oil
3 lbs	(1.4 kg) chicken wings
3 cups	(750 mL) carrots, grated
1 cup	(250 mL) mushrooms, sliced
1 cup	(250 mL) onions, minced
1	garlic clove, crushed
1 tbsp	(15 mL) parsley, chopped
1 cup	(250 mL) tomato juice
	salt and pepper

- Preheat oven to 350 °F (175 °C).
- In a skillet, heat oil. Sear chicken wings all over.
- Transfer to an ovenproof casserole dish. Add remaining ingredients. Cover. Cook in oven 35 minutes. Serve.

NUTRITION	
CALORIES PER SERVING: 534	
FAT: 37 g	CAL. FROM FAT: 62%
PROTEIN: 36 g	CHOLESTEROL: 142 mg
SODIUM: 413 mg	CARBOHYDRATES: 15 g

Three-way Chicken Wings

4 SERVINGS	
³/₄ cup	(180 mL) commercial oriental garlic sauce
³/₄ cup	(180 mL) barbecue commercial sauce
3 lbs	(1.4 kg) chicken wings
	salt and pepper

First way: stove-top cooking
- In a casserole dish, mix both sauces. Add chicken wings. Season to taste. Over moderate heat, simmer until wings are cooked. Serve.

Second way: charcoal-grill cooking
- In a bowl, mix both sauces. Generously brush over chicken wings. Season. Barbecue, basting often with sauce. Serve.

Third way: oven cooking
- Preheat oven to 450 °F (230 °C).
- In an ovenproof dish, mix both sauces. Add chicken wings. Season. Cook in oven 40 minutes or until wings are tender. Baste regularly with sauce. Serve.

VARIATION
- For an exotic touch, add ¹/₄ tsp (1 mL) ground ginger.

NUTRITION	
CALORIES PER SERVING: 476	
FAT: 30 g	CAL. FROM FAT: 58%
PROTEIN: 40 g	CHOLESTEROL: 142 mg
SODIUM: 1754 mg	CARBOHYDRATES: 9 g

Pork Stuffing

3 CUPS (750 mL)	
¹/₄ cup	(60 mL) margarine
1	onion, chopped
1	chicken heart, ground
1	chicken liver, ground
1	chicken gizzard, ground
1 lb	(450 g) ground pork
	salt and pepper
	poultry seasoning
1 cup	(250 mL) mashed potatoes

- In a skillet, melt margarine. Over high heat, lightly fry onion and giblets. Reduce heat. Continue cooking 5-8 minutes.
- Add pork. Season. Continue cooking 15-20 minutes. Fold in mashed potatoes.
- Stuff mixture into a 3-4 lb (1.4-1.8 kg) chicken. (Truss or close with small skewers.) Cook chicken according to your choice of recipe.

VARIATIONS
- Replace ground pork with pork sausages, and mashed potatoes with cooked rice.
- Add ¹/₂ cup (125 mL) apple sauce.
- Replace mashed potatoes with cooked couscous. Add a chopped sweet red pepper.
- Replace ground pork with ground ham, and mashed potatoes with tomato-flavored rice.

NUTRITION	
CALORIES PER SERVING: 352	
FAT: 24 g	CAL. FROM FAT: 63%
PROTEIN: 24 g	CHOLESTEROL: 127 mg
SODIUM: 268 mg	CARBOHYDRATES: 8 g

Chicken Livers with Bell Peppers

4 SERVINGS	
3 tbsp	(45 mL) butter or margarine
1 ¹/₂ lbs	(675 g) chicken livers
	salt and pepper
1	medium-size onion, minced
1	green bell pepper, cut into strips
1	sweet red pepper, cut into strips

- In a skillet, melt 2 tbsp (30 mL) butter. Sauté chicken livers. Season with salt and pepper. Over moderate heat, cook 3-4 minutes. Set aside.
- In a frying pan, melt remaining butter. Cook minced onion 2-3 minutes. Add peppers. Continue cooking 3 minutes.
- Fold vegetables into fried livers. Serve on a bed of fettucine with tomato sauce, if desired.

NUTRITION	
CALORIES PER SERVING: 310	
FAT: 15 g	CAL. FROM FAT: 45%
PROTEIN: 31 g	CHOLESTEROL: 770 mg
SODIUM: 267 mg	CARBOHYDRATES: 11 g

From let to right :
Chicken Livers with Bell Peppers,
Three-way Chicken Wings,
Carrot Chicken Wings

Old-fashioned Stuffed Roast Turkey

10-12 SERVINGS

1	10-12 lb (4.5-5.4 kg) turkey

Stuffing

4	bacon slices, diced
1	onion, finely chopped
5	celery stalks, minced
1 ½ lbs	(675 g) ground pork
	salt and pepper
1 ½ cups	(375 mL) mashed potatoes, without milk
2 tbsp	(30 mL) oil (optional)

- Preheat oven to 325 °F (160 °C).
- Wipe and trim turkey for cooking. Set aside.
- In a casserole dish, lightly cook bacon, onion and celery. Add pork. Season to taste. Cook 30 minutes, draining cooking juices regularly.

- Fold in mashed potatoes. Stuff turkey with hot mixture. Truss or close with small skewers.
- Line a roasting pan with aluminum foil. Transfer turkey to pan. Cook in oven 20-30 minutes per 1 lb (450 g).

- Remove stuffing from cooked turkey. Heat in hot oil, if desired.
- Transfer turkey to a large serving dish. Serve piping hot stuffing separately.

NUTRITION	
CALORIES PER SERVING: 804	
FAT: 44 g	CAL. FROM FAT: 51%
PROTEIN: 89 g	CHOLESTEROL: 300 mg
SODIUM: 397 mg	CARBOHYDRATES: 6 g

Creamy Turkey Mold

6-8 SERVINGS	
3	envelopes unflavored gelatin
1 ¼ cups	(300 mL) poultry broth
1 cup	(250 mL) mayonnaise
¼ cup	(60 mL) heavy cream
1 tbsp	(15 mL) lemon juice
1 ½ tsp	(7 mL) salt
¼ tsp	(1 mL) pepper
4 cups	(1 L) cooked turkey, diced
¾ cup	(180 mL) celery, diced
¼ cup	(60 mL) sweet red pepper, diced
¼ cup	(60 mL) green bell pepper, diced
½ cup	(125 mL) seedless red grapes, diced

- In a double-boiler, dissolve gelatin in poultry broth. Let stand to cool slightly.
- In a large bowl, mix mayonnaise, cream and lemon juice. Season with salt and pepper.
- In a second bowl, combine remaining ingredients. Set aside.
- Fold gelatin mixture into creamy mayonnaise. Add to turkey mixture, stirring well.
- Pour into an 8-cup (2 L) mold. Refrigerate 8 hours or until mixture has set. Unmold. Serve.

NUTRITION	
CALORIES PER SERVING: 434	
FAT: 29 g	CAL. FROM FAT: 56%
PROTEIN: 18 g	CHOLESTEROL: 59 mg
SODIUM: 691 mg	CARBOHYDRATES: 34 g

Turkey Croquettes

4 SERVINGS	
2 cups	(500 mL) cooked turkey, ground
10 oz	(284 mL) canned cream of chicken soup
1 tbsp	(15 mL) parsley, chopped
1	onion, finely chopped
1 tsp	(5 mL) lemon juice
1 ½ cups	(375 mL) cooked rice
1	egg
2 tbsp	(30 mL) milk
1 cup	(250 mL) bread crumbs
4 cups	(1 L) oil for frying

- In a bowl, mix first 6 ingredients. Refrigerate 1 hour.
- In a medium-size bowl, lightly beat together egg and milk. Set aside.
- Sprinkle bread crumbs onto a plate. Set aside.
- Remove turkey mixture from refrigerator. Shape into 12 patties. Dredge with bread crumbs. Dip in beaten egg and milk mixture. Dredge with bread crumbs once more.
- In a deep-fryer, heat oil to 400 °F (205 °C). Fry patties to a nice golden brown color. Serve with béchamel sauce, if desired.

NUTRITION	
CALORIES PER SERVING: 399	
FAT: 15 g	CAL. FROM FAT: 32%
PROTEIN: 23 g	CHOLESTEROL: 86 mg
SODIUM: 577 mg	CARBOHYDRATES: 47 g

Turkey Breast Casserole

6 SERVINGS	
2	turkey breasts, skinned, boned
	salt and pepper
2	zucchini, minced
1	onion, minced
8 oz	(225 g) mushrooms, minced
19 oz	(540 mL) tomato sauce
2	garlic cloves, chopped
1 tbsp	(15 mL) parsley, chopped
1/2 tsp	(2 mL) basil
1/2 tsp	(2 mL) oregano
	pinch of thyme

- Preheat oven to 350 °F (175 °C).
- In an ovenproof covered casserole dish, place turkey breasts. Season with salt and pepper. Top with vegetables.
- Pour in tomato sauce. Sprinkle with garlic, parsley and mixed herbs. Cover. Cook in oven 1 hour or so. Remove lid. Continue cooking 10 minutes. Serve.

NUTRITION	
CALORIES PER SERVING: 117	
FAT: 1 g	CAL. FROM FAT: 9%
PROTEIN: 16 g	CHOLESTEROL: 32 mg
SODIUM: 613 mg	CARBOHYDRATES: 12 g

Stuffed Turkey Breast

3-4 SERVINGS	
3 cups	(750 mL) whole wheat bread, diced
2 cups	(500 mL) chicken broth
1 cup	(250 mL) turkey giblets, ground
4.4 oz	(125 g) plain yogurt
1	onion, chopped
3 tbsp	(45 mL) almonds, chopped
1 tbsp	(15 mL) parsley, chopped
	pinch of sage
	pinch of thyme
	pinch of paprika
	pinch of ground clove
	salt and pepper
1	turkey breast, skinned, boned

- Preheat oven to 400 °F (205 °C).
- In a small bowl, pour 1/2 cup (125 mL) chicken broth over diced bread. Soak 5 minutes. Drain. Transfer bread to a large bowl. Mix in giblets, yogurt, onion, almonds, parsley and seasonings.
- Make an incision lengthwise across turkey breast. Stuff with bread mixture. Tie with a string. Place in a shallow casserole dish. Pour in remaining broth. Cover. Cook in oven 30 minutes.
- Lower oven temperature to 350 °F (175 °C). Continue cooking 1 hour, basting regularly. Transfer to a serving dish. Serve.

NUTRITION	
CALORIES PER SERVING: 682	
FAT: 17 g	CAL. FROM FAT: 22%
PROTEIN: 43 g	CHOLESTEROL: 201 mg
SODIUM: 1102 mg	CARBOHYDRATES: 96 g

Barbecued Turkey Leg

3-4 SERVINGS

1	whole turkey leg, skinned
3 tbsp	(45 mL) vegetable oil
	salt, pepper and paprika
1	small onion, finely chopped
1/2 cup	(125 mL) celery, diced
3/4 cup	(180 mL) red ketchup
1 cup	(250 mL) water
2 tbsp	(30 mL) Worcestershire sauce
1 tbsp	(15 mL) white vinegar
1 tbsp	(15 mL) brown sugar
1 tsp	(5 mL) dry mustard

- Brush turkey leg with 2 tbsp (30 mL) oil. Season.

- On a barbecue, place an oiled grid 3 inches (7.5 cm) from charcoal. Roast turkey leg 3 minutes each side.

- Raise grid to 6 inches (15 cm). Continue cooking 25 minutes or so, turning over meat regularly. Baste with a little oil, if needed.

- In a skillet, heat remaining oil. Lightly fry vegetables. Add remaining ingredients. Mix to a smooth sauce. Over low heat, simmer 15 minutes.

- Place turkey leg on a bed of rice. Coat with sauce. Serve with carrots and snow peas, if desired.

NUTRITION	
CALORIES PER SERVING: 356	
FAT: 17 g	CAL. FROM FAT: 42%
PROTEIN: 31 g	CHOLESTEROL: 100 mg
SODIUM: 779 mg	CARBOHYDRATES: 21 g

Brandied Turkey Legs

3-4 SERVINGS

1/2 cup	(125 mL) butter or margarine
2	turkey legs, skinned
1 oz	(30 mL) brandy
2 tbsp	(30 mL) shallots, minced
2 tbsp	(30 mL) parsley, chopped
1/4 tsp	(1 mL) thyme
	salt and pepper
1/2 cup	(125 mL) white wine
1/2 cup	(125 mL) heavy cream

- In a casserole dish, over low heat, melt butter. Lightly brown turkey legs all over. Continue cooking 15 minutes, turning meat from time to time.

- Pour in brandy. While stirring dish, flambé until flames extinguish.

- Mix in remaining ingredients, except cream. Cover. Simmer 45 minutes or until turkey is tender.

- Remove turkey legs from casserole dish. Fold cream into cooking juices. Stir to a smooth sauce.

- Transfer turkey legs to a serving dish. Ladle sauce on top. Serve.

NUTRITION	
CALORIES PER SERVING: 532	
FAT: 40 g	CAL. FROM FAT: 73%
PROTEIN: 31 g	CHOLESTEROL: 141 mg
SODIUM: 444 mg	CARBOHYDRATES: 3 g

Duck à l'Orange

4 SERVINGS	
1	5-lb (2.2 kg) duck, prepared
2 tbsp	(30 mL) butter
	pinch of nutmeg
	salt and pepper
1 cup	(250 mL) orange juice
3 tbsp	(45 mL) orange peel
1/2 cup	(125 mL) chicken broth
1/3 cup	(80 mL) honey

- Preheat oven to 350 °F (175 °C).

- Truss duck. Place in a roasting pan. Brush with butter. Season. Cook in oven 75 minutes, basting regularly with cooking juices.

- Meanwhile, in a casserole dish, mix remaining ingredients. Bring to a boil. Over low heat, simmer 30 minutes or until broth reduces by half.

- Remove duck from oven. Carve into portions. Coat with sauce. Serve.

NUTRITION	
CALORIES PER SERVING: 1332	
FAT: 152 g	CAL. FROM FAT: 75 %
PROTEIN: 40 g	CHOLESTEROL: 24 mg
SODIUM: 312 mg	CARBOHYDRATES: 22 g

Quails in Rum

2 SERVINGS	
4	quails, prepared
4 oz	(125 mL) brown rum
2 tbsp	(30 mL) honey
2 tbsp	(30 mL) chili sauce
	salt and pepper
3/4 cup	(180 mL) chicken broth

- Preheat oven to 350 °F (175 °C).

- In an ovenproof skillet, place quails. Set aside.

- In a bowl, mix rum, honey and chili sauce to a smooth sauce. Season with salt and pepper. Brush over quails. Cook in oven 30 minutes, basting with rum sauce every 5 minutes.

- Remove quails from skillet. Deglaze with chicken broth. Over high heat, let reduce 2 minutes.

- Transfer quails to a serving dish. Coat with sauce. Serve.

NUTRITION	
CALORIES PER SERVING: 655	
FAT: 28 g	CAL. FROM FAT: 48 %
PROTEIN: 45 g	CHOLESTEROL: 172 mg
SODIUM: 229 mg	CARBOHYDRATES: 23 g

Stuffed Quails

4 SERVINGS	
	stuffing of your choice, lukewarm *(p. 116)*
8	quails, prepared
1/4 cup	(60 mL) butter, softened
	salt and pepper
	sauce of your choice, hot

- Preheat oven to 350 °F (175 °C).

- Stuff quails. Truss or close with small skewers.

- In an ovenproof dish, place quails. Brush with softened butter. Season with salt and pepper. Cook in oven 30 minutes.

- Remove quails from oven. Coat with hot sauce. Serve.

NUTRITION	
CALORIES PER SERVING: 901	
FAT: 56 g	CAL. FROM FAT: 56 %
PROTEIN: 50 g	CHOLESTEROL: 198 mg
SODIUM: 1432 mg	CARBOHYDRATES: 44 g

Smoked Goose Salad

4 SERVINGS	
3 tbsp	(45 mL) virgin olive oil
1/4 cup	(60 mL) bacon, diced
1	smoked goose breast, skinned, cut into strips
	salt and pepper
1/3 cup	(80 mL) port wine
1/4 cup	(60 mL) wine vinegar
20 oz	(560 g) fresh spinach, washed, stalks removed

- In a skillet, heat 1/2 tsp (2 mL) oil. Over high heat, brown bacon 3 minutes. Mix in goose strips. Cook 3 minutes. Season with salt and pepper.

- Deglaze skillet with port wine and wine vinegar. Continue cooking until liquid reduces by half.

- Meanwhile, in a large salad bowl, combine spinach and remaining oil. Season with salt and pepper. Toss.

- Pour goose mixture over spinach. Toss once more. Serve.

NUTRITION	
CALORIES PER SERVING: 321	
FAT: 22 g	CAL. FROM FAT: 64 %
PROTEIN: 20 g	CHOLESTEROL: 60 mg
SODIUM: 411 mg	CARBOHYDRATES: 7 g

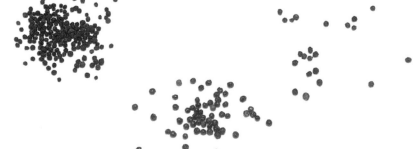

From top to bottom :
Duck à l'Orange
Quails in Rum,
Smoked Goose Salad

In days past, beef was often unjustly banished in low fat diets. It is true that it contains fat, as all meat does! Beef is, nevertheless, an excellent source of protein and iron, therefore it is part of a healthy and balanced diet.

To reduce fat intake choose lean cuts of beef. Remove the visible fat and use methods of cooking that use little or no fat.

In this section you will find dishes ranging from the timeless Classic Roast Beef (p.127) to the exotic Korean-style Beef Ribs (p.143). You are sure to find menu items to suit even the most discerning palate.

BEEF

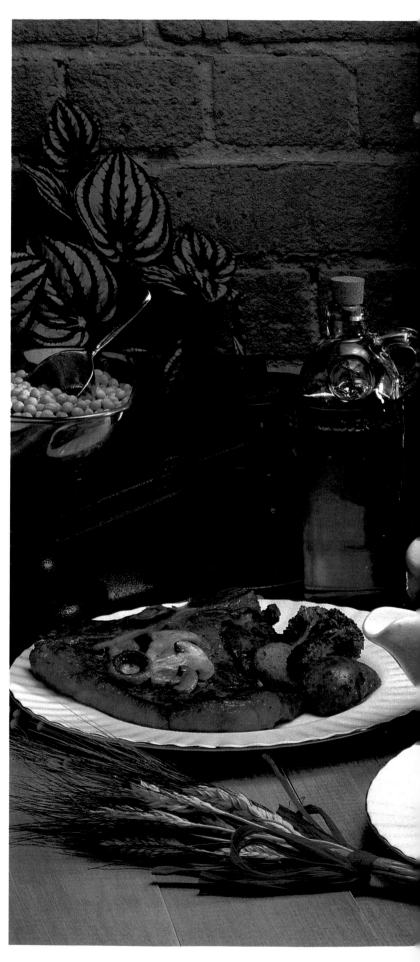

Favorite Roast Beef

6 SERVINGS	
2 tbsp	(30 mL) oil
1	4-lb (1.8 kg) rump roast
1	medium-size onion, coarsely chopped
1	small garlic clove, chopped
¼ cup	(60 mL) boiling water
	salt and pepper
3 tbsp	(45 mL) butter
3 tbsp	(45 mL) flour

- Preheat oven to 350 °F (175 °C).

- In an ovenproof casserole dish, heat oil. Sear roast all over 10 minutes or so.

- Add onion and garlic. Pour in boiling water. Season generously with salt and pepper. Cover. Cook in oven 2 hours or until roast is tender.

- Remove roast from dish. Let stand 5 minutes before carving.

- Meanwhile, degrease cooking juices. Set aside.

- In a casserole dish, melt butter. Sprinkle with flour. Cook until golden brown. While stirring, add 2 cups (500 mL) degreased cooking juices. Add water if juices are insufficient. Simmer until sauce thickens. Pour into a sauceboat.

- Serve roast with baked potatoes and cole slaw, if desired.

NUTRITION	
CALORIES PER SERVING: 645	
FAT: 48 g	CAL. FROM FAT: 55%
PROTEIN: 67 g	CHOLESTEROL: 191 mg
SODIUM: 322 mg	CARBOHYDRATES: 4 g

Roast Beef with Mushroom-Leek Sauce

4-6 SERVINGS	
1	small envelope leek soup mix
10 oz	(284 mL) canned cream of mushroom soup
	salt and pepper, to taste
1 ½ cups	(375 mL) water
1	3-4 lb (1.4-1.8 kg) inside round roast

- Preheat oven to 325 °F (160 °C).

- In a bowl, mix first 4 ingredients to a smooth sauce.

- In a small roasting pan, place roast. Pour sauce on top. Cover. Roast in oven 3 hours or so.

- Approximately 45 minutes before the end of cooking, adjust seasoning.

- Add ½ cup (125 mL) boiling water if sauce is too thick.

- Remove roast from pan. Let stand 5 minutes before carving.

- Meanwhile, degrease sauce.

- Ladle sauce over roast. Serve.

NUTRITION	
CALORIES PER SERVING: 652	
FAT: 40 g	CAL. FROM FAT: 56%
PROTEIN: 60 g	CHOLESTEROL: 181 mg
SODIUM: 945 mg	CARBOHYDRATES: 10 g

Recipe shown above

Classic Roast Beef

8 SERVINGS	
1	5-6 lb (2.2-2.6 kg) strip loin roast
4	bacon slices, halved (optional)
	salt and pepper
1/2 tsp	(2 mL) thyme
1 tsp	(5 mL) parsley, chopped
2 tbsp	(30 mL) flour (optional)
1/4 cup	(60 mL) water or beef broth (optional)

- Preheat oven to 325 °F (160 °C). If strip loin is lean, lard with bacon slices.

- In a roasting pan with a rack, place meat, fatty side up.

- Cook in oven 20 minutes per 1 lb (450 g) for rare meat, or 25-30 minutes for medium-rare. Baste often. Halfway through cooking, season.

- Transfer roast beef to a serving dish. Keep warm in oven 5 minutes before carving.

- If desired, make a sauce by sprinkling cooking juices with 2 tbsp (30 mL) flour. Brown. Fold in water. Simmer 4-5 minutes, stirring constantly. Strain sauce. Pour into a sauceboat.

- Surround roast beef with baked potatoes, green beans and carrots, if desired. Serve with sauce.

NUTRITION	
CALORIES PER SERVING: 582	
FAT: 39 g	CAL. FROM FAT: 60 %
PROTEIN: 57 g	CHOLESTEROL: 179 mg
SODIUM: 226 mg	CARBOHYDRATES: 2 g

Mexican Beef

4 SERVINGS	
2 tbsp	(30 mL) vegetable oil
1	2-lb (900 g) beef blade
1/2 cup	(125 mL) water
1/2 tsp	(2 mL) sugar
1 tsp	(5 mL) salt
1 tsp	(5 mL) cayenne
	pinch of pepper
28 oz	(796 mL) canned tomatoes, in their juice
1	green bell pepper, diced
1-2	carrots, sliced into rounds
1	large onion, chopped
1/2 cup	(125 mL) mushrooms, minced

- In a heavy-bottomed casserole dish, heat oil. Sear beef blade all over. Add remaining ingredients.

- Cover. Braise 75 minutes or until meat is cooked.

- Remove beef blade from dish. Carve into single portions.

- Return beef pieces to casserole dish. Over low heat, in cooking juices, simmer uncovered 10 minutes. Serve.

NUTRITION	
CALORIES PER SERVING: 605	
FAT: 45 g	CAL. FROM FAT: 66 %
PROTEIN: 34 g	CHOLESTEROL: 132 mg
SODIUM: 937 mg	CARBOHYDRATES: 17 g

Minute Pepper Steaks

4 SERVINGS	
4	7-oz (190 g) inside round steaks
¹/₂-1 tsp	(2-5 mL) pepper
3 tbsp	(45 mL) butter
1 tbsp	(15 mL) Worcestershire sauce
1 tbsp	(15 mL) lemon juice
¹/₄ tsp	(1 mL) celery salt
¹/₂	garlic clove, minced

- Rub steaks with generous amounts of pepper so seasoning will stick. Set aside.

- In a casserole dish, melt butter. Add remaining ingredients. Mix to a smooth sauce. Brush over steaks. Set remainder aside.

- In a large skillet, brown steaks 5 minutes or so. Do not overcook.

- Transfer steaks to individual plates. Coat with sauce. Serve.

NUTRITION	
CALORIES PER SERVING: 459	
FAT: 32 g	CAL. FROM FAT: 65%
PROTEIN: 38 g	CHOLESTEROL: 141 mg
SODIUM: 327 mg	CARBOHYDRATES: 1 g

Swiss Steak

4 SERVINGS	
2 tbsp	(30 mL) flour
¹/₂ tsp	(2 mL) seasoning salt
¹/₄ tsp	(1 mL) pepper
1	1-lb (450 g) blade or round steak, boned
1 tbsp	(15 mL) vegetable oil
¹/₄ tsp	(1 mL) dry mustard
¹/₂ tsp	(2 mL) Worcestershire sauce
¹/₄ cup	(60 mL) brown sugar
¹/₂ cup	(125 mL) ketchup
¹/₂ cup	(125 mL) water
1	onion, sliced

- Preheat oven to 350 °F (175 °C).

- In a plate, combine flour, salt and pepper. Dredge steak with mixture. With a meat mallet, pound steak so seasoned flour will stick. Set aside.

- In a large skillet, heat oil. Brown meat on both sides. Degrease skillet.

- In a small bowl, mix remaining ingredients, except onion. Pour over steak. Add onion slices. Cover. Braise in oven 1 hour or until steak is tender. Serve.

NUTRITION	
CALORIES PER SERVING: 360	
FAT: 17 g	CAL. FROM FAT: 43%
PROTEIN: 23 g	CHOLESTEROL: 67 mg
SODIUM: 768 mg	CARBOHYDRATES: 28 g

Porterhouse Steaks with Vegetables

4 SERVINGS

10	French shallots, peeled
2 tbsp	(30 mL) butter
3 cups	(750 mL) mushrooms, quartered
10 oz	(284 g) canned green beans, in their juice
10 oz	(284 g) canned asparagus, in their juice
	salt and pepper
4	tomatoes, halved
1 tbsp	(15 mL) oil
4	8-oz (225 g) Porterhouse steaks
3 oz	(90 mL) cognac

■ In a saucepan filled with lightly-salted boiling water, blanch shallots 2 minutes. Drain. Pat dry.

■ In a skillet, melt butter. Lightly brown shallots and mushrooms. Keep warm.

■ In a casserole dish, heat beans and asparagus in their juice. Season to taste with salt and pepper. Drain. Keep warm.

■ Preheat oven to BROIL.

■ Sprinkle tomato halves with pepper. Transfer to a baking sheet. Broil in oven 2-3 minutes. Keep warm.

■ In a skillet, heat oil. Sear steaks 5 minutes per side. Pour cognac over steaks. Flambé 30 seconds. In a warm serving dish, arrange steaks in a ring of vegetables. Serve.

NUTRITION	
CALORIES PER SERVING: 740	
FAT: 50 *g*	CAL. FROM FAT: 64%
PROTEIN: 38 *g*	CHOLESTEROL: 142 *mg*
SODIUM: 668 *mg*	CARBOHYDRATES: 25 *g*

Recipe shown above

Spicy Barbecued Steaks

2 SERVINGS

4 tsp	(20 mL) butter
2	strip loin steaks
2 tbsp	(30 mL) barbecue spices
	salt
1 oz	(30 mL) cognac
½ cup	(125 mL) red wine
1 tbsp	(15 mL) all-purpose flour
2 tbsp	(30 mL) sour cream

■ In a heavy-bottomed skillet, melt 1 tbsp (15 mL) butter. Over high heat, sear steaks 5 minutes each side. Season. Pour cognac over steaks. Flambé 30 seconds.

■ Transfer steaks to a warm serving dish. Keep warm.

■ Deglaze skillet with wine. Over high heat, reduce liquid by half.

■ Meanwhile, in a bowl, mix remaining butter and flour.

■ Stir kneaded butter and sour cream into wine sauce, mixing until smooth. Spoon over steaks. Serve.

NUTRITION	
CALORIES PER SERVING: 697	
FAT: 51 *g*	CAL. FROM FAT: 74%
PROTEIN: 34 *g*	CHOLESTEROL: 154 *mg*
SODIUM: 474 *mg*	CARBOHYDRATES: 7 *g*

Bourbon Rib Eye Steaks

4 SERVINGS	
2 tbsp	(30 mL) butter
4	6-oz (165 g) rib eye steaks
	salt and pepper
4 oz	(125 mL) bourbon or whiskey
1/2 cup	(125 mL) heavy cream

- In a skillet, melt butter. Sear steaks 3-5 minutes each side. Season with salt and pepper. Pour bourbon over steaks. Flambé 30 seconds.

- Remove steaks from skillet. Keep warm.

- Fold cream into steak cooking fat. Whisk to a smooth sauce. Bring to a boil. Remove immediately from heat. Spoon over steak. Serve.

NUTRITION	
CALORIES PER SERVING: 679	
FAT: 53 g	CAL. FROM FAT: 80%
PROTEIN: 29 g	CHOLESTEROL: 169 mg
SODIUM: 206 mg	CARBOHYDRATES: 1 g

Russian-style Beef

2 SERVINGS	
2	large potatoes, sliced
	salt and pepper
2	onions, sliced into rings
2	8-oz (225 g) round steaks
10 oz	(284 mL) canned cream of tomato soup
1	green bell pepper, minced

- Preheat oven to 325 °F (160 °C).

- Grease an ovenproof dish. Place half the potatoes over the bottom. Season with salt and pepper. Cover with half the onion slices. Arrange steaks on top. Cover with remaining onions, then potatoes.

- Pour tomato soup over dish. Sprinkle with bell pepper. Cover. Cook in oven 90 minutes or so.

- Approximately 15 minutes before the end of cooking, remove lid. Serve.

NUTRITION	
CALORIES PER SERVING: 801	
FAT: 30 g	CAL. FROM FAT: 33%
PROTEIN: 53 g	CHOLESTEROL: 134 mg
SODIUM: 1108 mg	CARBOHYDRATES: 82 g

Oven-baked Beef

6 SERVINGS	
1	garlic clove, chopped
1 tsp	(5 mL) marjoram
	salt and pepper
4 oz	(115 g) salted pork fat, diced
1	2-lb (900 g) chuck short rib steak
6	cloves
1 tbsp	(15 mL) vegetable oil
1 tbsp	(15 mL) butter
2 cups	(500 mL) beef broth
1	onion, chopped
3	carrots, sliced
1 cup	(250 mL) celery, chopped

- Preheat oven to 350 °F (175 °C).

- On a sheet of wax paper, sprinkle garlic, marjoram, salt and pepper. Dredge diced pork fat. Make incisions into beef slice. Stick diced pork fat and cloves into incisions.

- In an ovenproof casserole dish, heat oil and melt butter. Lightly brown beef slice on both sides. Pour in broth. Bring to a boil.

- Add onion, carrots and celery. Adjust seasoning. Cover. Braise in oven 90 minutes or until beef is tender. Serve.

VARIATION
- Use other beef cuts such as shoulder, blade, etc.

NUTRITION	
CALORIES PER SERVING: 553	
FAT: 43 g	CAL. FROM FAT: 70%
PROTEIN: 29 g	CHOLESTEROL: 115 mg
SODIUM: 187mg	CARBOHYDRATES: 12 g

Flank Steak with Candied Shallots

4 SERVINGS	
2 tsp	(10 mL) butter
16	French shallots, halved
2 tsp	(10 mL) hot mustard
4 oz	(125 mL) port wine
1/2 cup	(125 mL) beef broth
	salt and pepper
2 tbsp	(30 mL) vegetable oil
4	7-oz (190 g) flank steaks

- In a small saucepan, melt butter. Cook shallots 5 minutes. Mix. Stir in mustard and port. Over high heat, reduce liquid by half.

- Add broth to saucepan. Bring to a boil. Reduce by half. Season to taste with salt and pepper.

- Meanwhile, in a frying pan, heat oil. Cook steaks on both sides.

- Transfer steaks to individual plates. Garnish with shallot halves. Coat with port sauce. Serve.

Note : rare or medium done is recommended, since well-done flank steaks tend to be tough.

NUTRITION	
CALORIES PER SERVING: 526	
FAT: 30 g	CAL. FROM FAT: 53%
PROTEIN: 42 g	CHOLESTEROL: 107 mg
SODIUM: 250 mg	CARBOHYDRATES: 20 g

Recipe shown above

Festive Tournedos

6 SERVINGS

¹/₂ cup	(125 mL) butter
6	ripe tomatoes, stems removed
	salt and pepper, to taste
2	medium-size eggplants, peeled, sliced into rounds
¹/₂ cup	(125 mL) flour
4 cups	(1 L) oil for frying
2	onions, sliced into rings
¹/₄ cup	(60 mL) milk
6	4-oz (115 g) filets mignon
6	bacon slices
2 tbsp	(30 mL) oil
3	potatoes, halved, oven-baked
1 cup	(250 mL) beef broth
¹/₂ cup	white wine
	fresh parsley, chopped

- In a skillet, melt 3 tbsp (45 mL) butter. Add tomatoes. Season. Cover. Over moderate heat, cook 10 minutes, turning over once. Reserve tomatoes and their cooking juices separately.

- Sprinkle eggplant rounds with salt and 3 tbsp (45 mL) flour.

- In a deep-fryer, heat oil to 400 °F (205 °C). Fry eggplant 5 minutes or so.

- Dip onion rings in milk. Dredge with remaining flour. Set aside.

- Remove eggplant from deep-fryer. Drain. Set aside.

- In the same oil, fry onion rings 3 minutes. Remove from deep-fryer. Drain. Season to taste with salt.

- Wrap filets mignon in bacon. Tie with a string. In a skillet, melt 1 tbsp (15 mL) butter. Sear filets 4 minutes each side, turning over without pricking meat. Season with salt and pepper.

- Remove string and bacon. Continue cooking filets mignon 1 minute, rolling in cooking fat.

- In a large serving dish, set tomatoes in a crown. Place a filet on each one. Top with onion rings. In the center of dish, pile eggplants. Surround with potatoes. Keep warm.

- In filets cooking fat, pour beef broth and cooking juices from tomatoes. Over high heat, reduce to two-thirds. Off heat, stir in white wine and remaining butter. Pour into a sauceboat.

- Garnish with parsley. Serve.

Recipe shown above, top photograph

VARIATION

- Replace tomatoes with croutons, and baked potatoes with sautéed potatoes, as shown above.

NUTRITION	
CALORIES PER SERVING: 809	
FAT: 55 *g*	CAL. FROM FAT: 61%
PROTEIN: 29 *g*	CHOLESTEROL: 128 *mg*
SODIUM: 600 *mg*	CARBOHYDRATES: 50 *g*

Filets Mignons with Whipped Cream

4 SERVINGS	
4	6-oz (165 g) filets mignons
4	bacon slices
¹/₄ tsp	(1 mL) pepper
1 tsp	(5 mL) paprika
¹/₄ tsp	(1 mL) chili powder
1 cup	(250 mL) heavy cream
3 tbsp	(45 mL) ketchup
1 ¹/₂ oz	(45 mL) cognac

- Preheat oven to 325 °F (160 °C).
- Wrap each filet mignon with a bacon slice. Secure with a string or toothpick. Season.
- Place filets mignons in an ovenproof dish. Cover. Cook in oven 30 minutes.
- Meanwhile, in a mixer bowl, whip cream into soft peaks. Delicately fold in ketchup and cognac. Set aside at room temperature.
- Transfer filets mignons to individual plates. Garnish with whipped cream. Serve.

Recipe shown above

NUTRITION	
CALORIES PER SERVING: 757	
FAT: 64 *g*	CAL. FROM FAT: 79%
PROTEIN: 33 *g*	CHOLESTEROL: 207 *mg*
SODIUM: 340 *mg*	CARBOHYDRATES: 5 *g*

Quick Filets Mignons

4 SERVINGS	
¹/₄ cup	(60 mL) butter, melted
¹/₄ cup	(60 mL) soy sauce
4	8-oz (225 g) filets mignons

- Mix melted butter and soy sauce. Brush all over filets mignons.
- In a microwave-safe dish, place a filet mignon. Cook in oven 1 ¹/₂ minutes on MEDIUM-HIGH. Turn over. Continue cooking 1 ¹/₂ minutes. Remove filet mignon from dish. Set aside.
- Cook remaining filets mignons the same way.
- In the same dish, place all 4 filets mignons. Cook 1 minute, on MEDIUM-HIGH. Let stand 5 minutes. Serve.

NUTRITION	
CALORIES PER SERVING: 746	
FAT: 63 *g*	CAL. FROM FAT: 77%
PROTEIN: 41 *g*	CHOLESTEROL: 190 *mg*
SODIUM: 1252 *mg*	CARBOHYDRATES: 2*g*

Beefy Rice Hot Pot

6 SERVINGS	
2 tbsp	(30 mL) vegetable oil
8 oz	(225 g) rump beef, minced
4 oz	(115 g) fresh mushrooms, sliced
1/2 cup	(125 mL) onion, chopped
1/2 cup	(125 mL) celery, chopped
2 cups	(500 mL) water
10 oz	(284 mL) canned cream of mushroom soup
1 tsp	(5 mL) salt
1/8 tsp	(0.5 mL) pepper
2 1/2 cups	(625 mL) cooked rice
1 1/2 cups	(375 mL) cooked carrots, sliced
1 cup	(250 mL) canned green peas, drained

▪ In a 10-cup (2.5 L) cooking pot, heat oil. Lightly cook minced beef. Mix in mushrooms, onion and celery.

▪ Pour in water and cream of mushroom. Season with salt and pepper. Over low heat, cook uncovered until meat is tender.

▪ Stir in remaining ingredients. Simmer 20 minutes. Stir thoroughly. Serve.

NUTRITION	
CALORIES PER SERVING: 350	
FAT: 19 g	CAL. FROM FAT: 48%
PROTEIN: 11 g	CHOLESTEROL: 33 mg
SODIUM: 898 mg	CARBOHYDRATES: 34 g

Almond Beef

6 SERVINGS	
2 1/4 lbs	(1 kg) round steak, 1-inch (2.5 cm) thick
1/2 cup	(125 mL) chicken broth, heated
4 cups	(1 L) cabbage, finely chopped
6 tbsp	(90 mL) vegetable oil
1	garlic clove, crushed
2 tbsp	(30 mL) soy sauce
1 tsp	(5 mL) cornstarch
1/4 cup	(60 mL) cold chicken broth
1/2 cup	(125 mL) toasted slivered almonds

▪ Across the grain, cut beef steak into strips. Set aside.

▪ In a casserole dish, mix hot chicken broth and cabbage. Bring to a boil.

Cook 2 minutes. Drain cabbage, reserving cooking liquid. Keep warm.

▪ In a skillet, heat half the oil. Lightly fry garlic. Pour in soy sauce and 1/4 cup (60 mL) cooking liquid. Simmer 2 minutes.

▪ Dilute cornstarch in cold chicken broth. Fold into liquid mixture, stirring to a smooth sauce.

▪ In a large skillet, heat remaining oil. Fry meat 6 minutes. Pour in sauce. Simmer 5 minutes.

▪ Spoon beef and sauce over a bed of cabbage. Sprinkle with toasted almonds. Serve.

NUTRITION	
CALORIES PER SERVING: 529	
FAT: 40 g	CAL. FROM FAT: 68%
PROTEIN: 36 g	CHOLESTEROL: 101 mg
SODIUM: 442 mg	CARBOHYDRATES: 6 g

Maple-flavored Beef Stew

6-8 SERVINGS	
3 tbsp	(45 mL) oil
2 lbs	(900 g) beef cubes
1 cup	(250 mL) onions, minced
1	garlic clove, chopped
1/4 cup	(60 mL) flour
2 cups	(500 mL) beef broth
1/2 cup	(125 mL) red wine
1/2 cup	(125 mL) maple syrup
2 cups	(500 mL) tomatoes, coarsely chopped
1/4 tsp	(1 mL) fresh ginger, grated
1/2 tsp	(2 mL) salt
1/4 tsp	(1 mL) pepper
1 cup	(250 mL) celery, diced
3 cups	(750 mL) potatoes, peeled, diced
2 cups	(500 mL) carrots, diced

- Preheat oven to 350 °F (175 °C).
- In a casserole dish, heat oil. Sear beef cubes. Add onions and garlic. Continue cooking 1 minute. Remove from heat. Sprinkle with flour. Pour in broth. Add wine, maple syrup, tomatoes and ginger. Season with salt and pepper. Cover. Cook in oven 1 hour.
- Fold in remaining ingredients. Cover. Continue cooking in oven 1 hour. Serve.

NUTRITION	
CALORIES PER SERVING: 426	
FAT: 17 g	CAL. FROM FAT: 36 %
PROTEIN: 28 g	CHOLESTEROL: 66 mg
SODIUM: 252 mg	CARBOHYDRATES: 38 g

Filet Mignon Brochettes

4 SERVINGS	
8	1-oz (30 g) beef cubes
4	bacon slices, halved
2 tsp	(10 mL) butter
8	shallots, chopped
2 cups	(500 mL) cooked rice
	garlic salt, to taste
1 tbsp	(15 mL) soy sauce
1	large sausage, cut into 8 rounds
2	onions, quartered
8	cherry tomatoes
3 tbsp	(45 mL) peanut oil

- Wrap each beef cube with a half-slice bacon. Set aside.
- In a skillet, melt butter. Cook shallots 30 seconds until tender but not browned. Mix in cooked rice, garlic salt and soy sauce. Keep warm.
- Thread a beef cube, a sausage round, an onion quarter and a cherry tomato onto each skewer.
- In a large frying pan, heat oil. Cook brochettes all over until meat is tender.
- Spoon a bed of rice over 4 plates. Place 2 brochettes on each. Serve with a green salad, if desired.

NUTRITION	
CALORIES PER SERVING: 601	
FAT: 34 g	CAL. FROM FAT: 49 %
PROTEIN: 21 g	CHOLESTEROL: 57 mg
SODIUM: 561 mg	CARBOHYDRATES: 56 g

Recipe shown above

Beef Olé !

6 SERVINGS	
1	onion, chopped
2	garlic cloves
¹/₂ cup	(125 mL) shallots, chopped
¹/₄ cup	(60 mL) soy sauce
¹/₄ tsp	(1 mL) pepper
2 lbs	(900 g) beef, diced
3 tbsp	(45 mL) oil
¹/₃ cup	(80 mL) brown sugar
	water
2-4	whole chili peppers, chopped
2	green bell peppers, diced
6	large carrots, cut into sticks
4 cups	(1 L) tomato juice
3 cups	(750 mL) quick-cooking rice

- In a bowl, mix first 5 ingredients. Add beef cubes. Marinate in refrigerator 30 minutes, stirring from time to time.
- Remove beef cubes from refrigerator. Drain.
- In a Dutch oven, heat oil. Sprinkle with brown sugar, mixing well. Brown beef cubes all over. Add enough water to cover meat. Fold in remaining ingredients, except rice. Cover. Cook 1 hour or until beef is tender. Add rice. Cover. Simmer 15 minutes. Serve.

Recipe shown above

VARIATION

- Replace beef with chicken.

NUTRITION	
CALORIES PER SERVING: 635	
FAT: 20 *g*	CAL. FROM FAT: 29 %
PROTEIN: 39 *g*	CHOLESTEROL: 83 *mg*
SODIUM: 1382 *mg*	CARBOHYDRATES: 83*g*

Barbecue Beef Stew

8 SERVINGS	
3 lbs	(1.4 kg) beef, cut into 1-inch (2.5 cm) cubes
1 cup	(250 mL) commercial barbecue sauce, regular or garlic flavor
1 ¹/₂ cups	(375 mL) water
1 tsp	(5 mL) salt
8	small potatoes
8	carrots, cut into 1 ¹/₂-inch (3.75 cm) chunks
1	head of celery, cut into 1 ¹/₂-inch (3.75 cm) chunks
1	onion, cut into 8 wedges
3 tbsp	(45 mL) flour
¹/₃ cup	(80 mL) cold water

- In a dish, place beef cubes. Pour in barbecue sauce, mixing well. Marinate in refrigerator 3 hours.
- In a casserole dish, place beef and marinade. Add water and salt. Bring to a boil. Cover. Simmer 45 minutes.
- Add vegetables. Cover. Continue cooking 30 minutes or until beef and vegetables are tender.
- Meanwhile, dilute flour in cold water. Pour over beef mixture, stirring well.
- Bring to a boil. Stir until sauce thickens. Over low heat, simmer 15 minutes. Serve.

NUTRITION	
CALORIES PER SERVING: 569	
FAT: 16 *g*	CAL. FROM FAT: 25 %
PROTEIN: 43 *g*	CHOLESTEROL: 94 *mg*
SODIUM: 651 *mg*	CARBOHYDRATES: 63 *g*

Plum Beef Casserole

6 SERVINGS	
2 cups	(500 mL) red wine
½ cup	(125 mL) wine vinegar
1 tbsp	(15 mL) oil
2	carrots, sliced into rounds
1	onion, chopped
1	garlic clove, chopped
	herb bouquet
	salt and pepper
3 lbs	(1.4 kg) beef cubes
2 tbsp	(30 mL) butter
1 cup	(250 mL) beef broth
8 oz	(225 g) dried prunes
	lukewarm water

- In a large salad bowl, combine first 8 ingredients. Add beef cubes, mixing well. Marinate in refrigerator 12 hours.
- Remove beef cubes from refrigerator. Drain well, reserving marinade.
- In a skillet, melt butter. Lightly cook beef cubes. Pour in broth and marinade. Cover. Over low heat, cook 2 ½ hours.
- Meanwhile, cover prunes with lukewarm water. Let soak.
- Approximately 15 minutes before the end of cooking, add prunes to beef casserole.
- On a serving dish, arrange beef cubes in a ring of prunes. Serve.

NUTRITION	
CALORIES PER SERVING: 613	
FAT: 527 g	CAL. FROM FAT: 43%
PROTEIN: 50 g	CHOLESTEROL: 138 mg
SODIUM: 271 mg	CARBOHYDRATES: 28 g

Tomato Beef Stew

6 SERVINGS	
2 lbs	(900 g) beef cubes
¼ cup	(60 mL) granulated sugar
2 tbsp	(30 mL) oil
1	medium-size onion, chopped
28 oz	(796 mL) canned crushed tomatoes
	salt and pepper
1 tbsp	(15 mL) cornstarch
3 tbsp	(45 mL) cold water

- Roll beef cubes in sugar. Set aside.
- In a skillet, heat oil. Lightly fry onion and beef cubes all over.
- Transfer beef mixture to a casserole dish. Add tomatoes, mixing well. Season to taste with salt and pepper. Simmer 1 hour or so.
- In a bowl, dilute cornstarch in water. Fold into beef mixture. Stir until sauce thickens. Simmer 10 minutes. Serve.

NUTRITION	
CALORIES PER SERVING: 369	
FAT: 18 g	CAL. FROM FAT: 44%
PROTEIN: 33 g	CHOLESTEROL: 83 mg
SODIUM: 402 mg	CARBOHYDRATES: 17 g

Baked Beef Macaroni

4 SERVINGS

1 tbsp	(15 mL) oil
1 lb	(450 g) ground beef
1	small onion, chopped
1/2 cup	(125 mL) green bell pepper, chopped
8 oz	(227 mL) canned tomato sauce
8 oz	(227 mL) canned mushrooms, drained
8 oz	(227 mL) canned whole kernel corn
1/2 cup	(125 mL) pimento-stuffed olives, sliced
1 cup	(250 mL) cooked macaroni
	salt and pepper
1 cup	(250 mL) Mozzarella cheese, grated

- Preheat oven to 350 °F (175 °C).
- In a skillet, heat oil. Lightly cook ground beef, onion and bell pepper. Remove from skillet. Drain. Transfer to an oven-proof dish.
- Fold in remaining ingredients, except cheese. Top with Mozzarella.
- Cook in oven until cheese has melted. Serve.

NUTRITION	
CALORIES PER SERVING: 640	
FAT: 43 g	CAL. FROM FAT: 60%
PROTEIN: 31 g	CHOLESTEROL: 122 mg
SODIUM: 942 mg	CARBOHYDRATES: 34 g

Meat Loaf

4 SERVINGS

1 1/2 lbs	(675 g) ground beef
1	onion, chopped
3/4 cup	(180 mL) oatmeal
1	egg, beaten
1 cup	(250 mL) milk
	salt and pepper
1/3 cup	(80 mL) brown sugar
1/2 cup	(125 mL) ketchup
1 tsp	(5 mL) dry mustard

- Preheat oven to 350 °F (175 °C).
- In a bowl, mix first 5 ingredients. Season to taste with salt and pepper.
- Press mixture into a buttered loaf pan. Set aside.
- In a second bowl, blend brown sugar, ketchup and dry mustard until smooth. Spread over meat loaf.
- Cover pan with aluminum foil. Cook in oven 75 minutes, removing foil after 30 minutes. Serve.

NUTRITION	
CALORIES PER SERVING: 753	
FAT: 50 g	CAL. FROM FAT: 59%
PROTEIN: 35 g	CHOLESTEROL: 198 mg
SODIUM: 677 mg	CARBOHYDRATES: 42 g

Red Wine and Beef Hash

4 SERVINGS

1 tbsp	(15 mL) oil
1 1/2 lbs	(675 g) ground beef
2	onions, diced
2	garlic cloves, crushed
1	sweet red pepper, diced
1	carrot, diced
2	celery stalks, diced
3	tomatoes, cut into wedges
1/2 cup	(125 mL) dry red wine
10 oz	(284 mL) canned beef broth
1 tbsp	(15 mL) beef broth concentrate
	salt and pepper
1 tbsp	(15 mL) cornstarch
3 tbsp	(45 mL) cold water

- In a casserole dish, heat oil. Lightly brown ground beef. Remove from dish. Set aside.
- In beef cooking fat, sauté onions, garlic, pepper, carrot and celery 3-4 minutes.
- Fold in meat, tomatoes, red wine, beef broth and concentrate. Season to taste with salt and pepper. Simmer 30 minutes.
- In a small bowl, dilute cornstarch in cold water. Pour over beef hash, mixing well. Simmer 5 minutes, stirring occasionally. Serve.

NUTRITION	
CALORIES PER SERVING: 587	
FAT: 39 g	CAL. FROM FAT: 63%
PROTEIN: 33 g	CHOLESTEROL: 128 mg
SODIUM: 222 mg	CARBOHYDRATES: 20 g

California Casserole

4 SERVINGS

2 cups	(500 mL) potatoes, diced
2 tsp	(10 mL) salt
1/4 tsp	(1 mL) pepper
2 cups	(500 mL) celery, cut into diagonal slices
1 1/2 cups	(675 g) ground beef
1/2 cup	(125 mL) onion, finely chopped
1 cup	(250 mL) broccoli florets
10 oz	(284 mL) canned cream of tomato soup

- Preheat oven to 325 °F (160 °C).
- Line bottom of a lightly-greased casserole dish with diced potatoes. Season with salt and pepper.
- Cover with successive layers of celery, ground beef, onion and broccoli florets. Season with salt and pepper between layers.
- Pour in cream of tomato. Cover. Cook in oven 75 minutes. Serve.

NUTRITION	
CALORIES PER SERVING: 675	
FAT: 47 g	CAL. FROM FAT: 62%
PROTEIN: 33 g	CHOLESTEROL: 145 mg
SODIUM: 1620 mg	CARBOHYDRATES: 30 g

From top to bottom :
California Casserole,
Red Wine and Beef Hash,
Meat Loaf

Curried Meatballs

4 SERVINGS

1 lb	(450 g) ground beef
1/2 tsp	(2 mL) salt
	pinch of pepper
3/4 cup	(180 mL) bread crumbs
1	egg, beaten
1/4 cup	(60 mL) tomato juice
3/4 cup	(180 mL) onions, finely chopped
1 tbsp	(15 mL) oil
1 tbsp	(15 mL) butter
1/2 cup	(125 mL) celery, chopped
1 1/2 cups	(375 mL) apples, peeled, diced
1 tbsp	(15 mL) curry powder
3 tbsp	(45 mL) flour
	salt and pepper
10 oz	(284 mL) canned beef consommé
3/4 cup	(180 mL) water
1 tsp	(5 mL) sugar
1 tsp	(5 mL) lemon peel
1 tsp	(5 mL) lemon juice

- In a bowl, mix first 6 ingredients. Add 1/4 cup (60 mL) onions. Shape into meatballs.

- In a skillet, heat oil and melt butter. Lightly brown meatballs 10 minutes. Remove from skillet.

- In 1 tsp (5 mL) meatball cooking fat, over low heat, fry remaining onions, celery and apples 2 minutes. Season with curry. Cook 1 minute. Gradually add remaining ingredients. Cover. Simmer 1 hour.

- Add meatballs to sauce. Simmer 30 minutes. Serve.

NUTRITION	
CALORIES PER SERVING: 581	
FAT: 39 *g*	CAL. FROM FAT: 61%
PROTEIN: 24 *g*	CHOLESTEROL: 149 *mg*
SODIUM: 1026 *mg*	CARBOHYDRATES: 32 *g*

Cabbage Rolls

4 SERVINGS

12	red cabbage leaves
	boiling water
1 tbsp	(15 mL) vinegar
1 tbsp	(15 mL) oil
1 tbsp	(15 mL) butter
1 1/4 lbs	(565 g) ground beef
1	onion, chopped
1	egg, beaten
1 cup	(250 mL) cooked rice
2 tsp	(10 mL) salt
1/2 tsp	(2 mL) pepper
1/2 tsp	(2 mL) thyme
3 cups	(750 mL) tomato juice
1/4 cup	(60 mL) cold water
1 tbsp	(15 mL) lemon juice
1 tbsp	(15 mL) brown sugar
	salt and pepper, to taste

- Preheat oven to 350 °F (175 °C).

- In a casserole dish, place cabbage. Cover with boiling water. Fold in vinegar. Simmer 10 minutes. Drain.

- In a skillet, heat oil and melt butter. Lightly fry ground beef and onion. Off heat, fold egg and cooked rice into mixture. Season.

- On a flattened cabbage leaf, place 1/4 cup (60 mL) beef mixture. Roll sausage-like. Secure with a toothpick. Repeat for a total of 12 rolls.

- Transfer cabbage rolls to an ovenproof dish. Pour tomato juice, water and lemon juice over rolls. Season with brown sugar, salt and pepper. Cover. Cook in oven 1 hour. Serve.

NUTRITION	
CALORIES PER SERVING: 682	
FAT: 45 *g*	CAL. FROM FAT: 56%
PROTEIN: 29 *g*	CHOLESTEROL: 173 *mg*
SODIUM: 1874 *mg*	CARBOHYDRATES: 40 *g*

Rice-topped Shepherd's Pie

	4 SERVINGS
2 tsp	(10 mL) vegetable oil
2	carrots, diced
1	onion, chopped
1 lb	(450 g) ground beef
2/3 cup	(160 mL) beef broth
1 tbsp	(15 mL) tomato paste
1 tbsp	(15 mL) Worcestershire sauce
	salt and pepper
3/4 cup	(180 mL) fresh or frozen green peas
3 cups	(750 mL) cooked rice
1	egg, beaten
1 cup	(250 mL) Cheddar cheese, grated
1/2 cup	(125 mL) sour cream

- Preheat oven to BROIL.
- In an ovenproof 10-inch (25 cm) skillet, heat oil. Cook carrots and onion 3 minutes.
- Add ground beef. Continue cooking. Fold in broth, tomato paste and Worcestershire sauce. Season to taste with salt and pepper. Cook 5 minutes. Add green peas. Cook 1 minute.
- Meanwhile, in a bowl, combine rice, egg, grated cheese and sour cream. Spread over beef mixture.
- Broil in oven 7 minutes or until rice topping is quite hot. Serve.

NUTRITION	
CALORIES PER SERVING: 758	
FAT: 43 g	CAL. FROM FAT: 52%
PROTEIN: 36 g	CHOLESTEROL: 173 mg
SODIUM: 629 mg	CARBOHYDRATES: 54 g

Recipe shown above

Savory Beef Torte

	4 SERVINGS
1	9-inch (23 cm) pie crust, *(p. 334)* half-baked
2 tbsp	(30 mL) butter
1 cup	(250 mL) onions, finely chopped
1/4 cup	(60 mL) zucchini, diced
1 lb	(450 g) ground beef
2 tbsp	(30 mL) flour
3/4 tsp	(3 mL) salt
1/4 tsp	(1 mL) pepper
1 tbsp	(15 mL) Worcestershire sauce
1 cup	(250 mL) cottage cheese
2	eggs, beaten
	paprika, to taste

- Preheat oven to 350 °F (175 °C).
- Line a 9-inch (23 cm) pie pan with crust. Set aside.
- In a skillet, melt butter. Sauté onions and zucchini. Add ground beef. Cook until beef turns brown all over. Sprinkle with flour. Season with salt, pepper and Worcestershire sauce.
- Pour beef mixture into crust.
- In a bowl, mix cheese and eggs. Spread over beef. Sprinkle with paprika. Cook in oven 40 minutes. Serve.

NUTRITION	
CALORIES PER SERVING: 719	
FAT: 51 g	CAL. FROM FAT: 65%
PROTEIN: 33 g	CHOLESTEROL: 208 mg
SODIUM: 1121 mg	CARBOHYDRATES: 30 g

Simmered Beef Liver

4 SERVINGS

¼ cup	(60 mL) flour
¼ tsp	(1 mL) cayenne
	pinch of oregano
	pinch of garlic salt
	salt and pepper
1 lb	(450 g) beef liver, cut into strips
2 tbsp	(30 mL) butter
1	onion, finely chopped
14 oz	(398 mL) canned tomato sauce

- On a plate, combine flour and spices. Dredge liver strips. Set aside.
- In a skillet, melt butter. Fry onion and liver strips all over 2-3 minutes.
- Pour in tomato sauce. Simmer 20 minutes, stirring from time to time. Serve.

NUTRITION	
CALORIES PER SERVING: 285	
FAT: 10 g	CAL. FROM FAT: 33 %
PROTEIN: 25 g	CHOLESTEROL: 417 mg
SODIUM: 774 mg	CARBOHYDRATES: 23 g

Princess Beef Liver

4 SERVINGS

1 lb	(450 g) beef liver, sliced
1 cup	(250 mL) milk
1 cup	(250 mL) flour
3 tbsp	(45 mL) dry mustard
	salt and pepper
	pinch of parsley
1 tbsp	(15 mL) oil
1	medium-size onion, chopped
1	green bell pepper, chopped
2	celery stalks, minced
2	shallots, minced
1 tbsp	(15 mL) butter
½ cup	(125 mL) chicken broth
1 cup	(250 mL) cauliflower florets
12	mushrooms

- In a bowl, combine liver slices and milk. Soak in refrigerator 2 hours. Remove from refrigerator. Drain liver.
- In a plate, mix flour, mustard, salt, pepper and parsley. Dredge liver slices.
- In a frying pan, heat oil. Sauté onion, pepper, celery and shallots 5 minutes.
- Preheat oven to 350 °F (175 °C).
- In a skillet, melt butter. Sear liver slices on both sides.
- In an ovenproof dish, place liver and fried vegetables. Pour broth on top. Surround with cauliflower and mushrooms. Cover. Cook in oven 30 minutes. Serve.

NUTRITION	
CALORIES PER SERVING: 3444	
FAT: 15 g	CAL. FROM FAT: 30 %
PROTEIN: 30 g	CHOLESTEROL: 418 mg
SODIUM: 221 mg	CARBOHYDRATES: 46 g

Carpacio

4 SERVINGS

1 lb	(450 g) rib steak, prepared, minced (as for Chinese fondue)
1 tbsp	(15 mL) pepper, coarsely ground
1 tbsp	(15 mL) dill
1/2 tsp	(2 mL) sea salt
1/2 cup	(125 mL) mayonnaise
1 tbsp	(15 mL) hot mustard
1 tbsp	(15 mL) Meaux or old-fashioned mustard

- On 4 individual plates, spread beef slices as much as possible. Sprinkle with pep-per, dill and sea salt. Press seasonings into meat.
- Seal each plate with plastic wrap. Refrigerate 2 hours.
- Meanwhile, in a bowl, blend remaining ingredients. Set aside at room temperature.
- Remove beef slices from refrigerator. Spoon mayonnaise on top. Serve.

NUTRITION	
CALORIES PER SERVING: 508	
FAT: 48 g	CAL. FROM FAT: 83%
PROTEIN: 20 g	CHOLESTEROL: 84 mg
SODIUM: 549mg	CARBOHYDRATES: 2 g

Korean-style Beef Ribs

4 SERVINGS

2 1/4 lbs	(1 kg) beef ribs
4 cups	(1 L) cold water
2	garlic cloves, minced
2	mushrooms, minced
2	shallots, cut into 2-inch (5 cm) chunks
1 tsp	(5 mL) sesame seeds
1 tbsp	(15 mL) sugar
1 tbsp	(15 mL) soy sauce

- In a covered casserole dish, place beef ribs. Cover with water. Bring to a boil. Cover dish. Cook 2 hours or until liquid has reduced by half and meat is tender.
- Fold in remaining ingredients. Simmer 15 minutes.
- Remove beef ribs from dish. Drain well. Pour cooking juices into a sauceboat.
- Transfer beef ribs to a serving dish. Serve with cooking juices.

NUTRITION	
CALORIES PER SERVING: 702	
FAT: 58 g	CAL. FROM FAT: 76%
PROTEIN: 36 g	CHOLESTEROL: 152 mg
SODIUM: 382 mg	CARBOHYDRATES: 6 g

Veal is a lean and tasty meat when well prepared. Veal and Tomato Stir-fry (p.152) is an example of a dish that is both quick and nutritious. The Veal Meatballs (p. 156) recipe is a good alternative to the traditional meatball stew; it contains very little fat as well.

Without restriction, we can allow ourselves to add veal to our menu regularly. It is sure to provide the cook with many compliments from appreciative diners.

VEAL

Braised Roast Veal

6 SERVINGS

1	3-lb (1.4 kg) roast veal, boneless, rolled, larded with pork fat strips
2 tbsp	(30 mL) peanut oil
6	celery stalks, cut into 2-inch (5 cm) diagonal slices
6	medium-size carrots, cut into 2-inch (5 cm) diagonal slices
1	onion, minced
	salt and pepper
1 tsp	(5 mL) tarragon
2 tsp	(10 mL) butter, melted

▪ Preheat oven to 350 °F (175 °C).

▪ Over moderate heat, in a large skillet, heat oil. Sear roast veal all over.

▪ Meanwhile, in a saucepan filled with lightly-salted boiling water, blanch celery and carrots 1 minute. Drain. Set aside.

▪ In an ovenproof casserole dish, spread onion rings. Place roast on top. Season with salt and pepper. Add blanched vegetables. Sprinkle with tarragon. Baste with butter. Cook in oven 20 minutes. Lower temperature to 325 °F (160 °C). Continue cooking 1 hour or so, basting every 20 minutes.

▪ Transfer braised roast veal to a serving dish. Coat with cooking juices. Serve.

Recipe shown above

VARIATIONS

• Approximately 20 minutes before the end of cooking, add 10 oz (284 mL) canned artichoke hearts, drained.

• Vary herbs (thyme, parsley, savory, garlic) to taste.

NUTRITION	
CALORIES PER SERVING: 344	
FAT: 159 *g*	CAL. FROM FAT: 49 %
PROTEIN: 33 *g*	CHOLESTEROL: 135 *mg*
SODIUM: 293 *mg*	CARBOHYDRATES: 10 *g*

Bacon-wrapped Roast Veal

8 SERVINGS

1	4-lb (8 kg) loin roast veal, prepared
8	bacon slices
1	onion, chopped
1 tbsp	parsley, chopped
1	bay leaf

▪ Preheat oven to 325 °F (160 °C).

▪ Lard veal with bacon. In a pan, roast 30 minutes per 1 lb (450 g). Halfway through, add onion and seasonings. Baste with cooking juices, if needed.

▪ Around 30 minutes before the end, remove bacon. Set aside.

▪ Continue roasting veal until golden. Serve with bacon.

NUTRITION	
CALORIES PER SERVING: 311	
FAT: 10 *g*	CAL. FROM FAT: 31 %
PROTEIN: 50 *g*	CHOLESTEROL: 182 *mg*
SODIUM: 269 *mg*	CARBOHYDRATES: 2 *g*

Roast Veal with Chives

6 SERVINGS	
1	3-lb (1.4 kg) roast veal
3 tbsp	(45 mL) chives, chopped
1/2 tsp	(2 mL) thyme
1/2 tsp	(2 mL) black pepper
2 tbsp	(30 mL) lemon juice

- Preheat oven to 375 °F (190 °C).
- In a roasting pan lined with aluminum foil, place veal roast.
- Season. Sprinkle with lemon juice.
- Roast in oven 90 minutes or so. Serve.

NUTRITION	
CALORIES PER SERVING: 268	
FAT: 7 g	CAL. FROM FAT: 25 %
PROTEIN: 48 g	CHOLESTEROL: 177 mg
SODIUM: 143 mg	CARBOHYDRATES: 1 g

Stuffed Veal Breast

6-8 SERVINGS	
1	3-lb (1.4 kg) veal breast, boneless
2 cups	(500 mL) soft part of bread
1 cup	(250 mL) milk
1 lb	(450 g) veal, finely ground
2	eggs, beaten
1 1/2 cups	(375 mL) fresh spinach, finely chopped
2	tomatoes, seedless, cubed
	salt and pepper

- Preheat oven to 350 °F (175 °C).
- With a knife, slit breast lengthwise in order to form a cavity. Set aside.
- In a small bowl, soak bread in milk. Mix in remaining ingredients. Season to taste with salt and pepper.
- Stuff breast with bread mixture. Truss or close with small skewers.
- Transfer stuffed breast to a roasting pan. Roast uncovered in oven 90 minutes or so.
- Serve with carrots and potatoes, if desired.

NUTRITION	
CALORIES PER SERVING: 348	
FAT: 16 g	CAL. FROM FAT: 44 %
PROTEIN: 39 g	CHOLESTEROL: 196 mg
SODIUM: 260 mg	CARBOHYDRATES: 9 g

St-Denis Veal Chops

6 SERVINGS

6	veal chops, 1-inch (2.5 cm) thick
2 tbsp	(30 mL) flour
2 tbsp	(30 mL) oil
2 tbsp	(30 mL) butter
1	onion, chopped
1	carrot, minced
1	celery stalk, minced
¼ tsp	(1 mL) marjoram
¼ tsp	(1 mL) rosemary
	salt and pepper
2-3	ripe tomatoes, peeled, chopped
½ cup	(125 mL) beef broth
2 tbsp	(30 mL) butter, melted
1 tsp	(5 mL) lemon peel
1	garlic clove, chopped
2 tbsp	(30 mL) parsley, chopped

- Dredge chops with flour.
- In a casserole dish, heat oil and melt butter. Fry chops on both sides. Add onion, carrot and celery. Cook until golden. Season.
- Pour in tomatoes and broth. Cover. Over low heat, simmer 30 minutes. Add a little extra broth if sauce is too thick.
- Meanwhile, in a bowl, mix butter, lemon peel, garlic and parsley.
- A few minutes before the end of cooking, fold seasoned butter into sauce.
- Serve chops on a bed of noodles, if desired.

NUTRITION	
CALORIES PER SERVING: 366	
FAT: 24 *g*	CAL. FROM FAT: 60 %
PROTEIN: 26 *g*	CHOLESTEROL: 120 *mg*
SODIUM: 238 *mg*	CARBOHYDRATES: 11 *g*

Veal Chops Verdurette

6 SERVINGS

2 tbsp	(30 mL) butter
6	veal chops
1 tbsp	(15 mL) flour
2 cups	(500 mL) beef broth
2	onions, sliced into rings
6	lettuce leaves
3	tomatoes, sliced

- Preheat oven to 375 °F (190 °C).
- In a skillet, melt butter. Sear veal chops 2 minutes each side. Remove from skillet.
- Sprinkle veal cooking fat with flour, mixing well. Fold broth into mixture. Over low heat, simmer 4-5 minutes or until sauce thickens.
- Meanwhile, transfer veal chops to an ovenproof dish. Cover with successive layers of onions, lettuce leaves and tomatoes, ending with a second layer of lettuce.
- Pour in enough sauce to cover lettuce. If sauce is insufficient, add tomato juice. Cook in oven 2 hours. Serve.

VARIATION
- Replace lettuce with spinach.

NUTRITION	
CALORIES PER SERVING: 316	
FAT: 18 *g*	CAL. FROM FAT: 50 %
PROTEIN: 27 *g*	CHOLESTEROL: 114 *mg*
SODIUM: 167 *mg*	CARBOHYDRATES: 12 *g*

Veal Chops with Cheese

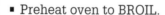

4 SERVINGS	
4	veal chops, prepared
2 tbsp	(30 mL) flour
2 tbsp	(30 mL) butter
	salt and pepper
4	Mozzarella cheese slices

- Preheat oven to BROIL.
- Dredge veal chops with flour. Set aside.
- In a skillet, over high heat, melt butter. Sear veal chops. Season with salt and pepper. Reduce heat. Cook veal chops 4-6 minutes each side. If needed, add a little water to avoid burning.
- Transfer veal chops to a roasting pan. Cover each one with a slice of Mozzarella. Broil in oven 3 minutes or until cheese has half-melted. Serve.

VARIATIONS
- Arrange on a bed of green peas. Surround with a crown of rice.

NUTRITION	
CALORIES PER SERVING: 629	
FAT: 45 g	CAL. FROM FAT: 65%
PROTEIN: 49 g	CHOLESTEROL: 215 mg
SODIUM: 679 mg	CARBOHYDRATES: 6 g

Veal Chops in Cream Sauce

4 SERVINGS	
1/2 cup	(125 mL) flour
	salt and pepper
4	veal chops
3 tbsp	(45 mL) butter
1	shallot, chopped
1	sweet red pepper, cut into strips
1 tsp	(5 mL) tarragon
1 cup	(250 mL) white wine
1/2 cup	(125 mL) light cream

- Preheat oven to 300 °F (150 °C).
- In a small bowl, mix flour, salt and pepper. Dredge chops with seasoned flour. Set aside.
- In a skillet, melt butter. Over moderate heat, cook veal chops 6 minutes or so each side. Remove chops from skillet. Transfer to a serving dish. Keep warm.
- In veal cooking fat, cook shallot, pepper and tarragon 3 minutes.
- Over high heat, deglaze skillet with white wine. Bring to a boil. Gently simmer 3 minutes. Fold cream into sauce. Spoon over veal chops. Serve.

NUTRITION	
CALORIES PER SERVING: 445	
FAT: 26 g	CAL. FROM FAT: 58%
PROTEIN: 27 g	CHOLESTEROL: 141 mg
SODIUM: 254 mg	CARBOHYDRATES: 16 g

Veal Tournedos in Shrimp Sauce

4 SERVINGS

2 tbsp	(30 mL) oil
2 tbsp	(30 mL) butter
4	4-oz (115 g) veal tournedos
3 tbsp	(45 mL) flour
3/4 cup	(180 mL) beef broth
1/2 cup	(125 mL) heavy cream
2 oz	(60 mL) sherry
3/4 tsp	(3 mL) salt
1/4 tsp	(1 mL) pepper
3/4 cup	(180 mL) baby shrimp

- In a skillet, heat oil and melt butter. Cook tournedos 5 minutes each side. Remove from skillet. Transfer to individual plates. Keep warm.

- Sprinkle veal cooking fat with flour, mixing well. While stirring, lightly brown 2 minutes. Slowly fold in broth, cream and sherry, mixing well. Season with salt and pepper. Over low heat, simmer 4 minutes.

- Add shrimp. Continue cooking 2 minutes. Coat tournedos with shrimp sauce. Serve.

VARIATIONS
- Replace beef broth with chicken broth.
- Replace sherry with cider or apple juice.

NUTRITION	
CALORIES PER SERVING: 423	
FAT: 32 g	CAL. FROM FAT: 70%
PROTEIN: 23 g	CHOLESTEROL: 154 mg
SODIUM: 570 mg	CARBOHYDRATES: 8 g

Veal Paupiettes

6-8 SERVINGS

3	hard-boiled eggs, chopped
12	black olives
3 tbsp	(45 mL) butter
8	veal scallops, very thinly sliced
8	thin ham slices
8	bacon slices
8	bay leaves
1/4 oz	(8 mL) cognac
2 tbsp	(30 mL) butter
1/4 cup	(60 mL) bacon, diced
1 cup	(250 mL) chicken broth
1/4 cup	(60 mL) onion, chopped
1	garlic clove, chopped
1/4 cup	(60 mL) carrots, diced

- Preheat oven to 350 °F (175 °C).
- In a large bowl, mix first 3 ingredients.
- Cover each veal scallop with a ham slice and 2 tbsp (30 mL) egg mixture. Roll. Wrap paupiettes lengthwise with a bacon slice. Tie with a string. Garnish with a bay leaf. Sprinkle with cognac. With a fork, prick paupiettes.
- In an ovenproof covered casserole dish, melt butter. Add veal paupiettes and diced bacon. Cook until golden brown.
- Fold in remaining ingredients. Cover. Cook in oven 45 minutes. Serve.

NUTRITION	
CALORIES PER SERVING: 638	
FAT: 37 g	CAL. FROM FAT: 54%
PROTEIN: 67 g	CHOLESTEROL: 300 mg
SODIUM: 2506 mg	CARBOHYDRATES: 6 g

Veal Medallions with Garbanzo Beans

4 SERVINGS

1/4 cup	(60 mL) butter
1 cup	(250 mL) canned garbanzo beans, rinsed, drained
1	French shallot, chopped
1	garlic clove, chopped
2 tbsp	(30 mL) parsley, chopped
1 tbsp	(15 mL) oil
8	2-oz (60 g) veal medallions
	salt and pepper
1 oz	(30 mL) cognac
1/2 cup	(125 mL) light cream

- In a skillet, melt half the butter. Sauté garbanzo beans a few minutes. Add shallot, garlic and half the parsley. Continue cooking 5 minutes, stirring occasionally. Remove mixture from skillet. Keep warm.

- In the same skillet, add remaining butter and oil. Cook veal medallions 5-7 minutes each side. Season with salt and pepper.

- Sprinkle with cognac. Flambé 30 seconds. Transfer medallions to individual plates. Keep warm.

- Mix cream into veal cooking fat. Over low heat, simmer 3 minutes.

- Top medallions with garbanzo bean mixture. Coat with sauce. Sprinkle with remaining chopped parsley. Serve.

NUTRITION	
CALORIES PER SERVING: 405	
FAT: 26 g	CAL. FROM FAT: 60%
PROTEIN: 22 g	CHOLESTEROL: 124 mg
SODIUM: 435 mg	CARBOHYDRATES: 17 g

Veal Scallopini with Zucchini

4 SERVINGS

4	4-oz (115 g) veal scallops
1/4 cup	(60 mL) whole wheat flour
2 tbsp	(30 mL) olive oil
	salt and pepper
1 tbsp	(15 mL) butter
1 cup	(250 mL) zucchini, julienned
2 tbsp	(30 mL) lemon juice
1/3 cup	(80 mL) dry white wine

- Preheat oven to 350 °F (175 °C).
- Dredge veal scallops with flour.
- In a skillet, heat oil. Sear veal scallops on both sides. Season to taste with salt and pepper. Transfer veal scallops to an ovenproof dish. Cook in oven 10 minutes or until veal is tender.
- In the same skillet, melt butter. While stirring, cook zucchini. As soon as zucchini change color, sprinkle in lemon juice and wine, mixing well. Continue cooking 2 minutes.
- Transfer veal scallops to individual plates. Top with zucchini mixture. Serve.

NUTRITION	
CALORIES PER SERVING: 248	
FAT: 15 g	CAL. FROM FAT: 56%
PROTEIN: 19 g	CHOLESTEROL: 81 mg
SODIUM: 150 mg	CARBOHYDRATES: 7 g

Clockwise from upper left :
Veal Paupiettes,
Veal Scallopini with Zucchini,
Veal Tournedos in Shrimp Sauce

Veal Strips with Mushrooms

6 SERVINGS

½ cup	(125 mL) flour
2 lbs	(900 g) veal, cut into strips
2 tbsp	(30 mL) butter
2	carrots, sliced into rounds
2	celery stalks, sliced
10 oz	(284 mL) canned cut green beans, drained
3 tbsp	(45 mL) soy sauce
2 cups	(500 mL) beef broth
	salt and pepper

- Preheat oven to 350 °F (175 °C).
- Set aside 1 tbsp (15 mL) flour for sauce. Dredge veal strips with remainder.
- In a frying pan, melt butter. Sear veal strips all over. Remove from skillet. Transfer to a covered ovenproof dish.
- Sprinkle veal cooking fat with reserved flour, mixing well. Add vegetables, soy sauce and broth. Season to taste with salt and pepper. Mix once more.
- Pour sauce over veal strips. Cover. Cook in oven 1 hour, stirring occasionally. If needed, add ½ cup (125 mL) broth during cooking. Serve on a bed of rice, if desired.

NUTRITION	
CALORIES PER SERVING: 280	
FAT: 13 *g*	CAL. FROM FAT: 43 %
PROTEIN: 25 *g*	CHOLESTEROL: 101 *mg*
SODIUM: 818 *mg*	CARBOHYDRATES: 15 *g*

Recipe shown above

Veal and Tomato Stir-fry

2 SERVINGS

2 tsp	(10 mL) olive oil
1 cup	(250 mL) onions, chopped
1 cup	(250 mL) mushrooms, minced
1	garlic clove, chopped
10 oz	(280 g) veal, cut into strips
2 cups	(500 mL) canned tomatoes, drained
2 tbsp	(30 mL) wine vinegar
1 tbsp	(15 mL) Dijon mustard
	salt and pepper
	parsley, chopped

- In a large non-stick skillet, heat oil. Cook onions, mushrooms and garlic 5 minutes or so.
- Add veal strips. Sear 5 minutes.
- Fold in remaining ingredients. Season to taste with salt and pepper. Over low heat, simmer 10 minutes or so.
- Spoon veal and vegetables over a bed of brown or wild rice, if desired. Garnish with parsley. Serve.

NUTRITION	
CALORIES PER SERVING: 688	
FAT: 27 *g*	CAL. FROM FAT: 31 %
PROTEIN: 50 *g*	CHOLESTEROL: 80 *mg*
SODIUM: 1200 *mg*	CARBOHYDRATES: 83 *g*

Veal Fricassée

4 SERVINGS	
¹⁄₄ cup	(60 mL) flour
1 tsp	(5 mL) salt
¹⁄₄ tsp	(1 mL) pepper
¹⁄₂ tsp	(2 mL) paprika
1 lb	(450 g) veal, cut into strips
1 cup	(250 mL) water
1 tbsp	(15 mL) Worcestershire sauce
2 tbsp	(30 mL) ketchup
2	medium-size carrots, sliced
1	leek, minced
1	potato, peeled, coarsely chopped
2	small onions, chopped
¹⁄₂ cup	(125 mL) frozen green peas

- In a plate, mix flour, salt pepper and paprika. Dredge veal strips.
- In a covered casserole dish, place veal strips. Add water, Worcestershire sauce and ketchup. Cover. Over low heat, simmer 30 minutes or until veal is tender.
- Add vegetables, except peas. Continue cooking 30 minutes or until vegetables are tender.
- Fold in peas. Simmer until peas are cooked. Serve.

NUTRITION	
CALORIES PER SERVING: 270	
FAT: 6 g	CAL. FROM FAT: 19%
PROTEIN: 20 g	CHOLESTEROL: 64 mg
SODIUM: 765 mg	CARBOHYDRATES: 35 g

Veal Fettucine

4 SERVINGS	
12 oz	(350 g) fettucine
12 oz	(350 g) veal, minced (as for Chinese fondue)
2 tbsp	(30 mL) vegetable oil
1	onion, chopped
1	garlic clove, chopped
1	green bell pepper, minced
1	sweet red pepper, minced
¹⁄₂ cup	(125 mL) beef broth
	salt and pepper

- In a saucepan filled with lightly-salted boiling water, cook fettucine.
- Meanwhile, in a covered skillet, heat oil. Sear veal slices. Remove from skillet. Set aside.
- In veal cooking fat, fry onion, garlic and bell pepper. Cover. Over low heat, cook until vegetables are tender-crisp.
- Mix in veal and beef broth. Season to taste with salt and pepper. Simmer 2 minutes.
- Drain fettucine. Spoon veal mixture over a bed of fettucine. Serve.

NUTRITION	
CALORIES PER SERVING: 493	
FAT: 13 g	CAL. FROM FAT: 24%
PROTEIN: 24 g	CHOLESTEROL: 50 mg
SODIUM: 105 mg	CARBOHYDRATES: 69 g

Veal Marengo

6 SERVINGS

3 tbsp	(45 mL) oil
3 lbs	(1.4 kg) veal, in cubes
2 tbsp	(30 mL) wheat flour
1 cup	(250 mL) beef broth
7 ½ oz	(213 mL) canned spicy tomato sauce
½ tsp	(2 mL) salt
¼ tsp	(1 mL) pepper
½ tsp	(2 mL) thyme
1 cup	(250 mL) onions, diced
2	garlic cloves, minced
1 tbsp	(15 mL) parsley, chopped
1	bay leaf
8 oz	(225 g) mushrooms, sliced

- In a microwave oven, preheat a baking dish 7 minutes, on HIGH. On same setting, heat oil 30 seconds. Sear veal cubes. Sprinkle with flour, mixing well. Fold in broth and tomato sauce. Cook 3-4 minutes, on HIGH. Stir once during cooking.

- Add remaining ingredients, except mushrooms. Cover. Cook 1 hour, on MEDIUM-HIGH. Stir once halfway through cooking.

- Remove from oven. Stir. Fold in mushrooms. Cover. Continue cooking 8-10 minutes or until veal is cooked. Let stand 5 minutes. Serve.

NUTRITION	
CALORIES PER SERVING: 366	
FAT: 14 g	CAL. FROM FAT: 35%
PROTEIN: 49 g	CHOLESTEROL: 193 mg
SODIUM: 508 mg	CARBOHYDRATES: 10 g

Veal Shepherd's Pie

4 SERVINGS

	juice of 1 lemon
8 oz	(225 g) mushrooms, sliced
1 tbsp	(15 mL) butter
3 cups	(750 mL) cooked veal, diced
10 oz	(284 mL) canned cream of chicken soup
	salt and pepper
2 cups	(500 mL) mashed potatoes
¼ cup	(60 mL) cheese, grated
2 tbsp	(30 mL) bread crumbs

- Preheat oven to 425 °F (220 °C).

- In a small bowl, sprinkle lemon juice over mushrooms.

- In a skillet, melt butter. Sauté mushrooms. Add diced veal and cream of chicken. Season to taste with salt and pepper. While stirring, continue cooking a few minutes.

- In an ovenproof buttered baking dish, spread veal mixture. Cover with mashed potatoes. Sprinkle with grated cheese and bread crumbs. Cook in oven 20 minutes. Serve.

NUTRITION	
CALORIES PER SERVING: 394	
FAT: 13 g	CAL. FROM FAT: 30%
PROTEIN: 42 g	CHOLESTEROL: 163 mg
SODIUM: 818 mg	CARBOHYDRATES: 28 g

Veal Stew with Onions and Mushrooms

6-8 SERVINGS	
3 lbs	(1.4 kg) veal, in cubes
1	onion, minced
2	carrots, diced
1	herb bouquet
	salt and pepper, to taste
3 tbsp	(45 mL) butter
1 lb	(450 g) mushrooms, minced
1/2 lb	(225 g) pearl onions
2 tbsp	(30 mL) flour
1	egg yolk
1 cup	(250 mL) light cream

- In a saucepan filled with lightly-salted boiling water, blanch veal cubes 5 minutes. Drain. Rinse. Return to saucepan. Cover with cold water. Bring to a boil. Skim off scum.

- Add onion, carrots and seasonings. Over low heat, simmer 1 hour.

- Remove veal cubes from saucepan. Set aside veal and cooking juices separately.

- In a skillet, melt 1 tbsp (15 mL) butter. Sauté mushrooms and pearl onions. Set aside.

- In the same skillet, melt remaining butter. Sprinkle with flour, mixing well. Slowly fold in veal cooking juices. Add egg yolk and cream. With a whisk, stir until sauce thickens.

- Place veal cubes in sauce. Add sautéed vegetables. Simmer 5 minutes. Serve.

NUTRITION	
CALORIES PER SERVING: 332	
FAT: 15 *g*	CAL. FROM FAT: 42 %
PROTEIN: 38 *g*	CHOLESTEROL: 201 *mg*
SODIUM: 297 *mg*	CARBOHYDRATES: 10 *g*

Recipe shown above

VARIATIONS
- Replace carrots with cauliflower or broccoli florets, as shown above.

- To cooking liquid, add 3 tbsp (45 mL) tomato paste.

Veal Meatballs

6 SERVINGS	
2 lbs	(900 g) ground veal
3	eggs
3	garlic cloves, chopped
½ cup	(125 mL) instant rice
	salt and pepper, to taste
½ cup	(125 mL) bread crumbs
4 cups	(1 L) ginger ale
1 ½ cups	(375 mL) chili sauce

- In a bowl, mix first 6 ingredients. With dampened hands, shape into 30 meatballs. Set aside.

- In a saucepan, combine ginger ale and chili sauce. Place meatballs in sauce. Over moderate heat, cook 2 hours or so.

- Serve with noodles or potatoes, if desired.

NUTRITION	
CALORIES PER SERVING: 386	
FAT: 13 g	CAL. FROM FAT: 31 %
PROTEIN: 34 g	CHOLESTEROL: 216 mg
SODIUM: 285 mg	CARBOHYDRATES: 31 g

Veal Patties in White Wine Sauce

4 SERVINGS	
2 lbs	(900 g) ground veal
1	egg
2 tbsp	(30 mL) onion, chopped
2 tbsp	(30 mL) capers, chopped
1 tbsp	(15 mL) parsley, chopped
1 tbsp	(15 mL) Worcestershire sauce
½ tsp	(2 mL) salt
	pinch of pepper
½ tsp	(2 mL) sage
2 tsp	(10 mL) olive oil
2 tsp	(10 mL) butter
1 cup	(250 mL) mushrooms, quartered
2 tbsp	(30 mL) shallots, chopped
2 tbsp	(30 mL) dry white wine

- In a bowl, mix first 9 ingredients. With dampened hands, shape into 8 patties. Set aside.

- In a skillet, heat oil and melt butter. Lightly brown patties. Remove from skillet. Set aside.

- In veal cooking fat, lightly cook mushroom quarters and shallots. Deglaze with white wine. Bring to a boil. Reduce heat. Place veal patties in skillet. Simmer 2-3 minutes. Serve.

NUTRITION	
CALORIES PER SERVING: 400	
FAT: 21 g	CAL. FROM FAT: 49 %
PROTEIN: 46 g	CHOLESTEROL: 237 mg
SODIUM: 567 mg	CARBOHYDRATES: 3 g

Veal Chili in Puff Pastry

2 SERVINGS	
1 tsp	(5 mL) vegetable oil
½ cup	(125 mL) onions, finely chopped
½ cup	(125 mL) green bell pepper, minced
2	garlic cloves, chopped
10 oz	(280 g) ground veal
1 tsp	(5 mL) chili powder
½ tsp	(2 mL) oregano
	pinch of salt
	a few drops of Tabasco sauce
¼ cup	(60 mL) canned red kidney beans, drained
½ cup	(125 mL) canned crushed tomatoes, drained
2 tbsp	(30 mL) tomato paste
2	commercial pastry shells

- In a skillet, heat oil. Sauté onions, pepper and garlic 5 minutes. Add veal. Season. While stirring, cook 3 minutes or until meat is brown all over.
- Fold in kidney beans, tomatoes and tomato paste. Simmer 10 minutes, stirring occasionally.
- Divide veal mixture among pastry shells. Serve.

NUTRITION	
CALORIES PER SERVING: 563	
FAT: 30 g	CAL. FROM FAT: 49 %
PROTEIN: 35 g	CHOLESTEROL: 116 mg
SODIUM: 664 mg	CARBOHYDRATES: 38 g

Recipe shown above

Veal Loaf

6 SERVINGS	
1 tsp	(5 mL) shortening
2	hard-boiled eggs, sliced
1 lb	(450 g) cooked veal, cut into strips
8 oz	(225 g) cooked ham, cut into strips
3	shallots, chopped
	salt and pepper, to taste
¼ tsp	(1 mL) nutmeg
	pinch of cayenne
1 tbsp	(15 mL) unflavored gelatin
¼ cup	(60 mL) cold water
1 ½ cups	(375 mL) chicken broth
¼ tsp	(1 mL) Tabasco sauce

- Rinse a bread pan under running cold water. Lightly grease with shortening. Place a few egg slices over bottom of pan. Cover with veal strips, ham strips and shallots. Season. Repeat last 3 steps until ingredients have been used.
- Let gelatin foam in cold water.
- In a saucepan, combine chicken broth and Tabasco sauce. Heat through. Stir in gelatin. Pour broth over meat. With a knife, make incisions so liquid penetrates all the way to bottom of pan. Refrigerate 12 hours.
- Unmold. Serve garnished with parsley, pepper strips and tomato slices, if desired.

NUTRITION	
CALORIES PER SERVING: 195	
FAT: 9 g	CAL. FROM FAT: 40 %
PROTEIN: 21 g	CHOLESTEROL: 125 mg
SODIUM: 653 mg	CARBOHYDRATES: 8 g

Veal Kidneys with Cranberries

4 SERVINGS	
1 lb	(450 g) veal kidneys, trimmed, cut into lobes
¹/₄ cup	(60 mL) whole wheat flour
3 tbsp	(45 mL) vegetable oil
1 cup	(250 mL) fresh or frozen cranberries
2 tbsp	(30 mL) raspberry vinegar
	salt and pepper
¹/₃ cup	(80 mL) beef broth
¹/₃ cup	(80 mL) chicken broth

- Preheat oven to 400 °F (205 °C).
- Dredge kidneys with flour.
- In an ovenproof skillet, over high heat, heat oil. Sear kidneys 5 minutes, stirring occasionally. Mix in cranberries. Sprinkle with raspberry vinegar. Cook 1 minute. Season to taste with salt and pepper.
- Pour both broths into skillet. Bring to a boil. Cook in oven 10 minutes or until kidneys are tender. Serve.

NUTRITION	
CALORIES PER SERVING: 298	
FAT: 16 *g*	CAL. FROM FAT: 49 %
PROTEIN: 22 *g*	CHOLESTEROL: 353 *mg*
SODIUM: 123 *mg*	CARBOHYDRATES: 16 *g*

Calf Sweetbreads Meunière

3-4 SERVINGS	
4 cups	(1 L) hot water
1 lb	(450 g) calf sweetbreads, trimmed
¹/₂ tsp	(2 mL) salt
3 tbsp	(45 mL) lemon juice
¹/₄ tsp	(1 mL) ground ginger
¹/₂ cup	(125 mL) butter
¹/₃ cup	(80 mL) bread crumbs
	parsley, chopped

- Preheat oven to BROIL.
- In a casserole dish, bring to a boil water, sweetbreads, salt, 1 tbsp (15 mL) lemon juice and ginger. Cover. Over low heat, simmer 20 minutes.
- Drain sweetbreads. Immerse in a bowl of ice-cold water. Remove filaments, veins and connective tissue. Slice in half lengthwise.
- In a small saucepan, over very low heat, melt butter. Baste sweetbreads. Dredge with bread crumbs. Set aside remaining melted butter.
- Transfer sweetbreads to a roasting pan with a rack. Brown in oven 4-5 minutes each side.
- Tip sweetbreads into a warm serving dish.
- In the same saucepan, combine butter and remaining lemon juice. Spoon over sweetbreads. Garnish with parsley. Serve.

VARIATIONS
- Serve on a bed of rice or mashed potatoes.

NUTRITION	
CALORIES PER SERVING: 679	
FAT: 31 *g*	CAL. FROM FAT: 38 %
PROTEIN: 58 *g*	CHOLESTEROL: 587 *mg*
SODIUM: 1383 *mg*	CARBOHYDRATES: 54 *g*

Braised Calf Tongue

2 SERVINGS	
2 tbsp	(30 mL) bacon, diced
1	small onion, minced
2 tbsp	(30 mL) butter
2 tbsp	(30 mL) flour
1 cup	(250 mL) beef broth
4	2-oz (60 g) cooked tongue slices
	salt and pepper
2 cups	(250 mL) mashed potatoes, hot

- In a small casserole dish, lightly brown bacon and onion. Fold in butter and flour. Pour broth into mixture. Simmer a few minutes.
- Add cooked tongue slices. Season to taste with salt and pepper. Continue cooking 10 minutes.
- Meanwhile, whip mashed potatoes until fluffy. Pipe a crown of mashed potatoes onto a serving dish.
- Pile braised tongue slices into the middle of potato crown. Serve.

VARIATION
- Serve with a tomato salad or mushrooms sautéed in butter.

NUTRITION	
CALORIES PER SERVING: 629	
FAT: 33 g	CAL. FROM FAT: 49 %
PROTEIN: 26 g	CHOLESTEROL: 157 mg
SODIUM: 858 mg	CARBOHYDRATES: 52 g

Calf Liver with Bacon

6 SERVINGS	
4 cups	(1 L) water
1 tbsp	(15 mL) vinegar
12	3-oz (96 g) veal liver slices
1/4 cup	(60 mL) flour
	salt and pepper, to taste
12	bacon slices

- Combine water and vinegar. Soak liver slices. Remove. Drain well.
- In a bowl, mix flour, salt and pepper. Dredge liver slices with seasoned flour. Set aside.
- In a skillet, cook bacon. Remove. Keep warm.
- In bacon drippings, sear floured liver slices 3-4 minutes each side
- Transfer liver slices to a serving dish. Garnish with bacon. Serve.

NUTRITION	
CALORIES PER SERVING: 320	
FAT: 14 g	CAL. FROM FAT: 40 %
PROTEIN: 35 g	CHOLESTEROL: 536 mg
SODIUM: 342 mg	CARBOHYDRATES: 12 g

W hy reserve lamb only
for special
occasions? This meat has a
unique flavour which can
be used in a thousand
recipes, as you will see
from the variety of dishes
in this chapter.

Marinated lamb is
delicious, notably in Roast
Lamb with Ginger (p.162):
prepared this way, it
contains little fat,
especially when it is baked
and grilled afterwards.

The recipes in this
section illustrate that
lamb is a delicious,
versatile meat suitable for
all types of dining.

LAMB

Roast Lamb with Ginger

6-8 SERVINGS	
2 tbsp	(30 mL) fresh ginger, finely chopped
1 tbsp	(15 mL) lemon peel
3	garlic cloves, minced
1 tsp	(5 mL) dried thyme
1/4 cup	(60 mL) flour
	salt and pepper
1/3 cup	(80 mL) fresh lemon juice
1	4 1/2-lb (2 kg) leg of lamb
3/4 cup	(180 mL) dry white wine or water
1 tbsp	(15 mL) cornstarch
2 tbsp	(30 mL) cold water

- Preheat oven to 450 °F (230 °C).

- In a small bowl, mix first 7 ingredients to a paste. Set aside. Cut outer fat from leg of lamb, leaving only a thin layer. Make incisions lengthwise across leg of lamb, 1/2-inch (1 cm) deep.

- Brush lamb with ginger mixture, ensuring that paste penetrates incisions. Cover. Refrigerate at least 3 hours or overnight.

- Transfer lamb to a roasting pan. Pour wine over meat. Roast in oven approximately 75 minutes or until inner temperature of meat reaches, according to meat thermometer, 130 °F (54 °C) for rare meat — or 140 °F (60 °C) for well-done meat. Baste often during cooking. Add water, if needed.

- Remove roast lamb from oven. Let stand 15 minutes under aluminum foil. Carve into thin slices. Keep warm.

- Degrease cooking juices. If needed, add wine or water. Bring to a boil, while scraping bottom of roasting pan.

- Meanwhile, dilute cornstarch in cold water. Fold into cooking juices. While stirring, cook until sauce thickens. Spoon over lamb slices. Serve.

NUTRITION	
CALORIES PER SERVING: 503	
FAT: 17 g	CAL. FROM FAT: 47%
PROTEIN: 37 g	CHOLESTEROL: 139 mg
SODIUM: 137 mg	CARBOHYDRATES: 6 g

Recipe shown above

Stuffed Leg of Lamb

6-8 SERVINGS	
2 tbsp	(30 mL) oil
2 lbs	(900 g) calf liver
2	onions, chopped
1/4 cup	(60 mL) parsley, chopped
2	mint leaves, finely chopped
2 cups	(500 mL) cooked rice
1 cup	(250 mL) apple sauce
1/2 cup	(125 mL) tomato sauce
1	4 1/2-lb (2 kg) leg of lamb
	pork fatback or bacon

- Preheat oven to 325 °F (160 °C).

(continued, next page)

- In a frying pan, heat oil. Cook calf liver.

- In a meat-grinder, mince liver, onions, parsley and mint.

- In a bowl, combine minced liver, rice, apple and tomato sauces. Mix in seasonings.

- Stuff leg of lamb with liver mixture. Cover with lard or bacon. Tie with a string.

- Transfer leg of lamb to a roasting pan. Roast uncovered in oven 30 minutes per 1 lb (450 g) of meat. Baste often.

- Transfer stuffed leg of lamb to a warm serving dish. Surround with a garnish of mint jelly or peeled orange slices, if desired. Serve.

NUTRITION	
CALORIES PER SERVING: 788	
FAT: 29 g	CAL. FROM FAT: 42%
PROTEIN: 60 g	CHOLESTEROL: 495 mg
SODIUM: 381 mg	CARBOHYDRATES: 29 g

Recipe shown above right

Dry Cider Leg of Lamb

8 SERVINGS

1	5-lb (2.2 kg) leg of lamb
1-2	garlic cloves, coarsely chopped

Marinade

2 cups	(500 mL) dry cider
1/2 cup	(125 mL) shallots, chopped
2 tsp	(10 mL) parsley, chopped
1/4 tsp	(1 mL) oregano
1 tsp	(5 mL) salt
1/2 tsp	(2 mL) pepper
1 tbsp	(15 mL) shortening
1 oz	(30 mL) calvados (optional)
2 tbsp	(30 mL) hot mustard
2 tbsp	(30 mL) butter, softened
2 tbsp	(30 mL) flour

- Preheat oven to 325 °F (160 °C).

- Trim and wipe leg of lamb. Make incisions lengthwise across leg of lamb. Insert garlic pieces into incisions.

- In a small bowl, mix marinade ingredients. Pour over lamb. Marinate in refrigerator 3 hours. Drain, reserving marinade.

- In a casserole dish, melt shortening. Sear lamb all over. Add calvados. Flambé. Sprinkle with a little marinade.

- Roast in oven 20 minutes per 1 lb (450 g) for rare meat — 25 minutes for well-done meat. Baste often.

- Remove lamb from oven. Keep warm. Place casserole dish over high heat. Degrease cooking juices. Add mustard and remaining marinade. Reduce heat.

- In a small bowl, blend softened butter and flour. Fold into marinade. Spoon over leg of lamb. Serve.

NUTRITION	
CALORIES PER SERVING: 611	
FAT: 23 g	CAL. FROM FAT: 50%
PROTEIN: 41 g	CHOLESTEROL: 162 mg
SODIUM: 473 mg	CARBOHYDRATES: 11 g

Recipe shown above left

Boning a Loin of Lamb

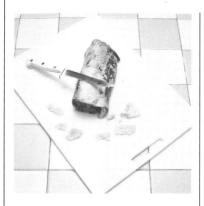

- With a knife, trim off as much fat as possible.

- Lay loin of lamb very flat, fatty side down. Slide knife between meat and bone.

- Press downwards following the bone.

- Once the bone has been detached on one side, fold it away in order to clear second side.

- Continue cutting along the bone until meat is fully severed, as shown above. Roll meat, tie with a string and cook, or stuff before rolling, as shown below.

Lamb Rolls with Watercress

4 SERVINGS		

Stuffing

1 cup	(250 mL) watercress, chopped
1	egg, beaten
3 tbsp	(45 mL) Parmesan cheese, grated
	salt and pepper
2	short loins of lamb, boned as in technique opposite
3 tbsp	(45 mL) peanut oil
3 tbsp	(45 mL) onion, chopped
3 tbsp	(45 mL) flour
1 cup	(250 mL) lamb or beef broth

- Preheat oven to 350 °F (175 °C).
- In a small bowl, mix stuffing ingredients.
- Cover each loin of lamb with half the stuffing. Roll tightly. Tie with a string.
- In a frying pan, heat oil. Lightly brown meat all over. Add onion. Season with salt and pepper. Cook 1 minute.
- Transfer lamb to an ovenproof dish. Roast in oven 12 minutes.
- Meanwhile, fold flour into lamb cooking fat, mixing until smooth. While stirring, add broth in 2 steps. Let liquid reduce by half. Set aside.
- Remove meat from oven. Let stand 5 minutes. Cut away string. Slice meat into 10 rounds. Place on a serving dish. Coat with sauce. Serve.

NUTRITION	
CALORIES PER SERVING: 800	
FAT: 71 g	CAL. FROM FAT: 81 %
PROTEIN: 31 g	CHOLESTEROL: 79 mg
SODIUM: 271 mg	CARBOHYDRATES: 8g

Tarragon Rack of Lamb

2 SERVINGS	
2 tbsp	(30 mL) oil
1	lamb rib roast, prepared
1/2 cup	(125 mL) semisweet white wine, heated
1	garlic clove, crushed
1/2 tsp	(2 mL) tarragon
	salt and pepper
1/2 cup	(125 mL) heavy cream
2 tbsp	(30 mL) capers

- Preheat oven to 400 °F (205 °C).

- In a frying pan, heat oil. Brown roast lamb all over.

- Transfer to an ovenproof dish. Pour in wine. Add garlic and tarragon. Season with salt and pepper. Roast in oven 10 minutes.

- Remove roast lamb from oven. Coat with cream. Sprinkle with capers. Roast in oven 20 minutes. Serve.

VARIATIONS
- Serve with green beans and mashed potatoes, or fried eggplant.

NUTRITION	
CALORIES PER SERVING: 986	
FAT: 93 g	CAL. FROM FAT: 88%
PROTEIN: 26 g	CHOLESTEROL: 208 mg
SODIUM: 285 mg	CARBOHYDRATES: 3 g

Surprise Rack of Lamb

4 SERVINGS	
1	garlic clove, chopped
3 tbsp	(45 mL) bread crumbs
1 tbsp	(15 mL) paprika
1 tbsp	(15 mL) hazelnuts, crumbled
1 tbsp	(15 mL) parsley, chopped
1 tbsp	(15 mL) mint, chopped
2	lamb rib roasts, prepared
	knobs of butter
	salt and pepper
1 tbsp	(15 mL) oil

- Preheat oven to 450 °F (230 °C).

- In a small bowl, combine garlic, bread crumbs, paprika, hazelnuts, parsley and mint. Set aside.

- Coat fatty side of lamb with half the bread crumb mixture. Dot with butter.

- In a skillet, heat oil. Sear roast lamb all over.

- Transfer roast lamb to an ovenproof dish. Season with salt and pepper. Roast in oven 15 minutes. Turn over once halfway through cooking.

- Remove from oven. Coat roast lamb with second half bread crumb mixture. Roast in oven 5 minutes. Serve.

NUTRITION	
CALORIES PER SERVING: 1324	
FAT: 121 g	CAL. FROM FAT: 83%
PROTEIN: 26 g	CHOLESTEROL: 208 mg
SODIUM: 285 mg	CARBOHYDRATES: 3 g

Lamb Chops in Puff Pastry

2 SERVINGS	
½ lb	(225 g) flaky pastry (p. 335)
2 tbsp	(30 mL) butter
3	shallots, minced
½ cup	(125 mL) canned sliced mushrooms, drained
2	ham slices, cut into thin strips
1 tsp	(5 mL) tomato paste
	salt and pepper
4	lamb chops, trimmed
½ oz	(15 mL) cognac, heated
1	egg, beaten

- Preheat oven to 400 °F (205 °C).

- Roll out pastry dough. Cut into 4 squares. Set aside.

- In a frying pan, melt half the butter. Lightly cook shallots, mushrooms and ham. Mix in tomato paste, salt and pepper. Set aside.

- In a skillet, melt remaining butter. Sear lamb chops on both sides. Sprinkle with cognac. Flambé.

- Place each lamb chop on a pastry square. Top with ham stuffing. Seal in pastry, leaving bone tips uncovered. Brush with beaten egg. Cook in oven 12 minutes or until dough turns golden brown. Serve.

Decoration
- Decorate bone tips with frills.

NUTRITION	
CALORIES PER SERVING: 1101	
FAT: 79g	CAL. FROM FAT: 62%
PROTEIN: 51 g	CHOLESTEROL: 813 mg
SODIUM: 1856 mg	CARBOHYDRATES: 47 g

Lamb Chops in Foil

3 SERVINGS	
3	potatoes, steamed in their skins
3	garlic cloves, chopped
2 tbsp	(30 mL) basil
2 tbsp	(30 mL) fresh parsley, chopped
	salt and pepper
1 tsp	(5 mL) oil
1 tsp	(5 mL) butter
6	lamb chops
2	onions, minced

- Preheat oven to 400 °F (205 °C).

- Peel steamed potatoes. Slice into rounds. Set aside.

- Cut 3 large squares of aluminum foil. Butter lightly. Set aside.

- In a small bowl, mix garlic, herbs, salt and pepper.

- In a non-stick frying pan, heat oil and melt butter. Lightly brown lamb chops. Set aside.

- In aluminum squares, spread layers of potato rounds. Place 2 lamb chops on each. Cover with onion slices. Sprinkle with mixed seasonings.

- Close aluminum foil, sealing in each serving. Cook in oven 30 minutes. Serve.

NUTRITION	
CALORIES PER SERVING: 849	
FAT: 52 g	CAL. FROM FAT: 55%
PROTEIN: 37 g	CHOLESTEROL: 138 mg
SODIUM: 196 mg	CARBOHYDRATES: 60 g

Piquant Lamb Chops

---
3 SERVINGS

Sauce

5 ½ oz	(156 mL)	tomato paste
2 tbsp	(30 mL)	brown sugar
¾ cup	(180 mL)	water
¼ cup	(60 mL)	vinegar
1 tsp	(5 mL)	salt
½ tsp	(2 mL)	dry mustard
2 tbsp	(30 mL)	vegetable oil
1		medium-size onion, chopped
1		garlic clove, chopped
1 tbsp	(15 mL)	lemon juice
6		lamb rib chops, trimmed

- Preheat oven to BROIL.
- In a bowl, mix sauce ingredients. Set aside.
- In a skillet, heat oil. Lightly brown onion and garlic. Mix in sauce and lemon juice. Set aside.
- Transfer lamb chops to a baking sheet. Place 4 inches (10 cm) from element. Broil 4-6 minutes each side.
- Place lamb chops on a serving dish. Coat with sauce. Serve.

NUTRITION	
CALORIES PER SERVING: 864	
FAT: 63 *g*	CAL. FROM FAT: 66%
PROTEIN: 49 *g*	CHOLESTEROL: 196 *mg*
SODIUM: 1282 *mg*	CARBOHYDRATES: 25 *g*

Mandarin Lamb Chops

---
4 SERVINGS
---

1 tbsp	(15 mL)	oil
8		lamb chops
2 tsp	(10 mL)	cornstarch
4 tsp	(20 mL)	cold water
1 cup	(250 mL)	cranberry juice
1 tbsp	(15 mL)	sugar
1 tsp	(5 mL)	salt
½ cup	(125 mL)	raisins
10 oz	(284 mL)	canned mandarin orange sections, drained

- In a skillet, heat oil. Sear lamb chops on both sides. Remove from skillet. Set aside.
- Dilute cornstarch in cold water. Set aside.
- Pour cranberry juice into skillet. Add cornstarch. Over low heat, cook until sauce thickens. Season with sugar and salt. Cook while stirring.
- Place lamb chops in sauce. Over low heat, simmer 25 minutes. Halfway through cooking, add raisins and mandarin oranges. Finish cooking. Serve.

NUTRITION	
CALORIES PER SERVING: 727	
FAT: 52 *g*	CAL. FROM FAT: 64%
PROTEIN: 31 *g*	CHOLESTEROL: 134 *mg*
SODIUM: 642 *mg*	CARBOHYDRATES: 34 *g*

Lamb Rolls with Apricot Sauce

	4 SERVINGS

Stuffing

1 cup	(250 mL) mashed sweet potatoes
1/4 cup	(60 mL) dried apricots, chopped
1 tbsp	(15 mL) molasses
8	thin slices of cooked roast lamb

Sauce

1 1/2 cups	(375 mL) apricot juice
1 tbsp	(15 mL) lemon juice
4 tsp	(20 mL) cornstarch
1/2 tsp	(2 mL) salt
	pinch of ginger
1/2 cup	(125 mL) golden raisins
2 tbsp	(30 mL) butter or margarine

- Preheat oven to 350 °F (175 °C).
- In a small bowl, combine stuffing ingredients. Divide stuffing among lamb slices. Roll. Secure with a wooden toothpick.
- Transfer lamb rolls to a cookie sheet. Cook in oven 15 minutes.
- Meanwhile, in a saucepan, blend sauce ingredients. Over low heat, while stirring, cook until sauce thickens. Add raisins and butter. Stir until butter melts. Pour apricot sauce over lamb rolls. Serve.

NUTRITION	
CALORIES PER SERVING: 680	
FAT: 129 g	CAL. FROM FAT: 39%
PROTEIN: 56 g	CHOLESTEROL: 196 mg
SODIUM: 583 mg	CARBOHYDRATES: 48 g

Mustardy Lamb Fillets

	4 SERVINGS

Sauce

2 tsp	(10 mL) flour
1/2 cup	(125 mL) white wine
1/2 cup	(125 mL) chicken broth
2 tsp	(10 mL) olive oil
2 tbsp	(30 mL) butter
16	lamb fillets
4	shallots, minced
1	garlic clove, crushed
2 tbsp	(30 mL) hot mustard

- In a bowl, dilute flour in wine and broth. Set aside.
- In a skillet, heat oil and melt butter. Lightly brown lamb fillets. Remove from skillet. Keep warm.
- In lamb cooking fat, sauté shallots and garlic. Fold in sauce. While stirring, let liquid reduce 5 minutes.
- Place lamb fillets in sauce. Simmer 5 minutes. Transfer fillets to a warm serving dish.
- Add mustard to sauce. Over high heat, cook 2 minutes while stirring constantly. Pour mustard sauce over fillets. Serve.

NUTRITION	
CALORIES PER SERVING: 367	
FAT: 86 g	CAL. FROM FAT: 72%
PROTEIN: 17 g	CHOLESTEROL: 80 mg
SODIUM: 211 mg	CARBOHYDRATES: 7 g

Recipe shown above

Minty Lamb Medallions with Pistachios

4 SERVINGS

2	lamb loins, boned
3 tbsp	(45 mL) whole wheat flour
3 tbsp	(45 mL) olive oil
¼ cup	(60 mL) pistachios, shelled
3 tbsp	(45 mL) mint jelly
1 cup	(250 mL) lamb or beef broth
	salt and pepper
	fresh mint leaves

- Cut lamb loins into 4 pieces. Flatten each piece to a medallion shape. Dredge with flour.

- Heat oil. Over high heat, sear medallions 3 minutes each side. Reduce heat. Continue cooking 2 minutes.

- Mix in pistachios and mint jelly. Fold in broth. Over high heat, bring to a boil. Let liquid reduce by half. Remove from heat. Let stand 3 minutes. Season with salt and pepper.

- Transfer to a serving dish. Garnish with fresh mint leaves. Serve.

NUTRITION	
CALORIES PER SERVING: 479	
FAT: 38g	CAL. FROM FAT: 71%
PROTEIN: 18 g	CHOLESTEROL: 71 mg
SODIUM: 86 mg	CARBOHYDRATES: 17 g

Lamb Medallions Provençal

4 SERVINGS

2	lamb loins, boned
3 tbsp	(45 mL) bread crumbs
3 tbsp	(45 mL) Parmesan cheese, grated
2	garlic cloves, chopped
1 tbsp	(15 mL) parsley, chopped
3 tbsp	(45 mL) olive oil
3 tbsp	(45 mL) tomato paste
1 cup	(250 mL) lamb or beef broth
	salt and pepper
	fresh parsley

- Cut lamb loins into 4 pieces. Flatten each to a medallion shape.

- Mix bread crumbs, Parmesan, garlic and parsley. Dredge medallions with mixture, pressing down so breading will stick to meat.

- In a skillet, heat oil. Lightly brown medallions 2 minutes each side. Reduce heat. Continue cooking 6 minutes.

- Mix in tomato paste. Pour lamb or beef stock into skillet. Over high heat, bring to a boil. Let liquid reduce by half. Season with salt and pepper. Remove from heat. Let stand 3 minutes. Garnish with fresh parsley. Serve.

Note : if lamb or beef stock is unavailable, replace with broth thickened using a roux or cornstarch.

NUTRITION	
CALORIES PER SERVING: 465	
FAT: 38 g	CAL. FROM FAT: 73%
PROTEIN: 21 g	CHOLESTEROL: 75 mg
SODIUM: 355 mg	CARBOHYDRATES: 11 g

Leftover Lamb Stew

4 SERVINGS	
2 tbsp	(30 mL) oil
1	large onion, chopped
1/2 cup	(125 mL) celery, minced
1	garlic clove, chopped
1	green bell pepper, diced
1	tomato, peeled, coarsely chopped
10 oz	(284 mL) canned tomato soup
	pinch of paprika
2 cups	(500 mL) leg of lamb, cooked, diced
	salt and pepper

- In a skillet, heat oil. Lightly brown onion. Add celery, garlic, bell pepper and tomato. Cook 5 minutes. Fold in tomato soup, paprika and meat. Season. Continue cooking 5 minutes.
- Serve on a bed of rice or macaroni.

NUTRITION	
CALORIES PER SERVING: 393	
FAT: 25 g	CAL. FROM FAT: 57%
PROTEIN: 32 g	CHOLESTEROL: 109 mg
SODIUM: 390 mg	CARBOHYDRATES: 10 g

Pork and Lamb Casserole

6-8 SERVINGS	
1 1/2 lbs	(675 g) potatoes, sliced
	salt and pepper
1 lb	(450 g) lamb shoulder, boned, cubed
1 lb	(450 g) pork shoulder, boned, cubed
2	onions, finely sliced
2/3 cup	(80 mL) white wine
2 tbsp	(30 mL) butter, diced

- Preheat oven to 375 °F (190 °C).
- Cover bottom of a buttered casserole dish with half the potato slices. Season with salt and pepper. Spread layers of lamb cubes, pork cubes and sliced onions. Pour in wine. Add remaining potatoes. Dot with butter. Cover. Cook in oven 75 minutes or until potatoes are golden brown. Serve.

NUTRITION	
CALORIES PER SERVING: 322	
FAT: 20g	CAL. FROM FAT: 59%
PROTEIN: 17 g	CHOLESTEROL: 15 mg
SODIUM: 134 mg	CARBOHYDRATES: 22 g

Shish-Kabobs

6-8 SERVINGS	
2 lbs	(900 g) leg of lamb or shoulder, cubed
1/2 cup	(125 mL) vegetable oil
1/4 cup	(60 mL) lemon juice
2	garlic cloves, crushed
1/2 cup	(125 mL) parsley, finely chopped
	salt and pepper

- Preheat oven to BROIL.
- In a shallow dish, combine all ingredients. Marinate meat 6 hours.
- Remove meat from marinade. Pat dry. Thread cubes onto skewers. Roast in oven 8-10 minutes or until meat is nicely browned. Rotate shish-kabobs 4 times during cooking. Serve.

VARIATION
- Barbecue shish-kabobs over charcoal.

NUTRITION	
CALORIES PER SERVING: 331	
FAT: 21 g	CAL. FROM FAT: 73%
PROTEIN: 16 g	CHOLESTEROL: 62 mg
SODIUM: 97 mg	CARBOHYDRATES: 1 g

Lamb with Bulgur

6 SERVINGS	
3 tbsp	(45 mL) vegetable oil
1 1/2 lbs	(675 g) lamb, in 2-inch (5 cm) cubes
1	onion, finely chopped
3 cups	(750 mL) water
1 cup	(250 mL) bulgur
19 oz	(540 mL) canned garbanzo beans, drained
1/2 tsp	(2 mL) salt
1/4 tsp	(1 mL) pepper
1/4 tsp	(1 mL) cinnamon

- In a casserole dish, heat oil. Lightly brown meat and onion. Add water. Bring to a boil. Reduce heat. Simmer around 45 minutes or until meat is tender. Add 1/2 cup (125 mL) water during cooking, if needed.
- Fold in bulgur, garbanzo beans and seasonings. Continue cooking 15 minutes. Serve this nourishing meal with pickles or yogurt, if desired.

NUTRITION	
CALORIES PER SERVING: 480	
FAT: 22 g	CAL. FROM FAT: 40%
PROTEIN: 28 g	CHOLESTEROL: 61 mg
SODIUM: 244 mg	CARBOHYDRATES: 45 g

Clockwise from upper left :
Leftover Lamb Stew, Pork and Lamb
Casserole, Shish-Kabobs, Lamb with Bulgur

Lamb Stew with Tomatoes and Onions

	4 SERVINGS
1 tbsp	(15 mL) vegetable oil
1 lb	(450 g) lamb cubes
2	onions, chopped
2	garlic cloves, minced
3 tbsp	(45 mL) butter
3 tbsp	(45 mL) flour
10 oz	(284 mL) canned tomato sauce
1/3 cup	(80 mL) water
1 tsp	(5 mL) red wine vinegar
	salt and pepper
2 tsp	(10 mL) fresh tarragon, finely chopped
2 tsp	(10 mL) fresh parsley, finely chopped
2 tsp	(10 mL) fresh fennel, finely chopped

- Over high heat, in a frying pan, heat oil. Sear lamb cubes. Reduce heat. Over low heat, brown meat 30 minutes. Mix in onion and garlic. Set aside.
- Preheat oven to 375 °F (190 °C)
- In a saucepan, melt butter. Fold in flour. Add in tomato sauce and water, stirring well. Season with vinegar, salt, pepper and herbs. Simmer 2-3 minutes.
- Transfer meat to an ovenproof dish. Cover with sauce. Cook in oven 6-7 minutes. Serve.

NUTRITION	
CALORIES PER SERVING: 333	
FAT: 18 g	CAL. FROM FAT: 49%
PROTEIN: 26 g	CHOLESTEROL: 97 mg
SODIUM: 684 mg	CARBOHYDRATES: 17 g

Lamb-stuffed Zucchini

	4 SERVINGS
Stuffing	
3 tbsp	(45 mL) butter
8 oz	(225 g) lamb shoulder, diced
1	onion, finely chopped
1/4 tsp	(1 mL) cinnamon
	salt and pepper
1/2 cup	(125 mL) pine nuts
8	medium-size unpeeled zucchini, halved lengthwise
2 cups	(500 mL) tomato sauce

- Preheat oven to 325°F (160 °C)
- In a skillet, melt butter. Lightly brown meat. Add remaining stuffing ingredients. Simmer 5 minutes or so. Set aside.
- Scoop out half the flesh from zucchini. Stuff with lamb mixture. Place in an ovenproof dish. Cover with tomato sauce. Cook in oven 40 minutes. Serve.

NUTRITION	
CALORIES PER SERVING: 316	
FAT: 20 g	CAL. FROM FAT: 52%
PROTEIN: 20 g	CHOLESTEROL: 60 mg
SODIUM: 963 mg	CARBOHYDRATES: 21 g

Curried Lamb

8 SERVINGS

19 oz	(540 mL) canned tomatoes, chopped, drained
2	onions, chopped
3	garlic cloves, chopped
¹/₄ cup	(60 mL) oil
2 ¹/₂ lbs	(1.2 kg) lamb cubes
1 tsp	(5 mL) ginger
¹/₂ tsp	(2 mL) coriander seeds
	pinch of thyme, chopped
2	bay leaves
¹/₄ tsp	(1 mL) crushed red peppers
¹/₈ tsp	(0.5 mL) clove
¹/₄ tsp	(1 mL) ground cumin
1 tsp	(5 mL) paprika
1 tsp	(5 mL) curcuma
	salt
1 ¹/₃ cups	(330 mL) water
2 ¹/₂ tsp	(12 mL) fresh coriander, chopped

- In a casserole dish, combine tomatoes, onions, garlic and oil. Over low heat, cook 10 minutes.

- Add lamb cubes and seasonings. Pour in water. Cover. Simmer 1 hour. Add coriander. Simmer 10 minutes. Serve on a bed of cinnamon-flavored white rice.

NUTRITION	
CALORIES PER SERVING: 288	
FAT: 15 g	CAL. FROM FAT: 46%
PROTEIN: 30 g	CHOLESTEROL: 92 mg
SODIUM: 258 mg	CARBOHYDRATES: 9 g

Recipe shown above

Lamb Quiche

4 SERVINGS

2 tbsp	(30 mL) butter
1	large onion, chopped
¹/₂ cup	(125 mL) mushrooms, sliced
¹/₄ tsp	(1 mL) dry mustard
1	9-inch (23 cm) pie crust *(p. 334)*
1 ¹/₂ cups	(375 mL) lamb, cooked, diced
¹/₂ cup	(125 mL) Parmesan cheese, grated
8 oz	(225 g) cream cheese, softened
1 cup	(250 mL) milk
3	eggs, beaten
1 tsp	(5 mL) salt
¹/₄ tsp	(1 mL) pepper
¹/₈ tsp	(0.5 mL) ground nutmeg
4	tomatoes, sliced

- Preheat oven to 400 °F (205 °C)

- In a frying pan, melt butter. Lightly cook onion, mushrooms and dry mustard. Set aside.

- Place meat in pie crust. Set aside.

- In a bowl, mix both cheeses. Add milk, eggs, salt, pepper and nutmeg. Fold in onion and mushroom mixture. Gently pour into pie crust. Cover with tomato slices. Bake in oven 10 minutes. Lower oven temperature to 350 °F (175 °C). Continue cooking 25 minutes. Remove quiche from oven. Serve.

NUTRITION	
CALORIES PER SERVING: 758	
FAT: 51 g	CAL. FROM FAT: 61%
PROTEIN: 37 g	CHOLESTEROL: 288 mg
SODIUM: 1424 mg	CARBOHYDRATES: 38 g

Spring Lamb Meatballs

4 SERVINGS	
1 lb	(450 g) ground lamb
2	eggs, beaten
4 oz	(115 g) Gruyère or Cheddar cheese
1	bread slice, crumbled
1 tsp	(5 mL) salt
1/2 tsp	(2 mL) pepper
	bread crumbs
1 tbsp	(15 mL) butter

- In a bowl, mix ground lamb, 1 egg, cheese, bread crumbs, salt and pepper. Shape into 32 small meatballs.
- Dip meatballs in remaining beaten egg. Dredge with bread crumbs.
- In a skillet, melt butter. Brown meatballs. Serve with a tossed salad, if desired.

NUTRITION	
CALORIES PER SERVING: 566	
FAT: 42 g	CAL. FROM FAT: 67%
PROTEIN: 32 g	CHOLESTEROL: 213 mg
SODIUM: 901 mg	CARBOHYDRATES: 14 g

Lemony Lamb Meatballs

6 SERVINGS	
1 1/2 lbs	(675 g) lean ground lamb
1/2 cup	(125 mL) unsalted crackers, crumbled
1	whole egg
1 tsp	(5 mL) dried basil
2 cups	(500 mL) water
2	cubes of beef broth
1 tbsp	(15 mL) cornstarch
2 tbsp	(30 mL) cold water
3 tbsp	(45 mL) lemon juice

- In a bowl, mix ground lamb, cracker crumbs, egg, salt, pepper and basil. Shape into 1 inch (2.5 cm) meatballs. Set aside.
- In a casserole dish, bring water to a boil. Dissolve beef broth cubes. Add meatballs. Cook 15 minutes. Remove meatballs. Keep warm.
- Meanwhile, dilute cornstarch in cold water. Add to lamb cooking broth. Bring to a boil. Cook 5 minutes. Fold in lemon juice. Pour over meatballs. Serve.

NUTRITION	
CALORIES PER SERVING: 377	
FAT: 28 g	CAL. FROM FAT: 67%
PROTEIN: 21 g	CHOLESTEROL: 113 mg
SODIUM: 369 mg	CARBOHYDRATES: 10 g

Lamb Patties

6-8 SERVING	
1 1/4 cups	(300 mL) bread crumbs
1 cup	(250 mL) milk
2	eggs, beaten
2 lbs	(900 g) ground lamb
	salt and pepper
6-8	bacon slices
1 tbsp	(15 mL) butter
6-8	pineapple slices
1 1/2 cups	(375 mL) mushrooms, quartered
1 tbsp	(15 mL) parsley, chopped

- In a bowl, soak bread in milk. Mix in eggs, lamb, salt and pepper. Refrigerate 1 hour.
- Shape into 6-8 patties. Wrap each one with a bacon slice. Secure with a toothpick.
- In a non-stick frying pan, brown patties 5 minutes or so on both sides. Keep warm.
- Meanwhile, in a frying pan, melt butter. Fry pineapple slices and mushrooms to a nice golden brown color.
- Place pineapple and lamb patties on a serving dish. Garnish with mushrooms. Sprinkle with parsley. Serve.

NUTRITION	
CALORIES PER SERVING: 870	
FAT: 38 g	CAL. FROM FAT: 37%
PROTEIN: 29 g	CHOLESTEROL: 142 mg
SODIUM: 411 mg	CARBOHYDRATES: 114 g

Lamb Meatloaf

6 SERVINGS	
1 1/2 lbs	(675 g) ground lamb
3/4 cup	(180 mL) cheese, grated
1	onion, chopped
3 tbsp	(45 mL) ketchup
2 tsp	(10 mL) Worcestershire sauce
	salt and pepper
1	egg, lightly beaten
1 lb	(450 g) bacon

- Preheat oven to 350 °F (175 °C)
- In a bowl, mix all ingredients, except bacon. Set aside.
- Line a loaf pan with bacon slices, so that bacon overlaps rim. Pour lamb mixture into pan. Fold bacon over meat, covering completely. Cook in oven 1 hour. Serve.

NUTRITION	
CALORIES PER SERVING: 842	
FAT: 69 g	CAL. FROM FAT: 75%
PROTEIN: 47 g	CHOLESTEROL: 192 mg
SODIUM: 1537 mg	CARBOHYDRATES: 5 g

Clockwise from upper left :
Spring Lamb Meatballs, Lamb Meatloaf,
Lemony Lamb Meatballs

LAMB **175**

oasted, ribbed, or as a
fillet, pork is easily
prepared and always
makes a successful meal.
Did you know that progress
in the pork industry has
enabled us to obtain leaner
pork? In addition, the
pork's fat is easy to remove
since it is mainly located
around the skin.

Pork is an excellent source
of protein and thiamine.

We have presented in
this chapter such recipes
as Mandarin Pork Stir-fry
(p. 186) and Roast Pork
in Spicy Apricot Sauce
(p. 178).

Don't hesitate to give in to
the delicious pork recipes
offered to you in this section.

PORK

Pork roast in Spicy Apricot Sauce

6 SERVINGS

3 lbs	(1.4 kg) pork roast, boned, rolled
8 oz	(227 mL) canned apricots, drained, chopped (reserve juice)
1 1/4 cups	(300 mL) water
2 1/2 tbsp	(38 mL) molasses
1 tsp	(5 mL) dry mustard
1 tsp	(5 mL) salt
1/4 tsp	(1 mL) pepper
2 tbsp	(30 mL) cornstarch
1 cup	(250 mL) chicken broth
1 tbsp	(15 mL) vinegar

- Preheat oven to 325 °F (160 °C).
- In an ovenproof dish, place roast. Set aside.
- In a bowl, blend apricot juice and water. Mix in molasses, mustard, salt and pepper.
- Pour sauce over roast. Cover. Cook in oven 2 hours or so, basting every 30 minutes.
- Approximately 30 minutes before the end of cooking, remove lid.
- Transfer roast to a warm serving dish. Keep warm.

- In a small bowl, dilute cornstarch in 3 tbsp (45 mL) chicken broth. Fold into cooking juices. Add remaining broth and vinegar. While stirring, bring to a boil.
- Fold in apricots. Adjust seasoning. Pour into a sauceboat.
- Serve roast and sauce with cauliflower or carrots, if desired.

VARIATIONS
- Serve cold with pasta salad or vegetables.
- Replace apricots with canned cherries, and chicken broth with beef broth.

NUTRITION	
CALORIES PER SERVING: 759	
FAT: 60 *g*	CAL. FROM FAT: 71%
PROTEIN: 40 *g*	CHOLESTEROL: 122 *mg*
SODIUM: 456 *mg*	CARBOHYDRATES: 15 *g*

Honey-glazed Pork Roast

8 SERVINGS	
¼ cup	(60 mL) honey
3 tbsp	(45 mL) soy sauce
1 tbsp	(15 mL) Dijon mustard
½ tsp	(2 mL) Tabasco sauce
1 tbsp	(15 mL) black peppercorns, crushed
1	2-lb (900 g) shoulder pork roast

- Preheat oven to 325 °F (160 °C).
- In a bowl, mix first 5 ingredients. Brush pork roast with generous amounts of honey mixture. Place in a roasting pan with a rack. Roast in oven 90 minutes.
- Remove roast from pan. Slice. Baste each slice with cooking juices.
- Return pork slices to roasting pan. Continue cooking in oven 10 minutes.
- Serve roast with steamed potatoes and string beans, if desired.

NUTRITION	
CALORIES PER SERVING: 239	
FAT: 15 g	CAL. FROM FAT: 58%
PROTEIN: 15 g	CHOLESTEROL: 60 mg
SODIUM: 466 mg	CARBOHYDRATES: 10 g

Old-fashioned Braised Pork Roast

8 SERVINGS	
2 tbsp	(30 mL) vegetable oil
1	5-lb (2 kg) shoulder pork roast
	salt and pepper
2	medium-size onions, quartered
1	garlic clove, crushed
1 ¼ cups	(300 mL) apple juice
3	medium-size potatoes, quartered
6	carrots, cut into sticks
1	small rutabaga, quartered
2	medium-size apples, peeled, quartered

- In a cooking pot, heat oil. Sear pork roast all over. Season with salt and pepper. Add onions, garlic and apple juice. Cover. Over low heat, cook 2 ½ -3 hours or until meat is tender. Transfer roast to a serving dish. Keep warm.
- To cooking juices, add remaining vegetables. Cover. Cook 15 minutes. Add apple quarters. Continue cooking 5 minutes or until vegetables are cooked.
- Serve roast with vegetable and apple medley.

VARIATION
- Replace apple juice with 1 bottle (341 mL) of beer.

NUTRITION	
CALORIES PER SERVING: 689	
FAT: 42 g	CAL. FROM FAT: 55%
PROTEIN: 47 g	CHOLESTEROL: 151 mg
SODIUM: 793 mg	CARBOHYDRATES: 40 g

Pork Chops with Tomatoes

4 SERVINGS	
4	pork chops, 3/4-inch (2 cm) thick
1 tbsp	(15 mL) prepared mustard
2 tbsp	(30 mL) butter
1/2 cup	(125 mL) onion, chopped
4	potatoes, peeled, sliced
19 oz	(540 mL) canned tomatoes, in their juice
2 tsp	(10 mL) salt
	pinch of pepper

- Brush pork chops with mustard.

- In a skillet, melt butter. Lightly cook onion. Add pork chops. Brown on each side.

- Fold in remaining ingredients. Cover. Over low heat, cook 1 hour. Serve.

NUTRITION	
CALORIES PER SERVING: 531	
FAT: 21 g	CAL. FROM FAT: 36%
PROTEIN: 30 g	CHOLESTEROL: 89 mg
SODIUM: 1433 mg	CARBOHYDRATES: 56 g

Baked Pork Chops

2 SERVINGS	
4	pork chops, 3/4-inch (2 cm) thick
1/3 cup	(80 mL) ketchup
1/4 cup	(60 mL) brown sugar
1/4 cup	(60 mL) onion, chopped
1/4 cup	(60 mL) celery, minced
	salt and pepper
3 tbsp	(45 mL) cold water

- Preheat oven to 325 °F (160 °C).

- On a non-stick baking sheet, place pork chops. Set aside.

- In a small bowl, mix remaining ingredients. Spread mixture over pork chops. Cover with aluminum foil. Bake in oven 75 minutes. Serve.

NUTRITION	
CALORIES PER SERVING: 618	
FAT: 30 g	CAL. FROM FAT: 43%
PROTEIN: 47 g	CHOLESTEROL: 147 mg
SODIUM: 793 mg	CARBOHYDRATES: 40 g

Barbecued Pork Chops

4 SERVINGS	
1 cup	(250 mL) cold water
3/4 cup	(180 mL) ketchup
2 tsp	(10 mL) vinegar
2 tbsp	(30 mL) Worcestershire sauce
3 tbsp	(45 mL) sugar
1 tbsp	(15 mL) butter
8	pork chops, 3/4-inch (2 cm) thick
	salt and pepper
3 tbsp	(45 mL) onion, chopped
2 tbsp	(30 mL) hot water

- In a bowl, mix first 5 ingredients to a sauce. Set aside.

- In a skillet, melt butter. Sear pork chops. Season with salt and pepper. Remove from skillet. Set aside.

- In pork cooking fat, sauté onion. Deglaze with hot water. Fold in sauce.

- Place pork chops in sauce. Bring to a boil. Cover. Over low heat, cook 50 minutes. Serve.

NUTRITION	
CALORIES PER SERVING: 581	
FAT: 32 g	CAL. FROM FAT: 51%
PROTEIN: 47 g	CHOLESTEROL: 155 mg
SODIUM: 800 mg	CARBOHYDRATES: 24 g

Pork Chops with Rice

4 SERVINGS	
2 tbsp	(30 mL) sunflower oil
8	pork chops, 1/2-inch (1.25 cm) thick
1	large onion, chopped
28 oz	(796 mL) canned tomatoes, in their juice
1 cup	(250 mL) quick-cooking rice
1/2 cup	(125 mL) water
	salt and pepper

- In a covered skillet, heat sunflower oil. Lightly brown pork chops. Remove from skillet. Set aside.

- In pork cooking fat, sauté onion. Place pork chops on top. Add tomatoes in their juice, rice and water. Cover. Over low heat, simmer 25-30 minutes or until meat is tender and rice is cooked. Season with salt and pepper. Serve.

NUTRITION	
CALORIES PER SERVING: 667	
FAT: 37 g	CAL. FROM FAT: 50%
PROTEIN: 50 g	CHOLESTEROL: 147 mg
SODIUM: 632 mg	CARBOHYDRATES: 32 g

*From top to bottom :
Barbecued Pork Chops,
Pork Chops with Rice,
Baked Pork Chops*

Braised Pork Chops

2 SERVINGS	
1 tsp	(5 mL) oil
2 tbsp	(30 mL) margarine
4	pork chops, 3/4-inch (2 cm) thick
3/4 cup	(180 mL) rice
1	small onion, chopped
1/2	green bell pepper, diced
1/4 tsp	(1 mL) sage
1/4 tsp	(1 mL) thyme
1	bay leaf
1 cup	(250 mL) canned tomatoes, drained
1 cup	(250 mL) chicken broth
	salt and pepper

- Preheat oven to 350 °F (175 °C).

- In a casserole dish, heat oil and melt margarine. Lightly brown pork chops. Remove from dish. Set aside.

- In pork cooking fat, lightly brown rice until it is coated in fat and changing color. Mix in remaining ingredients. Season to taste with salt and pepper.

- Place pork chops on rice mixture. Braise in oven 1 hour. Serve.

NUTRITION	
CALORIES PER SERVING: 941	
FAT: 46 g	CAL. FROM FAT: 44%
PROTEIN: 55 g	CHOLESTEROL: 153 mg
SODIUM: 678 mg	CARBOHYDRATES: 75 g

Pork Chops in Mushroom Sauce

6 SERVINGS	
1/4 cup	(60 mL) all-purpose flour
2 tsp	(10 mL) salt
1/4 tsp	(1 mL) pepper
1/2 tsp	(2 mL) paprika
6	pork chops, 3/4-inch (2 cm) thick
2 tbsp	(30 mL) oil or margarine
2	garlic cloves, crushed
10 oz	(284 mL) canned cream of mushroom soup
1 cup	(250 mL) water
3	potatoes, peeled, sliced
2	onions, sliced
	fresh parsley, chopped

- In a plate, mix flour, salt, pepper and paprika. Dredge pork chops with seasoned flour. Set aside.

- In a skillet, heat oil. Lightly brown pork chops 4 minutes each side. Add garlic, cream of mushroom and water. Over low heat, simmer 15 minutes.

- Cover pork chops with sliced potatoes and onion. Adjust seasoning. If needed, add enough water to cover meat and vegetables.

- Over low heat, continue cooking 30 minutes or until potatoes are done. Serve garnished with parsley.

NUTRITION	
CALORIES PER SERVING: 460	
FAT: 22 g	CAL. FROM FAT: 44%
PROTEIN: 28 g	CHOLESTEROL: 74 mg
SODIUM: 1208 mg	CARBOHYDRATES: 36 g

Tender Chops with Apple Stuffing

4 SERVINGS

4	pork chops, 1-inch (2.5 cm) thick

Apple Stuffing

2 cups	(500 mL) apples, peeled, chopped
1/4 cup	(60 mL) raisins
1	egg, beaten
2 tbsp	(30 mL) butter, melted
1/2 tsp	(2 mL) cinnamon
1/2 tsp	(2 mL) salt
1/8 tsp	(0.5 mL) pepper

Sweet Glaze

1/3 cup	(80 mL) currant jelly
2 tbsp	(30 mL) orange juice

- Slit chops lengthwise to form a cavity. Set aside.
- In a bowl, mix apple stuffing ingredients. Stuff pork chops with mixture. In a 12 x 8 x 2-inch (31 x 21 x 5 cm) microwave-safe dish, arrange chops star-like, with meaty parts pointing outwards. Set aside.
- In a bowl, mix glaze ingredients. Brush chops with half the glaze.
- Wrap dish in wax paper. Cook in microwave oven 35-40 minutes, on MEDIUM. After 15 minutes of cooking, half-rotate dish clockwise.
- Remove chops from oven. Let stand 5 minutes. Coat with remaining glaze. Serve.

NUTRITION	
CALORIES PER SERVING: 450	
FAT: 22 g	CAL. FROM FAT: 43 %
PROTEIN: 25 g	CHOLESTEROL: 134 mg
SODIUM: 409 mg	CARBOHYDRATES: 40 g

Pork Rack with Lentils

4 SERVINGS

1	4-rib pork loin
	salt and pepper
2 tbsp	(30 mL) shortening
1	onion, chopped
1	shallot, chopped
2	carrots, diced
1	turnip, diced
1 tbsp	(15 mL) all-purpose flour
14 oz	(398 mL) canned lentils, rinsed, drained
1	celery stalk, diced
1	garlic clove, chopped
1/4 cup	(60 mL) solid pork fat, diced
1	herb bouquet
	water

- Preheat oven to 350 °F (175 °C).
- Season pork loin with salt and pepper. Place in casserole dish. Roast in oven 75 minutes.
- Meanwhile, in a covered saucepan, melt shortening. Lightly brown onion, shallots, carrots and turnip. Sprinkle with flour, mixing well.
- Add lentils, celery, garlic, diced lard and herb bouquet. Season to taste with salt and pepper. Cover mixture with water. Simmer uncovered 20 minutes. Set aside.
- Approximately 15 minutes before the end of cooking, surround pork rack with lentil mixture. Serve.

NUTRITION	
CALORIES PER SERVING: 578	
FAT: 28 g	CAL. FROM FAT: 43 %
PROTEIN: 51 g	CHOLESTEROL: 108 mg
SODIUM: 224 mg	CARBOHYDRATES: 31 g

Barbecued Pork Scallops

8 SERVINGS	
3 tbsp	(45 mL) butter
8	5-oz (140 g) pork tenderloin servings
2	onions, chopped
2	green bell peppers, diced
1/2 cup	(125 mL) water
1/2 cup	(125 mL) ketchup
2 tbsp	(30 mL) vinegar
10 oz	(284 mL) canned cream of tomato soup
3 tbsp	(45 mL) brown sugar

- Preheat oven to 350 °F (175 °C).
- In a frying pan, melt butter. Sear pork scallops 2 minutes each side. Transfer to an ovenproof dish. Set aside.
- In pork cooking fat, sauté onions and bell peppers. Pour over scallops. Set aside.
- In a bowl, mix remaining ingredients to a sauce. Spoon over scallops. Cook in oven 1 hour.
- Serve pork scallops with mashed potatoes, a salad or a vegetable medley, if desired.

VARIATION
- Replace cream of tomato soup with canned whole tomatoes.
- Replace pork scallops with pork chops or steaks.

NUTRITION	
CALORIES PER SERVING: 280	
FAT: 12 g	CAL. FROM FAT: 38%
PROTEIN: 26 g	CHOLESTEROL: 70 mg
SODIUM: 527 mg	CARBOHYDRATES: 18 g

Zingy Pork Noisettes

2 SERVINGS	
4	2-oz (60 g) pork medallions
1/4 cup	(60 mL) flour
	pinch of salt
	pinch of pepper
2 tbsp	(30 mL) oil
2 tbsp	(30 mL) butter
2 tbsp	(30 mL) sugar
3 tbsp	(45 mL) lemon juice
3	shallots, chopped
1/4 cup	(60 mL) chicken broth

- Place pork medallions between 2 sheets of wax paper. With a rolling pin, flatten meat. Set aside.
- On a plate, mix flour, salt and pepper. Lightly dredge pork noisettes with seasoned flour.
- In a skillet, heat oil and melt butter. Lightly brown noisettes 2 minutes each side. Remove from skillet. Set aside.
- Degrease skillet. Mix in sugar and lemon juice. Over moderate heat, caramelize 2-3 minutes, stirring constantly. Fold in shallots and chicken broth.
- Place noisettes in sauce. Cook 2-3 minutes.
- Transfer pork noisettes to individual plates. Coat with lemon sauce. Serve.

NUTRITION	
CALORIES PER SERVING: 536	
FAT: 36 g	CAL. FROM FAT: 60%
PROTEIN: 20 g	CHOLESTEROL: 88 mg
SODIUM: 244 mg	CARBOHYDRATES: 34 g

Pork Tenderloins in Cream Sauce

4 SERVINGS	
1 ½ lbs	(675 g) pork tenderloins
	salt and pepper
2 tbsp	(30 mL) butter
1	onion, chopped
1 cup	(250 mL) mushrooms, minced
½ cup	(125 mL) white wine
2 tbsp	(30 mL) all-purpose flour
¾ cup	(180 mL) light cream

- Cut tenderloins into 4 servings. Season. Set aside.

- In a skillet, melt butter. Sear pork pieces 8 minutes or so each side.

- Add chopped onion and mushrooms. Sauté 2 minutes. Deglaze with white wine. Cover. Simmer 10 minutes.

- Meanwhile, in a small bowl, blend flour and cream. Set aside.

- Remove pork pieces from skillet. Carve each into 4-5 slices. Transfer to individual plates. Keep warm.

- Pour flour and cream mixture into skillet. While stirring, cook until sauce thickens. Pour over pork slices. Serve.

NUTRITION	
CALORIES PER SERVING: 395	
FAT: 20 g	CAL. FROM FAT: 49 %
PROTEIN: 38 g	CHOLESTEROL: 156 mg
SODIUM: 253 mg	CARBOHYDRATES: 9 g

Cognac Pork

4 SERVINGS	
1 tbsp	(15 mL) oil
1 tbsp	(15 mL) butter
2	pork tenderloins
1	onion, chopped
1	garlic clove, chopped
4 oz	(125 mL) cognac
2 tsp	(10 mL) butter, softened
2 tsp	(10 mL) all-purpose flour
2 cups	(500 mL) beef broth

- Preheat oven to 350 °F (175 °C).

- In a skillet, heat oil and 1 tbsp (15 mL) butter. Sear tenderloins. Remove cooking fat from skillet, except 1 tbsp (15 mL). Lightly brown onion and garlic. Mix in cognac. Simmer 3-5 minutes.

- Remove tenderloins from skillet. Transfer to a roasting pan. Cook in oven 30 minutes or until tenderloins are done.

- Meanwhile, in a small bowl, blend softened butter and flour to a paste. Set aside.

- In the same skillet, pour beef broth. Simmer until liquid reduces by one-third. Fold in butter and flour paste. Pass sauce through a sieve. Set aside.

- Carve each tenderloin in half. Arrange on individual plates. Coat with sauce. Serve with a vegetable medley, if desired.

NUTRITION	
CALORIES PER SERVING: 447	
FAT: 21 g	CAL. FROM FAT: 50 %
PROTEIN: 40 g	CHOLESTEROL: 141 mg
SODIUM: 193 mg	CARBOHYDRATES: 8 g

Mandarin Pork Stir-fry

6 SERVINGS	
1 tbsp	(15 mL) cornstarch
1/2 cup	(125 mL) chicken broth
2 tbsp	(30 mL) orange peel
2 tbsp	(30 mL) orange juice
2 tbsp	(30 mL) oil
1 cup	(250 mL) celery, sliced
1/2	green bell pepper, minced
1 tbsp	(15 mL) butter
1 cup	(250 mL) mushrooms
1 cup	(250 mL) snow peas
1/4 cup	(60 mL) shallots, chopped
1 lb	(450 g) pork, cut into strips
1	garlic clove, crushed
18 oz	(227 mL) canned mandarin oranges, drained

- In a small bowl, mix first 4 ingredients to a smooth sauce. Set aside.
- In a wok, heat 1 tbsp (15 mL) oil. Stir-fry celery 1 minute. Add bell pepper. Stir-fry 1 more minute.
- Add 1 tbsp (15 mL) butter. Once butter has melted, fold in mushrooms, snow peas and shallots. Stir-fry 1 minute. Remove vegetables from wok. Set aside.
- To vegetable cooking fat, add remaining oil. Stir-fry pork and garlic 6 minutes.
- Fold in vegetables, mandarin oranges and sauce. Reheat 1 minute. Serve on a bed of rice, if desired.

NUTRITION	
CALORIES PER SERVING: 254	
FAT: 17 g	CAL. FROM FAT: 58%
PROTEIN: 13 g	CHOLESTEROL: 46 mg
SODIUM: 131 mg	CARBOHYDRATES: 14 g

Pork Chop Suey

4-6 SERVINGS	
2 tbsp	(30 mL) butter
1/2 cup	(125 mL) onions, chopped
1 cup	(250 mL) leeks, chopped
1 cup	(250 mL) mushrooms, minced
1/4 cup	(60 mL) water chestnuts, sliced
2 cups	(500 mL) cooked pork, diced
2 cups	(500 mL) chicken broth
3 tbsp	(45 mL) soy sauce
8 oz	(225 g) bean sprouts
	salt and pepper

- In a skillet, melt butter. Sauté onions, leeks, mushrooms and water chestnuts. Add pork. Cook 5 minutes.
- Fold in remaining ingredients. Season to taste with salt and pepper. Bring to a boil. Over low heat, continue cooking 8 minutes. Serve.

NUTRITION	
CALORIES PER SERVING: 212	
FAT: 12 g	CAL. FROM FAT: 51%
PROTEIN: 16 g	CHOLESTEROL: 53 mg
SODIUM: 664 mg	CARBOHYDRATES: 11 g

Honey Mustard-glazed Spareribs

4 SERVINGS

3 lbs	(1.4 kg) spareribs
¼ cup	(60 mL) water
¼ cup	(60 mL) Dijon mustard
2 tbsp	(30 mL) dark brown sugar, packed
1 tbsp	(15 mL) honey
¼ tsp	(1 mL) dried rosemary, crumbled
	pinch of hot pepper flakes
	dash of Worcestershire sauce

- Carve ribs into individual servings. Place in a 12-cup (3 L) microwave-safe casserole dish. Add water.
- Cover. Cook in oven 5 minutes, on HIGH. Continue cooking 30-40 minutes, on MEDIUM-LOW.
- Meanwhile, in a bowl, mix remaining ingredients to a smooth sauce. Set aside.
- Once cooked, remove ribs from microwave oven. Transfer to a browning griddle. Brush with mustard sauce.
- On MEDIUM-HIGH, cook 10-15 minutes or until ribs turn golden brown and are nicely glazed. Serve with cole slaw, if desired.

NUTRITION	
CALORIES PER SERVING: 640	
FAT: 50 *g*	CAL. FROM FAT: 72 %
PROTEIN: 37 *g*	CHOLESTEROL: 165 *mg*
SODIUM: 351 *mg*	CARBOHYDRATES: 7 *g*

Recipe shown above

Pork Liver Fricassée

4 SERVINGS

2 tbsp	(30 mL) vegetable oil
1 lb	(450 g) pork liver, diced
1	onion, chopped
3	potatoes, peeled, diced
½ cup	(125 mL) water
1 cup	(250 mL) vegetable juice
	salt and pepper

- In a skillet, heat oil. Sear liver.
- Add onion. Cook lightly. Fold in remaining ingredients. Season to taste with salt and pepper. Bring to a boil.
- Cover. Over low heat, simmer 20 minutes or until potatoes are cooked. Serve.

NUTRITION	
CALORIES PER SERVING: 397	
FAT: 11 *g*	CAL. FROM FAT: 25 %
PROTEIN: 29 *mg*	CARBOHYDRATES: 342 *g*
SODIUM: 423 *mg*	CARBOHYDRATES: 45 *g*

Meatball Stew

6 SERVINGS

2 lbs	(900 g) ground pork
½ cup	(125 mL) bread crumbs
2	eggs, lightly beaten
½ cup	(125 mL) water
¼ tsp	(1 mL) mustard
1 tsp	(5 mL) dry mustard
1 tsp	(5 mL) salt
¼ tsp	(1 mL) pepper
¼ tsp	(1 mL) ground cloves
¼ tsp	(1 mL) cinnamon
2 tbsp	(30 mL) oil
½ cup	(125 mL) onions, chopped
2 cups	(500 mL) beef broth
3 tbsp	(45 mL) flour, browned
3 tbsp	(45 mL) cold water

- In a medium-size bowl, mix pork, bread crumbs, eggs, water and seasonings. Shape into meatballs. Set aside.

- In a skillet, heat oil. Sauté onions. Add meatballs. Brown lightly. Fold in broth. Cover. Over moderate heat, simmer 1 hour.

- In a small bowl, blend flour in cold water. Fold into stew, mixing well. Serve.

NUTRITION	
CALORIES PER SERVING: 604	
FAT: 40 g	CAL. FROM FAT: 61%
PROTEIN: 45 g	CHOLESTEROL: 208 mg
SODIUM: 579 mg	CARBOHYDRATES: 13 g

Deep Dish Vegetable Pork

6 SERVINGS

2 lbs	(900 g) ground pork, cooked
2	medium-size onions, sliced
2	carrots, sliced
2	potatoes, peeled, sliced
10 oz	(284 mL) canned tomato soup
10 oz	(284 mL) water
	salt and pepper

- Preheat oven to 325 °F (160 °C).

- In a deep rectangular pyrex dish, place cooked pork. Spread successive layers of half the onion, carrot and potato slices. Repeat.

- Pour soup and water on top. Season to taste with salt and pepper.

- Cook in oven around 90 minutes or until vegetables are tender. Serve.

NUTRITION	
CALORIES PER SERVING: 580	
FAT: 32 g	CAL. FROM FAT: 51%
PROTEIN: 42 g	CHOLESTEROL: 142 mg
SODIUM: 514 mg	CARBOHYDRATES: 29 g

Danish Pork Hash

8 SERVINGS

2 tbsp	(30 mL) butter
¾ cup	(180 mL) brown sugar
3 cup	(750 mL) cabbage, shredded
	salt and pepper
2 lbs	(900 g) ground pork
½ cup	(125 mL) red wine

- In a heavy-bottomed cooking pot, melt butter until golden. Mix in brown sugar. Cook until caramelized.

- Fold in cabbage. Season to taste with salt and pepper, mixing well. Place ground pork over cabbage. Pour in wine.

- Cover. Over very low heat, cook 2-3 hours, stirring often so mixture does not stick to bottom.

- Serve hot with potatoes and warm beets, or on a bed of rice, if desired.

VARIATION
- Replace brown sugar with maple syrup.

NUTRITION	
CALORIES PER SERVING: 457	
FAT: 26 g	CAL. FROM FAT: 54%
PROTEIN: 30 g	CHOLESTEROL: 114 mg
SODIUM: 145 mg	CARBOHYDRATES: 22 g

Pork Pasta Shells

6 SERVINGS

1 lb	(450 g) ground pork
1	small envelope onion soup mix
1 tsp	(5 ml) oregano
28 oz	(796 mL) canned whole tomatoes
2 cups	(500 mL) water
2 cups	(500 mL) jumbo pasta shells
1 cup	(250 mL) Mozzarella cheese, grated

- In a casserole dish, combine first 5 ingredients. Bring to a boil. Gently mix in pasta shells.

- Cover. Over low heat, simmer 20 minutes, stirring from time to time.

- Preheat oven to BROIL.

- Transfer pork mixture to an ovenproof serving dish. Sprinkle with cheese.

- Broil in oven until cheese turns a nice golden brown color. Serve.

NUTRITION	
CALORIES PER SERVING: 461	
FAT: 22 g	CAL. FROM FAT: 42%
PROTEIN: 30 g	CHOLESTEROL: 88 mg
SODIUM: 1003 mg	CARBOHYDRATES: 36 g

Clockwise from left :
Deep Dish Vegetable Pork,
Meatball Stew,
Danish Pork Hash

Easter Ham

8-10 SERVINGS

4 cups	(1 L) cold water
4 cups	(1 L) apple juice
2	carrots, coarsely chopped
4	onions, quartered
1	garlic clove, finely chopped
4	celery stalks, in chunks
1 tbsp	(15 mL) prepared mustard
¹⁄₂ cup	(125 mL) molasses or maple syrup
1	5-lb (2.2 kg) uncooked boneless ham
	orange marmalade
	pineapple slices
	maraschino cherries
	cloves
	fresh parsley, chopped

■ In a large casserole dish, combine first 8 ingredients. Bring to a boil. Cover. Over low heat, simmer 30 minutes.

■ Place ham in casserole dish. Cover. Simmer 50-60 minutes. Remove from heat. Let ham cool slightly in cooking juices.

■ Remove lukewarm ham from dish. Trim away rind and fat.

■ Preheat oven to 325 °F (160 °C).

■ Transfer ham to a roasting pan. Pour enough ham cooking juices to cover bottom of pan.

■ Brush ham with marmalade. Garnish with pineapple slices and cherries. Stick with cloves.

■ Roast in oven 30-45 minutes, basting occasionally.

■ Remove ham from oven. Transfer to a large serving dish. Sprinkle with chopped parsley. Serve hot.

VARIATIONS

• Replace pineapple with apricot halves, and cherries with seedless green grapes, as shown above.

• Replace apple juice with cranberry juice, and cherries with cranberries.

NUTRITION	
CALORIES PER SERVING: 829	
FAT: 26g	CAL. FROM FAT: 28%
PROTEIN: 42 g	CHOLESTEROL: 129 mg
SODIUM: 2856 mg	CARBOHYDRATES: 129 g

Ham Steaks

3 tbsp	(45 mL) white vinegar
3 tbsp	(45 mL) brown sugar
¼ tsp	(1 mL) ground clove
½ cup	(125 mL) water
2	cooked ham slices, ½-inch (1.25 cm) thick

- In a bowl, mix first 4 ingredients well.
- With a fork, prick ham slices all over. Place in a covered dish. Pour liquid mixture over ham.

- Cover. Marinate in refrigerator 1 hour.
- Preheat oven to BROIL.
- Remove ham from dish, reserving marinade.
- Transfer ham slices to a roasting pan with a rack. Broil in oven 4-5 minutes each side. Baste with marinade during cooking.
- Serve with sautéed potatoes and relish, if desired.

VARIATION
- Barbecue over charcoal for a delicious summer treat ! Use a burning hot, well-oiled grill.

NUTRITION	
CALORIES PER SERVING: 289	
FAT: 7 g	CAL. FROM FAT: 23 %
PROTEIN: 33 g	CHOLESTEROL: 77 mg
SODIUM: 2169 mg	CARBOHYDRATES: 22 g

Ham Turnovers

24 TURNOVERS

1	egg, beaten
1 tbsp	(15 mL) water
1 lb	(450 g) shortcrust pastry (p. 334)
3 cups	(750 mL) cooked ham, diced
2 tbsp	(30 mL) chili peppers, finely chopped
3 tbsp	(45 mL) onion, chopped
10 oz	(284 mL) canned cream of mushroom soup
	poppy or sesame seeds

- Preheat oven to 400 °F (205 °C).
- In a small bowl, mix egg and water. Set aside.
- With a rolling pin, flatten pastry. Cut into 5-inch (12.5 cm) rounds. Set aside.
- In a bowl, mix remaining ingredients, except poppy seeds. In the middle of each pastry round, place 3 tbsp (45 mL) ham mixture. Moisten edges. Fold into half-moons.
- With a fork, seal turnovers. Make small vents on top. Brush with beaten egg. Sprinkle with poppy seeds.
- Bake in oven 15-20 minutes or until turnovers are golden brown. Serve.

NUTRITION	
CALORIES PER SERVING: 132	
FAT: 8 g	CAL. FROM FAT: 57 %
PROTEIN: 5 g	CHOLESTEROL: 29 mg
SODIUM: 358 mg	CARBOHYDRATES: 9 g

Ham Meatloaf

8 SERVINGS

Meatloaf

2 ½ cups	(625 mL)	ground ham
1 cup	(250 mL)	ground veal
¼ cup	(60 mL)	lean ground pork
2 cups	(500 mL)	corn flakes
¼ cup	(60 mL)	honey
½ cup	(125 mL)	orange juice
½ tsp	(2 mL)	salt
½ tsp	(2 mL)	paprika
1 tsp	(5 mL)	prepared mustard
2		eggs, lightly beaten

Sauce

¼ cup	(60 mL)	honey
¼ cup	(60 mL)	prepared mustard

- Preheat oven to 350 °F (175 °C).
- In a large bowl, mix meatloaf ingredients. Pour into a 8 x 12-inch (20.5 x 30.5 cm) pyrex dish. Cook in oven 45 minutes.
- Meanwhile, in a small bowl, combine sauce ingredients. Set aside.
- Remove meatloaf from oven. Brush with sauce. Continue cooking in oven 15 minutes. Serve.

NUTRITION	
CALORIES PER SERVING: 364	
FAT: 20 *g*	CAL. FROM FAT: 48 %
PROTEIN: 21 *g*	CHOLESTEROL: 125 *mg*
SODIUM: 1231 *mg*	CARBOHYDRATES: 26 *g*

Sugar Ham Pie

4 SERVINGS

2		eggs, beaten
⅔ cup	(160 mL)	evaporated milk
1 tsp	(5 mL)	Worcestershire sauce
		pinch of pepper
¾ cup	(180 mL)	bread crumbs
3 cups	(750 mL)	ground ham, cooked
¾ tsp	(3 mL)	dry mustard
¾ tsp	(3 mL)	all-purpose flour
⅓ cup	(80 mL)	brown sugar
1 tbsp	(15 mL)	vinegar

- Preheat oven to 350 °F (175 °C). Butter a 9-inch (23 cm) pyrex pie pan. Set aside.
- In a bowl, blend first 5 ingredients. Fold in ham. Pour mixture into pie pan. Set aside.
- In a bowl, mix remaining ingredients until smooth.
- Pour over ham mixture. Bake in oven 1 hour. Serve with mashed potatoes and a tossed green salad, if desired.

NUTRITION	
CALORIES PER SERVING: 692	
FAT: 42 *g*	CAL. FROM FAT: 55 %
PROTEIN: 36 *g*	CHOLESTEROL: 223 *mg*
SODIUM: 2383 *mg*	CARBOHYDRATES: 41 *g*

Recipe shown above

Garnished Ham

4 SERVINGS

1	green bell pepper, sliced into rounds
1 tbsp	(15 mL) margarine or oil
1	medium-size onion, chopped
2 cups	(500 mL) cooked ham, diced
³/₄ cup	(180 mL) bread crumbs
¹/₂ cup	(125 mL) cheese, grated
10 oz	(284 mL) canned cream of mushroom soup
¹/₂ cup	(125 mL) milk
2	eggs, lightly beaten

- Preheat oven to 350 °F (175 °C).
- Reserve half the bell pepper for decoration.
- In a skillet, melt margarine. Sauté onion and remaining peppers. Fold in remaining ingredients, mixing well.
- Grease a square 8-inch (20.5 cm) baking dish.
- Pour ham mixture into dish. Bake in oven 1 hour or so.
- Remove from oven. Garnish with bell pepper rounds. Serve with broccoli, if desired.

NUTRITION	
CALORIES PER SERVING: 434	
FAT: 25 g	CAL. FROM FAT: 52 %
PROTEIN: 24 g	CHOLESTEROL: 151 mg
SODIUM: 1834 mg	CARBOHYDRATES: 28 g

Ham Noodles

4 SERVINGS

	water
1 tbsp	(15 mL) vegetable oil
1 tsp	(5 mL) salt
8 oz	(225 g) linguini
1 ¹/₂ cups	(375 mL) cooked ham, diced
2 tbsp	(30 mL) onion, chopped
2 tbsp	(30 mL) margarine
10 oz	(284 mL) canned cream of chicken soup
¹/₂ cup	(125 mL) green beans, cooked
¹/₂ cup	(125 mL) water
2 tbsp	(30 mL) bread crumbs

- In a microwave-safe casserole dish, combine water, oil and salt. Bring to a boil, on HIGH. Stir in linguini. Cook on MEDIUM until noodles are tender. Drain. Set aside.
- In a 6-cup (1.5 L) covered casserole dish, combine diced ham, onion and margarine. Cover. Cook 3 minutes, on HIGH.
- Fold in cream of chicken, green beans, linguini and ¹/₂ cup (125 mL) water.
- Cover. Cook 5 minutes, on HIGH. Stir once, halfway through cooking.
- Remove ham noodles from oven. Sprinkle with bread crumbs. Cover. Let stand 2-3 minutes. Serve.

NUTRITION	
CALORIES PER SERVING: 568	
FAT: 30 g	CAL. FROM FAT: 48 %
PROTEIN: 23 g	CHOLESTEROL: 62 mg
SODIUM: 1979 mg	CARBOHYDRATES: 50 g

Did you know that dieticians recommend consuming fish at least three times a week?

Fish has a lean and tender flesh. If battered and fried, however, fish may become very rich in fat and calories...Be careful!

This section offers you a variety of culinary discoveries such as Snail-stuffed Artichokes (p. 214) and Sole Florentine (p. 200). Never again will it be possible for us to associate "fish" with "punishment"!

FISH AND SEAFOOD

Salmon Medallions

4 SERVINGS

1 cup	(250 mL) mushrooms, minced
2	green onions, chopped
4	4-oz (115 g) fresh salmon filet medallions
½ cup	(125 mL) white wine
	salt and pepper
2	eggs, beaten
3 tbsp	(45 mL) butter
2 tsp	(10 mL) green peppercorns

- Preheat oven to 450 °F (230 °C).
- In an ovenproof dish, place mushrooms and green onions. Arrange salmon medallions on top. Sprinkle with wine. Season with salt and pepper. Cook in oven 10-15 minutes. Remove from oven. Keep salmon medallions warm.
- Fold a little salmon cooking juices into beaten eggs. Pour remaining juices into a small saucepan. Heat through. Fold in eggs, whisking until sauce thickens. Add butter. Spoon over salmon. Sprinkle with green peppercorns. Serve.

NUTRITION	
CALORIES PER SERVING: 272	
FAT: 15 g	CAL. FROM FAT: 53 %
PROTEIN: 26 g	CHOLESTEROL: 174 mg
SODIUM: 282 mg	CARBOHYDRATES: 3 g

Salmon Scallops with Sorrel Butter

4 SERVINGS

1	knob of butter
8	fresh or frozen large sorrel leaves, stalks removed, chopped
¼ cup	(60 mL) white vermouth
¼ cup	(60 mL) butter
1 lb	(450 g) salmon fillets, cut into scallops
	salt and pepper
	pinch of tarragon
2 tbsp	(30 mL) water
	sorrel leaves

- In a small saucepan, melt butter. Add sorrel leaves. Cover. Cook a few minutes or until sorrel leaves are limp.
- Sprinkle with vermouth. Cook uncovered until mixture turns to a purée. Over low heat, add butter. Stir until butter slowly melts. Keep warm.
- Season scallops with salt, pepper and tarragon.
- In a non-stick frying pan, pour water. Over high heat, cook scallops. Tip onto 4 warm plates. Coat with sorrel butter. Garnish with sorrel leaves. Serve.

VARIATION
- Steam salmon scallops.

NUTRITION	
CALORIES PER SERVING: 293	
FAT: 18 g	CAL. FROM FAT: 60 %
PROTEIN: 23 g	CHOLESTEROL: 97 mg
SODIUM: 323 mg	CARBOHYDRATES: 4 g

Baked Salmon

4 SERVINGS

4	4-oz (115 g) salmon steaks
2 tbsp	(30 mL) lemon juice
1/4 cup	(60 mL) green onions, chopped
	pepper, to taste
1	lemon, quartered or sliced
	parsley, chopped

- Preheat oven to 375 °F (190 °C).

- In an ovenproof dish, place salmon steaks. Sprinkle with lemon juice and green onions. Season with pepper.

- Bake in oven 30-45 minutes or until fish flakes easily when tested with a fork.

- Tip onto 4 plates. Garnish with sliced or quartered lemon. Sprinkle with parsley. Serve.

NUTRITION	
CALORIES PER SERVING: 182	
FAT: 5 g	CAL. FROM FAT: 22%
PROTEIN: 26 g	CHOLESTEROL: 59 mg
SODIUM: 146 mg	CARBOHYDRATES: 12 g

Recipe shown above

Salmon Pie

8-10 SERVINGS

4	shortcrust pastries (p. 334)
12 oz	(341 mL) canned salmon (reserve juice)
	milk
2 tbsp	(30 mL) butter
1/2 cup	(125 mL) celery, finely chopped
1	small onion, finely chopped
2 tbsp	(30 mL) flour
	salt and pepper
1 tbsp	(15 mL) parsley, chopped
	pinch of savory
1 tbsp	(15 mL) lemon juice
2	small potatoes, diced
1/2 cup	(125 mL) green peas
2	hard-boiled eggs, chopped

- Preheat oven to 350 °F (175 °C). Line 2 pie pans with crust.

- To salmon juice, add enough milk to make 2/3 cup (160 mL) liquid.

- In a saucepan, melt butter. Over moderate heat, sauté celery and onion 10 minutes or so. Fold in flour, salt and pepper. While stirring, add milk in a thin stream. Season with parsley, savory and lemon juice. Cook until sauce thickens.

- Fold in salmon, potatoes, green peas and eggs. Pour into pie crusts. Cover with remaining crusts. Pinch edges to seal. Make 4 vents in top crust. Bake in oven 20 minutes or until pies turn a nice golden brown color. Serve.

NUTRITION	
CALORIES PER SERVING: 297	
FAT: 14g	CAL. FROM FAT: 51%
PROTEIN: 13 g	CHOLESTEROL: 59 mg
SODIUM: 490 mg	CARBOHYDRATES: 31 g

Trout in Creamy Herb Sauce

3 SERVINGS	
Sauce	
1/2 cup	(125 mL) sour cream
2 tbsp	(30 mL) butter, melted
2 tsp	(10 mL) onion, chopped
1 tsp	(5 mL) dried dill
1/2 tsp	(2 mL) thyme
6	2-oz (60 g) trout fillets
	salt and pepper

- Preheat oven to 425 °F (220 °C).
- In a bowl, mix sauce ingredients. Set aside.
- In a buttered ovenproof dish, place fillets. Season lightly with salt and pepper. Coat with sauce. Cook uncovered in oven 15 minutes or until flesh turns opaque. Cover with aluminum foil for last 5 minutes of cooking. Serve.

NUTRITION	
CALORIES PER SERVING: 319	
FAT: 25 *g*	CAL. FROM FAT: 66 %
PROTEIN: 25 *g*	CHOLESTEROL: 103 *mg*
SODIUM: 276 *mg*	CARBOHYDRATES: 2 *g*

Trout Meunière

4 SERVINGS	
1/2 cup	(125 mL) butter
4	8-oz (225 g) trout, cleaned, patted dry
	salt
	flour
1 tbsp	(15 mL) vegetable oil
2 tbsp	(30 mL) butter
1/4 cup	(60 mL) parsley, coarsely chopped
2 tbsp	(30 mL) lemon juice

- In a saucepan, melt 1/2 cup (125 mL) butter. Skim fat. Pour clarified butter into a frying pan. Set aside.
- Season trout inside and out with salt. Dredge with flour. Shake off excess flour.
- Over moderate heat, in a large heavy-bottomed frying pan, heat oil and melt 2 tbsp (30 mL) butter. Cook trout 5-6 minutes each side.
- Transfer trout to a warm serving dish. Keep warm.
- In the same frying pan, heat clarified butter to a golden color.
- Sprinkle trout with parsley, lemon juice and melted butter. Serve at once.

NUTRITION	
CALORIES PER SERVING: 476	
FAT: 38 *g*	CAL. FROM FAT: 71 %
PROTEIN: 20 *g*	CHOLESTEROL: 126 *mg*
SODIUM: 384 *mg*	CARBOHYDRATES: 15 *g*

Mushroom-stuffed Trout

	4 SERVINGS	
2 tbsp	(30 mL) butter
2	onions, finely chopped
1	celery stalk, finely chopped
4 oz	(115 g) mushrooms, chopped
	salt and pepper
1 tbsp	(15 mL) bread crumbs
3 tbsp	(45 mL) heavy cream
1 tbsp	(15 mL) fresh fennel, chopped
1 tsp	(5 mL) chives, chopped
4	8-oz (225 g) trout, cleaned, patted dry
½ tsp	(2 mL) flour

- Preheat oven to 375 °F (190 °C).
- In a skillet, melt butter. Lightly sauté onions and celery. Over moderate heat, cook 3 minutes. Mix in mushrooms, salt, pepper and bread crumbs. Fold in cream, fennel and chives. Cook 3 minutes.
- Stuff trout with mixture. Close openings. Dredge stuffed trout with flour. Cook in oven 15 minutes. Serve.

NUTRITION	
CALORIES PER SERVING: 259	
FAT: 16 g	CAL. FROM FAT: 55%
PROTEIN: 20 g	CHOLESTEROL: 80 mg
SODIUM: 177 mg	CARBOHYDRATES: 10 g

Velvety-smooth Trout

	6 SERVINGS	
1 tbsp	(15 mL) vegetable oil
2 tbsp	(30 mL) butter
6	trout, 7-8 inches (18-20.5 cm) long, cleaned, patted dry
1 ½ cups	(375 mL) heavy cream
2	egg whites, in stiff peaks
1 tsp	(5 mL) onion salt
2 tsp	(10 mL) dried dill
	pepper
	paprika
½ cup	(125 mL) chives, chopped

- Preheat oven to 450 °F (230 °C).
- In a skillet, heat oil and melt butter. Lightly cook trout. Place in a buttered baking dish. Keep warm.
- Whip cream until peaks form. Gently fold in egg whites. Season with onion salt, dill and pepper. Pour over trout. Cook in oven 20 minutes.
- Sprinkle with paprika and chopped chives. Serve.

NUTRITION	
CALORIES PER SERVING: 392	
FAT: 34 g	CAL. FROM FAT: 77%
PROTEIN: 20 g	CHOLESTEROL: 141 mg
SODIUM: 391 mg	CARBOHYDRATES: 2 g

Sole with White Wine Sauce

4 SERVINGS

2	8-oz (225 g) sole fillets, halved
¹/₂ cup	(125 mL) celery leaves, coarsely chopped
1	onion, sliced
1	lemon, sliced
2 tbsp	(30 mL) parsley
¹/₄ tsp	(1 mL) pepper
	dots of butter
1 cup	(250 mL) white wine
4 tsp	(20 mL) kneaded butter
	parsley, lemon or shrimp

- Preheat oven to 350 °F (175 °C).
- Roll sole fillets. Secure with toothpicks. Place in an oven-proof stove-top dish. Top with celery leaves, onion and lemon slices. Season with parsley and pepper. Dot each serving with butter. Pour in wine. Cover. Cook in oven 10 minutes.
- Transfer fillets to a serving dish. Keep warm.
- Simmer cooking juices. Add kneaded butter, whisking until sauce thickens. Spoon over fish. Garnish with parsley, lemon or shrimp. Serve.

NUTRITION	
CALORIES PER SERVING: 229	
FAT: 10 g	CAL. FROM FAT: 46%
PROTEIN: 19 g	CHOLESTEROL: 26 mg
SODIUM: 181 mg	CARBOHYDRATES: 8 g

Shrimp-stuffed Sole

4 SERVINGS

Stuffing

1 cup	(250 mL) baby shrimp
1 tbsp	(15 mL) Italian bread crumbs
1 tbsp	(15 mL) milk
1 tbsp	(15 mL) butter
1 tbsp	(15 mL) chili sauce
1 tbsp	(15 mL) lemon juice
1 tbsp	(15 mL) shallot, chopped
¹/₄ cup	(60 mL) bread crumbs
2 tbsp	(30 mL) paprika
4	6-oz (165 g) sole fillets, cleaned, patted dry
2 tbsp	(30 mL) butter, melted

- In a small bowl, combine stuffing ingredients. Set aside.
- Mix bread crumbs and paprika. Set aside.
- Spread stuffing over fish fillets. Roll. Secure with a toothpick. Brush with melted butter. Dredge with bread crumb and paprika mixture.
- On a microwave-safe browning griddle, arrange rolls in a circle. On HIGH, cook in oven 7-9 minutes or until flesh turns opaque. Let stand 3 minutes. Coat with your choice of sauce. Serve.

NUTRITION	
CALORIES PER SERVING: 258	
FAT: 10 g	CAL. FROM FAT: 37%
PROTEIN: 32 g	CHOLESTEROL: 62 mg
SODIUM: 330 mg	CARBOHYDRATES: 8 g

Sole Florentine

4 SERVINGS

10 oz	(280 g) fresh spinach, stalks removed, washed, spin-dried
1 lb	(450 g) sole fillets
4 oz	(115 g) cream cheese, softened
	salt and pepper
1 tbsp	(15 mL) butter
1 tbsp	(15 mL) flour
¹/₂ cup	(125 mL) chicken broth
	paprika

- In a microwave-safe bowl, cook spinach 4 minutes, on HIGH. Drain if needed. In a shallow rectangular dish, pour spinach. Set aside.
- Spread each fillet with 1 tbsp (15 mL) cheese. Season with salt and pepper. Roll. Arrange fish over spinach. Cover with a punctured plastic wrap. Cook 6 minutes, on HIGH. Let stand 1 minute.
- In a pyrex measuring cup, melt butter. Add flour. Fold in broth. Cook 1-2 minutes, on HIGH. Blend in remaining cheese until smooth. Pour over fillets. Sprinkle with paprika. Serve with butter-flavored basmati rice, if desired.

NUTRITION	
CALORIES PER SERVING: 231	
FAT: 14 g	CAL. FROM FAT: 54%
PROTEIN: 21 g	CHOLESTEROL: 40 mg
SODIUM: 245 mg	CARBOHYDRATES: 6 g

Sole with Olives

4 SERVINGS

Sauce

8 oz	(225 g) Gruyère cheese, grated
¹/₄ cup	(60 mL) light cream or evaporated milk
12	pimento-stuffed olives, sliced
1 lb	(450 g) sole fillets
¹/₄ cup	(60 mL) vegetable oil
1 tbsp	(15 mL) vinegar or lemon juice
	salt and pepper
3 tbsp	(45 mL) bread crumbs

- In a bowl, mix sauce ingredients. Set aside.
- In a dish, marinate sole 1 hour in oil and vinegar. Drain. Pat dry.
- Preheat oven to 450 °F (230 °C).
- Transfer fillets to an oven-proof buttered dish. Season with salt and pepper. Coat with sauce. Sprinkle with bread crumbs. Cook in oven 10-12 minutes. Serve.

NUTRITION	
CALORIES PER SERVING: 490	
FAT: 35 g	CAL. FROM FAT: 65%
PROTEIN: 36 g	CHOLESTEROL: 67 mg
SODIUM: 452 mg	CARBOHYDRATES: 7 g

From top to bottom :
Sole with White Wine Sauce,
Shrimp-stuffed Sole,
Sole Florentine

Curried Tuna

6 SERVINGS	
6 oz	(165 g) canned tuna, drained (reserve juice)
1/2 cup	(125 mL) celery, chopped
1 cup	(250 mL) onion, chopped
1 cup	(250 mL) mushrooms, sliced
1 tsp	(5 mL) curry powder
10 oz	(284 mL) canned cream of chicken soup
1/3 cup	(80 mL) milk
	cooked rice, hot
1/3 cup	(80 mL) toasted slivered almonds
19 oz	(540 mL) canned peach slices, drained

- In a saucepan, bring tuna juice to a boil. Add celery, onion and mushrooms. Simmer until vegetables are tender.
- Fold in curry powder, cream of chicken and milk. Add tuna. Heat through.
- Serve on a bed of hot rice. Sprinkle with almonds. Surround with peach slices.

VARIATION
- Replace toasted almonds with grated coconut.

NUTRITION	
CALORIES PER SERVING: 282	
FAT: 7 g	CAL. FROM FAT: 23%
PROTEIN: 14 g	CHOLESTEROL: 14 mg
SODIUM: 488 mg	CARBOHYDRATES: 41 g

Tuna Kabobs

4 SERVINGS	

Dressing

1 cup	(250 mL) dry white wine
	juice and peel of 1/2 lemon
3 tbsp	(45 mL) olive oil
2 tbsp	(30 mL) tomato paste
1	garlic clove, crushed
1/2 tsp	(2 mL) sage
1 tsp	(5 mL) thyme
2 tsp	(10 mL) sugar
1/2 tsp	(2 mL) ground pepper
2	sweet red peppers, in chunks
16	1-oz (30 g) tuna cubes
	fresh fennel sprigs

- In a dish, mix marinade ingredients. Add tuna and bell peppers. Marinate 2 hours. Drain.
- Preheat oven to BROIL.
- Alternating with pepper chunks, thread tuna cubes onto skewers. Broil 3 minutes each side. Baste with marinade during cooking. Remove from oven. Garnish with fennel sprigs. Serve on a bed of rice, if desired.

VARIATION
- Barbecue over charcoals 12 minutes or so. Baste often with marinade, rotating kabobs from time to time.

NUTRITION	
CALORIES PER SERVING: 343	
FAT: 16 g	CAL. FROM FAT: 47%
PROTEIN: 28 g	CHOLESTEROL: 43 mg
SODIUM: 146 mg	CARBOHYDRATES: 13 g

Greek-style Haddock

	8-10 SERVINGS
3	green onions, chopped
1/4 cup	(60 mL) fresh parsley, chopped
3 tbsp	(45 mL) vegetable oil
2 tbsp	(30 mL) flour
1 tsp	(5 mL) paprika
1 tsp	(5 mL) salt
28 oz	(796 mL) canned tomatoes, in their juice
1/4 tsp	(1 mL) basil
1/2 tsp	(2 mL) salt
1/4 tsp	(1 mL) pepper
2 lbs	(900 g) fresh haddock fillets

- Preheat oven to 500 °F (260 °C).
- In a small bowl, mix green onions, parsley, oil, flour, paprika and salt. Set aside.
- In a buttered ovenproof dish, pour tomatoes. Season with basil, salt and pepper. Place fish on top. Sprinkle with green onion mixture. Cook in oven 15-18 minutes. Serve.

NUTRITION	
CALORIES PER SERVING: 155	
FAT: 5 g	CAL. FROM FAT: 29%
PROTEIN: 19 g	CHOLESTEROL: 52 mg
SODIUM: 552 mg	CARBOHYDRATES: 9 g

Recipe shown above

Haddock with Cheese

	4 SERVINGS
1/2 cup	(125 mL) Parmesan cheese, grated
1 tsp	(5 mL) salt
1/8 tsp	(0.5 mL) pepper
1 lb	(450 g) fresh or frozen haddock fillets
3/4 cup	(180 mL) flour
1/4 cup	(60 mL) shortening
	paprika

- On a sheet of wax paper, mix cheese, salt and pepper.
- Dredge haddock fillets with flour, then cheese.
- In a skillet, over moderate heat, melt shortening. Lightly brown fish 5-6 minutes on both sides. Sprinkle with paprika. Serve.

NUTRITION	
CALORIES PER SERVING: 355	
FAT: 18 g	CAL. FROM FAT: 45%
PROTEIN: 29 g	CHOLESTEROL: 75 mg
SODIUM: 845 mg	CARBOHYDRATES: 18 g

Sweet-and-sour Sole

8 SERVINGS

Sauce

1/2 cup	(125 mL) butter, melted
1 tbsp	(15 mL) lemon juice
1 tsp	(5 mL) Worcestershire sauce
1 tsp	(5 mL) prepared mustard
1 tsp	(5 mL) salt
	pinch of pepper
2 lbs	(900 g) fresh sole fillets
1/4 cup	(125 mL) bread crumbs

- Preheat oven to 350 °F (175 °C).
- In a small bowl, mix sauce ingredients. Set aside.
- Dredge fillets with bread crumbs. Place in a buttered ovenproof dish. Coat with sauce. Cook in oven 35 minutes or until fish flakes easily when tested with a fork. Serve.

NUTRITION	
CALORIES PER SERVING: 240	
FAT: 14 g	CAL. FROM FAT: 54%
PROTEIN: 24 g	CHOLESTEROL: 67 mg
SODIUM: 486 mg	CARBOHYDRATES: 3 g

Bass Meunière

6 SERVINGS

2	1-lb (450 g) bass, cleaned, patted dry
3 tbsp	(45 mL) flour
3 tbsp	(45 mL) vegetable oil
3 tbsp	(45 mL) butter
	salt and pepper
2 tbsp	(30 mL) butter
	juice of 1 lemon
1	lemon, sliced

- Lightly slash backs of fish. Dredge with flour.
- In a frying pan, heat oil and melt 3 tbsp (45 mL) butter. Over low heat, cook bass 5 minutes each side. Season with salt and pepper. Remove bass. Keep warm.
- In the same skillet, melt 2 tbsp (30 mL) butter. Add lemon juice.
- Transfer bass to a serving dish. Sprinkle with lemony butter. Garnish with lemon slices. Serve.

VARIATION
- For an economical alternative, substitute mullet.

NUTRITION	
CALORIES PER SERVING: 334	
FAT: 22 g	CAL. FROM FAT: 59%
PROTEIN: 29 g	CHOLESTEROL: 128 mg
SODIUM: 218 mg	CARBOHYDRATES: 5 g

Halibut with Tomatoes

4 SERVINGS

2 tbsp	(30 mL) olive oil
4	6-oz (165 g) halibut steaks
	salt and pepper
2 tbsp	(30 mL) onion, chopped
28 oz	(796 mL) canned spicy tomatoes, drained
1 tbsp	(15 mL) tomato paste
1 cup	(250 mL) fish broth or stock, heated
1	green bell pepper, minced
1	lemon, sliced

- Preheat oven to 350 °F (175 °C).
- In a skillet, heat 1 tbsp (15 mL) oil. Cook halibut steaks 3 minutes each side. Season. Remove from skillet. Transfer to an ovenproof dish. Continue cooking in oven 5-6 minutes.
- Meanwhile, in the same skillet, heat remaining oil. Cook onion 2 minutes. Add tomatoes, tomato paste, hot broth and bell peppers. Adjust seasoning. Cook 4 minutes.
- Spoon tomato sauce into a serving dish. Place halibut steaks on top. Garnish with lemon slices. Serve.

NUTRITION	
CALORIES PER SERVING: 327	
FAT: 13 g	CAL. FROM FAT: 35%
PROTEIN: 29 g	CHOLESTEROL: 128 mg
SODIUM: 218 mg	CARBOHYDRATES: 5 g

Sole with Leeks and Oranges

4 SERVINGS

3	leeks, cut into rounds
	salt and pepper
1 tbsp	(15 mL) olive oil
2	8-oz (225 g) sole fillets
1 cup	(250 mL) fresh-squeezed orange juice
	bay leaves, crumbled
1	tomato, sliced
1	orange, peeled, pith removed, sectioned
	parsley sprigs

- If using a conventional oven, preheat to 450 °F (230 °C).
- In a baking dish, spread leeks. Season with salt and pepper. Sprinkle with oil. Place fillets on top of leeks. Pour in orange juice. Sprinkle with bay leaves. Cover.
- Cook in oven 15 minutes or in microwave oven 4-5 minutes, on HIGH. Let stand 2 minutes. Serve fish coated with cooking juices. Surround with leek rounds and tomato slices. Garnish with orange sections and parsley.

NUTRITION	
CALORIES PER SERVING: 218	
FAT: 5 g	CAL. FROM FAT: 20%
PROTEIN: 22 g	CHOLESTEROL: 0 mg
SODIUM: 163 mg	CARBOHYDRATES: 24 g

Clockwise from upper left :
Halibut with Tomatoes,
Bass Meunière,
Sole with Leeks and Oranges

Flounder with Grapefruit

4 SERVINGS

2	1-lb (450 g) flounder fillets
1 tbsp	(15 mL) vinegar
1 tsp	(5 mL) parsley
1	bay leaf
2 tsp	(10 mL) butter
1	onion, chopped
1 cup	(250 mL) grapefruit juice
1 tbsp	(15 mL) capers
	salt and pepper
1	grapefruit, peeled, pith removed, sectioned

■ In a casserole dish, cover flounder with salted water. Add vinegar, parsley and bay leaf. Bring to a boil. Simmer 10-15 minutes. Remove flounder. Skin fish, detaching fillets. Transfer to a serving dish. Keep warm.

■ In a skillet, melt butter. Lightly cook onion. Add grapefruit juice and capers. Season. Bring to a boil. Simmer 1 minute. Spoon sauce over fish. Serve with grapefruit sections.

NUTRITION	
CALORIES PER SERVING: 231	
FAT: 3 g	CAL. FROM FAT: 13%
PROTEIN: 35 g	CHOLESTEROL: 5 mg
SODIUM: 191 mg	CARBOHYDRATES: 14 g

Removing Flounder Fillets

■ With a knife, loosen skin along one edge. Pull skin away from fillet, peeling completely. Use a knife, if needed.

■ Press knife against back bone. Slide blade along bone in order to fully release fillets.

■ Proceed in the same way to detach second side.

Roasted Monkfish

8 SERVINGS

1	2 ¹/₄-lb (1 kg) monkfish
2	garlic cloves, in pieces
6	bacon slices
	olive oil for basting
3 tbsp	(45 mL) olive oil
1 lb	(450 g) tomatoes, peeled, cut into wedges
10 oz	(280 g) mushrooms, minced
	savory and rosemary
	salt and pepper
¹/₄ cup	(60 mL) sour cream

- Preheat oven to 400 °F (205 °C).
- Stick flesh with garlic pieces. Wrap fish in bacon strips. Tie with a string. Brush with oil. Roast in oven 30 minutes or so. Turn over 3 times during cooking. Baste often with oil.
- In a skillet, heat 3 tbsp (45 mL) oil. Lightly brown tomatoes and mushrooms. Season to taste. Over low heat, cook vegetables. Fold in cream, mixing well. Spoon over monkfish. Serve.

VARIATION
- Barbecue monkfish over charcoal.

NUTRITION	
CALORIES PER SERVING: 223	
FAT: 13 g	CAL. FROM FAT: 52%
PROTEIN: 21 g	CHOLESTEROL: 39 mg
SODIUM: 120 mg	CARBOHYDRATES: 5 g

Perch in Creamy Fennel Sauce

8 SERVINGS

¹/₃ cup	(80 mL) bread crumbs
¹/₃ cup	(80 mL) rye flour
	salt and pepper
2 lbs	(900 g) perch fillets
¹/₄ cup	(60 mL) butter or margarine
Sauce	
¹/₃ cup	(80 mL) fennel, finely chopped
1 cup	(250 mL) heavy cream
1 tbsp	(15 mL) soy sauce

- Sprinkle a sheet of wax paper with bread crumbs, flour, salt and pepper. Dredge fish with mixture.
- In a frying pan, melt butter. Over moderate heat, lightly brown fish. Remove fillets from pan. Keep warm.
- In the same pan, add fennel and cream. Simmer until sauce thickens. Fold in soy sauce. Adjust seasoning.
- Pour sauce over a serving dish. Place fish on top. Serve with baked potatoes or rice, if desired.

NUTRITION	
CALORIES PER SERVING: 291	
FAT: 18 g	CAL. FROM FAT: 56%
PROTEIN: 24 g	CHOLESTEROL: 158 mg
SODIUM: 319 mg	CARBOHYDRATES: 8 g

Fish Surprise

6 SERVINGS	

Stuffing

2 cups	(500 mL) cooked fish, crumbled
1 tbsp	(15 mL) parsley, chopped
1/4 cup	(60 mL) soft part of bread
1	egg, beaten
2 tbsp	(30 mL) milk
1 tbsp	(15 mL) onion, finely chopped
2 tbsp	(30 mL) butter, melted
	salt and pepper
2 1/2 cups	(625 mL) long-grain rice, cooked
1 tbsp	(15 mL) parsley, chopped

- Preheat oven to 450 °F (230 °C).
- In a bowl, mix stuffing ingredients. Set aside.
- In a second bowl, combine rice and parsley. Set aside.
- In 6 greased ramekins or a muffin pan, divide half the rice mixture. Add stuffing. Top with remaining rice.
- Place ramekins in a large dish filled with water. Cook in oven 30 minutes. Unmold. Serve with a tomato sauce, if desired.

NUTRITION	
CALORIES PER SERVING: 215	
FAT: 6 g	CAL. FROM FAT: 26%
PROTEIN: 19 g	CHOLESTEROL: 59 mg
SODIUM: 286 mg	CARBOHYDRATES: 20 g

Tofu-stuffed Fish

8 SERVINGS	

Stuffing

2 tbsp	(30 mL) butter or margarine
2	garlic cloves, chopped
12	fresh mushrooms, chopped
1	onion, finely chopped
6 oz	(165 g) tofu, crumbled
1/4 cup	(60 mL) parsley, chopped
1/4 cup	(60 mL) bread crumbs
1/2 tsp	(2 mL) salt and pepper
8	white fish fillets
10 oz	(284 mL) canned cream of celery soup

- In a skillet, melt butter. Fry garlic, mushrooms and onion. Add tofu and parsley. Cook 2-3 minutes.
- Fold in bread crumbs, salt and pepper.
- Cover each fillet with around 2 tbsp (30 mL) stuffing. Roll fillets. Secure with toothpicks.
- Place fish in a skillet. Pour in cream of celery. Simmer 10 minutes or until fillets are cooked. If extra stuffing remains, fold into sauce during cooking. Serve.

NUTRITION	
CALORIES PER SERVING: 96	
FAT: 6 g	CAL. FROM FAT: 52%
PROTEIN: 3 g	CHOLESTEROL: 12 mg
SODIUM: 419 mg	CARBOHYDRATES: 9 g

Creole Fish

4-6 SERVINGS	
2 tsp	(10 mL) butter
¹/₂ cup	(125 mL) onion, chopped
¹/₂ cup	(125 mL) green bell pepper, chopped
¹/₂ cup	(125 mL) mushrooms, sliced
14 oz	(398 mL) canned crushed tomatoes, in their juice
1 tbsp	(15 mL) lemon juice
¹/₈ tsp	(0.5 mL) dry mustard
1	bay leaf
2	dashes of Tabasco sauce
	salt and pepper
1 lb	(450 g) fish fillets, cubed

▪ In a large skillet, melt butter. Sauté onion, bell pepper and mushrooms until vegetables are tender.

▪ Add tomatoes, lemon juice, mustard, bay leaf and Tabasco sauce. Season with salt and pepper. Bring to a boil. Simmer 30 minutes. Add fish. Cover. Cook 7-10 minutes. Serve in a deep serving dish.

NUTRITION	
CALORIES PER SERVING: 97	
FAT: 2 g	CAL. FROM FAT: 19 %
PROTEIN: 14 g	CHOLESTEROL: 36 mg
SODIUM: 211 mg	CARBOHYDRATES: 5 g

Recipe shown above

Fish au Gratin

4 SERVINGS	
2 tbsp	(30 mL) butter or margarine
2 tbsp	(30 mL) flour
¹/₂ tsp	(2 mL) salt
¹/₈ tsp	(0.5 mL) pepper
1 cup	(250 mL) milk
²/₃ cup	(160 mL) corn flakes, ground
2 cups	(500 mL) cooked fish, crumbled
1	hard-boiled egg, sliced
2 tsp	(10 mL) sweet red pepper, minced
1 tbsp	(15 mL) butter or margarine

▪ Preheat oven to 350 °F (175 °C).

▪ In a saucepan, melt butter. Fold in flour, salt and pepper. Gradually blend in milk, stirring until sauce thickens.

▪ In a 5-cup (1.25 L) ovenproof dish, spread half the corn flakes. Add fish, egg slices and bell pepper. Coat with sauce. Cover with remaining corn flakes. Dot with butter. Bake in oven 20-30 minutes. Serve.

NUTRITION	
CALORIES PER SERVING: 302	
FAT: 12 g	CAL. FROM FAT: 38 %
PROTEIN: 28 g	CHOLESTEROL: 104 mg
SODIUM: 863 mg	CARBOHYDRATES: 18 g

Fish Croquettes

4-6 SERVINGS

4 cups	(1 L) peanut oil
2 tbsp	(30 mL) butter
¼ cup	(60 mL) flour, sifted
	salt and pepper
1 cup	(250 mL) heavy cream
3 cups	(750 mL) fish (cod, trout, sole), crumbled
1	egg yolk, beaten
2	eggs, beaten
1 cup	(250 mL) bread crumbs

- In a deep-fryer, heat oil to 350 °F (175 °C).

- In a saucepan, melt butter. Add flour, salt and pepper, blending to a roux. Pour in cream. Over high heat, stir until sauce thickens. Remove from heat. Fold in fish and egg yolk, mixing well. Shape into 1-inch (2.5 cm) thick patties.

- Dip fish patties in beaten eggs. Dredge with bread crumbs. Fry 2 minutes, turning over a few times. Drain on a paper towel. Serve with your choice of sauce, salad or seasonal vegetables.

NUTRITION	
CALORIES PER SERVING: 438	
FAT: 27 g	CAL. FROM FAT: 56%
PROTEIN: 29 g	CHOLESTEROL: 188 mg
SODIUM: 549 mg	CARBOHYDRATES: 19 g

Recipe shown above

Healthy Fish Fillets

2 SERVINGS

2	4-oz (115 g) sole fillets
	milk
¼ cup	(60 mL) wheat germ
1 tbsp	(15 mL) cold first pressed oil

- Dip sole in milk. Dredge with wheat germ.

- Over high heat, in a non-stick frying pan, heat oil. Sear fillets. Serve.

NUTRITION	
CALORIES PER SERVING: 207	
FAT: 10 g	CAL. FROM FAT: 42%
PROTEIN: 21 g	CHOLESTEROL: 4 mg
SODIUM: 80 mg	CARBOHYDRATES: 9 g

Fish Burgers

2-4 SERVINGS

Stuffing

1/4 cup	(60 mL) onion, finely chopped
6 1/2 oz	(184 g) canned tuna flakes
1/4 cup	(60 mL) celery, finely chopped
1/2 cup	(125 mL) sweet pickles, finely chopped
1 tbsp	(15 mL) mayonnaise
2-4	hamburger buns
2-4	cheese slices

- Preheat oven to 450 °F (230 °C).
- In a bowl, mix stuffing ingredients. Divide mixture among hamburger buns. Top with cheese. Wrap individually in aluminum foil. Cook in oven or charcoal grill around 10 minutes. Serve.

NUTRITION	
CALORIES PER SERVING: 671	
FAT: 41 *g*	CAL. FROM FAT: 55 %
PROTEIN: 41 *g*	CHOLESTEROL: 122 *mg*
SODIUM: 1987 *mg*	CARBOHYDRATES: 122 *g*

Smoked Fish Omelette

4 SERVINGS

1 tbsp	(15 mL) butter
1 1/2 cups	(375 mL) smoked fish, in pieces
6	eggs
1 cup	(250 mL) milk
1 tsp	(5 mL) parsley, chopped
	salt and pepper
2 tbsp	(30 mL) butter

- In a frying pan, melt butter. Lightly cook fish.
- In a bowl, whip eggs. Fold in milk, fish and parsley. Season with salt and pepper, mixing well.
- In a frying pan, melt butter. Cook omelette to desired taste. Serve.

NUTRITION	
CALORIES PER SERVING: 312	
FAT: 21 *g*	CAL. FROM FAT: 61 %
PROTEIN: 26 *g*	CHOLESTEROL: 326 *mg*
SODIUM: 916 *mg*	CARBOHYDRATES: 4 *g*

Deep Sea Pot Pie

8 SERVINGS

1 1/2 cups	(375 mL) water
1 cup	(250 mL) onions, chopped
2 cups	(500 mL) potatoes, diced
1/2 cup	(125 mL) carrots, diced
1 cup	(250 mL) celery, diced
1/4 cup	(60 mL) green onions, chopped
8 oz	(225 g) scallops
8 oz	(225 g) lobster meat or crab meat
8 oz	(225 g) shrimp, shelled
1 tbsp	(15 mL) fish spices
	salt and pepper
1/2 cup	(125 mL) butter
5 oz	(142 mL) canned evaporated milk
4 tsp	(20 mL) cornstarch
1	shortcrust pastry (p. 334)

- Preheat oven to 350 °F (175 °C).

- In a casserole dish, pour water. Add vegetables. Boil 6-8 minutes. Add seafood. Simmer a few minutes. Add remaining ingredients, except pie crust. Continue cooking 5 minutes.

- Cover with pie crust. Bake in oven 30 minutes or until crust turns a nice golden brown color. Serve.

NUTRITION	
CALORIES PER SERVING: 358	
FAT: 19 g	CAL. FROM FAT: 48%
PROTEIN: 21 g	CHOLESTEROL: 125 mg
SODIUM: 377 mg	CARBOHYDRATES: 26 g

Seafood au Gratin

8 SERVINGS

3 tbsp	(45 mL) butter
2 tbsp	(30 mL) flour
2 cups	(500 mL) chicken broth, heated
2-3	shallots, chopped
10 oz	(284 mL) canned mushrooms, drained
1/2 cup	(125 mL) white wine
1 lb	(450 g) scallops
1 lb	(450 g) crab meat
1 lb	(450 g) cooked shrimp
1 cup	(250 mL) cheese, grated

- Preheat oven to 400 °F (205 °C).

- In a skillet, melt butter. Fold in flour. Gradually add chicken broth. Over high heat, whisk until sauce thickens.

- Mix in shallots, mushrooms and wine. Continue cooking 2 minutes. Fold in seafood. Transfer to a baking dish. Sprinkle with cheese. Bake in oven 10-12 minutes. Serve.

NUTRITION	
CALORIES PER SERVING: 312	
FAT: 12 g	CAL. FROM FAT: 36%
PROTEIN: 39 g	CHOLESTEROL: 209 mg
SODIUM: 703 mg	CARBOHYDRATES: 9 g

Crab Quiches

24 TARTS	
1 cup	(250 mL) canned crab meat, drained, in pieces
1 cup	(250 mL) Gruyère cheese, grated
4	shallots, minced
4	eggs, beaten
1 cup	(250 mL) light cream
1 tsp	(5 mL) paprika
	pinch of pepper
24	tart crusts (p. 334)

- Preheat oven to 375 °F (190 °C).
- In a bowl, mix crab, cheese and shallots. Set aside.
- In a second bowl, mix eggs, cream, paprika and pepper. Set aside.
- On a cookie sheet, place tarts. Spoon first mixture into crusts. Gently pour egg and cream mixture over crab. Bake in oven around 20 minutes. Serve.

NUTRITION	
CALORIES PER SERVING: 191	
FAT: 12 g	CAL. FROM FAT: 58%
PROTEIN: 6 g	CHOLESTEROL: 47 mg
SODIUM: 242 mg	CARBOHYDRATES: 15 g

Recipe shown above right

VARIATIONS
- Replace crab meat with canned drained oysters.
- Add 3 tbsp (45 mL) tomato paste at the same time as cream, as shown opposite.
- Add 1/4 cup (60 mL) finely-shredded spinach to egg and cream mixture, as shown bottom right.

Cheese-broiled Oysters

3 SERVINGS	
	coarse salt
24	fresh oysters, opened, drained
3 tbsp	(45 mL) butter
3 tbsp	(45 mL) flour
3 tbsp	(45 mL) Parmesan cheese, grated
	lemon juice

- Preheat oven to 400 °F (205 °C).
- Fill a roasting pan or cookie sheet with coarse salt. Wedge oysters in salt.
- In a small bowl, combine butter, flour and cheese. Spread mixture over oysters.
- Broil in oven 10 minutes. Sprinkle with a few drops of lemon juice. Serve.

NUTRITION	
CALORIES PER SERVING: 241	
FAT: 16 g	CAL. FROM FAT: 58%
PROTEIN: 12 g	CHOLESTEROL: 95 mg
SODIUM: 2351 mg	CARBOHYDRATES: 14 g

Snail-stuffed Artichokes

4 SERVINGS	
2 tbsp	(30 mL) butter
1	garlic clove, chopped
5 oz	(142 mL) canned snails
1/2 cup	(125 mL) celery, chopped
1/2 cup	(125 mL) shallots, chopped
10 oz	(284 mL) canned sliced mushrooms, drained
10 oz	(284 mL) canned artichoke hearts, drained
1 cup	(250 mL) cheese, grated

- Preheat oven to BROIL.
- In a skillet, melt butter. Lightly cook garlic, snails, celery, shallots and mushrooms for a few minutes.
- In an ovenproof dish, place artichokes. Top with snail mixture. Sprinkle with grated cheese. Broil in oven 6 minutes or so. Serve on a bed of buttered fresh pasta.

NUTRITION	
CALORIES PER SERVING: 260	
FAT: 16 g	CAL. FROM FAT: 52%
PROTEIN: 17 g	CHOLESTEROL: 45 mg
SODIUM: 616 mg	CARBOHYDRATES: 16 g

Mussels Ravigote

4 SERVINGS	
2 tbsp	(30 mL) butter
2 tbsp	(30 mL) red onion, chopped
1 1/2 cups	(375 mL) dry white wine
4 1/2 lbs	(2 kg) mussels, cleaned, soaked
1/2 cup	(125 mL) heavy cream
3 tbsp	(45 mL) capers, chopped
4	anchovy fillets, chopped
	sea salt
	fresh ground pepper

- In a casserole dish, melt butter. Lightly cook onion 3 minutes or so. Pour in wine. Bring to a boil. Add mussels. Cover. Reduce heat. Cook 2 minutes or so.
- Add cream, capers and anchovies. Season with salt and pepper, mixing well. Once mussels are cooked, remove with a slotted spoon. Transfer to 4 individual plates. Set aside.
- Bring cooking juices to a boil. While stirring, simmer until liquid thickens. Pour over mussels. Serve.

NUTRITION	
CALORIES PER SERVING: 663	
FAT: 29 g	CAL. FROM FAT: 43%
PROTEIN: 63 g	CHOLESTEROL: 203 mg
SODIUM: 1769 mg	CARBOHYDRATES: 21 g

Mussels in Beer Sauce

4 SERVINGS	
2 tbsp	(30 mL) butter
2 tbsp	(30 mL) French shallots, chopped
1 1/2 cups	(375 mL) brown beer
4 1/2 lbs	(2 kg) mussels, cleaned, soaked
3 tbsp	(45 mL) potato flour
1/2 cup	(125 mL) vegetable juice
	sea salt
	fresh ground pepper

- In a casserole dish, melt butter. Lightly cook shallots 3 minutes or so. Pour in beer. Bring to a boil. Add mussels. Cover. Reduce heat. Cook 5 minutes or so. Stir halfway through cooking.
- Once mussels are cooked, remove with a slotted spoon. Transfer to 4 individual plates. Set aside.
- Dilute potato flour in vegetable juice. Fold into cooking juices. Season to taste.
- Bring to a boil. While stirring, simmer until liquid thickens. Pour over mussels. Serve.

NUTRITION	
CALORIES PER SERVING: 564	
FAT: 17 g	CAL. FROM FAT: 29%
PROTEIN: 62 g	CHOLESTEROL: 158 mg
SODIUM: 1666 mg	CARBOHYDRATES: 31 g

Clockwise from upper left :
Mussels Ravigote, Cheese-broiled Oysters,
Snail-stuffed Artichokes

Ceviche

4 SERVINGS

1 lb	(450 g) seafood (shrimp, scallops, crab meat), cut into bite-size pieces
2 tbsp	(30 mL) vinegar
1/4 cup	(60 mL) fresh lime juice
1/4 cup	(60 mL) fresh lemon juice
8 oz	(225 g) ripe tomatoes, seeded, peeled, diced
4 oz	(115 g) pickled pearl onions, chopped
2 tbsp	(30 mL) light oil
1 tsp	(5 mL) fresh oregano or
1/2 tsp	(2 mL) dried oregano

- Wash seafood in cold water mixed with vinegar. Pat dry. Place in a glass or porcelain bowl. Sprinkle with lime and lemon juices. Marinate in refrigerator overnight, stirring occasionally. Add tomatoes, onions, oil and oregano.

- Transfer seafood mixture to serving bowls or scallop shells. Garnish with parsley. Serve.

VARIATION
- Serve ceviche with sliced fruit such as oranges.

NUTRITION	
CALORIES PER SERVING: 212	
FAT: 9 *g*	CAL. FROM FAT: 38%
PROTEIN: 24 *g*	CHOLESTEROL: 173 *mg*
SODIUM: 241 *mg*	CARBOHYDRATES: 9 *g*

Smoked Sturgeon with Mussels and Apples

4 SERVINGS

1	apple, quartered, minced
2 cups	(500 mL) water juice of 1/2 lemon
8 oz	(225 g) smoked sturgeon, minced
1 cup	(250 mL) smoked mussels, drained fresh ground pepper
2 tbsp	(30 mL) olive oil
2 tbsp	(30 mL) chives, chopped

- In a bowl, place apple slices. Pour in water. Sprinkle with lemon juice. Soak 1 minute. Drain.

- On a plate, arrange sturgeon slices, alternating with apple slices and smoked mussels. Season to taste with pepper. Sprinkle with oil and chives. Serve with a salad.

NUTRITION	
CALORIES PER SERVING: 223	
FAT: 11 *g*	CAL. FROM FAT: 44%
PROTEIN: 22 *g*	CHOLESTEROL: 91 *mg*
SODIUM: 348 *mg*	CARBOHYDRATES: 9 *g*

Shrimp Pasta

4-6 SERVINGS

1 lb	(450 g) spaghetti
3 tbsp	(45 mL) butter or margarine
1-2	carrots, cut into small sticks
	whites of 2 leeks, coarsely chopped
½ cup	(125 mL) green bell pepper, chopped
1 cup	(250 mL) mushrooms, minced
1	tomato, peeled, chopped
	pinch of nutmeg
	salt and pepper
1 lb	(450 g) medium-size shrimp, shelled
⅔ cup	(160 mL) whipped cream
	parsley, chopped

- Cook pasta following package instructions.
- Meanwhile, in a skillet, melt butter. Without browning, cook all vegetables, except tomato, until tender. Season. Mix in shrimp and tomato. Cook until shrimp become opaque and start to curl up. Fold in whipped cream. Over low heat, while stirring gently, heat through.
- Drain pasta. Transfer to a warm serving dish. Coat with sauce. Toss a little. Sprinkle with parsley. Serve.

VARIATIONS
- Replace spaghetti with linguini or egg noodles.

NUTRITION	
CALORIES PER SERVING: 484	
FAT: 13 g	CAL. FROM FAT: 25 %
PROTEIN: 26 g	CHOLESTEROL: 148 mg
SODIUM: 224 mg	CARBOHYDRATES: 64 g

Seafood Fettucine Verdi

6 SERVINGS

1 lb	(450 g) spinach fettucine
6 tbsp	(90 mL) olive oil
1	onion, minced
4	small carrots, minced
1	celery stalk, diced
	salt and pepper
	pinch of oregano
1 lb	(450 g) seafood, cut into bite-size pieces
¾ cup	(180 mL) dry white wine

- Cook pasta following package instructions.
- In a skillet, heat oil. Cook onion until tender but not browned. Add carrots and celery. Season with salt, pepper and oregano. Cook 4-5 minutes. Add seafood and wine. Over low heat, simmer until seafood is cooked. Pour over drained pasta. Serve.

VARIATIONS
- Add tomatoes at the same time as carrots.
- Replace onion with garlic, and oregano with basil.
- Replace seafood with fresh fish.

NUTRITION	
CALORIES PER SERVING: 524	
FAT: 18 g	CAL. FROM FAT: 31 %
PROTEIN: 25 g	CHOLESTEROL: 97 mg
SODIUM: 228 mg	CARBOHYDRATES: 62 g

Every now and then an occasion arises when you want to show off your culinary talents to the fullest. It may be special friends or the boss coming to dinner, an important birthday or anniversary.

Here is a collection of recipes for that celebration; dishes that speak volumes about how much you care. These are savory party dishes, to be sure, but they can serve just as well as the centerpieces of family dinners.

In this chapter you will find such delights as Bourguignon Fondue (p. 222) or Stuffed Goose Breast (p. 224).

This section will surely enable you to cope with any demand on your time or talents.

Braised Pork Roast

6-8 SERVINGS	
1	4-lb (1.8 kg) pork roast
1	bay leaf
1	clove
1 cup	(250 mL) chicken broth, heated
1 cup	(250 mL) beef broth, heated
1 cup	(250 mL) onion soup, heated

- Preheat oven to 350 °F (175 °C).

- In an ovenproof cooking pot, place pork. Add bay leaf, clove, both broths and onion soup. Cover. Braise in oven 2 hours or so.

- Approximately 30 minutes before the end of cooking, remove lid. Cook until brown. Serve with sautéed potatoes and a green salad, if desired.

NUTRITION	
CALORIES PER SERVING: 725	
FAT: 61 g	CAL. FROM FAT: 75 %
PROTEIN: 40 g	CHOLESTEROL: 124 mg
SODIUM: 231 mg	CARBOHYDRATES: 4 g

Lamb Tournedos with Mustard Sauce

4 SERVINGS	
1 tbsp	(15 mL) peanut oil
4	6-oz (165 g) lamb tournedos
	salt and pepper
2 tsp	(10 mL) French shallots, chopped
3 tbsp	(45 mL) hot mustard
1 cup	(250 mL) beef broth
1/2 tsp	(2 mL) tarragon, chopped
3 tbsp	(45 mL) sour cream

- Preheat oven to 225 °F (105 °C).

- In a frying pan, heat oil. Cook tournedos to desired taste. Turn over once only. Season with salt and pepper. Transfer tournedos to a baking sheet. Keep warm in oven.

- In hot frying pan, cook shallots 1 minute. Fold in mustard. Add beef broth and tarragon. Let liquid reduce by half.

- Add sour cream. Reduce heat. Return tournedos to pan. Turn over in sauce so meat is well-coated. Reheat without boiling. Serve.

NUTRITION	
CALORIES PER SERVING: 317	
FAT: 17 g	CAL. FROM FAT: 48 %
PROTEIN: 37 g	CHOLESTEROL: 119 mg
SODIUM: 312 mg	CARBOHYDRATES: 3 g

Cheesy Buffalo Steaks

4 SERVINGS	
1 tbsp	(15 mL) peanut oil
4	6-oz (165 g) buffalo steaks
1/4 tsp	(1 mL) fresh ground pepper
1/4 tsp	(1 mL) onion salt
3 oz	(90 g) Cheddar cheese, sliced
3 oz	(90 g) Mozzarella cheese, sliced

- Preheat oven to BROIL.
- In a frying pan, heat oil. Cook steaks slightly less than desired taste. Turn over only once during cooking. Season.
- Transfer steaks to a roasting pan. Cover with sliced cheese, alternating both kinds. Place in oven 4 inches (10 cm) from element. Broil around 2 minutes or until cheeses have melted. Serve.

NUTRITION	
CALORIES PER SERVING: 490	
FAT: 26 g	CAL. FROM FAT: 49%
PROTEIN: 60 g	CHOLESTEROL: 181 mg
SODIUM: 439 mg	CARBOHYDRATES: 1 g

Recipe shown above

Buffalo Meatballs with Sauce

8 SERVINGS	
2 cups	(500 mL) potatoes, grated
1 1/2 lbs	(675 g) ground buffalo meat
2/3 cup	(160 mL) onion, chopped
1 tsp	(5 mL) salt
1/4 tsp	(1 mL) pepper
1/4 tsp	(1 mL) garlic powder
1/4 cup	(60 mL) milk
1	egg, beaten
1/4 cup	(60 mL) butter
1/2 cup	(125 mL) water
3 tbsp	(45 mL) flour
2 1/2 cups	(625 mL) water
2 cups	(500 mL) sour cream
1 tsp	(5 mL) dill seeds
10 oz	(280 g) frozen green peas

- In a large bowl, mix first 8 ingredients. Shape into 1 1/2-inch (3.75 cm) meatballs.
- In a cast iron skillet, melt 1 tbsp (15 mL) butter. Brown meatballs. Pour in 1/2 cup (125 mL) water. Cover. Simmer 20 minutes. Remove meatballs. Keep warm.
- In the same skillet, melt remaining butter. Mix in flour. Add 2 1/2 cups (625 mL) water. While stirring, simmer until sauce thickens. Remove from heat. Add sour cream, dill and green peas. Heat through. Place meatballs in sauce. Mix well. Simmer 3 minutes. Serve.

NUTRITION	
CALORIES PER SERVING: 419	
FAT: 24 g	CAL. FROM FAT: 51%
PROTEIN: 31 g	CHOLESTEROL: 134 mg
SODIUM: 471 mg	CARBOHYDRATES: 19 g

Bourguignon Fondue

4 SERVINGS	
4 cups	(1 L) peanut oil
1	potato, sliced
2	garlic cloves
1 lb	(450 g) cubed beef

- In a fondue dish, pour oil. Add potato slices and garlic. Heat oil to 350 °F (175 °C).

- Arrange beef on a serving dish. Serve fondue with the following sauces :

NUTRITION	
CALORIES PER SERVING: 506	
FAT: 48 g	CAL. FROM FAT: 85 %
PROTEIN: 18 g	CHOLESTEROL: 68 mg
SODIUM: 57 mg	CARBOHYDRATES: 0 g

Cocktail Sauce

AROUND 1/2 CUP (125 mL)	
1/2 cup	(125 mL) chili sauce
1 tbsp	(15 mL) horseradish in vinegar
	dash of Worcestershire sauce

- In a small bowl, mix all ingredients.

Garlic Sauce

AROUND 1/2 CUP (125 mL)	
1/2 cup	(125 mL) mayonnaise
2	garlic cloves, chopped
	dash of Worcestershire sauce
	salt and pepper

- In a small bowl, mix all ingredients.

Parsley Sauce

AROUND 1/2 CUP (125 mL)	
1/2 cup	(125 mL) parsley, chopped
2 tsp	(10 mL) mayonnaise
	dash of Worcestershire sauce
	salt and pepper

- In a small bowl, mix all ingredients.

Tartar Sauce

AROUND 1/2 CUP (125 mL)	
1/2 cup	(125 mL) mayonnaise
2 tbsp	(30 mL) sour pickles, chopped
2 tsp	(10 mL) capers, chopped
1/4 tsp	(1 mL) garlic, chopped
	dash of Worcestershire sauce
1	anchovy fillet, chopped
	salt and pepper

- In a small bowl, mix all ingredients.

Curry Sauce

AROUND 1/2 CUP (125 mL)	
1/2 cup	(125 mL) mayonnaise
1 tbsp	(15 mL) chili sauce
1 tsp	(5 mL) curry powder
	dash of Worcestershire sauce
	salt and pepper

- In a small bowl, mix all ingredients.

Whiskey Sauce

AROUND 1/2 CUP (125 mL)	
1/2 cup	(125 mL) mayonnaise
1 tbsp	(15 mL) chili sauce
1/2 oz	(15 mL) whiskey
	dash of Worcestershire sauce
	salt and pepper

- In a small bowl, mix all ingredients.

Piquant Sauce

AROUND 1/2 CUP (125 mL)	
1/2 cup	(125 mL) pickled hot peppers, chopped
1 tbsp	(15 mL) chili sauce
1 tbsp	(15 mL) mayonnaise
	dash of Worcestershire sauce

- In a small bowl, mix all ingredients.

Onion Hash

AROUND 1/2 CUP (125 mL)	
1/4 cup	(60 mL) yellow onion, chopped
1/4 cup	(60 mL) red onion, chopped
2 tsp	(10 mL) virgin olive oil
2 tsp	(10 mL) parsley, chopped
	salt and pepper

- In a small bowl, mix all ingredients.

CALORIES PER SERVING OF SAUCES	
1 SERVING = 1 TABLESPOON	
COCKTAIL SAUCE : 17	GARLIC SAUCE : 99
PARSLEY SAUCE : 19	TARTAR SAUCE : 100
CURRY SAUCE : 100	WHISKEY SAUCE : 103
PIQUANT SAUCE : 16	ONION HASH : 13

Super Steak Tartar

2 SERVINGS	
10 oz	(284 g) very lean, freshly ground beef
2	egg yolks
1 tbsp	(15 mL) onion, chopped
2 tsp	(10 ml) cappers, chopped
2	anchovies, chopped
2 tsp	(10 mL) sour pickles, chopped
1/4 tsp	(1 ml) salt
1/4 tsp	(1 ml) black pepper
4 to 8	drops of Tabasco sauce
1 tsp	(5 mL) Worcestershire sauce

- Combine all the ingredients and shape in individual portions.

- Serve with french fries and mix vegetables. For a refined presentation, reserved the egg yolks and serve them in cracked shells on top of each portions.

NUTRITION	
CALORIES PER SERVING: 267	
FAT: 12 g	CAL. FROM FAT: 44 %
PROTEIN: 35 g	CHOLESTEROL: 298 mg
SODIUM: 633 mg	CARBOHYDRATES: 1 g

Stuffed Goose Breast

4 SERVINGS

1	1 ¼-lb (565 g) goose breast

Stuffing

3 oz	(90 g) liver pâté
¼ cup	(60 mL) mushrooms, minced
2 tbsp	(30 mL) vegetable oil
	salt and pepper
1	onion, sliced
1	garlic clove, chopped
1 cup	(250 mL) chicken broth, heated

- Preheat oven to 400 °F (205 °C).
- Make an incision lengthwise across goose breast, in order to form a cavity for stuffing.
- In a bowl, combine stuffing ingredients. Spoon into breast cavity. Close tightly with a string.
- In an ovenproof skillet, heat oil. Sear breast on both sides. Season with salt and pepper. Add onion slices and garlic. Roast in oven 30 minutes.
- Halfway through cooking, remove goose breast from oven. Degrease. Add chicken broth. Return to oven. Continue cooking. Carve into slices. Coat with cooking juices. Serve.

NUTRITION	
CALORIES PER SERVING: 292	
FAT: 15 *g*	CAL. FROM FAT: 48 %
PROTEIN: 31 *g*	CHOLESTEROL: 123 *mg*
SODIUM: 280 *mg*	CARBOHYDRATES: 7 *g*

Roasted Guinea-Fowl with Cherries

4 SERVINGS

1	4 ½-lb (2 kg) Guinea-fowl
3 tbsp	(45 mL) butter
	salt and pepper
19 oz	(540 mL) canned Bing cherries
¼ cup	(60 mL) honey
¼ cup	(60 mL) chicken broth
¼ tsp	(1 mL) thyme, chopped
2 tsp	(10 mL) parsley, chopped

- Preheat oven to 350 °F (175 °C).
- Truss fowl. Brush with butter. Season.
- Place in a roasting pan. Cook in oven 2 hours or so.
- Meanwhile, drain cherries, reserving their juice. Set aside cherries. Mix cherry juice with remaining ingredients. Pour over Guinea-fowl. Baste with cooking juices every 15 minutes. Around 15 minutes before the end of cooking, add cherries.
- Once fowl is cooked, remove from roasting pan. Degrease cooking juices. Bring to a boil. Simmer 5 minutes. Carve Guinea-fowl. Coat each serving with cooking juices. Serve.

NUTRITION	
CALORIES PER SERVING: 863	
FAT: 36 *g*	CAL. FROM FAT: 38 %
PROTEIN: 92 *g*	CHOLESTEROL: 302 *mg*
SODIUM: 367 *mg*	CARBOHYDRATES: 41 *g*

Pheasant in Wine Sauce

4 SERVINGS

1	4-lb (1.8 kg) pheasant, cut into 10 pieces
¹/₂ cup	(125 mL) wheat flour
¹/₄ cup	(60 mL) oil or butter
	salt and pepper
2 oz	(60 mL) calvados
2 cups	(500 mL) red wine
1 cup	(250 mL) chicken broth
¹/₄ tsp	(1 mL) thyme, chopped
2 tsp	(10 mL) parsley, chopped
2	bay leaves
¹/₂ cup	(125 mL) bacon, diced
¹/₄ cup	(60 mL) pearl onions
¹/₄ cup	(60 mL) mushrooms, halved

- Dredge each pheasant piece with flour twice.

- In a casserole dish, heat oil or melt butter. Sear pheasant pieces all over. Season with salt and pepper.

- Deglaze with calvados. Warm up a little. Flambé 30 seconds or so. Add wine, chicken broth and seasonings. Bring to a boil. Reduce heat. Simmer 50 minutes or so.

- Meanwhile, in a skillet, heat bacon. Add onions and mushrooms. Brown lightly. Degrease. Add to simmering pheasant. Serve with fresh pasta, if desired.

NUTRITION	
CALORIES PER SERVING: 934	
FAT: 58 g	CAL. FROM FAT: 67%
PROTEIN: 51 g	CHOLESTEROL: 264 mg
SODIUM: 602 mg	CARBOHYDRATES: 16 g

Cornish Game Hens with Cabbage

6 SERVINGS

3	cornish game hens, cut into halves
¹/₂ cup	(125 mL) flour
1 cup	(250 mL) bacon, diced
1	head of green cabbage, coarsely chopped
4-6	large onions, minced
¹/₂ tsp	(2 mL) thyme
	salt and pepper
¹/₂ cup	(125 mL) white wine or cider

- Dredge each cornish game hens piece with flour.

- In a heavy-bottomed cooking pot, heat bacon. Over low heat, brown hens pieces 25 minutes. Remove from pot. Set aside.

- In hot cooking pot, pour cabbage and onions. Cover. Cook 15 minutes, stirring often.

- Return hens to cooking pot. Season with thyme, salt and pepper. Add wine or cider. Cover. Simmer around 1 hour or until tender. Serve.

NUTRITION	
CALORIES PER SERVING: 724	
FAT: 43 g	CAL. FROM FAT: 55%
PROTEIN: 61 g	CHOLESTEROL: 122 mg
SODIUM: 776 mg	CARBOHYDRATES: 18 g

Rabbit Stew

4 SERVINGS

Marinade

1 ¹/₂ cups	(375 mL)	red wine
¹/₂ cup	(125 mL)	red wine vinegar
3		bay leaves
3		cloves
		pinch of salt
2		peppercorns
1 tbsp	(15 mL)	allspice
1		4-lb (1.8 kg) rabbit, cut into pieces
		flour
¹/₂ cup	(125 mL)	olive oil
2 lbs	(900 g)	pearl onions
2 lbs	(900 g)	tomatoes, peeled, crushed
2 tbsp	(30 mL)	sugar

- In a dish, combine marinade ingredients. Add rabbit pieces. Cover. Refrigerate 12-24 hours.

- Remove rabbit from marinade. Pat dry. Dredge with flour. Pass marinade through a sieve. Set aside.

- In a casserole dish, heat oil. Brown rabbit pieces all over. Remove from casserole dish. Set aside. Brown onion in rabbit cooking fat. Add tomatoes, sugar, marinade and rabbit pieces. Simmer around 1 hour or until meat is tender.

- Serve with potatoes sprinkled with chopped parsley, if desired.

VARIATION
- Replace pearl onions with 2 medium-size onions, sliced.

NUTRITION	
CALORIES PER SERVING: 983	
FAT: 54 *g*	CAL. FROM FAT: 47%
PROTEIN: 96 *g*	CHOLESTEROL: 259 *mg*
SODIUM: 854 *mg*	CARBOHYDRATES: 44 *g*

Sweet-and-sour Roast Venison

6-8 SERVINGS

		salt and pepper
1		boar rack
2 tbsp	(30 mL)	shortening
¹/₂ cup	(125 mL)	water
8 oz	(227 mL)	canned tomato sauce
2		onions, sliced
1		garlic clove, minced

Sauce

2 tbsp	(30 mL)	brown sugar
¹/₂ tsp	(2 mL)	dry mustard
¹/₂ cup	(125 mL)	lemon juice
¹/₄ cup	(60 mL)	vinegar
¹/₃ cup	(80 mL)	ketchup
1 tbsp	(15 mL)	Worcestershire sauce

- Rub salt and pepper into boar rack.

- In a cast iron cooking pot, melt shortening. Brown roast all over. Add water, tomato sauce, onions and garlic. Reduce heat. Simmer 30 minutes or so.

- Meanwhile, in a small bowl, mix sauce ingredients. Pour over roast. Continue cooking around 1 hour or until meat is tender. Serve.

NUTRITION	
CALORIES PER SERVING: 491	
FAT: 17 *g*	CAL. FROM FAT: 32%
PROTEIN: 68 *g*	CHOLESTEROL: 186 *mg*
SODIUM: 493 *mg*	CARBOHYDRATES: 14 *g*

Marinated Beef Steaks

4 SERVINGS

Marinade

1 cup	(250 mL) chili sauce
1 ½ cups	(375 mL) orange juice
¼ cup	(60 mL) onion, chopped
1 tsp	(5 mL) garlic, chopped
1 tbsp	(15 mL) Worcestershire sauce
1 tbsp	(15 mL) Dijon mustard
1 tsp	(5 mL) parsley, chopped
¼ cup	(60 mL) vegetable oil
1	1 ½-lb (675 g) beef steak, ½-inch (1.25 cm) thick

- In a bowl, mix marinade ingredients.
- Make diamond-shape incisions on both sides of steak. Place in a dish. Pour marinade over meat. Cover. Refrigerate at least 12 hours. Drain steak, reserving marinade.
- Preheat oven to BROIL.
- Transfer steak to a roasting pan with a rack. Place in oven 4 inches (10 cm) from element. Broil 4-5 minutes each side. Baste with marinade every 2 minutes. Serve with a salad, tomato slices and baked potatoes, if desired.

VARIATION
- Place steaks on an oiled charcoal grill. Barbecue 5-7 minutes each side. During cooking, baste often with marinade.

NUTRITION	
CALORIES PER SERVING: 493	
FAT: 24 *g*	CAL. FROM FAT: 45%
PROTEIN: 52 *g*	CHOLESTEROL: 140 *mg*
SODIUM: 221 *mg*	CARBOHYDRATES: 15 *g*

Gourmet Venison

8 SERVINGS

½ cup	(125 mL) flour
1 tsp	(5 mL) salt
½ tsp	(2 mL) pepper
2 tsp	(10 mL) nutmeg
2 lbs	(900 g) cubed venison (caribou, moose or deer)
3 tbsp	(45 mL) oil
1 tbsp	(15 mL) butter
2	large onions, minced
2	garlic cloves, chopped
1 tsp	(5 mL) brown sugar
1	bottle (341 mL) beer
1	bay leaf
	juice and peel of ½ orange

- Sprinkle a sheet of wax paper with flour, salt, pepper and nutmeg. Dredge venison cubes with mixture.
- In a cast iron cooking pot, heat oil and melt butter. Sear venison cubes 2-3 minutes all over. Remove from pot. Set aside. Sauté onions and garlic 4 minutes or so. Fold in brown sugar. Cook 1 minute.
- Return venison to cooking pot. Add beer, bay leaf, orange peel and juice. Bring to a boil. Reduce heat. Simmer 90 minutes. Add a little water if sauce is too thick. Serve.

NUTRITION	
CALORIES PER SERVING: 333	
FAT: 14 *g*	CAL. FROM FAT: 39%
PROTEIN: 35 *g*	CHOLESTEROL: 97 *mg*
SODIUM: 364 *mg*	CARBOHYDRATES: 13 *g*

Recipe shown above

Dieticians recommend we diminish our consumption of meat by replacing it with low fat substitutes. Tofu, eggs, nuts, cheeses, beans and legumes are all meat substitutes; they constitute an important source of proteins.

We have to be cautious when it comes to nuts and cheeses. They can be an even greater source of fat than meat. Let's not abuse eggs either; they contain a lot of cholesterol!

Add variety to your menu by incorporating a Vegetable Cheese Pie (p. 232) into your meal. Or try serving your guests an Eggplant Parmigiana (p. 233). We are sure you will find them delicious.

VEGETARIAN

Tofu on Rice

3-4 SERVINGS

2 cups	(500 mL) vegetable broth
2 tbsp	(30 mL) soy sauce
3/4 cup	(180 mL) brown rice
1 1/2 cups	(375 mL) vegetable broth
1 1/4 cups	(300 mL) water
1 cup	(250 mL) onion, chopped
1 1/2 cups	(375 mL) celery, chopped
1 cup	(250 mL) mushrooms, chopped
2 cups	(500 mL) tofu, diced
	tarragon, basil, thyme, rosemary, cayenne, to taste
4 tsp	(20 mL) cornstarch
1/4 cup	(60 mL) water
1	firm tomato, diced
2	green onions, chopped

■ In a saucepan, bring to a boil 2 cups (500 mL) vegetable broth and soy sauce. Add rice. Reduce heat to minimum. Continue cooking until rice is done.

■ In a second saucepan, combine 1 1/2 cups (375 mL) vegetable broth, water, onion, celery, mushrooms and tofu. Simmer 6 minutes. Season.

■ Dilute cornstarch in 1/4 cup (60 mL) water. Fold into tofu mixture. Stir until sauce thickens. Add tomato. Simmer 4 minutes. Serve on a bed of soy-flavored rice. Garnish with green onions. Serve with fresh vegetables, if desired.

NUTRITION	
CALORIES PER SERVING: 388	
FAT: 9 g	CAL. FROM FAT: 17 %
PROTEIN: 22 g	CHOLESTEROL: 1 mg
SODIUM: 811 mg	CARBOHYDRATES: 74 g

Tofu Stew

2 SERVINGS

2 cups	(500 mL) beef broth, degreased
1 1/2 cups	(375 mL) vegetable juice
12 oz	(350 g) tofu, diced
1 cup	(250 mL) turnip, cut into strips
1 cup	(250 mL) cauliflower florets
1/2	onion, chopped
1/2	green bell pepper, minced
1	carrot, cut into strips
1 tsp	(5 mL) onion powder
1 tsp	(5 mL) garlic powder
	salt and pepper

■ In a cooking pot, simmer all ingredients 30 minutes or so. Serve.

Recipe shown above

VARIATIONS
• Replace beef broth with chicken or vegetable broth.
• Replace cauliflower with broccoli, green bell pepper with sweet red pepper, turnip with parsnip.
• Replace vegetable juice with 3/4 cup (180 mL) orange juice and 3/4 cup (180 mL) cranberry juice.
• Sprinkle with 1/4 cup (60 mL) toasted sesame seeds.

NUTRITION	
CALORIES PER SERVING: 332	
FAT: 15 g	CAL. FROM FAT: 37 %
PROTEIN: 24 g	CHOLESTEROL: 15 mg
SODIUM: 822 mg	CARBOHYDRATES: 33 g

Tofu in Puff Pastry

3 SERVINGS

3 tbsp	(45 mL)	butter
3 tbsp	(45 mL)	flour
2 cups	(500 mL)	milk
1 tbsp	(15 mL)	butter
1		onion, minced
6		mushrooms, chopped
1/2 cup	(125 mL)	canned green peas, drained
6		pastry shells
1 tbsp	(15 mL)	onion powder
		pinch of garlic powder
1 tsp	(5 mL)	salt
		pinch of pepper
6 oz	(165 g)	tofu, crumbled

- Preheat oven to 350 °F (175 °C).
- In a saucepan, melt 3 tbsp (45 mL) butter. Fold in flour, mixing well. While stirring, cook 2 minutes. Add milk. Stir until sauce thickens.
- In a skillet, melt 1 tbsp (15 mL) butter. Lightly cook onion, mushrooms and green peas.
- Meanwhile, heat pastry shells in oven.
- Add vegetables to white sauce. Season with onion powder, garlic powder, salt and pepper. Add tofu.
- Remove pastry shells from oven. Spoon tofu mixture into shells. Serve.

NUTRITION	
CALORIES PER SERVING: 610	
FAT: 39 *g*	CAL. FROM FAT: 56 %
PROTEIN: 18 *g*	CHOLESTEROL: 96 *mg*
SODIUM: 1155 *mg*	CARBOHYDRATES: 51 *g*

Almond Tofu

8 SERVINGS

1/4 cup	(60 mL)	soy sauce
2 tbsp	(30 mL)	peanut butter
1/4 tsp	(1 mL)	garlic powder
1 tsp	(5 mL)	onion powder
1/2 tsp	(2 mL)	ginger
2 lbs	(900 g)	tofu, diced
2 tbsp	(30 mL)	vegetable oil
2 tbsp	(30 mL)	peanut oil
1		green bell pepper, diced
6-8		green onions, cut into 1-inch (2.5 cm) lengths
1 cup	(250 mL)	celery, cut into 1-inch (2.5 cm) lengths
5 oz	(142 mL)	water chestnuts, sliced
2 tbsp	(30 mL)	cornstarch
2 cups	(500 mL)	cold water
1/4 cup	(60 mL)	soy sauce
1/2 cup	(125 mL)	roasted almonds

- In a bowl, mix first 5 ingredients. Add tofu. Marinate 2 hours, stirring occasionally.
- In a skillet, heat vegetable oil. Pour in tofu and marinade. Cook tofu until all liquid is absorbed.
- In a second skillet, heat peanut oil. Cook vegetables and water chestnuts " al dente ".
- Meanwhile, dilute cornstarch in water and soy sauce. Pour over vegetables, mixing well. Over low heat, continue cooking until sauce thickens. Add tofu and almonds. Serve on a bed of rice, if desired.

NUTRITION	
CALORIES PER SERVING: 274	
FAT: 19 *g*	CAL. FROM FAT: 58 %
PROTEIN: 14 *g*	CHOLESTEROL: 0 *mg*
SODIUM: 1075 *mg*	CARBOHYDRATES: 17 *g*

Vegetable Tajine

4 SERVINGS

1 tbsp	(15 mL) oil
4	large onions, sliced, in rings
1	green bell pepper, minced
1	sweet red pepper, minced
3	medium-size zucchini, sliced into rounds
19 oz	(540 mL) canned spicy tomatoes
3	eggs, beaten
¹/₂ cup	(125 mL) Mozzarella cheese, grated

	thyme, basil, parsley, savory, celery salt, to taste
1 cup	(250 mL) Mozzarella cheese, grated

- Preheat oven to 350 °F (175 °C).

- In a cooking pot, heat oil. Lightly cook onions. Add bell peppers, zucchini and tomatoes. Over low heat, simmer.

- In a bowl, combine beaten eggs, ¹/₂ cup (125 mL) cheese and mixed herbs. Pour into cooking pot, mixing well.

- In a large greased pyrex dish, place vegetable mixture. Top with 1 cup (250 mL) cheese. Broil in oven 20-25 minutes. Serve with rice, if desired.

NUTRITION	
CALORIES PER SERVING: 319	
FAT: 18 g	CAL. FROM FAT: 49%
PROTEIN: 18 g	CHOLESTEROL: 175 mg
SODIUM: 536 mg	CARBOHYDRATES: 25 g

Vegetable Cheese Pie

6-8 SERVINGS

2 tbsp	(30 mL) vegetable oil
1	garlic clove, chopped
1 cup	(250 mL) zucchini, chopped
1 cup	(250 mL) celery, chopped
¹/₂ cup	(125 mL) carrots, grated
¹/₂ cup	(125 mL) mushrooms, sliced
¹/₂ cup	(125 mL) green bell pepper, chopped
1 cup	(250 mL) whole kernel corn
14 oz	(398 mL) canned tomato sauce
1 tbsp	(15 mL) brown sugar
1 tsp	(5 mL) oregano
¹/₂ tsp	(2 mL) salt
¹/₂ tsp	(2 mL) basil
	pinch of pepper

	pinch of allspice
2	shortcrust pastries (p. 334)
1 cup	(250 mL) Cheddar cheese, grated
1	egg and 1 tbsp (15 mL) water, beaten together

- Preheat oven to 325 °F (160 °C).

- In a large cooking pot heat oil. Cook garlic and vegetables, except corn, 3-5 minutes.

- Add tomato sauce, corn, brown sugar and seasonings. Cook 3-5 minutes.

- Line a pie pan with crust. Spread vegetables into crust. Sprinkle with cheese. Top with second pie crust. Brush with beaten egg. Bake in oven 30-40 minutes. Serve.

NUTRITION	
CALORIES PER SERVING: 345	
FAT: 21 g	CAL. FROM FAT: 54%
PROTEIN: 9 g	CHOLESTEROL: 37 mg
SODIUM: 833 mg	CARBOHYDRATES: 32 g

Eggplant Parmigiana

	4 SERVINGS
1	eggplant, in ½-inch (1.25 cm) thick slices
2	eggs, beaten
⅓ cup	(80 mL) whole wheat flour
¼ cup	(60 mL) olive oil
	salt and pepper
¼ tsp	(1 mL) oregano, chopped
¼ tsp	(1 mL) basil, chopped
½ tsp	(2 mL) chervil, chopped
1 tsp	(5 mL) parsley, chopped
2 cups	(500 mL) tomato sauce
8	Mozzarella cheese slices

- Preheat oven to 350 °F (175 °C).
- Dip eggplant slices in beaten egg. Dredge with flour.
- In a large frying pan, heat oil. Lightly brown eggplant slices on both sides. Season with salt and pepper.
- Transfer eggplant slices to a greased pyrex dish. Sprinkle with mixed herbs. Pour in tomato sauce. Top with cheese. Cook in oven around 15 minutes or until cheese has melted and starts to brown. Serve.

NUTRITION	
CALORIES PER SERVING: 969	
FAT: 72 g	CAL. FROM FAT: 66%
PROTEIN: 56 g	CHOLESTEROL: 294 mg
SODIUM: 1736 mg	CARBOHYDRATES: 28 g

Potato Cabbage Casserole

	4 SERVINGS
6	large potatoes, peeled, boiled
4 tsp	(20 mL) butter or margarine
⅔ cup	(160 mL) skim milk
2 ½ cups	(625 mL) green cabbage, minced, blanched
2 tsp	(10 mL) fresh parsley, chopped
	salt and pepper
1 tbsp	(15 mL) vegetable oil
1 cup	(250 mL) onion, finely chopped
1 cup	(250 mL) aged Cheddar cheese, grated

- Preheat oven to 350 °F (175 °C).
- In a blender or bowl, mash potatoes, butter and milk until smooth. Fold in cabbage, parsley, salt and pepper. Set aside.
- In a frying pan, heat oil. Cook onion until tender but not browned. Add to potato mixture.
- In a greased 10-cup (2.5 L) baking dish, spread a layer of mashed potatoes. Cover with half the cheese. Spread a second layer of mashed potatoes, then remaining cheese.
- Cook in oven 30-40 minutes or until cheese turns a nice golden brown color. Serve.

NUTRITION	
CALORIES PER SERVING: 538	
FAT: 17 g	CAL. FROM FAT: 28%
PROTEIN: 18 g	CHOLESTEROL: 41 mg
SODIUM: 293 mg	CARBOHYDRATES: 81 g

Meatless Spaghetti Sauce

AROUND 8 CUPS (2 L)

1/2 cup	(125 mL) vegetable oil or sesame oil
2	large onions, chopped
2 cups	(500 mL) celery, chopped
2 cups	(500 mL) fresh mushrooms, chopped
1/2 cup	(125 mL) soy beans, crushed
1 cup	(250 mL) sunflower seeds, chopped or ground
1 cup	(250 mL) peanuts, chopped

28 oz	(796 mL) canned tomatoes
10 oz	(284 mL) canned cream of tomato soup
19 oz	(540 mL) canned tomato juice
12 oz	(341 mL) canned tomato paste
2	leeks, minced
2	green bell peppers, finely chopped
4-6	garlic cloves, chopped
1 tbsp	(15 mL) honey
1/2 tsp	(2 mL) crushed red peppers

1/2 tsp	(2 mL) Tabasco sauce
2	pinches of parsley
3	bay leaves
1 tsp	(5 mL) sea salt
1/2 tsp	(2 mL) pepper
1 tsp	(5 mL) basil
1 tsp	(5 mL) thyme
1 tsp	(5 mL) oregano
1/2 tsp	(2 mL) cinnamon
1/2 tsp	(2 mL) ground cloves

- In a heavy-bottomed saucepan, heat oil. Cook onions, celery and mushrooms 4 minutes. Add soy beans, sunflower seeds and peanuts. Continue cooking 5 minutes.

- Pour in tomatoes, cream of tomato soup, tomato juice and paste. Add leeks and bell peppers. Bring to a boil. Simmer 10 minutes. Fold in garlic, honey, crushed red peppers and Tabasco sauce. Simmer 2 hours.

- Approximately 30 minutes before the end of cooking, add other seasonings. If sauce is too thick, add tomato juice. Serve on a bed of fresh pasta, cooked " al dente ".

NUTRITION	
CALORIES PER CUP: 387	
FAT: 28 g	CAL. FROM FAT: 61%
PROTEIN: 11 g	CHOLESTEROL: 0 mg
SODIUM: 817 mg	CARBOHYDRATES: 29 g

Vegetable-Pine Nut Tortellini

4 SERVINGS	
¼ cup	(60 mL) sweet red pepper, diced
¼ cup	(60 mL) green bell pepper, diced
¼ cup	(60 mL) turnip, diced
¼ cup	(60 mL) carrots, diced
1 lb	(450 g) spinach-stuffed tortellini
3 tbsp	(45 mL) olive oil
2	garlic cloves, chopped
¼ cup	(60 mL) pine nuts
1 cup	(250 mL) vegetable juice
	salt and pepper
	basil, finely shredded

- In a saucepan filled with lightly-salted boiling water, blanch vegetables 2 minutes or so. Remove with a slotted spoon. Cool under running cold water. Drain. Set aside.

- In the same boiling water, cook pasta following package instructions. Drain. Set aside.

- In a skillet, heat oil. Sauté vegetables, garlic and pine nuts. Stir until pine nuts start to brown lightly. Add vegetable juice. Season with salt and pepper. Bring to a boil. Add tortellini. While stirring, heat through. Garnish with basil. Serve.

NUTRITION	
CALORIES PER SERVING: 367	
FAT: 23 g	CAL. FROM FAT: 54%
PROTEIN: 13 g	CHOLESTEROL: 147 mg
SODIUM: 485 mg	CARBOHYDRATES: 30 g

Zucchini Noodles

4 SERVINGS	
1 lb	(450 g) fettucine
3	medium-size zucchini
3 tbsp	(45 mL) olive oil
2	garlic cloves, chopped
½ tsp	(2 mL) tarragon, chopped
	salt and pepper
½ cup	(125 mL) plain yogurt (optional)

- In a saucepan filled with lightly-salted boiling water, cook pasta following package instructions. Drain.

- Thinly slice zucchini lengthwise. Cut each slice into fettucini-like strips.

- In a large skillet, heat oil. Sauté zucchini and garlic, while stirring.

- In a colander, run fettucini under running hot water. Drain. Add to zucchini in skillet. Season with tarragon, salt and pepper. Continue cooking until pasta is hot. Add yogurt, if desired. Heat through 2 minutes. Serve.

NUTRITION	
CALORIES PER SERVING: 544	
FAT: 13 g	CAL. FROM FAT: 22%
PROTEIN: 17 g	CHOLESTEROL: 4 mg
SODIUM: 69 mg	CARBOHYDRATES: 89 g

New Wave Rice Pilaf

4-6 SERVINGS

¼ cup	(60 mL) peanut oil
¾ cup	(180 mL) brown long-grain rice
¾ cup	(180 mL) white long-grain rice
1 cup	(250 mL) hot water
2 cups	(500 mL) vegetable juice, heated
2	tomatoes, diced
1 cup	(250 mL) asparagus, minced
2	garlic cloves, chopped
10 oz	(284 mL) canned sliced mushrooms, drained
	salt and pepper

- Preheat oven to 350 °F (175 °C).

- In an ovenproof casserole dish, heat oil. Add brown and white rice. While stirring, cook 2 minutes. Mix in water and vegetable juice. Fold in tomatoes, asparagus, garlic and mushrooms. Season with salt and pepper. Cover. Cook in oven 45 minutes or so.

- Towards end of cooking, if mixture is too thick, add extra vegetable juice. If mixture is too liquid, cook uncovered 5-10 minutes. Serve.

NUTRITION	
CALORIES PER SERVING: 297	
FAT: 10 g	CAL. FROM FAT: 31 %
PROTEIN: 6 g	CHOLESTEROL: 0 mg
SODIUM: 519 mg	CARBOHYDRATES: 47 g

Recipe shown above

Fancy Rice

4-6 SERVINGS

Dressing

⅓ cup	(80 mL) vegetable oil
⅓ cup	(80 mL) lemon juice
1 tbsp	(15 mL) dry mustard
1 tsp	(5 mL) paprika
½ tsp	(2 mL) curry powder
¼ tsp	(1 mL) thyme
	salt and pepper
4 cups	(1 L) water, lightly-salted
2 cups	(500 mL) long-grain rice
2 tbsp	(30 mL) butter
1 cup	(250 mL) almonds
1 cup	(250 mL) cashews
1 cup	(250 mL) celery, finely chopped
5	green onions, chopped
2	avocados, diced
1	garlic clove, chopped

- In a bowl, mix dressing ingredients.

- In a saucepan, bring water to a boil. Cook rice following package instructions. Add dressing. Marinate in refrigerator 12 hours.

- In a frying pan, melt butter. Lightly brown almonds and cashews 3 minutes or so. Add vegetables, avocados and garlic. Fold into rice. Serve.

NUTRITION	
CALORIES PER SERVING: 643	
FAT: 40 g	CAL. FROM FAT: 53 %
PROTEIN: 12 g	CHOLESTEROL: 10 mg
SODIUM: 107 mg	CARBOHYDRATES: 67 g

Red Kidney Bean Chili

4-6 SERVINGS

2	celery stalks, diced
1	green bell pepper, minced
1	sweet red pepper, minced
2	carrots, minced
3 tbsp	(45 mL) butter
2	potatoes, cooked, diced
19 oz	(540 mL) canned tomatoes, in their juice
2 tbsp	(30 mL) tomato paste
2	19-oz (540 mL) cans of red kidney beans
2 tsp	(10 mL) parsley, chopped
1 tsp	(5 mL) basil, chopped
1/2 tsp	(2 mL) chili sauce
	salt and pepper

■ In a saucepan filled with lightly-salted boiling water, blanch celery, bell peppers and carrots 2 minutes. Drain.

■ In a large skillet, melt butter. Sauté all vegetables, except tomatoes, 4 minutes or so. Add tomatoes and tomato paste. Bring to a boil. Add beans and seasonings. Simmer 30 minutes.

■ Serve with whole wheat rolls or nachos, if desired.

NUTRITION	
CALORIES PER SERVING: 312	
FAT: 7 *g*	CAL. FROM FAT: 19%
PROTEIN: 13 *g*	CHOLESTEROL: 15 *mg*
SODIUM: 989 *mg*	CARBOHYDRATES: 53 *g*

Garbanzo Bean Loaf

3-4 SERVINGS

---

1 tbsp	(15 mL) butter or margarine
1	onion, chopped
2	garlic cloves, chopped
4	celery stalks, minced
2	tomatoes, minced
2 tbsp	(30 mL) tomato paste
19 oz	(540 mL) canned garbanzo beans, mashed
1	egg, beaten
1/2 cup	(125 mL) whole wheat bread crumbs
1/4 cup	(60 mL) fresh parsley, finely chopped
1 tsp	(5 mL) dried thyme
1 tsp	(5 mL) dried savory
	salt and pepper

■ Preheat oven to 375 °F (190 °C).

■ In a skillet, melt butter or margarine. Cook onion, garlic and celery until tender. Add tomatoes and tomato paste. Continue cooking 5 minutes.

■ In a large bowl, pour hot mixture. Add garbanzo beans, egg, bread crumbs and mixed herbs. Season with salt and pepper, mixing well. Pour into a greased loaf pan. Cover with aluminum foil. Bake in oven 1 hour or so.

■ Let stand a few minutes before unmolding. Serve with tomato sauce, if desired.

NUTRITION	
CALORIES PER SERVING: 302	
FAT: 7 *g*	CAL. FROM FAT: 19%
PROTEIN: 12 *g*	CHOLESTEROL: 53 *mg*
SODIUM: 683 *mg*	CARBOHYDRATES: 52 *g*

VEGETABLES

Dieticians recommend eating three to four portions of raw or cooked vegetables daily. Most vegetables are an excellent source of Vitamin A, Vitamin C and dietary fiber.

If we avoid adding butter, oil, or other fat, the vegetable dish can satisfy your hunger, while being a low source of calories.

In this chapter you will find succulent and beautiful ways to prepare vegetables. Selections range from the conventional Baked Potato (p. 261) to exotic Mediterranean Avocados (p. 243). With these delicious dishes, it's easy to enjoy eating healthy!

From top to bottom :
Artichoke Hearts in Tomato Sauce,
Garnished Artichoke Bottoms,
Artichoke Hearts with Blue Cheese

240 SIDE DISHES

Artichoke Hearts in Tomato Sauce

4 SERVINGS

12	artichoke hearts
1 cup	(250 mL) tomato juice
2 tsp	(10 mL) basil, chopped
2 tsp	(10 mL) tarragon, chopped
1	garlic clove, chopped
	salt and pepper

- In a bowl, mix all ingredients. Refrigerate overnight.
- The next day, remove artichoke hearts from marinade. Cut each one into quarters.
- Divide into 4 equal servings. Serve artichoke hearts covered in marinade.

CALORIES PER SERVING: 141	
FAT: 1 g	CAL. FROM FAT: 3%
PROTEIN: 10 g	CHOLESTEROL: 0 mg
SODIUM: 483 mg	CARBOHYDRATES: 32 g

Garnished Artichoke Bottoms

4 SERVINGS

1 tbsp	(15 mL) butter
1 cup	(250 mL) mushrooms, chopped
3 tbsp	(45 mL) sweet red pepper, chopped
1	garlic clove, chopped
2 tbsp	(30 mL) onion, chopped
	salt and pepper
1/4 cup	(60 mL) white wine
12	artichoke bottoms
3 tbsp	(45 mL) Parmesan cheese, grated

- Preheat oven to BROIL.
- In a frying pan, melt butter. Cook mushrooms, bell pepper, garlic and onion 4 minutes or so. Season with salt and pepper. Add white wine. Let reduce until liquid has almost all evaporated.
- Stuff artichoke bottoms with mixture. Sprinkle with Parmesan. Broil in oven around 4 minutes or until cheese starts to brown lightly. Serve.

CALORIES PER SERVING: 259	
FAT: 7 g	CAL. FROM FAT: 20%
PROTEIN: 16 g	CHOLESTEROL: 11 mg
SODIUM: 403 mg	CARBOHYDRATES: 42 g

Artichoke Hearts with Blue Cheese

4 SERVINGS

1/4 cup	(60 mL) plain yogurt
2 tbsp	(30 mL) Blue cheese, crumbled
1 tsp	(5 mL) lemon juice
1/4 tsp	(1 mL) garlic, chopped
	dash of Worcestershire sauce
	salt and pepper
12	artichoke hearts

- In a bowl, mix ingredients, except artichoke hearts.
- Drain artichoke hearts. Stuff with Blue cheese mixture. Serve.

CALORIES PER SERVING: 148	
FAT: 2 g	CAL. FROM FAT: 10%
PROTEIN: 10 g	CHOLESTEROL: 4 mg
SODIUM: 341 mg	CARBOHYDRATES: 29 g

Artichokes and asparagus are considered luxuries because of their high cost. At their best in spring, these vegetables are plentiful from the end of April until June. You will find them good value, and a welcome way to end the winter.

Asparagus in a Bundle

4 SERVINGS

16	fresh asparagus tips
2	bacon slices
	salt and pepper

- Peel asparagus.
- In a saucepan filled with lightly-salted boiling water, blanch asparagus 2 minutes. Remove from saucepan. Rinse under running cold water. Drain.
- Cut bacon slices in half. Place 4 asparagus on each bacon half-slice. Wrap bacon around asparagus. Secure with a wooden toothpick.
- Cook in microwave oven 6 minutes, on HIGH. Turn over 3 times during cooking. Let stand 3 minutes. Serve.

CALORIES PER SERVING: 51	
FAT: 2 g	CAL. FROM FAT: 28%
PROTEIN: 4 g	CHOLESTEROL: 3 mg
SODIUM: 142 mg	CARBOHYDRATES: 6 g

Asparagus with Apples

4 SERVINGS

16	fresh asparagus tips
2 tbsp	(30 mL) butter
1/2 cup	(125 mL) apple, diced
1	garlic clove, chopped
	pinch of nutmeg
	pinch of cinnamonr

- Peel asparagus. Trim away and reserve heads.
- In a saucepan filled with lightly-salted boiling water, blanch asparagus stems 2 minutes. Remove from saucepan. Rinse under running cold water. Drain. Dice stems.
- In a frying pan, melt butter. Cook diced asparagus, apple, garlic and seasonings 5 minutes or so.
- Meanwhile, blanch asparagus heads 4 minutes or so. Rinse under running cold water. Drain.
- Divide asparagus and apple mixture among 4 plates. Garnish each serving with 4 asparagus heads. Serve.

CALORIES PER SERVING: 92	
FAT: 16 g	CAL. FROM FAT: 53%
PROTEIN: 3 g	CHOLESTEROL: 15 mg
SODIUM: 105 mg	CARBOHYDRATES: 9 g

Marinated Asparagus

4 SERVINGS

24	canned asparagus tips, drained
1/2 cup	(125 mL) grapefruit juice
1/2 cup	(125 mL) white wine
2 tsp	(10 mL) fennel, chopped
2 tsp	(10 mL) tarragon, chopped
1	garlic clove, chopped
	salt and pepper

- In a bowl, mix all ingredients. Refrigerate overnight.
- The next day, remove asparagus from marinade. Place on a bed of finely shredded lettuce or cabbage, if desired. Coat with marinade. Serve.

CALORIES PER SERVING: 41	
FAT: 1 g	CAL. FROM FAT: 11%
PROTEIN: 8 g	CHOLESTEROL: 25 mg
SODIUM: 260 mg	CARBOHYDRATES: 13 g

From top to bottom : Asparagus in a Bundle, Asparagus with Apples, Marinated Asparagus

EGGPLANTS AND AVOCADOS

From top to bottom :
Fried Eggplant,
Garlicky Eggplant,
Cheese-broiled Eggplant

Fried Eggplant

4 SERVINGS

8	eggplant rounds, 1/2-inch (1.25 cm) thick
1/4 cup	(60 mL) whole wheat flour
2	eggs, beaten
1/4 cup	(60 mL) bread crumbs
1/2 cup	(125 mL) peanut oil
	salt and pepper

- Cut each eggplant round into 4 triangles. Dredge with flour. Dip in beaten eggs. Roll in bread crumbs.

- In a skillet, heat oil. Cook eggplant until golden brown. Remove from skillet. Drain on a paper towel. Season with salt and pepper. Serve with spicy mayonnaise.

CALORIES PER SERVING: 168	
FAT: 1o *g*	CAL. FROM FAT: 50 %
PROTEIN: 5 *g*	CHOLESTEROL: 92 *mg*
SODIUM: 110 *mg*	CARBOHYDRATES: 16 *g*

Garlicky Eggplant

4 SERVINGS

3 tbsp	(45 mL) olive oil
2 cups	(500 mL) egg-plant, diced
1/4 cup	(60 mL) celery, diced
1/4 cup	(60 mL) sweet red pepper, diced
3	garlic cloves, chopped
1/4 tsp	(1 mL) basil, chopped
	salt and pepper

- In a frying pan, heat oil. While stirring, cook vegetables 4 minutes or so.

- Add garlic and seasonings. Continue cooking 3 minutes or so. Serve.

CALORIES PER SERVING: 120	
FAT: 10 *g*	CAL. FROM FAT: 74 %
PROTEIN: 1 *g*	CHOLESTEROL: 0 *mg*
SODIUM: 31 *mg*	CARBOHYDRATES: 7 *g*

Cheese-broiled Eggplant

4 SERVINGS

2	small eggplants
2 tbsp	(30 mL) olive oil
1/4 cup	(60 mL) tomato sauce
	salt and pepper
1 cup	(250 mL) Mozza-rella cheese, grated

- Preheat oven to BROIL.

- Slice eggplants in half lengthwise. If needed, cut a thin slice from the rounded side of eggplant halves to prevent rolling.

- In a saucepan filled with lightly-salted boiling water, blanch eggplant 6 minutes. Remove from saucepan. Rinse under running cold water. Drain.

- On an ovenproof baking sheet, place eggplant halves. Brush with oil. Spoon equal amounts of tomato sauce over each. Season with salt and pepper. Top with grated cheese. Broil in oven around 4 minutes or until cheese starts to turn golden brown. Serve.

CALORIES PER SERVING: 203	
FAT: 14 *g*	CAL. FROM FAT: 60 %
PROTEIN: 8 *g*	CHOLESTEROL: 25 *mg*
SODIUM: 260 *mg*	CARBOHYDRATES: 13 *g*

Avocados and eggplants are more and more popular, and play an increasing part in our daily menu. The avocado is the most nutritious fruit to be found ; it is also the most fattening ! A half-avocado contains 150 calories. We therefore recommend moderation.

Avocado in Red Wine

4 SERVINGS	
2	avocados
1 cup	(250 mL) red wine
¹/₂ tsp	(2 mL) mint, chopped
1	garlic clove, chopped
1	French shallot, chopped
	salt and pepper

- Peel avocados. Remove pits. Dice avocado flesh.
- In a bowl, mix all ingredients. Refrigerate overnight.
- The next day, drain avocados, reserving red wine marinade to use as a salad dressing ingredient in another recipe. Serve avocados on a bed of finely-shredded lettuce or cabbage, if desired.

CALORIES PER SERVING: 168	
FAT: 11 g	CAL. FROM FAT: 73 %
PROTEIN: 2 g	CHOLESTEROL: 0 mg
SODIUM: 69 mg	CARBOHYDRATES: 8 g

Curried Avocado Fans

4 SERVINGS	
2	avocados
2 tbsp	(30 mL) lemon juice
¹/₂ cup	(125 mL) mayonnaise
1 tsp	(5 mL) curry
	dash of Worcestershire sauce
¹/₄ tsp	(1 mL) garlic, chopped

- Peel avocados. Cut in half lengthwise. Remove pits. Sprinkle with lemon juice so avocados are coated all over.
- Slice each avocado half into a fan shape. Arrange on a plate.
- Mix remaining ingredients to a sauce. Spoon over avocados. Serve.

CALORIES PER SERVING: 321	
FAT: 35 g	CAL. FROM FAT: 90 %
PROTEIN: 1 g	CHOLESTEROL: 10 mg
SODIUM: 166 mg	CARBOHYDRATES: 7 g

Mediterranean Avocados

4 SERVINGS	
2	avocados
³/₄ cup	(180 mL) plain yogurt
1	garlic clove, chopped
2	dashes of Worcestershire sauce
2 tbsp	(30 mL) lemon juice
¹/₄ cup	(60 mL) spinach leaves, finely shredded
	salt and pepper
1	tomato, finely sliced

- Peel avocados. Remove pits. Dice avocado flesh.
- In a bowl, mix all ingredients, except tomato slices. Refrigerate overnight.
- The next day, serve avocados on a bed of tomato slices.

CALORIES PER SERVING: 150	
FAT: 13 g	CAL. FROM FAT: 71 %
PROTEIN: 3 g	CHOLESTEROL: 5 mg
SODIUM: 77 mg	CARBOHYDRATES: 9 g

*From top to bottom :
Avocados in Red Wine,
Curried Avocado Fans,
Mediterranean Avocados*

BEETS AND BROCCOLI

Spicy Beets

4 SERVINGS	
2 cups	(500 mL) cooked beets, diced
1/2 cup	(125 mL) fennel bulb, diced
3 tbsp	(45 mL) butter
3	wild garlic cloves in vinegar, chopped
1 oz	(30 mL) pastis
	salt and pepper

- Drain beets.
- In a saucepan filled with lightly-salted boiling water, blanch fennel 3 minutes. Drain.
- In a frying pan, melt butter. Cook beets, fennel and wild garlic 4 minutes. Add pastis. Season with salt and pepper. Continue cooking 3 minutes or so. Serve.

NUTRITION	
CALORIES PER SERVING: 143	
FAT: 9 g	CAL. FROM FAT: 59%
PROTEIN: 2 g	CHOLESTEROL: 23 mg
SODIUM: 178 mg	CARBOHYDRATES: 12 g

Beets with Green Tomatoes

4 SERVINGS	
3	green tomatoes
3	beets
2 tbsp	(30 mL) red wine
2 tbsp	(30 mL) tarragon vinegar
3	garlic cloves, chopped
3 tbsp	(45 mL) onion, chopped
1/4 cup	(60 mL) olive oil
1 tsp	(5 mL) savory, chopped
	salt and pepper

- Cut each tomato into 8 wedges. Slice wedges in half.
- Cut beets into 1/4-inch (0.5 cm) thick slices. Cut each slice into half-moons.
- Mix remaining ingredients. Add vegetables. Marinate in refrigerator 2 days.
- Serve chilled or heat through beforehand.

NUTRITION	
CALORIES PER SERVING: 189	
FAT: 14 g	CAL. FROM FAT: 65%
PROTEIN: 3 g	CHOLESTEROL: 0 mg
SODIUM: 121 mg	CARBOHYDRATES: 14 g

Broccoli Brochettes

4 SERVINGS	
1 cup	(250 mL) broccoli florets
1 1/2 cups	(375 mL) chicken broth
2 tbsp	(30 mL) soy sauce
3 tbsp	(45 mL) butter
1	garlic clove, chopped
1/2 tsp	(2 mL) chervil, chopped
2 tsp	(10 mL) lemon juice

- Thread broccoli florets onto long wooden toothpicks or small skewers.
- In a saucepan, bring to a boil chicken broth and soy sauce. Over low heat, cook brochettes in broth 4 minutes or so.
- Meanwhile, in a small frying pan, melt butter. Add garlic and chervil. Bring to a froth. Pour in lemon juice. Remove from heat.
- Serve brochettes sprinkled with garlic butter.

NUTRITION	
CALORIES PER SERVING: 128	
FAT: 10 g	CAL. FROM FAT: 67%
PROTEIN: 3 g	CHOLESTEROL: 28 mg
SODIUM: 627 mg	CARBOHYDRATES: 8 g

Piquant Broccoli Florets

4 SERVINGS	
16	medium-size broccoli florets
1 cup	(250 mL) vegetable juice
1/4 tsp	(1 mL) chili powder
1/4 tsp	(1 mL) crushed red peppers
1 tbsp	(15 mL) lemon juice
1	garlic clove, chopped
2 tsp	(10 mL) cornstarch
2 tbsp	(30 mL) cold water
	salt and pepper

- In a saucepan filled with lightly-salted boiling water, blanch broccoli florets 5 minutes or so. Remove from saucepan. Drain. Set aside.
- In a small saucepan, bring vegetable juice to a boil. Reduce heat. Simmer 2 minutes. Mix in chili powder, crushed red peppers, lemon juice and garlic.
- Dilute cornstarch in cold water. Fold into mixture. Season with salt and pepper. Continue cooking around 3 minutes or until sauce thickens. Place broccoli in sauce. Reheat. Serve.

NUTRITION	
CALORIES PER SERVING: 25	
FAT: 1 g	CAL. FROM FAT: 6%
PROTEIN: 1 g	CHOLESTEROL: 0 mg
SODIUM: 273 mg	CARBOHYDRATES: 6 g

Clockwise from upper left :
Broccoli Brochettes,
Spicy Beets,
Piquant Broccoli Bouquets

Beets and broccoli are brightly-colored vegetables that make attractive side dishes. To keep both their color and nutritious value, they should be cooked in as little water as possible. Broccoli is an excellent source of vitamin C, and is also a good source of vitamin A and fiber.

CARROTS AND CELERY

From top to bottom :
Mustard Carrots,
Glazed Carrots,
Carrot Purée

Mustard Carrots

4 SERVINGS

1 ¹/₂ cups	(375 mL) carrots, diced
¹/₄ cup	(60 mL) sweet red pepper, diced
1 tbsp	(15 mL) peanut oil
2 tbsp	(30 mL) old-fashioned mustard
3 tbsp	(45 mL) chicken broth
	salt and pepper

- In a saucepan filled with lightly-salted boiling water, blanch carrots and sweet red peppers 3 minutes or so. Drain. Set aside.
- In a frying pan, heat oil. While stirring, cook vegetables 3 minutes or so. Add mustard, mixing well.
- Fold in chicken broth. Season with salt and pepper. Continue cooking 2 minutes or so. Serve.

CALORIES PER SERVING: 57	
FAT: 4 g	CAL. FROM FAT: 59 %
PROTEIN: 1 g	CHOLESTEROL: 1 mg
SODIUM: 154 mg	CARBOHYDRATES: 5 g

Glazed Carrots

4 SERVINGS

16	spring baby carrots
1 tbsp	(15 mL) butter
1 tbsp	(15 mL) honey
	salt and pepper
16	small parsley sprigs

- Brush carrots. Remove stems.
- In a saucepan filled with lightly-salted boiling water, blanch carrots 4 minutes or so. Drain. Set aside.
- In a frying pan, melt butter. Cook carrots 2 minutes or so. Add honey. Season with salt and pepper. While stirring, continue cooking until carrots are well-coated with melted honey.
- Divide carrots among 4 plates. Garnish the end of each carrot with a parsley sprig to imitate a stem. Serve.

CALORIES PER SERVING: 42	
FAT: 3 g	CAL. FROM FAT: 58 %
PROTEIN: 0g	CHOLESTEROL: 8 mg
SODIUM: 52 mg	CARBOHYDRATES: 5 g

Carrot Purée

8 SERVINGS

8	large carrots, peeled
3	medium-size potatoes, peeled
2 tbsp	(30 mL) butter
1 tbsp	(15 mL) milk
1	egg, beaten
¹/₄ tsp	(1 mL) ground nutmeg
¹/₂ tsp	(2 mL) chervil, chopped

- Preheat oven to 300 °F (150 °C).
- Cut vegetables into large chunks.
- In a saucepan filled with lightly-salted boiling water, cook carrots and potatoes 12 minutes or so. Remove from heat. Drain in a metal colander.
- Place colander on a baking sheet. Dry cooked vegetables in oven 10 minutes.
- In a bowl, mash vegetables. Add remaining ingredients. Mix to a smooth purée. Serve.

CALORIES PER SERVING: 160	
FAT: 3 g	CAL. FROM FAT: 17 %
PROTEIN: 4 g	CHOLESTEROL: 8 mg
SODIUM: 60 mg	CARBOHYDRATES: 31 g

Carrots are especially rich in vitamin A. This vitamin helps to maintain your night vision : recent studies show that it is also helpful in preventing certain types of cancer.

Celery is rarely used except to enhance the flavor of other dishes or as a snack to relieve hunger pains. Nevertheless, with its color and flavor, celery can easily become the main ingredient of an elegant and delicious dish.

Braised Celery with Tomatoes

4 SERVINGS	
12	celery stalks, cut into 4-inch (10 cm) lengths, with a little leaf
1 tbsp	(15 mL) butter
¼ tsp	(1 mL) garlic clove, chopped
¼ tsp	(1 mL) fennel seeds
1 cup	(250 mL) tomato juice
½ tsp	(2 mL) basil, chopped
	salt and pepper

■ In a saucepan filled with lightly-salted boiling water, blanch celery 1 minute or so. Drain.

■ In a small saucepan, melt butter. Cook celery, garlic and fennel seeds 1 minute or so. Add remaining ingredients. Bring to a boil. Reduce heat. Cover. Simmer 10 minutes or so. Serve.

CALORIES PER SERVING: 38	
FAT: 3 *g*	CAL. FROM FAT: 63 %
PROTEIN: 1 *g*	CHOLESTEROL: 8 *mg*
SODIUM: 302 *mg*	CARBOHYDRATES: 3 *g*

Oriental-style Celery

4 SERVINGS	
2 tbsp	(30 mL) peanut oil
1 cup	(250 mL) celery, cut into diagonal slices
¼ cup	(60 mL) oyster mushrooms, minced
8	miniature corn, diced
1	garlic clove, chopped
½ cup	(125 mL) chicken broth
1 tbsp	(15 mL) cornstarch
2 tbsp	(30 mL) cold water
	salt and pepper

■ In a large frying pan or wok, heat oil. Cook celery 2 minutes or so. Add oyster mushrooms, corn and garlic. Stir-fry 1 minute or so.

■ Fold in chicken broth. Continue cooking 2 minutes, stirring constantly.

■ In a small bowl, dilute cornstarch in cold water. Fold into mixture in pan. Season with salt and pepper, mixing well. Continue cooking until sauce thickens. Serve.

CALORIES PER SERVING: 170	
FAT: 7 *g*	CAL. FROM FAT: 40 %
PROTEIN: 8 *g*	CHOLESTEROL: 2 *mg*
SODIUM: 4106 *mg*	CARBOHYDRATES: 17 *g*

Celery in Virgin Oil

AROUND 2 CUPS (500 mL)	
2 cups	(500 mL) celery, diced
½ cup	(125 mL) virgin olive oil
¼ cup	(60 mL) onion, chopped
2 tsp	(10 mL) crushed red peppers
2	garlic cloves, chopped
¼ tsp	(1 mL) rosemary, chopped
¼ tsp	(1 mL) sea salt

■ In a saucepan filled with lightly-salted boiling water, blanch diced celery 3 minutes or so. Remove from heat. Drain. Set aside.

■ In a small saucepan, warm oil. Remove from heat. Add remaining ingredients, mixing well.

■ Transfer celery to a jar. Stir in seasoned oil. Shaking occasionally, keep at room temperature.

Note : marinated celery will keep up to 2 weeks.

CALORIES PER SERVING: 254	
FAT: 27 *g*	CAL. FROM FAT: 94 %
PROTEIN: 1 *g*	CHOLESTEROL: 0 *mg*
SODIUM: 165 *mg*	CARBOHYDRATES: 3 *g*

From top to bottom :
Braised Celery with Tomatoes,
Oriental-style Celery,
Celery in Virgin Oil

MUSHROOMS AND CABBAGE

From top to bottom :
Fried Oyster Mushrooms,
Mushrooms in Garlic Cream,
Greek Mushrooms

Fried Oyster Mushrooms

4 SERVINGS	
8 oz	(225 g) oyster mushrooms
1/4 cup	(60 mL) whole wheat flour
1/4 cup	(60 mL) peanut oil
1 tsp	(5 mL) sesame oil
1 tbsp	(15 mL) sesame seeds
	salt and pepper

- Dredge oyster mushrooms with flour. Shake off excess flour.
- In a frying pan, heat oils. Sauté mushrooms until golden brown. Remove from pan. Sprinkle with sesame seeds. Season with salt and pepper. Serve.

CALORIES PER SERVING: 188	
FAT: 16 g	CAL. FROM FAT: 76%
PROTEIN: 3 g	CHOLESTEROL: 0 mg
SODIUM: 47 mg	CARBOHYDRATES: 8 g

Mushrooms in Garlic Cream

4 SERVINGS	
12 oz	(341 mL) canned quartered mushrooms
2 tsp	(10 mL) butter
1/4 tsp	(1 mL) garlic, chopped
1/4 cup	(60 mL) heavy cream
	pinch of nutmeg
	salt and pepper

- Drain mushrooms.
- In a frying pan, melt butter. Cook garlic 1 minute. Mix in mushrooms. Continue cooking 1 minute.
- Fold in remaining ingredients. Continue cooking until cream thickens. Serve.

CALORIES PER SERVING: 89	
FAT: 8 g	CAL. FROM FAT: 72%
PROTEIN: 2 g	CHOLESTEROL: 26 mg
SODIUM: 431 mg	CARBOHYDRATES: 5 g

Greek Mushrooms

4 SERVINGS	
12 oz	(341 mL) canned sliced mushrooms
1 tbsp	(15 mL) olive oil
1/4 cup	(60 mL) onion, minced
2 tbsp	(30 mL) carrot, grated
1	garlic clove, chopped
1/2 cup	(125 mL) white wine
1/2 cup	(125 mL) tomato juice
2 tbsp	(30 mL) lemon juice
1	pinch of each, thyme, fennel, dill, chives, chopped
1	bay leaf
	salt and pepper

- Drain mushrooms.
- In a frying pan, heat oil. Cook onion, carrot and garlic 2 minutes. Mix in mushrooms. Continue cooking 1 minute.
- Fold in remaining ingredients. Continue cooking until liquid has reduced by at least one-third. Let vegetables cool in their cooking juices. Serve.

CALORIES PER SERVING: 83	
FAT: 4 g	CAL. FROM FAT: 46%
PROTEIN: 2 g	CHOLESTEROL: 0 mg
SODIUM: 4556 mg	CARBOHYDRATES: 8 g

Mushrooms are delicate and should be handled gently. Instead of washing them, use a brush to clean them carefully. This will also help to retain their full flavor. Mushrooms are a good source of potassium and phosphorus.

Mustardy Green Cabbage

4 SERVINGS	
3 tbsp	(45 mL) butter
2 cups	(500 mL) green cabbage, minced
1	garlic clove, chopped
1/4 cup	(60 mL) onion, chopped
1 tsp	(5 mL) dry mustard
1 cup	(250 mL) chicken broth
2 tsp	(10 mL) soy sauce
	salt and pepper

- In a casserole dish, melt butter. Without browning, cook cabbage, garlic and onion 4 minutes or so, stirring constantly.
- Add remaining ingredients, mixing well. Cover. Continue cooking until cabbage is tender. Serve.

CALORIES PER SERVING: 115	
FAT: 10 *g*	CAL. FROM FAT: 72%
PROTEIN: 2 *g*	CHOLESTEROL: 26 *mg*
SODIUM: 322 *mg*	CARBOHYDRATES: 6 *g*

Port-flavored Red Cabbage

4 SERVINGS	
3 tbsp	(45 mL) butter
2 cups	(500 mL) red cabbage, minced
1	garlic clove, chopped
1/4 cup	(60 mL) onion, chopped
1 oz	(30 mL) port wine
3 tbsp	(45 mL) wine vinegar
2 tsp	(10 mL) honey
	salt and pepper

- In a heavy-bottomed casserole dish, melt butter. Without browning, cook cabbage, garlic and onion 6 minutes or so, stirring constantly.
- Add in remaining ingredients, mixing well. Cover. Stirring occasionally, continue cooking until cabbage is tender. Serve.

CALORIES PER SERVING: 113	
FAT: 9 *g*	CAL. FROM FAT: 70%
PROTEIN: 1 *g*	CHOLESTEROL: 23 *mg*
SODIUM: 180 *mg*	CARBOHYDRATES: 8 *g*

Chinese Cabbage with Peanuts

4 SERVINGS	
3 tbsp	(45 mL) butter
2 cups	(500 mL) Chinese cabbage, minced
1	garlic clove, chopped
2 tbsp	(30 mL) onion, chopped
1/4 cup	(60 mL) peanuts
1/2 tsp	(2 mL) sesame oil
	salt and pepper

- In a heavy-bottomed casserole dish, melt butter. While stirring, cook cabbage, garlic, onion and peanuts 4 minutes or so.
- Add sesame oil. Season with salt and pepper, mixing well. Continue cooking 3 minutes. Serve.

CALORIES PER SERVING: 139	
FAT: 14 *g*	CAL. FROM FAT: 84%
PROTEIN: 3 *g*	CHOLESTEROL: 23 *mg*
SODIUM: 138 *mg*	CARBOHYDRATES: 3 *g*

From top to bottom :
Mustardy Green Cabbage,
Port-flavored Red Cabbage,
Chinese Cabbage with Peanuts

BRUSSEL SPROUTS AND CAULIFLOWER

From top to bottom :
Saffron Brussel Sprouts,
Brussel Sprouts with Prosciutto,
Brussel Sprouts with Shallots

Saffron Brussel Sprouts

4 SERVINGS	
2 cups	(500 mL) Brussel sprouts
3/4 cup	(180 mL) chicken broth
1/2 tsp	(2 mL) saffron
1/4 tsp	(1 mL) curry
	pinch of coriander, chopped
	salt and pepper
1 tbsp	(15 mL) corn-starch
2 tbsp	(30 mL) cold water

▪ In a saucepan filled with lightly-salted boiling water, blanch Brussel sprouts 4 minutes or so. Drain. Slice Brussel sprouts in half.

▪ In a small saucepan, bring chicken broth to a boil. Mix in seasonings. Add Brussel sprouts. Simmer 3 minutes.

▪ Dilute cornstarch in cold water. Fold into vegetables. Continue cooking until sauce thickens. Serve.

CALORIES PER SERVING: 56	
FAT: 1 g	CAL. FROM FAT: 17%
PROTEIN: 3 g	CHOLESTEROL: 2 mg
SODIUM: 72 mg	CARBOHYDRATES: 10 g

Brussel Sprouts with Prosciutto

4 SERVINGS	
2 cups	(500 mL) Brussel sprouts
1 tbsp	(15 mL) peanut oil
1/4 cup	(60 mL) Prosciutto ham, minced
1	garlic clove, chopped
	salt and pepper

▪ In a saucepan filled with lightly-salted boiling water, blanch Brussel sprouts 5 minutes or so. Drain. Slice Brussel sprouts in half.

▪ In a frying pan, heat oil. While stirring, cook Prosciutto 3 minutes or so.

▪ Add Brussel sprouts and garlic. Season with salt and pepper, mixing well. Continue cooking 3 minutes. Serve.

CALORIES PER SERVING: 89	
FAT: 5 g	CAL. FROM FAT: 46%
PROTEIN: 6 g	CHOLESTEROL: 10 mg
SODIUM: 444 mg	CARBOHYDRATES: 7 g

Brussel Sprouts with Shallots

4 SERVINGS	
2 cups	(500 mL) Brussel sprouts
1/4 cup	(60 mL) shallots, minced
1/4 cup	(60 mL) leek, minced
2 tbsp	(30 mL) peanut oil
1	garlic clove, chopped
	salt and pepper

▪ Slice Brussel sprouts in half.

▪ In a saucepan filled with lightly-salted boiling water, blanch Brussel sprouts and shallots 4 minutes or so. Add leek. Continue cooking 30 seconds. Drain.

▪ In a frying pan, heat oil. While stirring, cook garlic 1 minute. Add blanched vegetables. Season with salt and pepper, mixing well. Continue cooking 3 minutes. Serve.

CALORIES PER SERVING: 70	
FAT: 2 g	CAL. FROM FAT: 21%
PROTEIN: 4 g	CHOLESTEROL: 0 mg
SODIUM: 232 mg	CARBOHYDRATES: 9 g

Recent findings prove that cauliflower and other members of the cabbage family (cabbage, broccoli, Brussels sprouts) can reduce the risk of colon, oesophagus and stomach cancer. It is therefore recommended that you include cabbage as often as possible in your diet !

Cauliflower in Cream Sauce

4 SERVINGS

2 tbsp	(30 mL) butter
1 ½ cups	(375 mL) cauliflower florets
¾ cup	(180 mL) heavy cream
1 tsp	(5 mL) nutmeg
	salt and pepper

- In a frying pan, melt butter. While stirring, cook cauliflower florets 3 minutes.
- Mix in all remaining ingredients. Continue cooking until cream sauce thickens. Serve.

CALORIES PER SERVING: 217	
FAT: 22 g	CAL. FROM FAT: 91%
PROTEIN: 2 g	CHOLESTEROL: 77 mg
SODIUM: 130 mg	CARBOHYDRATES: 4 g

Florentine Cauliflower

4 SERVINGS

1 ½ cups	(375 mL) chicken broth
1 ½ cups	(375 mL) cauliflower florets
1	garlic clove, chopped
½ cup	(125 mL) spinach, finely shredded
	salt and pepper

- In a saucepan, mix chicken broth, cauliflower and garlic. Bring to a boil. Reduce heat. Half-cover saucepan. Simmer mixture 8 minutes or so.
- Add spinach. Season with salt and pepper, mixing well. Continue cooking 2 minutes or so. Serve.

CALORIES PER SERVING: 46	
FAT: 2 g	CAL. FROM FAT: 29%
PROTEIN: 2 g	CHOLESTEROL: 5 mg
SODIUM: 79 mg	CARBOHYDRATES: 7 g

Cauliflower with Mushrooms

4 SERVINGS

2 cups	(500 mL) cauliflower florets
¾ cup	(180 mL) canned cream of mushroom soup
¾ cup	(180 mL) milk
2 tbsp	(30 mL) Parmesan cheese, grated
1 tbsp	(15 mL) parsley, chopped
	fresh ground pepper

- In a saucepan filled with lightly-salted boiling water, blanch cauliflower florets 1 minute or so. Drain.
- In a saucepan, combine remaining ingredients. Bring to a boil. Reduce heat. Simmer 5 minutes. Add cauliflower florets. Continue cooking 4 minutes. Serve.

CALORIES PER SERVING: 104	
FAT: 6 g	CAL. FROM FAT: 52%
PROTEIN: 5 g	CHOLESTEROL: 9 mg
SODIUM: 479 mg	CARBOHYDRATES: 8 g

From top to bottom : Cauliflower in Cream Sauce, Florentine Cauliflower, Cauliflower with Mushrooms

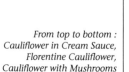

Cucumbers, Zucchini, Endives and Spinach

From top to bottom :
Egg-stuffed Cucumbers,
Zucchini Balls in Tomato Sauce,
Cream of Celery Zucchini

Egg-stuffed Cucumbers

4 SERVINGS

1	English cucumber
2	hard-boiled eggs, chopped
3 tbsp	(45 mL) mayonnaise
2 tsp	(10 mL) chili sauce
1 tbsp	(15 mL) parsley, chopped
	salt and pepper
1 tsp	(5 mL) pink peppercorns

- Trim ends off cucumber. Peel or flute cucumber. Cut into 2 equal sections. Slice each section in half lengthwise.

- With a spoon, scoop out seeds from cucumber sections.

- In a bowl, mix remaining ingredients. With a spoon or pastry bag, pipe egg mixture into cucumbers. Serve.

CALORIES PER SERVING: 128	
FAT: 11 *g*	CAL. FROM FAT: 74 %
PROTEIN: 4 *g*	CHOLESTEROL: 95 *mg*
SODIUM: 138 *mg*	CARBOHYDRATES: 5 *g*

Zucchini Balls in Tomato Sauce

4 SERVINGS

4	zucchini
1/2 cup	(125 mL) chicken broth
1/2 cup	(125 mL) tomato juice
1 tbsp	(15 mL) cornstarch
2 tbsp	(30 mL) cold water
	salt and pepper

- With a melon baller, shape zucchini into small balls.

- In a saucepan, bring to a boil chicken broth and tomato juice. Add zucchini. Cook 4 minutes.

- Dilute cornstarch in cold water. Fold into vegetable mixture. Continue cooking until sauce thickens. Serve.

CALORIES PER SERVING: 42	
FAT: 1 *g*	CAL. FROM FAT: 14 %
PROTEIN: 2 *g*	CHOLESTEROL: 2 *mg*
SODIUM: 165 *mg*	CARBOHYDRATES: 8 *g*

Cream of Celery Zucchini

8 SERVINGS

2 cups	(500 mL) zucchini, sliced
3/4 cup	(180 mL) canned cream of celery soup
3/4 cup	(180 mL) milk
1 tbsp	(15 mL) parsley, chopped
1 tsp	(5 mL) celery seeds
	pinch of nutmeg
	fresh ground pepper

- In a saucepan filled with lightly-salted boiling water, blanch zucchini 1 minute or so. Drain.

- In a saucepan, combine remaining ingredients. Bring to a boil. Reduce heat. Simmer 5 minutes. Add zucchini. Continue cooking 2 minutes. Serve.

CALORIES PER SERVING: 42	
FAT: 2 *g*	CAL. FROM FAT: 40 %
PROTEIN: 2 *g*	CHOLESTEROL: 6 *mg*
SODIUM: 194 *mg*	CARBOHYDRATES: 5 *g*

While cucumbers take on a new look, and zucchini and endives become "sophisticated", spinach has already had its moments of glory. Made famous by television's Popeye, spinach provides a good source of iron and folic acid. Since vitamin C helps absorption of the iron in spinach, we recommend that you serve citrus fruit in the same menu.

Pastis Endive

4 SERVINGS

3 tbsp	(45 mL) butter
5	heads of endive, minced
1/4 cup	(60 mL) onion, minced
1/4 cup	(60 mL) pastis
1/4 tsp	(1 mL) ground nutmeg
	salt and pepper

- In a frying pan, melt butter. Cook endives and onions 3 minutes or so.
- Add pastis and nutmeg. Season with salt and pepper, mixing well. Continue cooking until liquid has evaporated. Serve.

CALORIES PER SERVING: 227	
FAT: 10 *g*	CAL. FROM FAT: 41 %
PROTEIN: 7 *g*	CHOLESTEROL: 23 *mg*
SODIUM: 290 *mg*	CARBOHYDRATES: 24 *g*

Wilted Spinach with Mushrooms

4 SERVINGS

2 tbsp	(30 mL) butter
1	garlic clove, chopped
2 tbsp	(30 mL) French shallots, chopped
1 cup	(250 mL) mushrooms, quartered
1/2 cup	(125 mL) white vermouth
3 cups	(750 mL) spinach, washed, stalks removed
	salt and pepper

- In a large frying pan, melt butter. Cook garlic and shallots 2 minutes or so. Add mushrooms. Continue cooking 2 minutes.
- Pour vermouth into pan. Add spinach. Season with salt and pepper. While stirring, continue cooking until spinach is limp and liquid has almost all evaporated. Serve.

CALORIES PER SERVING: 115	
FAT: 6 *g*	CAL. FROM FAT: 65 %
PROTEIN: 2 *g*	CHOLESTEROL: 15 *mg*
SODIUM: 114 *mg*	CARBOHYDRATES: 6 *g*

Spinach with Sauce

4 SERVINGS

3/4 cup	(180 mL) vegetable juice
1	garlic clove, chopped
2 cups	(500 mL) spinach, finely shredded
2 tsp	(10 mL) cornstarch
4 tsp	(20 mL) cold water
1/4 tsp	(1 mL) ground nutmeg
	salt and pepper
1	hard-boiled egg, chopped

- In a saucepan, bring vegetable juice to a boil. Mix in garlic and spinach. Over low heat, continue cooking 2 minutes or so.
- Dilute cornstarch in cold water. Pour into saucepan, mixing well. Season. While stirring, continue cooking until sauce thickens. Divide spinach among 4 plates. Sprinkle with chopped egg.

CALORIES PER SERVING: 36	
FAT: 1 *g*	CAL. FROM FAT: 30 %
PROTEIN: 2g	CHOLESTEROL: 45 *mg*
SODIUM: 240 *mg*	CARBOHYDRATES: 4 *g*

From top to bottom :
Pastis Endive,
Wilted Spinach with Mushrooms,
Spinach with Sauce

Green beans, corn, turnip and parsnip

Hot Buttered Bean Salad

4 SERVINGS

³/₄ cup	(180 mL) cut green beans
³/₄ cup	(180 mL) cut yellow wax beans
2 tbsp	(30 mL) butter
¹/₄ cup	(60 mL) tomato, diced
1	garlic clove, chopped
1 tbsp	(15 mL) basil leaves, minced
1 tbsp	(15 mL) spinach leaves, minced
1 tbsp	(15 mL) watercress leaves, minced
	salt and pepper

- In a saucepan filled with lightly-salted boiling water, blanch string beans 1 minute. Drain.

- In a frying pan, melt butter. Cook beans 3 minutes or so. Add remaining ingredients. While stirring, continue cooking 4 minutes or so. Serve.

NUTRITION	
CALORIES PER SERVING: 67	
FAT: 6 g	CAL. FROM FAT: 73 %
PROTEIN: 1 g	CHOLESTEROL: 15 mg
SODIUM: 108 mg	CARBOHYDRATES: 4 g

Corn Stroganoff

4 SERVINGS

2 tbsp	(30 mL) butter
1 ¹/₂ cups	(375 mL) whole kernel corn
¹/₄ cup	(60 mL) onion, minced
1	garlic clove, chopped
3 tbsp	(45 mL) chicken broth
	salt and pepper
3 tbsp	(45 mL) sour cream

- In a frying pan, melt butter. While stirring, cook corn, onion and garlic 3 minutes or so.

- Add chicken broth. Season with salt and pepper. Fold in sour cream. Continue cooking 2 minutes. Serve.

NUTRITION	
CALORIES PER SERVING: 135	
FAT: 9 g	CAL. FROM FAT: 53 %
PROTEIN: 3 g	CHOLESTEROL: 21 mg
SODIUM: 150 mg	CARBOHYDRATES: 14 g

Two-tone Turnip

4 SERVINGS

³/₄ cup	(60 mL) turnip, diced
³/₄ cup	(60 mL) rabioles, diced
2 tbsp	(30 mL) butter
1 tbsp	(15 mL) honey
1 tbsp	(15 mL) toasted sesame seeds
	salt and pepper

- In a saucepan filled with lightly-salted boiling water, blanch turnip and rabioles 5 minutes or so. Drain.

- In a frying pan, melt butter. Cook turnip and rabioles 3 minutes or so. Add remaining ingredients. While stirring, continue cooking 3 minutes. Serve.

NUTRITION	
CALORIES PER SERVING: 103	
FAT: 7 g	CAL. FROM FAT: 58 %
PROTEIN: 1 g	CHOLESTEROL: 15 mg
SODIUM: 118 mg	CARBOHYDRATES: 10 g

Roasted Parsnip

4 SERVINGS

2 cups	(500 mL) parsnip, sliced
1 cup	(250 mL) peanut oil
1	garlic clove, chopped
2 tsp	(10 mL) celery seeds
	salt and pepper

- In a saucepan filled with lightly-salted boiling water, blanch sliced parsnip 1 minute or so. Drain. Dry with a paper towel.

- In a heavy-bottomed casserole dish, heat oil. Add garlic. In 2 steps, fry sliced parsnip until golden brown. Remove. Shake off excess oil. Transfer to a serving dish. Sprinkle with celery seeds. Season with salt and pepper. Serve.

NUTRITION	
CALORIES PER SERVING: 107	
FAT: 7 g	CAL. FROM FAT: 58 %
PROTEIN: 1 g	CHOLESTEROL: 0 mg
SODIUM: 11 mg	CARBOHYDRATES: 52 g

Clockwise from right :
Roasted Parsnip,
Two-tone Turnip,
Hot Buttered Bean Salad

Green or yellow string beans are as popular as turnips and a mainstay of our traditional vegetable stews. Lately, several exotic recipes have helped us rediscover their many uses.

As for parsnip, many remain unfamiliar with this close relative of the carrot and the turnip. Corn has no such problem : its color and vitamins have made it a favorite of North Americans. Corn is also a good source of vitamin C, potassium and fiber. Calorie-wise, it compares to the potato.

ONIONS AND LEEKS

Onion Rings with Sesame Seeds

6 SERVINGS	
2 cups	(500 mL) peanut oil
2 tbsp	(30 mL) sesame oil
4	onions, sliced
1/2 cup	(125 mL) whole wheat flour
2 tbsp	(30 mL) sesame seeds, ground
2	eggs, beaten

- In a deep-fryer, heat oils to 400 °F (205 °C).
- Separate onion into rings. Mix flour and sesame seeds. Dip each onion ring in beaten eggs. Dredge twice in flour and sesame seed mixture.
- Fry onion rings until golden brown. Serve.

CALORIES PER SERVING: 154	
FAT: 9 g	CAL. FROM FAT: 48%
PROTEIN: 1 g	CHOLESTEROL: 23 mg
SODIUM: 89 mg	CARBOHYDRATES: 20 g

Spicy Onions

4 SERVINGS	
3	onions
1 tbsp	(15 mL) olive oil
1/4 tsp	(1 mL) curry
1/4 tsp	(1 mL) paprika
1/4 tsp	(1 mL) onion, powder
1/4 tsp	(1 mL) garlic salt
1/4 tsp	(1 mL) parsley, chopped
	dash of Worcestershire sauce

- Cut each onion into 8 wedges.
- In a microwave-safe dish, mix all ingredients. Cook in oven 5 minutes, on HIGH. Stir once halfway through cooking. Let stand 2 minutes. Serve.

CALORIES PER SERVING: 74	
FAT: 4 g	CAL. FROM FAT: 42%
PROTEIN: 1 g	CHOLESTEROL: 0 mg
SODIUM: 5 mg	CARBOHYDRATES: 10 g

Candied Red Onions

4 SERVINGS	
3 tbsp	(45 mL) butter
1 1/2 cups	(375 mL) red onions, minced
1	garlic clove, chopped
1 tbsp	(15 mL) wine vinegar
2 tbsp	(30 mL) honey
2 tbsp	(30 mL) sugar

- In a heavy-bottomed casserole dish, melt butter. While stirring, cook onions and garlic 5 minutes or so.
- Mix in wine vinegar, honey and sugar. Over low heat, continue cooking 15 minutes. Stir occasionally. Once onions are thoroughly candied, remove from heat. Serve lukewarm or chilled.

CALORIES PER SERVING: 154	
FAT: 9 g	CAL. FROM FAT: 48%
PROTEIN: 1 g	CHOLESTEROL: 23 mg
SODIUM: 89 mg	CARBOHYDRATES: 20 g

From top to bottom :
Onion Rings with Sesame Seeds,
Spicy Onions,
Candied Red Onions

Jack-of-all-trades, the onion is included in almost all cooked recipes, bringing its distinctive flavor to meat, salad, pasta and other favorites. Why not try it on its own, as a side dish to accompany roasted fish, for example.

In their shape, leeks remind us of large green onions. While leeks first became popular as a main staple of our homemade soups, their strong flavor enhances more and more of our daily menu.

Leeks in Cream of Brie

4 SERVINGS

	whites of 6 leeks, cut into 4-inch (10 cm) lengths
2 tsp	(10 mL) butter
1 tbsp	(15 mL) onion, chopped
³/₄ cup	(180 mL) heavy cream
1 oz	(30 g) Brie cheese
	pinch of nutmeg
	salt and pepper

• In a saucepan filled with lightly-salted boiling water, blanch leeks 6 minutes or so. Drain. Set aside.

• In a frying pan, melt butter. Cook chopped onion 1 minute. Fold in cream. Continue cooking 2 minutes.

• Meanwhile, remove crust from Brie. Fold cheese into cream sauce. Season with nutmeg, salt and pepper. While stirring, continue cooking until Brie has completely melted. Reheat leeks in sauce. Serve.

CALORIES PER SERVING: 245	
FAT: 21 *g*	CAL. FROM FAT: 73 %
PROTEIN: 4 *g*	CHOLESTEROL: 73 *mg*
SODIUM: 142 *mg*	CARBOHYDRATES: 13 *g*

Wilted Leeks with Raisins

4 SERVINGS

2 cups	(500 mL) leeks, minced
2 tbsp	(30 mL) butter
¹/₄ cup	(60 mL) raisins
1 cup	(250 mL) white wine
2 tsp	(10 mL) chives, chopped
	salt and pepper

• In a saucepan filled with lightly-salted boiling water, blanch leeks 1 minute or so. Drain. Set aside.

• In a frying pan, melt butter. Lightly cook leeks 2 minutes. Add remaining ingredients. While stirring, continue cooking until liquid has all evaporated. Serve.

CALORIES PER SERVING: 132	
FAT: 6 *g*	CAL. FROM FAT: 53 %
PROTEIN: 1 *g*	CHOLESTEROL: 15 *mg*
SODIUM: 111 *mg*	CARBOHYDRATES: 11 *g*

Leeks Alfredo

4 SERVINGS

2 cups	(500 mL) leeks, minced
¹/₄ cup	(60 mL) bacon, minced
1 cup	(250 mL) béchamel sauce
2 tbsp	(30 mL) Parmesan cheese, grated
	salt and pepper

• In a saucepan filled with lightly-salted boiling water, blanch leeks 1 minute or so. Drain. Set aside.

• In a frying pan, cook bacon. Degrease pan. Cook leeks with bacon 1 minute. Add remaining ingredients. While stirring, cook until béchamel is hot and mixture is well-blended. Serve.

CALORIES PER SERVING: 201	
FAT: 13 *g*	CAL. FROM FAT: 59 %
PROTEIN: 9 *g*	CHOLESTEROL: 31 *mg*
SODIUM: 408 *mg*	CARBOHYDRATES: 12 *g*

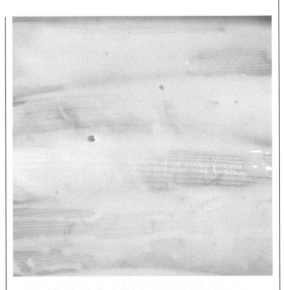

From top to bottom :
Leeks in Cream of Brie,
Wilted Leeks with Raisins,
Leeks Alfredo

GREEN PEAS AND BELL PEPPERS

Gourmet Peas Lyonnais

	4 SERVINGS
2 tbsp	(30 mL) butter
1/2 cup	(125 mL) onions, minced
1 1/2 cups	(375 mL) snow peas, minced
1/4 cup	(60 mL) chicken broth
1/4 cup	(60 mL) cooked bacon, crumbled
	pinch of rosemary
	pinch of thyme
	salt and pepper

- In a large frying pan, melt butter. Cook onions 1 minute. Mix in snow peas. While stirring, continue cooking 3 minutes or so.
- Add remaining ingredients, mixing well. Continue cooking 2 minutes. Serve.

CALORIES PER SERVING: 173	
FAT: 13 g	CAL. FROM FAT: 69%
PROTEIN: 7 g	CHOLESTEROL: 29 mg
SODIUM: 476 mg	CARBOHYDRATES: 7 g

Medley Extravaganza

	4 SERVINGS
1/4 cup	(60 mL) carrots
1/4 cup	(60 mL) turnip
1/4 cup	(60 mL) parsnip
1/4 cup	(60 mL) zucchini
1/4 cup	(60 mL) green peas
1/4 cup	(60 mL) whole kernel corn
	salt and pepper

- With a small melon baller, shape carrots, turnip, parsnip and zucchini into pearls.
- In a saucepan filled with lightly-salted boiling water, blanch vegetables 3 minutes or so. Drain. Season. Serve.

VARIATION
- Blanch vegetables only 1 minute. Cook in 2 tbsp (30 mL) butter 3 minutes. Season. Serve.

CALORIES PER SERVING: 27	
FAT: 1 g	CAL. FROM FAT: 5%
PROTEIN: 1 g	CHOLESTEROL: 0 mg
SODIUM: 53 mg	CARBOHYDRATES: 6 g

Green Peas in Piquant Sauce

	4 SERVINGS
2 cups	(500 mL) green peas
3/4 cup	(180 mL) chicken broth
2 tbsp	(30 mL) chili sauce
1/2 tsp	(2 mL) crushed red peppers
2	drops of Tabasco sauce
	pinch of salt
	paprika

- In a small saucepan, mix all ingredients, except paprika. Bring to a boil. Reduce heat. Simmer 5 minutes. Serve green peas sprinkled with paprika.

CALORIES PER SERVING: 78	
FAT: 1 g	CAL. FROM FAT: 12%
PROTEIN: 5 g	CHOLESTEROL: 2 mg
SODIUM: 48 mg	CARBOHYDRATES: 13 g

From top to bottom :
Gourmet Peas Lyonnais,
Medley Extravaganza,
Green Peas in Piquant Sauce

Over time, green peas have proven their versatility as the main ingredient of many dishes. Both fresh and frozen peas offer vivid color and good nutritional value ; they should be our first choice.

Bell peppers are a good source of vitamin C. Local markets now offer this favorite vegetable in its wide range of colors for a lively, exotic touch. Sweet or hot, fresh or cooked, bell peppers lend themselves readily to many dishes.

Lemony Green Bell Peppers

4 SERVINGS

2	green bell peppers, minced
2 tbsp	(30 mL) butter
3 tbsp	(45 mL) lemon juice
1 tbsp	(15 mL) lemon peel, grated
	salt and pepper

- In a saucepan filled with lightly-salted boiling water, blanch bell peppers 2 minutes or so. Drain. Set aside.
- In a frying pan, melt butter. Cook bell peppers 2 minutes. Add lemon juice and peel. Season with salt and pepper, mixing well. While stirring, continue cooking 2 minutes. Serve.

CALORIES PER SERVING: 62	
FAT: 6 g	CAL. FROM FAT: 78%
PROTEIN: 0 g	CHOLESTEROL: 15 mg
SODIUM: 103 mg	CARBOHYDRATES: 3 g

Roasted Bell Peppers

6 SERVINGS

1	green bell pepper
1	sweet red pepper
1	yellow pepper
½ cup	(125 mL) olive oil
3 tbsp	(45 mL) soy sauce
1	garlic clove, chopped
	fresh ground pepper

- Cut bell peppers into thick slices (one for each face of pepper).
- Mix all remaining ingredients. Marinate sliced bell peppers in mixture 20 minutes.
- Preheat barbecue or oven to BROIL.
- Remove bell peppers from marinade. Shake off excess liquid. Do not dry.
- Barbecue bell peppers 3 minutes each side or broil in oven 4 minutes each side. Baste with marinade twice during cooking. Serve.

CALORIES PER SERVING: 30	
FAT: 2 g	CAL. FROM FAT: 65%
PROTEIN: 0 g	CHOLESTEROL: 0 mg
SODIUM: 58 mg	CARBOHYDRATES: 2 g

Sautéed Bell Peppers

4 SERVINGS

1	green bell pepper, diced
1	sweet red pepper, diced
2 tbsp	(30 mL) butter
1	garlic clove, chopped
1 tsp	(5 mL) French shallot, chopped
	salt and pepper

- In a saucepan filled with lightly-salted boiling water, blanch bell peppers 1 minute or so. Drain. Set aside.
- In a frying pan, melt butter. Cook garlic and shallot 1 minute. Add bell peppers. Season with salt and pepper, mixing well. Continue cooking 2 minutes. Serve.

CALORIES PER SERVING: 59	
FAT: 6 g	CAL. FROM FAT: 84%
PROTEIN: 0 g	CHOLESTEROL: 15 mg
SODIUM: 103 mg	CARBOHYDRATES: 2 g

From top to bottom :
Lemony Green Bell Peppers,
Roasted Bell Peppers,
Sautéed Bell Peppers

POTATOES

From top to bottom :
Potatoes on a Bed of Bean Sprouts,
Ham and Potato Purée,
Sautéed Potatoes

Potatoes on a Bed of Bean Sprouts

4 SERVINGS	
1 ½ cups	(375 mL) chicken broth
1 ½ cups	(375 mL) potatoes, diced
¼ cup	(60 mL) pearl onions
1 tsp	(5 mL) tarragon, chopped
	fresh ground pepper
1 ½ cups	(375 mL) bean sprouts, blanched, hot

• In a saucepan, bring chicken broth to a boil. Add potatoes and onions. Cook around 6 minutes or until vegetables are tender. In the last minute of cooking, add tarragon and pepper.

• On 4 plates, arrange a bed of bean sprouts. Top with cooked vegetables. Sprinkle with hot chicken broth. Serve.

CALORIES PER SERVING: 104	
FAT: 2 g	CAL. FROM FAT: 14%
PROTEIN: 4 g	CHOLESTEROL: 5 mg
SODIUM: 54 mg	CARBOHYDRATES: 20 g

Ham and Potato Purée

AROUND 4 CUPS (1 L)	
1 lb	(450 g) potatoes, peeled
½ cup	(125 mL) cooked ham, ground
1 tbsp	(15 mL) chives, chopped
1 tbsp	(15 mL) parsley, chopped
½ tsp	(2 mL) salt
2 tbsp	(30 mL) butter
2 tbsp	(30 mL) milk
1	egg, beaten
¼ tsp	(1 mL) ground nutmeg
	salt and pepper

• Preheat oven to 300 °F (150 °C).

• Cut potatoes into large pieces. In a saucepan filled with lightly-salted boiling water, cook potatoes 12 minutes or so. Drain in a metal colander. Place colander on a baking sheet. Dry cooked vegetables in oven 10 minutes.

• In a bowl, mash potatoes. Add remaining ingredients. Mix to a smooth purée. Serve.

CALORIES PER SERVING: 216	
FAT: 13 g	CAL. FROM FAT: 54%
PROTEIN: 8 g	CHOLESTEROL: 81 mg
SODIUM: 748 mg	CARBOHYDRATES: 17 g

Sautéed Potatoes

4 SERVINGS	
2 cups	(500 mL) potatoes, diced
2 tbsp	(30 mL) peanut oil
1 tbsp	(15 mL) butter
½ cup	(125 mL) cooked bacon, crumbled
1	garlic clove, chopped
½ tsp	(1 mL) rosemary, chopped
1 tsp	(5 mL) parsley, chopped
	salt and pepper

• In a saucepan filled with lightly-salted boiling water, blanch potatoes 3 minutes or so. Drain. Pat dry.

• In a large frying pan, heat oil until smoky. Sauté potatoes, stirring often so they turn a slight golden color all over. Mix in remaining ingredients. While stirring, continue cooking until potatoes are nicely browned. Serve.

CALORIES PER SERVING: 156	
FAT: 10 g	CAL. FROM FAT: 55%
PROTEIN: 2 g	CHOLESTEROL: 8 mg
SODIUM: 34 mg	CARBOHYDRATES: 16 g

Economical, nutritious and versatile, potatoes are available all year round, and are a good source of potassium. When eaten with their skin, potatoes also provide necessary fiber.

Potatoes in Mornay Sauce

4 SERVINGS

2 cups	(500 mL) potatoes, sliced
3/4 cup	(180 mL) béchamel sauce
3 tbsp	(45 mL) Parmesan cheese, grated
1/4 tsp	(1 mL) sage, chopped
	salt and pepper

- In a saucepan filled with lightly-salted boiling water, blanch sliced potatoes 4 minutes or so. Drain.

- Meanwhile, in a saucepan, combine remaining ingredients. Bring to boiling point, removing from heat as soon as sauce starts to bubble.

- Mix in potatoes. Over very low heat, simmer 5 minutes or so. Serve.

CALORIES PER SERVING: 163	
FAT: 6 *g*	CAL. FROM FAT: 35 %
PROTEIN: 6 g	CHOLESTEROL: 20 *mg*
SODIUM: 197 *mg*	CARBOHYDRATES: 21 *g*

Oven Fries

4 SERVINGS

2 tbsp	(30 mL) peanut oil
1 tbsp	(15 mL) sesame oil
1/4 tsp	(1 mL) sea salt
1/8 tsp	(0.5 mL) fresh ground pepper
1/2 tsp	(2 mL) basil, chopped
1/2 tsp	(2 mL) chervil, chopped
1/2 tsp	(2 mL) paprika
3 cups	(750 mL) potatoes, cut into sticks

- Preheat oven to 425 °F (220 °C).

- In a large bowl, combine all ingredients, except potatoes. Mix well. Add potatoes. Turn over until potatoes are evenly coated with mixture.

- In a roasting pan, spread a single layer of potato sticks. Cook in oven around 30 minutes or until fries are browned. Turn over 3-4 times during cooking. Serve.

CALORIES PER SERVING: 232	
FAT: 19 *g*	CAL. FROM FAT: 73 %
PROTEIN: 2 g	CHOLESTEROL: 0 *mg*
SODIUM: 185 *mg*	CARBOHYDRATES: 15 *g*

Baked Potatoes

4 SERVINGS

4	medium-size potatoes
1/2 cup	(125 mL) plain yogurt
3 tbsp	(45 mL) pimento-stuffed olives, chopped
1 tsp	(5 mL) parsley, chopped
1 tbsp	(15 mL) green onions, chopped
	salt and pepper

- With a fork. prick potatoes 3-4 times. Place in the middle of a microwave-safe dish. Cook potatoes 14-16 minutes, on HIGH.

- Meanwhile, mix remaining ingredients. Once potatoes are cooked, cut one side of each potato crosswise. Pry apart. Spoon olive yogurt into the middle. Serve.

CALORIES PER SERVING: 239	
FAT: 2 *g*	CAL. FROM FAT: 17 %
PROTEIN: 7 g	CHOLESTEROL: 4 *mg*
SODIUM: 141 *mg*	CARBOHYDRATES: 50 *g*

From top to bottom :
Potatoes in Mornay Sauce,
Oven Fries,
Baked Potatoes

TOMATOES

Cherry Tomatoes Provençale

8 TOMATOES

3 tbsp	(45 mL) breadcrumbs
2 tsp	(10 mL) parsley, chopped
1	garlic clove, chopped
	salt and pepper
2 tsp	(10 mL) vegetable oil
8	cherry tomatoes, halved
2 tsp	(10 mL) Parmesan cheese, grated

- Preheat oven to 400 °F (205 °C).

- In a bowl, combine breadcrumbs, parsley, garlic, salt and pepper.

- Lighly coat each tomato half with oil, then cover with breadcrumb mixture, sprinkle with Parmesan and bake for 5 minutes.

NUTRITION	
CALORIES PER SERVING: 116	
FAT: 4 g	CAL. FROM FAT: 28 %
PROTEIN: 4 g	CHOLESTEROL: 1 mg
SODIUM: 83 mg	CARBOHYDRATES: 19 g

Tomatoes au Gratin

4 TO 6 SERVINGS

3 tbsp	(45 mL) olive oil
4	large tomatoes, cut into 1/2 inch (2 cm) thick slices
1 tbsp	(15 mL) oregano or marjoram
2 tbsp	(30 mL) capers
1/4 tsp	(1 mL) salt
	pepper
1/4 cup	(60 mL) breadcrumbs
1/4 cup	(60 mL) Parmesan cheese, grated

- Preheat oven to 450 °F (220 °C).

- Coat a baking with 1 tbsp (15 ml) olive oil and spread half the tomato slices in bottom, then sprinkle with oregano and add half the capers, Seasson with salt and pepper.

- Arrange rest of tomatoes and capers over mixture. Sprinkle with breadcrumbs and cheese, and coat with rest of olive oil. Bake for 15 minutes. Serve hot or cold.

NUTRITION	
CALORIES PER SERVING: 111	
FAT: 8 g	CAL. FROM FAT: 65 %
PROTEIN: 3 g	CHOLESTEROL: 3 mg
SODIUM: 215 mg	CARBOHYDRATES: 7 g

Garnished Tomatoes

6 SERVINGS

6	tomatoes
1/4 cup	(60 mL) broccoli florets, blanched
1/4 cup	(60 mL) cauliflower florets, blanched
1/4 cup	(60 mL) spinach leaves, shredded
1/4 cup	(60 mL) Mozzarella cheese, grated
1	garlic clove, chopped
2 tbsp	(30 mL) olive oil
	salt and pepper

- Preheat oven to 350 °F (175 °C).

- Slice off tops from tomatoes. With a spoon, scoop out pulp, reserving around 1/4 cup (60 mL) pulp.

- Mix reserved pulp with remaining ingredients. Stuff tomatoes with mixture. Cook in oven 20 minutes or so. Serve.

NUTRITION	
CALORIES PER SERVING: 83	
FAT: 6 g	CAL. FROM FAT: 62 %
PROTEIN: 2 g	CHOLESTEROL: 4 mg
SODIUM: 34 mg	CARBOHYDRATES: 6 g

Tomato Crêpes

4 SERVINGS

2	large tomatoes
3 tbsp	(45 mL) olive oil
3 tbsp	(45 mL) basil leaves, finely shredded
2 tbsp	(30 mL) black olives, chopped
	salt and pepper
16	small slices of Bocconcini cheese
4	small crêpes (p. 380)

- Cut each tomato into 8 slices.

- Mix oil, basil and olives. Season with salt and pepper.

- Spread sliced tomatoes and cheese on a large baking sheet. Sprinkle evenly with oil mixture. Let stand 30 minutes.

- In the middle of each crêpe, arrange 4 tomato slices and 4 cheese slices so they overlap. Fold crêpes. Serve cold, or warm in oven.

NUTRITION	
CALORIES PER SERVING: 258	
FAT: 22 g	CAL. FROM FAT: 76 %
PROTEIN: 4 g	CHOLESTEROL: 56 mg
SODIUM: 210 mg	CARBOHYDRATES: 12 g

From top to bottom :
Garnished Tomatoes,
Tomato Crêpes

The tomato's unique red color has made it a staple in the presentation of many dishes. Especially sweet and juicy in July and August, the tomato is the versatile companion of both our everyday meals and special-occasion menus.

BEANS, CONDIMENTS, CEREALS AND PASTA

From top to bottom :
Lima Beans with Basil,
Orange-flavored Couscous,
Pesto

Lima Beans with Basil

6 SERVINGS	
2 tbsp	(30 mL) butter
2 tbsp	(30 mL) green onions, chopped
14 oz	(398 mL) canned Lima beans, drained
3 tbsp	(45 mL) parsley, chopped
1 tsp	(5 mL) basil, chopped
	salt and pepper
1	tomato, diced

■ In a frying pan, melt butter. Cook green onions 1 minute. Add Lima beans, parsley and basil. Season. Continue cooking 5 minutes or so, stirring occasionally. Add diced tomato. Continue cooking 1 minute. Serve.

CALORIES PER SERVING: 126	
FAT: 4 g	CAL. FROM FAT: 28 %
PROTEIN: 6 g	CHOLESTEROL: 10 mg
SODIUM: 78 mg	CARBOHYDRATES: 10 g

Orange-flavored Couscous

6 SERVINGS	
1 cup	(250 mL) couscous
1/2 cup	(125 mL) orange juice
3/4 cup	(180 mL) water
1/2 tsp	(2 mL) orange peel
1 tbsp	(15 mL) sliced almond
1 tsp	(5 mL) honey
	pinch of cinnamon
	salt and pepper

■ In a microwave-safe dish, mix all ingredients. Let stand 8 minutes. Cover. Cook 6 minutes, on HIGH. Stir halfway through cooking.

■ Let stand 6 minutes. Fluff with a fork. Serve.

CALORIES PER SERVING: 135	
FAT: 1 g	CAL. FROM FAT: 6 %
PROTEIN: 4 g	CHOLESTEROL: 0 mg
SODIUM: 34 mg	CARBOHYDRATES: 27 g

Pesto

AROUND 1 CUP (250 mL)	
2 1/2 cups	(625 mL) basil leaves
3 tbsp	(45 mL) virgin olive oil
3 tbsp	(45 mL) pine nuts
3	garlic cloves, chopped
	salt and pepper
	roasted pine nuts

■ Wash, then spin-dry basil leaves.

■ In a large frying pan, heat 1 tbsp (15 mL) oil. Cook pine nuts and garlic 30 seconds or until lightly browned. Add basil. While stirring, continue cooking until basil leaves are limp. Remove from heat.

■ Add remaining oil. Season with salt and pepper. With a pestle or blender, purée mixture. Garnish with roasted pine nuts. Serve.

CALORIES PER CUP (250 mL): 590	
FAT: 60 g	CAL. FROM FAT: 85 %
PROTEIN: 12 g	CHOLESTEROL: 0 mg
SODIUM: 183 mg	CARBOHYDRATES: 12 g

By virtue of their fiber content, legumes and cereals have become the stars of health-food cooking. They provide a welcome health bonus and are featured in most foreign cuisines... Pesto, hummus and other dishes blend familiar ingredients in entirely new ways, for an exotic touch.

Pasta is not fattening ! If weight becomes a worry, make a habit of serving pasta with low-fat sauces.

Parsley Hash

AROUND 1 CUP (250 ML)	
3/4 cup	(180 mL) fresh parsley, chopped
3 tbsp	(45 mL) onion, chopped
3 tbsp	(45 mL) black olives, chopped
2	garlic cloves, chopped
2 tbsp	(30 mL) olive oil
	salt and pepper

- Mix all ingredients. Serve.

CALORIES PER CUP (250 ML): 356	
FAT: 30 *g*	CAL. FROM FAT: 86 %
PROTEIN: 0 *g*	CHOLESTEROL: 0 *mg*
SODIUM: 456 *mg*	CARBOHYDRATES: 12 *g*

Radish Yogurt Sauce

AROUND 1 CUP (250 ML)	
1/4 cup	(60 mL) radishes
3/4 cup	(180 mL) plain yogurt
1 tbsp	(15 mL) fennel leaves, chopped
2	dashes of Worcestershire sauce
2 tsp	(10 mL) lemon juice
	salt and pepper

- Coarsely chop radishes.
- Mix all ingredients. Serve.

CALORIES PER CUP (250 ML): 112	
FAT: 4 *g*	CAL. FROM FAT: 44 %
PROTEIN: 8 *g*	CHOLESTEROL: 20 *mg*
SODIUM: 276 *mg*	CARBOHYDRATES: 12 *g*

Hummus

AROUND 1 CUP (250 ML)	
3 tbsp	(45 mL) butter
3/4 cup	(180 mL) egg-plant, peeled, diced
3/4 cup	(180 mL) canned garbanzo beans, drained
2	garlic cloves, chopped
1/4 cup	(60 mL) onion, chopped
	salt and pepper

- In a large skillet, melt butter. Cook diced egg-plant and garbanzo beans 5 minutes or so. Add garlic and onion. Season with salt and pepper. While stirring, continue cooking 5 minutes.
- Remove from heat. Purée in blender. Serve.

CALORIES PER CUP (250 ML): 551	
FAT: 36 *g*	CAL. FROM FAT: 58 %
PROTEIN: 11 *g*	CHOLESTEROL: 92 *mg*
SODIUM: 889 *mg*	CARBOHYDRATES: 49 *g*

*From top to bottom :
Parsley Hash,
Radish Yogurt Sauce,
Hummus*

Egg-fried Rice

8 SERVINGS

2 cups	(500 mL) long-grain rice
2 cups	(500 mL) chicken broth
2 cups	(500 mL) water
2 tbsp	(30 mL) Worcestershire sauce
1 tbsp	(15 mL) margarine
2 tsp	(10 mL) salt
2	garlic cloves, chopped
3 tbsp	(45 mL) vegetable oil
3 cups	(750 mL) fresh vegetables (carrots, onions, peppers, celery, zucchini), chopped
5	eggs, lightly beaten

- In a large saucepan, combine first 7 ingredients. Bring to a boil. Reduce heat. Cover. Simmer 20 minutes.

- In a wok or large skillet, heat 1 tbsp (15 mL) oil. Stir-fry vegetables until tender-crisp. Remove. Set aside.

- Add 1 tbsp (15 mL) oil into wok. While stirring, cook eggs. Remove. Set aside with vegetables.

- Pour remaining oil into wok. Add rice, vegetables and eggs. Stir-fry to reheat mixture. Serve.

CALORIES PER SERVING: 320	
FAT: 11 g	CAL. FROM FAT: 30%
PROTEIN: 9 g	CHOLESTEROL: 118 mg
SODIUM: 845 mg	CARBOHYDRATES: 48 g

VARIATIONS

- When combining all ingredients, add 1 cup (250 mL) cooked ham, diced.

- When combining all ingredients, add 1 cup (250 mL) cooked salmon, diced, as shown above right.

- When combining all ingredients, add 1/4 cup (60 mL) chili sauce, as shown above left.

- Replace 1/2 cup (125 mL) long-grain rice with equal amount wild rice — previously soaked 6 hours in 1 cup (250 mL) water —, as shown above center.

Watercress and Apple Pasta

4 SERVINGS	
8 oz	(225 g) pasta, of your choice
1 tbsp	(15 mL) olive oil
1 tbsp	(15 mL) butter
1/2 cup	(125 mL) watercress, chopped
1/4 cup	(60 mL) apple, diced

- Cook pasta following package instructions. Drain.

- In a large frying pan, heat oil and melt butter. Lightly cook watercress and apple. Add pasta. Season, mixing well. Continue cooking until pasta is quite hot. Serve.

CALORIES PER SERVING: 270	
FAT: 7 g	CAL. FROM FAT: 24%
PROTEIN: 7 g	CHOLESTEROL: 8 mg
SODIUM: 79 mg	CARBOHYDRATES: 43 g

Recipe shown above left

Spinach Pasta

4 SERVINGS	
8 oz	(225 g) spinach pasta
1 tbsp	(15 mL) olive oil
1 tbsp	(15 mL) butter
1/2 cup	(125 mL) spinach leaves, finely shredded
1	garlic clove, chopped

- Cook pasta following package instructions. Drain.

- In a large frying pan, heat oil and melt butter. Lightly cook spinach and garlic. Add pasta. Season, mixing well. Continue cooking until pasta is quite hot. Serve.

CALORIES PER SERVING: 221	
FAT: 7 g	CAL. FROM FAT: 30%
PROTEIN: 7 g	CHOLESTEROL: 49 mg
SODIUM: 93 mg	CARBOHYDRATES: 32 g

Recipe shown above center

Tomato Pasta

4 SERVINGS	
8 oz	(225 g) pasta, of your choice
1 tbsp	(15 mL) olive oil
1 tbsp	(15 mL) butter
1/4 cup	(60 mL) tomato, diced
2 tbsp	(30 mL) chili sauce

- Cook pasta following package instructions. Drain.

- In a large frying pan, heat oil and melt butter. Lightly cook tomato. Add chili sauce and pasta. Season, mixing well. Continue cooking until pasta is quite hot. Serve.

CALORIES PER SERVING: 270	
FAT: 7 g	CAL. FROM FAT: 24%
PROTEIN: 7 g	CHOLESTEROL: 8 mg
SODIUM: 79 mg	CARBOHYDRATES: 43 g

Recipe shown above right

Three-seed Pasta

4 SERVINGS	
8 oz	(225 g) pasta, of your choice
1 tbsp	(15 mL) olive oil
1 tbsp	(15 mL) butter
1 tbsp	(15 mL) sesame seeds
1 tbsp	(15 mL) fennel seeds
1 tbsp	(15 mL) poppy seeds

- Cook pasta following package instructions. Drain.

- In a large frying pan, heat oil and melt butter. Lightly roast seeds. Add pasta. Season, mixing well. Continue cooking until pasta is quite hot. Serve.

CALORIES PER SERVING: 295	
FAT: 9 g	CAL. FROM FAT: 29%
PROTEIN: 8 g	CHOLESTEROL: 8 mg
SODIUM: 79 mg	CARBOHYDRATES: 44 g

Salads bring variety and color to your diet. Vegetables, rice, pasta, beans and legumes, nuts, and other ingredients enable you to create a salad as colourful as it is nutritious.

In this chapter you will find excellent suggestions for salad side dishes and salad meals. In fact, salads such as Garbanzo Bean Salad (p. 282) that contain protein such as meat, cheese or beans can be served as a main course.

SALADS

Watercress Salad

4 SERVINGS		
2 cups	(500 mL)	watercress
1/2 cup	(125 mL)	zucchini, minced
1/4 cup	(60 mL)	pickles, minced

Dressing

1/3 cup	(80 mL)	plain yogurt
1		garlic clove, chopped
1 tbsp	(15 mL)	lemon juice
1 tsp	(5 mL)	dill, chopped
		salt and pepper
4		curly lettuce leaves

- In a salad bowl, arrange watercress, sliced zucchini and pickles.
- In a bowl, mix yogurt, garlic, lemon juice and dill. Season with salt and pepper. Pour dressing over salad. Serve on a bed of lettuce.

NUTRITION	
CALORIES PER SERVING: 23	
FAT: 1 g	CAL. FROM FAT: 25 %
PROTEIN: 2 g	CHOLESTEROL: 2 mg
SODIUM: 251 mg	CARBOHYDRATES: 3 g

Garden Salad

4 SERVINGS		
1		head of Boston lettuce, hand-torn
3		tomatoes, diced
2		carrots, grated
1/4 cup	(60 mL)	cooked beets, sliced

Dressing

3 tbsp	(45 mL)	fresh basil, chopped
2 tbsp	(30 mL)	fennel leaves, chopped
1/4 cup	(60 mL)	virgin olive oil
3 tbsp	(45 mL)	cider vinegar
		salt and pepper

- In a salad bowl, mix vegetables.
- In a small bowl, mix dressing ingredients. Pour over vegetables. Serve.

NUTRITION	
CALORIES PER SERVING: 184	
FAT: 14 g	CAL. FROM FAT: 64 %
PROTEIN: 3 g	CHOLESTEROL: 0 mg
SODIUM: 81 mg	CARBOHYDRATES: 15 g

Endive Duet Salad

---
6 SERVINGS

1	head of curly endive, hand-torn
3	heads of endive, minced
2	green apples, diced

Dressing

2 tbsp	(30 mL) walnuts, chopped
1/4 cup	(60 mL) olive oil
2 tsp	(10 mL) hot mustard
2 tbsp	(30 mL) wine vinegar
1 oz	(30 mL) port wine
1 tsp	(5 mL) crushed red peppers
	salt and pepper

■ In a salad bowl, mix both kinds of endive. Cover with diced apples.

■ In a small airtight jar, combine dressing ingredients. Seal jar. Shake vigorously. Pour dressing over salad, tossing gently. Serve.

NUTRITION	
CALORIES PER SERVING: 164	
FAT: 10 *g*	CAL. FROM FAT: 53%
PROTEIN: 4 *g*	CHOLESTEROL: 0 *mg*
SODIUM: 116 *mg*	CARBOHYDRATES: 16 *g*

Easy Salad

---
6 SERVINGS
---

2 cups	(500 mL) spinach, stalks removed
1	head of Boston lettuce, hand-torn
2	green onions, chopped
6	cauliflower florets, blanched
4	radishes, minced
1	celery stalk, minced
6	broccoli florets, blanched

Dressing

1/4 cup	(60 mL) vinegar
1 tbsp	(15 mL) sugar
1/3 cup	(80 mL) ketchup
1/2 cup	(125 mL) vegetable oil
	salt and pepper

■ In a bowl, mix vegetables. Refrigerate 1 hour.

■ In an airtight container, mix dressing ingredients. Seal jar. Shake vigorously. Refrigerate 1 hour. Pour dressing over vegetables. Serve.

NUTRITION	
CALORIES PER SERVING: 285	
FAT: 19 *g*	CAL. FROM FAT: 55%
PROTEIN: 9 *g*	CHOLESTEROL: 0 *mg*
SODIUM: 273 *mg*	CARBOHYDRATES: 26 *g*

Garnished Green Salad

4 SERVINGS	
1	head of Boston lettuce, hand-torn
3 tbsp	(45 mL) onion, finely chopped
1	celery stalk, chopped
3 tbsp	(45 mL) green bell pepper, chopped
1	green onion, chopped
1 cup	(250 mL) alfalfa sprouts
1/4 cup	(60 mL) Cheddar cheese, diced
1	hard-boiled egg, sliced

Dressing

3 tbsp	(45 mL) mayonnaise
1 tbsp	(15 mL) vinegar
2 tbsp	(30 mL) sunflower oil
1 tbsp	(15 mL) brown sugar

- In a salad bowl, arrange vegetables, cheese and egg slices decoratively.
- In a jar, mix dressing ingredients. When ready to serve only, pour over salad.

NUTRITION	
CALORIES PER SERVING: 229	
FAT: 19 *g*	CAL. FROM FAT: 72%
PROTEIN: 6 *g*	CHOLESTEROL: 56 *mg*
SODIUM: 139 *mg*	CARBOHYDRATES: 11 *g*

Chilled Salad

8 SERVINGS	
1	small head of curly lettuce, hand-torn
10 oz	(280 g) fresh spinach, stalks removed
10 oz	(284 mL) canned green peas, drained
2 cups	(500 mL) cheese, grated
1	green onion, chopped
1 cup	(250 mL) cooked bacon, crumbled
6	hard-boiled eggs, sliced

Dressing

1 cup	(250 mL) mayonnaise
1 cup	(250 mL) sour cream or plain yogurt
3 tbsp	(45 mL) soy sauce
	salt and pepper

- In a rectangular dish, spread successive layers of lettuce, spinach, green peas, cheese, green onion, bacon and eggs.
- In a bowl, mix dressing ingredients. Pour over salad. Cover with aluminum foil. Refrigerate 12 hours. Serve.

NUTRITION	
CALORIES PER SERVING: 586	
FAT: 52 *g*	CAL. FROM FAT: 77%
PROTEIN: 24 *g*	CHOLESTEROL: 205 *mg*
SODIUM: 1389 *mg*	CARBOHYDRATES: 10 *g*

Caesar Salad

10-12 SERVINGS

8 oz	(225 g) bacon, diced
4	bread slices, diced

Dressing

6 tbsp	(90 mL) vegetable oil
2 tbsp	(30 mL) vinegar
1 tbsp	(15 mL) olive oil
1 tbsp	(15 mL) lemon juice
1 tsp	(5 mL) salt

1 tsp	(5 mL) tarragon
	pinch of sugar
	pinch of pepper
	pinch of dry mustard
	drop of Tabasco sauce
	dash of Worcestershire sauce
1 tsp	(5 mL) parsley
1 tsp	(5 mL) garlic, chopped
1	egg

2	heads of Romaine lettuce
3/4 cup	(180 mL) fresh Parmesan cheese, grated
1/2 cup	(125 mL) parsley, chopped
6	anchovy fillets, chopped
3	hard-boiled eggs, quartered

- In a frying pan, cook bacon until crisp. Drain. Set aside. In bacon drippings, toast diced bread.

- In a large bowl, mix dressing ingredients with a wooden spoon.

- When ready to serve only, tear lettuce over dressing.

- Sprinkle with Parmesan. Add bacon and croutons. Garnish with parsley, anchovies and quartered eggs. Toss. Serve.

NUTRITION	
CALORIES PER SERVING: 272	
FAT: 21 *g*	CAL. FROM FAT: 70 %
PROTEIN: 13 *g*	CHOLESTEROL: 84 *mg*
SODIUM: 742 *mg*	CARBOHYDRATES: 7 *g*

Surprise Salad

8-10 SERVINGS	
10 oz	(280 g) spinach, stalks removed
2	heads of Boston lettuce, hand-torn
4-5	French shallots, chopped
2	oranges, peeled, diced
1	avocado, peeled, pitted, diced

Dressing

1/4 cup	(60 mL) lemon juice
2 tsp	(10 mL) orange juice
1 tsp	(5 mL) orange peel, grated
2 tbsp	(30 mL) sugar
1 tsp	(5 mL) salt
1 tsp	(5 mL) dry mustard
1 tsp	(5 mL) paprika
1/2 tsp	(2 mL) celery seeds
2/3 cup	(160 mL) vegetable oil

- In a large serving dish, arrange fruit and vegetables decoratively.
- Mix dressing ingredients. Pour over fruit and vegetables. Serve.

NUTRITION	
CALORIES PER SERVING: 203	
FAT: 17 g	CAL. FROM FAT: 72%
PROTEIN: 3 g	CHOLESTEROL: 0 mg
SODIUM: 238 mg	CARBOHYDRATES: 0 g

Autumn Salad

6 SERVINGS	
2	tomatoes, diced
10 oz	(284 mL) canned palm hearts, drained, sliced into rounds
1	head of curly lettuce, hand-torn
1	small carrot, grated
1	celery stalk, minced
1	red apple, diced

Dressing

1/2 cup	(125 mL) plain yogurt
1 tsp	(5 mL) hot mustard
1 tbsp	(15 mL) olive oil
1 tsp	(5 mL) honey
1/2 tsp	(2 mL) wine vinegar
3 tbsp	(45 mL) lemon juice
	pinch of salt

- In a salad bowl, arrange vegetables and diced apple.
- In a small bowl, mix dressing ingredients. Pour over salad, tossing gently. Serve.

NUTRITION	
CALORIES PER SERVING: 126	
FAT: 3 g	CAL. FROM FAT: 21%
PROTEIN: 3 g	CHOLESTEROL: 2 mg
SODIUM: 66 mg	CARBOHYDRATES: 25 g

Mixed Salad

4 SERVINGS	
2 cups	(500 mL) bean sprouts, rinsed, drained
2 cups	(500 mL) spinach, stalks removed, finely shredded
1 cup	(250 mL) fresh mushrooms, sliced
1/2 cup	(125 mL) green onions, chopped
3	celery stalks, chopped
1/3 cup	(80 mL) raisins
3	parsley sprigs, chopped
1 cup	(250 mL) unsalted sunflower seeds

Dressing

3 tbsp	(45 mL) soy sauce
3 tbsp	(45 mL) vegetable oil
1	garlic clove, chopped
1 tsp	(5 mL) lemon juice

- In a salad bowl, mix vegetables, raisins and parsley. Add sunflower seeds.
- In a small bowl, mix dressing ingredients. When ready to serve only, pour over salad.

NUTRITION	
CALORIES PER SERVING: 403	
FAT: 22 g	CAL. FROM FAT: 44%
PROTEIN: 19 g	CHOLESTEROL: 0 mg
SODIUM: 1026 mg	CARBOHYDRATES: 44 g

Mushroom Salad Florentine

4 SERVINGS	
3 cups	(750 mL) spinach, stalks removed
1 cup	(250 mL) mushrooms, minced

Dressing

3 tbsp	(45 mL) lemon juice
2 tsp	(10 mL) olive oil
1/2 tsp	(2 mL) fresh basil, chopped
1/2 tsp	(2 mL) sugar
1/2	garlic clove, chopped
1/4 tsp	(1 mL) pepper
1 tsp	(5 mL) hot mustard
1/8 tsp	(0.5 mL) salt

- In a salad bowl, mix spinach and mushrooms.
- In a small bowl, mix dressing ingredients. Pour over vegetables. Toss salad. Serve.

NUTRITION	
CALORIES PER SERVING: 37	
FAT: 2 g	CAL. FROM FAT: 53%
PROTEIN: 1 g	CHOLESTEROL: 0 mg
SODIUM: 1027 mg	CARBOHYDRATES: 44 g

From top to bottom :
Autumn Salad,
Surprise Salad,
Mixed Salad

Cole Slaw

10 SERVINGS

Dressing

¹/₂ cup	(125 mL)	vegetable oil
¹/₂ cup	(125 mL)	vinegar
¹/₄ cup	(60 mL)	granulated sugar
1 tsp	(5 mL)	prepared mustard
1 tsp	(5 mL)	salt
1 tsp	(5 mL)	celery seeds
1		large head of cabbage, finely chopped
1		onion, sliced into rings
2		carrots, grated
1 tbsp	(15 mL)	parsley, finely chopped

- In a 5-cup (1.25 L) saucepan, bring dressing ingredients to a boil. Simmer 1 minute. Let cool. Refrigerate 2 hours before serving.

- In a salad bowl, mix vegetables and parsley. Pour dressing over cole slaw. Serve.

NUTRITION	
CALORIES PER SERVING: 143	
FAT: 11 *g*	CAL. FROM FAT: 67%
PROTEIN: 1 *g*	CHOLESTEROL: 0 *mg*
SODIUM: 241 *mg*	CARBOHYDRATES: 11 *g*

Recipe shown above

Jellied Broccoli Ring

4 SERVINGS

3 oz	(90 g)	lemon jelly powder
1 ¹/₄ cups	(300 mL)	boiling water
3 tbsp	(45 mL)	vinegar
2 tsp	(10 mL)	sugar
3 tbsp	(45 mL)	commercial Italian dressing
1 ¹/₂ cups	(375 mL)	broccoli florets
¹/₄ cup	(60 mL)	celery, finely chopped
2 tbsp	(30 mL)	onion, finely chopped
		salt, pepper and paprika
		lettuce leaves
1		tomato, quartered

- In a bowl, dissolve jelly powder in boiling water. Let cool. Add vinegar, sugar and dressing. Stirring occasionally, refrigerate until jelly sets to an egg white consistency. Add broccoli, celery, onion, salt, pepper and paprika.

- In a ring mold oiled, then rinsed under cold water, pour mixture. Refrigerate around 2 hours or until mixture has set.

- Unmold on a bed of lettuce. Garnish with tomato wedges. Serve as a salad or as a condiment to accompany cold cuts.

NUTRITION	
CALORIES PER SERVING: 165	
FAT: 6 *g*	CAL. FROM FAT: 29%
PROTEIN: 4 *g*	CHOLESTEROL: 0 *mg*
SODIUM: 204 *mg*	CARBOHYDRATES: 27 *g*

Exotic Eggplant Salad

4 SERVINGS	

Dressing

1 cup	(250 mL) sour cream
1/2 tsp	(2 mL) hot mustard
1 tsp	(5 mL) lemon juice
1/2	garlic clove, crushed pinch of pepper
1/4 tsp	(1 mL) salt
1	fresh pineapple
2 tbsp	(30 mL) butter
2 1/2 cups	(625 mL) unpeeled eggplant, diced
2 1/2 cups	(625 mL) cooked rice, chilled
1 cup	(250 mL) celery, sliced
1/2 cup	(125 mL) green onions, chopped

- In a bowl, mix dressing ingredients. Set aside.
- Cut pineapple lengthwise, starting from crown. Remove core (hard center). Scoop out pulp, reserving shells intact. Dice pulp.
- In a skillet, melt butter. Cook eggplant until slightly browned.
- In a large bowl, mix diced pineapple and eggplant with rice, celery and green onions. Fold in dressing, mixing well. Spoon into pineapple shells.
- Cut into servings in front of guests. Serve.

NUTRITION	
CALORIES PER SERVING: 441	
FAT: 19 *g*	CAL. FROM FAT: 38 %
PROTEIN: 7 *g*	CHOLESTEROL: 41 *mg*
SODIUM: 260 *mg*	CARBOHYDRATES: 64 *g*

Fruit Salad

6-8 SERVINGS	

Dressing

1/2 cup	(125 mL) raspberry vinegar
1/4 cup	(60 mL) vegetable oil
1/4 cup	(60 mL) liquid honey
1 tbsp	(15 mL) lime juice
2 cups	(500 mL) spinach, stalks removed
1	small head of Romaine lettuce, hand-torn
1	head of Boston lettuce, hand-torn
1 1/2 cups	(375 mL) pineapple, in chunks
1/2	cantaloupe, shaped into small balls
3	grapefruit, peeled, sectioned
1 1/2 cups	(375 mL) seedless green grapes
2	apples, diced
1 cup	(250 mL) strawberries or raspberries
3/4 cup	(180 mL) ham or Prosciutto, julienned

- In a small bowl, mix dressing ingredients. Set aside.
- In a glass bowl, arrange a bed of spinach and lettuce. Nestle fruit and ham on top.
- When ready to serve only, pour raspberry dressing over salad. Serve.

NUTRITION	
CALORIES PER SERVING: 225	
FAT: 8 *g*	CAL. FROM FAT: 30 %
PROTEIN: 6 *g*	CHOLESTEROL: 6 *mg*
SODIUM: 207 *mg*	CARBOHYDRATES: 37 *g*

Corn Salad

4-6 SERVINGS		

Dressing

1/2 cup	(125 mL) mayonnaise
2 tbsp	(30 mL) milk
2 tbsp	(30 mL) vinegar
2 tbsp	(30 mL) sugar
	salt and pepper
14 oz	(398 mL) canned whole kernel corn, drained
1/2 cup	(125 mL) green bell pepper, diced
1/2 cup	(125 mL) sweet red pepper, diced
1/2 cup	(125 mL) celery, minced into diagonal slices
1	carrot, grated
3	green onions, chopped

- In a bowl, mix dressing ingredients. Set aside.
- In a salad bowl, mix vegetables. Pour dressing over salad. Toss. Serve.

NUTRITION	
CALORIES PER SERVING: 238	
FAT: 17 g	CAL. FROM FAT: 57%
PROTEIN: 4 g	CHOLESTEROL: 7 mg
SODIUM: 171 mg	CARBOHYDRATES: 24 g

Vegetable Salad

8-10 SERVINGS		

Dressing

1 cup	(250 mL) granulated sugar
1 cup	(250 mL) vinegar
3/4 cup	(180 mL) vegetable oil
1 tbsp	(15 mL) prepared mustard
1 tsp	(5 mL) celery seeds
1 tsp	(5 mL) salt
1/2 cup	(125 mL) broccoli florets
1/2 cup	(125 mL) cauliflower florets
1/4 cup	(60 mL) green bell pepper, diced
1	carrot, sliced
1 cup	(250 mL) mushrooms, quartered
1/2 cup	(125 mL) cucumber, sliced
1/4 cup	(60 mL) onion, chopped
1	head of red cabbage, minced

- In a small saucepan, combine dressing ingredients. Bring to a boil. Let cool 30 minutes or so. Set aside.
- In a saucepan filled with lightly-salted boiling water, blanch broccoli, cauliflower, bell pepper and carrot 1 minute. Drain. Let cool.
- In a salad bowl, mix all vegetables. Pour dressing over salad. Serve.

NUTRITION	
CALORIES PER SERVING: 257	
FAT: 17 g	CAL. FROM FAT: 56%
PROTEIN: 2 g	CHOLESTEROL: 0 mg
SODIUM: 856 mg	CARBOHYDRATES: 50 g

Asparagus Salad

4 SERVINGS		

Dressing

1/2 cup	(125 mL) corn oil
1/4 cup	(60 mL) lemon juice
3 tbsp	(45 mL) wine vinegar
1 tsp	(5 mL) hot mustard
1 tsp	(5 mL) French shallots, finely chopped
	salt and pepper
1 lb	(450 g) green asparagus tips, peeled, trimmed 1 inch (2.5 cm) from base

- In a bowl, mix dressing ingredients. Set aside.
- In a saucepan, pour 2 inches (5 cm) cold water. Lightly season with salt. Bring to a boil. Add asparagus. Half-cover saucepan. Over moderate heat, cook 10 minutes. Drain.
- On a serving dish, arrange asparagus. Coat with dressing. Serve.

NUTRITION	
CALORIES PER SERVING: 265	
FAT: 27 g	CAL. FROM FAT: 89%
PROTEIN: 2 g	CHOLESTEROL: 0 mg
SODIUM: 62 mg	CARBOHYDRATES: 6 g

Potato Salad

4-6 SERVINGS		

3 cups	(750 mL) potatoes, cooked in their skin, diced
1 cup	(250 mL) celery, diced
3 tbsp	(45 mL) red onion, chopped
1/4 cup	(60 mL) parsley, finely chopped
1/4 cup	(60 mL) sweet pickles, chopped
3/4 cup	(180 mL) mayonnaise
2 tsp	(10 mL) salt
1/4 tsp	(1 mL) paprika

- In a bowl, mix ingredients. Serve.

NUTRITION	
CALORIES PER SERVING: 286	
FAT: 24 g	CAL. FROM FAT: 70%
PROTEIN: 2 g	CHOLESTEROL: 10 mg
SODIUM: 982 mg	CARBOHYDRATES: 21 g

Clockwise from upper left :
Vegetable Salad,
Corn Salad,
Potato Salad

Five-Vegetable Rice Salad

4 SERVINGS	
1 cup	(250 mL) cooked rice
3/4 cup	(180 mL) carrots, chopped
1/4 cup	(60 mL) celery, finely chopped
1/4 cup	(60 mL) mushrooms, finely chopped
1/4 cup	(60 mL) green bell pepper, finely chopped
1/4 cup	(60 mL) sweet red pepper, chopped
1/2 tsp	(2 mL) celery salt
1/2 tsp	(2 mL) curry powder
1/2 tsp	(2 mL) garlic salt
	fresh ground pepper

Dressing

2 tbsp	(30 mL) mayonnaise
1 tsp	(5 mL) water
2 tsp	(10 mL) prepared mustard

- In a large bowl, mix rice, vegetables and seasonings.
- In a small bowl, mix dressing ingredients. Pour over rice and vegetables. Serve.

NUTRITION	
CALORIES PER SERVING: 128	
FAT: 6 g	CAL. FROM FAT: 43 %
PROTEIN: 2 g	CHOLESTEROL: 2 mg
SODIUM: 538 mg	CARBOHYDRATES: 17 g

Crispy-crunchy Salad

4-6 SERVINGS	
2 cups	(500 mL) cooked rice
2 cups	(500 mL) spinach, finely shredded
1 cup	(250 mL) bean sprouts
3	celery stalks, minced into diagonal slices
1 cup	(250 mL) mushrooms, quartered
1	green bell pepper, cut into strips
1/2 cup	(125 mL) green onions, chopped
1 cup	(250 mL) peanuts
1/3 cup	(80 mL) raisins
3	parsley sprigs, chopped

Dressing

1/2 cup	(125 mL) peanut oil
1/4 cup	(60 mL) soy sauce
1	garlic clove, crushed
1/4 tsp	(1 mL) celery pepper

- In a large bowl, mix all ingredients, except for dressing.
- In a small bowl, mix dressing ingredients.
- Approximately 30 minutes before serving, pour dressing over salad. Serve.

NUTRITION	
CALORIES PER SERVING: 517	
FAT: 32 g	CAL. FROM FAT: 52 %
PROTEIN: 17 g	CHOLESTEROL: 0 mg
SODIUM: 856 mg	CARBOHYDRATES: 50 g

Brown Rice Salad

6-8 SERVINGS	
3 cups	(750 mL) cooked brown rice, drained
1/2 cup	(125 mL) green onions, chopped
1 cup	(250 mL) zucchini, cut into rounds, blanched
10 oz	(284 mL) canned green peas, drained

Dressing

1/2 cup	(125 mL) vegetable oil
2 tbsp	(30 mL) soy sauce
1 tbsp	(15 mL) vinegar
2 tsp	(10 mL) curry powder
1 tsp	(5 mL) celery seeds
1 tsp	(5 mL) salt

- In a bowl, mix rice and vegetables.
- In a small bowl, mix dressing ingredients. Pour over rice and vegetables. Refrigerate 4 hours. Serve chilled.

NUTRITION	
CALORIES PER SERVING: 229	
FAT: 15 *g*	CAL. FROM FAT: 56 %
PROTEIN: 3 *g*	CHOLESTEROL: 0 *mg*
SODIUM: 624 *mg*	CARBOHYDRATES: 22 *g*

Rice Salad with Cottage Cheese

6-8 SERVINGS	
3 cups	(750 mL) cooked rice
2	carrots, grated
1/4 cup	(60 mL) celery, finely chopped
1/4 cup	(60 mL) sweet red pepper, diced
1/4 cup	(60 mL) parsley, chopped

Dressing

1 cup	(250 mL) cottage cheese
1 cup	(250 mL) sour cream salt and pepper

- In a salad bowl, mix rice, vegetables and parsley.
- In a small bowl, mix dressing ingredients. Pour over salad, mixing well. Serve.

NUTRITION	
CALORIES PER SERVING: 188	
FAT: 7 *g*	CAL. FROM FAT: 33 %
PROTEIN: 7 *g*	CHOLESTEROL: 15 *mg*
SODIUM: 163 *mg*	CARBOHYDRATES: 24 *g*

Recipe shown above

Garbanzo Bean Salad

---

2 SERVINGS

1/2 cup	(125 mL) canned garbanzo beans, drained
1/2 cup	(125 mL) celery, chopped
1/2 cup	(125 mL) tomatoes, chopped
1/2 cup	(125 mL) cucumber, peeled, seeded, chopped
2 tbsp	(30 mL) wine vinegar
1 tbsp	(15 mL) fresh parsley, chopped
1 tbsp	(15 mL) fresh lemon juice
2 tsp	(10 mL) vegetable oil
1	garlic clove, chopped or
1/8 tsp	(0.5 mL) garlic powder
1/2 tsp	(2 mL) hot mustard
	salt and pepper

- In a salad bowl, mix all ingredients.
- Cover. Stirring occasionally, refrigerate until salad is chilled. Serve.

NUTRITION	
CALORIES PER SERVING: 143	
FAT: 6 g	CAL. FROM FAT: 33 %
PROTEIN: 4 g	CHOLESTEROL: 0 mg
SODIUM: 322 mg	CARBOHYDRATES: 21 g

Red Kidney Bean Salad

4-6 SERVINGS

Dressing

1 tbsp	(15 mL) rice vinegar
1 tbsp	(15 mL) fresh lime juice
1 tsp	(5 mL) honey
1 tsp	(5 mL) vegetable oil
	salt and pepper
1 cup	(250 mL) canned red kidney beans, drained
1	orange, peeled, sectioned
1/4 cup	(60 mL) red onion, sliced, in rings
1/4 cup	(60 mL) celery, sliced
1/4 cup	(60 mL) green bell pepper, diced
1/4 cup	(60 mL) sweet red pepper, diced
8	lettuce leaves

- In a small bowl, mix dressing ingredients.
- In a medium-size bowl, mix beans, orange, onion, celery and bell peppers.
- Line a serving dish with lettuce leaves. Pile bean salad into the middle. Pour dressing on top. Serve.

NUTRITION	
CALORIES PER SERVING: 64	
FAT: 1 g	CAL. FROM FAT: 13 %
PROTEIN: 3 g	CHOLESTEROL: 0 mg
SODIUM: 181 mg	CARBOHYDRATES: 12 g

Italian Salad

8-10 SERVINGS

1 1/2 cups	(375 mL) medium-size pasta shells, cooked, cooled
1 cup	(250 mL) cucumber, halved lengthwise, sliced
1 cup	(250 mL) cooked ham, cut into strips
1/2 cup	(125 mL) celery, sliced
1/4 cup	(60 mL) green onions, chopped
1/2 cup	(125 mL) commercial creamy Italian dressing
1	head of lettuce, hand-torn
3	heads of endive, minced
1	tomato, quartered
2	Mozzarella cheese slices, cut into strips
	Parmesan cheese, grated

- In a bowl, combine pasta, cucumber, ham, celery and green onions. Mix with a little dressing. Refrigerate.
- When ready to serve only, place lettuce and endive into a salad bowl. Add pasta mixture. Toss gently. Garnish with tomato wedges and cheese strips. Sprinkle with Parmesan. Serve dressing on the side.

NUTRITION	
CALORIES PER SERVING: 251	
FAT: 17 g	CAL. FROM FAT: 59%
PROTEIN: 12 g	CHOLESTEROL: 37 mg
SODIUM: 518 mg	CARBOHYDRATES: 14 g

Salmon Salad

4-6 SERVINGS

1 cup	(250 mL) fusilli or large spirals
1 1/2 cups	(375 mL) frozen green peas, rinsed, drained
1 cup	(250 mL) Swiss cheese, diced
7 1/2 oz	(213 mL) canned red salmon, drained, in pieces
1/2 cup	(125 mL) carrot, grated
1/2 cup	(125 mL) commercial creamy cucumber dressing

- Cook pasta following package instructions. Drain. Rinse under cold water.
- In a large bowl, gently toss all ingredients. Serve.

NUTRITION	
CALORIES PER SERVING: 316	
FAT: 19 g	CAL. FROM FAT: 53%
PROTEIN: 17 g	CHOLESTEROL: 38 mg
SODIUM: 531 mg	CARBOHYDRATES: 21 g

Adults have to take two to four portions of dairy products daily.

Cheeses represent an excellent source of protein and calcium. Certain cheeses contain a higher amount of fat and should be consumed in moderation. The fat content of cheese is almost always indicated on the packaging.

The cheese trays and recipes that are presented to you in this chapter invite you to experiment with cheese as a menu addition.

CHEESES

CHEESE BOARDS

Cheeses fall into 7 types or " families " which are based on texture and sharpness : fresh (cottage, ricotta...), soft (Brie, Camembert, Livarot, Munster...), semi-soft (Oka, Saint-Paulin...), Hard (Cheddar, Emmenthal, Gouda, Gruyère, Jarlsberg...), Hard-grating (Parmesan, Romano...), Blue (Danish Blue, Cambozola, Gorgonzola, Roquefort...) and Goat cheeses.

A cheese board is the best way to experiment with cheese at any time of the year, and is suitable for any occasion.

When preparing your cheese board, allow 2-3 oz (60-90 g) of cheese for each guest. Add up servings, then divide by the total number of cheeses you plan to serve. This simple calculation will tell you the exact amount of cheese needed.

The cheese boards presented here follow every golden rule, varying tastes and textures for distinct yet pleasing contrasts.

A cheese board with bread, crackers and fresh fruit will add that exciting touch to any family meal or friendly get-together.

THREE-CHEESE BOARD
- Brie
- Roquefort
- Oka

FOUR-CHEESE BOARD
- Camembert
- Danish Blue
- Goat cheese
- Saint-Paulin

FIVE-CHEESE BOARD
- Aged Cheddar
- Cambozola
- Goat cheese
- Munster
- Saint-André

FIVE-CHEESE BOARD
- Livarot
- Emmenthal
- Gouda
- Black-pepper Rondelé
- Gorgonzola

SIX-CHEESE BOARD
- Brie
- Goat cheese
- Danish Blue
- Oka
- Gruyère
- Saint-Paulin

VERY SHARP CHEESE BOARD
- Roquefort
- Maroilles
- Crottin de chèvre
- Cambozola

MILD CHEESE BOARD
- Mild Cheddar
- Mixed Herb double cream cheese
- Saint-Paulin
- Jarlsberg

Herb and Oil Goat Cheese

4 SERVINGS

1 cup	(250 mL) virgin olive oil
1	small fresh rosemary sprig
1	garlic clove, chopped
1	fresh thyme sprig
3	fresh tarragon sprigs
1/4 tsp	(1 mL) crushed red peppers
1/8 tsp	(0.5 mL) fresh ground pepper
4	2-oz (60 g) goat cheese slices

- In a jar, mix all ingredients, except goat cheese.
- Place sliced cheese into seasoned oil so that it is coated all over. If needed, add a little oil.
- Marinate cheese 4-10 days before serving.

NUTRITION	
CALORIES PER SERVING: 333	
FAT: 27 g	CAL. FROM FAT: 73%
PROTEIN: 18 g	CHOLESTEROL: 60 mg
SODIUM: 200 mg	CARBOHYDRATES: 5 g

Sweet Brie

4 SERVINGS

4	2-oz (60 g) Brie cheese wedges
1/4 cup	(60 mL) clover honey
1/4 cup	(60 mL) walnuts, coarsely chopped

- Preheat oven to BROIL.
- Place a wedge of Brie in each of 4 individual baking dishes. Drizzle 1 tbsp (15 mL) clover honey over cheese. Sprinkle with chopped walnuts.
- Broil in oven around 4 minutes or until cheese wedges have half-melted. Serve.

NUTRITION	
CALORIES PER SERVING: 265	
FAT: 17 g	CAL. FROM FAT: 56%
PROTEIN: 12 g	CHOLESTEROL: 57 mg
SODIUM: 358 mg	CARBOHYDRATES: 18 g

Marinated Cheese

4 SERVINGS

4 oz	(115 g) Emmenthal cheese, diced
4 oz	(115 g) Mozzarella cheese, diced
1 cup	(250 mL) rosé wine
2 oz	(60 mL) port wine
1 oz	(30 mL) blackcurrant liqueur

- In a jar, combine all ingredients. Marinate 4-7 days.
- Drain diced cheeses. Serve.

NUTRITION	
CALORIES PER SERVING: 283	
FAT: 15 g	CAL. FROM FAT: 62%
PROTEIN: 14 g	CHOLESTEROL: 51 mg
SODIUM: 195 mg	CARBOHYDRATES: 6 g

Blue Cheese Mashed in Port Wine

4 SERVINGS

4	2-oz (60 g) Blue cheese wedges
1/2 cup	(125 mL) spinach, finely shredded
	fresh ground pepper
4	1-oz (30 mL) glasses of port wine

- On 4 salad plates, place 1 wedge Blue cheese. Garnish on one side with shredded spinach. Season with pepper, according to the individual preference of each guest.
- Serve port wine so guests can pour a little wine over cheese, then lightly mash it with a fork. Cheese is to be enjoyed while sipping remaining port wine.

NUTRITION	
CALORIES PER SERVING: 246	
FAT: 16 g	CAL. FROM FAT: 68%
PROTEIN: 12 g	CHOLESTEROL: 43 mg
SODIUM: 796 mg	CARBOHYDRATES: 5 g

Clockwise from upper left :
Herb and Oil Goat Cheese,
Blue Cheese Mashed in Port Wine,
Sweet Brie

DESSERTS AND PASTRIES

Do we have to reject pies, cakes, and sweets under the pretext that they are rich in fat and calories? People who are health conscious are asking themselves this question. As far as we are concerned, desserts can be part of a nutritious diet, if we indulge in small portions, savoring every bite.

Desserts make our meal more enjoyable. For better nutrition, choose selections with a fruit or dairy base, reserving the creamy desserts for special occasions. Picking desserts which are low in fat and sugar also helps to maintain a nutritious menu.

We can often reduce the sugar in a recipe by one-third without altering the texture and quality of the dessert. It is more difficult, however, to reduce the fat as it imparts tenderness and lightness.

Even if dieticians recommend fresh fruit to complete the meal, they are not opposed when we give in to temptation… with moderation!

C akes and spongecakes
are offered in this
section. Indulge without
remorse in the Sugarless
Tomato Cake (p. 306) or the
Applesauce Cake (p. 304).

As for other desserts, it
is "wise", notably in terms
of counting calories, to
avoid whipped cream.
Limit the quantity of nuts
or reduce by half the
mayonnaise, replacing it
with natural yogurt.

We can also use light
cream cheese and skim
milk in all the desserts that
call for these ingredients,
therefore reducing fat
content and calories.

CAKES

Spongecakes

Vanilla Spongecake, Basic Recipe

1 SPONGECAKE	
5	eggs
3/4 cup	(180 mL) sugar
1 cup	(250 mL) all-purpose flour
1/2 tsp	(2 mL) baking powder
3 tbsp	(45 mL) butter, melted
1 tsp	(5 mL) vanilla extract

NUTRITION	
CALORIES PER SERVING: 209	
FAT: 7 g	CAL. FROM FAT: 31%
PROTEIN: 5 g	CHOLESTEROL: 126 mg
SODIUM: 100 mg	CARBOHYDRATES: 31 g

- Preheat oven to 350 °F (175 °C). Butter and flour a 9-inch (23 cm) springform cake pan. Set aside.

- Place a stainless-steel bowl over a saucepan filled with simmering hot water. In bowl, beat eggs and sugar 5 minutes or until mixture thickens. Off heat, continue beating until mixture cools slightly. Set aside.

- In a second bowl, sift flour and baking powder. Fold into beaten egg mixture.

- With a spatula or whisk, gently fold in melted butter and vanilla extract. Pour batter into cake pan.

- Bake in oven 25-35 minutes. Remove from oven. Detach cake from pan by running a small knife around sides. Let cool 5 minutes. Undo cake pan. Turn out cake onto a wire rack or cookie sheet sprinkled with sugar. Let stand until cold.

VARIATIONS

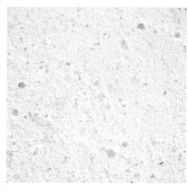

LEMON SPONGECAKE

- Replace vanilla with 1 tsp (5 mL) grated lemon peel, 1 tbsp (15 mL) lemon juice and 2 drops yellow food coloring.

ORANGE SPONGECAKE

- Replace vanilla with 2 tsp (10 mL) grated orange peel, 1/2 tsp (2 mL) orange blossom or 1 tbsp (15 mL) orange juice. Add 2 drops orange food coloring (optional).

COFFEE SPONGECAKE

- To butter, add 2 tbsp (30 mL) instant coffee.

CHOCOLATE FUDGE SPONGECAKE

- Melt 4 oz (115 g) semisweet chocolate. Let cool. Fold in after melted butter.

NUT SPONGECAKE

- Add 3/4 cup (180 mL) chopped nuts of your choice (almonds, hazelnuts, pecans, pistachios, etc.) before melted butter.

CHOCOLATE CHIP SPONGECAKE

- Into flour, fold 1/2 cup (125 mL) grated semisweet chocolate.

COCOA SPONGECAKE

- In a bowl, mix flour with 3 tbsp (45 mL) cocoa. Fold in 2 tsp (10 mL) vegetable oil and 2 drops red food coloring (optional), at the same time as melted butter.

SESAME SEED SPONGECAKE

- Into flour, fold ¹/₂ cup (125 mL) toasted sesame seeds.

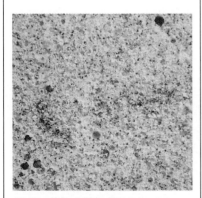

POPPY SEED SPONGECAKE

- Into flour, fold ¹/₂ cup (125 mL) poppy seeds.

SPICE SPONGECAKE

- Into flour, fold 2 tsp (10 mL) mixed ground spices (cinnamon, clove, nutmeg, etc).

TOMATO SPONGECAKE

- Add ¹/₄ cup (60 mL) tomato paste at the same time as butter.

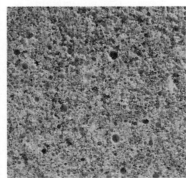

MIXED HERB SPONGECAKE

- Add your choice of ¹/₄ cup (60 mL) mixed herbs (basil, thyme, etc.) before melted butter.

Cake Roll

- To make a cake roll, follow basic spongecake recipe, reducing butter to 4 tsp (20 mL). Proceed according to basic method. All spongecake variations suggested here are suitable. Bake as follows :

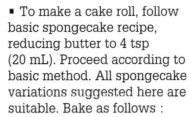

- *Butter a 15 x 10-inch (38 x 25 cm) cookie sheet. Cover with buttered ovenproof wax paper. Set aside. Preheat oven to 375 °F (190 °C).*
- *Prepare spongecake following method but reducing butter.*

- *Pour batter onto cookie sheet. Spread evenly with a spatula. Bake in oven 12 minutes or so.*
- *Remove from oven. Turn out onto a towel sprinkled with sugar — or with cocoa for a chocolate roll.*

- *Unmold cake. Wait 2-3 minutes, then carefully peel away wax paper. (If paper sticks to cake, moisten with a brush dipped in very cold water.)*

- *With a serrated knife, finely trim cake to remove crusty edge and make rolling easier.*

- *Roll up cake, enclosing towel. Let cool on a rack.*
- *Prepare garnish. Proceed according to a recipe on the following pages.*

Rich and Famous Roll

8 SERVINGS	
1 cup	(250 mL) cream cheese, softened
2	ripe bananas
1 tbsp	(15 mL) orange peel, grated
1/2 cup	(125 mL) chocolate chips
3 tbsp	(45 mL) Grand Marnier
1	cake roll - chocolate chip spongecake (p. 294)
2 cups	(500 mL) orange butter cream (p. 331)
1	orange, peeled, thinly sliced
2 cups	(500 mL) orange sauce (p. 416)

- In a mixer bowl, beat cheese until fluffy. Add bananas. Beat at moderate speed. Fold in peel, chocolate and Grand Marnier.

- Unroll cold cake. Evenly spread with mixture. Gently roll again.

- Cover with orange butter cream. Decorate top with orange slices. Refrigerate 1 hour. Serve with orange sauce.

VARIATION
- Use a nut spongecake. Replace peel with 3 tbsp (45 mL) chopped nuts. Garnish with peanut and chocolate butter cream (p. 331), and nuts.

NUTRITION	
CALORIES PER SERVING: 632	
FAT: 45 g	CAL. FROM FAT: 63%
PROTEIN: 6 g	CHOLESTEROL: 168 mg
SODIUM: 521 mg	CARBOHYDRATES: 52 g

Creamy Fruit Roll

8 SERVINGS	
2 cups	(500 mL) strawberries, raspberries or blueberries
1 cup	(250 mL) custard (p. 412)
1 1/2 cups	(375 mL) whipped cream
1	cake roll - poppy seed spongecake (p. 295)
2/3 cup	(160 mL) apricot glaze (p. 414)

- In a bowl, mix half the fruit with custard and 1/2 cup (125 mL) whipped cream. Set aside.

- Unroll cold cake. Spread with mixture. Gently roll again.

- Arrange remaining fruit on top of cake. Cover with glaze.

- Using a pasty bag with a fluted nozzle, decorate with whipped cream. Refrigerate 1 hour before serving.

VARIATIONS
- Moisten spongecake with 1/4 cup (60 mL) fruit liqueur. Garnish with icing sugar and slivered almonds.

NUTRITION	
CALORIES PER SERVING: 351	
FAT: 12 g	CAL. FROM FAT: 29%
PROTEIN: 6 g	CHOLESTEROL: 123 mg
SODIUM: 184 mg	CARBOHYDRATES: 58 g

Viennese Coffee Roll

8 SERVINGS	
4 tsp	(20 mL) cornstarch
1/2 cup	(125 mL) very strong coffee
2 oz	(60 mL) Irish cream liqueur or cognac
1	cake roll - coffee spongecake *(p. 294)*
2 cups	(500 mL) whipped cream
1 tbsp	(15 mL) ground cinnamon
2 cups	(500 mL) mocha butter cream *(p. 331)*
1/4 cup	(60 mL) cocoa
24	chocolate-covered coffee beans

- In a saucepan, dilute cornstarch in coffee. Heat until mixture thickens. Fold in Irish cream liqueur. Set aside.
- Unroll cold cake. Brush with coffee mixture, spreading evenly. Cover with whipped cream. Sprinkle with cinnamon. Gently roll again.
- With a spatula, spread mocha butter cream over cake. Dust with cocoa. Decorate each serving with 3 chocolate-covered coffee beans. Serve with ice cream or fruit coulis *(pp. 414-415)*.

NUTRITION	
CALORIES PER SERVING: 697	
FAT: 55 *g*	CAL. FROM FAT: 70%
PROTEIN: 7 *g*	CHOLESTEROL: 200 *mg*
SODIUM: 533 *mg*	CARBOHYDRATES: 46 *g*

Triple Chocolate Roll

8 SERVINGS	
1	cake roll - chocolate fudge spongecake *(p. 294)*
1/2 cup	(125 mL) raspberry jam
3 cups	(750 mL) chocolate butter cream *(p. 331)*
1 cup	(250 mL) chocolate shavings *(p. 330)*
2 cups	(500 mL) chocolate sauce *(p. 416)*

- Unroll cold cake. Spread successive layers of raspberry jam and one-third chocolate butter cream. Sprinkle with chocolate shavings. Gently roll again.
- With a spatula, frost cake with remaining butter cream. Decorate with remaining chocolate shavings. Serve with chocolate sauce.

VARIATIONS
- Use white chocolate shavings or chocolate chips. Decorate with almonds and cherries. Vary fruit jam flavors.

NUTRITION	
CALORIES PER SERVING: 1609	
FAT: 75 *g*	CAL. FROM FAT: 37%
PROTEIN: 13 *g*	CHOLESTEROL: 274 *mg*
SODIUM: 399 *mg*	CARBOHYDRATES: 274 *g*

Swiss Roll

8 SERVINGS	
1	cake roll - vanilla spongecake (p. 294)
1 cup	(250 mL) strawberry jam
1 1/2 cups	(375 mL) Chantilly cream (p. 413)
1/2 cup	(125 mL) icing sugar

- Unroll cold cake. Spread successive layers of strawberry jam and Chantilly cream. Gently roll again.

- Dust with icing sugar. Serve with fresh fruit or fruit salad, if desired.

Recipe shown opposite

MAPLE SYRUP ROLL

- In a bowl, whip 1 cup (250 mL) heavy cream until soft peaks form. Gently fold in 1/2 cup (125 mL) maple syrup.

Replace vanilla spongecake with orange spongecake, jam with maple syrup, and Chantilly cream with maple-flavored whipped cream. Dust with 1/2 cup (125 mL) cocoa. Serve with maple syrup, if desired.

NUTRITION	
CALORIES PER SERVING: 428	
FAT: 14 g	CAL. FROM FAT: 28%
PROTEIN: 5 g	CHOLESTEROL: 103 mg
SODIUM: 177 mg	CARBOHYDRATES: 74 g

Recipe shown opposite

NUTRITION	
CALORIES PER SERVING: 449	
FAT: 24 g	CAL. FROM FAT: 46%
PROTEIN: 6 g	CHOLESTEROL: 121 mg
SODIUM: 193 mg	CARBOHYDRATES: 55 g

Hazelnut Roll

8 SERVINGS	
1	cake roll - nut spongecake (p. 294)
1/2 cup	(125 mL) commercial hazelnut chocolate spread
2 cups	(250 mL) chocolate Chantilly cream (p. 413)
2/3 cup	(160 mL) hazelnuts

- Unroll cold cake. Cover with hazelnut chocolate spread, then 1/2 cup (125 mL) chocolate Chantilly cream. Gently roll again. Frost cake with remaining chocolate Chantilly cream. Decorate with hazelnuts.

Christmas Log

8 SERVINGS

1 cup	(250 mL) cherry jam or canned pitted cherries
1 oz	(30 mL) rum
1	cake roll - cocoa spongecake *(p. 295)*
2 ½ cups	(625 mL) whipped cream
2 cups	(500 mL) mocha butter cream *(p. 331)*
¼ cup	(60 mL) commercial chocolate syrup
¼ cup	(60 mL) cocoa
6	green almond paste holly leaves *(p. 330)*
12	very red currants or small cherries
2-3	meringue mushrooms *(p. 330)*

- In a bowl, mix cherry jam and rum.

- Unroll cold cake. Spread with jam. Cover with half the whipped cream. Gently roll again.

- Trim a 1 to 2-inch (2.5 to 5 cm) diagonal slice off one end of roll. Set aside for use to simulate a tree knot.

- With a spatula, spread a layer of mocha butter cream over cake, reserving ¼ cup (60 mL) to cover knot. Do not frost log ends. Place knot on top of log. Coat sides with remaining mocha butter cream. With a spatula, mark log and knot with ridges to imitate bark.

- With a spatula, spread remaining whipped cream over log ends and on top of knot. Using a pastry bag with a very small nozzle, pipe swirls of chocolate onto whipped cream. With a small knife, draw lines perpendicular to spiral.

- Using a sieve, lightly dust cocoa over contour of log.

- Decorate with holly, red currants and meringue mushrooms.

VARIATIONS
- Use different flavors of spongecake, cream or jam. Vary fruit.

NUTRITION	
CALORIES PER SERVING: 873	
FAT: 49 *g*	CAL. FROM FAT: 48%
PROTEIN: 9 *g*	CHOLESTEROL: 188 *mg*
SODIUM: 462 *mg*	CARBOHYDRATES: 109 *g*

- *Spread a layer of mocha butter cream over cake, reserving some to cover knot.*

- *Place knot on top of log. Coat sides with remaining mocha butter cream. Mark with ridges to imitate bark.*

- *Trim a 1 to 2-inch (2.5 to 5 cm) diagonal slice off one end of roll. Set aside for use to simulate a tree knot.*

- *Pipe swirls of chocolate onto whipped cream. Draw lines perpendicular to spiral.*

Freezer Cake

6 SERVINGS

1	orange spongecake (p. 294)
2 oz	(60 mL) orange liqueur
1 ¼ cups	(300 mL) Chantilly cream (p. 413)
¾ cup	(180 mL) oranges, peeled, pith removed, sectioned
1 ¼ cups	(300 mL) Chantilly cream
	orange slices and peel

- Slice spongecake into 2 layers. Line bottom of a 9-inch (23 cm) springform cake pan with first layer. Moisten with 1 oz (30 mL) orange liqueur. Set aside.
- In a bowl, mix 1 ¼ cups (300 mL) Chantilly cream and oranges. Spread over first layer. Cover with second spongecake layer. Moisten with remaining liqueur. Seal cake pan in plastic wrap. Freeze at least 2 hours.
- Remove from freezer. Unclip pan. Unmold cake. Cover top and sides with 1 ¼ cups (300 mL) Chantilly cream. Freeze 1 more hour or so.
- Before serving, decorate with orange slices and peel.

NUTRITION	
CALORIES PER SERVING: 417	
FAT: 16 g	CAL. FROM FAT: 35%
PROTEIN: 6 g	CHOLESTEROL: 128 mg
SODIUM: 210 mg	CARBOHYDRATES: 60 g

Recipe shown above

CHOCOLATE FREEZER CAKE
- Replace orange spongecake with cocoa spongecake (p. 295), first part Chantilly cream with chocolate mousse (p. 399), and oranges with chocolate shavings and curls (p. 330), as shown opposite.

BLUEBERRY FREEZER CAKE
- Replace oranges with fresh or frozen blueberries, and orange liqueur with blueberry liqueur. Decorate with fresh blueberries, as shown opposite.

Angel-food Cake

6 SERVINGS

1	vanilla spongecake *(p. 294)*
2	egg whites
2 1/2 cups	(625 mL) Chantilly cream *(p. 413)*
12 oz	(341 mL) canned peach slices
	roasted almonds

- Prepare spongecake following basic recipe. Beat egg whites until stiff. Gently fold into batter. Bake in oven.
- Remove from oven. Slice spongecake into 2 layers.

- Mix 1 cup (250 mL) Chantilly cream and half the peaches. Spread over first cake layer. Cover with second layer.
- Frost cake with remaining Chantilly cream. Arrange remaining peaches on top. Decorate sides with roasted almonds. Refrigerate at least 1 hour.

VARIATIONS
- Use different flavors of spongecake. Flavor Chantilly cream with almond or orange liqueur. Vary fruit. Garnish contour of cake with poppy seeds.

NUTRITION	
CALORIES PER SERVING: 635	
FAT: 35 *g*	CAL. FROM FAT: 48%
PROTEIN: 10 *g*	CHOLESTEROL: 178 *mg*
SODIUM: 257 *mg*	CARBOHYDRATES: 74 *g*

Madeltorte Cake

8-10 SERVINGS

1 1/4 cups	(330 mL) pastry flour
1 tsp	(5 mL) baking powder
1/3 cup	(80 mL) sugar
1/2 cup	(125 mL) butter, softened
1	egg, lightly beaten

Topping

1/2 cup	(125 mL) butter, softened
1/2 cup	(125 mL) fine sugar
2	eggs
1/2 tsp	(2 mL) almond extract
1 cup	(250 mL) nuts, finely chopped

Icing

1/2 cup	(125 mL) raspberry jam
1/4 cup	(60 mL) icing sugar
1 tsp	(5 mL) lemon juice

- In a bowl, mix dry ingredients. Add butter and egg. Press mixture over bottom of a springform cake pan. Cover. Refrigerate 30 minutes.
- Preheat oven to 350 °F (175 °C).

Topping

- In a large bowl, cream butter and sugar. Fold in eggs and almond extract. Add nuts.
- Pour into pan, on top of cooled batter. Bake in oven 1 hour.
- Let cool 1 hour.

Icing

- Brush jam over top of cake. In a bowl, mix icing sugar and lemon juice. Frost cake. Decorate with fruit.

NUTRITION	
CALORIES PER SERVING: 440	
FAT: 28 *g*	CAL. FROM FAT: 55%
PROTEIN: 6 *g*	CHOLESTEROL: 104 *mg*
SODIUM: 246 *mg*	CARBOHYDRATES: 45 *g*

Orange Chiffon Cake

8-10 SERVINGS	
1 1/4 cups	(300 mL) pastry flour, sifted
3/4 cup	(180 mL) sugar
2 tsp	(10 mL) baking powder
1/2 tsp	(2 mL) salt
1/4 cup	(60 mL) corn oil
3	egg yolks
1/3 cup	(80 mL) orange juice
2 tsp	(10 mL) orange peel, grated
3	egg whites
1/4 tsp	(1 mL) cream of tartar
2 cups	(500 mL) raspberry butter cream (p. 331)
	fresh fruit

- Preheat oven to 325 °F (160 °C).
- In a bowl, mix dry ingredients. Make a well in the center. Pour in oil, egg yolks, orange juice and peel. Mix until smooth. Set aside.
- In a second bowl, beat egg whites and cream of tartar until soft peaks form.

- Gently add to first mixture by folding batter over egg whites. Pour into an unbuttered 9-inch (23 cm) square cake pan or ring mold. Bake in oven 1 hour or until springy to the touch.
- Remove from oven. Turn out onto a wire rack or towel sprinkled with sugar. Let cool before unmolding. Cover with butter cream. Garnish with fresh fruit.

NUTRITION	
CALORIES PER SERVING: 351	
FAT: 7 g	CAL. FROM FAT: 18%
PROTEIN: 4 g	CHOLESTEROL: 64 mg
SODIUM: 224 mg	CARBOHYDRATES: 71 g

Recipe shown above left

Deluxe Banana Cake

8-10 SERVINGS	
2 tbsp	(30 mL) corn syrup
2/3 cup	(160 mL) sugar
2	large eggs, beaten
2/3 cup	(160 mL) sunflower oil
2/3 cup	(160 mL) milk
2	bananas, mashed
1 1/4 cups	(300 mL) flour
2 tbsp	(30 mL) cocoa
1 tsp	(5 mL) baking powder
1 tsp	(5 mL) baking soda

Icing

1/4 cup	(60 mL) butter, melted
2 tbsp	(30 mL) milk
	few drops of vanilla extract
3 cups	(750 mL) icing sugar
3 tbsp	(45 mL) cocoa
1	banana, sliced
	lemon juice

- Preheat oven to 350 °F (175 °). Butter and flour a 9 x 13-inch (23 x 33 cm) cake pan or star-shape mold.
- In a large bowl, mix corn syrup, sugar, eggs, oil, milk and bananas.
- In a second bowl, sift together dry ingredients. Fold into first mixture. Pour into cake pan. Bake in oven 1 hour. Let cool.

Icing

- In a bowl, mix butter, milk and vanilla extract. Add icing sugar and cocoa, mixing until smooth. Spread over cake.
- Dip sliced banana in lemon juice to prevent discoloration. Arrange on top of cake.

NUTRITION	
CALORIES PER SERVING: 480	
FAT: 21 g	CAL. FROM FAT: 39%
PROTEIN: 4 g	CHOLESTEROL: 52 mg
SODIUM: 233 mg	CARBOHYDRATES: 72 g

Recipe shown above right

Upside-down Pear Cake

8-10 SERVINGS

¼ cup	(60 mL) shortening
14 oz	(398 mL) canned pear halves
½ cup	(125 mL) brown sugar
1	egg
½ cup	(125 mL) milk
1 cup	(250 mL) all-purpose flour
2 tsp	(10 mL) baking powder
	pinch of salt

- Preheat oven to 375 °F (190 °C). Butter an 8-inch (20 cm) round deep cake pan. Set aside.

- In a saucepan, melt shortening. Spread over bottom of pan. Line with pear halves. Add brown sugar.

- Beat egg and milk. Sift in flour, baking powder and salt, mixing well. Pour into pan, over pear halves.

- Bake in oven 1 hour or so. Immediately turn out onto a plate. While cake is still warm, pour fruit coulis (pp. 414-415) into center of pears, if desired. Garnish with your choice of fruit.

NUTRITION	
CALORIES PER SERVING: 176	
FAT: 6 g	CAL. FROM FAT: 31 %
PROTEIN: 2 g	CHOLESTEROL: 20 mg
SODIUM: 104 mg	CARBOHYDRATES: 29 g

Recipe shown above left

Upside-down Apple Cake

8-10 SERVINGS

¼ cup	(60 mL) butter
¾ cup	(180 mL) brown sugar
3	apples
½ tsp	(2 mL) cinnamon

Batter

¼ cup	(60 mL) butter, melted
⅓ cup	(80 mL) sugar
1	egg
¼ cup	(60 mL) molasses
1 cup	(250 mL) flour
1 tsp	(5 mL) baking powder
½ tsp	(2 mL) baking soda
⅛ tsp	(0.5 mL) salt
⅓ cup	(80 mL) boiling water

- If using a conventional oven, preheat to 325 °F (160 °C).

- In a saucepan, melt butter and brown sugar. Coat bottom of a square 9-inch (23 cm) pyrex dish.

- Peel apples, if desired. Cut into thick slices. Remove core. Place into mold. Sprinkle with cinnamon.

Batter

- In a bowl, cream butter and sugar. Fold in egg and molasses. Set aside.

- In a second bowl, sift dry ingredients. Fold into first mixture. While stirring, blend in boiling water. Pour into dish, on top of apples. Bake in conventional oven 40 minutes, or in microwave oven 12 minutes, on HIGH.

- Remove from oven. Immediately turn out onto a plate. Let drain. Serve warm.

NUTRITION	
CALORIES PER SERVING: 227	
FAT: 6 g	CAL. FROM FAT: 21 %
PROTEIN: 2 g	CHOLESTEROL: 31 mg
SODIUM: 191 mg	CARBOHYDRATES: 44 g

Recipe shown above right

Banana Cake

8-10 SERVINGS

½ cup	(125 mL) margarine
¼ cup	(60 mL) sugar
½ cup	(125 mL) brown sugar, well-packed
2	eggs, beaten
1 tsp	(5 mL) vanilla extract
2 cups	(500 mL) flour
2 tsp	(10 mL) baking powder
¼ tsp	(1 mL) baking soda
¼ tsp	(1 mL) salt
1 cup	(250 mL) bananas, mashed
1 cup	(250 mL) milk
½ cup	(125 mL) nuts, chopped

Icing

1 ⅓ cups	(330 mL) icing sugar
2 tbsp	(30 mL) milk
¼ tsp	(1 mL) vanilla extract
	pinch of salt
	nuts, chopped

- Preheat oven to 350 °F (175 °C). Butter a 10-inch (25 cm) ring mold. Set aside.

- In a bowl, mix first 3 ingredients. Stir in eggs and vanilla. Set aside.

- In a second bowl, sift dry ingredients. Add to first mixture, alternating with bananas and milk. Fold in nuts.

- Pour into pan. Bake in oven 30-35 minutes.

- Let cool. Unmold onto a serving dish. Set aside.

Icing

- In a bowl, sift icing sugar. Fold in milk, vanilla extract and salt.

- Pour icing over cake. Decorate with chopped nuts.

NUTRITION	
CALORIES PER SERVING: 428	
FAT: 19 *g*	CAL. FROM FAT: 39 %
PROTEIN: 7 *g*	CHOLESTEROL: 40 *mg*
SODIUM: 308 *mg*	CARBOHYDRATES: 59 *g*

Recipe shown above left

Applesauce Cake

8-10 SERVINGS

1 ¾ cups	(425 mL) apple sauce
1 cup	(250 mL) sugar
1 cup	(250 mL) mayonnaise
½ cup	(125 mL) milk
1 tsp	(5 mL) vanilla extract
3 cups	(750 mL) all-purpose flour
2 tsp	(10 mL) baking soda
½ tsp	(2 mL) salt
2 tsp	(10 mL) cinnamon
½ tsp	(2 mL) nutmeg
1 cup	(250 mL) nuts, chopped
½ cup	(250 mL) raisins

- Preheat oven to 350 °F (175 °C). Butter and flour a 9-inch (23 cm) cake pan. Set aside.

- In a mixer bowl, at low speed, beat first 5 ingredients.

- In a second bowl, sift together flour, baking soda, salt, cinnamon and nutmeg. Fold into first mixture. Increase speed. Beat 2 minutes.

- Fold in nuts and raisins. Pour into pan. Bake in oven 30-35 minutes or until a knife inserted in the middle comes out clean.

- Let cool slightly. Serve warm with ice cream or whipped cream, if desired.

NUTRITION	
CALORIES PER SERVING: 526	
FAT: 28 *g*	CAL. FROM FAT: 45 %
PROTEIN: 7 *g*	CHOLESTEROL: 9 *mg*
SODIUM: 494 *mg*	CARBOHYDRATES: 67 *g*

Recipe shown above right

Dream Cake

16 SERVINGS

2 cups	(500 mL) flour, sifted
1 cup	(250 mL) brown sugar
1 cup	(250 mL) butter, in pieces

Garnish

²/₃ cup	(160 mL) milk
¹/₃ tsp	(1.5 mL) vanilla extract
1 ¹/₄ cups	(300 mL) grated coconut
¹/₃ cup	(80 mL) walnuts
¹/₄ cup	(60 mL) red and green candied cherries, sliced

- Preheat oven to 350 °F (175 °C). Butter a square 8-inch (20 cm) cake pan. Set aside.

- In a bowl, mix flour and brown sugar. Work in butter pieces until smooth. Pour into pan. Bake in oven 10 minutes. Set aside.

Garnish

- In a bowl, mix all ingredients. Spread into pan, over first mixture.

- Bake in oven around 20 minutes or until garnish browns lightly. Let cool. Serve.

NUTRITION	
CALORIES PER SERVING: 244	
FAT: 14 *g*	CAL. FROM FAT: 51%
PROTEIN: 2 *g*	CHOLESTEROL: 32 *mg*
SODIUM: 143 *mg*	CARBOHYDRATES: 29 *g*

Recipe shown above right

Coconut-frosted Date Cake

8-10 SERVINGS

¹/₂ cup	(125 mL) butter
1 cup	(250 mL) sugar
1 cup	(250 mL) dates, cut into pieces
1 cup	(250 mL) boiling water
1 tsp	(5 mL) vanilla extract
1	egg
1 ¹/₂ cups	(375 mL) flour
1 tsp	(5 mL) baking powder
¹/₄ tsp	(1 mL) baking soda

Icing

1 cup	(250 mL) brown sugar
¹/₄ cup	(60 mL) sugar
6 tbsp	(90 mL) butter
5 tbsp	(75 mL) grated coconut

- Preheat oven to 350 °F (175 °C).

- In a bowl, mix butter, sugar, dates, water, vanilla extract and egg. Set aside.

- In a second bowl, sift dry ingredients. Fold into first mixture.

- Pour into an unbuttered 9-inch (23 cm) cake pan. Bake in oven 35-40 minutes.

Icing

- In a saucepan, over high heat, boil all ingredients until a drop tipped into cold water turns to a soft ball. Spread over warm cake. Decorate with sliced dates, if desired.

NUTRITION	
CALORIES PER SERVING: 451	
FAT: 17 *g*	CAL. FROM FAT: 34%
PROTEIN: 3 *g*	CHOLESTEROL: 61 *mg*
SODIUM: 251 *mg*	CARBOHYDRATES: 74 *g*

Recipe shown above left

Potato-Chocolate Cake

8 SERVINGS

1 cup	(250 mL)	butter
1 1/2 cups	(375 mL)	sugar
4		eggs, beaten
3 oz	(90 mL)	unsweetened chocolate
1 cup	(250 mL)	mashed potatoes, cooled
1 tsp	(5 mL)	cinnamon
1 tsp	(5 mL)	nutmeg
2 cups	(500 mL)	unbleached flour, sifted twice
1 tsp	(5 mL)	baking soda
1 cup	(250 mL)	sour milk
3/4 cup	(180 mL)	nuts, chopped

- Preheat oven to 350 °F (175 °C). Butter a chimney mold. Set aside.

- In a bowl, cream butter. Vigorously stir in sugar until light and fluffy. Mix in beaten eggs. Set aside.

- In a double-boiler, melt chocolate. Remove from heat. Let cool. Add to first mixture with potatoes, cinnamon and nutmeg.

- In a bowl, sift flour and baking soda. Fold into first mixture, alternating with sour milk. Mix in nuts. Pour into mold. Bake in oven 45 minutes.

- Let cool. Unmold. Serve with raspberry jam and whipped cream, if desired.

NUTRITION	
CALORIES PER SERVING: 666	
FAT: 39 g	CAL. FROM FAT: 51%
PROTEIN: 11 g	CHOLESTEROL: 154 mg
SODIUM: 512 mg	CARBOHYDRATES: 274 g

Sugarless Tomato Cake

8 SERVINGS

1/3 cup	(80 mL)	vegetable oil
1		egg
1/2 cup	(125 mL)	puréed tomatoes or seeded tomatoes, coarsely chopped
1/2 tsp	(2 mL)	vanilla extract
1 1/2 cups	(375 mL)	whole wheat flour, sifted
1/2 tsp	(2 mL)	baking soda
		pinch of sea salt
1/8 tsp	(0.5 mL)	nutmeg
1/4 tsp	(1 mL)	cinnamon
1/2 cup	(125 mL)	nuts, chopped
2-3		fresh tomatoes, seeded, chopped
		whipped cream

- Preheat oven to 325 °F (160 °C). Butter and flour a 9-inch (23 cm) cake pan. Set aside.

- In a bowl, whisk oil and egg. Add puréed tomatoes and vanilla extract. Set aside.

- In a second bowl, mix remaining ingredients, except whipped cream. Fold into first mixture. Pour into mold. Bake in oven 50 minutes.

- Garnish with whipped cream. Serve.

NUTRITION	
CALORIES PER SERVING: 288	
FAT: 21 g	CAL. FROM FAT: 62%
PROTEIN: 6 g	CHOLESTEROL: 43 mg
SODIUM: 114 mg	CARBOHYDRATES: 23 g

Recipe shown above

Zucchini Cake

8 SERVINGS

3	eggs
1 ½ cups	(375 mL) sugar
1 ½ cups	(375 mL) cream cheese, softened
1 tsp	(5 mL) vanilla extract
3 cups	(750 mL) unbleached flour, sifted twice
1 tbsp	(15 mL) baking powder
1 tsp	(5 mL) salt
1 tsp	(5 mL) nutmeg
⅓ cup	(80 mL) walnuts, chopped
1 cup	(250 mL) vegetable oil
2 cups	(500 mL) zucchini, grated

Lemon sauce

1	egg
¼ cup	(60 mL) lemon juice
1 tbsp	(15 mL) lemon peel, grated
2 tbsp	(30 mL) all-purpose flour
1 cup	(250 mL) sugar
1 tsp	(5 mL) butter, melted

- Preheat oven to 350 °F (175 °C). Butter a round deep cake pan. Set aside.

- In a bowl, mix eggs, sugar, cheese and vanilla extract. Set aside.

- In a second bowl, sift dry ingredients. Add nuts. Fold into first mixture, one-third at a time. Blend in oil, in 2 steps. Gently mix in zucchini. Pour into pan.

- Bake in oven 1 hour. Let cool.

Lemon sauce
- In a bowl, beat egg, lemon juice and peel until creamy smooth.

- In a second bowl, mix flour and sugar. Fold into first mixture. Add melted butter.

- Pour into a saucepan. While stirring, bring to a boil. Cover. Remove from heat. Let cool, stirring occasionally. Pour over cake.

NUTRITION	
CALORIES PER SERVING: 863	
FAT: 46 g	CAL. FROM FAT: 47%
PROTEIN: 12 g	CHOLESTEROL: 139 mg
SODIUM: 563 mg	CARBOHYDRATES: 104 g

Recipe shown above right
Above left : New-Age Carrot Cake

New-Age Carrot Cake

8-10 SERVINGS

1 ¼ cups	(300 mL) raw carrots, finely grated
1 cup	(250 mL) brown sugar
½ cup	(125 mL) oil
2	eggs
1 ½ cups	(375 mL) flour
1 tsp	(5 mL) baking powder
1 tsp	(5 mL) baking soda
½ tsp	(2 mL) salt
½ tsp	(2 mL) cinnamon
½ tsp	(2 mL) nutmeg
½ tsp	(2 mL) ginger
¾ cup	(180 mL) apple sauce
¼ cup	(60 mL) raisins

Icing

¼ cup	(60 mL) butter
½ cup	(125 mL) cream cheese, softened
½ tsp	(2 mL) vanilla extract
2 ½ cups	(625 mL) icing sugar

- Preheat oven to 350 °F (175 °C). Butter a 9-inch (23 cm) cake pan.

- In a bowl, mix carrots and sugar. Fold in oil, then eggs.

- In a second bowl, sift dry ingredients. Add all at once to first mixture. Fold in apple sauce and raisins. Pour into pan. Bake in oven 30-35 minutes.

Icing
- In a bowl, mix all ingredients. Whip until smooth. Spread over cold cake.

NUTRITION	
CALORIES PER SERVING: 489	
FAT: 21 g	CAL. FROM FAT: 37%
PROTEIN: 4 g	CHOLESTEROL: 61 mg
SODIUM: 374 mg	CARBOHYDRATES: 74 g

Fruitcake

2 CAKES

1/2 cup	(125 mL) almonds, julienned
2 cups	(500 mL) candied cherries
1 cup	(250 mL) candied fruit peel, chopped
2 cups	(500 mL) raisins
1 cup	(250 mL) currants
1 cup	(250 mL) fruit liqueur, of your choice
2 cups	(500 mL) flour
1/2 tsp	(2 mL) baking soda
1/2 tsp	(2 mL) salt
1 tsp	(5 mL) clove
1 tsp	(5 mL) cinnamon
1 tsp	(5 mL) allspice

3/4 cup	(180 mL) molasses
3/4 cup	(180 mL) apple juice
1 cup	(250 mL) butter
2 cups	(500 mL) brown sugar
6	eggs

- In a bowl, macerate almonds and fruit in liqueur 24 hours.
- Preheat oven to 275 °F (135 °C). Butter and line with wax paper your choice of pan (see sizes further on).
- In a bowl, sift dry ingredients. Set aside.
- In a second bowl, mix molasses and apple juice. Set aside.
- In a third bowl, whip butter, brown sugar and eggs. Fold in dry ingredients, alternating with molasses mixture. Add macerated fruit and liqueur. Pour into pans.

- Bake in oven 2 hours for a 8 1/2 x 4 1/2 x 2 1/2-inch (21 x 11 x 6 cm) loaf pan, 3 hours for a 10-inch (25 cm) ring mold, or 1 hour at 300 °F (150° C) for muffin pans.
- Remove from oven. Unmold. Let stand 10 minutes before peeling off wax paper. Once cake is cold, wrap in liqueur-soaked cheesecloth, then aluminum foil. Store in a cool place.

Note : at its best if baked at least 3 months ahead of time, fruitcake is good up to a year.

NUTRITION	
CALORIES PER SERVING: 540	
FAT: 15 g	CAL. FROM FAT: 26 %
PROTEIN: 6 g	CHOLESTEROL: 99 mg
SODIUM: 285 mg	CARBOHYDRATES: 91 g

Recipe shown above

Rhubarb Strawberry Ring

8 SERVINGS

5 tbsp	(75 mL) shortening
3/4 cup	(180 mL) sugar
2	eggs
2 cups	(500 mL) pastry flour
1 tsp	(5 mL) baking powder
	pinch of salt
3 tbsp	(45 mL) milk
1/2 tsp	(2 mL) vanilla extract
1 cup	(250 mL) rhubarb, diced
1/2 cup	(125 mL) strawberries, sliced

- Preheat oven to 375 °F (190 °C). Butter and flour a chimney mold. Set aside.
- In a bowl, beat shortening and sugar until creamy smooth. Beat in eggs, one at a time.
- In a second bowl, sift flour, baking powder and salt.
- In a third bowl, mix milk and vanilla extract. Fold dry ingredients into first mixture, alternating with vanilla-flavored milk. Add rhubarb and strawberries. Pour into mold. Bake in oven 40 minutes.

Recipe shown left, opposite page

VARIATIONS
- Coat with maple syrup. Replace rhubarb with cranberries.

NUTRITION	
CALORIES PER SERVING: 268	
FAT: 10 g	CAL. FROM FAT: 32 %
PROTEIN: 4 g	CHOLESTEROL: 47 mg
SODIUM: 80 mg	CARBOHYDRATES: 42 g

Pumpkin Cake

8-10 SERVINGS

3 cups	(750 mL) unbleached flour, sifted twice
2 tsp	(10 mL) baking soda
1/4 tsp	(1 mL) salt
1 tsp	(5 mL) cinnamon
1/2 tsp	(2 mL) clove
1/2 cup	(125 mL) margarine
3/4 cup	(180 mL) brown sugar
2	eggs, beaten
2 cups	(500 mL) pumpkin, mashed

Coconut frosting

1/4 cup	(60 mL) brown sugar
5 tbsp	(75 mL) flour
1/4 tsp	(1 mL) salt
3	egg yolks, beaten
2 cups	(500 mL) milk
1 cup	(250 mL) grated coconut
1/2 tsp	(2 mL) vanilla extract

- Preheat oven to 325 °F (160 °C). Butter and flour a 9 x 5-inch (23 x 13 cm) cake pan. Set aside.
- In a bowl, sift dry ingredients. Set aside.
- In a second bowl, whip margarine and brown sugar until creamy smooth. Fold in eggs. Whip in dry ingredients, alternating with mashed pumpkin. Pour into pan. Bake 1 hour. Unmold onto a wire rack.

Coconut frosting

- In a saucepan, mix brown sugar, flour and salt. Fold in egg yolks. Gradually blend in milk. While stirring, bring to a boil.
- Off heat, add coconut and vanilla extract. Let cool, stirring occasionally to prevent a skin forming. Spread over cake.

NUTRITION	
CALORIES PER SERVING: 428	
FAT: 16 g	CAL. FROM FAT: 33%
PROTEIN: 9 g	CHOLESTEROL: 107 mg
SODIUM: 533 mg	CARBOHYDRATES: 63 g

Recipe shown above right

Quick 'n' Easy Fruitcake

8 SERVINGS	
4 cups	(1 L) fresh, frozen or canned fruit
2	eggs
2 tsp	(10 mL) vanilla extract
1 1/4 cups	(300 mL) brown sugar
3/4 cup	(180 mL) oil
1 cup	(250 mL) flour
1 tsp	(5 mL) baking powder
1/2 tsp	(2 mL) salt
2 tsp	(10 mL) cinnamon

- Preheat oven to 350 °F (175 °C). Butter and line with wax paper an 8 x 12-inch (20 x 30 cm) cake pan.

- In a bowl, mix fruit, eggs, vanilla extract, brown sugar and oil.

- In a second bowl, sift together dry ingredients. Stir into liquid mixture.

- Bake in oven 50 minutes or so. Let cool in pan.

VARIATIONS
- To batter, add grated coconut, chopped nuts or dates. Frost with icing made from 3 oz (90 g) cream cheese, 1 tsp (5 mL) butter, 1 tsp (5 mL) vanilla extract and 1 1/2 cups (375 mL) icing sugar. Serve with coulis *(pp. 414-415)* or custard sauce *(p. 413)*.

NUTRITION	
CALORIES PER SERVING: 510	
FAT: 22 g	CAL. FROM FAT: 38%
PROTEIN: 5 g	CHOLESTEROL: 46 mg
SODIUM: 210 mg	CARBOHYDRATES: 77 g

Recipe shown above

Carrot Cake

8 SERVINGS	
3/4 cup	(180 mL) flour
1 tsp	(5 mL) baking powder
1/2 tsp	(2 mL) baking soda
3/4 cup	(180 mL) brown sugar
1/2 cup	(125 mL) oil
2	eggs
1 cup	(250 mL) raw carrots, grated

Caramel sauce

1 cup	(250 mL) corn syrup
1 cup	(250 mL) brown sugar
1/2 cup	(125 mL) butter, softened
1 1/2 tbsp	(22 mL) cornstarch
1 cup	(250 mL) heavy cream

- In a bowl, sift flour, baking powder and baking soda. Set aside.

- In a second bowl, mix brown sugar, oil and eggs. Fold in dry ingredients and carrots. Pour into an un-buttered pyrex dish. Bake in microwave oven 5 minutes on MEDIUM, then 2 minutes on HIGH. Let stand 8 minutes.

Caramel sauce
- In a microwave-safe bowl, mix all ingredients, except cream. Cook 5 minutes, on HIGH.

- Blend in cream. Pour over cake at once or let cool.

NUTRITION	
CALORIES PER SERVING: 686	
FAT: 37 g	CAL. FROM FAT: 47%
PROTEIN: 3 g	CHOLESTEROL: 117 mg
SODIUM: 316 mg	CARBOHYDRATES: 90 g

Mocha Cake

8 SERVINGS

¹/₄ cup	(60 mL) sugar
¹/₂ cup	(125 mL) strong coffee
2 oz	(60 mL) Irish cream liqueur
1	coffee spongecake (p. 294) **or cocoa spongecake** (p. 295)
1 ¹/₄ cups	(300 mL) mocha butter cream (p. 331)
1 ¹/₄ cups	(300 mL) chocolate Chantilly cream (p. 413)
¹/₄ cup	(60 mL) roasted coffee beans
¹/₄ cup	(60 mL) icing sugar

- Dissolve sugar in coffee. Add Irish cream liqueur. Set aside.

- Slice spongecake into 3 layers. Brush first layer with ¹/₂ cup (60 mL) coffee mixture. Spread with half the butter cream. Place second layer on top. Brush with ¹/₄ cup (60 mL) coffee mixture. Spread with remaining butter cream. Cover with third spongecake layer, then remaining coffee mixture.

- Spread chocolate Chantilly cream over top and sides of cake. Decorate with coffee beans. Dust with icing sugar. Refrigerate at least 1 hour before serving.

NUTRITION	
CALORIES PER SERVING: 496	
FAT: 30 g	CAL. FROM FAT: 55%
PROTEIN: 4 g	CHOLESTEROL: 145 mg
SODIUM: 344 mg	CARBOHYDRATES: 50 g

Recipe shown above left

Devil's Cake

8 SERVINGS

1	cocoa spongecake (p. 295)
1	chocolate chip spongecake (p. 294)
1 ¹/₂ cups	(375 mL) chocolate butter cream (p. 331)
1 ¹/₂ cups	(375 mL) chocolate Chantilly cream (p. 413)
¹/₂ cup	(125 mL) chocolate shavings (p. 330)
¹/₃ cup	(80 mL) cocoa
1 ¹/₂ cups	(375 mL) chocolate sauce (p. 416)

- Slice each spongecake into 2 layers. Spread ¹/₂ cup (125 mL) chocolate butter cream over first cocoa layer. Cover with successive layers of chocolate chip spongecake, ¹/₂ cup (125 mL) chocolate butter cream, second chocolate chip spongecake, then ¹/₂ cup (125 mL) chocolate butter cream. End with second cocoa spongecake layer. Refrigerate at least 1 hour.

- Remove from refrigerator. Cover top and sides of cake with chocolate Chantilly cream and chocolate shavings. Dust with cocoa. Pipe swirls of Chantilly cream onto cake, if desired. Serve with chocolate sauce.

NUTRITION	
CALORIES PER SERVING: 1199	
FAT: 53 g	CAL. FROM FAT: 36%
PROTEIN: 13 g	CHOLESTEROL: 161 mg
SODIUM: 436 mg	CARBOHYDRATES: 202 g

Black Forest Cake

8 SERVINGS	
14 oz	(398 mL) canned Bing cherries
½ cup	(125 mL) sugar
1 tbsp	(15 mL) cornstarch
2 oz	(60 mL) kirsch
1	chocolate fudge spongecake (p. 294) or cocoa spongecake (p. 295)
2 ½ cups	(625 mL) Chantilly cream (p. 413)
8	fresh cherries
1 cup	(250 mL) chocolate shavings (p. 330)
2 tbsp	(30 mL) icing sugar

- Drain cherries, reserving juice.

- In a small saucepan, melt sugar in a little cherry juice.

- In a small bowl, dilute cornstarch in remaining cherry juice. Fold into syrup in saucepan. While stirring, bring to a boil. Remove from heat. Let cool. Add kirsch.

- Slice spongecake into 3 layers. With a pastry brush, spread one-third cherry syrup over first layer. Top with ⅔ cup (160 mL) Chantilly cream, then half the cherries.

- Cover with second sponge-cake layer. Brush with second-third cherry syrup. Spread with ⅔ cup (160 mL) Chantilly cream, then remaining cherries. End with last spongecake layer, then remaining cherry syrup.

- Cover top and sides of cake with Chantilly cream. Using a pastry bag with a fluted nozzle, pipe swirls of whipped cream onto cake. Add a fresh cherry to each. Garnish sides of cake with chocolate shavings. Place a few shavings on top of cake. Dust with icing sugar.

- Refrigerate 1 hour or so before serving.

NUTRITION	
CALORIES PER SERVING: 1366	
FAT: 80 g	CAL. FROM FAT: 47%
PROTEIN: 14 g	CHOLESTEROL: 133 mg
SODIUM: 206 mg	CARBOHYDRATES: 193 g

Recipe shown, opposite page

- *Cover with second sponge-cake layer. Brush with second-third cherry syrup.*

- *Top with Chantilly cream, then cherries.*

- *Using a pastry bag with a fluted nozzle, pipe swirls of whipped cream onto cake.*

- *Garnish sides of cake with chocolate shavings.*

Saint-Honoré

8 SERVINGS

1 lb	(450 g) flaky pastry (p. 335)
2	eggs, beaten
2 cups	(500 mL) puff paste (p. 356)
2 oz	(60 mL) Grand Marnier
3 cups	(750 mL) Chantilly cream (p. 412)
1 ½ cups	(375 mL) custard (p. 412)
9	puff shells (p. 356)
1 ½ cups	(375 mL) whipped cream
½ cup	(125 mL) semisweet chocolate, melted
1 cup	(250 mL) canned peaches, drained
2 tbsp	(30 mL) orange peel, grated
	icing sugar (optional)

- Preheat oven to 400 °F (205 °C).

- Roll out flaky pastry to a circle, 9-inch (23 cm) wide by ¼-inch (0.5 cm) thick. Butter, then moisten a cookie sheet. Transfer pastry to cookie sheet.

- Prick with a fork. Brush with beaten egg.

- Using a pastry bag with a plain nozzle, pipe a crown of puff paste along edge of pastry crust. Starting from the center, spiral puff paste onto pastry. Brush with beaten egg. Bake in oven 20 minutes. Let cool.

- In a bowl, mix Grand Marnier, half the Chantilly cream and all of the custard. Set aside.

- With a pencil, punch a hole under each puff. Using a pastry bag with a plain nozzle, stuff with Grand Marnier cream.

- Spread a layer of Grand Marnier cream into the center of cold cake.

- Dip puff bottoms in chocolate. Set around crown, reserving 1 puff for center decoration. Arrange peaches over cream layer. Cover with remaining Grand Marnier cream, then Chantilly cream. Sprinkle with orange peel. Place last puff in the center of Saint-Honoré. Dust with icing sugar, if desired. Serve at once or refrigerate.

- Using a pastry bag with a plain nozzle, pipe a crown of puff paste along edge of pastry crust. Starting from the center, spiral puff paste onto pastry.

- With a pencil, punch a hole under each puff. Using a pastry bag with a plain nozzle, stuff with Grand Marnier cream.

NUTRITION	
CALORIES PER SERVING: 1319	
FAT: 92 g	CAL. FROM FAT: 63 %
PROTEIN: 18 g	CHOLESTEROL: 253 mg
SODIUM: 446 mg	CARBOHYDRATES: 104 g

- Dip puff bottoms in chocolate. Set around crown, reserving 1 puff for center decoration.

- Cover with remaining Grand Marnier cream, then Chantilly cream.

CHOCOLATE SAINT-HONORÉ

- Replace Chantilly cream with chocolate Chantilly cream *(p. 413)*.
- Replace peaches with ²/₃ cup (160 mL) chocolate shavings *(p. 330)*, and orange peel with ¹/₄ cup (60 mL) grated coconut.
- Dip puff crowns in 2 cups (500 mL) melted chocolate.

Recipe shown above

SURPRISE SAINT-HONORÉ

- Replace alcohol with 3 tbsp (45 mL) grenadine. Color Chantilly cream with 2 drops red food coloring.
- Replace peaches with ²/₃ cup (160 mL) candy-covered chocolate, and orange peel with ¹/₂ cup (125 mL) chocolate shavings *(p. 330)*. The perfect cake for a child's birthday !

NUTTY SAINT-HONORÉ

- To custard, add ¹/₄ cup (60 mL) almond powder. Decorate with ¹/₂ cup (125 mL) slivered almonds, hazelnuts, walnuts or pistachios.

CHEESECAKES

Rise-and-shine Cheesecake

Crust

3/4 cup	(180 mL) all-purpose flour or whole wheat flour
3 tbsp	(45 mL) brown sugar
1 tbsp	(15 mL) orange peel, finely grated
6 tbsp	(90 mL) butter
1	egg yolk, beaten

Filling

2 1/2 cups	(625 mL) cream cheese, softened
1 tbsp	(15 mL) orange peel, finely grated
1 cup	(250 mL) sugar
1/2 tsp	(2 mL) orange blossom or vanilla extract
3	eggs
1/4 cup	(60 mL) orange juice
2	large oranges, peeled, pith removed, sectioned
1 cup	(250 mL) orange glaze (p. 414)

Crust

- Preheat oven to 400 °F (205 °C). Butter bottom of a springform cake pan. Set aside.

- In a bowl, mix flour, brown sugar and orange peel. Fold in butter, mixing until granular. Blend in egg yolk.

- Press one-third crust over bottom of pan. Wrap remainder, setting aside. Bake bottom crust (without sides of pan) around 7 minutes or until golden brown. Remove from oven.

- Butter sides of pan. Attach to bottom. Line with a 2-inch (5 cm) border of crust. Set aside.

Filling

- Lower oven temperature to 375 °F (190 °C).

- In a large bowl, whip cheese and orange peel until creamy smooth. Fold in sugar, orange blossom, eggs and orange juice. Pour into pan. Bake in oven 40-50 minutes.

- Remove from oven. Let cool 15 minutes. Release spring. Run a knife along sides of pan. Let cool 30 minutes. Unclip pan. Let cool 1 more hour. Garnish with orange sections. Cover with orange glaze. Refrigerate 1 hour. Decorate with fresh mint before serving, if desired.

NUTRITION	
CALORIES PER SERVING: 504	
FAT: 29 g	CAL. FROM FAT: 50%
PROTEIN: 8 g	CHOLESTEROL: 157 mg
SODIUM: 274 mg	CARBOHYDRATES: 58 g

Classic Cheesecake

Crust

1 1/2 cups	(375 mL) Graham cracker crumbs
3 tbsp	(45 mL) brown sugar
1/2 cup	(125 mL) butter, melted

Filling

1 cup	(250 mL) cottage cheese
1 lb	(450 g) cream cheese, softened
1 cup	(250 mL) sugar
2 tbsp	(30 mL) all-purpose flour
2 tsp	(10 mL) vanilla extract
3	eggs
1/4 cup	(60 mL) milk
1 cup	(250 mL) sour cream
1 cup	(250 mL) strawberries, sliced

Crust

- Butter an 8-inch (20 cm) springform cake pan. Set aside.

- In a bowl, mix Graham cracker crumbs, brown sugar and butter. Press over bottom and along sides of pan. Set aside.

Filling

- Preheat oven to 375 °F (190 °C).

- In a large bowl, whip cottage cheese until smooth. Fold in cream cheese, sugar, flour and vanilla extract. Stir in eggs. With a spatula, add milk. Pour into pan.

- Bake in oven 45-55 minutes.

- Remove from oven. Spread sour cream over cake. Let cool 30 minutes before unmolding. Refrigerate 3-4 hours. Decorate with strawberries. Serve.

Recipe shown, opposite page

VARIATIONS

- Replace strawberries with blueberries or kiwis.

- Sprinkle grated coconut over cake.

NUTRITION	
CALORIES PER SERVING: 501	
FAT: 33 g	CAL. FROM FAT: 59%
PROTEIN: 11 g	CHOLESTEROL: 142 mg
SODIUM: 472 mg	CARBOHYDRATES: 40 g

Hazelnut Cheesecake

8-10 SERVINGS

Crust

1 cup	(250 mL)	Graham cracker crumbs
3/4 cup	(180 mL)	nuts, chopped
1/3 cup	(80 mL)	brown sugar
1/3 cup	(80 mL)	margarine or butter, melted

Filling

1 1/2 cups	(375 mL)	cream cheese, softened
3/4 cup	(180 mL)	commercial hazelnut chocolate spread
3		eggs
3 tbsp	(45 mL)	heavy cream
2/3 cup	(160 mL)	plain yogurt

Crust

- Butter a springform cake pan. In a bowl, mix Graham cracker crumbs, nuts, sugar and butter. Press over bottom and along sides of pan.

Filling

- Preheat oven to 350 °F (175 °C).

- In a bowl, whip cheese into soft peaks. Fold in 1/2 cup (125 mL) hazelnut chocolate spread. Add eggs and cream, mixing lightly. Pour into pan. Bake in oven 35-45 minutes.

- Let cake cool on a wire rack 15 minutes.

- In a bowl, mix yogurt and remaining hazelnut chocolate spread. Smooth over cake. Unclip pan. Let cool 90 minutes.

NUTRITION	
CALORIES PER SERVING: 439	
FAT: 31 g	CAL. FROM FAT: 62 %
PROTEIN: 8 g	CHOLESTEROL: 117 mg
SODIUM: 308 mg	CARBOHYDRATES: 34 g

Recipe shown opposite left

Choco-coco Cheesecake

8-10 SERVINGS

Crust

1 cup	(250 mL)	Graham cracker crumbs
2/3 cup	(160 mL)	grated coconut
1/3 cup	(125 mL)	butter
2 tbsp	(30 mL)	cocoa

Filling

2 1/2 cups	(675 mL)	cream cheese, softened
1 1/2 cups	(375 mL)	sugar
2 tbsp	(30 mL)	flour
4		eggs
1/3 cup	(80 mL)	heavy cream
1 tbsp	(15 mL)	vanilla extract
1/2 cup	(125 mL)	semisweet chocolate, melted
1/3 cup	(80 mL)	grated coconut
2 oz	(60 g)	chocolate
2 tsp	(10 mL)	shortening

Crust

- Butter a springform cake pan. In a bowl, mix Graham cracker crumbs, coconut, butter and cocoa. Press mixture over bottom and along sides of pan.

Filling

- Preheat oven to 325 °F (165 °C).

- In a large bowl, whip cream cheese until smooth. Set aside.

- In a second bowl, mix sugar and flour. Fold into cheese. Add eggs, mixing well.

- In a third bowl, mix cream and vanilla extract. Fold in melted chocolate and grated coconut.

- Pour into pan. Bake in oven 1 hour or so.

- Let cake cool on a wire rack 15 minutes. Release spring. Run a knife along sides of pan. Let cool 30 minutes. Unclip pan. Refrigerate 2 hours.

- Meanwhile, in a small saucepan, melt chocolate and shortening. Remove cake from refrigerator. Pour chocolate over cake, in a spiral. With a knife, decorate by tracing lines across cake. Refrigerate 15 minutes before serving.

NUTRITION	
CALORIES PER SERVING: 602	
FAT: 41 g	CAL. FROM FAT: 60 %
PROTEIN: 9 g	CHOLESTEROL: 163 mg
SODIUM: 355 mg	CARBOHYDRATES: 53 g

Recipe shown above right

Cheesecake in a Minute

8-10 SERVINGS

Crust

1 1/2 cups	(375 mL) Graham cracker crumbs
1/4 cup	(60 mL) brown sugar
1/2 cup	(125 mL) butter or margarine, melted

Filling

1/3 cup	(80 mL) fruit juice
1 1/2	envelopes unflavored gelatin
1 cup	(250 mL) cream cheese, softened
2/3 cup	(160 mL) sugar
1 cup	(250 mL) cottage cheese, drained
1 tbsp	(15 mL) vanilla extract
1 cup	(250 mL) whipped cream
3	kiwis, sliced
1	orange, peeled, pith removed, sectioned
1	apple, sliced
1/4 cup	(60 mL) pecans

Crust

- Preheat oven to 350 °F (175 °C). Butter a springform cake pan. Set aside.

- In a bowl, mix Graham cracker crumbs, brown sugar and butter. Press mixture over bottom and along sides of pan. Bake in oven 9 minutes or so. Set aside to cool.

Filling

- In a small saucepan, while stirring, heat fruit juice and gelatin until gelatin dissolves fully. Set aside.

- In a bowl, whip cream cheese and sugar until soft peaks form. Fold in cottage cheese. Set aside.

- While gelatin mixture is still liquid, add vanilla. Pour into cheese mixture, beating vigorously. With a spatula, gently fold in whipped cream. Pour into crust. Refrigerate 2-3 hours (or freeze 1 hour). Unmold cake. Garnish with fruit and pecans.

NUTRITION	
CALORIES PER SERVING: 424	
FAT: 24 g	CAL. FROM FAT: 51%
PROTEIN: 13 g	CHOLESTEROL: 68 mg
SODIUM: 387 mg	CARBOHYDRATES: 39 g

VARIATIONS

- Vary fruit combinations (raspberries, red currants and blueberries, as shown above) and fruit juices.

- Replace fruit juice with water or milk, and gelatin envelopes with your choice of jelly powder. Garnish with chopped nuts.

Rum Mocha Cheesecake

8-10 SERVINGS

Crust

1 ½ cups	(375 mL) oatmeal cookies, crumbled
⅓ cup	(80 mL) butter or margarine
2 tsp	(10 mL) cocoa

Filling

2 tbsp	(30 mL) instant coffee
2 oz	(60 mL) dark rum
2 ¾ cups	(680 mL) cream cheese, softened
1 cup	(250 mL) brown sugar
⅔ cup	(160 mL) semisweet chocolate, melted, lukewarm
2 tbsp	(30 mL) all-purpose flour
1 tbsp	(15 mL) vanilla extract
3	eggs
1 ½ cups	(375 mL) sour cream
½ cup	(125 mL) pistachios or almonds

Crust
- Butter a springform cake pan. Set aside.
- In a small bowl, mix cookie crumbs, butter and cream. Press over bottom and along sides of pan, up to 1 ½ inches (3.75 cm) from top. Set aside.

Filling
- Preheat oven to 375 °F (190 °C).
- In a bowl, dissolve coffee in rum. Set aside.
- In a mixer bowl, lightly whip cream cheese, brown sugar, chocolate and flour. Fold in vanilla extract and eggs. Mix at low speed.

- With a spatula, fold in rum and coffee mixture. Pour into pan.
- Bake in oven 45-55 minutes or until center of cake has set.
- Remove from oven. Let cool 10 minutes. Detach cake by running a knife along sides of pan. Unclip pan. Let cool 2 hours. Cover cake with sour cream. Decorate with pistachios or almonds. Refrigerate at least 2 hours before serving.

VARIATIONS
- Garnish cake with whipped cream dusted with cocoa.
- Serve cake on a sauce or coulis *(pp. 414-417)*.

NUTRITION	
CALORIES PER SERVING: 703	
FAT: 48 *g*	CAL. FROM FAT: 61 %
PROTEIN: 11 *g*	CHOLESTEROL: 139 *mg*
SODIUM: 436 *mg*	CARBOHYDRATES: 59 *g*

Peachy Cheesecake

6 SERVINGS

Crust

³/₄ cup	(180 mL) flour
3 tbsp	(45 mL) brown sugar
2 tbsp	(30 mL) orange peel, grated
¹/₄ cup	(60 mL) butter
1	egg yolk, beaten

Filling

3 ¹/₂ cups	(875 mL) canned peaches
2 cups	(500 mL) cream cheese, softened
¹/₂ cup	(125 mL) sugar
2 tbsp	(30 mL) flour
4	eggs
¹/₂ cup	(125 mL) peach juice
1 tsp	(5 mL) vanilla extract
²/₃ cup	(160 mL) apricot glaze *(p. 414)*

- Preheat oven to 375 °F (190 °C).

Crust

- Butter bottom of a spring-form cake pan. Set aside.

- In a bowl, mix flour, sugar and orange peel. Add butter, mixing until granular.

- Fold in egg yolk. Press one-third of crust over bottom of pan. Wrap remainder, setting aside.

- Bake bottom crust (without sides of pan) around 6 minutes or until golden brown. Remove from oven. Let cool.

- Butter sides of pan. Attach to bottom. Line with crust, up to 2 inches (5 cm) from top. Set aside.

Filling

- Reserve 3 peach halves for decoration. Finely chop remainder.

- In a large bowl, whip cheese until creamy.

- In a second bowl, combine sugar and flour. Fold into cheese. Mix in eggs. Fold in chopped peaches, peach juice and vanilla extract, whipping slightly. Pour into pan. Bake in oven 40-50 minutes.

- Let cool 15 minutes. Unmold. Decorate cake with sliced peaches. Cover with apricot glaze. Refrigerate 3-6 hours.

NUTRITION	
CALORIES PER SERVING: 752	
FAT: 38 *g*	CAL. FROM FAT: 44 %
PROTEIN: 13 *g*	CHOLESTEROL: 261 *mg*
SODIUM: 365 *mg*	CARBOHYDRATES: 96 *g*

VARIATIONS

- Use oranges, removing peel and pith (as shown above), apricots, nectarines or litchis. Vary fruit juices. Decorate with almonds.

Melt-in-your-mouth Raspberry Cheesecake

8-10 SERVINGS

Crust

³/₄ cup	(180 mL) all-purpose flour
3 tbsp	(45 mL) sugar
1 tsp	(5 mL) lemon peel, finely grated
6 tbsp	(90 mL) butter or margarine
1	egg yolk, beaten
4	drops of vanilla extract

Filling

24 oz	(675 g) cream cheese, softened
1 tbsp	(15 mL) lemon peel, finely grated
1 cup	(250 mL) sugar
2 tbsp	(30 mL) all-purpose flour
2	eggs
1	egg yolk
1 tsp	(5 mL) vanilla extract
¹/₄ cup	(60 mL) milk
3 cups	(750 mL) raspberries
1 cup	(250 mL) raspberry glaze (p. 414)

- Preheat oven to 375 °F (190 °C).

Crust
- Butter bottom of a spring-form cake pan. Set aside.

- In a bowl, mix flour, sugar and lemon peel. Add butter, mixing until granular. Set aside.

- In a second bowl, whip egg yolk and vanilla extract. Fold into pastry crust. Press one-third over bottom of pan. Wrap remainder, setting aside.

- Bake bottom crust (without sides of pan) around 6 minutes or until golden brown. Remove from oven. Let cool.

- Butter sides of pan. Attach to bottom. Line with crust, up to 2 inches (5 cm) from top. Set aside.

Filling
- In a large bowl, whip cheese and lemon peel until creamy. Fold in sugar and flour. Whip. Set aside.

- In a second bowl, mix 2 eggs, egg yolk and vanilla extract. Fold into cheese mixture. With a spatula, lightly blend in milk. Pour into crust. Bake in oven 30-40 minutes.

- Remove from oven. Let cool 30 minutes. Unclip pan. Let cake cool 30 more minutes. Wrap cake. Refrigerate 2-3 hours.

- Remove cake from refrigerator. Decorate with raspberries. Cover with raspberry glaze. Return to refrigerator until glaze sets. Serve.

VARIATION
- Cover raspberries with 1 ¹/₂ cups (375 mL) Chantilly cream (p. 413).

NUTRITION	
CALORIES PER SERVING: 559	
FAT: 33 g	CAL. FROM FAT: 52 %
PROTEIN: 9 g	CHOLESTEROL: 173 mg
SODIUM: 297 mg	CARBOHYDRATES: 60 g

Chocolate Chip Cheesecake

8-10 SERVINGS

Crust

1 ²/₃ cups	(410 mL) Graham cracker crumbs
¹/₃ cup	(80 mL) walnuts, chopped
¹/₂ cup	(125 mL) butter or margarine, melted

Filling

2 ³/₄ cups	(675 mL) cream cheese, softened
1 cup	(250 mL) sugar
2 tbsp	(30 mL) all-purpose flour
3 tbsp	(45 mL) cocoa
1 tsp	(5 mL) vanilla extract
2	eggs
1	egg yolk
¹/₄ cup	(60 mL) heavy cream
²/₃ cup	(160 mL) chocolate chips
1 cup	(250 mL) strawberry glaze (p. 414)
12	cherries
	chocolate shavings (p. 330)

Crust

- Butter bottom of a springform cake pan. Set aside.

- In a bowl, mix Graham cracker crumbs, nuts and butter. Press mixture over bottom and along sides of pan, up to 2 inches (5 cm) from top. Set aside.

Filling

- Preheat oven to 375 °F (190 °C).

- In a large bowl, whip cream cheese, sugar, flour and cocoa until creamy smooth.

- Fold in vanilla extract and eggs, whipping lightly. With a spatula, mix in cream and chocolate chips. Pour into pan. Bake in oven 40-50 minutes.

- Remove from oven. Let cake cool 15 minutes. Release spring. Run a knife along sides of pan. Let cool 30 minutes. Unclip pan. Cover cake with strawberry glaze. Decorate with red cherries and chocolate shavings. Refrigerate at least 4 hours.

NUTRITION	
CALORIES PER SERVING: 1134	
FAT: 66 *g*	CAL. FROM FAT: 50%
PROTEIN: 14 *g*	CHOLESTEROL: 159 *mg*
SODIUM: 450 *mg*	CARBOHYDRATES: 137 *g*

VARIATION

- Decorate with fresh strawberries dipped in melted chocolate and chocolate Chantilly cream (p. 413), as shown above.

SHORTCAKES

Strawberry Shortcake, Basic Recipe

	8 SERVINGS
1	9-inch (23 cm) vanilla spongecake (p. 294)
¹/₂ cup	(125 mL) Grand Marnier-flavored syrup (p. 414)
1 cup	(250 mL) custard (p. 412)
3 cups	(750 mL) fresh strawberries, rinsed, hulled
3 cups	(750 mL) Chantilly cream (p. 413)
²/₃ cup	(160 mL) strawberry glaze (p. 414)

- Slice spongecake into 2 equal layers. Brush each layer with syrup. Garnish first layer with custard. Top with 2 cups (500 mL) strawberries, then 1 cup (250 mL) Chantilly cream. Cover with second spongecake layer. With a spatula, coat shortcake with Chantilly cream.

- Dip remaining strawberries in strawberry glaze. Set in a crown on top of shortcake. Using a spatula or pastry bag with a fluted nozzle, decorate center of shortcake with remaining Chantilly cream.

- Refrigerate or serve at once.

NUTRITION	
CALORIES PER SERVING: 590	
FAT: 28 g	CAL. FROM FAT: 42%
PROTEIN: 8 g	CHOLESTEROL: 184 mg
SODIUM: 220 mg	CARBOHYDRATES: 78 g

Coconut Banana Shortcake

	8 SERVINGS
1	nut spongecake (p. 294)
¹/₂ cup	(125 mL) rum syrup (p. 414)
3	bananas, sliced
1 cup	(250 mL) maraschino cherries
²/₃ cup	(160 mL) apricot glaze (p. 414)
1 cup	(250 mL) grated coconut, toasted

- Prepare shortcake following basic recipe but replacing vanilla spongecake with nut spongecake, Grand Marnier-flavored syrup with rum syrup, strawberries with bananas and cherries, and strawberry glaze with apricot glaze.

- Arrange 2 sliced bananas and half the cherries on custard. Garnish top of cake with remaining fruit. Cover with apricot glaze. Sprinkle shortcake with coconut.

NUTRITION	
CALORIES PER SERVING: 359	
FAT: 5 g	CAL. FROM FAT: 12%
PROTEIN: 4 g	CHOLESTEROL: 58 mg
SODIUM: 188 mg	CARBOHYDRATES: 76 g

Chocolate Pear Shortcake

	8 SERVINGS
1	chocolate fudge spongecake (p. 294)
2 ¹/₂ cups	(625 mL) canned pear halves
¹/₂ cup	(125 mL) rum syrup (p. 414)
1 cup	(250 mL) custard (p. 412)
3 cups	(750 mL) chocolate Chantilly cream (p. 413)
4 oz	(115 g) semisweet chocolate
¹/₄ cup	(60 mL) butter

- Prepare shortcake following basic recipe but replacing vanilla spongecake with chocolate spongecake. Set aside 8 pear halves for decoration. Brush 2 cake layers with rum syrup. Spread first layer with custard, remaining pears and chocolate Chantilly cream. Cover with second cake layer. Coat with chocolate Chantilly cream.

- In a double-boiler, melt chocolate. Add butter. Mix off heat.

- Dip 8 reserved pear halves in melted chocolate. Place symmetrically on top of cake. Garnish with chocolate Chantilly cream.

NUTRITION	
CALORIES PER SERVING: 657	
FAT: 38 g	CAL. FROM FAT: 50%
PROTEIN: 8 g	CHOLESTEROL: 199 mg
SODIUM: 272 mg	CARBOHYDRATES: 74 g

Recipe shown above

Blueberry Shortcake

8 SERVINGS	
1	poppy seed spongecake (p. 295)
3 ½ cups	(875 mL) blueberries
⅔ cup	(160 mL) apricot glaze (p. 414)
2 tbsp	(30 mL) poppy seeds

- Prepare shortcake following basic recipe but replacing vanilla spongecake with poppy seed spongecake, strawberries with blueberries, and strawberry glaze with apricot glaze. Arrange blueberries in the center of cake. Cover with apricot glaze. Sprinkle sides of shortcake with poppy seeds.

NUTRITION	
CALORIES PER SERVING: 560	
FAT: 26 g	CAL. FROM FAT: 41%
PROTEIN: 8 g	CHOLESTEROL: 23 mg
SODIUM: 198 mg	CARBOHYDRATES: 77 g

Recipe shown above left

Pineapple Shortcake

8 SERVINGS	
1	orange spongecake (p. 294)
18	canned pineapple slices
½ cup	(125 mL) cocoa

- Prepare shortcake following basic recipe but replacing vanilla spongecake with orange spongecake, strawberries with pineapple, and strawberry glaze with cocoa.
- Reserve 6 pineapple slices for decoration. Arrange on top of assembled shortcake. Sprinkle shortcake with cocoa.

NUTRITION	
CALORIES PER SERVING: 367	
FAT: 7 g	CAL. FROM FAT: 14%
PROTEIN: 5 g	CHOLESTEROL: 43 mg
SODIUM: 187 mg	CARBOHYDRATES: 67 g

Recipe shown above right

Peach 'n' Almond Shortcake

8 SERVINGS	
1	nut spongecake (p. 294)
3 cups	(750 mL) canned peach halves, drained
½ cup	(125 mL) honey
¾ cup	(180 mL) almond powder

- Prepare shortcake following basic recipe but replacing vanilla spongecake with nut sponge-cake, strawberries with peaches, and strawberry glaze with honey.
- Reserve 8 peach halves for decoration. Dip in honey. Dredge with almond powder. Arrange on top of assembled shortcake.

NUTRITION	
CALORIES PER SERVING: 448	
FAT: 20 g	CAL. FROM FAT: 39%
PROTEIN: 10 g	CHOLESTEROL: 56 mg
SODIUM: 220 mg	CARBOHYDRATES: 69 g

Raspberry Shortcake

8 SERVINGS	
1	basic recipe shortcake
3 ½ cups	(875 mL) fresh raspberries
⅔ cup	(160 mL) slivered almonds

- Prepare shortcake following basic recipe but replacing strawberries with raspberries.
- Arrange raspberries in the center of shortcake. Cover with strawberry glaze. Garnish sides with slivered almonds.

NUTRITION	
CALORIES PER SERVING: 402	
FAT: 18 g	CAL. FROM FAT: 38%
PROTEIN: 11 g	CHOLESTEROL: 62 mg
SODIUM: 199 mg	CARBOHYDRATES: 59 g

Charlotte Bavarian Cream

ABOUT 3 ½ CUPS (875 ML)	
1 cup	(250 mL) milk
1 cup	(250 mL) sugar
4	egg yolks
1	envelope unflavored gelatin
3 tbsp	(45 mL) cold water
½ tsp	(2 mL) vanilla or other extract
1 cup	(250 mL) whipped cream

- In a saucepan, bring milk and half the sugar to a boil.

- In a bowl, beat egg yolks with remaining sugar. Add boiling milk. Return to pan, over heat. With a wooden spatula, stir until cream thickens. Do not let boil.

- Meanwhile, in a bowl, let gelatin foam in cold water. Add to cream. Let cool. For quicker results, dip bottom of saucepan in a bowl of ice-cold water, stirring gently until cream has cooled.

NUTRITION	
CALORIES PER SERVING: 217	
FAT: 9 g	CAL. FROM FAT: 37%
PROTEIN: 8 g	CHOLESTEROL: 131 mg
SODIUM: 30 mg	CARBOHYDRATES: 27 g

- Once cream starts to thicken, add vanilla extract. Fold in whipped cream.

Note : charlotte should be ready to receive Bavarian cream, since gelatin will set completely in a matter of minutes.

BAVARIAN STRAWBERRY CREAM
- Into boiling milk, fold ½ cup (125 mL) puréed strawberries.

BAVARIAN COFFEE CREAM
- Into boiling milk, fold 3 tbsp (45 mL) instant coffee.

BAVARIAN CHOCOLATE CREAM
- Before boiling milk, blend in ¼ cup (60 mL) cocoa.

KIRSCH-FLAVORED BAVARIAN CREAM
- Into basic recipe, fold 1 oz (30 mL) kirsch at the same time as vanilla extract.

American-style Russian Charlotte

8-10 SERVINGS	
1	vanilla spongecake (p. 294) or 9-inch (23 cm) commercial sponge cake
3 tbsp	(45 mL) raspberry or blueberry jam
3 cups	(750 mL) Grand Marnier-flavored light cream (p. 413)
36	ladyfingers (p. 447)
1 ¼ cups	(300 mL) fruit salad or fresh fruit
1 ½ cups	(375 mL) Chantilly cream (p. 413)

- Slice spongecake into 2 equal layers. Over first layer, spread jam, then a thin coat of light cream. Cover with second spongecake. Coat top and sides with light cream.

- Trim off one end of ladyfingers. Surround charlotte with upright cookies, rounded tip up. Add another coat of light cream to top of charlotte. Spread a layer of fruit salad or fresh fruit. Pipe swirls of Chantilly cream over fruit. Decorate with fresh fruit, if desired.

NUTRITION	
CALORIES PER SERVING: 583	
FAT: 29 g	CAL. FROM FAT: 44%
PROTEIN: 10 g	CHOLESTEROL: 275 mg
SODIUM: 219 mg	CARBOHYDRATES: 72 g

Coconut Strawberry Charlotte

8-10 SERVINGS

1	vanilla spongecake (p. 294)
1/4 cup	(60 mL) strawberry jam
2/3 cup	(160 mL) grated coconut
2 cups	(500 mL) Bavarian strawberry cream (p. 326)
3	drops of red food coloring (optional)
2 cups	(500 mL) Chantilly cream (p. 413)
36	cocoa ladyfingers (p. 447)
3/4 cup	(180 mL) fresh strawberries

- Slice spongecake into 2 equal layers.

- Place first layer into the bottom of a mold. Brush with jam. Sprinkle with half the grated coconut. Cover with Bavarian cream. Top with second cake layer. Refrigerate 1 hour.

- Remove from refrigerator. Unmold. Add food coloring to Chantilly cream, if desired.

- With a spatula, coat charlotte with Chantilly cream. Surround charlotte with a row of ladyfingers. Using a pastry bag, pipe remaining Chantilly cream onto charlotte. Decorate with strawberries. Sprinkle with remaining grated coconut.

NUTRITION	
CALORIES PER SERVING: 634	
FAT: 37 g	CAL. FROM FAT: 52 %
PROTEIN: 9 g	CHOLESTEROL: 304 mg
SODIUM: 227 mg	CARBOHYDRATES: 68 g

Chocolate Coffee Charlotte

8-10 SERVINGS

1 oz	(30 mL) rum
1/4 cup	(60 mL) honey
1	cocoa spongecake (p. 295)
2 cups	(500 mL) Bavarian coffee cream (p. 326)
2 cups	(500 mL) chocolate Chantilly cream (p. 413)
36	cigars (p. 360) chocolate shavings (p. 330)

- In a bowl, mix rum and honey. Slice spongecake into 2 equal layers. Place first layer into the bottom of a mold. Brush with rum mixture. Top with Bavarian coffee cream. Cover with second spongecake layer.

- Let set in refrigerator 1 hour. Remove from refrigerator. Unmold.

- With a spatula, coat charlotte with chocolate Chantilly cream. Surround with a row of cigars tightly squeezed together. Using a pastry bag, pipe remaining Chantilly cream on top of charlotte. Decorate with chocolate shavings.

NUTRITION	
CALORIES PER SERVING: 964	
FAT: 59 g	CAL. FROM FAT: 53 %
PROTEIN: 12 g	CHOLESTEROL: 304 mg
SODIUM: 222 mg	CARBOHYDRATES: 107 g

Individual Charlottes

---

6 SERVINGS

2 cups	(500 mL) spongecake *(p. 294)* **or commercial sponge cake, diced**
5 tbsp	(75 mL) kirsch syrup *(p. 414)*
¼ cup	(60 mL) raspberry jam
2 cups	(500 mL) light cream *(p. 413)*
9	ladyfingers *(p. 447)*
1 ½ cups	(375 mL) Chantilly cream *(p. 413)*
6	raspberries
6	mint leaves

■ Into bottom of 6 dessert cups, arrange a few pieces of cake moistened with kirsch syrup.

■ Pour 2 tsp (10 mL) raspberry jam into each cup. Using a spoon or pastry bag, fill three-quarters with light cream. Cut ladyfingers in half. Place 3 ladyfingers against sides of each cup, rounded tip up. Using a pastry bag with a medium-size fluted nozzle, pipe a swirl of Chantilly cream onto each charlotte. Decorate with a raspberry and a mint leaf.

VARIATIONS
• Use different jam flavors and any other fresh or canned fruit.

NUTRITION	
CALORIES PER SERVING: 732	
FAT: 36 *g*	CAL. FROM FAT: 44 %
PROTEIN: 11 *g*	CHOLESTEROL: 251 *mg*
SODIUM: 276 *mg*	CARBOHYDRATES: 93 *g*

Small Apple Nut Charlottes

---

8 SERVINGS

2 cups	(500 mL) vanilla spongecake *(p. 294)* **or cocoa spongecake** *(p. 295)*, **diced**
2 cups	(500 mL) apple sauce
1 tbsp	(15 mL) ground cinnamon
2 cups	(500 mL) light cream *(p. 413)*
24	ladyfingers *(p. 447)*
1 cup	(250 mL) Chantilly cream *(p. 413)*
½ cup	(125 mL) nuts, chopped

■ In successive layers, divide diced spongecake, apple sauce, cinnamon and light cream among 8 molds or dessert cups. Cut ladyfingers in half. Line 6 ladyfingers against sides of each cup, rounded tip up.

■ Using a pastry bag with a medium-size fluted nozzle, pipe a swirl of Chantilly cream onto each charlotte. Sprinkle with 1 tbsp (15 mL) chopped nuts. Serve.

VARIATIONS
• Moisten sponge dices with alcohol. Garnish bottom of dessert cups with chopped dried fruit or sweet chocolate bread. Replace apple sauce with jam or puréed rhubarb, peach or pear, and nuts with hazelnuts or almonds.

NUTRITION	
CALORIES PER SERVING: 599	
FAT: 29 *g*	CAL. FROM FAT: 43 %
PROTEIN: 11 *g*	CHOLESTEROL: 248 *mg*
SODIUM: 229 *mg*	CARBOHYDRATES: 76 *g*

St-Placide Charlotte

	8-10 SERVINGS
1	Swiss roll (p. 298)
1 cup	(250 mL) canned apricot halves
2 cups	(500 mL) Bavarian strawberry cream (p. 326)
1 cup	(250 mL) apricots, cut into pieces
1 cup	(250 mL) Chantilly cream (p. 413)
1/2 cup	(125 mL) roasted almonds, crumbled
1	cocoa spongecake, 3/4-inch (1.75 cm) thick (p. 295)
1/2 cup	(125 mL) apricot glaze (p. 414)

- Cut cake roll into 1/2-inch (1.25 cm) thick slices.
- Line a round deep mold with cake slices, alternating with apricot halves.
- In a bowl, mix Bavarian cream and apricots. Pour into mold.
- In a second bowl, mix Chantilly cream with half the almonds. Pour into mold. Cover with cocoa spongecake. Refrigerate 1 hour. Unmold. Cover charlotte with apricot glaze. Sprinkle sides with almond crumbs.

VARIATIONS
- Replace apricots with pears, litchis or grated coconut.

NUTRITION	
CALORIES PER SERVING: 681	
FAT: 40 g	CAL. FROM FAT: 52%
PROTEIN: 9 g	CHOLESTEROL: 215 mg
SODIUM: 270 mg	CARBOHYDRATES: 75 g

Island Charlotte

	8-10 SERVINGS
1	cocoa spongecake (p. 295)
1/4 cup	(60 mL) strawberry jam
1	envelope unflavored gelatin
2 cups	(500 mL) strawberry yogurt, at room temperature
1/2 cup	(125 mL) dried figs, chopped
2 cups	(500 mL) Chantilly cream (p. 413)
24	chocolate-covered wafers
1/2 cup	(125 mL) fresh figs, sliced

- Slice spongecake into 2 equal layers. Place first layer into a mold. Brush with jam. Set aside.
- In a bowl, dissolve gelatin in a little water. Fold into yogurt, stirring vigorously. Add figs. Pour over spongecake in mold. Cover with second spongecake layer. Refrigerate 1 hour.
- Remove from refrigerator. Unmold. With a spatula, coat charlotte with Chantilly cream. Press wafers around charlotte. Using a pastry bag, pipe Chantilly cream onto charlotte. Decorate with fresh figs. Serve.

VARIATIONS
- Decorate with fresh strawberries. Vary yogurt flavors.

NUTRITION	
CALORIES PER SERVING: 464	
FAT: 18 g	CAL. FROM FAT: 34%
PROTEIN: 11 g	CHOLESTEROL: 97 mg
SODIUM: 253 mg	CARBOHYDRATES: 68 g

Royal Charlotte

	8-10 SERVINGS
18	Swiss roll slices, 1/2-inch (1.25 cm) thick (p. 298)
1 cup	(250 mL) fruit salad, drained
2 cups	(500 mL) kirsch-flavored Bavarian cream (p. 326)
1	spongecake of your choice, 9-inch (23 cm) wide by 1/2-inch (1.25 cm) thick (pp. 294 -295)
1/2 cup	(125 mL) apricot glaze (p. 414)
	fresh mint leaves
	strawberry, raspberry or blueberry coulis (p. 415)

- Line a 9-inch (23 cm) round deep mold with cake slices. Set aside.
- In a bowl, mix fruit salad and Bavarian cream. Pour into mold, over cake. Cover with spongecake. Refrigerate 3 hours.
- Unmold over cardboard. Spread apricot glaze all over cake. Decorate with fresh mint. Serve charlotte with fresh fruit or coulis.

NUTRITION	
CALORIES PER SERVING: 627	
FAT: 29 g	CAL. FROM FAT: 41%
PROTEIN: 8 g	CHOLESTEROL: 190 mg
SODIUM: 257 mg	CARBOHYDRATES: 86 g

Recipe shown above

Decorations and Frostings

Icing Sugar Decorations

- Lay paper strips side by side on top of cake. Using a fine sieve, dust with icing sugar.

- Gently remove paper strips.

- For fancier results, make your own paper cut-outs or use a decorative paper doily.

Almond Paste Holly Leaves

- Color some almond paste by adding a few drops green food coloring. Roll out to a 1/8-inch (0.25 cm) thickness.

- Cut paste into 1 x 2-inch (2.5 x 5 cm) rectangles. With a small round pastry cutter, trim edges to imitate holly.

- With a knife, make right-angled marks to imitate nervures.

Meringue Mushrooms

- Using a pastry bag, squeeze mushroom stems and caps onto a cookie sheet lined with pastry paper. Dry in oven 30 minutes at 175 °F (85 °C).

- Carve a small hole under each mushroom cap. Sprinkle in a few drops of melted chocolate. Join with stems. Let chocolate set.

- Decorate mushrooms with melted chocolate, icing sugar, jam, etc.

Chocolate Curls and Shavings

- Onto a pastry sheet, pour 1 1/2 cups (375 mL) melted chocolate. With a narrow spatula, spread evenly. Let harden.

- With a large spatula, scrape chocolate from bottom of pan to make curls and shavings.

Butter Cream

ABOUT 2 CUPS (500 mL)	
1 cup	(250 mL) unsalted butter
4 cups	(1 L) icing sugar
3	egg yolks
¼ cup	(60 mL) heavy cream
2 tsp	(10 mL) vanilla extract

- In a large bowl, cream butter around 8 minutes or until light and fluffy. While beating, sift in icing sugar a little at a time. Add eggs one by one, whipping vigorously between additions. Fold in cream and vanilla. Continue beating until smooth.

CHOCOLATE BUTTER CREAM

- In a double-boiler, melt 5 oz (140 g) unsweetened chocolate. Let cool until lukewarm. Add to butter cream. Beat until smooth.

PEANUT AND CHOCOLATE BUTTER CREAM

- In a double-boiler, melt 4 oz (115 g) unsweetened chocolate. Let cool until lukewarm. Fold into butter cream. Add ¹⁄₃ cup (80 mL) peanut butter. Beat until smooth.

◀ NUTRITION	
CALORIES PER SERVING: 507	
FAT: 29 g	CAL. FROM FAT: 51%
PROTEIN: 1 g	CHOLESTEROL: 156 mg
SODIUM: 9 mg	CARBOHYDRATES: 61 g

MOCHA BUTTER CREAM

- In a double-boiler, melt 2 oz (60 g) unsweetened chocolate. Let cool until lukewarm.

  Dissolve 3 tbsp (45 mL) instant coffee in 3 tbsp (45 mL) hot water. Let cool until lukewarm.

  Replace cream and vanilla in basic recipe with these ingredients.

ORANGE BUTTER CREAM

- In basic recipe for butter cream, replace heavy cream with 1 tbsp (15 mL) orange peel, 2 tbsp (30 mL) Grand Marnier and 2 tbsp (30 mL) orange juice.

RASPBERRY BUTTER CREAM

- In basic recipe for butter cream, replace heavy cream with 5 tbsp (75 mL) raspberries and 1 tbsp (15 mL) lemon juice.

Recipes shown above, left to right : Orange Butter Cream, Chocolate Butter Cream, Raspberry Butter Cream, Mocha Butter Cream

Pies have the undesirable reputation of containing much fat and calories! The pie crust is very rich in fat. To lighten your pies, you may eliminate the top crust and, even better, replace the bottom one with a graham wafer crust.

Notice the Yogurt Sugar Pie (p. 336), an original and interesting recipe, especially when we avoid the top crust. Decorate it with lattice strips on the top of the filling. St-Louis Apple Tart (p. 343) is another good choice where the pastry cream can be lightened by reducing the quantity of sugar and by using skim milk.

PIES AND TARTS

Shortcrust Pastry

FOR 2 PIE CRUSTS OR 8 TARTS	
5 tbsp	(75 mL) cold water
1 tbsp	(15 mL) sugar
1 tsp	(5 mL) salt
²/₃ cup	(160 mL) shortening
2 cups	(500 mL) flour

- In a bowl, dissolve sugar and salt in water.

- In a second bowl, mix shortening and flour until granular. Make a well in the center.

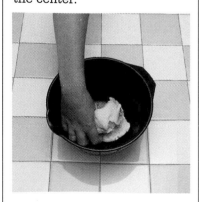

- Pour liquid mixture into well. Gently hand-mix, without kneading.
- Seal dough in plastic wrap. Refrigerate at least 15 minutes.

Sugar Crust Pastry

FOR 2 PIE CRUSTS OR 8 TARTS	
¹/₂ cup	(125 mL) butter
1 cup	(250 mL) icing sugar
1	small egg
3	drops of vanilla extract
1 ¹/₄ cups	(300 mL) flour

- In a mixer bowl, cream butter. Fold in icing sugar, mixing until granular. Mix in egg and vanilla extract.

- With a spatula, fold in flour without over-mixing.
- Wrap dough. Refrigerate.

Rolling, Fitting and Baking Pies and Tarts

- *Preheat oven to 400 °F (205 °C). Butter a pie pan or tart molds.*
- *Remove dough from refrigerator. Roll out and divide into two 9-inch (23 cm) crusts. Wrap up excess dough. Refrigerate.*
- *Flour a clean, even surface. Shape dough into a ball. With a rolling pin, gently flatten dough. If dough tends to stick, lightly flour rolling pin. Roll out dough to a ¹/₈-inch (0.25 cm) thickness.*
- *Roll dough around pin, to place more easily into pie pan. Unfold over pan.*

- *Lift up pan. Drop flat onto working surface, so dough settles into pan by itself.*
- *With the blunt edge of a knife, trim away excess dough.*

◀◀	NUTRITION
CALORIES PER PIE: 1084	
FAT: 68 g	CAL. FROM FAT: 58%
PROTEIN: 12 g	CHOLESTEROL: 0 mg
SODIUM: 267 mg	CARBOHYDRATES: 25 g

◀	NUTRITION
CALORIES PER PIE: 942	
FAT: 48 g	CAL. FROM FAT: 45%
PROTEIN: 12 g	CHOLESTEROL: 209 mg
SODIUM: 596 mg	CARBOHYDRATES: 120 g

- *To make lining easier, arrange molds star-like. Place pie crust on top. Roll pin over molds to trim off excess dough. Pinch dough so it will bind to molds.*

- *Fashion your choice of edges : with fingers, as shown above, or with a knife, as shown below. Let stand 15 minutes before cooking. Bake in oven 15 minutes or so.*

Flaky Pastry

AROUND 2 LBS (900 g)	
½ cup	(125 mL) butter
2 ½ cups	(625 mL) all-purpose flour
1 tsp	(5 mL) salt
1 cup	(250 mL) ice-cold water

Forming

1 ¼ cups	(300 mL) cold butter, in a 4-inch (10 cm) square

- In a bowl, cream butter. Fold in flour and salt, mixing until granular. Make a well in the center. Pour in water. With a spatula, gently glide flour into water.

- With hands, knead 4-5 times until dough is smooth and no longer sticks to hands. Shape into a ball.

- Transfer dough to a floured cookie sheet. Cover with plastic wrap. Refrigerate at least 20 minutes.

NUTRITION	
CALORIES PER SERVING: 286	
FAT: 15 *g*	CAL. FROM FAT: 47%
PROTEIN: 16 *g*	CHOLESTEROL: 75 *mg*
SODIUM: 634 *mg*	CARBOHYDRATES: 22 *g*

Rolling Pastry

1. Remove butter and dough from refrigerator.

2. Deeply mark dough with a cross-shape incision.

3. With hands, unfold each cross section outwards.

4. With a rolling pin, flatten dough into a cross. Place butter square in the center.

5. Fold in all 4 dough sections to seal in butter.

6. Flour lightly. Roll out dough into a 15 x 8-inch (40 x 20 cm) rectangle. With a pastry brush, remove excess flour.

7. Fold in rectangle, bringing both ends toward the center, to form a 8-inch (20 cm) square. Brush away excess flour once more.

8. Fold in two to make 4 layers of dough.

9. Wrap. Refrigerate at least 45 minutes.

- *Remove from refrigerator. Repeat steps 6 through 9 to make 8 layers of dough. For even flakier results, roll a third time. Return dough to refrigerator. Chill at least 8 hours before baking.*

Country Pie

6-8 SERVINGS

2	9-inch (23 cm) pie crusts (p. 334)
1/3 cup	(80 mL) raspberry jam
1/2 cup	(125 mL) rolled oats
1 1/2 cups	(375 mL) brown sugar
	pinch of salt
1/2 cup	(125 mL) semisweet chocolate chips
2/3 cup	(160 mL) milk
2 tbsp	(30 mL) butter, melted

- Preheat oven to 350 °F (175 °C). Line a pie pan with crust.

- Spread jam over crust. Set aside.

- In a bowl, mix rolled oats, brown sugar, salt and chocolate chips. Fold in milk and melted butter. Pour into crust.

- With a brush, moisten edges of dough. Cover with second crust. Pinch edges to seal.

- Bake in oven 25 minutes. Serve warm or chilled. Garnish with ice cream or yogurt, if desired.

NUTRITION	
CALORIES PER SERVING: 512	
FAT: 20 g	CAL. FROM FAT: 34%
PROTEIN: 5 g	CHOLESTEROL: 10 mg
SODIUM: 370 mg	CARBOHYDRATES: 82 g

Maple Syrup Pie

6-8 SERVINGS

1/2 cup	(125 mL) cornstarch
1/2 cup	(125 mL) water
3	egg yolks
2 cups	(500 mL) brown sugar
1 1/2 cups	(375 mL) maple syrup
1/2 cup	(125 mL) butter
1/3 cup	(80 mL) nuts, chopped
1 tsp	(5 mL) vanilla extract
1	9-inch (23 cm) baked pie crust (p. 334) or Graham cracker crumb crust
	whipped cream
	nuts, chopped

- In a bowl, dilute cornstarch in water. Mix in egg yolks.

- In a saucepan, over moderate heat, melt brown sugar in maple syrup. Fold in cornstarch, mixing until thick and creamy. Over low heat, continue cooking 3 minutes, while stirring.

- Off heat, mix in butter, chopped nuts and vanilla extract. Pour into crust. Refrigerate 2 hours. Garnish with whipped cream and chopped nuts. Serve.

VARIATION
- Replace nuts with currants.

NUTRITION	
CALORIES PER SERVING: 760	
FAT: 33 g	CAL. FROM FAT: 39%
PROTEIN: 6 g	CHOLESTEROL: 131 mg
SODIUM: 299 mg	CARBOHYDRATES: 114 g

Yogurt Sugar Pie

6-8 SERVINGS

2	9-inch (23 cm) pie crusts (p. 334)
1 3/4 cups	(425 mL) brown sugar
1 cup	(250 mL) plain yogurt
4 tsp	(20 mL) all-purpose flour
4 tsp	(20 mL) butter
1	egg
1 tsp	(5 mL) vanilla extract
2	eggs, beaten

- Preheat oven to 350 °F (175 °C). Line a pie pan with crust. Set aside.

- In a bowl, mix brown sugar and yogurt. Set aside.

- In a second bowl, mix flour, butter, egg and vanilla extract. Blend into first mixture. Pour into crust.

- Cover with remaining crust. Make a few incisions into top to let cooking steam escape. Brush with beaten eggs. Bake in oven 50 minutes or so.

NUTRITION	
CALORIES PER SERVING: 455	
FAT: 17 g	CAL. FROM FAT: 32%
PROTEIN: 6 g	CHOLESTEROL: 77 mg
SODIUM: 363 mg	CARBOHYDRATES: 72 g

Pecan Pie

6-8 SERVINGS

1	9-inch (23 cm) pie crust *(p. 334)*
1 ⅓ cups	(330 mL) brown sugar
½ cup	(125 mL) condensed milk
2	eggs
2 tbsp	(30 mL) all-purpose flour
2 tsp	(10 mL) vanilla extract
1 tbsp	(15 mL) butter, melted
⅔ cup	(160 mL) pecans

- Preheat oven to 350 °F (175 °C). Line a pie pan with crust. Set aside.

- In a bowl, mix brown sugar and condensed milk. Fold in eggs, flour, vanilla extract and melted butter. Pour into crust. Arrange pecans on top.

- Bake in oven 25-30 minutes.

APPLE SUGAR PIE
- On top of pie, arrange concentric circles of thinly-sliced apples. Bake in oven.

NUTRITION	
CALORIES PER SERVING: 370	
FAT: 13 *g*	CAL. FROM FAT: 32%
PROTEIN: 5 *g*	CHOLESTEROL: 56 *mg*
SODIUM: 212 *mg*	CARBOHYDRATES: 59 *g*

Sugar Pie

6-8 SERVINGS

1	9-inch (23 cm) pie crust *(p. 334)*
2 tbsp	(30 mL) cornstarch
2 tbsp	(30 mL) flour
¾ cup	(180 mL) light cream
1 ¼ cups	(300 mL) brown sugar
⅔ cup	(160 mL) heavy cream
1 tsp	(5 mL) vanilla extract
4 tsp	(20 mL) butter
	whipped cream (optional)

- Preheat oven to 350 °F (175 °C). Line a pie pan with crust. Set aside.

- In a bowl, mix cornstarch, flour and half the light cream. Whisk until creamy. Set aside.

- In a saucepan, mix brown sugar, heavy cream and remaining light cream. Bring to a boil.

- Whisking vigorously, fold in cornstarch and flour mixture. Off heat, scrape sides of pan while whisking. Return to heat. Continue whisking until bubbly. Off heat, fold in vanilla extract and butter. Pour into mold. Bake in oven 20-30 minutes. Let cool slightly or fully. Serve with whipped cream, if desired.

Recipe shown above, top photograph
Variation
- Cover with crust or dough strips in a lattice pattern, as shown above, bottom photograph.

NUTRITION	
CALORIES PER SERVING: 375	
FAT: 20 *g*	CAL. FROM FAT: 47%
PROTEIN: 3 *g*	CHOLESTEROL: 47 *mg*
SODIUM: 195 *mg*	CARBOHYDRATES: 48 *g*

Chocolate Fudge Pie

6-8 SERVINGS

1	9-inch (23 cm) pie crust (p. 334)
6 oz	(165 g) dark unsweetened chocolate
1 cup	(250 mL) butter
1 ½ cups	(375 mL) sugar
⅓ cup	(80 mL) all-purpose flour
7	eggs
1 tsp	(5 mL) vanilla extract

- Preheat oven to 350 °F (175 °C).

- Butter and flour a springform pie pan. Line with crust. Bake in oven 15 minutes. Let cool.

- In a double-boiler, melt chocolate and butter, stirring often. Let cool.

- In a bowl, beat sugar, flour, eggs and vanilla extract until smooth and creamy. Fold into chocolate mixture. Pour into crust. Bake in oven 25-35 minutes. Let cool. Unmold.

Recipe shown opposite left

VARIATION

- Replace vanilla with 4 drops orange blossom and 3 tbsp (45 mL) grated orange peel.

NUTRITION	
CALORIES PER SERVING: 633	
FAT: 44 g	CAL. FROM FAT: 60 %
PROTEIN: 9 g	CHOLESTEROL: 222 mg
SODIUM: 428 mg	CARBOHYDRATES: 58 g

Minute Chocolate Pie

6-8 SERVINGS

2 cups	(500 mL) milk
⅔ cup	(160 mL) sugar
4 oz	(115 g) unsweetened chocolate
4	egg yolks
2 tbsp	(30 mL) cornstarch
2 tbsp	(30 mL) butter
1 tsp	(5 mL) vanilla extract
1	9-inch (23 cm) pie crust, baked (p. 334)
2 cups	(500 mL) whipped cream
2 tbsp	(30 mL) cocoa

- In a saucepan, heat 1 ½ cups (375 mL) milk and half the sugar.

- Meanwhile, in a double-boiler, melt chocolate. Fold into warm milk.

- In a bowl, combine remaining sugar and egg yolks. Add remaining milk and cornstarch, mixing until creamy smooth. While whisking, pour into boiling milk.

- Once mixture starts to bubble, remove from heat. Mix in butter and vanilla. Pour into baked crust.

- Let cool. Decorate with whipped cream. Dust with cocoa.

Recipe shown above right

VARIATIONS

- Add ⅔ cup (160 mL) grated coconut at the same time as butter and vanilla.

- Replace whipped cream with your choice of ice cream.

NUTRITION	
CALORIES PER SERVING: 446	
FAT: 33 g	CAL. FROM FAT: 62 %
PROTEIN: 7 g	CHOLESTEROL: 163 mg
SODIUM: 222 mg	CARBOHYDRATES: 37 g

Peanut Butter Pie

8-10 SERVINGS

1	Graham cracker crumb crust
2 ½ cups	(625 mL) smooth peanut butter
2 ½ cups	(625 mL) cream cheese, softened
2 cups	(500 mL) sugar
3 tbsp	(45 mL) butter, melted
2 tsp	(10 mL) vanilla extract
½ tsp	(2 mL) ground cinnamon
1 ½ cups	(375 mL) whipped cream
¾ cup	(180 mL) semisweet chocolate, finely chopped
5 tbsp	(75 mL) strong coffee, heated
	peanuts

▪ Line a 9-inch (23 cm) springform pie pan with Graham cracker crumb crust. Set aside.

▪ In a food processor, beat peanut butter, cream cheese, sugar, melted butter, vanilla extract and cinnamon 2-3 minutes or until smooth.

▪ With a spatula, fold in whipped cream a little at a time. Pour into crust. Smooth surface with a spatula. Refrigerate 3-5 hours or until filling has set.

▪ In a double-boiler, melt chocolate and coffee, mixing well. Let chocolate cool 5 minutes or so. Pour lukewarm mixture over cold pie. Refrigerate 15-25 minutes.

▪ Unmold using a small knife warmed in hot water. Run knife along sides of pan. Release spring. Garnish with peanuts. Serve.

NUTRITION	
CALORIES PER SERVING: 1064	
FAT: 76 g	CAL. FROM FAT: 62%
PROTEIN: 24 g	CHOLESTEROL: 96 mg
SODIUM: 654 mg	CARBOHYDRATES: 83 g

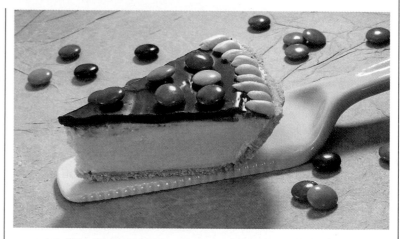

VARIATIONS

• Decorate pie with candy-covered chocolate, as shown above.

• Use crunchy peanut butter.

Upside-down Pistachio Pie

6-8 SERVINGS	
2	9-inch (23 cm) pie crusts (p. 334)
1/3 cup	(80 mL) water
1/2 cup	(125 mL) brown sugar
1/4 cup	(60 mL) honey
1/4 cup	(60 mL) butter
2 cups	(500 mL) pistachios, chopped
1/2 cup	(125 mL) heavy cream
1/3 cup	(80 mL) raspberry jam
1 oz	(30 mL) blackcurrant liqueur
	pistachios

- Line a springform pie pan with crust so dough slightly exceeds rim.

- In a saucepan, bring to a boil water, brown sugar and honey. Mix until brown sugar dissolves. Reduce heat. Simmer 25 minutes.

- Fold in butter, pistachios and cream. Simmer at least 15 minutes. Pour into crust.

- Preheat oven to 400 °F (205 °C).

- Moisten edges of dough. Cover with second crust, so dough also slightly exceeds rim. Pinch edges. Bake in oven 30-35 minutes. Let cool. Unmold.

- In a saucepan, melt together jam and blackcurrant liqueur. Brush over pie. Decorate with pistachios.

NUTRITION	
CALORIES PER SERVING: 530	
FAT: 32 g	CAL. FROM FAT: 54%
PROTEIN: 7 g	CHOLESTEROL: 36 mg
SODIUM: 368 mg	CARBOHYDRATES: 56 g

VARIATION
- Replace raspberry jam with blackcurrant jam.

Upside-down Pear and Pastis Pie

6-8 SERVINGS

3 tbsp	(45 mL) butter
¼ cup	(60 mL) sugar
16	canned pear halves
2 oz	(60 mL) pastis
1	flaky pastry crust
	(p. 335)
	vanilla ice cream (optional)

- Preheat oven to 350 °F (175 °C). Butter a flameproof 8-inch (20.5 cm) wide by 2-inch (5 cm) deep cake pan. Sprinkle with sugar.

- In bottom of pan, arrange a circle of pears, rounded side down. Over very high heat, caramelize pears and sugar, rotating pan occasionally. Remove from heat after 3 minutes.

- Pour in pastis. Return to heat. Flambé. Remove from heat once flames have extinguished. Cover with crust. Pinch edges. Bake in oven 25-35 minutes.

- Remove from oven. Let cool until lukewarm. Slightly tip pan over a bowl to retrieve cooking syrup. Set aside.

- Turn out pie over a plate. Serve warm with cooking syrup and vanilla ice cream, if desired.

NUTRITION	
CALORIES PER SERVING: 454	
FAT: 12 *g*	CAL. FROM FAT: 24 %
PROTEIN: 3 *g*	CHOLESTEROL: 11 *mg*
SODIUM: 185 *mg*	CARBOHYDRATES: 84 *g*

VARIATIONS

- Replace pears and pastis with peaches and orange liqueur (as shown opposite), pineapples and rum (as shown bottom right), apples and kirsch, strawberries and vodka, etc.

Pumpkin Pie

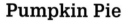

6-8 SERVINGS

1	9-inch (23 cm) pie crust (p. 334)
1 cup	(250 mL) pumpkin, cooked
³/₄ cup	(180 mL) grated coconut
¹/₂ cup	(125 mL) sugar
	pinch of ground nutmeg
¹/₂ tsp	(2 mL) ground cinnamon
¹/₄ tsp	(1 mL) allspice
2 tbsp	(30 mL) butter, melted
¹/₂ tsp	(2 mL) vanilla extract
2	eggs, lightly beaten
1 cup	(250 mL) milk, heated
1 cup	(250 mL) whipped cream

■ Preheat oven to 350 °F (190 °C). Line a pie pan with crust. Set aside.

■ In a bowl, mix pumpkin, grated coconut and sugar. Add spices.

■ In a second bowl, mix butter, vanilla extract, eggs and milk. Fold into pumpkin mixture. Pour into crust. Bake in oven 40-50 minutes.

■ Let cool. Decorate with whipped cream.

NUTRITION	
CALORIES PER SERVING: 304	
FAT: 19 g	CAL. FROM FAT: 55 %
PROTEIN: 5 g	CHOLESTEROL: 78 mg
SODIUM: 228 mg	CARBOHYDRATES: 31 g

Apple Rhubarb Tart

6-8 SERVINGS

1	9-inch (23 cm) pie crust (p. 334)
3 cups	(750 mL) rhubarb, cut into pieces
²/₃ cup	(160 mL) sugar
¹/₄ cup	(60 mL) water
³/₄ cup	(180 mL) heavy cream
¹/₂ cup	(125 mL) sugar
4	eggs
¹/₄ cup	(60 mL) all-purpose flour
1 tsp	(5 mL) vanilla extract
1 tsp	(5 mL) dark rum
2	apples, peeled, very thinly sliced
¹/₂ cup	(125 mL) apricot glaze (p. 414)

■ Preheat oven to 350 °F (175 °C). Line a springform pan with crust.

■ In a saucepan, bring to a boil rhubarb, ²/₃ cup (160 mL) sugar and water. Cover. Boil 5 minutes. Remove from heat. Let cool.

■ In a bowl, half-whip cream. Add remaining sugar, eggs, flour, vanilla extract and rum. Whip fully. Fold in cooked rhubarb. Pour into crust. Cover with sliced apples.

■ Bake in oven 35 minutes. Lower oven temperature to 300 °F (150 °C). Bake 5 minutes. Remove from oven. Let cool. Cover with apricot glaze.

NUTRITION	
CALORIES PER SERVING: 410	
FAT: 17 g	CAL. FROM FAT: 36 %
PROTEIN: 5 g	CHOLESTEROL: 122 mg
SODIUM: 191 mg	CARBOHYDRATES: 62 g

St-Louis Apple Tart

6-8 SERVINGS	
1	9-inch (23 cm) pie crust (p. 334)
³/₄ cup	(180 mL) custard (p. 412)
2	apples, peeled, finely sliced
¹/₂ cup	(125 mL) apricot glaze (p. 414)

■ Preheat oven to 375 °F (190 °C). Line a pie pan with crust. Set aside.

■ Spread custard into crust. Arrange concentric circles of apples over custard.

■ Bake in oven 30 minutes or so. Let cool 10 minutes. Cover with apricot glaze.

Recipe shown above left and right

VARIATIONS
• Flavor custard with almond liqueur. Garnish pie with roasted sliced almonds.

NUTRITION	
CALORIES PER SERVING: 190	
FAT: 7 g	CAL. FROM FAT: 34%
PROTEIN: 3 g	CHOLESTEROL: 26 mg
SODIUM: 173 mg	CARBOHYDRATES: 30 g

Apple Cream Pie

6-8 SERVINGS	
1	9-inch (23 cm) pie crust (p. 334)
4	apples, peeled, finely sliced
2	egg yolks
4 tsp	(20 mL) sugar
2	drops of vanilla extract
²/₃ cup	(160 mL) heavy cream
¹/₂ cup	(125 mL) apricot glaze (p. 414) **(optional)**

■ Preheat oven to 375 °F (190 °C). Line a pie pan with crust. Set aside.

■ Arrange concentric circles of apples over crust. Bake in oven 20 minutes.

■ Meanwhile, in a bowl, mix egg yolks, sugar and vanilla extract. Fold in cream.

■ Remove pie from oven. Cover with cream mixture. Return to oven approximately 20 minutes or until top is golden brown. Let cool 10 minutes.

■ Unmold. Cover with apricot glaze, if desired.

VARIATIONS
• Decorate pie with slivered almonds or grated Cheddar cheese.

NUTRITION	
CALORIES PER SERVING: 287	
FAT: 15 g	CAL. FROM FAT: 45%
PROTEIN: 3 g	CHOLESTEROL: 80 mg
SODIUM: 163 mg	CARBOHYDRATES: 38 g

Lime Tart

6-8 SERVINGS	
4	eggs
2	egg yolks
1 cup	(250 mL) sugar
1 cup	(250 mL) lime juice
2	drops of green food coloring (optional)
1 cups	(250 mL) butter, melted
1	9-inch (23 cm) pie crust, baked (p. 334)

- Preheat oven to 300 °F (150 °C).

- In a bowl, vigorously beat together eggs and sugar. Whip in lime juice, food coloring and melted butter. Pour into crust.

- Bake in oven 20 minutes or until pie filling has set. Let cool. Serve.

NUTRITION	
CALORIES PER SERVING: 452	
FAT: 32 g	CAL. FROM FAT: 63 %
PROTEIN: 5 g	CHOLESTEROL: 206 mg
SODIUM: 406 mg	CARBOHYDRATES: 38 g

Lemon Meringue Pie

6-8 SERVINGS	
	juice of 5 lemons
	peel of 5 lemons, grated
1 ¼ cups	(300 mL) sugar
6	egg yolks
⅓ cup	(80 mL) butter, melted
1	9-inch (23 cm) pie crust, baked (p. 334)
3 cups	(750 mL) unbaked meringue (p. 358)

- In a saucepan, mix lemon juice and peel with sugar. While stirring, bring to a boil. Remove from heat. Let cool.

- In a bowl, beat eggs, gradually folding in lemon mixture. In a double-boiler, stirring occasionally, cook around 45 minutes or until thick and creamy. Off heat, fold in butter. Let cool completely. Pour into crust.

- Preheat oven to BROIL.

- Using a pastry bag with a fluted nozzle, pipe meringue onto pie. Lightly brown in oven 1-2 minutes. Serve.

VARIATIONS
- Color meringue with 2 drops yellow food coloring. After cooking, sprinkle with grated coconut, icing sugar or cocoa. Replace lemon with lime.

NUTRITION	
CALORIES PER SERVING: 489	
FAT: 18 g	CAL. FROM FAT: 31 %
PROTEIN: 5 g	CHOLESTEROL: 180 mg
SODIUM: 244 mg	CARBOHYDRATES: 83 g

Orange Pie

6-8 SERVINGS

1	9-inch (23 cm) pie crust (p. 334)
1/3 cup	(80 mL) cornstarch
3	egg yolks
2/3 cup	(160 mL) orange juice
3 tbsp	(45 mL) orange peel
1 1/3 cups	(330 mL) sugar
2/3 cup	(160 mL) apricot juice
2	drops of orange food coloring (optional)
2/3 cup	(160 mL) orange, peeled, pith removed, sectioned
2/3 cup	(160 mL) apricot halves
2 tbsp	(30 mL) lemon juice
2 tbsp	(30 mL) butter nuts, chopped
2 cups	(500 mL) unbaked meringue (p. 358)

■ Preheat oven to 350 °F (175 °C). Line a springform pan with crust. Bake in oven 20-30 minutes. Set aside.

■ In a bowl, mix cornstarch and egg yolks until creamy. Set aside.

■ In a second bowl, mix orange juice, orange peel, sugar, apricot juice and food coloring, if desired. Fold 1/2 cup (125 mL) liquid into cornstarch and egg mixture. Set aside.

■ In a saucepan, bring remaining liquid to a boil. Fold in cornstarch and egg mixture. Stir until thickened.

■ Off heat, add fruit. Gently stirring with a spatula, bring back to a boil. Off heat, mix in lemon juice and butter. Let cool.

■ Preheat oven to BROIL.

■ Pour lukewarm filling into crust. Sprinkle with chopped nuts. Cover with meringue. Lightly brown in oven 1-2 minutes. Unmold.

VARIATIONS

• Replace nuts with almonds, and meringue with whipped cream (do not broil in oven). Decorate with fruit.

NUTRITION	
CALORIES PER SERVING: 509	
FAT: 11 g	CAL. FROM FAT: 19%
PROTEIN: 5 g	CHOLESTEROL: 87 mg
SODIUM: 193 mg	CARBOHYDRATES: 101 g

Garden Fruit Tart

6-8 SERVINGS

1	9-inch (23 cm) pie crust, baked (p. 334)
½ cup	(125 mL) raspberry jam
1 ½ cups	(375 mL) custard (p. 412)
2 cups	(500 mL) fresh fruit
2 cups	(500 mL) Chantilly cream (p. 413)
½ cup	(125 mL) slivered almonds

- In cold crust, spread successive layers of raspberry jam, custard and fruit.
- Using a pastry bag with a fluted nozzle, garnish with Chantilly cream. Sprinkle with slivered almonds. Refrigerate 20 minutes or so. Serve.

VARIATIONS
- Use a commercial sponge-cake crust.
- Replace raspberry jam with other flavors of jam (apple, strawberry, blueberry), with marmalade, etc.
- Sprinkle pie with grated coconut, poppy seeds, chopped peanuts, chocolate chips or shavings, etc.

NUTRITION	
CALORIES PER SERVING: 489	
FAT: 28 g	CAL. FROM FAT: 51%
PROTEIN: 8 g	CHOLESTEROL: 113 mg
SODIUM: 226 mg	CARBOHYDRATES: 53 g

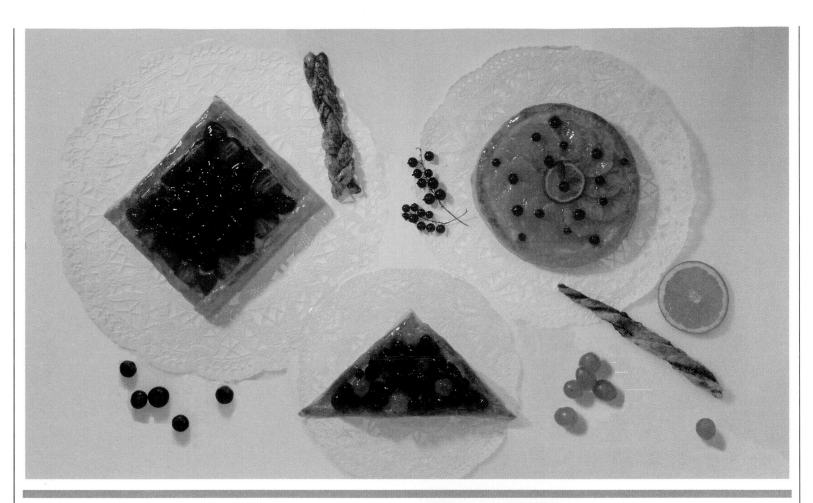

Seasonal Fruit Pastries

6 SERVINGS

1 lb	(450 g) puff pastry (p. 335)
1	egg, beaten
1 ½ cups	(375 mL) custard (p. 412)
1 ½ cups	(375 mL) fresh fruit
½ cup	(125 mL) apricot glaze (p. 414)

- Preheat oven to 375 °F (190 °C).

- Roll out dough to an ⅛-inch (0.25 cm) thickness. Using a pastry cutter, cut into squares, triangles, etc. With a fork, prick dough. Set aside.

- Roll out dough trimmings to make ½-inch (1.25 cm) wide strips, long enough to circle each pastry.

- Moisten pastry and contour strips. Gently press strips over pastry edges so they stick.

- Transfer to a slightly-dampened cookie sheet. Brush contour strips with beaten egg. Let stand 15 minutes.

- Bake in oven 15-20 minutes. Check often to insure crust does not burn.

- Remove from oven. Let cool completely. Fill with custard. Garnish with fruit. Brush with glaze. Refrigerate at least 2 hours. Serve.

NUTRITION	
CALORIES PER SERVING: 527	
FAT: 24 *g*	CAL. FROM FAT: 40 %
PROTEIN: 10 *g*	CHOLESTEROL: 144 *mg*
SODIUM: 191 *mg*	CARBOHYDRATES: 70 *g*

Recipe shown above

Chocolate-glazed Pear Tart

6-8 SERVINGS

4 cups	(1 L) water
1 ½ cups	(375 mL) sugar
10	fresh pears, peeled, cored, halved lengthwise
½ cup	(125 mL) marmalade
1	9-inch (23 cm) pie crust, baked (p. 334)
10 oz	(280 g) semisweet dark chocolate
2 tbsp	(30 mL) butter
½ cup	(125 mL) heavy cream

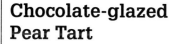

- In a saucepan, over high heat, bring to a boil water and sugar. Add pears. Over low heat, cook 20 minutes. Remove from heat. Cover. Let stand 1 hour.

- Spread marmalade into crust. Arrange concentric circles of pears over marmalade.

- In a double-boiler, melt chocolate. Fold in butter and cream. Warm a little. Drizzle over pears. Serve lukewarm.

NUTRITION	
CALORIES PER SERVING: 701	
FAT: 26 g	CAL. FROM FAT: 31 %
PROTEIN: 4 g	CHOLESTEROL: 28 mg
SODIUM: 191 mg	CARBOHYDRATES: 125 g

Marshmallow Fruit Pie

6-8 SERVINGS

Crust

1 ½ cups	(375 mL) Graham cracker crumbs
½ cup	(125 mL) margarine or butter, melted
¼ cup	(60 mL) brown sugar

Garnish

24	marshmallows
¼ cup	(60 mL) milk
1 ½ cups	(375 mL) fresh or canned fruit, drained
⅓ cup	(80 mL) sweet chocolate chips
½ cup	(125 mL) whipped cream
1 cup	(250 mL) chocolate Chantilly cream (p. 413)

- Preheat oven to 350 °F (175 °C).

- In a bowl, mix crust ingredients. Press over bottom of a 9-inch (23 cm) pie pan. Bake 7-9 minutes.

- In a double-boiler, melt marshmallows in milk, stirring constantly. Fold in fruit and chocolate chips. Let cool fully. With a spatula, fold in whipped cream. Spread into crust.

- Refrigerate 3-5 hours. Cover with chocolate Chantilly cream. Serve.

VARIATIONS
- Replace Chantilly cream with cocoa, strawberries or raspberries.

NUTRITION	
CALORIES PER SERVING: 859	
FAT: 27 g	CAL. FROM FAT: 27 %
PROTEIN: 9 g	CHOLESTEROL: 41 mg
SODIUM: 375 mg	CARBOHYDRATES: 154 g

Almond Custard Tarts

8 TARTS

2 oz	(60 g) almond paste
5 tbsp	(75 mL) sugar
2	eggs (1 egg separated)
1/4 cup	(60 mL) butter
1/2 tsp	(2 mL) almond extract
3/4 cup	(180 mL) flour
1/4 cup	(60 mL) heavy cream
1	basic recipe sugar crust pastry (p. 334)
8 tsp	(40 mL) raspberry jam
1 cup	(250 mL) dried fruit and candied cherries
1/2 cup	(125 mL) apricot glaze (p. 414)

- Preheat oven to 325 °F (160 °C).

- In a mixer bowl, at moderate speed, cream almond paste, sugar and one egg white until smooth. Gradually add butter. Scraping sides, mix to a soft paste. Gradually fold in remaining eggs and almond extract.

- Add flour all at once. At low speed, mix until flour is absorbed. Avoid over-mixing. Gently blend in cream. Refrigerate.

- Line tart molds with crust. Pour 1 tsp (5 mL) jam into each mold. Cover with cold almond mixture. Bake in oven 15-20 minutes.

- Remove from oven. Garnish with dried fruit and candied cherries. Cover with apricot glaze. Serve.

NUTRITION	
CALORIES PER SERVING: 535	
FAT: 27 *g*	CAL. FROM FAT: 44 %
PROTEIN: 7 *g*	CHOLESTEROL: 105 *mg*
SODIUM: 182 *mg*	CARBOHYDRATES: 69 *g*

Recipe shown above

Tart Variations

8 TARTS

1	basic recipe sugar crust pastry (p. 334)
	your choice of filling for a 9-inch (23 cm) pie

- Preheat oven to 325 °F (160 °C). Line tart molds with crust. Set aside.

- Prepare your choice of filling. Pour into molds. Bake in oven 15-20 minutes.

- Let cool completely. Garnish with whipped cream and cocoa, if desired.

Recipe shown above : Maple Syrup Tarts (filling on p. 336)

Walnut Tarts

8 TARTS

1	basic recipe sugar crust pastry (p. 334)
3 tbsp	(45 mL) butter
1/3 cup	(80 mL) all-purpose flour
1 cup	(250 mL) maple syrup
1 cup	(250 mL) hot water
1/2 tsp	(2 mL) vanilla extract
	walnuts
1 cup	(250 mL) whipped cream
1/4 cup	(60 mL) cocoa

▪ Preheat oven to 350 °F (175 °C). Line tart molds with crust. Bake in oven 15 minutes.

▪ In a saucepan, melt butter. Add flour. Mix until butter is absorbed. Add syrup and hot water. While stirring, bring to a boil. Reduce heat. Simmer 7 minutes or until mixture thickens and becomes translucent. Stir occasionally.

▪ Remove from heat. Let cool completely. Mix in vanilla extract. Pour into molds.

▪ Garnish each tart with walnuts, 2 tbsp (30 mL) whipped cream and cocoa. Serve.

VARIATIONS
• To maple syrup, add 1/2 cup (125 mL) currants.

NUTRITION	
CALORIES PER SERVING: 459	
FAT: 25 g	CAL. FROM FAT: 49%
PROTEIN: 5 g	CHOLESTEROL: 65 mg
SODIUM: 142 mg	CARBOHYDRATES: 55 g

Fruit Tarts

8 TARTS

1	basic recipe sugar crust pastry (p. 334)
1 3/4 cups	(430 mL) custard (p. 412)
1 1/4 cups	(300 mL) fresh or canned fruit, drained
2/3 cup	(160 mL) apricot glaze (p. 414)

▪ Preheat oven to 375 °F (190 °C). Line tart molds with crust. Bake in oven 15 minutes or so. Remove from oven. Let cool completely.

▪ Garnish with custard. Decorate with fruit. Cover with apricot glaze.

VARIATION
• Pour 1 tsp (5 mL) jam into bottom of each baked crust. Garnish with custard.

NUTRITION	
CALORIES PER SERVING: 405	
FAT: 18 g	CAL. FROM FAT: 39%
PROTEIN: 7 g	CHOLESTEROL: 94 mg
SODIUM: 146 mg	CARBOHYDRATES: 56 g

Bavarian Tarts

8 TARTS	
1	basic recipe sugar crust pastry *(p. 334)*
1	small box raspberry jelly powder
1 cup	(250 mL) boiling water
1 cup	(250 mL) milk
¹/₄ cup	(60 mL) sour cream
8	maraschino cherries

- Preheat oven to 400 °F (205 °C).

- Roll out and trim dough. Line 8 tart molds. Bake in oven 15 minutes or so.

- In a bowl, dissolve jelly powder in boiling water. Let cool until lukewarm. Mix in milk. Let stand until mixture has half-set. Pour into molds. Refrigerate until jelly is quite firm.

- Garnish each tart with sour cream. Decorate with a cherry.

VARIATIONS
- Use different powder jelly flavors and fruit, according to season.

NUTRITION	
CALORIES PER SERVING: 608	
FAT: 18 *g*	CAL. FROM FAT: 26 %
PROTEIN: 6 *g*	CHOLESTEROL: 41 *mg*
SODIUM: 256 *mg*	CARBOHYDRATES: 108 *g*

Minute Fruit Tarts

8 TARTS	
1	basic recipe sugar crust pastry *(p. 334)*
2 cups	(500 mL) vanilla instant pudding
4	mandarin oranges or clementines, peeled, pith removed, sectioned
2	pears, slivered
2	peaches, slivered
1	kiwi, sliced
³/₄ cup	(180 mL) apple jelly

- Preheat oven to 400 °F (205 °C).

- Roll out and trim dough. Line 8 tart molds. Bake in oven 15 minutes or so.

- Prepare instant pudding following package instructions. Divide among crusts.

- Cover with peeled mandarin oranges without their pith, sliced pears, peaches and kiwi.

- In a saucepan, melt apple jelly. With a brush, glaze fruit. Refrigerate 1 hour. Serve.

Recipe shown above

VARIATIONS
- Vary fruit, pudding flavors and jelly.
- Garnish with whipped cream and chocolate vermicelli.

NUTRITION	
CALORIES PER SERVING: 566	
FAT: 16 *g*	CAL. FROM FAT: 24 %
PROTEIN: 4 *g*	CHOLESTEROL: 33 *mg*
SODIUM: 834 *mg*	CARBOHYDRATES: 106 *g*

Raspberry Flan

6-8 SERVINGS

1 cup	(250 mL) frozen raspberries, drained
1	9-inch (23 cm) pie crust, baked (p. 334)

Custard

2 cups	(500 mL) milk
½ cup	(125 mL) sugar
4	eggs
1 tsp	(5 mL) vanilla extract
	cocoa

- Preheat oven to 325 °F (160 °C).

- Pour raspberries into cold crust. Set aside.

- In a saucepan, heat milk and sugar until smoky. Lightly beat in eggs and vanilla extract. Strain, pouring over raspberries in crust.

- Bake in oven 45 minutes or so. Let cool or chill in refrigerator. Dust with cocoa. Serve.

NUTRITION	
CALORIES PER SERVING: 253	
FAT: 10 g	CAL. FROM FAT: 36%
PROTEIN: 6 g	CHOLESTEROL: 100 mg
SODIUM: 203 mg	CARBOHYDRATES: 34 g

PEACH FLAN

- Replace raspberries with 7 canned peach halves, and vanilla extract with rum extract.

BLUEBERRY FLAN

- Replace raspberries with fresh or frozen blueberries, and vanilla extract with blackcurrant liqueur.

THREE-FRUIT FLAN

- Replace raspberries with 1 fresh sliced kiwi, 4 canned pear halves and 8 canned apricot halves. Replace vanilla extract with almond extract.

- *Pour raspberries into cold crust.*

- *In a saucepan, heat milk and sugar until smoky. Lightly beat in eggs and vanilla extract.*

- *Strain, pouring over raspberries in crust.*

- *Let cool or chill in refrigerator. Dust with cocoa. Serve.*

PASTRIES

Puffs, babas, donuts and whipped cream...wc find here something that will satisfy every sweet tooth. But we cannot allow ourselves to have too many! Unfortunately, all those little sweets are filled with fat and sugar.

If you are trying to keep your intake of unwanted calories low, try placing these delectable goodies at the end of a meal where the main course was especially low in calories.

PUFFS

Puff Paste

AROUND 24 PUFFS OR 12 ÉCLAIRS	
1 cup	(250 mL) water
1/2 cup	(125 mL) butter or shortening
1/2 tsp	(2 mL) salt
1 tbsp	(15 mL) sugar
1 cup	(250 mL) all-purpose flour
4	eggs
1	egg, beaten

- Preheat oven to 400 °F (205 °C).

- In a saucepan, bring to a boil water, butter, salt and sugar. Remove from heat.

- Pour in flour all at once. With a wooden spatula, mix until well-blended.

- Return to heat in order to dry paste. Mix constantly to avoid burning.

- Remove from heat. Transfer paste to a bowl. Let cool 5 minutes, stirring occasionally.

- Fold in eggs one at a time, until paste is smooth and glossy.

- Using a pastry bag with a medium-size fluted nozzle, squeeze 1-inch (2.5 cm) puffs or 4 x 1-inch (10 x 2.5 cm) éclairs onto a buttered cookie sheet.

- Lightly brush with beaten egg. (Do not let egg drip onto cookie sheet.) Bake in oven 25-30 minutes. Let puffs cool fully before stuffing.

NUTRITION	
CALORIES PER RECIPE: 1730	
FAT: 130 g	CAL. FROM FAT: 65%
PROTEIN: 40 g	CHOLESTEROL: 910 mg
SODIUM: 1340 mg	CARBOHYDRATES: 110 g

- *Pour in flour all at once.*

- *With a wooden spatula, mix until well-blended.*

- *Fold in eggs one at a time, until paste is smooth and glossy.*

- *Using a pastry bag with a medium-size fluted nozzle, squeeze puffs onto a buttered cookie sheet.*

- *Squeeze 4 x 1-inch (10 x 2.5 cm) éclairs onto a buttered cookie sheet.*

Chocolate Éclairs

10 ÉCLAIRS	
10	éclairs, baked, cooled
2 cups	(500 mL) chocolate Chantilly cream (p. 413)
²/₃ cup	(160 mL) cocoa

- Slice each éclair in half lengthwise.

- Using a pastry bag with a fluted nozzle, pipe 3 tbsp (45 mL) chocolate Chantilly cream into first half. Cover with second half of éclair.

- Using a sieve, dust éclairs with cocoa. Serve.

VARIATION
- Dust with icing sugar and cocoa.

NUTRITION	
CALORIES PER SERVING: 420	
FAT: 32 g	CAL. FROM FAT: 66%
PROTEIN: 6 g	CHOLESTEROL: 48 mg
SODIUM: 142 mg	CARBOHYDRATES: 31 g

Cream Profiteroles

18 PUFFS	
18	puffs, baked, cooled
1 ³/₄ cups	(425 mL) Chantilly cream (p. 413)
6 oz	(165 g) semisweet chocolate
¹/₂ cup	(125 mL) grated coconut

- With a pencil, punch a hole in each puff. Using a pastry bag with a very small nozzle, stuff with Chantilly cream. Set aside.

- In a double-boiler, melt chocolate. Dip puff crowns in melted chocolate. Sprinkle at once with grated coconut.

VARIATION
- Stuff with flavored custard (p. 412). Dip in white chocolate. Sprinkle with chocolate vermicelli.

NUTRITION	
CALORIES PER SERVING: 386	
FAT: 26 g	CAL. FROM FAT: 63%
PROTEIN: 5 g	CHOLESTEROL: 24 mg
SODIUM: 135 mg	CARBOHYDRATES: 32 g

MERINGUES

Perfect Meringue, Basic Recipe

3 CUPS (750 mL)

½ cup	(125 mL) egg whites
⅔ cup	(160 mL) sugar
½ cup	(125 mL) icing sugar
	pinch of cream of tartar
2	drops of vanilla extract

- Preheat oven to 250 °F (120 °C).

- In a large mixer bowl, mix all ingredients, except vanilla extract. (Make sure bowl is quite dry and that no particles of egg yolk remain in whites.) At maximum speed, beat 3-5 minutes or until meringue rises and soft peaks form.

- Add vanilla extract. At low speed, mix 7 minutes or until meringue is smooth, glossy and stiff.

- Form into rosettes, spirals or cups.

VARIATION
- To meringue, add a few drops food coloring at the same time as vanilla extract.

NUTRITION	
CALORIES PER RECIPE: 808	
FAT: 0 g	CAL. FROM FAT: 0 %
PROTEIN: 16 g	CHOLESTEROL: 0 mg
SODIUM: 200 mg	CARBOHYDRATES: 192 g

- *Mix all ingredients, except vanilla extract.*

- *At maximum speed, beat until meringue rises and soft peaks form.*

- *Beat once more until meringue is smooth, glossy and stiff.*

Shaping and Baking Meringues

Rosettes

- Using a pastry bag with a fluted nozzle, squeeze 24 small meringue rosettes onto a cookie sheet. Bake in oven 30 minutes. Let cool fully.

Spirals

- Using a pastry bag with a fluted nozzle, squeeze 10 meringue spirals onto a cookie sheet. Bake in oven 30 minutes. Let cool fully. Garnish.

Cups

- Using a pastry bag with a fluted nozzle, squeeze six 2 ½-inch (5 cm) meringue circles onto a cookie sheet.

- In concentric circles, squeeze more meringue onto and around each circle. Form into cups, 1 ½-inch (3.75 cm) high. Bake in oven 30 minutes.

Cream Rosettes

18 ROSETTES	
36	rosettes, baked, cooled
2 cups	(500 mL) Chantilly cream *(p. 413)*
1/4 cup	(60 mL) cocoa

- Sandwich 2 tbsp (30 mL) Chantilly cream between 2 cold rosette bottoms. Repeat until all rosettes are joined in pairs. Dust with cocoa.

VARIATION
- Use chocolate Chantilly cream *(p. 413)*.

NUTRITION	
CALORIES PER ROSETTE: 175	
FAT: 7 *g*	CAL. FROM FAT: 37%
PROTEIN: 2 *g*	CHOLESTEROL: 27 *mg*
SODIUM: 26 *mg*	CARBOHYDRATES: 27 *g*

Chocolate Spirals

10 SPIRALS	
8 oz	(225 g) semisweet chocolate
10	spirals, baked, cooled
1/2 cup	(125 mL) grated coconut

- In a double-boiler, melt chocolate. Dip spirals in melted chocolate. Sprinkle each spiral with 1 tbsp (15 mL) grated coconut.

VARIATIONS
- Replace vanilla extract with almond, orange or lemon extract. Sprinkle with almonds, hazelnuts or chopped nuts.

NUTRITION	
CALORIES PER SPIRAL: 210	
FAT: 8 *g*	CAL. FROM FAT: 32%
PROTEIN: 2 *g*	CHOLESTEROL: 0 *mg*
SODIUM: 34 *mg*	CARBOHYDRATES: 36 *g*

Party Meringues

6 CUPS	
6	cups, baked, cooled
1 1/2 cups	(375 mL) custard *(p. 412)*
3/4 cup	(180 mL) commercial hazelnut chocolate spread
1 1/2 cups	(375 mL) raspberries

- Garnish each cup with 1/4 cup (60 mL) custard. Cover with successive layers of hazelnut chocolate spread, then raspberries.

NUTRITION	
CALORIES PER SERVING: 276	
FAT: 4 *g*	CAL. FROM FAT: 10%
PROTEIN: 7 *g*	CHOLESTEROL: 70 *mg*
SODIUM: 109 *mg*	CARBOHYDRATES: 66 *g*

VARIATIONS
- Serve on your choice of coulis *(pp. 414-415)* or custard sauce *(p. 413)*. Vary fruit : blueberries, strawberries, etc. Garnish with Chantilly cream *(p. 413)* or sprinkle with cocoa, grated coconut or chopped nuts.

WAFERS

Wafer Paste

8 LARGE OR 12 SMALL WAFERS	
¼ cup	(60 mL) butter
¾ cup	(180 mL) icing sugar
4	egg whites
¾ cup	(180 ml) all-purpose flour
½ tsp	(2 mL) almond extract

- Preheat oven to 375 °F (190 °C). Butter cookie sheets. Set aside.

- In a saucepan, melt butter. Let cool until lukewarm.

- In a bowl, whisk remaining ingredients. Fold in lukewarm butter, mixing until smooth.

- On a cookie sheet, ladle 3 tbsp (45 mL) paste to form a wafer around 5 inches (12.5 cm) in diameter. Allow 2 wafers per cookie sheet. Bake in oven 12-15 minutes.

- Remove from oven. With a spatula, lift wafers. Lay over a rolling pin so they will cool into a rounded shape, or shape into tulips, cones or cigars.

Note : wafers will keep a long time if stored in a dry place.

NUTRITION	
CALORIES PER LARGE WAFER: 145	
FAT: 6 g	CAL. FROM FAT: 36%
PROTEIN: 3 g	CHOLESTEROL: 15 mg
SODIUM: 86 mg	CARBOHYDRATES: 20 g

VARIATIONS
- Make smaller wafers, using 2 tbsp (30 mL) paste for each.
- Sprinkle each wafer with 1 tbsp (15 mL) slivered almonds. Fold in two.
- *On a cookie sheet, ladle*

paste. With a spoon, spread evenly.

- *Lay wafers over rolling pin so they will cool into a rounded shape.*

Tulips

- *Removing wafers from oven, lay into muffin-pan cups, soup bowls or upside-down over a glass, so they form a cup. Crimp up edges to create flower shapes. Let cool.*

Cones

- *Roll each wafer around a wooden spoon to create a cone shape. Let cool.*

Cigars

- *Roll each wafer around a wooden spoon handle to form cigars.*

Strawberry Chocolate Tulips

4 TULIPS	
4	tulips
1 cup	(250 mL) custard *(p. 412)*
1 cup	(250 mL) fresh strawberries, washed, hulled, sliced
1/2 cup	(125 mL) chocolate sauce *(p. 416)*
1/2 cup	(125 mL) Chantilly cream *(p. 413)*

- Garnish each tulip with 1/4 cup (60 mL) custard and 1/4 cup (60 mL) strawberries. Cover with 2 tbsp (30 mL) chocolate sauce.

- Using a pastry bag or spoon, decorate with a swirl of Chantilly cream.

VARIATIONS
- Use chocolate Chantilly cream *(p. 413)*. Vary fruit, custard flavors *(p. 412)* and sauces *(pp. 416-417)*. Sprinkle with nuts.
- Use tulips as dessert cups for ice cream, sherbet or pudding.

NUTRITION ▲	
CALORIES PER SERVING: 250	
FAT: 13 *g*	CAL. FROM FAT: 38%
PROTEIN: 6 *g*	CHOLESTEROL: 100 *mg*
SODIUM: 122 *mg*	CARBOHYDRATES: 40 *g*

NUTRITION ▶	
CALORIES PER SERVING: 374	
FAT: 24 *g*	CAL. FROM FAT: 54%
PROTEIN: 4 *g*	CHOLESTEROL: 61 *mg*
SODIUM: 69 *mg*	CARBOHYDRATES: 42 *g*

Fruity Chocolate Cones

4 CONES	
3 oz	(90 g) semisweet dark chocolate
4	cones
1 cup	(250 mL) fruit salad, drained
1 cup	(250 mL) Chantilly cream *(p. 413)*

- In a double-boiler, melt chocolate. Dip cone ends in melted chocolate.

- In a bowl, mix fruit salad and Chantilly cream. Pour into cones.

VARIATION
- Replace dark chocolate with white chocolate.

Chocolate Cigars

4 CIGARS	
3 oz	(90 g) semisweet chocolate
4	cigars

- In a double-boiler, melt chocolate. Dip cigar ends in melted chocolate.

- Cigars are ideal to accompany ice cream, sherbet or pudding.

VARIATIONS
- Using a pastry bag with a very small nozzle, stuff cigars with whipped cream or any other filling.

NUTRITION	
CALORIES PER SERVING: 127	
FAT: 7 *g*	CAL. FROM FAT: 46%
PROTEIN: 1 *g*	CHOLESTEROL: 0 *mg*
SODIUM: 37 *mg*	CARBOHYDRATES: 18 *g*

TURNOVERS

Fruit Filling

3 CUPS (750 mL)	
1/3 cup	(80 mL) cornstarch
2 cups	(500 mL) fruit juice
1/2 cup	(125 mL) sugar
1 tsp	(5 mL) vanilla extract
1 tsp	(5 mL) cinnamon
1 cup	(250 mL) fresh or frozen fruit, in chunks

■ In a bowl, dilute cornstarch in 1/2 cup (125 mL) fruit juice. Set aside.

■ In a saucepan, heat remaining fruit juice, sugar, vanilla extract and cinnamon. Add fruit. Bring to a boil. Let mixture boil 1 minute.

■ Add fruit juice and cornstarch mixture. Stirring vigorously, boil until mixture bubbles. Off heat, continue stirring 2 minutes. Let cool.

NUTRITION	
CALORIES PER 1/4 CUP: 88	
FAT: 1 g	CAL. FROM FAT: 1%
PROTEIN: 1 g	CHOLESTEROL: 0 mg
SODIUM: 10 mg	CARBOHYDRATES: 22 g

Fruit Turnovers

12 TURNOVERS	
2 lbs	(900 g) flaky pastry (p. 335)
3 cups	(750 mL) fruit filling
1	egg, beaten

■ Preheat oven to 350 °F (175 °C).

■ Roll out flaky pastry to a 1/4-inch (0.5 cm) thickness. Cut into 4 x 6-inch (9 x 14 cm) ovals. With a pastry brush, moisten oval edges with water. Spoon 1/4 cup (60 mL) fruit filling into the center of each. Fold turnovers, pinching edges to seal. With a knife, cut small notches into edges.

■ Transfer turnovers to a buttered dampened cookie sheet. With a brush, glaze turnovers with beaten egg. Let stand 15 minutes before cooking. Bake in oven 20 minutes. Let cool.

VARIATIONS

• With a pencil, punch a hole in baked, then cooled, turnovers. Using a pastry bag, stuff with Chantilly cream (p. 413).

• Decorate with Chantilly cream. Garnish with fresh fruit or serve on a coulis (pp. 414-415).

NUTRITION	
CALORIES PER SERVING: 520	
FAT: 21 g	CAL. FROM FAT: 35%
PROTEIN: 5 g	CHOLESTEROL: 59 mg
SODIUM: 154 mg	CARBOHYDRATES: 82 g

■ *Roll out flaky pastry to a 1/4-inch (0.5 cm) thickness. Cut into 4 x 6-inch (9 x 14 cm) ovals.*

■ *With a pastry brush, moisten oval edges with water.*

■ *Spoon 1/4 cup (60 mL) fruit filling into the center of each pastry oval.*

■ *Fold turnovers, pinching edges to seal. With a knife, cut small notches into edges.*

SAVARINS AND BABAS

Savarin Paste

1 SAVARIN	
1	envelope active dry yeast
1/2 cup	(125 mL) lukewarm water or milk
3	eggs
2 tbsp	(30 mL) sugar
1 tsp	(5 mL) salt
1 5/8 cups	(400 mL) all-purpose flour
7 tbsp	(105 mL) butter, melted, cooled

- Preheat oven to 375 °F (190 °C). Butter a savarin mold. Set aside.

- In a bowl, mix yeast with 1/4 cup (60 mL) water. Set aside.

- In a mixer bowl, beat eggs, remaining water, sugar and salt. At low speed, while folding in flour, mix 5 minutes. At high speed, beat until dough clears sides of bowl. Add melted butter, in a thin stream. Pour dough into savarin mold.

- Cover dough with a damp dish-towel. Put in a warm and humid place, draft-free. Let dough rise around 1 hour or until it has doubled in size.

- Bake in oven 25-30 minutes or until a knife inserted into the middle comes out clean.

- Remove from oven. Let stand 10 minutes on a rack. Unmold. Let cool.

NUTRITION	
CALORIES PER RECIPE: 230	
FAT: 12 g	CAL. FROM FAT: 48%
PROTEIN: 6 g	CHOLESTEROL: 98 mg
SODIUM: 397 mg	CARBOHYDRATES: 24 g

- *At high speed, beat until dough clears sides of bowl. Add melted butter, in a thin stream.*

- *Pour dough into savarin mold.*

- *Let dough rise around 1 hour or until it has doubled in size.*

Baba Paste

10 LARGE OR 20 SMALL BABAS	
1/2 cup	(125 mL) currants
4 oz	(125 mL) rum
1	basic recipe savarin paste

- Macerate currants in rum 2 hours.

- Preheat oven to 375 °F (190 °C). Butter a 10-muffin pan or 20 baba molds.

- Prepare savarin paste, folding in currants at the same time as melted butter.

- Fill two-thirds of each mold with savarin paste. Let dough rise 30 minutes in a warm and humid place.

- Bake in oven 15-20 minutes. Let cool on a rack 20 minutes.

NUTRITION	
CALORIES PER SERVING: 239	
FAT: 12 g	CAL. FROM FAT: 51%
PROTEIN: 3 g	CHOLESTEROL: 27 mg
SODIUM: 71 mg	CARBOHYDRATES: 24 g

Savarin

8-10 SERVINGS

1	savarin, cooled
1 1/2 cups	(375 mL) rum syrup (p. 414)
2 cups	(500 mL) fresh raspberries
3/4 cup	(180 mL) apricot glaze (p. 414)
1/4 cup	(60 mL) icing sugar

- With a fork, prick savarin so it will easily soak in syrup.

- Pour rum syrup over savarin, 1/2 cup (125 mL) at a time. Repeat twice, at 15 minute intervals.

- Garnish center of savarin with whole raspberries. Cover fruit and savarin with apricot glaze. Dust with icing sugar. Serve.

VARIATIONS

- Garnish savarin with other fruit. Sprinkle with chopped nuts, slivered almonds, pistachios or grated coconut.

NUTRITION	
CALORIES PER SERVING: 371	
FAT: 12 g	CAL. FROM FAT: 31%
PROTEIN: 3 g	CHOLESTEROL: 27 mg
SODIUM: 80 mg	CARBOHYDRATES: 60 g

Babas

10 LARGE OR 20 SMALL BABAS

10	large babas, cooled
	or
20	small babas, cooled
1 cup	(250 mL) rum syrup (p. 414)
3/4 cup	(180 mL) apricot glaze (p. 414)
1/4 cup	(60 mL) icing sugar

- Moisten babas with rum syrup. Cover with apricot glaze. Dust with icing sugar.

VARIATIONS

- Serve babas with whipped cream and caramel pecan sauce (p. 416). Serve on a coulis (pp. 414-415), with fresh fruit on the side. Sprinkle with chopped nuts or grated coconut.

NUTRITION	
CALORIES PER SERVING: 360	
FAT: 12 g	CAL. FROM FAT: 31%
PROTEIN: 3 g	CHOLESTEROL: 27 mg
SODIUM: 80 mg	CARBOHYDRATES: 57 g

DOUGHNUTS

Chocolate-Coconut Doughnuts

AROUND 2 DOZEN	
1	envelope active dry yeast
1 cup	(250 mL) lukewarm water
1 tsp	(5 mL) salt
1/4 cup	(60 mL) sugar
1	egg
1/2 tsp	(2 mL) lemon extract
5 cups	(1.25 L) flour
1/4 cup	(60 mL) butter or shortening
	oil for frying
2 cups	(500 mL) semisweet chocolate, melted
1/4 cup	(60 mL) grated coconut

- In a bowl, dilute yeast in half the water. Set aside.

- In a second bowl, dissolve salt and sugar in remaining water. Fold in egg and lemon extract. Mix in flour and butter. Add diluted yeast.

- Knead dough 8 minutes or so. Let rise 30 minutes.

NUTRITION	
CALORIES PER DOUGHNUT: 205	
FAT: 8 g	CAL. FROM FAT: 34%
PROTEIN: 4 g	CHOLESTEROL: 13 mg
SODIUM: 115 mg	CARBOHYDRATES: 32 g

- Punch down dough to force out air and stop fermentation. Let rise 10 more minutes. With a cookie cutter, cut into 3-inch (7.5 cm) rounds. Transfer doughnuts to a lightly-floured cookie sheet. Put in a warm closed place 30 minutes.

- Heat oil to 400 °F (205 °C). Deep fry doughnuts. Let cool. Dip one side in melted chocolate. Sprinkle with grated coconut.

VARIATION

- With a pencil, punch a hole in one side of doughnuts. Using a pastry bag with a small nozzle, stuff doughnuts with apple sauce or jam. Dust with icing sugar and cinnamon.

Lemon Doughnuts

AROUND 2 DOZEN	
1/4 cup	(60 mL) sugar
1/2 tsp	(2 mL) salt
1 cup	(250 mL) milk
2	eggs
	peel of 2 lemons, grated
2 1/2 cups	(625 mL) flour
1 tbsp	(15 mL) baking powder
1/4 cup	(60 mL) butter
	oil for frying

- In a bowl, dissolve sugar and salt into milk. Fold in eggs and lemon peel, beating lightly. Set aside.

- In a second bowl, sift flour and baking powder. Fold in butter. Lightly mix until granular. Make a well in the center. Add liquid mixture, mixing until creamy.

- With a rolling pin, flatten dough to a 1/4-inch (0.5 cm) thickness. Cut dough with a doughnut cutter or two different-size cutters.

- Heat oil to 400 °F (205 °C). Fry doughnuts to a nice golden brown color. Let cool. Dust with sugar, icing sugar, cinnamon, cocoa or commercial crystallized sugar.

NUTRITION	
CALORIES PER DOUGHNUT: 100	
FAT: 4 g	CAL. FROM FAT: 40%
PROTEIN: 2 g	CHOLESTEROL: 22 mg
SODIUM: 119 mg	CARBOHYDRATES: 13 g

- *Mix until creamy.*

- *With a rolling pin, flatten dough to a 1/4-inch (0.5 cm) thickness. Cut dough with a doughnut cutter or two different-size cutters.*

- *Deep-fry in oil heated to 400 °F (205 °C), until doughnuts turn golden brown.*

COATED FRUIT

Rhubarb Fritters

6 SERVINGS	
2	egg yolks
1 cup	(250 mL) flat beer, at room temperature
1 tbsp	(15 mL) butter, melted
1 tsp	(5 mL) vanilla extract
1 ¼ cups	(300 mL) all-purpose flour
3 tbsp	(45 mL) sugar
¼ tsp	(1 mL) salt
2	egg whites
1 cup	(250 mL) icing sugar
2 cups	(500 mL) vegetable oil
6	rhubarb stalks, in bite-size pieces

- In a bowl, beat egg yolks, beer, butter and vanilla extract. Set aside.
- In a second bowl, sift flour, sugar and salt. Fold into first mixture. Mix to a smooth batter. Cover. Refrigerate 1 hour.
- In a third bowl, beat egg whites and 2 tbsp (30 mL) icing sugar until peaks form.
- Remove batter from refrigerator. Gently fold in beaten egg whites. Set aside.
- In a saucepan, heat oil to 360 °F (180 °C).
- Dredge rhubarb with remaining icing sugar. Dip in batter. Fry 3 minutes or until golden brown.
- Drain on a paper towel to soak away excess oil. Dust with brown or white sugar. Serve hot.

VARIATION
- Replace rhubarb with pineapple slices rolled in cocoa and icing sugar.

NUTRITION	
CALORIES PER SERVING: 375	
FAT: 11 g	CAL. FROM FAT: 27%
PROTEIN: 7 g	CHOLESTEROL: 76 mg
SODIUM: 142 mg	CARBOHYDRATES: 60 g

Candy Apples

6 SERVINGS	
6	apples
6	wooden sticks
2 cups	(500 mL) sugar
1 ½ cups	(375 mL) corn syrup
1 cup	(250 mL) water
2 tbsp	(30 mL) ground cinnamon
6	drops of Tabasco sauce
6	drops of red food coloring (optional)

- Wash and pat dry apples. Remove stems. Insert wooden sticks one-third way up apples.
- In a saucepan, mix sugar, corn syrup, water, cinnamon, Tabasco and food coloring, if desired. Bring to a boil, stirring at regular intervals. Place a candy thermometer in mixture. Without stirring, boil until temperature reaches 300 °F (150 °C). Remove from heat.
- Dip each apple in candy, rotating rapidly to coat fully. Keep apple suspended over saucepan to drain excess candy.
- Place on a roasting pan covered with aluminum foil. Let candy harden. Serve.

NUTRITION	
CALORIES PER SERVING: 570	
FAT: 1 g	CAL. FROM FAT: 1%
PROTEIN: 0 g	CHOLESTEROL: 0 mg
SODIUM: 59 mg	CARBOHYDRATES: 151 g

Double Chocolate Fruit

14 TREATS	
14	fresh fruit pieces
6 oz	(165 g) semisweet dark chocolate
1 1/2 oz	(45 g) white chocolate
3/4 cup	(180 mL) Grand Marnier-flavored light cream (p. 413)
	fresh mint (optional)

- Line a roasting pan with wax paper. Set aside.
- Wash fruit in cold water. Pat dry. Set aside.
- In a double-boiler, melt semisweet dark chocolate.
- Dip fruit two-thirds in chocolate. Place in roasting pan. Set aside.
- In a double-boiler, melt white chocolate. Dip in ends of a fork. Drizzle chocolate over fruit, in a zigzag motion.
- Refrigerate around 10 minutes or until chocolate hardens.
- Serve on a platter with light cream on the side. Decorate with mint leaves, if desired.

NUTRITION	
CALORIES PER TREAT: 142	
FAT: 7 g	CAL. FROM FAT: 41%
PROTEIN: 2 g	CHOLESTEROL: 11 mg
SODIUM: 9 mg	CARBOHYDRATES: 21 g

Love Bites

6 SERVINGS	
24	fresh cherries, with their stem
12 oz	(375 mL) white rum
1/2 lb	(225 g) semisweet chocolate

- Wash cherries in cold water. Drain. Pat dry.
- In a large preserve jar, loosely place cherries. Pour in rum. Seal airtight. Macerate 15 days in refrigerator.
- Remove from refrigerator. Drain cherries. Pat dry with a paper towel. Set aside.
- In a double-boiler, melt chocolate. Dip cherries halfway in melted chocolate. Place on wax paper. Wait for chocolate to set. Dip cherries once more in melted chocolate. Refrigerate until chocolate hardens.

NUTRITION	
CALORIES PER SERVING: 213	
FAT: 7 g	CAL. FROM FAT: 29%
PROTEIN: 3 g	CHOLESTEROL: 0 mg
SODIUM: 4 mg	CARBOHYDRATES: 37 g

TREATS

Chocolate Truffles

AROUND 40 TRUFFLES	
¹/₄ cup	(60 mL) butter
³/₄ cup	(180 mL) heavy cream
1 tbsp	(15 mL) sugar
2 tsp	(10 mL) brandy
7 oz	(190 g) semisweet chocolate, grated
1 oz	(30 g) unsweetened chocolate, grated
	cocoa, icing sugar or granulated sugar

- In a saucepan, mix butter, cream and sugar. Bring to a boil.

- Off heat, add brandy and both chocolates. Mix until chocolate has fully melted.

- Refrigerate 3-4 hours or until paste is quite firm.

- Shape into balls, using 1 tbsp (15 mL) paste for each. Roll in cocoa, icing sugar or granulated sugar. Refrigerate or freeze in an airtight container.

NUTRITION	
CALORIES PER TRUFFLE: 56	
FAT: 5 g	CAL. FROM FAT: 70%
PROTEIN: 0 g	CHOLESTEROL: 9 mg
SODIUM: 14 mg	CARBOHYDRATES: 4 g

Recipe shown opposite page, left side

Mashmallow Brownies

30 SQUARES	
¹/₂ cup	(125 mL) butter
¹/₄ cup	(60 mL) cocoa
1 cup	(250 mL) sugar
2	eggs
¹/₂ tsp	(2 mL) vanilla extract
³/₄ cup	(180 mL) all-purpose flour
¹/₂ tsp	(2 mL) baking powder
¹/₄ tsp	(1 mL) salt
³/₄ cup	(180 mL) walnuts, chopped
20	large marshmallows

- Preheat oven to 350 °F (175 °C). Butter a 9 x 13-inch (23 x 33 cm) baking pan.

- In a large saucepan, melt butter. Fold in cocoa. Off heat, mix in sugar, eggs and vanilla extract. Set aside.

- In a bowl, sift flour, baking powder and salt. Add to cocoa mixture. Fold in nuts. Spread evenly into pan. Bake in oven 20 minutes.

- Remove from oven 7 minutes before the end. Cover with marshmallows. Return to oven so marshmallows will melt.

- Let cool 15 minutes. Cut into squares. Serve.

NUTRITION	
CALORIES PER SQUARE: 84	
FAT: 4 g	CAL. FROM FAT: 40%
PROTEIN: 12 g	CHOLESTEROL: 20 mg
SODIUM: 61 mg	CARBOHYDRATES: 12 g

Recipe shown above

Butterscotch Roses

8 ROSES	
³/₄ cup	(180 mL) butter
1 ¹/₄ cups	(300 mL) brown sugar
¹/₂ cup	(125 mL) nuts, chopped
2 cups	(500 mL) flour
1 tbsp	(15 mL) baking powder
¹/₂ tsp	(2 mL) salt
¹/₄ cup	(60 mL) shortening
⁷/₈ cup	(210 mL) milk

- Preheat oven to 425 °F (220 °C). Butter 8 large muffin-pan cups. Set aside.

- In a bowl, cream butter and brown sugar. Mix in nuts. Spoon 1 tbsp (15 mL) mixture into each cup. Set aside remainder.

- In a bowl, sift flour, baking powder and salt. Mix in shortening until granular. Make a well in the center. Pour in milk. With a fork, gently mix to a soft dough.

- Flour a clean, even surface. Roll out dough to a square, 12-inch (30 cm) wide by ¹/₄-inch (0.5 cm) thick. Spread remaining caramel mixture over dough. Roll.

- Slice into 8 rounds. Place over caramel in muffin cups.

- Bake in oven 20 minutes or so. Unmold at once.

NUTRITION	
CALORIES PER ROSE: 522	
FAT: 30 g	CAL. FROM FAT: 50%
PROTEIN: 6 g	CHOLESTEROL: 50 mg
SODIUM: 471 mg	CARBOHYDRATES: 61 g

Recipe shown above

Heavenly Fruit Bars

---

18 BARS

1st layer

¹/₃ cup	(80 mL)	butter
¹/₃ cup	(80 mL)	brown sugar, well-packed
¹/₂ cup	(125 mL)	all-purpose flour
³/₄ cup	(180 mL)	commercial puffed rice
¹/₄ tsp	(1 mL)	baking soda

2nd layer

2		eggs
¹/₄ cup	(60 mL)	heavy cream
1 tsp	(5 mL)	vanilla extract
¹/₂ cup	(125 mL)	brown sugar
¹/₂ cup	(125 mL)	raisins
¹/₂ cup	(125 mL)	red cherries, halved
¹/₂ cup	(125 mL)	nuts, chopped
¹/₂ cup	(125 mL)	grated coconut

3rd layer

¹/₂ cup	(125 mL)	semisweet chocolate chips
¹/₄ cup	(60 mL)	butter
1 ¹/₄ cups	(300 mL)	commercial puffed rice

1st layer

▪ In a bowl, cream butter and brown sugar. Fold in flour, puffed rice and baking soda. Press mixture over bottom of a square 9-inch (23 cm) baking pan. Set aside.

2nd layer

▪ Preheat oven to 350 °F (175 °C).

▪ In a large bowl, beat eggs, cream and vanilla extract. Fold in brown sugar. Mix in fruit and nuts. Pour over first mixture in pan. Bake in oven 12-15 minutes.

3rd layer

▪ In a double-boiler, melt chocolate chips. Fold in butter as soon as chocolate has melted. Mix in puffed rice.

▪ Remove bars from oven. With a spatula, cover with chocolate mixture. Refrigerate 1 hour.

▪ Cut into 4 ¹/₂ x 1-inch (10 x 2.5 cm) bars.

NUTRITION	
CALORIES PER BAR: 207	
FAT: 12 *g*	CAL. FROM FAT: 52 %
PROTEIN: 2 *g*	CHOLESTEROL: 41 *mg*
SODIUM: 96 *mg*	CARBOHYDRATES: 24 *g*

Crispy Nut Squares

24 SQUARES	
1 cup	(250 mL) peanut butter
1 cup	(250 mL) brown sugar
1 cup	(250 mL) corn syrup
1 cup	(250 mL) walnuts
2 cups	(500 mL) commercial puffed rice
2 cups	(500 mL) commercial corn flakes
1/2 cup	(125 mL) chocolate chips
1/2 cup	(125 mL) caramel chips

- Butter a baking pan.
- In a large saucepan, bring to a boil peanut butter, brown sugar and corn syrup. Boil 2 minutes.
- Off heat, mix in nuts and cereal. Spread mixture into roasting pan. Set aside.
- In a double-boiler, melt chocolate and caramel chips. Spread evenly over first mixture. Refrigerate 20 minutes before cutting into squares.

VARIATIONS
- Use crunchy peanut butter, hazelnuts, almonds, pistachios, etc.

NUTRITION	
CALORIES PER SQUARE: 192	
FAT: 8 g	CAL. FROM FAT: 33%
PROTEIN: 3 g	CHOLESTEROL: 0 mg
SODIUM: 90 mg	CARBOHYDRATES: 31 g

Maple Squares

16 SQUARES	
1/2 cup	(125 mL) butter
1 cup	(250 mL) all-purpose flour
1/2 cup	(125 mL) brown sugar
2/3 cup	(160 mL) brown sugar
1 cup	(250 mL) maple syrup
2	eggs, beaten
1/4 cup	(60 mL) butter, melted
1/2 tsp	(2 mL) salt
1/2 cup	(125 mL) nuts, chopped
1/2 tsp	(2 mL) vanilla or maple extract
3 tbsp	(45 mL) flour

- Preheat oven to 350 °F (175 °C). Butter a square 8-inch (20.5 cm) baking pan.
- In a bowl, mix flour and 1/2 cup (125 mL) brown sugar. Press over bottom of pan. Bake in oven 20 minutes.
- In a saucepan, mix 2/3 cup (160 mL) brown sugar and maple syrup. Bring to a boil. Simmer 5 minutes.
- Remove from heat. Let cool. Add eggs. Fold in remaining ingredients. Pour over first mixture. Bake in oven 30 minutes.
- Let cool. Cut into squares or use a cookie cutter.

NUTRITION	
CALORIES PER SQUARE: 257	
FAT: 12 g	CAL. FROM FAT: 40%
PROTEIN: 2 g	CHOLESTEROL: 46 mg
SODIUM: 169 mg	CARBOHYDRATES: 37 g

Chocolate Oat Squares

16 SQUARES

¼ cup	(60 mL) butter
2 cups	(500 mL) sugar
½ cup	(125 mL) cocoa
½ cup	(125 mL) milk
1 tsp	(5 mL) vanilla extract
2 cups	(500 mL) rolled oats
¼ cup	(60 mL) commercial hazelnut chocolate spread

- Butter a square 8-inch (20.5 cm) baking pan. Set aside.
- In a saucepan, mix all ingredients, except rolled oats and spread. Heat until sugar has melted. Boil 1 minute.
- Off heat, mix in rolled oats and spread. Pour into pan. Refrigerate 20 minutes before cutting into squares.

NUTRITION	
CALORIES PER SQUARE: 179	
FAT: 4 g	CAL. FROM FAT: 19%
PROTEIN: 3 g	CHOLESTEROL: 9 mg
SODIUM: 36 mg	CARBOHYDRATES: 36 g

Healthy Date Squares

36 SQUARES

1 ½ cups	(375 mL) water
2 cups	(500 mL) dates, chopped
1 tbsp	(15 mL) lemon juice
¾ cup	(180 mL) butter
1 cup	(250 mL) brown sugar
¾ cup	(180 mL) whole wheat flour
½ cup	(125 mL) all-purpose flour
¾ cup	(180 mL) bran flakes
½ cup	(125 mL) rolled oats
½ tsp	(2 mL) baking soda
½ tsp	(2 mL) salt

- Preheat oven to 400 °F (205 °C). Butter a square 9-inch (23 cm) baking pan. Set aside.
- In a saucepan, bring to a boil water, dates and lemon juice. Reduce heat. While stirring, simmer until mixture thickens slightly. Set aside.
- In a bowl, cream butter and brown sugar. Fold in remaining ingredients.
- Over bottom of pan, press two-thirds of mixture. Cover with date mixture. Pour remaining third on top.
- Bake in oven 25 minutes or until golden brown. Remove from oven. Let stand 15 minutes before cutting into squares.

NUTRITION	
CALORIES PER SQUARE: 103	
FAT: 4 g	CAL. FROM FAT: 33%
PROTEIN: 1 g	CHOLESTEROL: 10 mg
SODIUM: 89 mg	CARBOHYDRATES: 17 g

Divine Treats

24 TREATS

1 cup	(250 mL) marmalade
1	cake roll - orange spongecake (p. 294)
1 lb	(450 g) commercial almond paste
1 oz	(30 mL) Grand Marnier
6	drops of yellow food coloring (optional)
1	drop of red food coloring (optional)
1/4 cup	(60 mL) hot water
2 cups	(500 mL) icing sugar
1/4 cup	(60 mL) maple syrup
	pistachios, halved

- Spread marmalade over cold cake. Set aside.
- In a large bowl, moisten almond paste with Grand Marnier. Set aside.
- Dilute food coloring in hot water, if desired. Mix in icing sugar and maple syrup. Set aside.
- With a rolling pin, flatten almond paste to cake size. Place on top of cake. With a serrated knife, trim off a 1/2-inch (1 cm) border around cake to make straight, even edges. Cut into 24 rectangles.

- Place a cake rack over a cookie sheet. Transfer a few cake pieces to rack. Coat with syrup. Decorate with pistachios. Repeat with other cake pieces, retrieving syrup from cookie sheet each time.

VARIATIONS
- Use different flavors of spongecake (pp. 294-295) and jam. Vary alcohols, food coloring and garnish. Cut into triangles, squares or use a cookie cutter.

NUTRITION	
CALORIES PER TREAT: 231	
FAT: 6 g	CAL. FROM FAT: 24%
PROTEIN: 4 g	CHOLESTEROL: 19 mg
SODIUM: 50 mg	CARBOHYDRATES: 42 g

- *Spread marmalade over cold cake.*

- *With a rolling pin, flatten almond paste to cake size.*

- *With a serrated knife, trim off a 1/2-inch (1 cm) border around cake to make straight, even edges. Cut into 24 rectangles.*

- *Place a few cake pieces on rack. Coat with syrup.*

Hazelnut Half-moons

24 TREATS

1/3 cup	(80 mL) icing sugar
1 cup	(250 mL) almond paste
5	drops of red food coloring (optional)
1/2 cup	(125 mL) commercial hazelnut chocolate spread
4 oz	(115 g) semisweet chocolate

▪ Sprinkle a clean, even surface with icing sugar. Knead almond paste. Fold in food coloring, if desired.

▪ With a rolling pin, flatten paste into a 1/4-inch (0.5 cm) thick rectangle. Cut rectangle into 2 equal parts. Smooth spread over first half. Cover with second half. Refrigerate 5-10 minutes.

▪ In a double-boiler, melt chocolate.

▪ Remove paste from refrigerator. With a glass, cut into circles then, using a knife, carve into half-moons.

▪ Dip one side of half-moons in melted chocolate. Let drain on a cookie sheet. Set aside until chocolate hardens. Sprinkle with icing sugar or sliced hazelnuts, if desired. Serve.

NUTRITION	
CALORIES PER TREAT: 80	
FAT: 4 g	CAL. FROM FAT: 40 %
PROTEIN: 1 g	CHOLESTEROL: 0 mg
SODIUM: 5 mg	CARBOHYDRATES: 12 g

Chocolate Fig Clusters

24 TREATS

1/2 cup	(125 mL) butter
1 cup	(250 mL) brown sugar
1	egg, beaten
1 tsp	(5 mL) vanilla extract
1 cup	(250 mL) figs, chopped
2 cups	(500 mL) commercial puffed rice
12 oz	(350 g) semisweet chocolate
1/4 cup	(60 mL) grated coconut

▪ In a saucepan, cream butter and brown sugar. Fold in egg and vanilla extract. Mix in figs.

▪ Over moderate heat, while stirring, cook 5-7 minutes or until brown sugar and butter have melted.

▪ Off heat, mix in puffed rice. Let cool slightly. Shape into balls, using 2 tbsp (30 mL) mixture for each. Refrigerate.

▪ In a double-boiler, melt chocolate. Mix in coconut.

▪ Remove balls from refrigerator. Using a fork, dip each ball in chocolate. Drain. Let cool on a cookie sheet.

NUTRITION	
CALORIES PER TREAT: 153	
FAT: 8 g	CAL. FROM FAT: 46 %
PROTEIN: 1 g	CHOLESTEROL: 18 mg
SODIUM: 48 mg	CARBOHYDRATES: 21 g

Dried Fruit Candy

20 TREATS

1 cup	(250 mL) dates
1 cup	(250 mL) currants
1/2 cup	(125 mL) nuts
1/3 cup	(80 mL) grated coconut
10	red cherries, halved
1 cup	(250 mL) sugar

▪ In a meat-grinder or food processor, chop all ingredients, except cherries, to a sticky, granular paste. Shape into small balls.

▪ Press a half-cherry into each ball. Roll in sugar. Serve at once or refrigerate.

NUTRITION	
CALORIES PER TREAT: 112	
FAT: 2 g	CAL. FROM FAT: 19%
PROTEIN: 1 g	CHOLESTEROL: 0 mg
SODIUM: 4 mg	CARBOHYDRATES: 23g

Coconut Rum Balls

24 TREATS

1 cup	(250 mL) almond paste
3/4 cup	(180 mL) grated coconut
1/2 oz	(15 mL) rum
1 tbsp	(15 mL) cocoa
6 oz	(165 g) semisweet chocolate

▪ In a large bowl, mix almond paste, 1/2 cup (125 mL) grated coconut, rum and cocoa until well-blended. Shape into 24 balls.

▪ In a double-boiler, melt chocolate. Using a fork, dip balls in chocolate. Drain on a cookie sheet. While chocolate is still lukewarm, sprinkle with remaining grated coconut. Let chocolate harden 5 minutes. Serve.

NUTRITION	
CALORIES PER TREAT: 72	
FAT: 4 g	CAL. FROM FAT: 52%
PROTEIN: 1 g	CHOLESTEROL: 0 mg
SODIUM: 7 mg	CARBOHYDRATES: 8 g

Irish Coffee Balls

24 TREATS

2 tsp	(10 mL) instant coffee
1/2 oz	(15 mL) Irish cream liqueur
1 cup	(250 mL) almond paste, at room temperature
6 oz	(165 g) semisweet chocolate
1/4 cup	(60 mL) chocolate vermicelli

▪ In a bowl, dilute coffee in liqueur. Fold in almond paste, mixing until all liquid is absorbed. Shape into 24 balls. Set aside.

▪ In a double-boiler, melt chocolate. Using a fork, dip balls in chocolate. Drain on a cookie sheet. Sprinkle with chocolate vermicelli. Let chocolate harden 5 minutes. Serve.

VARIATIONS
• Use different alcohols.

NUTRITION	
CALORIES PER TREAT: 149	
FAT: 10 g	CAL. FROM FAT: 53%
PROTEIN: 2 g	CHOLESTEROL: 0 mg
SODIUM: 4 mg	CARBOHYDRATES: 17 g

Almond Chocolate Treats

24 TREATS

1/4 cup	(60 mL) icing sugar
1 cup	(250 mL) almond paste
8 oz	(225 g) semisweet chocolate
24	white almonds

▪ Sprinkle a clean, even surface with icing sugar. With a rolling pin, flatten almond paste to a 1/2-inch (1.25 cm) thick rectangle. Cut into 24 small squares.

▪ In a double-boiler, melt chocolate. Using a fork, dip squares in melted chocolate.

▪ Drain on a cookie sheet. Decorate with an almond. Let chocolate harden. Serve.

NUTRITION	
CALORIES PER TREAT: 99	
FAT: 6 g	CAL. FROM FAT: 50%
PROTEIN: 2 g	CHOLESTEROL: 0 mg
SODIUM: 2 mg	CARBOHYDRATES: 12 g

CRÊPES, TRIFLES, SOUFFLÉS, MOUSSES...

These delicious crêpes are a nutritious choice when we choose a fruit, cheese, or nut filling, instead of a chocolate and whipped cream filling. Cover your crêpes with a fruit syrup or yogurt instead of a caramel or chocolate sauce. You may also replace the jam contained in certain crêpes with stewed fruit.

In this section, we present light, delicious mousses, without fat and without added sugar. Take care to rinse the canned fruit used in the recipe Tutti-Frutti Mousse (p. 400) and the sugar content will be reduced.

CRÊPES

Crêpes, Basic Recipe

AROUND 20 CRÊPES

1 cup	(250 mL) all-purpose flour
1/2 tsp	(2 mL) salt
1/4 cup	(60 mL) sugar
1 1/3 cups	(330 mL) milk
2	eggs, beaten
	vanilla extract
2 tbsp	(30 mL) butter, melted

- In a bowl, sift flour. Make a well in the center. Set aside.

- In a second bowl, dilute salt and sugar in milk. Fold in beaten eggs. Mix in a few drops of vanilla extract.

- Pour into the center of well. With a whisk, gradually fold liquid mixture into flour until creamy smooth.

- Mix in melted butter. Refrigerate 1 hour or so.

- In a frying pan, ladle batter, 2-3 tbsp (30-45 mL) for each crêpe. Over high heat, cook crêpes. Flip once surface starts to bubble, and crêpe seems to loosen from pan. Cook second side 1 minute or so.

Note : crêpes may be kept frozen up to 2 months.

CITRUS CRÊPES
- Add 2 tbsp (30 mL) citrus peel to batter.

CHOCOLATE CRÊPES
- Replace 1/4 cup (60 mL) flour with 1/2 cup (125 mL) cocoa.

NUTRITION	
CALORIES PER SERVING: 59	
FAT: 2 g	CAL. FROM FAT: 33%
PROTEIN: 2 g	CHOLESTEROL: 24 mg
SODIUM: 78 mg	CARBOHYDRATES: 8 g

- *Pour liquid into well. Mix with a whisk.*

- *In a frying pan, ladle batter, 2-3 tbsp (30-45 mL) for each crêpe.*

- *Over high heat, cook crêpes. Flip once surface starts to bubble, and crêpe seems to loosen from pan. Cook second side 1 minute or so.*

- *Crêpes come in different flavors (plain or chocolate), and shapes : four- or eightfold, square-shaped, rolled, ...*

- *To make crêpe bundles, first spoon filling into center of crêpes. Fold in edges to enclose filling. Tie with orange peel.*

Cheesy Orange Crêpes

10 SERVINGS

1 cup	(250 mL) cottage cheese
½ cup	(125 mL) cream cheese, softened
1	egg
1 tbsp	(15 mL) sugar
1 tbsp	(15 mL) orange peel, grated
10	crêpes (p. 380)
2 tsp	(10 mL) butter
	icing sugar
2 cups	(500 mL) orange sauce (p. 416)

■ In a large bowl, mix both cheeses, egg, sugar and orange peel until smooth.

■ Divide mixture by spooning into the center of crêpes. Fold two sides of each crêpe toward center. Tuck remaining two sides over top, package-like. Set aside.

■ In a large frying pan, over moderate heat, melt butter. Place crêpes in pan. Lightly brown both sides 2 minutes or so. Dust with icing sugar. Serve hot with orange sauce.

NUTRITION	
CALORIES PER SERVING: 148	
FAT: 6 g	CAL. FROM FAT: 39%
PROTEIN: 7 g	CHOLESTEROL: 37 mg
SODIUM: 260 mg	CARBOHYDRATES: 16 g

Nutty Fudge Crêpes

6 SERVINGS

⅓ cup	(80 mL) cream cheese, softened
¾ cup	(180 mL) Ricotta cheese
⅔ cup	(160 mL) sweet chocolate chips
2 tbsp	(30 mL) orange peel
6	crêpes (p. 380)
½ cup	(125 mL) walnuts, finely chopped

■ If using a conventional oven, preheat to 350 °F (175 °C).

■ In a bowl, beat cream cheese 2 minutes. Fold in Ricotta cheese. Add chocolate chips and orange peel. Spoon over each crêpe.

■ Fold crêpes in four. Sprinkle with chopped nuts. Transfer to a cookie sheet. Cook in microwave oven 2 minutes on HIGH, or 5 minutes in conventional oven. Serve hot.

NUTRITION	
CALORIES PER SERVING: 322	
FAT: 18 g	CAL. FROM FAT: 49%
PROTEIN: 8 g	CHOLESTEROL: 45 mg
SODIUM: 121 mg	CARBOHYDRATES: 35 g

Barbary Crêpes

6 SERVINGS

½ cup	(125 mL) raspberry jam
6	fresh or canned pears, peeled, cored, minced
6	crêpes (p. 380)
1 ½ cups	(375 mL) chocolate sauce (p. 416)
½ cup	(125 mL) grated coconut

- Spread successive layers of jam then pears over crêpes.
- Roll crêpes. Pour chocolate sauce on top. Sprinkle with grated coconut. Serve.

Recipe shown above

VARIATIONS
- Replace pears with litchis, bananas or kiwis.

NUTRITION	
CALORIES PER SERVING: 414	
FAT: 5 g	CAL. FROM FAT: 8 %
PROTEIN: 8 g	CHOLESTEROL: 16 mg
SODIUM: 251 mg	CARBOHYDRATES: 14 g

Ice Cream Crêpes with Almonds and Blueberries

6 SERVINGS

1 cup	(250 mL) vanilla ice cream
6	crêpes (p. 380)
½ cup	(125 mL) slivered almonds
¾ cup	(180 mL) fresh blueberries
	icing sugar

- Scoop equal amount of ice cream into the center of each crêpe. Sprinkle with slivered almonds. Divide blueberries among crêpes.
- Fold each crêpe. Dust with icing sugar. Serve.

VARIATIONS
- Vary ice cream flavors to suit your fancy.

NUTRITION	
CALORIES PER SERVING: 204	
FAT: 9 g	CAL. FROM FAT: 37 %
PROTEIN: 5 g	CHOLESTEROL: 25 mg
SODIUM: 205 mg	CARBOHYDRATES: 27 g

Lucifer Crêpes

6 SERVINGS

3 tbsp	(45 mL) butter
3 tbsp	(45 mL) sugar
1/3 cup	(80 mL) orange juice
2 tbsp	(30 mL) lemon juice
6	crêpes (p. 380)
2 tbsp	(30 mL) orange peel, grated
2 oz	(60 mL) Grand Marnier

- In a large frying pan, melt butter and sugar. Add orange and lemon juices. Simmer 7 minutes.
- Fold crêpes in four. Place in frying pan. Cook 2 minutes. Add orange peel. Set aside.
- In a small saucepan, heat Grand Marnier. Pour over crêpes. Flambé, stirring pan until flames extinguish.

Recipe shown above

VARIATIONS
- Replace orange juice with cherry juice, lemon juice with 2 tbsp (30 mL) lemon peel, and Grand Marnier with sherry.
- Replace orange juice with passion-fruit juice, lemon juice with 3 tbsp (45 mL) grated coconut, and Grand Marnier with brandy.

NUTRITION	
CALORIES PER SERVING: 207	
FAT: 7 g	CAL. FROM FAT: 33%
PROTEIN: 3 g	CHOLESTEROL: 31 mg
SODIUM: 344 mg	CARBOHYDRATES: 29 g

Angel-food Crêpes

4 SERVINGS

1 cup	(250 mL) cream cheese, softened
1/4 cup	(60 mL) brown sugar
3/4 cup	(180 mL) dates, chopped
4	crêpes (p. 380)
2 oz	(60 mL) sherry, heated
4	red cherries

- In a bowl, whip cheese and brown sugar. Mix in dates. Divide mixture among crêpes.
- Fold crêpes in four.
- Place in a frying pan. Warm up. Pour sherry over crêpes. Flambé. Decorate each crêpe with a cherry. Serve hot.

Recipe shown above

VARIATIONS
- Replace dates with 1/2 cup (125 mL) dried figs or apricots, and 1/4 cup (60 mL) chopped pecans.

NUTRITION	
CALORIES PER SERVING: 468	
FAT: 21 g	CAL. FROM FAT: 41%
PROTEIN: 8 g	CHOLESTEROL: 80 mg
SODIUM: 466 mg	CARBOHYDRATES: 61 g

Summer Crêpes

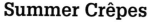

8 SERVINGS	
½	cantaloupe, finely sliced
½	honeydew melon, finely sliced
8	crêpes *(p. 380)*
1 cup	(250 mL) honey
2 tbsp	(30 mL) fresh ginger, grated
	ground cinnamon
	melon balls

- Divide sliced cantaloupe and honeydew melon among crêpes. Drizzle honey over fruit. Sprinkle with ginger.
- Fold crêpes. Dust with cinnamon.
- Garnish with melon balls, shaped with a melon baller.

NUTRITION	
CALORIES PER SERVING: 242	
FAT: 1 *g*	CAL. FROM FAT: 4%
PROTEIN: 3 *g*	CHOLESTEROL: 12 *mg*
SODIUM: 229 *mg*	CARBOHYDRATES: 60 *g*

Minty Raspberry Crêpes

6 SERVINGS	
1 cup	(250 mL) whipped cream
⅓ cup	(80 mL) fresh mint, coarsely chopped
6	crêpes *(p. 380)*
1 ¼ cups	(300 mL) fresh raspberries
	icing sugar

- In a bowl, gently mix whipped cream and mint.
- Divide raspberries, then whipped cream, among crêpes.
- Fold crêpes. Dust with icing sugar. Refrigerate or serve at once.

NUTRITION	
CALORIES PER SERVING: 145	
FAT: 8 *g*	CAL. FROM FAT: 51%
PROTEIN: 2 *g*	CHOLESTEROL: 38 *mg*
SODIUM: 198 *mg*	CARBOHYDRATES: 16 *g*

Strawberry Chocolate Crêpes

6 SERVINGS

¼ cup	(60 mL) strawberry jam
6	chocolate crêpes (p. 380)
¾ cup	(180 mL) Chantilly cream (p. 413)
½ cup	(125 mL) fresh strawberries, sliced
¼ cup	(60 mL) banana, sliced
	icing sugar
	cranberry-strawberry coulis (p. 415)

▪ Spoon equal amount of jam over each crêpe. Set aside.

▪ In a bowl, mix Chantilly cream, strawberries and sliced banana. Divide mixture among crêpes.

▪ Roll crêpes. Dust with icing sugar. Serve with coulis.

Recipe shown above

VARIATION
• Serve with chocolate sauce (p. 416).

NUTRITION	
CALORIES PER SERVING: 349	
FAT: 9 *g*	CAL. FROM FAT: 23%
PROTEIN: 3 *g*	CHOLESTEROL: 42 *mg*
SODIUM: 247 *mg*	CARBOHYDRATES: 67 *g*

Chilled Upside-down Crêpes

8 SERVINGS

½ cup	(125 mL) fresh strawberries, sliced
½ cup	(125 mL) sweet chocolate chips
12	crêpes (p. 380)
½ cup	(60 mL) Grand Marnier-flavored syrup (p. 414)
1 ½ cups	(375 mL) strawberry ice cream, softened
2 tbsp	(30 mL) orange peel

▪ In a bowl, mix strawberries and chocolate chips. Set aside.

▪ Lay a crêpe into bottom of a cake pan slightly larger than crêpes.

▪ Coat with 1 tsp (5 mL) Grand Marnier syrup. Spread with 2 tbsp (30 mL) ice cream. Sprinkle 1 tbsp (15 mL) strawberry and chocolate chip mixture on top. Cover with a crêpe.

▪ Repeat until ingredients have been used.

▪ Freeze 2-3 hours. Remove from freezer. Unmold onto a serving dish (if needed, dip bottom of pan 30 seconds in hot water).

▪ Sprinkle with orange peel. Cut into triangular wedges. Serve with your choice of sauce (pp. 416-417).

NUTRITION	
CALORIES PER SERVING: 236	
FAT: 7 *g*	CAL. FROM FAT: 28%
PROTEIN: 4 *g*	CHOLESTEROL: 23 *mg*
SODIUM: 302 *mg*	CARBOHYDRATES: 39 *g*

Crêpe Tort

	8-10 SERVINGS
1 ¹/₂ cups	(375 mL) commercial hazelnut chocolate spread
3 tbsp	(45 mL) lemon peel
1 tbsp	(15 mL) butter
1 cup	(250 mL) hazelnuts or walnuts, chopped
¹/₂ cup	(125 mL) brown sugar
6	crêpes (p. 380)
6	chocolate crêpes (p. 380)
1 cup	(250 mL) sour cream or plain yogurt

- In a bowl, mix spread and lemon peel. Set aside.

- In a frying pan, melt butter. Add hazelnuts and brown sugar. Mix until brown sugar has melted and caramelized. Set aside.

- Lay a plain crêpe over a dessert platter. Cover with 2 tbsp (30 mL) hazelnut spread mixture, then 2 tbsp (30 mL) caramelized mixture. Top with a chocolate crêpe. Repeat this way until all crêpes have been stacked. Cover tort with sour cream. Serve.

NUTRITION	
CALORIES PER SERVING: 287	
FAT: 11 g	CAL. FROM FAT: 29%
PROTEIN: 6 g	CHOLESTEROL: 18 mg
SODIUM: 280 mg	CARBOHYDRATES: 55 g

Recipe shown above

Apple-stuffed Crêpes

	6 SERVINGS
1 cup	(250 mL) apples, in chunks
1 cup	(250 mL) apple sauce
2 tsp	(10 mL) cinnamon
6	crêpes (p. 380)
3 tbsp	(45 mL) pecans, chopped
1 cup	(250 mL) whipped cream

- In a bowl, mix apples, apple sauce and cinnamon. Divide mixture among crêpes.

- Roll crêpes. Decorate each one with chopped pecans and whipped cream.

NUTRITION	
CALORIES PER SERVING: 183	
FAT: 9 g	CAL. FROM FAT: 45%
PROTEIN: 2 g	CHOLESTEROL: 38 mg
SODIUM: 199 mg	CARBOHYDRATES: 24 g

Island Crêpes

6 SERVINGS

28 oz	(796 mL) canned apricot halves
1 tbsp	(15 mL) lemon peel, grated
⅓ cup	(80 mL) butter or margarine
2 tbsp	(30 mL) sugar
2 oz	(60 mL) dark rum
	pinch of salt
6	crêpes *(p. 380)*
2 oz	(60 mL) orange liqueur

- Set aside 12 apricot halves.

- In a bowl, mash remaining apricots and their syrup with lemon peel. Pour into a large frying pan. Add butter, sugar, rum and salt. Over moderate heat, simmer 2 minutes.

- Fold crêpes in four. Place in pan. Divide reserved apricots among crêpes. Cook until quite hot.

- In a saucepan, warm orange liqueur 30 seconds. Pour over crêpes. Flambé. Serve.

NUTRITION	
CALORIES PER SERVING: 326	
FAT: 16 *g*	CAL. FROM FAT: 49 %
PROTEIN: 3 *g*	CHOLESTEROL: 10 *mg*
SODIUM: 395 *mg*	CARBOHYDRATES: 35 *g*

VARIATIONS
- Replace apricots with prunes (as shown opposite), peaches, nectarines, or pears (as shown bottom right). Vary liqueurs.

TRIFLES

Banana Chiffon Trifle

8 SERVINGS	
1/2	envelope unflavored gelatin
	water
1 cup	(250 mL) ripe bananas, mashed
1 tbsp	(15 mL) lemon juice
1 tbsp	(15 mL) lemon peel
2	egg whites
1/3 cup	(80 mL) sugar
1 cup	(250 mL) whipped cream
2 cups	(500 mL) white bread cubes
2/3 cup	(160 mL) chestnut purée
1/3 cup	(80 mL) commercial chocolate syrup
1 1/2 cups	(375 mL) peanut and chocolate butter cream (p. 331)
1 tbsp	(15 mL) cocoa
1/2 cup	(125 mL) hazelnuts

Banana Chiffon Cream

▪ Following package instructions, let gelatin foam in a little water. Set aside.

▪ In a large bowl, mix mashed bananas with lemon juice and peel. Set aside.

▪ In the top half of a double-boiler, whip egg whites and sugar to a foamy meringue. Add gelatin. Whip mixture until gelatin dissolves. Remove from double-boiler. Let cool.

▪ With a spatula, fold whipped cream into meringue, alternating with banana purée. Refrigerate 1 hour or so.

Assembly

▪ In a large bowl, place half the bread cubes. Spread half the chestnut purée on top. Pour in banana chiffon cream. Cover with remaining bread cubes. Refrigerate 1 hour or so.

▪ Remove from refrigerator. Spread remaining chestnut purée over bread. Coat with chocolate syrup. Using a spatula or pastry bag, pipe peanut and chocolate butter cream all over trifle. Dust with cocoa. Decorate with hazelnuts. Refrigerate 1 more hour. Serve.

NUTRITION	
CALORIES PER SERVING: 393	
FAT: 31 g	CAL. FROM FAT: 66%
PROTEIN: 6 g	CHOLESTEROL: 80 mg
SODIUM: 294 mg	CARBOHYDRATES: 30 g

Coffee Amaretto Trifle

6 SERVINGS	
2 cups	(500 mL) vanilla spongecake (p. 294), cubed
3 oz	(90 mL) almond liqueur
3 cups	(750 mL) coffee custard (p. 412), lukewarm
1 cup	(250 mL) whipped cream
1/3 cup	(80 mL) roasted sliced almonds

▪ In a bowl, moisten half the spongecake cubes with half the almond liqueur. Cover with half the custard, remaining spongecake cubes, then remaining custard. Refrigerate 1 hour.

▪ Using a pastry bag with a fluted nozzle, cover trifle with whipped cream. Decorate with almonds. Refrigerate 3 hours. Serve.

NUTRITION	
CALORIES PER SERVING: 409	
FAT: 20 g	CAL. FROM FAT: 45%
PROTEIN: 11 g	CHOLESTEROL: 205 mg
SODIUM: 205 mg	CARBOHYDRATES: 44 g

Orange Trifle

6 SERVINGS	
2 cups	(500 mL) vanilla **spongecake** (p. 294), **cubed**
²/₃ cup	(160 mL) dried **apricots, in chunks**
2 cups	(500 mL) orange **custard** (p. 412)
¹/₃ cup	(80 mL) orange **marmalade**
³/₄ cup	(180 mL) oranges, **peeled, pith removed, sectioned**
1 cup	(250 mL) whipped **cream**
2 tbsp	(30 mL) orange peel, **grated**
¹/₄ cup	(60 mL) roasted sliced **almonds**

■ In a large bowl, spread successive layers of half the spongecake cubes, half the apricots and half the orange custard. Cover with marmalade. Repeat first 3 steps. Arrange half the orange sections over custard.

■ Cover with a layer of whipped cream. Decorate with remaining orange sections, orange peel and sliced almonds. Refrigerate.

Recipe shown above

VARIATIONS
● Decorate with different nuts or fruit (fresh or dried). Replace marmalade with jam.

NUTRITION	
CALORIES PER SERVING: 407	
FAT: 16 *g*	CAL. FROM FAT: 35%
PROTEIN: 9 *g*	CHOLESTEROL: 159 *mg*
SODIUM: 174 *mg*	CARBOHYDRATES: 59 *g*

Surprise Trifle

6-8 SERVINGS	
2 cups	(500 mL) chocolate **vanilla sandwich cookies, crumbled**
1 cup	(250 mL) chocolate **custard** (p. 412)
1 cup	(250 mL) vanilla ice **cream**
1 cup	(250 mL) Chantilly **cream** (p. 413)
¹/₂ cup	(125 mL) candy-**covered chocolate**

■ Mix crumbled cookies, custard and ice cream.

■ Pour into a serving bowl. Cover. Freeze 1 hour or so.

■ Remove from freezer. Garnish with Chantilly cream. Sprinkle with candy-covered chocolate.

■ Serve at once so trifle remains a little frozen.

NUTRITION	
CALORIES PER SERVING: 330	
FAT: 19 *g*	CAL. FROM FAT: 51%
PROTEIN: 5 *g*	CHOLESTEROL: 75 *mg*
SODIUM: 134 *mg*	CARBOHYDRATES: 37 *g*

Frosty Trifle

6-8 SERVINGS

1	orange spongecake (p. 294)
2 cups	(500 mL) Grand Marnier-flavored light cream (p. 413)
1 cup	(250 mL) strawberry sherbet (p. 406)
³/₄ cup	(180 mL) strawberries, sliced
¹/₂ cup	(125 mL) strawberry jam
1 cup	(250 mL) whipped cream
¹/₃ cup	(80 mL) cocoa
1 ¹/₃ cups	(375 mL) custard sauce (p. 413)

- Cut spongecake into very small cubes.
- In a large bowl, mix spongecake cubes with flavored light cream.
- In a large serving bowl, place half the spongecake mixture. Cover with small spoonfuls of sherbet, alternating with sliced strawberries. Top with remaining spongecake mixture. Using a pastry bag, garnish with whipped cream.
- Cover. Refrigerate 2-3 hours.
- Remove trifle from refrigerator 15 minutes or so before serving.
- Divide into servings. Dust with cocoa. Decorate with mint leaves and whole strawberries, if desired. Serve with custard sauce.

NUTRITION	
CALORIES PER SERVING: 438	
FAT: 22 g	CAL. FROM FAT: 44%
PROTEIN: 8 g	CHOLESTEROL: 177 mg
SODIUM: 211 mg	CARBOHYDRATES: 53 g

Country Trifle

6 SERVINGS

2 cups	(500 mL) raisin bread (p. 421), cut into 1-inch (2.5 cm) cubes
1 cup	(250 mL) fresh strawberries
¹/₂ cup	(125 mL) brown sugar
1 cup	(250 mL) heavy cream
2 cups	(500 mL) Chantilly cream (p. 413)

- In a bowl, spread successive layers of half the bread cubes, one-third the raspberries, half the brown sugar, half the cream and half the Chantilly cream. Repeat first 4 steps.

- Using a spatula or pastry bag with a nozzle, spread second half Chantilly cream. Refrigerate 2 hours. Serve.

Recipe shown above

VARIATION
- Replace raisin bread with whole wheat or rye bread.

NUTRITION	
CALORIES PER SERVING: 675	
FAT: 40 g	CAL. FROM FAT: 52%
PROTEIN: 10 g	CHOLESTEROL: 135 mg
SODIUM: 370 mg	CARBOHYDRATES: 73 g

Chocolate Chip Cookie Trifle

6 SERVINGS

2 ¼ cups	(560 mL) chocolate chip cookies, crumbled
⅔ cup	(160 mL) sweet chocolate chips
2 cups	(500 mL) custard, hot (p. 412)
1 cup	(250 mL) chocolate Chantilly cream (p. 413)
¼ cup	(60 mL) grated coconut

- In a bowl, spread successive layers of one-third crumbled cookies, half the chocolate chips and half the custard. Repeat all 3 steps. Top with remaining cookies. Refrigerate 1 hour.

- Using a pastry bag with a fluted nozzle, decorate with chocolate Chantilly cream. Sprinkle with coconut. Refrigerate 1 hour. Serve.

VARIATIONS
- Replace chocolate chips with sliced strawberries, whole blueberries, raisins or dates.

NUTRITION	
CALORIES PER SERVING: 776	
FAT: 43 *g*	CAL. FROM FAT: 49%
PROTEIN: 12 *g*	CHOLESTEROL: 180 *mg*
SODIUM: 283 *mg*	CARBOHYDRATES: 92 *g*

Black Forest Trifle

6 SERVINGS

1 ½ cups	(375 mL) cocoa spongecake (p. 295), cubed
⅔ cup	(160 mL) Bing cherries
⅓ cup	(80 mL) Grand Marnier-flavored syrup (p. 414) or maple syrup
2 cups	(500 mL) Chantilly cream (p. 413)
½ cup	(125 mL) chocolate shavings (p. 330)

- In a bowl, spread successive layers of half the cocoa spongecake cubes, half the cherries, half the syrup and half the Chantilly cream. Repeat first 3 steps.

- Using a spatula or pastry bag with a fluted nozzle, spread remaining Chantilly cream. Decorate with chocolate shavings. Refrigerate 2 hours. Serve.

NUTRITION	
CALORIES PER SERVING: 987	
FAT: 62 *g*	CAL. FROM FAT: 52%
PROTEIN: 9 *g*	CHOLESTEROL: 119 *mg*
SODIUM: 152 *mg*	CARBOHYDRATES: 177 *g*

Pineapple Trifle

6 SERVINGS	
1	envelope unflavored gelatin
1 cup	(250 mL) pineapple juice
1	small box pineapple jelly powder
1 cup	(250 mL) boiling water
1	commercial angel-food cake
2 cups	(500 mL) heavy cream
19 oz	(540 mL) canned pineapple chunks
	mint leaves (optional)

▪ In a bowl, let gelatin foam in pineapple juice. Set aside.

▪ In a second bowl, dissolve powder jelly in boiling water. Fold in gelatin and pineapple juice mixture. Let cool until half-set.

▪ Meanwhile, cut angel-food cake into small cubes. Set aside.

▪ Whip cream. Fold in half-set jelly.

▪ Over the bottom of a buttered chimney mold, spread successive layers of half the cake cubes, half the pineapple chunks and half the whipped cream and jelly mixture. Repeat all 3 steps. Refrigerate 4 hours or so.

▪ Remove from refrigerator. Unmold trifle over a serving dish. Garnish with mint leaves, if desired. Serve.

VARIATIONS
• Use other jelly powder flavors and fruit.

NUTRITION	
CALORIES PER SERVING: 672	
FAT: 32 g	CAL. FROM FAT: 41 %
PROTEIN: 14 g	CHOLESTEROL: 186 mg
SODIUM: 261 mg	CARBOHYDRATES: 87 g

Fruit Trifle

4 SERVINGS	
1 ¹/₃ cups	(330 mL) fruitcake (p. 308), cubed
2 cups	(500 mL) flavored light cream (p. 413)
³/₄ cup	(180 mL) Chantilly cream (p. 413)
	mint leaves (optional)

▪ In a large bowl, spread successive layers of half the fruitcake cubes and half the light cream. Repeat both steps.

▪ Using a pastry bag with a fluted nozzle, garnish with Chantilly cream. Refrigerate 8 hours. Decorate with mint, if desired. Serve.

NUTRITION	
CALORIES PER SERVING: 657	
FAT: 44 g	CAL. FROM FAT: 59 %
PROTEIN: 7 g	CHOLESTEROL: 147 mg
SODIUM: 184 mg	CARBOHYDRATES: 62 g

Recipe shown above

Chocolate-Sherry Trifle

6 SERVINGS	
1 cup	(250 mL) macaroons, crumbled
2 oz	(60 mL) sherry
1 ½ cups	(375 mL) cocoa spongecake (p. 295), diced
1 ¼ cups	(300 mL) chocolate custard (p. 412)
½ cup	(125 mL) jam, of your choice
1 ¾ cups	(425 mL) chocolate Chantilly cream (p. 413)
	icing sugar (optional)

▪ In a bowl, moisten half the macaroons with sherry. Set aside.

▪ In a large bowl, spread successive layers of sponge-cake cubes, chocolate custard and jam. Cover with some sherry-flavored macaroons, then half the chocolate Chantilly cream. Sprinkle remaining macaroons.

▪ Using a pastry bag with a fluted nozzle, pipe remaining chocolate Chantilly cream over trifle. With a sieve, dust with icing sugar, if desired. Refrigerate 8 hours. Serve.

VARIATIONS
• Vary spongecake flavors and alcohols.

NUTRITION	
CALORIES PER SERVING: 620	
FAT: 28 g	CAL. FROM FAT: 40%
PROTEIN: 9 g	CHOLESTEROL: 167 mg
SODIUM: 280 mg	CARBOHYDRATES: 86 g

Maple Nut Trifle

4 SERVINGS	
2 cups	(500 mL) Genoa bread (p. 424), cut into ½-inch (1.25 cm) cubes
¾ cup	(180 mL) maple syrup
1 ¾ cups	(425 mL) custard, hot (p. 412)
1 cup	(250 mL) Chantilly cream (p. 413)
¼ cup	(60 mL) walnuts, chopped

▪ In a bowl, moisten bread cubes with maple syrup.

▪ In a large bowl, spread successive layers of half the bread cubes and half the custard. Repeat both steps. Let cool.

▪ Using a pastry bag with a fluted nozzle, pipe Chantilly cream rosettes or zigzags onto trifle. Decorate with chopped walnuts. Refrigerate 12 hours. Serve.

NUTRITION	
CALORIES PER SERVING: 797	
FAT: 28 g	CAL. FROM FAT: 31%
PROTEIN: 17 g	CHOLESTEROL: 183 mg
SODIUM: 588 mg	CARBOHYDRATES: 123 g

SOUFFLÉS

Chocolate Soufflé

4 SERVINGS

2 tbsp	(30 mL) cornstarch
³/4 cup	(180 mL) milk
4 oz	(115 g) unsweetened chocolate
¹/2 cup	(125 mL) sugar
1 tsp	(5 mL) vanilla extract
4	egg yolks
5	egg whites
¹/4 tsp	(1 mL) cream of tartar

- Preheat oven to 350 °F (175 °C). Butter and sugar a soufflé dish.

- Dilute cornstarch in ¹/4 cup (60 mL) milk. Set aside.

- In a saucepan, while stirring, heat remaining milk, chocolate, sugar and vanilla extract. Add diluted cornstarch. Over high heat, vigorously whisk 2 minutes or until mixture thickens and starts to bubble. Remove from heat. Let cool completely.

- In a bowl, beat egg yolks 5 minutes or so. Add 3 tbsp (45 mL) chocolate mixture. Fold into chocolate in saucepan. Set aside.

- In a second bowl, beat egg whites and cream of tartar until stiff peaks form. With a whisk, gently fold in chocolate mixture.

- Pour into soufflé dish. Bake in oven 45-50 minutes. Serve with whipped cream, if desired.

NUTRITION	
CALORIES PER SERVING: 373	
FAT: 22 g	CAL. FROM FAT: 49%
PROTEIN: 12 g	CHOLESTEROL: 219 mg
SODIUM: 102 mg	CARBOHYDRATES: 40 g

Chilled Chocolate-Orange Soufflé

4 SERVINGS

Chocolate layer

1	envelope unflavored gelatin
2 tbsp	(30 mL) sugar
2	eggs, separated
³/4 cup	(180 mL) milk
3 tbsp	(45 mL) milk chocolate, coarsely chopped

Orange layer

1	envelope unflavored gelatin
2 tbsp	(30 mL) sugar
2	eggs, separated
³/4 cup	(180 mL) orange juice
1 tsp	(5 mL) orange peel
¹/4 cup	(60 mL) sugar

Chocolate Layer

- In a saucepan, mix gelatin and sugar.

- In a bowl, beat egg yolks and milk. Combine with gelatin. Over low heat, while stirring, warm up 3-4 minutes or until mixture thickens and gelatin dissolves.

- Off heat, add chocolate. Stir until chocolate has melted. Set aside.

(continued on next page)

Orange Layer

- In a saucepan, mix gelatin and 2 tbsp (30 mL) sugar.

- In a bowl, beat egg yolks with orange juice and peel. Fold into gelatin. Over low heat, while stirring, warm up 3-4 minutes or until mixture thickens and gelatin dissolves.

- Remove from heat. Let cool until gelatin starts to set.

Assembly

- In a bowl, beat 4 egg whites and ¼ cup (60 mL) sugar into soft peaks. Divide mixture in half.

- With a spatula, gently fold first half into chocolate mixture and second half into orange mixture.

- Pour chocolate mixture into soufflé mold. Cover with orange layer. Refrigerate 1 hour until soufflé sets.

- Garnish with orange sections dipped in chocolate.

Recipe shown opposite page, top photograph

NUTRITION	
CALORIES PER SERVING: 329	
FAT: 8 *g*	CAL. FROM FAT: 22 %
PROTEIN: 28 *g*	CHOLESTEROL: 191 *mg*
SODIUM: 104 *mg*	CARBOHYDRATES: 37 *g*

NUTRITION ▶	
CALORIES PER SERVING: 387	
FAT: 23 *g*	CAL. FROM FAT: 51 %
PROTEIN: 7 *g*	CHOLESTEROL: 144 *mg*
SODIUM: 67 *mg*	CARBOHYDRATES: 42 *g*

Cold Soufflé Milanese

4-6 SERVINGS		
2 cups	(500 mL)	light cream
1 tbsp	(15 mL)	gelatin
¼ cup	(60 mL)	lemon juice
3		eggs, separated
1 cup	(250 mL)	sugar
1		lemon peel, grated
		slivered almonds
		pistachios

- In a bowl, whip cream. Set aside in refrigerator.

- Fit soufflé dish with a 2-inch (5 cm) ovenproof paper collar.

- In a bowl, dissolve gelatin in half the lemon juice. Set aside.

- In the top part of a double-boiler, whip egg yolks, sugar, second half of lemon juice and peel until thickened. Add dissolved gelatin. Let cool.

- In a second bowl, beat egg whites until peaks form. Gently fold into egg yolks, alternating with whipped cream. Pour into mold. Refrigerate 1 hour until soufflé sets.

- Remove paper collar. Decorate contour with slivered almonds and pistachios.

Recipe shown above, top photograph

VARIATIONS

- Replace lemon with limes. Decorate with cocoa, hazelnuts, coconut or poppy seeds.

Recipe shown above, bottom photograph

Grand Marnier Soufflé

4 SERVINGS

³/₄ cup	(180 mL)	milk
¹/₃ cup	(80 mL)	sugar
		peel of 1 orange
3 tbsp	(45 mL)	butter
¹/₃ cup	(80 mL)	flour
4		eggs, separated
1 oz	(30 mL)	Grand Marnier
2 tbsp	(30 mL)	orange juice
		icing sugar

- Preheat oven to 375 °F (190 °C). Butter and sugar 4 ramekins.

- In a saucepan, bring to a boil milk, sugar and orange peel. Set aside.

- In a second saucepan, melt butter. With a whisk, blend in flour until mixture turns to a roux.

- Whisk boiling milk into flour mixture. Bring to a boil. Cook 1-2 minutes until thickened. Remove from heat. Let cool 2-3 minutes. Add egg yolks, Grand Marnier and orange juice. Set aside.

- In a bowl, beat egg whites until peaks form. With a spatula, fold into first mixture. Fill ramekins, up to ¹/₂-inch (1.25 cm) from top. Bake 15-20 minutes. Approximately 5 minutes before the end of cooking, dust soufflé with icing sugar.

NUTRITION	
CALORIES PER SERVING: 307	
FAT: 14 g	CAL. FROM FAT: 44%
PROTEIN: 8 g	CHOLESTEROL: 212 mg
SODIUM: 163 mg	CARBOHYDRATES: 33 g

Banana-Litchi Soufflé

4 SERVINGS

2 tbsp	(30 mL)	butter
2 tbsp	(30 mL)	cornstarch
		pinch of salt
1 cup	(250 mL)	bananas, mashed
¹/₃ cup	(80 mL)	litchis, chopped
¹/₂ oz	(15 mL)	dark rum
1 tbsp	(15 mL)	lime juice
1 tsp	(5 mL)	lime peel, grated
3		egg yolks
¹/₂ cup	(125 mL)	sugar
5		egg whites

- Preheat oven to 350 °F (175 °C). Butter and sugar 4 ramekins or a soufflé dish.

- In a saucepan, melt butter with cornstarch and salt. Add mashed bananas and litchis. Over low heat, while stirring, cook 3 minutes or until mixture thickens. Add rum, lime juice and peel. Remove from heat. Set aside.

- In a bowl, beat egg yolks and sugar. Fold in fruit mixture. Set aside.

- In a second bowl, beat egg whites until soft peaks form. With a spatula, gently fold into first mixture. Pour into soufflé dish. Bake in oven around 35 minutes (or 25 minutes for ramekins).

NUTRITION	
CALORIES PER SERVING: 275	
FAT: 10 g	CAL. FROM FAT: 32%
PROTEIN: 7 g	CHOLESTEROL: 175 mg
SODIUM: 166 mg	CARBOHYDRATES: 40 g

Peach 'n' Almond Soufflé

4 SERVINGS

¹/₂ cup	(125 mL) egg whites
¹/₃ cup	(80 mL) sugar
	pinch of cream of tartar (optional)
4	egg yolks
1 cup	(250 mL) peaches, mashed
3 tbsp	(45 mL) cornstarch
¹/₃ cup	(80 mL) slivered white almonds
2 tbsp	(30 mL) lemon juice
	pinch of salt
¹/₂ oz	(15 mL) almond liqueur
2	drops of orange food coloring (optional)
	icing sugar

- Preheat oven to 375 °F (190 °C). Butter and sugar 4 ramekins or a soufflé dish.
- In a bowl, beat first 3 ingredients until peaks form.
- In a second bowl, combine remaining ingredients, except icing sugar. Gently fold in egg whites. Pour into soufflé dish. Bake in oven 35 minutes (or 25 minutes for ramekins).
- Carefully remove from oven. Dust with icing sugar. Serve.

Recipe shown above

VARIATIONS
- Replace peaches with apricots or mangoes.

NUTRITION	
CALORIES PER SERVING: 251	
FAT: 10 *g*	CAL. FROM FAT: 37%
PROTEIN: 9 *g*	CHOLESTEROL: 213 *mg*
SODIUM: 90 *mg*	CARBOHYDRATES: 31 *g*

Plum Soufflé

4 SERVINGS

	water
2 cups	(500 mL) pitted dried prunes
1 tbsp	(15 mL) butter
1 tbsp	(15 mL) flour
	peel of 1 lemon, grated
¹/₂ tsp	(2 mL) cinnamon
4	egg whites
¹/₂ tsp	(2 mL) salt
¹/₂ cup	(125 mL) sugar
	icing sugar (optional)

- In water, soak prunes 3-4 hours.
- Preheat oven to 400 °F (205 °C). Butter and sugar a soufflé dish. Set aside.
- Drain prunes. Pour into a bowl. Purée. Mix in butter, flour, lemon peel and cinnamon. Set aside.
- In a second bowl, beat egg whites and salt until stiff peaks form. Gently fold in previous mixture. Pour into soufflé dish.
- Bake in oven 30 minutes. Serve warm, dusted with icing sugar, if desired.

VARIATIONS
- Replace prunes with other dried fruit.

NUTRITION	
CALORIES PER SERVING: 322	
FAT: 3 *g*	CAL. FROM FAT: 8%
PROTEIN: 6 *g*	CHOLESTEROL: 8 *mg*
SODIUM: 353 *mg*	CARBOHYDRATES: 73 *g*

Mousses, Jellies and Puddings

Cherry Cheese Mousse

8 SERVINGS	
1 lb	(450 g) cream cheese, softened
1	small box lime jelly powder
2 cups	(500 mL) boiling water
1 cup	(250 mL) cold water
2 1/2 cups	(625 mL) cherries, pitted
1	small box cherry jelly powder
1 cup	(250 mL) cherry juice

- In a food processor, beat cream cheese until smooth. Set aside.
- Dissolve lime jelly powder in 1 cup (250 mL) boiling water. Add cold water and cherries. Fold into cream cheese.
- Pour into a springform mold or divide among dessert cups. Refrigerate.
- Dissolve cherry jelly powder in 1 cup (250 mL) boiling water. Add cherry juice. Let cool.
- Remove first mixture from refrigerator. Top with cherry jelly. Refrigerate at least 1 more hour before serving.

NUTRITION	
CALORIES PER SERVING: 328	
FAT: 20 g	CAL. FROM FAT: 54 %
PROTEIN: 7 g	CHOLESTEROL: 62 mg
SODIUM: 225 mg	CARBOHYDRATES: 31 g

Coffee Mousse

4 SERVINGS	
1	envelope unflavored gelatin
3/4 cup	(180 mL) water
2 tsp	(10 mL) instant coffee
3/4 cup	(180 mL) sugar
4	egg yolks
1 1/2 cups	(375 mL) whipped cream
1/4 cup	(60 mL) sour cream
12	coffee beans

- In a bowl, dissolve gelatin in a little water.
- In a saucepan, heat water, instant coffee and sugar. Whip in dissolved gelatin and egg yolks.
- Remove from heat. Dip bottom of saucepan in cold water for speedier cooling. Whip until mixture has cooled. Fold in whipped cream as soon as gelatin starts to set.
- Pour into dessert cups. Refrigerate 15 minutes.
- Garnish each cup with 1 tbsp (15 mL) sour cream and 3 coffee beans. Serve.

Recipe shown above

VARIATIONS
- Garnish with chocolate Chantilly cream *(p. 413)*, as shown. Dust with icing sugar or cocoa. Decorate with grated coconut or chopped nuts.

NUTRITION	
CALORIES PER SERVING: 429	
FAT: 25 g	CAL. FROM FAT: 51 %
PROTEIN: 14 g	CHOLESTEROL: 280 mg
SODIUM: 44 mg	CARBOHYDRATES: 40 g

Maple Mousse

4 SERVINGS	
3/4 cup	(180 mL) maple syrup
1	envelope unflavored gelatin
3 tbsp	(45 mL) cold water
3	large egg yolks
2 cups	(500 mL) heavy cream
1/2 oz	(15 mL) dark rum
1/4 cup	(60 mL) roasted almonds

▪ In a heavy-bottomed saucepan, over low heat, warm maple syrup.

▪ Meanwhile, in a bowl, dissolve gelatin in cold water. Let stand 5 minutes. Dip bottom of bowl in hot water until gelatin has dissolved completely.

▪ While stirring, fold in maple syrup. Remove from heat. Set aside.

▪ In a second bowl, whip egg yolks until creamy. Fold into maple syrup. Beat until mixture has cooled.

▪ In a third bowl, whip cream. Fold into maple syrup, reserving a little whipped cream for decoration. Pour into a large bowl or individual dessert cups. Refrigerate 2 hours or until mousse has set.

▪ Fold dark rum into remaining whipped cream. Garnish mousse. Sprinkle with roasted almonds.

NUTRITION	
CALORIES PER SERVING: 718	
FAT: 54 g	CAL. FROM FAT: 66%
PROTEIN: 17 g	CHOLESTEROL: 323 mg
SODIUM: 67 mg	CARBOHYDRATES: 45 g

Chocolate Mousse

6 SERVINGS	
1	envelope unflavored gelatin
1/4 cup	(60 mL) water
3	egg whites
1/3 cup	(80 mL) sugar
1	drop of red food coloring (optional)
4 oz	(115 g) semisweet chocolate
2 cups	(500 mL) whipped cream

▪ In a small bowl, dissolve gelatin in water. Set aside.

▪ In a double-boiler, warm egg whites and sugar until sugar has fully dissolved.

▪ In a mixer bowl, beat egg whites until peaks form. Add dissolved gelatin and food coloring.

▪ In a saucepan, over low heat, melt chocolate. Fold into egg white mixture. With a spatula, gently fold in half the whipped cream. Pour into dessert cups. Refrigerate 20 minutes.

▪ Decorate each cup with a swirl of whipped cream. Sprinkle with cocoa or chocolate shavings, if desired.

VARIATIONS
• Decorate with strawberries, cherries, raspberries or bananas dipped in icing sugar or cocoa.

NUTRITION	
CALORIES PER SERVING: 304	
FAT: 20 g	CAL. FROM FAT: 57%
PROTEIN: 10 g	CHOLESTEROL: 54 mg
SODIUM: 52 mg	CARBOHYDRATES: 24 g

Tutti-Frutti Mousse

4 SERVINGS

1/2	banana
6	canned pear halves, drained
6	canned peach halves, drained
1 tsp	(5 mL) lemon juice
1	envelope unflavored gelatin
2 tbsp	(30 mL) water
2	egg whites
	fresh fruit
	fresh mint leaves

- In a food processor, purée fruit with lemon juice. Set aside.
- In a small saucepan, dissolve gelatin in water. Warm up a little.
- In a mixer bowl, beat eggs until peaks form. Gently fold in fruit purée and gelatin.
- Pour into dessert cups. Decorate with fresh fruit and mint. Serve.

NUTRITION	
CALORIES PER SERVING: 410	
FAT: 2 g	CAL. FROM FAT: 3%
PROTEIN: 17 g	CHOLESTEROL: 1 mg
SODIUM: 25 mg	CARBOHYDRATES: 35 g

Blueberry-Banana Mousse

4 SERVINGS

1 1/2	envelopes unflavored gelatin
1/4 cup	(60 mL) orange juice
1 1/2 cups	(375 mL) blueberries
3	bananas, mashed
3 tbsp	(45 mL) plain yogurt

- In a small saucepan, dissolve gelatin in orange juice. Warm up a little.
- In a mixer bowl, mix all ingredients to a smooth, creamy mousse.
- Divide among dessert cups. Decorate with fresh fruit, if desired. Serve.

VARIATIONS
- Decorate with walnuts. Serve with small cakes or wafers.

NUTRITION	
CALORIES PER SERVING: 203	
FAT: 1 g	CAL. FROM FAT: 5%
PROTEIN: 17 g	CHOLESTEROL: 1 mg
SODIUM: 25 mg	CARBOHYDRATES: 35 g

Rhubarb Mousse

8 SERVINGS	
2 cups	(500 mL) rhubarb, cubed
1/4 cup	(60 mL) sugar
2	envelopes unflavored gelatin
1/4 cup	(60 mL) cold water
1/4 cup	(60 mL) boiling water
3 cups	(750 mL) vanilla ice cream
1 tsp	(5 mL) lemon peel
1/2 tsp	(2 mL) nutmeg

- In a saucepan, cook rhubarb and sugar 10 minutes.
- In a bowl, dissolve gelatin in cold water. Add boiling water. Mix until gelatin dissolves completely. Fold in sweetened rhubarb. Let cool slightly. Mix in remaining ingredients. Refrigerate 1 hour.
- Garnish with whipped cream and julienned rhubarb, if desired.

NUTRITION	
CALORIES PER SERVING: 169	
FAT: 6 g	CAL. FROM FAT: 29 %
PROTEIN: 12 g	CHOLESTEROL: 22 mg
SODIUM: 52 mg	CARBOHYDRATES: 19 g

Strawberry Mousse

6 SERVINGS	
1 1/2	envelopes unflavored gelatin
3 cups	(750 mL) frozen strawberries, thawed, drained (reserve syrup)
1 cup	(250 mL) plain yogurt
1 cup	(250 mL) heavy cream
1/4 cup	(60 mL) sugar

Stawberry sauce
	water
1 tbsp	(15 mL) cornstarch
2 tsp	(10 mL) orange peel

- In a bowl, dissolve gelatin in 1/4 cup (60 mL) strawberry syrup. Let stand 5 minutes. Dip bottom of bowl in hot water until gelatin dissolves completely. Fold in strawberries and yogurt. Set aside.
- In a second bowl, whip cream and sugar. Add to strawberries as soon as gelatin starts to set. Pour into dessert cups. Refrigerate.

Strawberry sauce
- Add enough water to remaining strawberry syrup to make 1 cup (250 mL) liquid.
- Pour into saucepan. Warm over low heat. Add cornstarch diluted in a little water. Mix until sauce thickens. Add orange peel. Let cool until lukewarm. Divide among dessert cups.

NUTRITION	
CALORIES PER SERVING: 338	
FAT: 16 g	CAL. FROM FAT: 41 %
PROTEIN: 13 g	CHOLESTEROL: 59 mg
SODIUM: 45 mg	CARBOHYDRATES: 40 g

Fruit Mold

12 SERVINGS

2	boxes lime jelly powder
2	boxes strawberry jelly powder
2	boxes orange jelly powder
	water
1 cup	(250 mL) honeydew melon balls
1 cup	(250 mL) strawberries, halved
1 cup	(250 mL) oranges, peeled, pith removed, sectioned

- Individually dissolve each jelly powder flavor in 1 ½ cups (375 mL) water (do not follow package instructions). Pour lime jelly into a springform pan. Cover with melon balls shaped with a melon baller. Refrigerate 30-50 minutes or until jelly has set.
- Remove from refrigerator. Proceed the same way with other jelly flavors and fruit. Refrigerate 30-50 minutes between layers. Once jelly mold is assembled, refrigerate 2 hours.
- Dip pan 15 seconds in hot water to unmold more easily. Unclip pan. Turn over a serving dish. Unmold. Cut with a knife previously warmed in hot water.

Recipe shown above

VARIATIONS
- Vary fruit and jelly powder flavors.

NUTRITION	
CALORIES PER SERVING: 173	
FAT: 0 *g*	CAL. FROM FAT: 0 %
PROTEIN: 4 *g*	CHOLESTEROL: 0 *mg*
SODIUM: 116 *mg*	CARBOHYDRATES: 41 *g*

Apricot Cups

6 SERVINGS

12	canned apricot halves, drained — reserve ¾ cup (180 mL) syrup
1 ½	envelopes unflavored gelatin
2 cups	(500 mL) water
2 oz	(60 mL) orange liqueur

- Place 2 apricot halves into each dessert cup.
- In a bowl, dissolve gelatin in water. If needed, warm up a little.
- Mix in apricot syrup and orange liqueur. Pour into cups over apricots. Refrigerate 2 hours.
- Unmold after dipping bottom of cups 15 seconds in hot water.

Recipe shown above, on top of fruit mold

VARIATIONS
- Serve with a coulis *(pp. 414-415)*, custard sauce *(p. 413)* or whipped cream.
- Replace 2 apricot halves with 1 peach half.

NUTRITION	
CALORIES PER SERVING: 387	
FAT: 1 *g*	CAL. FROM FAT: 1 %
PROTEIN: 13 *g*	CHOLESTEROL: 0 *mg*
SODIUM: 23 *mg*	CARBOHYDRATES: 84 *g*

Cherry Surprisexs

12 TREATS

1	box strawberry jelly powder
1 1/2 cups	(375 mL) water
12	red cherries, with their stem

- In a bowl, dissolve jelly powder in water.
- Place cherries in sections of an ice-cube tray. Cover with diluted jelly. Refrigerate until set.
- Unmold after dipping bottom of tray 15 seconds in hot water.

NUTRITION	
CALORIES PER TREAT: 139	
FAT: 1 g	CAL. FROM FAT: 9%
PROTEIN: 2 g	CHOLESTEROL: 0 mg
SODIUM: 20 mg	CARBOHYDRATES: 31 g

Recipe shown above left

Orangy Litchis

8 SERVINGS

1	box orange jelly powder
1 1/2 cups	(375 mL) water
8	litchis
	peel of 3 oranges, grated

- In a bowl, dissolve jelly powder in water.
- Roll each litchi in orange peel. Place into the middle of a dessert cup. Top with diluted jelly. Refrigerate until set.
- Unmold after dipping bottom of cups 15 seconds in hot water.

NUTRITION	
CALORIES PER SERVING: 98	
FAT: 1 g	CAL. FROM FAT: 3%
PROTEIN: 2 g	CHOLESTEROL: 0 mg
SODIUM: 33 mg	CARBOHYDRATES: 25 g

Fruit Bavarian Cream

8 SERVINGS

1	box jelly powder, your choice of flavor
1	envelope unflavored gelatin
4 cups	(1 L) vanilla ice cream
	fresh fruit

- In a bowl, prepare jelly powder following package instructions. Fold in gelatin.
- In a second bowl, soften ice cream. Fold into jelly. Add fruit.
- Pour into small ramekins. Refrigerate at least 4 hours or until set.

NUTRITION	
CALORIES PER SERVING: 223	
FAT: 7 g	CAL. FROM FAT: 29%
PROTEIN: 9 g	CHOLESTEROL: 29 mg
SODIUM: 86 mg	CARBOHYDRATES: 33 g

Recipe shown above right

Stuffed Cantaloupes

4 SERVINGS

2	ripe cantaloupes
2 cups	(500 mL) red grapes
1	box jelly powder, your choice of flavor
	water
	Chantilly cream *(p. 413)*

- Slice cantaloupes and grapes in half. Remove seeds.
- Prepare jelly powder following package instructions.
- Divide grapes among cantaloupe halves. Cover with jelly. Refrigerate 30-60 minutes or until set.
- Remove from refrigerator. Garnish with Chantilly cream.

NUTRITION	
CALORIES PER SERVING: 203	
FAT: 5 g	CAL. FROM FAT: 19%
PROTEIN: 4 g	CHOLESTEROL: 15 mg
SODIUM: 75 mg	CARBOHYDRATES: 40 g

Butterscotch Cobbler

10 SERVINGS	
¹⁄₄ cup	(60 mL) butter, softened
³⁄₄ cup	(180 mL) sugar
1	egg
1 ¹⁄₂ cups	(375 mL) all-purpose flour
1 tbsp	(15 mL) baking powder
¹⁄₂ tsp	(2 mL) salt
³⁄₄ cup	(180 mL) milk
¹⁄₂ tsp	(2 mL) vanilla extract
¹⁄₂ cup	(125 mL) grated coconut

Sauce

2 cups	(500 mL) brown sugar
1 cup	(250 mL) water
2 tsp	(10 mL) butter

- Preheat oven to 350 °F (175 °C).
- In a bowl, whip butter. Fold in sugar and egg. In a second bowl, sift flour, baking powder and salt. Set aside.
- In a third bowl, mix milk and vanilla extract. Fold in first mixture, alternating with dry ingredients.
- Pour into a square 8-inch (20.5 cm) cake pan. Sprinkle with coconut. Bake 25-30 minutes or until cake is golden brown.

Sauce
- In a saucepan, while stirring, heat all ingredients 8-10 minutes. Serve with cold or warm cake.

NUTRITION	
CALORIES PER SERVING: 375	
FAT: 8 *g*	CAL. FROM FAT: 18 %
PROTEIN: 3 *g*	CHOLESTEROL: 35 *mg*
SODIUM: 312 *mg*	CARBOHYDRATES: 75 *g*

Banana Pudding

4-6 SERVINGS	
1 tbsp	(15 mL) cornstarch
2 cups	(500 mL) milk
¹⁄₂ cup	(125 mL) grated coconut
2	bananas, sliced
3	egg yolks
¹⁄₂ cup	(125 mL) sugar
1 tsp	(5 mL) vanilla extract
2 tbsp	(30 mL) orange peel
1	basic recipe meringue *(p. 358)*

- Preheat oven to 450 °F (230 °C).
- In a bowl, dilute cornstarch in a little milk. Set aside.
- In a small saucepan, warm remaining milk. Add diluted cornstarch. Let mixture thicken. Add grated coconut and sliced bananas. Cook 1 minute. Set aside.
- In a bowl, beat egg yolks, sugar, vanilla extract and orange peel. Fold into hot mixture.
- Pour into a square dish. Top with meringue. Bake in oven 3 minutes or until meringue is golden brown. Serve.

NUTRITION	
CALORIES PER SERVING: 257	
FAT: 7 *g*	CAL. FROM FAT: 25 %
PROTEIN: 6 *g*	CHOLESTEROL: 117 *mg*
SODIUM: 87 *mg*	CARBOHYDRATES: 42 *g*

Pineapple Rice Pudding

6-8 SERVINGS

1 cup	(250 mL) heavy cream
1/2 cup	(125 mL) water
1/2 cup	(125 mL) instant rice
14 oz	(398 mL) canned crushed pineapples, well-drained
1/2 cup	(125 mL) sugar
	strawberries, sliced
	poppy seeds

- In a bowl, whip cream until stiff peaks form. Refrigerate.

- In a saucepan, bring water to a boil. Add rice. Cook 5 minutes. Remove from heat. Let cool. Refrigerate.

- In a bowl, mix all ingredients, except strawberries and poppy seeds.

- Divide among dessert cups. Garnish with fresh strawberries. Sprinkle with poppy seeds.

VARIATIONS
- Use other fruit or well-drained fruit salad.

NUTRITION	
CALORIES PER SERVING: 214	
FAT: 12 g	CAL. FROM FAT: 47%
PROTEIN: 2 g	CHOLESTEROL: 41 mg
SODIUM: 13 mg	CARBOHYDRATES: 28 g

Orange Liqueur Crème Brûlée

4 SERVINGS

2	eggs
3-4	egg yolks
1 1/2 cups	(375 mL) light cream
1/4 cup	(60 mL) sugar
1 1/2 oz	(45 mL) orange liqueur
4 tsp	(20 mL) orange peel
1 1/3 cups	(330 mL) apricots, in pieces
2 tbsp	(30 mL) brown sugar

- Preheat oven to 325 °F (160 °C).

- In a bowl, beat eggs, cream and sugar. Fold in orange liqueur and peel. Set aside.

- Place 1/3 cup (80 mL) apricot pieces in each of 4 ramekins. Cover with egg mixture. Bake in oven 35 minutes.

- Remove from oven. Let cool slightly.

- Meanwhile, increase oven temperature to BROIL.

- Dust with brown sugar. Broil 3-5 minutes until caramelized. Serve lukewarm.

VARIATIONS
- Use pineapple, bananas, raspberries and different liqueurs.

NUTRITION	
CALORIES PER SERVING: 388	
FAT: 24 g	CAL. FROM FAT: 57%
PROTEIN: 8 g	CHOLESTEROL: 311 mg
SODIUM: 71 mg	CARBOHYDRATES: 33 g

SHERBETS

Grapefruit Sherbet

3 CUPS (750 mL)

1/2 cup	(125 mL) powdered milk
2 cups	(500 mL) grapefruit juice
1 cup	(250 mL) pink grapefruit, peeled, pith removed, sectioned

- In a bowl, mix powdered milk and grapefruit juice. Freeze around 2 hours or until mixture hardens.
- In a blender, whip frozen juice and grapefruit sections until smooth. Pour into an airtight container. Freeze until mixture hardens again. Let sherbet soften a little before serving.

VARIATIONS
- Use orange juice and an orange, peeled and pith removed (as shown opposite) ; or lemon juice and a lime, peeled and pith removed. For lemon lime sherbet, add 1/2 cup (125 mL) icing sugar to cut acidity.
- Add 1-2 tbsp (15-30 mL) orange liqueur or pastis.

(Refer to sherbet technique on p. 92)

NUTRITION	
CALORIES PER SERVING: 97	
FAT: 3 g	CAL. FROM FAT: 27%
PROTEIN: 3 g	CHOLESTEROL: 10 mg
SODIUM: 40 mg	CARBOHYDRATES: 15 g

Strawberry Sherbet

2 1/2 CUPS (625 mL)

1 cup	(250 mL) strawberry, raspberry or mixed-berry juice
2 cups	(500 mL) frozen strawberries
1/2 cup	(125 mL) icing sugar
1 tbsp	(15 mL) lemon juice
1/2 oz	(15 mL) vodka

- In a food processor, mix all ingredients until smooth. Pour into an airtight container. Freeze 2 hours.
- Remove from freezer. Whip again. Return to freezer until firm. Serve with fruit or wafers, if desired.

NUTRITION	
CALORIES PER SERVING: 195	
FAT: 1 g	CAL. FROM FAT: 1%
PROTEIN: 1 g	CHOLESTEROL: 0 mg
SODIUM: 2 mg	CARBOHYDRATES: 48 g

Melon Sherbet

3 CUPS (750 mL)

2 cups	(500 mL) cantaloupe
2 cups	(500 mL) honeydew melon
2 tbsp	(30 mL) lemon juice
1 oz	(30 mL) pastis (optional)
2/3 cup	(160 mL) icing sugar

- In a food processor, mix all ingredients until smooth. Pour into an airtight container. Freeze 2 hours or so. Whip again in food processor.
- Freeze 2 more hours. Serve.

NUTRITION	
CALORIES PER SERVING: 67	
FAT: 1 *g*	CAL. FROM FAT: 1%
PROTEIN: 0 *g*	CHOLESTEROL: 0 *mg*
SODIUM: 4 *mg*	CARBOHYDRATES: 15 *g*

Recipe shown above left

Passion Sherbet

4 SERVINGS

1 1/4 cups	(300 mL) sugar
	juice of 2 oranges and of 2 limes
	flesh of 2 ripe passion fruits
1	egg white
1/2 tsp	(2 mL) vanilla extract

- In a saucepan, bring to a boil sugar and fruit juices. Simmer 5 minutes. Let cool.
- Purée passion fruits. Fold into fruit syrup.
- Pour into an airtight container. Freeze 2 hours. Remove from freezer. Beat egg white and vanilla until stiff peaks form. Fold into sherbet. Serve.

NUTRITION	
CALORIES PER SERVING: 270	
FAT: 10 *g*	CAL. FROM FAT: 0%
PROTEIN: 1 *g*	CHOLESTEROL: 0 *mg*
SODIUM: 16 *mg*	CARBOHYDRATES: 68 *g*

Sherbet Terrine

9 SERVINGS

1/2	recipe strawberry sherbet *(p. 406)*
1/2	recipe banana-kiwi frozen yogurt *(p. 408)*
1/2	recipe passion sherbet

- Line a loaf pan with wax paper.
- Spread successive layers of 3 sherbet flavors. Cover with aluminum foil. Freeze 3 hours.
- Dip bottom of pan 15 seconds or so in hot water. Turn over a level surface. Unmold.

- Cut from top to bottom into 1-inch (2.5 cm) thick slices. Wrap carefully. Freeze.

Recipe shown above right

VARIATIONS
- Use different sherbet flavors.
- Decorate with a mint leaf. Serve with your choice of coulis *(pp. 414-415)*.

NUTRITION	
CALORIES PER SERVING: 146	
FAT: 5 *g*	CAL. FROM FAT: 31%
PROTEIN: 1 *g*	CHOLESTEROL: 18 *mg*
SODIUM: 12 *mg*	CARBOHYDRATES: 25 *g*

FROSTY TREATS

Raspberry Frozen Yogurt

AROUND 2 ½ CUPS (625 mL)	
1 ½ cups	(375 mL) plain yogurt
2 cups	(500 mL) raspberries
½ cup	(125 mL) sugar
1 tbsp	(15 mL) lemon juice
½ tbsp	(7 mL) lemon peel, grated
½ oz	(15 mL) Grand Marnier or other liqueur (optional)

- In a food processor, mix all ingredients until creamy. Pour into a large airtight container. Freeze around 2 hours or until mixture looks granular but not frozen solid.

- Pour again into food processor. Grind until creamy. Freeze once more so mixture hardens.

- Before serving, let soften 10 minutes or so. Grind again for a creamier texture, if desired.

- Serve in tulips *(p. 360)* or on a fruit coulis *(pp. 414-415)*, with fresh fruit and mint, if desired.

PEACH-APRICOT FROZEN YOGURT
- Replace raspberries with pitted peaches and apricots.

BANANA-KIWI FROZEN YOGURT
- Replace raspberries with sliced bananas and kiwis. Flavor with rum.

BLACKBERRY-BLUEBERRY FROZEN YOGURT
- Replace raspberries with blueberries and blackberries.

PINEAPPLE-PEAR FROZEN YOGURT
- Replace raspberries with canned sliced pineapple and pears. Drain fruit thoroughly before adding to recipe.

CHERRY FROZEN YOGURT
- Replace raspberries with fresh pitted cherries.

NUTRITION	
CALORIES PER SERVING: 192	
FAT: 3 *g*	CAL. FROM FAT: 15 %
PROTEIN: 4 *g*	CHOLESTEROL: 11 *mg*
SODIUM: 40 *mg*	CARBOHYDRATES: 38 *g*

Nutty Frozen Yogurt

AROUND 2 ½ CUPS (625 mL)	
1 ½ cups	(375 mL) plain yogurt
½ cup	(125 mL) commercial hazelnut chocolate spread
½ cup	(125 mL) nuts
¼ cup	(60 mL) sugar
2 tbsp	(30 mL) orange juice
1 tbsp	(15 mL) orange peel, grated

- In a food processor, mix all ingredients. Proceed according to recipe for raspberry frozen yogurt.

VARIATIONS
- Use almonds, hazelnuts, grated coconut, walnuts, pecans or pistachios.

NUTRITION	
CALORIES PER SERVING: 267	
FAT: 13 *g*	CAL. FROM FAT: 37 %
PROTEIN: 7 *g*	CHOLESTEROL: 11 *mg*
SODIUM: 61 *mg*	CARBOHYDRATES: 44 *g*

Nutty Chocolate-Cheese Frozen Mousse

AROUND 4 CUPS (1 L)	
4	egg yolks
¼ cup	(60 mL) sugar
1 cup	(250 mL) Ricotta cheese, at room temperature
⅔ cup	(160 mL) semisweet chocolate, melted, at room temperature
2 cups	(500 mL) whipped cream
¾ cup	(180 mL) nuts, chopped

- Line an 8 x 4-inch (20.5 x 10 cm) loaf pan with wax paper.

- In a mixer bowl, beat egg yolks and sugar until smooth. Set aside.

- In a bowl, beat Ricotta cheese and melted chocolate. Fold in egg yolk mixture, whipping constantly.

- Gently fold in whipped cream and ½ cup (125 mL) nuts. Pour into pan. Freeze at least 4 hours.

- When ready to serve only, unmold mousse by briefly dipping bottom of pan in hot water. Turn over a serving dish. Remove wax paper. Sprinkle with remaining chopped nuts.

- Slice. Serve with a coulis *(pp. 414-415)* or a sauce *(pp. 416-417)*.

NUTRITION	
CALORIES PER SERVING: 267	
FAT: 13 *g*	CAL. FROM FAT: 37 %
PROTEIN: 7 *g*	CHOLESTEROL: 11 *mg*
SODIUM: 61 *mg*	CARBOHYDRATES: 44 *g*

*Clockwise from upper left, frozen yogurt flavors :
Raspberry, Banana-Kiwi, Blackberry-Blueberry, Peach-Apricot, Pineapple-Pear, Cherry*

JAMS AND MARMALADES

Garden Strawberry Jam

AROUND 5 CUPS (1.25 L)

1 tbsp	(15 mL) hot water
1/2 tsp	(2 mL) lemon juice
1/2 tsp	(2 mL) white vinegar
4 cups	(1 L) strawberries, hulled
3 cups	(750 mL) sugar

- In a saucepan, bring to a boil water, lemon juice and vinegar. Add strawberries. Cover. Remove from heat. Macerate 2 minutes.
- Add sugar. Bring back to a boil. Over moderate heat, cook 20 minutes or so.

CALORIES PER 2 TBSP: 62	
FAT: 1 g	CAL. FROM FAT: 0 %
PROTEIN: 0 g	CHOLESTEROL: 0 mg
SODIUM: 0 mg	CARBOHYDRATES: 16 g

Blueberry-Rhubarb Jam

AROUND 8 CUPS (2 L)

8 cups	(2 L) fresh blueberries
4 cups	(1 L) rhubarb, cut into 1/2-inch (1.25 cm) pieces
1 cup	(250 mL) water
4 cups	(1 L) sugar

- In a large saucepan, mix fruit and water. Over moderate heat, cook uncovered 10-12 minutes.
- Add sugar, mixing lightly. Bring to a boil. Let mixture boil uncovered 10 minutes or so.

CALORIES PER 2 TBSP: 62	
FAT: 1 g	CAL. FROM FAT: 0 %
PROTEIN: 0 g	CHOLESTEROL: 0 mg
SODIUM: 2 mg	CARBOHYDRATES: 15 g

Nutty Apricot Jam

AROUND 6 CUPS (1.5 L)

8 cups	(2 L) apricots, pitted, in pieces
4 cups	(1 L) sugar
1 1/2 cups	(375 mL) nuts, chopped
2 tbsp	(30 mL) lemon juice

- In a large saucepan, mix all ingredients. Bring to a boil. Let mixture boil uncovered around 10 minutes or until thickened to a jam.

CALORIES PER 2 TBSP: 103	
FAT: 3 g	CAL. FROM FAT: 21 %
PROTEIN: 1 g	CHOLESTEROL: 0 mg
SODIUM: 1 mg	CARBOHYDRATES: 20 g

Rhubarb Jam

AROUND 8 CUPS (2 L)

6 cups	(1.5 L) rhubarb
4 cups	(1 L) sugar
2	oranges, peeled, pith removed, coarsely chopped
1/2 cup	(125 mL) lemon juice
1 tbsp	(15 mL) lemon peel, grated

- In a bowl, combine rhubarb and sugar. Let stand overnight.
- In a large saucepan, without covering, cook all ingredients around 10 minutes or until mixture thickens.

CALORIES PER 2 TBSP: 52	
FAT: 0 g	CAL. FROM FAT: 0 %
PROTEIN: 0 g	CHOLESTEROL: 0 mg
SODIUM: 1 mg	CARBOHYDRATES: 14 g

Strawberry-Rhubarb Jam

AROUND 10 CUPS (2.5 L)

6 cups	(1.5 L) fresh strawberries, hulled, crushed
4 cups	(1 L) rhubarb, cut into 1/2-inch (1.25 cm) pieces
6 cups	(1.5 L) sugar

- In a large saucepan, bring fruit to a boil. Over moderate heat, cook uncovered 15 minutes.
- Add sugar, mixing lightly. Boil uncovered around 10 minutes or until thickened to a jam.
- Pour into warm sterilized jars. Let cool slightly. Seal.

VARIATION
- Replace strawberries and rhubarb with 8 cups (2 L) crushed raspberries and 1 1/2 cups (375 mL) coconut.

CALORIES PER 2 TBSP: 62	
FAT: 1 g	CAL. FROM FAT: 0 %
PROTEIN: 0 g	CHOLESTEROL: 0 mg
SODIUM: 0 mg	CARBOHYDRATES: 16 g

Pumpkin Marmalade

AROUND 4 CUPS (1 L)

3	unpeeled oranges, sectioned
1	unpeeled lemon, sectioned
2 cups	(500 mL) sugar
3 cups	(750 mL) pumpkin flesh, seeded

- In a food processor, chop citrus fruit. Set aside.
- In a large saucepan, bring to a boil sugar and pumpkin. Add citrus fruit.
- Over moderate heat, stirring often, cook uncovered 45-50 minutes until mixture thickens.

CALORIES PER SERVING: 141	
FAT: 1 g	CAL. FROM FAT: 1 %
PROTEIN: 0 g	CHOLESTEROL: 0 mg
SODIUM: 16 mg	CARBOHYDRATES: 2 g

Pear 'n' Almond Marmalade

AROUND 6 CUPS (1.5 L)

10 cups	(2.5 L) pears, sliced
6 cups	(1.5 L) sugar
	juice and grated peel of 2 lemons
1 1/2 cups	(375 mL) slivered white almonds
1 tsp	(5 mL) ginger, chopped

- In a large saucepan, alternating ingredients, pour pears, sugar, juice, lemon peel and almonds.
- Add ginger. Bring to a boil. Stirring often, let mixture boil uncovered 45-50 minutes until thickened.

CALORIES PER SERVING: 144	
FAT: 2 g	CAL. FROM FAT: 11 %
PROTEIN: 1 g	CHOLESTEROL: 0 mg
SODIUM: 3 mg	CARBOHYDRATES: 33 g

CREAMS AND CUSTARDS

Custard

AROUND 1 ¾ CUPS (425 mL)

2 cups	(500 mL) milk
⅔ cup	(160 mL) sugar
3	egg yolks
¼ cup	(60 mL) cornstarch
2 tbsp	(30 mL) unsalted butter
½ tsp	(2 mL) vanilla extract

- In a saucepan, heat milk and sugar. Set aside.
- In a bowl, whip egg yolks and cornstarch. Dilute in ⅓ cup (80 mL) hot milk mixture. Set aside.
- Bring to a boil remaining sweetened milk. Beat into egg yolk mixture.
- Pour into saucepan. Cook 1 minute or so, whisking vigorously.
- Off heat, whisk in butter and vanilla until creamy smooth. Let cool until lukewarm. Refrigerate.

NUTRITION	
CALORIES PER 2 TBSP: 96	
FAT: 4 g	CAL. FROM FAT: 38%
PROTEIN: 2 g	CHOLESTEROL: 55 mg
SODIUM: 19 mg	CARBOHYDRATES: 13 g

COFFEE CUSTARD
- Into hot milk, fold 2 tbsp (30 mL) instant coffee.

CHOCOLATE CUSTARD
- Into hot milk, fold 3 tbsp (45 mL) cocoa.

ALMOND CUSTARD
- Into hot milk, fold 1 tsp (5 mL) almond extract. To chilled custard, add 3 tbsp (45 mL) roasted sliced almonds.

RUM RAISIN CUSTARD
- Into hot milk, fold 1 tsp (5 mL) rum extract and 3 tbsp (45 mL) raisins.

ORANGE CUSTARD
- Into hot milk, fold grated peel of 2 oranges.

PEAR CUSTARD
- Into hot milk, fold 1 tsp (5 mL) pear brandy. To chilled custard, add 3 tbsp (45 mL) canned pears, chopped.

Clockwise from bottom left, custard flavors : Plain, Chocolate, Coffee, Orange

Almond Cream

AROUND 2 ½ CUPS (625 mL)

2 cups	(500 mL) heavy cream
½ tsp	(2 mL) almond extract
3 tbsp	(45 mL) roasted slivered almonds

- Refrigerate cream and mixer bowl.
- In mixer bowl, at moderate speed, whip cream a few minutes. Add extract. At high speed, whip until stiff peaks form. Fold in almonds.

CHOCOLATE WHIPPED CREAM
- Replace extract and almonds with 2 tbsp (30 mL) commercial chocolate syrup.

NUTRITION	
CALORIES PER 2 TBSP: 89	
FAT: 9 g	CAL. FROM FAT: 93%
PROTEIN: 1 g	CHOLESTEROL: 33 mg
SODIUM: 9 mg	CARBOHYDRATES: 1 g

Recipe shown above, upper row

Chantilly Cream

AROUND 2 ½ CUPS (625 mL)

2 cups	(500 mL) heavy cream
½ cup	(125 mL) icing sugar
½ tsp	(2 mL) vanilla extract

- Refrigerate cream and mixer bowl.
- In mixer bowl, at moderate speed, whip all ingredients a few minutes. Increase speed to high, whipping until stiff peaks form. Refrigerate unused Chantilly cream.

Recipe shown above, bottom left

CHOCOLATE CHANTILLY CREAM
- Gently fold ⅓ cup (80 mL) cocoa into whipped mixture.

NUTRITION	
CALORIES PER 2 TBSP: 94	
FAT: 9 g	CAL. FROM FAT: 83%
PROTEIN: 0 g	CHOLESTEROL: 33 mg
SODIUM: 9 mg	CARBOHYDRATES: 4 g

Custard Sauce

AROUND 2 ½ CUPS (625 mL)

2 cups	(500 mL) milk
4	egg yolks
½ cup	(125 mL) sugar
1 tsp	(5 mL) vanilla extract

- In a double-boiler, bring milk to a boil. Set aside.
- In a mixer bowl, at high speed, whip remaining ingredients until thick and creamy. Fold into milk. While stirring, cook until sauce thickens.
- Pass hot sauce through a sieve. Serve warm or cold.

NUTRITION	
CALORIES PER 2 TBSP: 47	
FAT: 2 g	CAL. FROM FAT: 35%
PROTEIN: 1 g	CHOLESTEROL: 46 mg
SODIUM: 13 mg	CARBOHYDRATES: 6 g

Light Cream

AROUND 2 CUPS (500 mL)

1 cup	(250 mL) whipped cream
1 cup	(250 mL) custard (p. 412)

- In a bowl, mix whipped cream and custard until smooth.

Recipe shown above, bottom right

FLAVORED LIGHT CREAM
- Into mixture, fold 1 oz (30 mL) liqueur or alcohol of your choice.

NUTRITION	
CALORIES PER 2 TBSP: 43	
FAT: 4 g	CAL. FROM FAT: 73%
PROTEIN: 1 g	CHOLESTEROL: 28 mg
SODIUM: 16 mg	CARBOHYDRATES: 2 g

PURÉES AND SAUCES

Apricot Glaze

AROUND 1 CUP (250 mL)	
³/₄ cup	(180 mL) apricot jam
3 tbsp	(45 mL) water

- With a spatula, strain apricot jam over a small saucepan.
- Over low heat, melt jam. Let cool 2 minutes. Stir in water.
- With a pastry brush, glaze your choice of cake, baba or pastry. (If glaze is too thick to spread easily, add a little water ; if too runny, add a little strained jam.)

Recipe shown opposite

VARIATIONS
- Use strawberry, raspberry, cherry or other fruit jam. Add a few drops red or yellow food coloring, if desired.
- Replace water with rum or any other alcohol or liqueur.

CALORIES PER 2 TBSP: 73	
FAT: 1 g	CAL. FROM FAT: 1 %
PROTEIN: 0 g	CHOLESTEROL: 0 mg
SODIUM: 12 mg	CARBOHYDRATES: 19 g

Rum Syrup

AROUND 1 ¹/₂ CUPS (375 mL)	
³/₄ cup	(180 mL) water
1 cup	(250 mL) sugar
1	orange section
3 oz	(90 mL) dark rum

- In a saucepan, bring to a boil water, sugar and orange. Without stirring, simmer 3 minutes.
- Remove from heat. Let cool 5 minutes. Add rum. Remove orange section.

VARIATIONS
- Replace orange section with a half-lemon, and rum with Grand Marnier, kirsch or any other liqueur.

CALORIES PER 2 TBSP: 81	
FAT: 0 g	CAL. FROM FAT: 0 %
PROTEIN: 0 g	CHOLESTEROL: 0 mg
SODIUM: 1 mg	CARBOHYDRATES: 17 g

Green Grape Coulis

AROUND 3 CUPS (750 mL)	
²/₃ cup	(160 mL) water
³/₄ cup	(180 mL) sugar
2 cups	(500 mL) green grapes
2 tbsp	(30 mL) lemon juice
2 tbsp	(30 mL) cornstarch

- In a saucepan, bring to a boil water and sugar. Add grapes and lemon juice. Simmer 3 minutes.
- Dilute cornstarch in a little water. Pour into saucepan. Cook 1 minute, stirring constantly.
- For a smoother coulis, run mixture through blender, then a sieve. Serve cold.

CALORIES PER 2 TBSP: 35	
FAT: 1 g	CAL. FROM FAT: 1 %
PROTEIN: 0 g	CHOLESTEROL: 0 mg
SODIUM: 1 mg	CARBOHYDRATES: 9 g

Plum Coulis

AROUND 3 CUPS (750 mL)	
²/₃ cup	(160 mL) water
³/₄ cup	(180 mL) sugar
2 cups	(500 mL) canned prunes
2 tbsp	(30 mL) lemon juice
2 tbsp	(30 mL) cornstarch

- In a saucepan, bring to a boil water and sugar. Add prunes and lemon juice. Simmer 3 minutes.
- Dilute cornstarch in a little water. Pour into saucepan. Cook 1 minute, stirring constantly.
- For a smoother coulis, run mixture through blender, then a sieve. Serve cold.

CALORIES PER 2 TBSP: 56	
FAT: 1 g	CAL. FROM FAT: 1 %
PROTEIN: 0 g	CHOLESTEROL: 0 mg
SODIUM: 1 mg	CARBOHYDRATES: 15 g

Strawberry-Cranberry Coulis

AROUND 3 CUPS (750 mL)

²/₃ cup	(160 mL)	water
³/₄ cup	(180 mL)	sugar
1 cup	(250 mL)	strawberries
1 cup	(250 mL)	cranberries
2 tbsp	(30 mL)	cranberry juice
2 tbsp	(30 mL)	cornstarch

- In a saucepan, bring to a boil water and sugar. Add fruit and cranberry juice. Simmer 3 minutes.
- Dilute cornstarch in a little water. Pour into saucepan. Cook 1 minute, stirring constantly.
- For a smoother coulis, run mixture through blender, then a sieve. Serve cold.

CALORIES PER 2 TBSP: 31	
FAT: 1 g	CAL. FROM FAT: 1%
PROTEIN: 0 g	CHOLESTEROL: 0 mg
SODIUM: 0 mg	CARBOHYDRATES: 8 g

Peach-Mango Coulis

AROUND 3 CUPS (750 mL)

²/₃ cup	(160 mL)	water
³/₄ cup	(180 mL)	sugar
1 cup	(250 mL)	each, peaches and mangoes, chopped
2 tbsp	(30 mL)	peach juice
2 tbsp	(30 mL)	cornstarch

- In a saucepan, bring to a boil water and sugar. Add fruit and juice. Simmer 3 minutes.
- Dilute cornstarch in a little water. Pour into saucepan. Cook 1 minute, stirring constantly.
- For a smoother coulis, run mixture through blender, then a sieve. Serve cold.

CALORIES PER 2 TBSP: 31	
FAT: 1 g	CAL. FROM FAT: 1%
PROTEIN: 0 g	CHOLESTEROL: 0 mg
SODIUM: 0 mg	CARBOHYDRATES: 8 g

Kiwi Coulis

AROUND 3 CUPS (750 mL)

²/₃ cup	(160 mL)	water
³/₄ cup	(180 mL)	sugar
2 cups	(500 mL)	ripe kiwis, peeled
2 tbsp	(30 mL)	orange juice
2 tbsp	(30 mL)	cornstarch

- In a saucepan, bring to a boil water and sugar. Add kiwis and orange juice. Simmer 3 minutes.
- Dilute cornstarch in a little water. Pour into saucepan. Cook 1 minute, stirring constantly.
- For a smoother coulis, run mixture through blender, then a sieve. Serve cold.

CALORIES PER 2 TBSP: 38	
FAT: 1 g	CAL. FROM FAT: 2%
PROTEIN: 0 g	CHOLESTEROL: 0 mg
SODIUM: 1 mg	CARBOHYDRATES: 9 g

Blueberry-Cherry Coulis

AROUND 3 CUPS (750 mL)

²/₃ cup	(160 mL)	water
³/₄ cup	(180 mL)	sugar
1 cup	(250 mL)	blueberries
1 cup	(250 mL)	cherries
2 tbsp	(30 mL)	cherry juice
2 tbsp	(30 mL)	cornstarch

- In a saucepan, bring to a boil water and sugar. Add fruit and cherry juice. Simmer 3 minutes.
- Dilute cornstarch in a little water. Pour into saucepan. Cook 1 minute, stirring constantly.
- For a smoother coulis, run mixture through blender, then a sieve. Serve cold.

CALORIES PER 2 TBSP: 35	
FAT: 1 g	CAL. FROM FAT: 2%
PROTEIN: 0 g	CHOLESTEROL: 0 mg
SODIUM: 1 mg	CARBOHYDRATES: 9 g

Chocolate Sauce

AROUND 2 1/2 CUP (625 mL)	
12 oz	(350 g) semisweet chocolate
1 tbsp	(15 mL) cocoa
1 cup	(250 mL) heavy cream

- In a double-boiler, while stirring, heat all ingredients to a smooth sauce.
- Serve hot or lukewarm.

PIRATE CHOCOLATE SAUCE
- Off heat, add 3 tbsp (45 mL) dark rum to cooked sauce.

CALORIES PER 2 TBSP: 122	
FAT: 9 g	CAL. FROM FAT: 64%
PROTEIN: 1 g	CHOLESTEROL: 16 mg
SODIUM: 6 mg	CARBOHYDRATES: 1 g

Caramel Pecan Sauce

AROUND 2 CUPS (500 mL)	
1/3 cup	(80 mL) butter
2/3 cup	(160 mL) pecans, chopped
1 1/4 cups	(300 mL) brown sugar
1 1/4 cups	(300 mL) heavy cream

- In a saucepan, over moderate heat, melt butter. While stirring, roast pecans around 7 minutes or until they turn a light golden brown.
- Stir in brown sugar and cream. Over low heat, simmer 3 minutes or so, stirring constantly. Remove from heat. Let cool slightly. Serve.

CALORIES PER 2 TBSP: 178	
FAT: 21 g	CAL. FROM FAT: 60%
PROTEIN: 1 g	CHOLESTEROL: 36 mg
SODIUM: 52 mg	CARBOHYDRATES: 18 g

Grand Marnier Sauce

AROUND 1 1/2 CUPS (375 mL)	
1 cup	(250 mL) milk
1	egg
3 tbsp	(45 mL) sugar
	pinch of salt
1 oz	(30 mL) Grand Marnier
1/4 cup	(60 mL) pistachios (optional)

- In a double-boiler, while whisking vigorously, heat milk, egg, sugar and salt until thickened.
- Off heat, add Grand Marnier. Fold in pistachios, if desired.

CALORIES PER 2 TBSP: 46	
FAT: 2 g	CAL. FROM FAT: 36%
PROTEIN: 1 g	CHOLESTEROL: 18 mg
SODIUM: 26 mg	CARBOHYDRATES: 5 g

Orange Sauce

AROUND 2 CUPS (500 mL)	
2 tbsp	(30 mL) cornstarch
2 cups	(500 mL) orange juice
3/4 cup	(180 mL) sugar
1 1/2 cups	(375 mL) oranges, peeled, pith removed, sectioned

- In a bowl, dissolve cornstarch in 1/3 cup (80 mL) orange juice.
- In a saucepan, bring to a boil remaining orange juice and sugar. Off heat, whisk in diluted cornstarch.
- Bring back to a boil. Remove from heat. Let cool slightly. Fold in orange sections. Serve.

CALORIES PER 2 TBSP: 60	
FAT: 1 g	CAL. FROM FAT: 1%
PROTEIN: 10 g	CHOLESTEROL: 11 mg
SODIUM: 486 mg	CARBOHYDRATES: 32 g

Lemon Sauce

AROUND 1 ½ CUPS (375 mL)		
½ cup	(125 mL) water
⅓ cup	(80 mL) sugar
⅓ cup	(80 mL) lemon peel
1 tbsp	(15 mL) cornstarch
1 cup	(250 mL) lemon juice

- In a saucepan, boil water, sugar and lemon peel 5 minutes.
- Meanwhile, dissolve cornstarch in lemon juice. While stirring, fold into boiling liquid mixture in a thin stream. Cook until sauce thickens, stirring constantly.
- Remove from heat. Let cool. Serve.

CALORIES PER 2 TBSP: 31	
FAT: 1 g	CAL. FROM FAT: 1 %
PROTEIN: 0 g	CHOLESTEROL: 0 mg
SODIUM: 1 mg	CARBOHYDRATES: 8 g

Maple Nut Sauce

AROUND 2 CUPS (500 mL)		
1 cup	(250 mL) water
1 cup	(250 mL) maple syrup
1 tbsp	(15 mL) cornstarch
2	drops of vanilla extract
½ cup	(125 mL) nuts, chopped

- In a saucepan, bring water to a boil. Add maple syrup.
- In a small bowl, dissolve cornstarch in 1 tbsp (15 mL) cold water. Fold into liquid mixture. Cook 4 minutes or until sauce thickens.
- Mix in vanilla extract and nuts. Serve hot or cold.

CALORIES PER 2 TBSP: 81	
FAT: 3 g	CAL. FROM FAT: 27 %
PROTEIN: 1 g	CHOLESTEROL: 0 mg
SODIUM: 2 mg	CARBOHYDRATES: 15 g

Spicy Sauce

AROUND 2 CUPS (500 mL)		
2 cups	(500 mL) milk
½ cup	(125 mL) sugar
1	cinnamon stick
1	egg yolk
1 tbsp	(15 mL) cornstarch
1 tsp	(5 mL) ginger
	pinch of nutmeg

- In a saucepan, boil milk and sugar. Add cinnamon.
- In a bowl, whip together egg yolk and cornstarch. Fold in 3 tbsp (45 mL) hot milk. Stir into saucepan. Over low heat, cook 2 minutes or until sauce thickens.
- Add spices, mixing well. Serve cold.

CALORIES PER 2 TBSP: 50	
FAT: 1 g	CAL. FROM FAT: 24 %
PROTEIN: 1 g	CHOLESTEROL: 17 mg
SODIUM: 16 mg	CARBOHYDRATES: 9 g

Mocha Coffee Sauce

AROUND 2 CUPS (500 mL)		
2 cups	(500 mL) strong coffee
½ cup	(125 mL) sugar
1 tbsp	(15 mL) cocoa
2 tbsp	(30 mL) cornstarch
3 tbsp	(45 mL) cold water

- In a saucepan, boil coffee, sugar and cocoa.
- Meanwhile, dissolve cornstarch in water. Fold into liquid mixture. Cook 4 minutes or until sauce thickens. Serve hot or cold.

CALORIES PER 2 TBSP: 29	
FAT: 1 g	CAL. FROM FAT: 2 %
PROTEIN: 0 g	CHOLESTEROL: 0 mg
SODIUM: 1 mg	CARBOHYDRATES: 7 g

How can one resist the incomparable aroma of hot, homemade bread? Give in without worrying about unwanted calories: bread contributes to a well-balanced diet.

Breads and muffins that contain whole-wheat flour, bran, nuts, vegetables and dried fruit are excellent and delicious sources of fiber. For breakfast, snacks, or for dessert, what an enjoyable way to complete your fiber intake for the day!

We find, in this section, a tasty Bran Loaf (p. 422) recommended because of the dietary fiber it contains. Not only is it good for you, it tastes fantastic as well.

BAKERY

BREADS

Classic White Bread, Basic Recipe

1 LOAF

1	envelope yeast
2 tbsp	(30 mL) sugar
1/4 cup	(60 mL) lukewarm water
1 cup	(250 mL) milk
1 tsp	(5 mL) salt
3 tbsp	(45 mL) butter
3 cups	(750 mL) all-purpose flour
2 tbsp	(30 mL) oil
1	egg, beaten

- Preheat oven to 375 °F (190 °C).

- In a large bowl, dissolve yeast and 4 pinches sugar in water. Let stand 10 minutes.

- In a saucepan, boil milk 1 minute. Remove from heat. Add remaining sugar, salt and butter. Let cool.

- Fold in diluted yeast. Add flour. Mix to a smooth, sticky dough.

- Flour a clean, even surface. Adding flour as needed, knead dough around 10 minutes or until it is smooth and no longer sticks to hands.

- In a stainless-steel bowl, pour oil. Add dough. Roll dough in oil to prevent drying. Cover with wax paper. Let rise 1 hour in a warm, humid place.

- Punch down dough. Line an unbuttered 9 x 5-inch (23 x 13 cm) loaf pan. Let dough rise to three-quarters of pan. Brush with beaten egg. Bake in oven 30-40 minutes. Remove from oven. Let stand 10 minutes before unmolding.

NUTRITION	
CALORIES PER LOAF: 2252	
FAT: 78 g	CAL. FROM FAT: 31 %
PROTEIN: 57 g	CHOLESTEROL: 306 mg
SODIUM: 2668 mg	CARBOHYDRATES: 328 g

VARIATIONS

BLUEBERRY BREAD
- Into flour, fold 1 cup (250 mL) blueberries.

NUT BREAD
- Into flour, fold 3/4 cup (180 mL) chopped nuts.

EARLY-BIRD BREAD
- Into flour, fold 2/3 cup (160 mL) dried apricots and 3 tbsp (45 mL) grated lemon peel.

GRANDFATHER BREAD
- Into flour, fold 1 cup (250 mL) dried fig, chopped into large pieces.

RASPBERRY BREAD
- Into flour, fold 1 cup (250 mL) fresh halved raspberries. Increase sugar to 1/4 cup (60 mL).

SESAME SEED BREAD
- Into flour, fold 1/2 cup (125 mL) toasted sesame seeds.

POPPY SEED BREAD
- Into flour, fold 1/2 cup (125 mL) poppy seeds.

CHOCOLATE CHIP BREAD
- Into flour, fold 1 cup (250 mL) semisweet chocolate chunks, or 1 cup (250 mL) chocolate chips.

COCONUT BREAD
- Into flour, fold 3/4 cup (180 mL) grated coconut.

COFFEE BREAD
- Into hot milk, fold 1/4 cup (60 mL) instant coffee.

APPLE CINNAMON BREAD

- In a skillet, over high heat, melt 1 tsp (5 mL) butter. Sauté 1 cup (250 mL) cubed apples and 2 tsp (10 mL) cinnamon. Fold into basic recipe at the same time as flour.

ORANGE CARROT BREAD

- Into flour, fold 1 cup (250 mL) grated carrots and ¼ cup (60 mL) grated orange peel.

TOMATO BREAD

- Into hot milk, fold 3 tbsp (45 mL) tomato paste. Into flour, fold ¾ cup (180 mL) seeded diced tomatoes.

RAISIN BREAD

- Into flour, fold ¾ cup (180 mL) currants.

SPICY BREAD

- Into flour, fold 1 tbsp (15 mL) mixed ground spices (cinnamon, clove, nutmeg, pepper).

CHOCOLATE BREAD

- Fold ½ cup (125 mL) cocoa at the same time as flour. Increase butter to ¼ cup (60 mL) and sugar to 3 tbsp (45 mL).

GREEN ONION BREAD

- In a skillet, melt 2 tbsp (30 mL) butter and 1 tbsp (15 mL) brown sugar. Sauté 1 ½ cups (375 mL) minced green onions. Fold into basic recipe at the same time as flour.

Perfect Bread Rolls

9 ROLLS	
2 ½ cups	(625 mL) flour
1 tsp	(5 mL) salt
2 tbsp	(30 mL) sugar
1	envelope yeast
	pinch of sugar
¾ cup	(180 mL) lukewarm water
2 tbsp	(30 mL) oil
1	egg, beaten
2 tbsp	(30 mL) whole wheat flour

- Preheat oven to 400 °F (205 °C).

- In a bowl, sift together flour, salt and 2 tsp (10 mL) sugar.

- In a large bowl, dissolve yeast and remaining sugar in lukewarm water. Wait 10 minutes. Add sifted ingredients all at once. Mix until smooth.

- Flour a clean, even surface. Knead dough 5 minutes or so.

- In a stainless-steel bowl, pour oil. Add dough. Roll dough in oil to prevent drying. Cover with wax paper. Let rise 1 hour in a warm, humid place.

- Punch down dough. Shape into 9 small balls. Place on an oiled baking sheet, 2 inches (5 cm) apart. Let rise in a warm, humid place until dough doubles in size. Brush with beaten egg. Sprinkle with whole wheat flour. Bake in oven 10 minutes or so.

VARIATIONS

- Replace whole wheat flour with grated cheese, coconut, almonds, seeds (pumpkin, sunflower, fennel, dill, coriander) or peppercorns.

- Sprinkle baking sheet with seeds or nuts.

NUTRITION	
CALORIES PER ROLL: 180	
FAT: 4 g	CAL. FROM FAT: 20 %
PROTEIN: 5 g	CHOLESTEROL: 20 mg
SODIUM: 260 mg	CARBOHYDRATES: 31 g

Whole Wheat Bread

1 LOAF

1	envelope yeast
7 tbsp	(105 mL) lukewarm water
5 tbsp	(75 mL) milk
1 tsp	(5 mL) molasses
1 cup	(250 mL) whole wheat flour
1/4 cup	(60 mL) whole wheat
3 tbsp	(45 mL) all-purpose flour
1 tbsp	(15 mL) brown sugar
1 tsp	(5 mL) salt
1 tbsp	(15 mL) butter

- Preheat oven to 375 °F (190 °C). Butter a 9 x 5-inch (23 x 13 cm) loaf pan. Set aside.
- In a large bowl, dissolve yeast in water. Add milk and molasses. Let stand 10 minutes.
- In a second bowl, mix remaining ingredients, except butter. Fold into diluted yeast.
- Knead lightly. Add butter. Knead 5 minutes. Let rise 1 hour.
- Punch down dough. Pour into loaf pan. Let dough rise to top of pan. Sprinkle with 1 tsp (5 mL) flour.
- Bake in oven 20-30 minutes. Remove from oven. Let cool 10 minutes before unmolding.

NUTRITION	
CALORIES PER LOAF: 825	
FAT: 17 g	CAL. FROM FAT: 18%
PROTEIN: 29 g	CHOLESTEROL: 41 mg
SODIUM: 177mg	CARBOHYDRATES: 149 g

Bran Loaf

1 LOAF

1	envelope yeast
1 cup	(250 mL) water
4 tsp	(20 mL) sugar
1 tsp	(5 mL) salt
1 cup	(250 mL) whole wheat flour
2 1/2 cups	(625 mL) all-purpose flour
3 tbsp	(45 mL) bran
1 tbsp	(15 mL) butter

- Preheat oven to 200 °F (95 °C). Place a saucepan filled with hot water on bottom rack. Butter a 9 x 5-inch (23 x 13 cm) loaf pan. Set aside.
- In a cup, dissolve yeast in 1/2 cup (125 mL) lukewarm water. Set aside.
- In a second cup, pour remaining lukewarm water. Dissolve sugar and salt. Set aside.
- In a bowl, lightly mix both kinds of flour, bran and butter. Fold in 2 liquid mixtures.
- Knead dough until lukewarm. Add a little flour. Let rise in oven 20 minutes.
- Remove dough from bowl. Punch down. Place in loaf pan. Return to oven until dough doubles in size.
- Remove bread and water-filled saucepan from oven. Increase temperature to 375 °F (190 °C). Return bread to oven. Bake on top rack 30 minutes.

NUTRITION	
CALORIES PER LOAF: 1769	
FAT: 18 g	CAL. FROM FAT: 9%
PROTEIN: 55 g	CHOLESTEROL: 31 mg
SODIUM: 2273 mg	CARBOHYDRATES: 354 g

Braided Egg Bread

---
1 LOAF

2	envelopes yeast
1 cup	(250 mL) lukewarm water
1/3 cup	(80 mL) milk
2 tsp	(10 mL) salt
3 tbsp	(45 mL) sugar
3 tbsp	(45 mL) butter, melted
2	eggs, beaten
4 cups	(1 L) all-purpose flour

■ Preheat oven to 200 °F (95 °C). Place a saucepan filled with hot water on bottom rack.

■ In a large bowl, dissolve yeast in lukewarm water. Let stand 10 minutes. Fold in remaining ingredients, except eggs and flour.

■ Mix in three-quarters of beaten eggs. Knead in flour. Place in oven. Let dough rise 30 minutes.

■ Punch down dough. Let rise in oven 15 more minutes.

■ Divide dough into 3 rolls. Braid together. Place on a buttered baking sheet. Return to oven until braid doubles in size.

■ Remove bread and water-filled saucepan from oven. Increase temperature to 375 °F (190 °C). Brush with remaining beaten egg. Return braid to oven. Bake on top rack 20-30 minutes.

NUTRITION	
CALORIES PER LOAF: 2514	
FAT: 51 g	CAL. FROM FAT: 19%
PROTEIN: 74 g	CHOLESTEROL: 469 mg
SODIUM: 9987 mg	CARBOHYDRATES: 433 g

Beer-Barley Bread

---
1 LOAF

1	envelope yeast
1 cup	(250 mL) lukewarm water
1 tsp	(5 mL) salt
1 tbsp	(15 mL) brown sugar
3 tbsp	(45 mL) barley
1 tbsp	(15 mL) butter
4 cups	(1 L) all-purpose flour
1 tbsp	(15 mL) butter
1 tbsp	(15 mL) beer
2 tbsp	(30 mL) oil

■ Preheat oven to 200 °F (95 °C). Place a saucepan filled with hot water on bottom rack. Butter a round or 9 x 5-inch (23 x 13 cm) loaf pan. Set aside.

■ In a large bowl, dissolve yeast in water. Let froth 5 minutes.

■ Fold in remaining ingredients, except oil. Knead with a little flour 5 minutes. Place in oven. Let rise 1 hour.

■ Punch down dough. Let rise 30 minutes.

■ Coat dough with oil. Place in loaf pan. Return to oven. Let rise until dough doubles in size.

■ Remove bread and water-filled saucepan from oven. Increase temperature to 375 °F (190 °C). Return bread to oven. Bake on top rack 45 minutes. Let stand 10 minutes before unmolding.

NUTRITION	
CALORIES PER LOAF: 2442	
FAT: 56 g	CAL. FROM FAT: 21%
PROTEIN: 61 g	CHOLESTEROL: 61 mg
SODIUM: 261 mg	CARBOHYDRATES: 417 g

Cherry Nut Loaf

1 LOAF	
2 cups	(500 mL) flour
1 cup	(250 mL) sugar
1 tbsp	(15 mL) baking powder
1/2 tsp	(2 mL) salt
2	eggs
1/4 cup	(60 mL) cherry juice
3/4 cup	(180 mL) milk
3 tbsp	(45 mL) sunflower or vegetable oil
1/4 tsp	(1 mL) almond extract
1 cup	(250 mL) canned pitted cherries, drained, halved
1/2 cup	(125 mL) walnuts, chopped

- Preheat oven to 350 °F (175 °C). Butter a 9 x 5-inch (23 x 13 cm) loaf pan.
- In a bowl, sift dry ingredients. Make a well in the center. Set aside.
- In a second bowl, beat eggs, cherry juice, milk, oil and almond extract. Pour into well. Beat vigorously to a smooth, creamy dough. Set aside.
- Lightly dredge cherries and nuts with flour. Fold into dough.
- Bake in oven 1 hour or so.

VARIATION
- Replace cherries with raspberries.

NUTRITION	
CALORIES PER LOAF: 2536	
FAT: 67 g	CAL. FROM FAT: 23%
PROTEIN: 49 g	CHOLESTEROL: 391 mg
SODIUM: 2367 mg	CARBOHYDRATES: 444 g

Genoa Buns

6 BUNS	
6 tbsp	(90 mL) butter
1 cup	(250 mL) sugar
1 cup	(250 mL) almond powder
4	large eggs
1 oz	(30 mL) rum
1/2 tsp	(2 mL) vanilla extract
1/2 cup	(125 mL) flour
2 tsp	(10 mL) baking powder
1 tsp	(5 mL) cornstarch

- Preheat oven to 350 °F (175 °C). Butter a muffin pan. Set aside.
- In a bowl, beat first 3 ingredients. While mixing, add eggs one at a time. Set aside.
- In a second bowl, combine rum and vanilla extract. Fold into first mixture. Set aside.
- In a third bowl, sift dry ingredients. Fold into liquid mixture.
- Pour dough into cups. Bake in oven 30-35 minutes. Serve hot or cold.

NUTRITION	
CALORIES PER BUN: 388	
FAT: 20 g	CAL. FROM FAT: 46%
PROTEIN: 7 g	CHOLESTEROL: 153 mg
SODIUM: 274 mg	CARBOHYDRATES: 45 g

Trapper Bread

2 LOAVES

1 tsp	(5 mL) sugar
½ cup	(125 mL) lukewarm water
1	envelope yeast
2 cups	(500 mL) boiling water
3 tbsp	(45 mL) butter
1 cup	(250 mL) rolled oats
2 tsp	(10 mL) salt
½ cup	(125 mL) molasses
1 cup	(250 mL) whole wheat flour
4 cups	(1 L) all-purpose flour
2 tbsp	(30 mL) oil

▪ Preheat oven to 200 °F (95 °C). Place a saucepan filled with hot water on bottom rack. Oil a cookie sheet. Set aside.

▪ In a small bowl, mix sugar, lukewarm water and yeast. Let froth 15 minutes.

▪ In a large bowl, pour boiling water, butter, rolled oats and salt. Stir a little. Fold in yeast. Gradually add molasses, whole wheat flour and 2 cups (500 mL) all-purpose flour until dough is smooth and sticky.

▪ Flour a clean, even surface with 1 cup (250 mL) all-purpose flour. Spread dough. Knead 10 minutes or so.

▪ Once dough has fully absorbed flour, add remaining flour in 2 steps. Dough is ready when it no longer sticks to fingers.

▪ Transfer to cookie sheet. Coat dough with oil. Place on oven top rack. Let rise 90 minutes or so. Remove from oven. Punch down dough. Knead 5 more minutes. Return to oven 20 minutes.

▪ Oil 2 loaf pans measuring 9 x 5 inches (23 x 13 cm) or 12 x 3 ½ inches (30.5 x 9 cm).

▪ Remove dough from oven. Divide in half. Place in pans. Set aside.

▪ Remove water-filled saucepan from oven. Increase oven temperature to 375 °F (190 °C). Return bread to oven. Bake 1 hour or so. Let stand 10 minutes before unmolding. Serve hot or cold.

Note : this very nourishing bread will keep easily if wrapped in aluminum foil or sealed in a plastic bag.

NUTRITION	
CALORIES PER LOAF: 1784	
FAT: 37 g	CAL. FROM FAT: 19%
PROTEIN: 43 g	CHOLESTEROL: 46 mg
SODIUM: 2357 mg	CARBOHYDRATES: 322 g

Healthy Date Loaf

	1 LOAF
1 cup	(250 mL) bran flakes
1 ¹/₂ cups	(375 mL) dates, chopped
1 ¹/₂ cups	(375 mL) boiling water
¹/₂ cup	(125 mL) all-purpose flour
¹/₂ cup	(125 mL) whole wheat flour
¹/₂ tsp	(2 mL) baking soda
1 tsp	(5 mL) baking powder
¹/₂ tsp	(2 mL) salt
1	egg
¹/₄ cup	(60 mL) molasses

- Preheat oven to 300 °F (150°C). Butter a loaf pan. Set aside.
- In a bowl, pour bran flakes, dates and boiling water. Let stand 30 minutes.
- In a second bowl, sift remaining dry ingredients. Set aside.
- In a third bowl, beat egg. Add molasses. Beat until mixture thickens. Gradually fold in dry ingredients, alternating with bran and date mixture. Pour into pan.
- Bake in oven 50-60 minutes. Remove from oven. Let cool slightly. Unmold. Serve.

NUTRITION	
CALORIES PER LOAF: 1663	
FAT: 9 g	CAL. FROM FAT: 4%
PROTEIN: 38 g	CHOLESTEROL: 181 mg
SODIUM: 3136 mg	CARBOHYDRATES: 190 g

Corn Bread

	1 LOAF
1 cup	(250 mL) all-purpose flour
¹/₄ cup	(60 mL) sugar
4 tsp	(20 mL) baking powder
4 tsp	(20 mL) salt
1 cup	(250 mL) cornmeal
1	egg
1 cup	(250 mL) milk
¹/₄ cup	(60 mL) butter, melted

- Preheat oven to 375 °F (190 °C). Butter a 9 x 5-inch (23 x 13 cm) loaf pan. Set aside.
- In a bowl, sift first 4 ingredients. Mix in cornmeal. Make a well in the center. Set aside.
- In a second bowl, beat egg. Fold in milk and butter. Pour liquid into the center of well. With a spatula, glide flour towards center of bowl. Mix to a smooth dough.
- Pour dough into pan. Cover with wax paper. Let stand 20 minutes.
- Bake in oven 25-30 minutes. Serve hot or cold.

APPLE CORN BREAD
- Proceed following corn bread recipe. Cover dough with 2 apples, peeled and sliced. Sprinkle with 2 tbsp (30 mL) brown sugar and 1 tsp (5 mL) cinnamon. Bake as instructed.

NUTRITION	
CALORIES PER LOAF: 177	
FAT: 61 g	CAL. FROM FAT: 31%
PROTEIN: 38 g	CHOLESTEROL: 337 mg
SODIUM: 9998 mg	CARBOHYDRATES: 269 g

Poppy Seed Minute Bread

1 LOAF		
2 tbsp	(30 mL)	shortening
1 cup	(250 mL)	sugar
1		egg
2/3 cup	(160 mL)	milk
1 tsp	(5 mL)	vanilla extract
1 1/2 cups	(375 mL)	whole wheat flour
2 tsp	(10 mL)	baking powder
1/2 tsp	(2 mL)	salt
1/4 cup	(60 mL)	poppy seeds

- Preheat oven to 350 °F (175 °C). Butter a 9 x 5 x 3-inch (23 x 13 x 7 cm) loaf pan. Set aside.
- In a bowl, cream shortening. Fold in sugar and egg.
- In a second bowl, whip milk and vanilla extract. Set aside.
- In a third bowl, mix remaining ingredients. Gradually fold in shortening, alternating with vanilla-flavored milk. Pour into pan.
- Bake in oven 50-60 minutes or until crust turns golden brown. Remove from oven. Let cool 10 minutes before unmolding.

NUTRITION	
CALORIES PER LOAF: 1980	
FAT: 54 *g*	CAL. FROM FAT: 24%
PROTEIN: 42 *g*	CHOLESTEROL: 203 *mg*
SODIUM: 1944 *mg*	CARBOHYDRATES: 350 *g*

Cheese Bread

1 LOAF		
2 cups	(500 mL)	all-purpose flour
4 tsp	(20 mL)	baking powder
1 1/2 tsp	(7 mL)	salt
1 cup	(250 mL)	mild Cheddar cheese, grated
2		eggs
1 cup	(250 mL)	milk
1/4 cup	(60 mL)	vegetable oil

- Preheat oven to 350 °F (175 °C). Butter a 9 x 5-inch (23 x 13 cm) loaf pan. Set aside.
- In a bowl, sift dry ingredients. Fold in Cheddar cheese. Make a well in the center. Set aside.
- In a second bowl, beat eggs. Fold in milk and oil, whisking constantly. Pour liquid mixture into the center of well.
- With a spatula, gently glide flour towards center of bowl. Mix with a wooden spoon. Do not knead. Pour dough into pan. Cover with wax paper. Let stand 20 minutes.
- Bake in oven 50-60 minutes. Unmold. Serve hot, cold or toasted.

NUTRITION	
CALORIES PER LOAF: 2133	
FAT: 111 *g*	CAL. FROM FAT: 47%
PROTEIN: 73 *g*	CHOLESTEROL: 518 *mg*
SODIUM: 5583 *mg*	CARBOHYDRATES: 209 *g*

DANISH PASTRIES

Quick Danish Pastries

6-8 PASTRIES

¹/₄ cup	(60 mL) butter
¹/₂ cup	(125 mL) brown sugar
2 tbsp	(30 mL) corn syrup
¹/₂ cup	(125 mL) pecans, halved
¹/₄ cup	(60 mL) maraschino cherries, quartered
10 oz	(280 g) commercial butter roll dough

- Place a glass in the center of a round 9-inch (23 cm) microwave-safe dish. Spread butter around glass. Melt in oven 30-45 seconds, on HIGH.

- Remove from oven. Sprinkle butter with brown sugar. Gently mix in corn syrup. Garnish with pecans and cherries. Arrange rolls on top, petal-like. Cook 6-8 minutes, on MEDIUM.

- Remove from oven. Pull out glass. Turn pastries over a serving dish. Let stand a few minutes so syrup will trickle down and around pastries. Serve lukewarm.

NUTRITION	
CALORIES PER PASTRY: 300	
FAT: 18 g	CAL. FROM FAT: 52 %
PROTEIN: 2 g	CHOLESTEROL: 36 mg
SODIUM: 126 mg	CARBOHYDRATES: 35 g

Individual Danish Pastries

2 DOZEN

¹/₃ cup	(80 mL) sugar
1 tsp	(5 mL) salt
³/₄ cup	(180 mL) water
1	envelope yeast
5	eggs
2 ¹/₂ cups	(625 mL) flour
1 ¹/₄ cups	(300 mL) butter
1	egg, beaten

- In a bowl, dissolve sugar and salt in half the water.

- In a second bowl, dissolve yeast in remaining water. Mix in eggs and flour. Add salted sweetened water.

- Knead dough until it leaves sides of bowl. Add butter in small pieces. Continue kneading until creamy. Transfer to a bowl. Let stand at least 12 hours.

- Preheat oven to 200 °F (95 °C). Place a saucepan filled with hot water on bottom rack. Butter small muffin-pan cups.

- Divide dough into 24 portions. Place in muffin cups. Let dough rise in oven 45 minutes or so.

- Remove pastries and water-filled saucepan from oven. Increase temperature to 375 °F (190 °C). Brush pastry with beaten egg. Return to oven. Bake 30 minutes.

NUTRITION	
CALORIES PER PASTRY: 159	
FAT: 11 g	CAL. FROM FAT: 60 %
PROTEIN: 3 g	CHOLESTEROL: 71 mg
SODIUM: 199 mg	CARBOHYDRATES: 13 g

Large Fruit Pastries

12 SERVINGS

1	basic recipe individual Danish pastries
3 tbsp	(45 mL) melted butter or custard (p. 412)
1 cup	(250 mL) candied fruit, chopped
1 cup	(250 mL) apricot jam
¹/₂ cup	(125 mL) grated coconut or chocolate vermicelli

- Preheat oven to 350 °F (175 °C). Butter 2 round 9-inch (23 cm) pans. Line each pan with 1 ¹/₄ cups (300 mL) Danish dough. Set aside.

- With a rolling pin, flatten remaining dough until 23 ¹/₂-inch (60 cm) long by 14-inch (36 cm) wide.

- With a brush, spread melted butter or custard over rolled-out dough. Sprinkle with candied fruit. Roll. Cut into 1-inch (2.5 cm) thick slices. Lay flat inside pans, leaving spreading space. Let rise.

- Bake in oven 40 minutes. Unmold. Brush with apricot jam. Sprinkle with coconut or chocolate vermicelli.

Recipe shown above

VARIATIONS

- Replace candied fruit with dried fruit (bananas, apricots, apples) or nuts.

NUTRITION	
CALORIES PER SERVING: 342	
FAT: 22 g	CAL. FROM FAT: 57 %
PROTEIN: 4 g	CHOLESTEROL: 148 mg
SODIUM: 430 mg	CARBOHYDRATES: 34 g

Jiffy Danish

12 PASTRIES

1	envelope active dry yeast
¹/₄ cup	(60 mL) sugar
¹/₄ cup	(60 mL) lukewarm water
³/₄ cup	(180 mL) partly-skimmed milk
3 ¹/₄ cups	(810 mL) all-purpose flour
¹/₄ tsp	(2 mL) salt
²/₃ cup	(160 mL) butter, melted
1	egg, lightly beaten
²/₃ cup	(160 mL) brown sugar
1 tbsp	(15 mL) ground cinnamon
¹/₂ cup	(125 mL) raisins
¹/₂ cup	(125 mL) pecans, chopped
	honey (optional)

- Preheat oven to 375 °F (190 °C).

- In a bowl, mix yeast and half the sugar in a little water. Set aside.

- In a saucepan, heat remaining water and milk. Fold into yeast mixture. Add remaining sugar, flour, salt, ¹/₄ cup (60 mL) butter and egg. Mix until dough leaves sides of bowl.

- Knead dough on a clean floured surface until smooth and elastic. Cover. Let rise 10 minutes.

- Roll out dough to a 14-inch (38 cm) square. Bruch with remaining butter. Set aside.

- In a bowl, mix brown sugar and cinnamon. Spread over dough. Sprinkle with raisins and pecans. Roll dough. Cut into 12 slices

- Place in large muffin-pan cups. Let rise until dough doubles in size. Bake in oven 18-20 minutes.

- Remove from oven. Unmold. Let cool.

- In a saucepan, heat honey. Brush over pastries, if desired.

NUTRITION	
CALORIES PER PASTRY: 335	
FAT: 13 *g*	CAL. FROM FAT: 33 %
PROTEIN: 5 *g*	CHOLESTEROL: 43 *mg*
SODIUM: 167 *mg*	CARBOHYDRATES: 52 *g*

VARIATIONS
- Replace raisins with apple sauce, strawberry or raspberry jam, or whole blueberries.

MUFFINS

Upside-down Whole Wheat Muffins

12 LARGE MUFFINS	
1/2 cup	(125 mL) brown sugar
1/4 cup	(60 mL) margarine
1/2 cup	(125 mL) pecans, chopped
2	eggs
3/4 cup	(180 mL) milk
1/2 cup	(125 mL) margarine, melted
1 1/2 cups	(375 mL) all-purpose flour
1 cup	(250 mL) whole wheat flour
1/3 cup	(80 mL) icing sugar
2 tbsp	(30 mL) baking soda
1 tsp	(5 mL) ground cinnamon
1/2 tsp	(2 mL) salt

- Preheat oven to 400 °F (205 °C). Butter or line large muffin-pan cups with paper cups.
- Place 2 tsp (10 mL) brown sugar and 1 tsp (5 mL) margarine in each cup. Melt in oven 2 minutes or so. Remove from oven. Divide pecans among cups. Set aside.
- In a bowl, beat eggs with a fork. Add milk and melted margarine. Set aside.
- In a second bowl, sift dry ingredients. Add egg mixture, stirring only as needed to moisten dry ingredients.
- Spoon batter into cups until full. Bake in oven 20 minutes or so. Remove. Turn over a rack at once. Serve warm.

NUTRITION	
CALORIES PER MUFFIN: 276	
FAT: 15 g	CAL. FROM FAT: 46%
PROTEIN: 5 g	CHOLESTEROL: 33 mg
SODIUM: 872 mg	CARBOHYDRATES: 33 g

Coffee Break Muffins

8 LARGE MUFFINS	
1	egg
1 1/4 cups	(300 mL) milk
1/2 cup	(125 mL) margarine, melted
2 1/2 cups	(625 mL) flour
1/2 cup	(125 mL) icing sugar
1 tbsp	(15 mL) baking powder
1 tsp	(5 mL) salt
1/4 cup	(60 mL) brown sugar
1/4 cup	(60 mL) nuts, chopped
1 tbsp	(15 mL) flour
1 tbsp	(15 mL) margarine
1 tsp	(5 mL) cinnamon

- Preheat oven to 400 °F (205 °C). Butter or line large muffin-pan cups with paper cups. Set aside.
- In a bowl, beat egg. Mix in milk and melted margarine. Set aside.
- In a second bowl, mix flour, icing sugar, baking powder and salt. Add egg mixture, stirring only as needed to moisten dry ingredients.
- In a third bowl, mix brown sugar, nuts, flour, margarine and cinnamon. Set aside.
- Pour first mixture into muffin cups until half-full. Spoon 1 tbsp (15 mL) brown sugar and nut mixture in the center of each muffin. Fill cups with remaining batter. Bake in oven 20 minutes or so.

NUTRITION	
CALORIES PER MUFFIN: 375	
FAT: 17 g	CAL. FROM FAT: 42%
PROTEIN: 7 g	CHOLESTEROL: 28 mg
SODIUM: 582 mg	CARBOHYDRATES: 48 g

Orange-Carrot Muffins

6 LARGE MUFFINS

1 cup	(250 mL) flour
1/2 cup	(125 mL) raisins
1/4 cup	(60 mL) wheat bran
1/4 cup	(60 mL) brown sugar
1/2 tsp	(2 mL) baking powder
	pinch of salt
1	egg
1/3 cup	(80 mL) oil
1/4 cup	(60 mL) margarine, melted
1/4 cup	(60 mL) molasses
2 tbsp	(30 mL) orange juice
2 tsp	(10 mL) orange peel
1 cup	(250 mL) carrots, grated

Pecan Topping

3 tbsp	(45 mL) pecans, chopped
3 tbsp	(45 mL) brown sugar
1/4 tsp	(1 mL) cinnamon

- Butter or line a microwave-safe muffin pan with doubled paper cups. Set aside.
- In a large bowl, mix dry ingredients.
- In a second bowl, beat egg, oil, margarine, molasses and orange juice. Fold in orange peel and carrots. Mix into dry ingredients. Fill cups to two-thirds. Set aside.
- In a bowl, mix topping ingredients. Divide among muffins.
- In microwave oven, bake 6 muffins at a time, 2 minutes on HIGH. Half-rotate pan after 1 minute. Let stand 5 minutes before serving.

NUTRITION	
CALORIES PER MUFFIN: 411	
FAT: 21 *g*	CAL. FROM FAT: 45%
PROTEIN: 3 *g*	CHOLESTEROL: 0 *mg*
SODIUM: 160 *mg*	CARBOHYDRATES: 55 *g*

Garden Oat Muffins

12 LARGE MUFFINS

1 1/2 cups	(375 mL) fast-cooking rolled oats
1 1/2 cups	(375 mL) milk
1	egg
1/2 cup	(125 mL) margarine, melted
1 cup	(250 mL) all-purpose flour
1 cup	(250 mL) whole wheat flour
1/2 cup	(125 mL) brown sugar
1 tbsp	(15 mL) baking powder
1 tsp	(5 mL) salt
1 tsp	(5 mL) cinnamon
1/2 tsp	(2 mL) nutmeg
1 cup	(250 mL) carrots, grated
1 cup	(250 mL) zucchini, grated

- Preheat oven to 400 °F (205 °C). Butter or line large muffin-pan cups with paper cups. Set aside.
- In a bowl, pour rolled oats and milk. Let stand 5 minutes. Mix in egg and margarine. Set aside.
- In a second bowl, mix both kinds of flour, brown sugar, baking powder and spices. Fold in liquid ingredients, stirring only as needed to moisten dry ingredients. Mix in vegetables.
- Spoon batter into muffin cups until full. Bake in oven 20 minutes or so.

VARIATION
- Replace one of the vegetables with grated beets.

NUTRITION	
CALORIES PER SERVING: 243	
FAT: 10 *g*	CAL. FROM FAT: 36%
PROTEIN: 6 *g*	CHOLESTEROL: 19 *mg*
SODIUM: 384 *mg*	CARBOHYDRATES: 34 *g*

Delicious Parmesan Muffins

12 SMALL MUFFINS	
1	egg
1 cup	(250 mL) milk
1/2 cup	(125 mL) plain yogurt
1/2 cup	(125 mL) margarine, melted
2 1/2 cups	(625 mL) flour
1 tbsp	(15 mL) baking powder
1 tsp	(5 mL) salt
1/2 cup	(125 mL) Parmesan cheese, grated
1/4 cup	(60 mL) sugar
1/2 tsp	(2 mL) dried basil

- Preheat oven to 400 °F (205 °C). Butter or line muffin pans with paper cups. Set aside.

- In a bowl, beat egg with a fork. Mix in milk, yogurt and margarine. Set aside.

- In a second bowl, mix flour, baking powder, salt, Parmesan, sugar and basil. Add liquid mixture, stirring only as needed to moisten dry ingredients.

- Spoon batter into muffin cups until full. Bake in oven 20 minutes or so.

NUTRITION	
CALORIES PER MUFFIN: 222	
FAT: 10 g	CAL. FROM FAT: 42%
PROTEIN: 6 g	CHOLESTEROL: 22 mg
SODIUM: 455 mg	CARBOHYDRATES: 26 g

Apple-Cheddar Muffins

12 LARGE MUFFINS	
1	egg
1 1/4 cups	(300 mL) milk
1/4 cup	(60 mL) margarine, melted
2 1/2 cups	(625 mL) flour
1/4 cup	(60 mL) icing sugar
1 tbsp	(15 mL) baking powder
1 tsp	(5 mL) salt
1 cup	(250 mL) unpeeled apple, grated
1 1/2 cups	(300 mL) aged Cheddar cheese, grated

- Preheat oven to 400 °F (205 °C). Butter or line large muffin-pan cups with paper cups. Set aside.

- In a bowl, beat egg, milk and margarine. Set aside.

- In a second bowl, mix flour, icing sugar, baking powder and salt. Fold in liquid ingredients, stirring only as needed to moisten dry ingredients. Add apple and 1 cup (250 mL) cheese.

- Fill muffin cups to the top. Sprinkle with remaining Cheddar cheese. Bake in oven 20 minutes or so.

NUTRITION	
CALORIES PER MUFFIN: 222	
FAT: 10 g	CAL. FROM FAT: 41%
PROTEIN: 8 g	CHOLESTEROL: 33 mg
SODIUM: 418 mg	CARBOHYDRATES: 25 g

Marmalade-Cheese Muffins

8 LARGE MUFFINS

2 cups	(500 mL)	flour
2 tsp	(10 mL)	baking powder
1/4 tsp	(1 mL)	salt
1/3 cup	(80 mL)	margarine
2/3 cup	(160 mL)	brown sugar
1		egg
2 tsp	(10 mL)	orange peel
2/3 cup	(160 mL)	milk
1/2 cup	(125 mL)	cream cheese, softened
2 tbsp	(30 mL)	icing sugar
1/2 cup	(125 mL)	orange marmalade
3 tbsp	(45 mL)	nuts, chopped

- Preheat oven to 375 °F (190 °C). Butter or line large muffin-pan cups with paper cups. Set aside.

- In a bowl, mix flour, baking powder and salt. Set aside.

- In a second bowl, whip margarine and brown sugar. Fold in egg and orange peel. Gradually mix in flour mixture and milk. Set aside.

- In a third bowl, mix cream cheese and icing sugar. Set aside.

- Half-fill muffin cups with first mixture. In the center of each muffin, spoon 4 tsp (20 mL) cheese mixture, then 1 tbsp (15 mL) marmalade.

- Fill muffin cups with remaining batter. Garnish with chopped nuts. Bake in oven 25-30 minutes.

NUTRITION	
CALORIES PER MUFFIN: 398	
FAT: 16 g	CAL. FROM FAT: 35 %
PROTEIN: 6 g	CHOLESTEROL: 41 mg
SODIUM: 324 mg	CARBOHYDRATES: 59 g

Recipe shown above

VARIATIONS

- Replace marmalade with prune, raspberry or blueberry jam, as shown above.

Chocolate-Mocha Muffins

1 cup	(250 mL) semisweet chocolate chips
1 tbsp	(15 mL) instant coffee
1/4 cup	(60 mL) margarine
1 1/4 cups	(300 mL) milk
1	egg
2 1/2 cups	(625 mL) flour
1/3 cup	(80 mL) icing sugar
1 tbsp	(15 mL) baking powder
1/2 tsp	(2 mL) salt

- Preheat oven to 400 °F (205 °C). Butter or line large muffin-pan cups with paper cups. Set aside.

- In a saucepan, over low heat, warm half the chocolate chips with coffee, margarine and milk. Whip until smooth. Let cool.

- In a large bowl, beat egg. Fold in dry ingredients. Add cold chocolate mixture, stirring only as needed to moisten batter. Lightly mix in remaining chocolate chips.

- Spoon batter into muffin cups until full. Bake in oven 20 minutes or so.

NUTRITION	
CALORIES PER MUFFIN: 378	
FAT: 16 g	CAL. FROM FAT: 37 %
PROTEIN: 7 g	CHOLESTEROL: 28 mg
SODIUM: 365 mg	CARBOHYDRATES: 55 g

Danish Cream Cheese Muffins

1	egg
1 3/4 cups	(425 mL) milk
1/2 cup	(125 mL) margarine, melted
1 tsp	(5 mL) lemon peel, grated
2 1/2 cups	(625 mL) flour
1 tsp	(5 mL) baking powder
1 tbsp	(15 mL) salt
1/2 cup	(125 mL) sugar
1/2 cup	(125 mL) cream cheese, softened
2 tbsp	(30 mL) icing sugar
1 tbsp	(15 mL) lemon juice

- Preheat oven to 400 °F (205 °C). Butter or line large muffin-pan cups with paper cups. Set aside.

- In a bowl, beat egg. Mix in milk, margarine and lemon peel.

- In a second bowl, mix flour, baking powder, salt and sugar. Fold in liquid mixture, stirring only as needed to moisten dry ingredients.

- In a third bowl, mix cream cheese, icing sugar and lemon juice until creamy. Set aside.

- Half-fill muffin cups with first mixture. Spoon 1 tsp (5 mL) cheese mixture in the center of each muffin. Fill muffin cups with remaining batter. Bake in oven 20 minutes.

NUTRITION	
CALORIES PER MUFFIN: 395	
FAT: 19 g	CAL. FROM FAT: 43 %
PROTEIN: 8 g	CHOLESTEROL: 45 mg
SODIUM: 1054 mg	CARBOHYDRATES: 49 g

Raisin Bran Muffins

8 LARGE MUFFINS

2 ½ cups	(625 mL)	bran flakes
1 cup	(250 mL)	partly-skimmed milk
1		egg, beaten
¼ cup	(60 mL)	margarine, melted
⅔ cup	(160 mL)	molasses
1 cup	(250 mL)	flour
1 tsp	(5 mL)	salt
½ cup	(125 mL)	raisins

- Preheat oven to 400 °F (205 °C). Butter or line large muffin-pan cups with paper cups. Set aside.
- In a bowl, soak bran flakes in milk until softened. Add beaten egg, margarine and molasses. Set aside.
- In a second bowl, mix dry ingredients. With a fork, fold into liquid mixture. Pour into cups. Bake in oven 20 minutes.

VARIATION
- Replace raisins with 1 ½ cups (375 mL) dried apple pieces.

NUTRITION	
CALORIES PER MUFFIN: 295	
FAT: 7 g	CAL. FROM FAT: 20 %
PROTEIN: 7 g	CHOLESTEROL: 24 mg
SODIUM: 6705 mg	CARBOHYDRATES: 59 g

Pineapple-Carrot Muffins

12 MUFFINS

2 cups	(500 mL)	flour
⅓ cup	(80 mL)	brown sugar
1 tbsp	(15 mL)	baking powder
2 tbsp	(30 mL)	sugar
½ tsp	(2 mL)	cinnamon
½ tsp	(2 mL)	ginger
½ tsp	(2 mL)	nutmeg
½ tsp	(2 mL)	clove
½ tsp	(2 mL)	salt
1 cup	(250 mL)	canned pineapple chunks, in their syrup
		milk
1		egg, beaten
¾ cup	(180 mL)	carrots, finely grated
⅓ cup	(80 mL)	oil
½ tsp	(2 mL)	vanilla extract

- Preheat oven to 400 °F (205 °C). Butter or line large muffin-pan cups with paper cups. Set aside.
- In a bowl, mix dry ingredients. Make a well in the center. Set aside.
- Strain pineapple over a second bowl, reserving syrup. Add enough milk to pineapple syrup to make ¾ cup (180 mL) liquid.
- Fold egg, carrots, oil, vanilla extract and pineapple chunks into syrup and milk mixture. Pour all at once into dry ingredients. With a fork, mix until batter is well-moistened.
- Pour into cups. Bake in oven 20-25 minutes.

NUTRITION	
CALORIES PER MUFFIN: 190	
FAT: 7 g	CAL. FROM FAT: 32 %
PROTEIN: 3 g	CHOLESTEROL: 16 mg
SODIUM: 191 mg	CARBOHYDRATES: 30 g

Yogurt Muffins

12 MUFFINS	
1 cup	(250 mL) plain yogurt or sour cream
1 tsp	(5 mL) baking soda
½ cup	(125 mL) butter
2	eggs
1 tsp	(5 mL) vanilla extract
2 cups	(500 mL) flour
½ tsp	(2 mL) baking powder
½ tsp	(2 mL) salt
1 cup	(250 mL) sugar
¾ cup	(180 mL) chocolate chips

Topping

¼ cup	(60 mL) chocolate chips
2 tbsp	(30 mL) nuts, chopped
2 tbsp	(30 mL) brown sugar
1 tsp	(5 mL) ground cinnamon

- Preheat oven to 350 °F (175 °C). Butter muffin pans. Set aside.
- In a bowl, mix yogurt and baking soda. Set aside.
- In a second bowl, beat butter. Add eggs one at a time, then vanilla extract. Set aside.
- In a large bowl, mix flour, baking powder, salt and sugar. Pour in yogurt mixture, stirring only as needed to moisten dry ingredients. Lightly mix in chocolate chips. Pour into cups.
- Mix topping ingredients. Spoon equal amounts over muffins. Bake in oven 30-35 minutes.

NUTRITION	
CALORIES PER MUFFIN: 338	
FAT: 15 g	CAL. FROM FAT: 40 %
PROTEIN: 5 g	CHOLESTEROL: 53 mg
SODIUM: 305 mg	CARBOHYDRATES: 48 g

Orange-Chocolate Muffins

12 LARGE MUFFINS	
1	egg
1 cup	(250 mL) milk
½ cup	(125 mL) margarine, melted
½ tsp	(2 mL) orange peel, grated
¼ cup	(60 mL) orange juice
1 ½ cups	(375 mL) all-purpose flour
1 cup	(250 mL) whole wheat flour
½ cup	(125 mL) icing sugar
1 tbsp	(15 mL) baking powder
½ tsp	(2 mL) salt
½ cup	(125 mL) semisweet chocolate chips

- Preheat oven to 400 °F (205 °C). Butter or line large muffin-pan cups with paper cups. Set aside.
- In a bowl, beat egg. Mix in milk, margarine, orange peel and juice. Set aside.
- In a large bowl, mix both kinds of flour, icing sugar, baking powder and salt. Pour in liquid ingredients, stirring only as needed to moisten dry ingredients. Lightly mix in chocolate chips.
- Spoon batter into muffin cups until full. Bake in oven 20 minutes or so.

NUTRITION	
CALORIES PER MUFFIN: 243	
FAT: 12 g	CAL. FROM FAT: 42 %
PROTEIN: 5 g	CHOLESTEROL: 18 mg
SODIUM: 285 mg	CARBOHYDRATES: 32 g

Recipe shown above

Multigrain Maple Syrup Muffins

18 MUFFINS

1 cup	(250 mL) rolled oats
³/₄ cup	(180 mL) wheat germ
¹/₂ cup	(125 mL) natural bran
¹/₂ tsp	(2 mL) salt
¹/₂ tsp	(2 mL) ground cinnamon
1 cup	(250 mL) buttermilk or sour milk
³/₄ cup	(180 mL) maple syrup
2	eggs, beaten
¹/₂ cup	(125 mL) oil
1 cup	(250 mL) flour
2 tsp	(10 mL) baking powder
1 tsp	(5 mL) baking soda
¹/₂ cup	(125 mL) raisins

- Preheat oven to 375 °F (190 °C). Butter muffin pans. Set aside.

- In a bowl, mix first 6 ingredients. Let stand 15 minutes. Add maple syrup, eggs and oil. Set aside.

- In a second bowl, mix flour, baking powder and baking soda. Fold into first mixture, stirring only as needed to moisten batter. Add raisins.

- Fill muffin cups until three-quarter full. Bake in oven 20-25 minutes. Remove from oven. Let stand 10 minutes before unmolding.

NUTRITION	
CALORIES PER MUFFIN: 176	
FAT: 8 *g*	CAL. FROM FAT: 37 %
PROTEIN: 4 *g*	CHOLESTEROL: 21 *mg*
SODIUM: 192 *mg*	CARBOHYDRATES: 25 *g*

Lemon Twist Blueberry Muffins

12 MUFFINS

1 tbsp	(15 mL) lemon juice
1 cup	(250 mL) milk
1	egg, beaten
¹/₄ cup	(60 mL) vegetable oil
¹/₄ cup	(60 mL) molasses
1 cup	(250 mL) natural bran
³/₄ cup	(180 mL) whole wheat flour
³/₄ cup	(180 mL) flour
1 ¹/₂ tsp	(7 mL) baking powder
¹/₂ tsp	(2 mL) baking soda
¹/₃ cup	(80 mL) brown sugar, well-packed
1 ¹/₂ tsp	(7 mL) lemon peel
1 cup	(250 mL) fresh or frozen blueberries

- Preheat oven to 375 °F (190 °C). Butter or line muffin pans with paper cups. Set aside.

- In a bowl, mix lemon juice and milk. Let milk sour 1 minute. Stir in egg, vegetable oil and molasses. Set aside.

- In a second bowl, mix dry ingredients. Fold in liquid mixture and blueberries, stirring only as needed to moisten dry ingredients.

- Spoon into cups. Bake in oven 20-25 minutes or until firm to the touch.

NUTRITION	
CALORIES PER MUFFIN: 171	
FAT: 6 *g*	CAL. FROM FAT: 30 %
PROTEIN: 4 *g*	CHOLESTEROL: 18 *mg*
SODIUM: 119 *mg*	CARBOHYDRATES: 28 *g*

COOKIES

Dried Fruit Oatmeal Cookies

AROUND 2 DOZEN

1/3 cup	(80 mL)	shortening
1/2 cup	(125 mL)	sugar
1/2 cup	(125 mL)	brown sugar
1		egg
1/2 cup	(125 mL)	all-purpose flour
1/2 tsp	(2 mL)	baking soda
1/4 tsp	(1 mL)	salt
1/4 cup	(60 mL)	dried prunes, chopped
1/2 cup	(125 mL)	currants
1/2 cup	(125 mL)	oatmeal

- In a bowl, cream shortening, sugar and brown sugar. Whisk in egg. Set aside.

- In a second bowl, sift together all-purpose flour, baking soda and salt. Fold into liquid mixture. Add prunes, currants and oatmeal, mixing well.

- Shape dough into 2 rolls. Wrap in wax paper. Refrigerate 1 hour.

- Preheat oven to 350 °F (175 °C). Butter a cookie sheet.

- Remove dough from refrigerator. Slice each roll into 12 cookies. Place on a cookie sheet. Bake in oven 15 minutes or so.

NUTRITION	
CALORIES PER COOKIE: 89	
FAT: 3 g	CAL. FROM FAT: 31%
PROTEIN: 1 g	CHOLESTEROL: 8 mg
SODIUM: 70 mg	CARBOHYDRATES: 15 g

Orange Cookies

AROUND 1 1/2 DOZEN

2 cups	(500 mL)	flour
4 tsp	(20 mL)	baking powder
		pinch of salt
1 cup	(250 mL)	sugar
1		egg, beaten
1/2 cup	(125 mL)	butter, softened
		peel of 1 orange
1/4 cup	(60 mL)	orange juice
18		whole almonds

- Preheat oven to 375 °F (190 °C).

- In a bowl, sift together dry ingredients. Add remaining ingredients, except almonds. Mix to a smooth dough.

- With a rolling pin, flatten dough to a 1/4-inch (0.5 cm) thickness. Cut cookies using a cookie cutter or knife. Press an almond into each cookie.

- Bake in oven 10 minutes.

VARIATIONS

- Replace orange peel and juice with grapefruit, lemon or lime peel and juice.

NUTRITION	
CALORIES PER COOKIE: 149	
FAT: 6 g	CAL. FROM FAT: 35%
PROTEIN: 2 g	CHOLESTEROL: 24 mg
SODIUM: 143 mg	CARBOHYDRATES: 23 g

AROUND 3 DOZEN

2 1/2 cups	(625 mL)	flour
1/2 cup	(125 mL)	sugar
1		egg
1 cup	(250 mL)	butter

Decoration

3		eggs, beaten
1/2 cup	(125 mL)	sugar
1 1/2 cups	(375 mL)	almond powder
20		candied cherries, halved

- Preheat oven to 425 °F (220 °C). Butter a cookie sheet. Set aside.

- In a large bowl, sift flour. Make a well in the center. Pour in sugar and egg. Set aside.

- Finely dice butter. Sprinkle over flour. With a pastry blender or two knives used scissor-fashion, mix until granular. Wrap dough. Refrigerate 30 minutes.

- Flour a clean, even surface. Roll out dough to 1/8-inch (0.25 cm) thickness. With a floured glass rim, cut dough into rounds. Arrange on a cookie sheet.

- Brush each cookie with beaten egg. Dust with sugar and almond powder. Decorate with a half-cherry.

- Bake in oven 8 minutes or so. Serve.

NUTRITION	
CALORIES PER COOKIE: 305	
FAT: 7 g	CAL. FROM FAT: 21%
PROTEIN: 2 g	CHOLESTEROL: 34 mg
SODIUM: 125 mg	CARBOHYDRATES: 60 g

VARIATIONS

- Cut dough into squares, triangles, diamond shapes or half-moons.

- Sprinkle baked cookies with cocoa. Dip in melted chocolate or brush with honey. Decorate with chopped pistachios or sliced almonds.

- Sandwich cookies in pairs with jam.

Recipes shown, opposite page

Jam Thimble Cookies

¹/₂ cup	(125 mL) brown sugar, well-packed
2 tbsp	(30 mL) sugar
¹/₂ cup	(125 mL) shortening
1	egg
¹/₄ cup	(60 mL) cold water
¹/₂ tsp	(2 mL) vanilla extract
1 ¹/₂ cups	(375 mL) all-purpose flour
¹/₂ tsp	(2 mL) baking soda
1 tsp	(5 ml) salt
1 cup	(250 mL) grated coconut
1 ¹/₂ cups	(375 mL) jam, of your choice
¹/₃ cup	(80 mL) icing sugar

- Preheat oven to 375 °F (190 °C). Butter a cookie sheet. Set aside.

- In a bowl, cream brown sugar, sugar and shortening. Mix in egg, water and vanilla extract. Set aside.

- In a second bowl, mix flour, baking soda, salt and coconut. Fold into first mixture.

- Spoon dough on a cookie sheet, pressing down to form thick rounds. Using the back of a table spoon, mark a deep indentation in the center of each cookie. Fill with 1 tbsp (15 mL) jam.

- Bake in oven 10-12 minutes. Remove from oven. Dust with icing sugar.

NUTRITION	
CALORIES PER COOKIE: 160	
FAT: 6 g	CAL. FROM FAT: 30 %
PROTEIN: 1 g	CHOLESTEROL: 8 mg
SODIUM: 135 mg	CARBOHYDRATES: 28 g

Almond Cookies

¹/₂ cup	(125 mL) shortening
¹/₂ cup	(125 mL) sugar
2 tbsp	(30 mL) corn syrup
2 tbsp	(30 mL) almond extract
2	eggs
1 ¹/₂ cups	(375 mL) all-purpose flour
³/₄ tsp	(3 mL) baking soda
¹/₄ tsp	(1 mL) salt
24	almond halves

- Preheat oven to 375 °F (190 °C).

- In a bowl, cream shortening and sugar. Fold in syrup, almond extract and 1 egg.

- In a second bowl, sift together flour, baking soda and salt. Fold into liquid mixture. Mix until dough is smooth and leaves sides of bowl.

- Shape into approximately 24 small balls, 1-inch (2.5 cm) round. Place on an unbuttered cookie sheet. Set aside.

- In a small bowl, beat remaining egg. Dip 24 almond halves in beaten egg. Lightly press one into each cookie. Bake in oven 15-20 minutes.

NUTRITION	
CALORIES PER COOKIE: 97	
FAT: 5 g	CAL. FROM FAT: 47 %
PROTEIN: 1 g	CHOLESTEROL: 15 mg
SODIUM: 67 mg	CARBOHYDRATES: 12 g

Chocolate Pecan Cookies

AROUND **4** DOZEN

1 cup	(250 mL) shortening
1 cup	(250 mL) brown sugar, well-packed
1/2 cup	(125 mL) sugar
2	eggs
1 tsp	(5 mL) vanilla extract
3 tbsp	(45 mL) orange peel, grated
2 cups	(500 mL) whole wheat flour
1 tsp	(5 mL) baking soda
1/2 tsp	(2 mL) salt
1 cup	(250 mL) pecans, chopped
1 cup	(250 mL) chocolate chips

- Preheat oven to 375 °F (190 °C).

- In a bowl, cream shortening, brown sugar and sugar. Mix in eggs, vanilla extract and orange peel.

- In a second bowl, sift flour, baking soda and salt. Fold into liquid mixture. Add pecans and chocolate chips.

- Shape dough into 1-inch (2.5 cm) balls. Place on an unbuttered cookie sheet. Using the bottom of a glass coated with icing sugar, flatten balls into nice, even rounds. Bake in oven 8-10 minutes.

NUTRITION	
CALORIES PER COOKIE: 227	
FAT: 13 *g*	CAL. FROM FAT: 51 %
PROTEIN: 2 *g*	CHOLESTEROL: 15 *mg*
SODIUM: 107 *mg*	CARBOHYDRATES: 27 *g*

Chewy Apple Cookies

AROUND **2** DOZEN

1/2 cup	(125 mL) butter
1 1/2 cups	(375 mL) brown sugar
1	egg
2 cups	(500 mL) apples, cut into small pieces
1/2 cup	(125 mL) dried apricots, cut into chunks
1/4 cup	(60 mL) apple juice
1/2 tsp	(2 mL) lemon juice
2 cups	(500 mL) whole wheat flour
1 tsp	(5 mL) baking soda
1/2 tsp	(2 mL) salt
1/4 tsp	(1 mL) ground clove
1/2 tsp	(2 mL) cinnamon

- Preheat oven to 350 °F (175 °C). Butter a cookie sheet. Set aside.

- In a bowl, cream butter, brown sugar and egg. Mix in apples, apricots, apple juice and lemon juice.

- In a second bowl, sift together dry ingredients. Fold into first mixture.

- Spoon dough on a cookie sheet, using 2 tbsp (30 mL) dough for each cookie. Bake in oven 10-12 minutes. Serve lukewarm.

NUTRITION	
CALORIES PER COOKIE: 135	
FAT: 4 *g*	CAL. FROM FAT: 27 %
PROTEIN: 2 *g*	CHOLESTEROL: 18 *mg*
SODIUM: 144 *mg*	CARBOHYDRATES: 24 *g*

Peanut Butter Cookies

AROUND 3 DOZEN

¹/₂ cup	(125 mL) shortening
¹/₂ cup	(125 mL) sugar
¹/₂ cup	(125 mL) brown sugar
¹/₂ cup	(125 mL) peanut butter
1	egg
¹/₂ tsp	(2 mL) vanilla extract
1 ³/₄ cups	(425 mL) all-purpose flour
1 tsp	(5 mL) baking soda
¹/₂ tsp	(2 mL) salt
36	peanuts

- Preheat oven to 375 °F (190 °C). Butter a cookie sheet. Set aside.

- In a bowl, cream shortening, sugar and brown sugar. Fold in peanut butter, egg and vanilla extract.

- In a second bowl, sift flour, baking soda and salt. Fold into first mixture. Mix to a smooth dough.

- Shape dough into 1-inch (2.5 cm) balls. Using a fork previously dipped in hot water, lightly flatten balls. Decorate each one with a peanut. Bake in oven 10-12 minutes.

NUTRITION	
CALORIES PER COOKIE: 104	
FAT: 6 *g*	CAL. FROM FAT: 49 %
PROTEIN: 2 *g*	CHOLESTEROL: 5 *mg*
SODIUM: 85 *mg*	CARBOHYDRATES: 11 *g*

Dried Fruit Delight

AROUND 2 DOZEN

2 ¹/₂ cups	(625 mL) all-purpose flour
1 tsp	(5 mL) baking powder
¹/₂ tsp	(2 mL) baking soda
¹/₂ tsp	(2 mL) salt
¹/₃ cup	(80 mL) butter, softened
1 cup	(250 mL) sugar
2	eggs
3 tbsp	(45 mL) milk
1 cup	(250 mL) nuts, chopped
1 cup	(250 mL) dates, chopped
¹/₂ cup	(125 mL) candied cherries, chopped

- Preheat oven to 375 °F (190 °C). Butter a cookie sheet. Set aside.

- In a bowl, sift flour, baking powder, baking soda and salt. Set aside.

- In a second bowl, mix butter, sugar, eggs and milk. Fold in sifted ingredients. Mix in nuts, dates and cherries.

- Shape dough into 1-inch (2.5 cm) balls. Place on a cookie sheet. Bake in oven 12 minutes.

- Remove from oven. Let cool. Serve.

VARIATIONS
- Use different candied fruit and nuts.

NUTRITION	
CALORIES PER COOKIE: 171	
FAT: 6 *g*	CAL. FROM FAT: 33 %
PROTEIN: 3 *g*	CHOLESTEROL: 22 *mg*
SODIUM: 121 *mg*	CARBOHYDRATES: 27 *g*

Raisin Cookies

AROUND 4 DOZEN

1 cup	(250 mL) water
1 cup	(250 mL) raisins
4 cups	(1 L) all-purpose flour
1 ½ tsp	(7 mL) baking powder
1 tsp	(5 mL) baking soda
1 tsp	(5 mL) salt
1 cup	(250 mL) oil
2 cups	(500 mL) sugar
3	eggs
1 tsp	(5 mL) vanilla extract

- Preheat oven to 220 °F (425 °C). Butter 2 cookie sheets. Set aside.
- In a saucepan, bring to a boil water and raisins.
- In a bowl, sift flour, baking powder, baking soda and salt. Set aside.
- In a second bowl, whip oil, sugar, eggs and vanilla extract 2 minutes. Gradually fold in first 2 mixtures. Avoid over-mixing. Spoon dough on cookie sheets, using 2 tbsp (30 mL) dough for each cookie. Bake on top oven rack 10 minutes.
- Remove from oven. Let cool.

NUTRITION	
CALORIES PER COOKIE: 124	
FAT: 5 g	CAL. FROM FAT: 35 %
PROTEIN: 2 g	CHOLESTEROL: 11 mg
SODIUM: 88 mg	CARBOHYDRATES: 19 g

Prairie Cookies

AROUND 2 DOZEN

⅓ cup	(80 mL) brown sugar
⅓ cup	(80 mL) butter, softened
½ cup	(125 mL) heavy cream
1	egg, beaten
½ cup	(125 mL) flour
1 ½ cups	(375 mL) rolled oats
½ cup	(125 mL) sunflower seeds
½ cup	(125 mL) raisins
⅔ cup	(160 mL) chocolate chips
½ cup	(125 mL) slivered almonds

- Preheat oven to 350 °F (175 °C). Butter a cookie sheet. Set aside.
- In a bowl, mix brown sugar and butter. Add cream and egg. Whip until mixture thickens. Fold in remaining ingredients, mixing well.
- Spoon dough on cookie sheet, using 2 tbsp (30 mL) dough for each cookie.
- Bake on top oven rack 20 minutes.

VARIATIONS
- Use white chocolate or carob chips. Replace almonds with chopped nuts.

NUTRITION	
CALORIES PER COOKIE: 144	
FAT: 9 g	CAL. FROM FAT: 52 %
PROTEIN: 3 g	CHOLESTEROL: 21 mg
SODIUM: 33 mg	CARBOHYDRATES: 16 g

Chocolate Chip Cookies

AROUND 3-4 DOZEN	
2 cups	(500 mL) butter
³/₄ cup	(180 mL) sugar
³/₄ cup	(180 mL) brown sugar
3	eggs
4 cups	(1 L) all-purpose flour
2 tsp	(10 mL) baking soda
1 tbsp	(15 mL) salt
2 ¹/₂ cups	(625 mL) chocolate chips

- Preheat oven to 350 °F (175 °C).

- In a bowl, cream butter. Fold in sugar, brown sugar and eggs. Set aside.

- In a second bowl, sift together flour, baking soda and salt. Fold into butter mixture. Add chocolate chips.

- Shape dough into rolls. Slice into ¹/₂-inch (1.25 cm) thick rounds. To avoid burning cookies, double thickness of cookie sheet (by placing 2 cookie sheets one on top of the other) or lower oven temperature. Bake in oven 6 minutes. Serve.

NUTRITION	
CALORIES PER COOKIE: 189	
FAT: 11 *g*	CAL. FROM FAT: 52%
PROTEIN: 2 *g*	CHOLESTEROL: 32 *mg*
SODIUM: 269 *mg*	CARBOHYDRATES: 22 *g*

Recipe shown above

CHOCOLATE-JAM COOKIES

- Before placing in oven, mark a deep indentation in the center of each dough round. Fill with your choice of jam or marmalade.

Recipe shown opposite

Granola Cookies

AROUND 4 DOZEN

³/₄ cup	(180 mL) butter or margarine
1 ¹/₂ cups	(375 mL) brown sugar
3	eggs
1 tsp	(5 mL) vanilla extract
1 cup	(250 mL) all-purpose flour
1 cup	(250 mL) rolled oats
¹/₄ cup	(60 mL) wheat germ
1 tsp	(5 mL) baking soda
¹/₂ tsp	(2 mL) salt
³/₄ cup	(180 mL) grated coconut
³/₄ cup	(180 mL) dried figs, chopped
¹/₂ cup	(125 mL) nuts, chopped

■ Preheat oven to 350 °F (175 °C). Butter cookie sheets. Set aside.

■ In a bowl, cream butter and brown sugar. Mix in eggs and vanilla extract. Set aside.

■ In a second bowl, mix flour, rolled oats, wheat germ, baking soda and salt. Fold into first mixture. Mix in coconut, figs and nuts.

■ Spoon dough on cookie sheets. Bake in oven 12-15 minutes.

NUTRITION	
CALORIES PER COOKIE: 79	
FAT: 4 g	CAL. FROM FAT: 41%
PROTEIN: 1 g	CHOLESTEROL: 19 mg
SODIUM: 87 mg	CARBOHYDRATES: 11 g

Recipe shown above

Dough Cookies

AROUND 1 DOZEN

¹/₄ cup	(60 mL) butter
¹/₄ cup	(60 mL) brown sugar
¹/₂ cup	(125 mL) sour cream
2 cups	(500 mL) all-purpose flour
2 tsp	(10 mL) baking powder
¹/₂ tsp	(2 mL) baking soda
¹/₂ tsp	(2 mL) salt
²/₃ cup	(160 mL) decoration of your choice : nuts, dried fruit, chocolate pieces
1	egg, beaten
	icing sugar or cocoa

■ Preheat oven to 375 °F (190 °C). Butter a cookie sheet. Set aside.

■ In a bowl, cream butter and brown sugar. Mix in sour cream.

■ In a second bowl, sift flour, baking powder, baking soda and salt. Fold into first mixture. Mix to a smooth dough.

■ Roll out dough. Cut cookies with a knife or cookie cutter. Top with your choice of decoration. Brush with beaten egg. Place on cookie sheet. Bake in oven 12 minutes.

■ Dust with icing sugar or cocoa before serving.

NUTRITION	
CALORIES PER COOKIE: 202	
FAT: 11 g	CAL. FROM FAT: 47%
PROTEIN: 4 g	CHOLESTEROL: 30 mg
SODIUM: 253 mg	CARBOHYDRATES: 23 g

Shortbread

AROUND 2 DOZEN	
1 cup	(250 mL) unsalted butter, softened
1 1/4 cups	(300 mL) sugar
1	egg
3	egg yolks
1 tbsp	(15 mL) almond extract
2 3/4 cups	(675 mL) all-purpose flour
1/2 cup	(125 mL) cornstarch
	nuts or candied fruit, chopped

- Preheat oven to 350 °F (175 °C).

- In a large mixer bowl, whip butter and sugar. Fold in whole egg, egg yolks and almond extract, beating well.

- In a second bowl, sift flour and cornstarch. Gradually fold into first mixture, stirring constantly to a smooth dough.

- Using a pastry bag with a fluted nozzle, pipe dough onto an unbuttered cookie sheet, 1 inch (2.5 cm) apart. Decorate with nuts or candied fruit. Bake in oven 10-12 minutes or until cookies turn golden brown. Let cool.

NUTRITION	
CALORIES PER COOKIE: 195	
FAT: 10 g	CAL. FROM FAT: 46%
PROTEIN: 3 g	CHOLESTEROL: 56 mg
SODIUM: 5 mg	CARBOHYDRATES: 24 g

Rolled Butter Cookies

AROUND 2 DOZEN	
3/4 cup	(180 mL) salted butter, softened
1 1/4 cups	(300 mL) sugar
3	egg yolks
1 tsp	(5 mL) almond extract
2 1/2 cups	(625 mL) flour, sifted

- Preheat oven to 350 °F (175 °C). Butter a cookie sheet. Set aside.

- In a large mixer bowl, cream butter and 3/4 cup (180 mL) sugar. Fold in egg yolks and almond extract. Mix in flour. Cover. Refrigerate 40 minutes.

- Remove dough from refrigerator. Shape into two 1 1/2-inch (3.75 cm) wide rolls. Dredge with remaining sugar. Seal in plastic wrap. Refrigerate 20 more minutes.

- Cut rolls into 1/4-inch (0.5 cm) thick slices. Place on a cookie sheet. Bake in oven 10 minutes or so. Let cool. Serve.

VARIATION
- Dredge roll with almond powder instead of sugar.

NUTRITION	
CALORIES PER SERVING: 146	
FAT: 6 g	CAL. FROM FAT: 40%
PROTEIN: 2 g	CHOLESTEROL: 42 mg
SODIUM: 59 mg	CARBOHYDRATES: 20 g

Ladyfingers

AROUND **4** DOZEN

8	egg yolks
1	egg
2 cups	(500 mL) meringue, in stiff peaks *(p. 358)*
1 ¼ cups	(375 mL) flour

- Preheat oven to 425 °F (220 °C).
- In a bowl, beat egg yolks and egg. With a whisk, gradually fold in meringue, alternating with flour. Avoid over-mixing. Using a pastry bag with a plain nozzle, pipe 3-inch (7.5 cm) long fingers onto an unbuttered cookie sheet, spacing them 1 inch (2.5 cm) apart. For a charlotte border, space ¼ inch (0.5 cm) apart only. Bake in oven 5-8 minutes.
- Let cookies cool.

NUTRITION	
CALORIES PER COOKIE: 41	
FAT: 1 *g*	CAL. FROM FAT: 22 %
PROTEIN: 1 *g*	CHOLESTEROL: 39 *mg*
SODIUM: 7 *mg*	CARBOHYDRATES: 7 *g*

COCOA LADYFINGERS
- Reduce flour to ¾ cup (180 mL) and add ¼ cup (60 mL) cocoa.

CHOCOLATE-DIPPED LADYFINGERS
- Dip cold ladyfingers in ½ cup (125 mL) melted chocolate.

Forming Ladyfingers

- *Using a pastry bag with a plain nozzle, pipe 3-inch (7.5 cm) long fingers onto an unbuttered cookie sheet, spacing them 1 inch (2.5 cm) apart.*

Charlotte Border

- *On cookie sheet, space fingers ¼ inch (0.5 cm) apart only, so cookies join into a strip while baking.*

- *Baked charlotte border and ladyfingers.*

CHOCOLATE-DIPPED LADYFINGERS
- Dip cold ladyfingers in melted chocolate.

Cheese Rusks

AROUND **1** DOZEN

4 cups	(1 L) flour
4 tsp	(20 mL) baking powder
2 tsp	(10 mL) salt
¼ cup	(60 mL) butter
⅓ cup	(80 mL) Cheddar cheese, grated
1 ½ cups	(375 mL) milk
⅓ cup	(80 mL) Parmesan cheese, grated

- In a bowl, sift together flour, baking powder and salt. Add butter, mixing until granular. Fold in Cheddar cheese. Pour in milk. Mix until dough leaves sides of bowl. Refrigerate 1 hour.
- Preheat oven to 400 °F (205 °C). Butter a cookie sheet. Set aside.
- On a floured surface, roll out dough to a ½-inch (1.25 cm) thickness. Cut into squares with a knife or cookie cutter. Place on a cookie sheet. Sprinkle with grated Parmesan. Bake in oven 15 minutes or so.

VARIATIONS
- Use different cheeses.

NUTRITION	
CALORIES PER COOKIE: 230	
FAT: 7 *g*	CAL. FROM FAT: 28 %
PROTEIN: 7 *g*	CHOLESTEROL: 20 *mg*
SODIUM: 602 *mg*	CARBOHYDRATES: 34 *g*

For a menu to be well-balanced, it must contain at least one portion of each of the following groups: grain products, fruits and vegetables, dairy products, meat and substitutes. The nutrients that are rich in fat and sugar are usually not favored by dieticians. This doesn't mean that we have to eliminate them from our menu; try to consume them in moderation only.

Discover, in this chapter, wonderful, innovative menus composed of recipes from this book. We are sure your family and guests will leave the table with satisfied smiles and many compliments to the cook.

MENUS

HOW TO PLAN MENUS

A WORD FROM THE CHEF

The following chapter is devoted to simplifying the art of creating menus for all types of occasion. These menus appear under 4 headings : standard menus ; theme menus ; buffets ; and healthy menus.

*All of the recipes featured in **Family Favorites** will help build your reputation as a gourmet and a chef !*

However, the quality and originality of the recipes that you serve do not alone ensure success. You must also learn to plan your menus based on some simple guidelines, which are here outlined for your benefit.

BLUEPRINT TO A SUCCESSFUL MENU

How food tastes is one thing, how it looks is another ! Because we all " eat " with our eyes first, dishes should be attractive – stimulating our appetite with the play of colors, shapes and textures.

Standard Menus

DO'S

- *Vary the color of sauces served in one meal.*

- *Make use of various garnishes, both in single dishes and throughout a meal.*

- *Combine dishes requiring different cooking methods.*

DON'TS

- *Never serve more than one dish of the same meat, poultry, fish or seafood.*

- *Never use similar garnishes in one meal.*
  ***Example :** Greek-style Haddock (p. 203) and Greek Mushrooms (p. 248)*

- *Never combine a dish with a sauce from the same family.*
  ***Example :** mayonnaise and tartar sauce*

- *Never include two dishes of a similar nature.*
  ***Example :** Leek Soup (p. 30) and Leeks Alfredo (p. 257)*

- *Never plan a menu with dishes requiring the same preparation.*
  ***Example** : Egg Balls (p. 21) and Meatball Stew (p. 188)*

Theme Menus

While the basic rules outlined in Standard Menus let you plan everyday meals with confidence, they may be disregarded at times. By its very nature, a theme menu calls for a certain repetition in ingredients and preparation methods.

EXAMPLES

- *A summer menu may include more than one charcoal-grilled dish.*

- *A summer menu may feature many dishes in which seasonal vegetables and fruit play a major part.*

- *A festival-type menu, by definition, calls for several dishes using similar ingredients.*

Buffets

Buffets are also governed by different guidelines. Here, aesthetic considerations prevail.

On the one hand, colors, decorations and garnishes should be varied. On the other hand, since a great many dishes are served, any attempt to avoid a repetition of ingredients or preparation methods is not only doomed, but useless. Therefore, the basic rule is **harmony** : *harmony of colors ; harmony of presentation ; harmony of flavors.*

A WORD FROM THE DIETICIAN

Eating healthy, balanced meals has become a positive goal for many of us, one which can be easily achieved by choosing our food from the 4 food groups. When planning menus, we need only add or remove some foods from each of the groups to arrive at healthy eating !

Let's look at how a standard menu may be modified to provide nutrients from the 4 food groups.

Standard Menu

Leek Soup
30
Chicken in Peach Sauce
104
Garnished Green Salad
272

BECOMES

Healthy Menu

Leek Soup
30
Chicken in Peach Sauce
104
Spinach Pasta
267
Garnished Green Salad
272
Raspberry Frozen Yogurt
408

PLANNING A HEALTHY MENU

according to the 4 food groups

- *3* servings Vegetables and Fruit
- *1* serving Meat and Alternatives
- *1* serving Grain Products
- *1* serving Milk Products

HEALTHY MENUS

For a menu to be considered a " healthy menu ", it must meet the following 4 requirements. It must :

- *include foods from the 4 food groups,*
- *be low in fat,*
- *be high in necessary vitamins and minerals,*
- *be high in complex glucid and fiber.*

Healthy Menu

EXAMPLE 1

Good Health Soup
30

Roast Veal with Chives
147

Cheesy Spinach Rice
76

Glazed Carrots
246

Healthy Date Squares
373

THE 4 FOOD GROUPS

To feel good about yourself, eat well, and eat healthily.

Enjoy a variety of foods from each group every day, and choose lower-fat foods more often.

Grain Products

Choose whole grain and enriched products more often.

Vegetables and Fruit

Choose dark green and orange vegetables and orange fruit more often.

Milk Products

Choose lower-fat milk products more often.

Meat and Alternatives

Choose leaner meat, poultry and fish, as well as legumes, more often.

Other foods

Other foods and beverages that are not part of any food group may also bring flavor and fun to your menus. However, some of these are higher in fat or calories.

Use these foods in moderation.

How many servings from each food group do you need ?

Because people need different amounts of food, choices from the 4 food groups should include :

Grain Products
5-12 servings per day

Vegetables and Fruit
5-10 servings per day

Meat and Alternatives
2-3 servings per day

Milk Products
2-4 servings per day

Children 4-9 years : 2-3 servings
Youth 10-16 years : 3-4 servings
Adults : 2-4 servings
Pregnant and nursing women : 3-4 servings

The numbers of servings you need every day from the 4 food groups and other foods depends on your age, body size, gender and activity level. This number increases during pregnancy and nursing.

Healthy Menu

EXAMPLE 2

Tomato Fondue
75

Baked Salmon
197

Piquant Broccoli Florets
244

Potatoes in Mornay Sauce
261

Fruit Salad
277

Too many servings !

This may seem like a lot of food ! Start by checking your real needs. It may be that you are already eating more servings than you realize. For example, a plate of spaghetti can count as 3-4 servings of grain products and a juice " box " as 2 servings of vegetables and fruit.

What is one serving ?

A rule of thumb exists to determine a single serving of each food in the 4 food groups.

For example, in grain products :
1 slice of bread = 1 serving ;
1 bagel, pita bread or bread
roll = 2 servings.

Servings from Meat and Alternatives vary in size. For example :
1 serving = 2-4 oz (50-100 g) of meat, poultry or fish.

This way, child-size servings will be smaller than adult-size servings.

Energy = Calories

You need food for energy. Energy is measured in Calories, Kilocalories (kcal) or Kilojoules (kJ). So the more calories you eat, the more energy you have. If you choose foods and determine servings using the information provided in this chapter, you will get between 1800-3200 Calories each day.

If you don't eat much, it's important to choose your food wisely. For example, women should choose foods high in iron such as beef and game meat, whole grain or enriched cereals, and legumes.

If you eat smaller servings but are hungry or if you are trying to lose weight, you may need to increase the number of servings from the 4 food groups and other foods.

Everyday menus

When planning balanced meals, the golden rule of the 4 food groups must be applied. Should your menu not include one of these food groups, you may add this missing food on the side at mealtimes or as a snack later on.

Three-course menus

Leek Soup
30

Chicken in Peach Sauce
104

Garnished Green Salad
272

Stuffed Salad Rolls
86

Garbanzo Bean Salad
282

Peach Flan
352

Avocado Pear Surprise
60

Beef Olé !
136

Chilled Salad
272

Vegetable Chowder
39

Minty Lamb Medallions with Pistachios
169

Summer Crêpes
384

Cream of Lettuce Soup
33

Greek-style Haddock
203

Corn Salad
278

Deviled Chicken Fricassée
113

Brown Rice Salad
281

Chocolate Chip Cookie Trifle
391

Carrot and Parsnip Soup
32

Ham Steaks
191

Butterscotch Cobbler
404

Chicken Liver Soup
36

Barbecued Pork Chops
180

Fruit Salad
277

Russian Salad
57

Deep Sea Pot Pie
212

Small Apple Nut Charlottes
328

Veal Fricassée
153

Easy Salad
271

Ice-Cream Crêpes with
Almonds and Blueberries
382

Spinach Soup with Dumplings
36

Curried Meatballs
140

Grapefruit Sherbet
406

Poached Egg in a Cone
68

Creole Chicken
107

Fruit Trifle
392

Cheesy Fish Soup
47

Fish Burgers
211

Tutti-Frutti Mousse
400

Vegetable-Pine Nut
Tortellini
235

Watercress Salad
270

Marshmallow
Fruit Pie
348

WEEKEND MENUS

You can never ignore the importance of choosing foods from the 4 food groups. Each group plays an essential part in healthy eating, providing various combinations of vitamins and minerals. Omitting these may lead to health problems, can affect your skin and hair, cause fatigue, and so on.

FOUR OR FIVE-COURSE MENUS

Fennel Soup
31

Liver Pâté Tart
68

Coq au Vin
112

Chocolate Coffee
Charlotte
327

Parmesan Fondue
81

Tomato Beef Stew
137

Caesar Salad
273

Pineapple Shortcake
325

HOLIDAY MENUS

CHRISTMAS EVE BUFFET

Tomatoes Tapenade
20
Small Cheese Puffs
20
Shrimp Canapés
26

Broccoli Quiche
73
Mussels in Beer Sauce
214
Garnished Ham
193

Spicy Beets	*244*
Gourmet Peas Lyonnais	*258*

Potato Salad
278
Mushroom Salad Florentine
274

Double Chocolate Fruit
369
Chocolate Truffles
370
Christmas Log
299

CHRISTMAS DAY LUNCH

Green Pea Soup
40
Quail Fricassée in Orange Sauce
88
Savory Beef Torte
141

Ham and Potato Purée	*260*
Broccoli Brochettes	*244*
Mustard Carrots	*246*

Watercress Salad
270
Coconut-Strawberry Charlotte
327

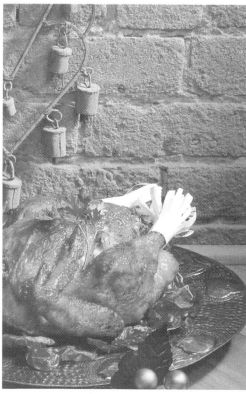

CHRISTMAS DAY DINNER

Menu 1

Cream of Carrot Soup
38
Norwegian Salmon
66
Trou Normand
96
Old-fashioned Stuffed Roast Turkey
118

Sautéed Potatoes	*260*
Hot Buttered Bean Salad	*254*
Garnished Tomatoes	*262*

Chilled Salad
272
Cheese Board
286
Fruitcake
308

Menu 2

Oyster Chowder
44
Caviar Tart
68
Veal Meatballs in Peach Sauce
87
Muscadet Wine Sherbet
92
Roasted Guinea-Fowl with Cherries
224

Egg-fried Rice	*266*
Fried Oyster Mushrooms	*248*
Carrot Purée	*246*

Jellied Broccoli Ring
276
Blue Cheese Mashed in Port Wine
288
Royal Charlotte
329

New Year's Eve Buffet

Small Cheese Puffs
20

Prosciutto Breadsticks
22

Canapés
26

Aspic
60

Vegetable Pie
72

Sausage Rolls
88

Salmon Salad
283

Crispy-crunchy Salad
280

Fruity Chocolate Cones
361

Love Bites
369

Chocolate Fig Clusters
375

New Year's Day Lunch

Asparagus Velouté
with Croutons
38

Smoked Salmon Mousse
65

Pork Rack with Lentils
183

Baked Potatoes
261

Onion Rings with Sesame Seeds
256

Two-tone Turnip
254

Mixed Salad
274

Classic Cheesecake
316

New Year's Day Dinner

Pesto Soup
36

Shrimp Mold
62

Beet Crêpes
78

Frosted Berries
95

Duck à l'Orange
122

Pastis Endive   *253*
Medley Extravaganza   *258*
Ham and Potato Purée   *260*

Mushroom Salad Florentine
274

Saint-Honoré
314

New Year's Day Buffet

Golden Cheese Toast
25

Pâté-stuffed Mushrooms
24

Oyster Crackers
22

Veal Loaf
157

Stuffed Turkey Breast
120

Saffron Brussels Sprouts   *250*
Mustard Carrots   *246*

Potato Salad
278

Garnished Green Salad
272

Cheese Board
286

Frosted Berries
95

Divine Treats
374

Cream Profiteroles
357

SPECIAL-OCCASION MENUS

Party menus and buffets are more elaborate and often much higher in fat and calories than everyday menus featured in this book.

For this reason, the following menus should be reserved for special occasions only.

EASTER LUNCH

Menu 1

Fennel Soup
31

Pineapple Islands
63

Sugar Ham Pie
192

Candied Red Onions	*256*
Lemony Green Bell Peppers	*259*
Sautéed Potatoes	*260*

Jellied Broccoli Ring
276

Deluxe Banana Cake
302

Menu 2

Cream of Carrot Soup
38

Stuffed Peaches
59

Mushroom-stuffed Trout
199

Potatoes in Mornay Sauce	*261*
Zucchini Balls	
in Tomato Sauce	*252*

Surprise Salad
274

Upside-down Pear
and Pastis Pie
341

EASTER DINNER

Menu 1

Leek Soup
30

Stuffed Tomatoes
65

Bacon-wrapped Plantain Bananas
73

Trou Normand
96

Easter Ham
190

Broccoli Brochettes	*244*
Medley Extravaganza	*258*
Baked Potatoes	*261*

Caesar Salad
273

Chocolate Pear Shortcake
324

Menu 2 ▪ Buffet

Canapés
26

Tomatoes Tapenade
20

Cheese Twists
25

Easter Ham (variation)
190

Artichoke Hearts
in Tomato Sauce   *240*
Marinated Asparagus   *241*

Five-Vegetable Rice Salad
280

Chilled Salad
272

Cheese Board
286

Chocolate Truffles
370

Hazelnut Half-moons
375

Dried Fruit Candy
376

Coconut Rum Balls
376

MOTHER'S DAY DINNER

Menu 1

Cream of Lettuce Soup
33

Hearts Vinaigrette
55

Roast Beef with
Mushroom-Leek Sauce
126

Baked Potatoes   *261*
Garnished Tomatoes   *262*

Garden Salad
270

Pineapple Trifle
392

Menu 2

Oyster Chowder
44

Asparagus au Gratin
74

Salmon Scallops with Sorrel Butter
196

Spinach Pasta   *267*
Sautéed Bell Peppers   *259*

Fruit Salad
277

Hazelnut Cheesecake
318

FATHER'S DAY DINNER

Menu 1

Green Bell Pepper Soup
48

Fiesta Nachos
80

Stuffed Leg of Lamb
162

Baked Potatoes   *261*
Green Peas in Piquant Sauce   *258*
Brussels Sprouts with Prosciutto   *250*

Caesar Salad
273

Garden Fruit Tart
346

Menu 2

Asparagus Rolls
53

Parmesan Fondue
81

Minute Pepper Steaks
128

Oven Fries   *261*
Leeks Alfredo   *257*
Mustard Carrots   *246*

Garnished Green Salad
272

Strawberry Sherbet
406

BUFFETS AND BRUNCHES

BRUNCHES

Cheese boards provide a pleasant finishing touch to party buffets – which often lack milk products. However, yogurt is a more suitable alternative for weekday menus.

Color and Health Tips :

1   If no fruit was served during the meal, the addition of juicy grapes or other seasonal fruit will enhance any cheese board.

2   If no grain products were included in the menu, whole wheat bread rolls and cheese are a perfect match !

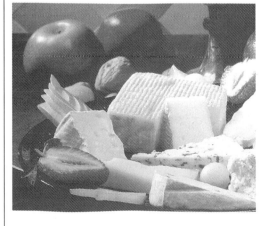

Brunch 1

Sweet-and-sour Soup
42

Carpacio
143

Ceviche
216

Smoked Fish Omelette
211

Veal Shepherd's Pie
154

Fancy Rice	*236*
Port-flavored Red Cabbage	*249*
Wilted Leeks with Raisins	*257*

Autumn Salad
274

Cheese Board
286

Chocolate Soufflé
394

Brunch 2

Crab Chowder
46

Golden Cheese Toast
25

Surprise Snail Kabobs
22

Vegetable Pie
72

Chicken-stuffed Mushrooms
77

Veal Loaf
157

Potatoes in Mornay Sauce	*261*
Tomato Crêpes	*262*

Italian Salad
283

Marinated Cheese
288

New-Age
Carrot Cake
307

BUFFETS

Buffet 1 ▪ Cold

Egg Balls
21

Small Cheese Puffs
20

Ham-and-Cheese Wheels
58

Shrimp New Orleans
66

Deviled Egg Trio
68

Veggie Pâté
76

Tomato Crêpes
262

Salmon Salad
283

Mushroom Salad Florentine
274

Cheese Board
286

Rhubarb Fritters
368

Marshmallow Brownies
370

Buffet 2

Prosciutto Breadsticks
22

Chicken Salad in Mini Pita Breads
22

Apricot-glazed Ham Meatballs
24

Cheese Twists
25

Smoked Oyster Pears
63

Tender-crisp Chicken Croquettes
115

Veal Chili in Puff Pastry
157

Garbanzo Bean Salad
282

Vegetable Salad
278

Seasonal Fruit Pastries
347

Buffet 4

Shrimp Mold
62

Antipasto
56

Cheesy Rice Cakes
79

Stuffed Salad Rolls
86

Cabbage Rolls
140

Sugar Ham Pie
192

Smoked Goose Salad
122

Potato Salad
278

Egg-stuffed Cucumbers
252

Creamy Fruit Roll
296

A critical aspect of buffet planning is food preservation. Dishes with mayonnaise or meat should never be kept at room temperature longer than 1 hour. They must also be prepared no more than 24 hours ahead of time, and should be kept chilled until ready to serve.

GRAND AND GOURMET MENUS

GRAND MENUS

SEVEN-COURSE MENUS

Menu 1

Pesto Soup
36

Scallop Entrée
67

Asparagus Mimosa
74

Honeydew Granita
92

Veal Medallions
with Garbanzo Beans
150

Easy Salad
271

Nutty Fudge
Crêpes
381

Menu 2

Good Health Soup
30

Carrot and Apricot Molds
56

Trou Normand
96

Shrimp-stuffed Sole
200

Mushroom Salad Florentine
274

Sweet Brie
288

Tutti-Frutti Mousse
400

EIGHT-COURSE MENUS

Menu 2

Shrimp Chowder
44

Hearts Vinaigrette
55

Cheese Rolls
81

Frosted Berries
95

Minty Lamb Medallions
with Pistachios
169

Garnished Green Salad
272

Marinated Cheese
288

Orange Liqueur Crème Brûlée
405

Menu 2

Pumpkin Soup
48

Cauliflower Crêpes
78

Muscadet Wine Sherbet
92

Stuffed Quails
122

Garden Salad
270

Frozen Fruit Cups
95

Cheese Board
286

Savarin
365

GOURMET MENUS

NINE-COURSE MENUS

Smoked Cod Soup
45

Cucumber in Minty Sauce
54

Quail Fricassée in Orange Sauce
88

Trou Normand
96

Calf Sweetbreads Meunière
158

Watercress Salad
270

Frosted Berries
95

Blue Cheese Mashed in Port Wine
288

Passion Sherbet
407

TEN-COURSE MENUS

Asparagus Velouté
with Croutons
38

Spicy Crab-stuffed Avocados
64

Chicken-stuffed
Mushrooms
77

Muscadet Wine Sherbet
92

Lamb Rolls with Watercress
164

Endive Duet Salad
271

Herb and Oil
Goat Cheese
288

Frozen Fruit Cups
95

Chocolate Truffles
370

Banana-Litchi Soufflé
396

Main index

In the main index, recipes are first listed by chapter, then alphabetized within each section.

The index follows the usual course of a meal, starting with appetizers to end with desserts.

Soups
AND APPETIZERS

SWEET
INTERMISSION

MAIN
DISHES

Side dishes

Salads

Cheeses

DESSERTS AND PASTRIES

SUPPLEMENTARY INDEX

The Supplementary Index was created to facilitate the location of certain recipes. Here's was it contains:

1 Recipes Out of Chapter

Certain recipes can have, in their title, the name of a section or chapter without being found within it. The Beef Mousse recipe, for example, is found in the Cold Appetizers chapter, but is not seen in the Beef chapter.

The Supplementary Index, under the Beef chapter heading, corrects this situation and allows you to trace this recipe and others in the book that are filed out of their category, using the key words that appear in their titles.

2 Recipes by Theme

The Supplementary Index also regroups certain recipes that appear in different places in the book. All of the Variety Meat, for example, is united under this title in the Supplementary Index, although they are found in different chapters in the Main Index.

3 Recipes Filed by Main Ingredient

The Supplementary Index identifies many recipes from the book according to the main ingredients that it contains; consequently, the same recipe that contains coffee and chocolate is found in two places in the Supplementary Index: under Coffee, as well as under Chocolate.

VARIETY MEAT

BEEF

COFFEE

CARAMEL

CHOCOLATE

CHEESES

FRUIT

Apples

Apricots

Avocados

Bananas

Marshmallows

Vegetables

LEGUMES

HONEY

NUTS AND SEEDS

PASTA

PORK

FISH AND SEAFOOD

RICE AND CEREALS